Curriculum Planning

FOR BETTER TEACHING AND LEARNING

by J. Galen Saylor

Professor of Secondary Education
and Chairman of the Department
University of Nebraska

and William M. Alexander

Professor of Education
George Peabody College
for Teachers

Foreword by Hollis L. Caswell

President, Teachers College
Columbia University

Holt, Rinehart and Winston • *New York*

Eighth Printing, December, 1960

27721-0114

Foreword

Continuing study of the curriculum in American schools is highly important. Not only is it essential that prospective teachers have a good understanding of curriculum principles and practices before undertaking the responsibilities of teaching; it is important also that teachers in service constantly review and refine their conceptions of what the curriculum should be. This is especially true in American schools because of the great pioneering undertaking in which we are engaged in attempting to provide appropriate education for all the children of all the people extending through the elementary and secondary periods in a common program. Great progress has been made toward this goal, but many problems remain to be solved.

This book should prove highly useful in achieving such a purpose, both for teachers in service and teachers in training. It is comprehensive in scope, treating the major issues and problems of curriculum development that are encountered in public school systems. The currently most significant theories and practices are presented with clarity and effectiveness.

One feature of the book which is noteworthy, and which will con tribute greatly to its use for teaching purposes, is the care taken by the authors to present various positions on curriculum issues fairly. At the same time they make perfectly clear their own position. The rather common practices in writings on the curriculum of setting up straw men and knocking them down and of taking a doctrinaire position are generally avoided. This should encourage those who use the book to think through their own positions on curriculum issues.

Reading lists are provided with each chapter. They are carefully selected, and annotations contribute to ease of use.

The authors bring to their analysis a wide background of experience. Curriculum director, director of research, school administrator, college teacher, consultant to workshop groups and curriculum committees, and participant in the activities of national and regional education associations indicate the breadth of experience upon which the authors draw.

I take particular personal pleasure in writing this foreword since both of the authors did their doctoral work under my guidance.

HOLLIS L. CASWELL

New York
May, 1954

Preface

Curriculum Planning: For Better Teaching and Learning is a comprehensive treatment of principles, problems, and practices in the planning of curriculum and teaching. We have aimed to prepare a book which will give some direction to all professional personnel concerned with guiding better educational programs for children and youth in elementary and secondary schools.

In order to help readers fully understand the complex processes of curriculum planning, we have drawn upon such foundation fields as philosophy, sociology, and psychology for the basic principles. We have particularly tried to present theories and practices which are consistent with modern knowledge about learning. A great deal of material has been included to explain specific problems and practices of planning in the classroom situation. Moreover, the entire book has been made as readable and usable as possible by the inclusion of a considerable number of illustrations, both narrative and photographic, drawings, charts, and tables. Each chapter also includes a selected, annotated list of materials for further study.

Certain basic beliefs have been paramount in our preparation and organization of materials for this book:

1. That better curriculum planning for children and youth in American elementary and secondary schools is essential and can be accomplished through the processes of planning we present.

2. That we who plan the curriculum—all of us associated with the education of children and youth—must consider fully many factors which affect the framework and day-by-day development of the curriculum.

3. That the real goal of curriculum planning is better learning and, therefore, that the development of better learning experiences is the central purpose of all curriculum planning.

4. That participation by all concerned, with full attention to evaluative data, is the method whereby fundamentally better curriculum planning will occur.

In developing these basic beliefs, we have organized the book in five parts:

> part 1—WHY IS BETTER CURRICULUM PLANNING NEEDED?
>
> part 2—WHAT MAJOR FACTORS MUST BE CONSIDERED IN CURRICULUM PLANNING?
>
> part 3—HOW SHALL THE CURRICULUM FRAMEWORK BE ORGANIZED?
>
> part 4—HOW SHALL WE PLAN THE CURRICULUM FOR BETTER TEACHING?
>
> part 5—HOW SHALL CURRICULUM PLANNING BE ORGANIZED AND EVALUATED?

Although those who plan curriculums may not always approach their problems in the logical order suggested by these titles, we believe our book should show this logic and make clear the procedures at each step and the relationship of all stages of curriculum planning.

We wish to express appreciation to the various publishers who have generously given permission to quote from certain of their copyrighted publications; to the school systems which have made photographs and other materials available to us; and to the Cooperative Study in Elementary Education of the Southern Association of Colleges and Secondary Schools, and the Association for Supervision and Curriculum Development, National Education Association, for the use of photographs from their files.

We should also like to express our appreciation to the many teachers we have taught and from whom we learned as well, to the colleagues in the school systems and teacher education institutions in which we have worked, and to the other professional co-workers whose questions and suggestions have helped our thinking on curriculum matters.

J. G. S.

W. M. A.

Lincoln, Nebraska
Coral Gables, Florida
May 1, 1954

Table of Contents

List of Figures

List of Tables

WHY IS BETTER
CURRICULUM PLANNING NEEDED?

We believe that all who work for good education should promote and engage in more and better curriculum planning. Current curriculum practice in American schools has some inadequacies, inequalities, and other deficiencies we would like to see eliminated. These lacks are due in part to many unresolved issues in curriculum planning. These issues will not be resolved nor our curriculum problems solved, we believe, until there is much wider and more continued participation in curriculum planning. If education is to be responsive to changes and problems in our culture, then informed curriculum planning is essential to all present and future educational programs. That is, we need better curriculum planning both to provide for presently unrecognized and unmet needs in education, and also to solve new educational problems as they arise.

In Part 1 our purpose is to present these problems and issues of curriculum planning which make necessary better curriculum planning by school personnel. Chapter 1 identifies and describes the problems of curriculum practice in American elementary and secondary schools. Chapter 2 analyzes several basic issues in curriculum planning and concludes with a statement of desirable characteristics of better planning processes.

chapter 1

Curriculum Practices in American Schools

This chapter defines needs for curriculum planning through a brief review and appraisal of current practices in American schools. Certain introductory concepts need to be understood as a basis for this review and appraisal, and are explained in the following sections dealing with what the curriculum is and what it includes.

WHAT IS THE CURRICULUM?

The curriculum is frequently considered to be those things we wish children to learn in school. Thus the multiplication table, the principles of democracy, and the use of the dictionary are parts of the curriculum. Overlooked by this concept, however, are many learnings which boys and girls acquire in school that are not so deliberately planned. For example, they learn to dislike school, to cheat, to play truant. Sometimes these negative learnings result from the very experiences teachers plan for directly opposing purposes. Whether or not teachers mean for them to do so, pupils also learn how to secure the approval of their peers and their teachers. That is, boys and girls may learn many things they select themselves. It must be recognized that teachers can plan learning experiences but that they cannot be positive of outcomes or learnings. The curriculum includes school experiences through which learners may achieve the ends sought by their teachers.

The term "school experience" is also significant in our concept of the curriculum. Does learning result only from experiences which occur in school? Pupils really acquire very few generalized learnings—that is, skills, understandings, or attitudes used in different situations—from one or more specific school experiences. Such learnings result from things seen and heard and done in a variety of situations. However, experiences in school frequently influence learnings outside. For example, interests in reading developed in school may influence the choice of magazines

3

and books to read out of school. On the other hand, a distaste for reading created by schoolbooks which are too difficult or uninteresting may
result in a child's tendency to avoid books altogether outside school. In
both cases, learning out of school is influenced by that in school.

To summarize, it is known: (1) that learning results from experience; (2) that the school provides experiences for learning purposes;
and (3) that many experiences outside school and resultant learnings
are influenced by or otherwise related to those which occur in school.
To promote desirable learning, teachers must arrange learning experiences in school and utilize related ones out of school. What results from
planning (or the lack thereof), whether or not it comes out as intended,
is the curriculum. The better the planning, the more likely that the
learnings desired will occur. To put it another way, the school curriculum is the total effort of the school to bring about desired outcomes in
school and in out-of-school situations. In short, the curriculum is the
school's program for learners.

This broad concept of the curriculum rules out of correct usage other
definitions which have been and are still used. The list of subjects offered
in a particular grade or school is frequently referred to as the curriculum, but this definition excludes the many things that occur in school
outside these classes. More properly, the subject offering of the school is
the "program of studies." For example, a sample program of studies of
a metropolitan high school is reproduced in Table 1. In high schools,
reference is frequently made to the "college preparatory curriculum,"
"industrial arts curriculum," "commercial curriculum," and so forth.
Here again the term is used to describe a particular set of subjects, and
the more appropriate reference would be to the college-preparatory program of studies, the industrial-arts program of studies, and the like.

Frequently a result of curriculum planning is a compilation of suggested subject matter, experiences, and materials for a particular subject
or curriculum area. This compilation, usually a mimeographed or
printed publication, is sometimes called "a curriculum." A "course of
study" or "teachers' guide" is a more appropriate term.

In secondary schools particularly, a large group of experiences have
been called "extracurricular" or "co-curricular." The clubs, athletics,
student organizations, publications, and other activities which occupy
such an important place in the high school pupil's schedule are not outside his program but are as much a part as are classes in algebra and
history. Similarly, the experiences that elementary and secondary pupils
have in the "activity program" or "activity period" are important phases
of their curriculums. So are the guidance tests and interviews, the assembly, the social program, the safety patrol, and other efforts of the

school to bring about learning which are sometimes referred to as being outside the "regular" program. In the curriculum, too, are the "co-op" work jobs, the excursions, the community surveys and campaigns, and other events which occur out of school but which are sponsored or supervised or chaperoned or prepared for by the schools. So is the listening and seeing and reading which pupils do as a result of teacher guidance in the choice of radio and television programs, library and museum facilities, and other out-of-school resources.

PLATE 1. THE CURRICULUM INCLUDES MANY TYPES OF EXPERIENCES. *In a single primary room there may be as many types of experience as there are children. (Courtesy of the Fulton County Schools, Atlanta, Georgia)*

The curriculum is the sum total of the school's efforts to influence learning, whether in the classroom, on the playground, or out of school. Whether the efforts result in the learnings that teachers desire depends on the many factors which affect the individual pupil's interaction with the situations arranged. Whether the experiences had correlate or conflict with those that pupils have outside the school must also be answered for each individual. The significant conclusion for the teachers is that everything they do to stimulate and direct pupils' experience and subsequent learning must be considered in curriculum planning.

WHAT DOES THE CURRICULUM INCLUDE?

Although great curriculum uniformity is not characteristic of American schools, there are similarities to be noted in the types of curriculum experiences, their patterns of organization, and, despite diversity of

TABLE 1

A Sample Program of Studies (John Marshall High School, Richmond, Virginia)

(Subjects printed in capitals are required. All subjects carry a credit of one year unless stated otherwise. Sixteen units plus Physical Education or Military are required for graduation. Subject prerequisites are printed in parentheses by studies requiring them except for vocational courses.)

NINTH YEAR

ENGLISH	1 and 2
SOCIAL STUDIES	1 and 2
GENERAL MATHEMATICS or ALGEBRA	1 and 2
PHYSICAL EDUCATION or MILITARY	1 and 2
Art	1 and 2
Home Economics	1 and 2
Industrial Arts	
General Metal (M D 1)	1 and 2
Mechanical Drawing	1 and 2
Woodwork	1 and 2
Junior Business Training	1 and 2
Latin, French, Spanish	1 and 2
Music	
Military Band	1 and 2
Orchestra	1 and 2
Voice	1 and 2
Science or Physical Geography	1 and 2

TENTH YEAR

ENGLISH	3 and 4
PHYSICAL EDUCATION or MILITARY	1 and 2
Art	May continue or begin
Biology or Physical Geography	1 and 2
Business Education	
Business Mathematics	1 and 2
Typewriting	1 and 2
History	3 and 4
Home Economics	May continue or begin
Industrial Arts	
Ceramics	1 and 2
Electricity	1 and 2
General Metal (M D 1)	1 and 2
Mechanical Drawing	1 and 2
Mechanical Drawing (1 yr Math)	3 and 4
Woodwork	1 and 2

Latin, French, Spanish	3 and 4
	(May begin 1 and 2)
Mathematics	
Algebra	1 and 2
Geometry (Alg 1, 2)	1 and 2
Practical Mathematics	1 and 2
Military	May continue or begin
Music	
Military Band	May continue or begin
Orchestra	May continue or begin
Voice	May continue or begin

ELEVENTH YEAR

ENGLISH	5 and 6
HISTORY	5 and 6
Art	May continue or begin
Business Education	
Bookkeeping	1 and 2
Shorthand	1 and 2
Typewriting	3 and 4 or 1 and 2
Consumer Problems	1 and 2
Diversified Occupations	1 and 2 (2 units)
Driver Training	¼ unit
Home Economics	
Clothing (Home Ec 1, 2)	1 and 2
Foods (Home Ec 1, 2)	1 and 2
Home Economics	May continue or begin
Industrial Arts	
Ceramics	1 and 2
Electricity	1 and 2
Jewelry	1 and 2
Mechanical Drawing	1 and 2
Mechanical Drawing (1 yr Math)	3 and 4
Woodwork	1 and 2
Latin, French, Spanish	3 and 4
	(May continue 5 and 6, May begin 1 and 2)
Mathematics	
Algebra	1 and 2
Algebra (Geom 1, 2)	3 and 4
Geometry (Alg 1, 2)	1 and 2

TABLE 1 *continued*

Military   May continue or begin

Music

   Military Band   May continue or begin

   Orchestra   May continue or begin

   Voice   May continue or begin

Science

   Chemistry (Alg 1, 2)   1 and 2

   Physics (Alg 1, 2)   1 and 2

Speech (Eng 1-5)   1 (½ unit)

Vocational Courses (Three periods daily)

   Vocational Auto Mechanics

                  1 and 2 (2 units)

   Vocational Comercial Art

                  1 and 2 (2 units)

   Vocational Drafting   1 and 2 (2 units)

   Vocational Electricity   1 and 2 (2 units)

   Vocational Machine Shop

                  1 and 2 (2 units)

   Vocational Printing   1 and 2 (2 units)

   Vocational Sheet Metal   1 and 2 (2 units)

TWELFTH YEAR

ENGLISH   7 and 8

GOVERNMENT   ½ unit

Art   May continue or begin

Business Education

   Bookkeeping   3 and 4 or 1 and 2

   Clerical Practice (Typ 1, 2)

             1 and 2 (½ unit

             for 1 without 2)

   Filing (Typ 1, 2)   ½ unit

   Shorthand *with*

      Secretarial Practice   1 and 2

   Typewriting   3 and 4 or 1 and 2

Driver Training   ¼ unit

Home Economics

   Clothing (Home Ec 1, 2)

            3 and 4 or 1 and 2

   Foods (Home Ec 1, 2)   1 and 2

   General Home Economics   1 and 2

Industrial Arts

   Ceramics   1 and 2

   Jewelry   1 and 2

   Mechanical Drawing (1 yr Math) 3 and 4

   Mechanical Drawing   1 and 2

Latin, French, Spanish   3 and 4

             (May continue 5, 6)

             (May continue 7, 8)

Mathematics

   Algebra   1 and 2

   Algebra (Alg 1, 2; Geom 1, 2)   3 and 4

   Geometry (Alg 1, 2)   1 and 2

Senior Arithmetic   ½ unit

Trigonometry (Geom 1, 2; Alg 1-4) ½ unit

Military   May continue or begin

Modern Problems   ½ unit

Music

   Military Band   May continue or begin

   Orchestra   May continue or begin

   Voice   May continue or begin

Part-Time Work Experience

   Diversified Occupations

       3 and 4 or 1 and 2 (2 units)

   Retail Training   1 and 2 (2 units)

   Vocational Office Practice

          1 and 2 (1½ units)

Science

   Chemistry (Alg 1, 2)   1 and 2

   Physics (Alg 1, 2)   1 and 2

Speech (Eng 1-5)

    1 and 2 (½ unit for 1 without 2)

Vocational Courses (Three periods daily)

   Vocational Auto Mechanics

             3 and 4 (2 units)

   Vocational Commercial Art

             3 and 4 (2 units)

   Vocational Drafting   3 and 4 (2 units)

   Vocational Electricity 3 and 4 (2 units)

   Vocational Machine Shop

             3 and 4 (2 units)

   Vocational Printing   3 and 4 (2 units)

   Vocational Sheet Metal

             3 and 4 (2 units)

Source: "Graduation Requirements and Courses Offered, 1951" (Richmond, Va.: John Marshall High School, 1951), pp. 3–6. Mimeographed. Reprinted by permission of Principal Fred B. Dixon.

provision and emphasis, their relationship to certain broad categories or areas. These matters of curriculum practice are described in this section.

Types of Curriculum Experiences

In the light of the concepts of the curriculum and related terms just presented, it is now possible to identify the kinds of experiences included in the curriculum. This may be done, first, in terms of the nature of the activities included, and, second, in terms of their physical location.

The scope of activities in the curriculum is potentially as broad as that of life itself. Actually, because of limitations of facilities, tradition, and imagination, activities are too frequently restricted to reading, writing, speaking, and listening. Also, of course, the maturity of children determines the nature of experiences in which they may appropriately engage. The range of possible activities includes the following, in addition to the basic sensory activities of touch, taste, and smell:

Reading: Books, magazines, pamphlets, newspapers, letters, signs and directions, charts, graphs, maps

Writing: Letters, stories, poems, essays, advertisements, newspaper articles, reports, minutes, summaries, outlines, notes

Seeing: Pictures, paintings, photographs, drawings, filmstrips, slides, movies, television, museum pieces, demonstrations, animals, plants, nature specimens, scientific apparatus, tools, machinery, farms, businesses, industries, institutions, processes, persons, groups, dramatic presentations

Listening: Directions, stories, conversation, discussion, speeches, plays, music, recordings, radio, movies

Talking: Answering and asking questions, conversation, reporting, discussing, debating, speaking formally

Creating: Drawings, paintings, clay modeling, woodworking, metalworking, cartoons, cooking, clothing, murals, floats, playhouses, friezes, maps, charts

Playing: Dramatic play, rhythms, games, dances

Practicing: Reading, writing, spelling, number skills, memorizing, study skills, music skills, art skills, use of tools and machines, typing, cooking, sewing, farm operations

Problem-solving: Reflecting, experimenting, demonstrating, calculating, evaluating, generalizing.

From the standpoint of location, curriculum experiences may occur in the classroom, general or specialized, in various all-school facilities, or out of school. In the classroom, almost any of the types just described may occur, although the traditional ones are reading, writing, and reciting (talking). All-school facilities for learning include the assembly room, visual-aids room, library, study halls, cafeteria, gymnasium, playground, social rooms, museum rooms, and others. Out-of-school experiences include the group excursions which are directly guided by the school and also the individual pupil's use of the learning situations available in churches, theaters, libraries, museums, parks, social centers, and homes.

Thus the experiences which may be included in the curriculum are necessarily limited only by the scope of activities appropriate and possible for children and by the resources of school and community. In practice, they may also be limited by parent indifference or opposition, restrictive school policies and schedules, costs, size of groups and of rooms, and by the lack of training, experience, and imagination of teachers.

Organization of Curriculum Experiences

The experiences of learners may be categorized in various ways. Although many deviations have been developed, the conventional organization is by "subjects." Subjects vary in breadth from such a very broad body of knowledge as language arts to such a specific one as mechanical drawing. Because of this variation related subjects are frequently referred to as being in an "area"; thus, reading and writing are in the language arts area and mechanical drawing and woodworking in the industrial arts area.

The traditional distinction between the "curriculum" (subjects) and the "extracurriculum" (activities) seems unacceptable because of the fallacious implication regarding the respective place and worth of subjects and activities. In the following section of this chapter, we use the term "curriculum experiences" to include both the conventional subjects and the so-called "extracurricular" activities.

A problem of curriculum planning of particular importance in day-to-day classroom teaching, whether in subjects, broad fields, core, or some other over-all pattern, is the organization of instruction. Traditionally instruction has been organized by "lessons" or perhaps by textbook divisions such as chapters, units, or parts. Teaching that is organized in better conformance to principles of learning includes related experiences in a basic division usually called a "unit of work," or "unit of experience," or "instructional unit." In this book we are using the term "instructional unit" or "unit of work" or just "unit" to designate the basic divisions of curriculum and teaching, regardless of the types of organizing centers involved. That is, we conceive of the job of curriculum planning as including the development of instructional units. Chapter 12 deals directly with this task.

Diversity of Curriculum Practices

If the United States had a highly centralized school system with a relatively uniform school program throughout the country, it would be simple to explain what the curriculum includes. Under the American philosophy of education, however, great centralization and uniformity are unacceptable. In the first place, the Constitution has been interpreted to make education a function of the states rather than of the federal government. Furthermore, within the states the principle of local initiative —that is, the responsibility of each community to develop a system of schools adapted to its needs—has had considerable influence. Most important, the democratic philosophy as applied in education has meant that no one set of ideologies, principles, and laws, except those of democracy, should be imposed as the curriculum of all our schools. By and large, American public schools do exhibit great differences. They range in size from a handful of pupils in isolated rural sections to metropolitan high schools enrolling several thousand pupils; in expenditures from less than $100 a pupil annually to more than $500; and in program of studies from a very narrow curriculum of the "three R's" in the elementary school and a minimum list of academic subjects in high school to an elementary program including twenty to thirty subjects and to a high school listing over two hundred named subjects. Also, the elementary school may or may not include the kindergarten and grades seven and eight; there may or may not be a junior high school, and if there is it may include grades six, seven, eight, or seven and eight, or seven, eight and nine; and the high school may include grades seven through twelve, nine through twelve, seven, eight, nine through eleven, or ten through twelve (senior high). In recent years some communities have added junior or community colleges, including grades eleven through fourteen or thirteen and fourteen.

Common Curriculum Areas

It is inevitable that these schools, so variously supported and organized, offer programs which exhibit great differences. Most place heavy emphasis on the subjects, but many have developed other emphases in curriculum organization (see Part 3). Some provide a wide range of out-of-classroom activities and facilities; others are highly academic. Some make extensive efforts to relate school and out-of-school experiences, others function with little regard to the home and community life of children and youth. However, various factors—among them, educational purposes, the division of knowledge into subjects, tradition, the force of college-preparatory requirements, and the influence of national commissions and publications—have resulted in a fairly common group of curriculum areas.

These common areas can be identified by analysis of school programs according to two factors: (1) apparent major behavioral changes or abilities sought; (2) major divisions of the school program. In general, because of the conventional subject organization of the curriculum, a major purpose such as facility in the skills of communication is paralleled by a division of the school program such as language arts. That is, every community expects its schools to teach children to read and write —to communicate—and experiences in this area are always provided by the school. Equally uniform is the expectation of the ability to use number skills, to think in quantitative terms; therefore attention is given to numbers or arithmetic in the curriculum. The schools of every community also provide experiences for the understanding and improvement of social living and of health practices, although wide variations occur in how these areas are developed. Most curriculums also include learning opportunities in science and in the creative and aesthetic fields. Somewhat less uniformly but fairly commonly at the elementary and early secondary levels attention is given to developing certain general work skills, and particularly in the upper high school years to certain special interests relating to further training or work.

In the following sections frequent reference is made to the programs of the schools in these areas, with some note of the range of practice in their nature, organization, and occurrence. Table 2 shows general practice regarding the provision of experience in each area by grade levels —whether generally provided all pupils, or usually on an elective basis, or varying greatly among schools.

APPRAISING CURRENT CURRICULUM PRACTICE

In order to identify the problems prevalent in current curriculum practice it seems necessary to have some basis for appraising the curriculum. Accordingly we present in Table 3 a check list of some characteristics of a good curriculum and then describe how the curriculums of schools in general do and do not exhibit each characteristic. The problems of current practice thus revealed are later summarized and related to the plan and contents of this book.

To appraise completely and accurately the curriculum practices of our many thousands of elementary and secondary schools is an impossible task. We believe that it is a desirable step for educational workers to appraise the curriculums of their own schools, and that the check list in Table 3 will be helpful for this purpose. It may even be difficult to appraise the curriculum of one school because of the differences observed between individual classrooms and teachers, but careful application of this guide to a school's total program should yield valid and important conclusions as to the goodness of the curriculum.

TABLE 2

Provision of Areas of Curriculum Experience

AREA	EXTENT OF PROVISION BY GRADE LEVEL			
	Primary	Intermediate	Junior High	Senior High
Communication Skills	Usually	Usually	Usually	Usually
Social Living	Usually	Usually	Usually	Usually
Quantitative Thinking	Usually	Usually	Usually	Elective
Science	Varies	Varies	Usually	Elective
Health	Usually	Usually	Usually	Usually
Creative and Aesthetic	Varies	Varies	Usually	Elective
Work Skills and Techniques	Varies	Varies	Usually	Elective
Special Interests	Little	Little	Elective	Elective

Note: "Usually" should be interpreted as meaning that some experiences in this area are usually provided at some grade if not all grades of this level to all pupils.

In introducing this appraisal section, we should emphasize the great pride that American educators and the public in general can justifiably take in the amazing achievements made in our relatively short educational history. The American school curriculum *is* good, we believe. As we note shortcomings in the following pages, we in no way mean to detract from the good that has been accomplished and now exists. The American school system is a very significant and complex feature of our entire democratic organization, and its contributions to general social advancement cannot be minimized. As educators we are aware of the heavy obligation of the schools to continue these contributions, and are anxious therefore that this book be a source of help to all persons who share the responsibility of planning the school program. Since the greatest concern must be to make improvements wherever possible, this appraisal deals more with shortcomings than achievements of the present curriculum.

Does the Curriculum Develop Social Understandings?

Several curriculum areas are largely or entirely devoted to the development of understandings about society, social problems, and social relationships. Skills for communication with one's fellows are prerequisites of successful social living, and instruction in them in one form or another is almost universal in each year of school. The entire area of social living, which also includes a variety of experiences at every grade level, should be directly related to the purpose of social understandings. Much of the material in science units and classes can be, and frequently is, approached with regard to the influence of scientific development on human welfare. Health, even when approached through problems of personal health and hygiene, is a matter of social concern and may be so developed. Many curriculum experiences in the areas of work skills and special interests also give attention to such questions as the social conditions and problems of workers, the relations of vocations and social and governmental policies, and social aspects of various leisure-time activities.

Despite the dominance of social understandings as a curriculum aim, we Americans have to admit that our social literacy is not all it could be. The misinformation, ignorance, and lack of informed opinion of the general public—all products to some degree of schooling—is well known. A 1948 study of opinion polls, carried on during a five-year period by national polling organizations, revealed that those who could not answer questions indicating factual knowledge of various kinds amounted to nearly 50 per cent of the sample population.[1] The widespread failure of our citizens to even cast their votes suggests a major job for citizenship education. The moral irresponsibility of some adults indicates a further inadequacy of education for social living. Our continued social problems of a wide variety—crime, delinquency, housing, racial and religious intolerance, economic conflict, inadequate support of schools and other social institutions, broken homes—all are evidence of the need for better education to develop social understanding.

Certainly the school curriculum cannot be blamed for all our social ills. Indeed, we school people can probably take much credit for the social progress Americans have made. Our only point is that it cannot be assumed that the present school program is adequate when there remains so much room for social improvement. And many deficiencies can be found in the programs of individual schools. Only a minority of schools are likely to show evidence of pupil participation in the government and

[1] Helen Crossley and George Kerry Smith, "What the Polls Show," *Educational Leadership,* 6:77 (November), 1948.

TABLE 3

A Check List for Appraising a School's Curriculum

(To be used as a guide for study of a particular school's total program for learners)

CRITERIA	APPRAISAL ITEMS TO NOTE STRENGTHS—WEAKNESSES —NEEDS

I. A GOOD CURRICULUM DEVELOPS SOCIAL UNDERSTANDINGS

A. The school program includes opportunity for pupils to participate in the government and other institutional functions of the school.

B. Social studies and other classes emphasize understandings of social backgrounds and problems as appropriate to pupils' maturities.

C. Children acquire facts and skills required for making group and individual decisions and judgments.

D. Rules and regulations recognize the rights and responsibilities of both groups and individuals.

E. The school activities exemplify social principles discussed in classrooms.

II. A GOOD CURRICULUM PROMOTES MAXIMUM PERSONAL DEVELOPMENT

A. Teachers have adequate information about each learner.

B. Learning situations provide maximum consideration to the unique characteristics of each learner.

C. The school determines individual interests and abilities through varied exploratory experiences.

D. The program fosters desirable personality traits.

E. Provision is made for the various phases of individual development—emotional, social, intellectual, physical.

F. The curriculum promotes individual development rather than conformity to some hypothetical standard of development.

G. The school offers a wide range of special-interest opportunities.

III. A GOOD CURRICULUM PROMOTES CONTINUITY OF EXPERIENCE

A. Classroom practices indicate concern for the maturity and learning sequence of each learner.

B. Teachers consult interests, past experiences, and other leads from learners in planning next experiences.

C. Teachers identify the relationships between present, past, and future experiences of a related type.

D. Teachers of the same learners, and past and present teachers of the same learners, exchange information regarding these learners' experiences.

E. If repeated, group experiences, such as excursions, serve different purposes.

TABLE 3 *continued*

IV. A GOOD CURRICULUM PROVIDES FOR ALL EDUCATIONAL GOALS

   A. The faculty has defined comprehensive educational goals.
   B. The total curriculum provides learning experiences for achieving each goal.
   C. In planning the experiences of pupils from year to year, teachers consider the total scope of goals.
   D. Teachers select instructional units in terms of the specific goals to be served.
   E. Goal-serving experiences provide for the varying abilities and needs of all learners.

V. A GOOD CURRICULUM MAINTAINS BALANCE AMONG ALL GOALS

   A. The school program provides for attention to each goal commensurate with its importance.
   B. The total plan of curriculum areas, required and elective subjects, and school activities reflects careful planning with respect to all goals.
   C. Guidance of each individual provides for him a program which is well balanced in terms of his needs and capacities.
   D. The school plant and facilities provide for attention to each goal commensurate with its importance.

VI. A GOOD CURRICULUM EMERGES IN LEARNING SITUATIONS

   A. Written curriculum plans encourage curriculum development in learning situations according to their unique possibilities.
   B. The plans for instructional units include alternative procedures and provision for pupil-teacher planning.
   C. The selection of learning experiences reflects careful pre-planning by teachers and equally careful attention to the demands of the learning situation.
   D. Pupil-teacher relations encourage pupil participation in the planning of learning experiences.
   E. The teaching and learning groups modify their plans as needs arise.

VII. A GOOD CURRICULUM USES EFFECTIVE LEARNING EXPERIENCES AND NEEDED RESOURCES

   A. Learning experiences employ the most effective situations available.
   B. Learning experiences are planned and developed so that pupils see purpose, meaning, and significance in each activity.
   C. Learners select their own materials and activities as frequently as possible and desirable.
   D. Learning experiences utilize all needed resources that are available.
   E. Teachers use resources as efficiently as possible to bring about maximum outcomes of the learning experience.

other institutional functions of the school. Many would not rate high on the criterion that "the school activities exemplify social principles discussed in classrooms." Our observations indicate that poor, frequently undemocratic processes prevail in many schools in the choice of pupil leaders, in the determination of school rules and regulations, in the development of plans in classes, clubs, and councils. Possibly the chief deficiency of many school curriculums is their failure to use the organized life of the school and the social groups of the classroom to develop appropriate understandings of how individuals operate cooperatively and successfully as group members.

Much of the social learning in school seems to occur without deliberate direction by the school. Adequate curriculum plans would provide for more group situations in school to be developed so as to bring about respect for principles of group organization and procedure as well as for understanding of how these principles are cooperatively applied. Schools are challenged to become real laboratories for developing social learning. As this opportunity is used, boys and girls learn how to respect and appreciate democracy by living democratically, to respect individuals for their own worth rather than according to artificial criteria, and to achieve social recognition by constructive acts.

Does the Curriculum Promote Optimum Personal Development?

Certain phases of the curriculum are deliberately planned to achieve the aim of personal development. In 1950 thirty-three states required by law or state board regulation that health be included in the secondary school curriculum; at that time, high schools in only four states did not have health instruction available either as a required or an elective subject. Although what "included" means is generally a matter for interpretation by local schools, this survey reported that health instruction had been increasing and that the quality of instruction had been improving.[2] Formal drills and calisthenics have declined in importance in physical education, the general program being increasingly concerned with developing interests in recreational activities. In addition to games corresponding to interests at particular levels of maturity, activities which carry over into adult recreation are introduced as soon as children can enjoy them. Concern is also exhibited for physical development through the selection of experiences in the light of the physical maturities and needs of children included.

Modern schools also serve needs of personal development through a

[2] See H. F. Kilander, *Health Instruction in the Secondary Schools* (U. S. Office of Education Pamphlet No. 110; Washington, D.C.: Government Printing Office, 1951), pp. 1–6.

wide variety of opportunities for creative and aesthetic expression and for development of special interests. In the area of creative and aesthetic experiences, the emphasis in both art and music education has been changing from skills and techniques alone to include appreciation and creativity. Especially in the elementary grades, language arts, dramatization, rhythms, and dancing offer rich opportunity for self-expression and the development of interest. In the high school, a great variety of elective courses and "extracurricular" activities helps youth develop rich, abiding interests.

Perhaps one of the most significant movements toward optimum personal development of learners has been that of child study and guidance. Great progress has been made in the refinement of techniques for learning about individual differences. In most schools significant data are available about pupils; in some, various types of special services are available to help individuals with many problems of mental, social, emotional, and physical development. There is a tragic gap, however, between knowledge of individual differences and what is done about them. Despite the known wide variations in learning ability and achievement, some type of standard expectations is still maintained in most school curriculums.

It is known, for example, that the range of a random group of six-year-olds entering the first grade will be about four years in general mental development, and that this range will have increased to about eight years by the time the same children have become twelve-year-olds. Furthermore, efforts to group such children homogeneously by ability will result in only about a 20 per cent reduction of the range of reading ability, for example.[3] The implications follow that individual children in a particular age or grade group must be expected to achieve quite different levels, that each child's level of achievement is determined by his unique characteristics, and that any expectation of optimum next levels must therefore be in terms of individual learners.

What are the common conflicting practices? Their underlying assumptions are stated succinctly by Cook as follows:

> The idea of homogeneous groups of pupils receiving uniform instruction by mass educational techniques dies hard. The assumptions persist: that grade levels signify rather definite stages of educational achievement, that the course of study for a grade is the prescribed academic requirement to be administered uniformly to all pupils, that all pupils in a grade should be capable of coping successfully with the work outlined for that grade, that a pupil should not be promoted to a grade until he is able to do the work outlined for that

[3] Walter W. Cook, "Individual Differences and Curriculum Practice," *Journal of Educational Psychology,* 39:141–143 (March), 1948.

grade, that when individual differences are provided for, all pupils can be brought up to standard, that maintaining a passing mark results in homogeneous instructional groups, and that when relative homogeneity of a class does not prevail, it is the result of poor teaching or lax standards.[4]

More specifically, here are some gaps between what is known and what is done about individual differences in many situations:

1. Although children in the same learning group differ in rates of learning, all in the group are frequently assigned the same job—that is, the same arithmetic problems, spelling words, textbook exercises, and the like—to be accomplished by the same deadline.

2. Although children in a particular group may be expected to differ in reading ability, they are made to read the same textbooks with the expectation that each will understand the material almost equally well.

3. Children entering a grade or a class will be at different levels of development and will continue developing at different rates, but they are expected to achieve the same level of development in skills and understandings by the end of the year. In fact, they are sometimes promoted only if they have achieved such a level.

4. Although each learner's characteristics and needs are different, "minimum essentials" are defined in terms of skills, facts, understandings, or projects for all members of a particular learning group.

5. The optimum progress of each pupil will be different from that of any other pupil, but his progress is compared with some assumed average or ideal called a "standard" and he is given marks according to comparison of the level attained with the standard. Thus a transfer pupil who enters Grade 2 as a nonreader but learns beginning reading during the year would in some situations be considered as below the standard and retained for a second year so that he might ultimately be promoted to Grade 3 as a child of third-grade reading ability.

6. It is known that individuals learn differently, but teachers give uniform tests to measure how much has been learned of what is included on the test, and then compare results of different children with some assumed standard. In some schools test scores of 100 per cent are still regarded as the ideal, but 75 per cent is used as a standard of accomplishment. Hence the pupil who may have been able to score 75 per cent originally and now scores 100 per cent is considered above average and the one who would have scored 0 per cent originally and now scores 50 per cent is below average. Which pupil has made greater progress in terms of whatever the test evaluates?

---

[4] *Ibid.*, p. 141. Reprinted by permission of Warwick & York, Inc.

7. Although children are known to have widely varying needs, interests, and abilities, schools compel them to engage in activities that may be appropriate to only a limited number of needs, interests, and abilities. Specifically, learning activities in many classrooms are confined to reading, answering questions, and writing papers.

The list above could be extended, but it suffices to indicate the size of the gap between what is known about personal development and what is done in many situations. Although this gap is being closed in an encouraging number of schools and classrooms, it probably remains the widest and the most difficult to bridge in American education. Every curriculum plan must resolve the issue of individual differences versus group standards. Difficult as the resolution may be in the face of tradition, limited facilities, and large classes, it is certain that the school program will not move from the "mass educational techniques" cited above without curriculum planning which recognizes the facts of individual differences and provides means for dealing with these differences.

Does the Curriculum Promote Continuity of Experience?

Continuity of experience or proper sequence of learning is a consistent aim of curriculum planning. Within each of the curriculum areas some order of learning experiences is generally considered desirable, and grade placement through courses of study, textbooks, uniform assignments, and other devices has been widely used to fix the sequence. Unfortunately, such devices assume that continuity of experience can be fixed for a group, whereas real sequence is an individual matter.

In some curriculum areas, mostly those in which the development of skills is emphasized, the individual nature of sequence in learning has also been recognized, and instruction has been planned so as to help each learner proceed step by step in accordance with his previous experiences and abilities. Thus in better elementary school practice wide variations in reading ability are expected, and each child is helped from where he is through successive steps in the sequence of reading skills.

However, observation of school practices in teaching the skills indicates great variations in the extent to which continuity of experience is developed. Such practices as the following ones, which are frequently observed, seem clearly in conflict with the basic principle of building one experience upon another, or continuity:

1. Boys and girls are required to drill on spelling words from some published list or spelling text without regard to whether these words have meaning for the children concerned.

2. Children are required to solve problems in arithmetic textbooks

or workbooks without regard to whether they really understand the problems, and to memorize tables of measures not used by children.

3. Pupils are made to memorize rules of grammar applying to usage which is not within their experience.

4. Drills on the use of the dictionary, reference books, tables of contents, and indexes are conducted through meaningless processes instead of in connection with information learners wish to secure.

5. The writing of letters, paragraphs, and so forth is based on uniform directions applying to written forms outside the pupils' experience, and in advance of their recognition of the purpose of these forms.

6. Exercises to develop facility in particular skills such as reading maps, using charts, or interpreting tables are assigned uniformly without reference to pupils' readiness and need for these skills.

The criterion of continuity of learning experience is violated in several ways other than in the teaching of skills. Continuity may be horizontal as well as vertical, and many learners are constantly moving from one experience to another and unrelated one because of departmentalized schedules and fixed time allotments. The lack of relationship of experiences in and out of school as well as from classroom to classroom interferes with the learner's own sequence of experience. Abrupt changes in school schedules created by outside demands or administrative necessity also violate continuity of learning. Repetition—of the same excursion or film or other activity from class to class or from year to year—is another deterrent to continuity.

However, the chief violation we observe regarding this criterion is in the great reliance that many curriculum plans place on the assumption that all learners follow the same sequence of experience. That is, the patterns of grade placement assume that all learners in a particular grade should have the same experience at the same time. The fact is that all learners of a particular grade not only should not, but indeed cannot, have the same experience at the same time. Because of the relationship of previous experiences to new ones and the variety of backgrounds of individual learners, it is virtually impossible for all members of a particular group to have identical interactions with their environmental stimuli, that is, to have the same experiences. For example, even an experience as interesting as the excursion of a first-grade group to the farm has different meanings to learners because of the varied experiential backgrounds they have for understanding what they see in this new environment. To summarize, continuity of experience is a criterion for application to each learner, and the usual curriculum plans which assume identical progress of individuals make a fallacious assumption regarding the nature of learning and experience.

One of the most favorable developments in current curriculum practice is the variety of means being employed to help teachers understand the experiential backgrounds of boys and girls. The use of cumulative records and other data, conferences of teachers having the same pupils in departmentalized programs, and conferences of past and present teachers of the same learners are increasingly employed to help teachers take learners from the point where they are. Such practices are in the direction of helping to develop a proper continuity of experience for each person. Exchange of information among teachers also helps to reduce repetitious experiences which militate against achievement of progressively higher levels of understanding. Parent-teacher planning is also being used more and more, especially in elementary schools, to promote a proper continuity of experiences in and out of school. School-wide planning too, is helping to provide desirable continuity throughout many schools.

Does the Curriculum Provide for All Educational Goals?

As indicated in Chapter 7, the recent history of the school curriculum is primarily one of trying to achieve wider educational goals. In addition to the three R's, which constituted almost its entire curriculum at one time, the elementary school now provides experiences in citizenship, physical, health, and safety education, in science, in creative and aesthetic areas, and in work skills. In addition to its traditional program of subjects for college-preparatory purposes, the secondary school offers a wide variety of courses in each curriculum area to provide for special interests and a range of activities designed to meet the needs of all youth. Although we give a more extensive list of goals in Chapter 7, we may note here that the youth who has completed the twelfth grade of an American school system should have attained some degree of facility in the following curriculum areas:

1. The skills of communication
2. Operations involving numbers and quantitative thinking
3. Relations with other people
4. Interpretation of scientific phenomena, and use of the scientific method of thinking
5. Care of the individual's health
6. Creative expression and the appreciation of aesthetic qualities
7. General skills and techniques of work
8. Special, individual interests relating to future activities

How well his curriculum has provided for his educational needs is another matter, of course. We believe that in theory almost any educational goal might be attacked in one or more of the usual curriculum areas but that in practice such definite patterns of subject matter have developed for most areas as to limit consideration of any need not directly related. Thus, many of the goals we list in Chapter 7, such as the following, which are commonly agreed upon, may not even be considered in many school programs: achieving emotional stability, preparing for marriage and family life, developing understandings needed by consumers, planning for economic independence. Furthermore, there is reason to doubt whether the usual curriculum areas generally achieve success in meeting the educational needs to which they directly aim. In the first place, there is great diversity of practice in the extent to which these areas are developed in the curriculum. For example, the special-interest areas included in the curriculum are greatly limited in many schools. Similarly, provisions in the areas of social living, health, creative and aesthetic experiences, and work skills vary from an inadequate minimum to very comprehensive programs. For youth whose experiences are in the limited programs, the needs to which these areas would be directed are served at best only partially.

In the second place, certain facts offer conclusive evidence that for the adult population the needs have not been met whether or not the schools alone are to be blamed. Thus, the estimated 10,000,000 persons in the United States who are unable to read and write well enough to qualify as competent citizens give evidence that communication skills have not been developed to a maximum level. Poor reading, speaking, and writing habits are matters of common observation. The widespread reading of inferior literature indicates need for improving the entire program of instruction in reading for leisure. Inadequacies of education for social living have already been noted. Draft rejections for health reasons place some blame on the school health program. The known susceptibility of millions of adults to propaganda and superstition is evidence of neglect of the development of scientific thinking. The dominance of commercialized recreation of questionable aesthetic value suggests neglect in the creative and aesthetic field. The poor work skills of large numbers of homemakers indicate inadequate experience in the elementary jobs to be done "around the house." The frustration that many youth have in securing and holding jobs points to the need for more vocational guidance and preparation in the special-interests areas.

Although some of the current literature of education—and even articles in popular magazines—criticizes the curriculum for failing to meet fundamental educational needs, it is difficult to substantiate the charge objectively and statistically. There are almost as many statements of needs as there are writers in the curriculum field, and comprehensive statistical data regarding how well the schools meet specific needs are lacking. However, common observation generally validates the criticisms. For example, did your school meet your own educational needs adequately? The facts are that our educational needs are considerably more extensive than the school program has as yet been able to approach in any comprehensive fashion, and that such approaches as have been made do not succeed with all individuals.

Probably the most complete data on opinions of recent graduates, parents, and teachers regarding the effectiveness of schools in meeting fundamental needs have been gathered in Illinois. Extensive "opinionnaires" were used in sixty Illinois communities participating in the Illinois Secondary School Curriculum Program to determine what recent graduates, parents, and teachers thought about the relationship of the programs of their particular schools to fifty-six life needs of youth. These needs were variously subsumed under such headings as making a living, managing personal finances wisely, living healthfully and safely, developing an effective personality, spending leisure time wholesomely and enjoyably, taking an effective part in civic affairs, preparing for a happy marriage and intelligent home management, and making effective use of educational opportunities. A partial summary of the findings of this comprehensive study follows:

a. From half to all of the recent graduates (the last three graduating classes in the 60 Illinois communities included in the study) said that they were already encountering all but two (marriage and parenthood) of the 56 life problems.

b. The parents in these 60 Illinois communities overwhelmingly endorsed the idea that it is the proper job of the high school to give help to pupils in reference to their immediate and soon-to-be encountered life problems:
   1) Over half of the parents endorsed all of the 56 life problems around which the study centered. . . .
   3) Three fourths or more thus endorsed 70% of these life problems.

c. The teacher "vote" was even higher:
   1) Over half of the high school teachers in these communities endorsed all of the life problems around which the study centered as being the proper concern of the high school. . . .
   3) Three fourths or more of the teachers likewise endorsed 90% of these life problems.

d. But here is how the recent graduates appraised their schools' performance:

  1) Only one of these 56 life problems had been treated with reasonable
  adequacy by the high school in the opinion of as many as three
  fourths of the recent graduates. . . .

  3) Only 23 of these 56 life problems had been given reasonably adequate treatment in the opinion of as many as half of these respondents.

e. And here is the teachers' over-all appraisal:

  1) Only one of the 56 life problems of youth had been treated with
  reasonable adequacy by the high school in the opinion of as many
  as three fourths of the teachers in the schools in question. . . .

  3) Only nine of the 56 life problems of youth had been given reasonably adequate treatments in the opinion of as many as half of the
  teachers.[5]

This study gives adequate evidence that, for the communities studied,
neither recent graduates nor teachers felt that the schools were meeting
the needs which both they and the parents felt the schools should serve.
We believe that evidence elsewhere would support the same conclusion
and, further, that this points to the need for curriculum planning. Indeed, the recommendation made by the Illinois study was that there
should be in each community "a local in-service action study designed to
help the total faculty, in concert with a panel of its parents and pupil
leaders" to carry on a program of comprehensive curriculum planning.[6]
Although the many successful curriculum improvement efforts of
past decades have been concerned with all levels of the school program,
recent criticisms by educators have most frequently been directed toward
the secondary school. This is to be explained in part by the relatively
recent development of universal secondary education. However, educators
cannot afford to be complacent about the elementary school program. A
recent publication on evaluation in elementary education makes this
point:

  The progress achieved in elementary education during the first fifty
  years of this century is a tribute to the men and women who demonstrated in productive action their faith in democracy, and who believed in equal educational opportunities for all American children.

[5] Harold C. Hand, *Prospectus of the Local Area Consensus Studies* (Circular Series
A, No. 51, Illinois Secondary School Curriculum Program, Bulletin No. 15; Springfield,
Ill.: Superintendent of Public Instruction, State of Illinois, March, 1951), pp. 5–6.
Reprinted by permission of the Superintendent.
  [6] *Ibid.,* p. 8.

. . . Adults can be pleased with this accomplishment, but they dare not discontinue their efforts to secure improvements in elementary education. Continuous evaluation must be made of the goals and practices of the schools with reference to such persistent and pressing problems as the impact of applied science on American life, the continuing international crisis, and the increased school population.[7]

Does the Curriculum Maintain Balance among All Goals?

In applying the criterion of balance, one again runs into the inconsistency between curriculum plans for groups and the needs of individual learners. Thus curriculum plans may incorporate provisions for all educational goals and suggest requirements, time allotments, and other means of ensuring balanced attention to each goal. But in the learning situation one individual needs far more time than another to acquire skill in speaking, for example. Not all teachers interpret suggestions as such; sometimes very fine suggestions are considered to be requirements so that all pupils are held to a uniform learning procedure which creates lack of balance for many individuals.

Not all curriculum plans provide means whereby teachers may attempt to maintain balance among the goals. Inadequate school facilities and other limitations may make impossible planning for the science, health, and creative and aesthetic areas, for example, in elementary schools or for the work skills and special-interests areas in secondary schools. Science is still in the process of being included in the elementary school curriculum, and there are many obstacles to overcome: teachers' fears of being unable to do an adequate job, the relatively poor preparation of elementary teachers in science, the inadequacy of equipment and supplies. One can visit schools in America in which the physical arrangements indicate almost complete neglect of pupils' health and safety, and others in which every care has been taken to make the school environment as healthful as possible. Similarly, the range of health instruction is from no services and no systematic instruction to complete health units with medical personnel employed by the schools and a definite program of health instruction.

Although experiences in any curriculum area may have creative and aesthetic possibilities, classroom observation indicates the widest variation in the extent to which these possibilities are utilized. Even systematic provision of experiences in art, music, literature, dramatization, rhythms, and dancing is woefully inadequate in many schools. Regarding work skills and techniques, one finds elementary school children in some cen-

[7] Harold G. Shane and E. T. McSwain, *Evaluation and the Elementary Curriculum* (New York: Henry Holt and Company, Inc., 1951), pp. 3–4. Reprinted by permission of Henry Holt and Company, Inc.

ters carrying on worth-while construction activities but in others lacking any facilities for learning to use tools. Junior high schools typically offer exploratory experiences in industrial arts and homemaking, but many American school children are still having highly academic experiences in Grades 7 and 8 and on through their four-year high schools. A study in 1947 showed that 54 per cent of a sample group of high schools had some

PLATE 2. ELEMENTARY SCHOOL CHILDREN LIKE SCIENCE. *They find resources for studying science all about them. (Courtesy of the Fort Worth, Texas, Public Schools)*

kind of work-experience program for their pupils, but even in these schools many pupils did not participate in the program.[8] Although many high schools offer vocational subjects, the enrollment is elective and only a portion of high school students have an opportunity to learn basic work skills and techniques included even in the prevocational courses. Participation in the activity program is determined by many factors, such as the activities offered, the time at which they are available, the expenses in-

[8] American Association of School Administrators, *The Expanding Role of Education* (Twenty-sixth Yearbook; Washington, D.C.: The Association, 1948), p. 164.

volved, and the conflict with classes. Hence it is to be reiterated that whether a learner's curriculum is balanced among all educational goals is determined in large part by the facilities of the school he attends, the comprehensiveness of its program, and the relationship of that program to social aims and his individual needs.

One of the chief reasons for a lack of balance in learners' educational programs is the influence of college-preparatory emphases and traditions. Although affecting most directly the high school curriculum, these factors also push down into the elementary school indirectly because of the pressure that high school requirements sometimes place on the elementary grades to give priorities to the more academic learnings such as grammar exercises. The basic factors regarding the college-preparatory influence are well known: the high school originally recognized as its basic function the preparation of its highly selected and relatively small population for college; the colleges considered certain subjects, especially mathematics, foreign languages, English, and history, as essential for college success, and these subjects were generally required by the high schools; now that three out of every four youth of high school age attend high school and only about one of every three who graduate (or about one of every six who attend) go to college, the pattern of subjects once required is still taken by most youth, regardless of future destinations. These are the facts. The gap between knowledge and practice comes at two points: (1) knowledge of the new population should result in less emphasis for all pupils on subjects considered of value only as preparation for further study; (2) knowledge of what is required for success in college brings into question the validity of previous assumptions regarding a desirable program of studies for college-bound youth.

As to the first point, less emphasis is given the college-preparatory pattern than was true a generation ago. Alternative programs of study are offered in larger high schools. The pupil who follows a college-preparatory pattern often does so now at the insistence of his parents rather than because of the advice of the high school counselors. In some states efforts are being made by colleges and high schools to remove the pressure of uniform requirements for recommended graduates of approved high schools. Many colleges have modified their requirements. However, small high schools unable to offer optional programs frequently offer only highly academic courses, and many colleges still have very definite course requirements for admission. The fact remains that large numbers of high school youth who never go to college pursue a program of studies that is highly academic in nature and which offers too little opportunity for the general education and exploratory experiences that these youth need.

We may question also the basic assumption underlying college entrance requirements—that certain subjects prepare for college better
than others. That this assumption continues may be implied from the
common requirement as late as 1946 by a majority of colleges and universities of four years of English in high school, one year of algebra, one
year of plane geometry, two years of a foreign language, one year of
natural science, and one year of social studies.[9] But research has found no
particular relationship between the pattern of subjects taken in high
school and success in college. The first major research in this area was the
Eight-Year Study, beginning in 1932 and conducted under the auspices
of the Commission on the Relation of School and College of the Progressive Education Association. By agreement with certain colleges, thirty
secondary schools departed from the usual preparatory programs. The
records in college of 1,475 graduates of these thirty high schools were
compared with those of matched graduates of conventional high schools.
The two groups were compared on many criteria of college success, and
there was no evidence that the graduates who had taken the traditional
preparatory programs were more successful. In fact, the graduates of the
experimental programs exceeded in several respects, such as total grade
average, academic and nonacademic honors, leadership abilities, and interest in current affairs.[10] Leonard's review of various studies dealing
with the relation of college success and college entrance requirements
concluded: "Clearly the assumption that college success depends on pursuing any prescribed subjects in high school cannot longer be accepted by
thinking people." [11] It is clear that curriculum planning lags far behind
the evidence as to what is college preparation. This point was definitely
established by a 1949 review of a wide sampling of reports of researches
dealing with factors related to scholastic success in colleges of arts and
sciences and teachers colleges. This comprehensive review reached the
following conclusions:

> The data reveal that many colleges are basing their entrance re-
> quirements on factors which do not have adequate value in predict-
> ing success in college, and therefore deny entrance to many students
> who should be admitted. The absence of any significant correlation
> between amount and pattern of high school subjects and college
> scholarship persists in spite of the broadening of high school
> curricula to include vocational subjects and the reluctance of

[9] Benjamin Fine, *Admission to American Colleges* (New York: Harper & Brothers,
1946), p. 54.
[10] See Wilford M. Aiken, *The Story of the Eight-Year Study* (New York: Harper &
Brothers, 1942), pp. 111–112, for the detailed comparisons.
[11] J. Paul Leonard, "Can We Face the Evidence on College-Entrance Requirements?" *School Review*, 53:332 (June), 1945.

colleges to vary in a corresponding degree from the original scholastic curriculum heavily loaded with verbal training.[12]

Does the Curriculum Emerge in Learning Situations?

Wide variations exist from classroom to classroom as well as from school to school in relation to the criterion of flexibility. Resourceful teachers can be observed guiding group discussion and planning so skillfully that plans are made and modified as needs arise. Curriculum-planning groups in many school systems are developing resource units from which teachers secure suggestions for activities and materials to be explored cooperatively with learners in classroom situations.

Contrary observations, however, show that pupil-teacher planning in many situations is nonexistent or poorly executed. In some relatively few instances, pupil-teacher planning is interpreted by teachers to mean that no preplanning is necessary, and the observer sees utter confusion. Many teachers lack the skills of discussion leadership. Resource units are not available in most school situations, and some teachers also lack experience in preparing their own unit plans with or without the guidance of resource units.

Flexibility is greatly limited in many situations by the restrictive nature of ground-to-be-covered requirements or, perhaps more often, by traditional notions that such requirements exist. Courses of study which prescribe specific units to be studied at particular times definitely restrict teachers in modifying plans for their classes. The practice of adopting and using uniform textbooks is a restriction of major importance if funds are lacking with which to purchase supplementary and alternative materials. Regulations regarding the number of minutes that particular subjects are to be taught each day or week create severe difficulties for teachers in adjusting plans to unexpected needs. Even questions and criticisms by supervisors which imply that teachers are failing to cover the ground are frequently cited by teachers as reasons for an inflexible curriculum. Grade and departmental examinations in elementary and secondary schools sometimes have the force of narrowing teaching to the skills and understandings on which learners are to be examined.

Schedules perhaps constitute the major barrier to a flexible curriculum. Under the departmentalized program which characterizes secondary schools and still prevails in some elementary schools, pupils are constantly moving from one classroom situation to another and planning must always anticipate the possible frustration of the need for more or less time

[12] Harley F. Garrett, "A Review and Interpretation of Investigations of Factors Related to Scholastic Success in Colleges of Arts and Science and Teachers Colleges," *Journal of Experimental Education,* 18:130 (December), 1949.

than the bell permits. Even in the self-contained classroom of the elementary school, undue concern for so-called "minimum essentials," time allotments, and daily time schedules may make for inflexibility. However, the schedule problem is being solved in some schools by core-curriculum plans with their provision of longer periods, unit plans for departmentalized work, skillful use of records of previous class sessions, and arrangements for schedule modifications to fit particular time demands for an excursion or other experience.

Our conception of an emergent curriculum is based on the point of view that democratic classroom procedures result in better learning on the part of pupils. A recent study of democratic procedures in elementary classrooms cited the following characteristics of a democratic classroom:

A) There is evidence of pupil purposes.

B) Freedom exists through standards established by the group, for the group welfare.

C) Pupils participate in planning and evaluating their work.

D) In the curriculum there is emphasis upon pupil growth rather than upon subject matter acquisition *per se.*

E) Students are given the opportunity of governing themselves, with adult guidance.

F) There is an atmosphere of cooperation, of sharing, of helping, of group welfare.

G) A flexible classroom schedule exists.

H) Wholesome teacher-pupil, pupil-pupil, and teacher-administrator relationships exist.

I) There is school-community cooperation.[13]

Evaluative measures used to determine the extent to which practices in a sample of 65 elementary classrooms were democratic, as defined by these criteria, gave an average "democraticness" score of 61 per cent, with the range within classes on all items of 39 to 89 per cent, and, on the item of pupil participation in planning and evaluating their work, an average score of 61 per cent.[14] Our own observation indicates that a flexible curriculum as evidenced by effective pupil participation in planning is certainly not to be found in a higher proportion of American classrooms than shown in this study. The evident fact is that current curriculum practice has not yet succeeded in putting into full operation those principles of democracy and learning which place high value on the active participation of learners in curriculum planning. These principles and

[13] Mary Beatrice Dalton, "Classroom Democracy—Functionally Defined and Measured" (unpublished doctoral dissertation; St. Louis, Mo.: Washington University, June, 1949), p. 5.

[14] *Ibid.,* p. 123.

their implementation are discussed more fully at many points in this book (see especially Chapters 6 and 13).

Does the Curriculum Use Effective Learning Experiences and Needed Resources?

The hold of the recitation method of teaching is perhaps as conclusive evidence as can be found of the gap between knowledge of learning theory and the practice of teaching, especially in secondary education. As early as 1912 an investigation of the recitation threw into light its almost ridiculous reliance on a long series of minute questions as a teaching device.[15] Thayer's book, optimistically entitled *The Passing of the Recitation,* appeared in 1928. Yet there is reason to believe that the recitation is still a very usual procedure in secondary school classrooms. Burton's observations of teaching practices led to the following conclusion:

> Vigorous pointed criticisms of the formal question-and-answer recitation for forty years has had little effect upon the so-called practical teacher. Precise surveys show, unhappily, that this type of recitation based on memorized material still predominates in school. The recitation as commonly used is probably the most fantastic of the vestigial remains of outmoded methods which still operate in the school.[16]

We may note the following ways in which the recitation procedure violates the principle of flexibility:

1. Every individual is unique, having different capacities, interests, and needs—but the recitation procedure assumes that all students will learn certain subject matter at the same time.

2. Individuals learn most effectively through attempting to solve problems of their own—but the recitation procedure gives them little opportunity to propose or investigate their own problems.

3. The function of a teacher is primarily that of guiding learners to identify and solve significant problems—but in the recitation both the identification and the solution of problems are already determined by teacher, textbook, or other authority.

We should also note that the recitation procedure is not confined to secondary schools. In elementary schools it is sometimes used in certain curriculum areas, especially social studies, science, and language; more-

---

[15] Romiett Stevens, *The Question as a Measure of Efficiency* (Teachers College Contributions to Education No. 48; New York: Bureau of Publications, Teachers College, Columbia University, 1912).

[16] William H. Burton, "Implications for Organization of Instruction and Instructional Adjuncts," Chapter IX in *Learning and Instruction* (Forty-ninth Yearbook of the National Society for the Study of Education, Part I; Chicago: The University of Chicago Press, 1950), p. 237.

over, the drill procedures which predominate in many elementary class-rooms at all levels are essentially the same type of memorize-recite expe-riences. Drill we believe to have a very important place in the curriculum, but only in keeping with its relationship to the learning process. Skills are learned in three steps: first, the learner must wish to acquire the skill; second, he must understand how to use it; and third, and only after the first and second steps, he needs whatever amount of practice or drill is required to attain the desired level of efficiency in the process. The ineffec-tive teaching of skills we have already noted is generally due to violations of these steps in elementary and secondary classrooms, for learners are frequently forced to try to practice skills they neither want to learn nor understand how to do. We must therefore regard the widespread use of drill procedures, workbooks, exercises in memory work, and the like, on a uniform basis as a problem for curriculum planning.

Despite the foregoing criticisms of classroom procedure, there must be noted the steady increase of interest in in-service education activities to help teachers plan more effective procedures, in publications for the same purpose, and in the reports of experimentation in classroom pro-cedures. Most encouraging is the great increase in the past two decades in the types and numbers of resources for learning used in American schools (see Chapter 14). Great expansion has occurred in the use of community resources, in the number of attractive and stimulating classrooms and other school facilities, and especially in the use of audiovisual aids of all sorts. Library facilities have expanded, classroom libraries have been de-veloped, and wonderful progress has been made by publishers in the de-velopment of attractive textbooks and other printed materials. That further improvement is needed in regard to resources is indicated by evidence of inadequate expenditures for instructional supplies and mate-rials in many systems and the wide variations in expenditures for this purpose between schools,[17] and especially by the great differences evident in teachers' know-how for making wise use of the available resources.[18]

SUMMARY: PROBLEMS OF CURRENT CURRICULUM PRACTICE

The foregoing appraisal of current curriculum practice has revealed many problems for effective curriculum planning to solve. Since the re-mainder of this book is devoted to principles and practices of such curric-

[17] See Educational Research Service, "Per Pupil Expenditures for Instructional Materials and Supplies, 1950–51, in 107 School Systems" (Washington, D.C.: National Education Association, November, 1952).

[18] See, for many helpful illustrations on the use of resources in the learning environ-ment, Association for Supervision and Curriculum Development, *Creating a Good Environment for Learning* (1954 Yearbook; Washington, D.C.: The Association, 1954).

ulum planning, we are summarizing here the problems we have noted and pointing out their relationships to the organization of our book.

Need for Understanding Basic Concepts of Curriculum and Curriculum Planning

We believe that educational workers in general need more uniform understanding of basic concepts of curriculum and curriculum planning. For example, the following confusions have been noted in the foregoing section:

1. Different meanings attached to the term "curriculum" and related concepts with resultant differences in practice

2. Inconsistent interpretations of the relation of the curriculum to learning and experience

3. The tendency to plan curriculums through the development of requirements of ground to be covered, schedules, and other prescriptive measures

4. Conflicting practices of teachers, parents, and others guiding the development of the same learners in relation to planning learning experiences

We hope that the definitions and evaluative statements in Chapter 1 have already helped the reader to clear up any such confusions. Chapter 2 continues the treatment of basic concepts by defining the major issues to be faced in curriculum planning and then stating our point of view as to desirable characteristics of processes of curriculum planning needed to resolve such issues. Thus Part 1, composed of Chapters 1 and 2, is devoted to the general topic, "Why Is Better Curriculum Planning Needed?"

Need for Analysis of Basic Factors in Curriculum Planning

We believe that many problems of current curriculum practice follow from the failure of those who plan and develop the curriculum to give careful consideration to certain basic factors. Some of the problems we have noted are these:

1. Lack of adherence to sound principles of learning in the planning and development of the curriculum

2. Inequalities in the curriculum due to inconsistent evaluation of educational goals in different schools and classrooms

3. Maintenance of uniform expectations which ignore the nature of the individual and the learning process

4. Lack of formulation of educational goals

5. Neglect of fundamental needs of children and youth

6. Influence of factors, such as ground-to-be-covered requirements,

college-preparatory traditions, and community pressures, out of proportion to their importance

7. Failure to utilize educational research and experimentation in curriculum planning

Part 2 of this book is devoted to analysis of the basic factors which
we believe must be considered in planning and developing the curriculum. Thus Chapter 3 identifies in detail several forces related to the historical and legal foundations of American education. Chapter 4 describes
the relationships of social aims to curriculum planning with particular
reference to the implications of the democratic philosophy. Chapter 5
deals with the nature of the individual as a factor in curriculum planning,
and Chapter 6 with the relationship of learning principles and processes
to the development of the curriculum. Chapter 7 gives consideration to
the problem of determining goals or outcomes of the curriculum.

Need for Planning of the Curriculum Framework

Such problems as the following, which we have noted in the current curriculum practices of American elementary and secondary schools, suggest
to us the need for more careful planning of the curriculum framework
within school systems and individual schools:

 1. Inconsistent plans for "curricular" and "extracurricular" experi-
    ences of learners
 2. Inequalities in the provision of basic curriculum areas
 3. Lack of a deliberate plan to achieve social learnings and other
    outcomes through use of the school situation
 4. Curriculum plans developed on the basis of group rather than
    individual expectations
 5. Lack of provision for continuity of learning experiences
 6. Neglect of important outcomes in administrative regulations
    governing learning situations
 7. Lack of relationship between learning experiences in and out
    of school

Part 3 of this book deals with the question, "How Shall the Curriculum Framework Be Organized?" and presents principles and practices
related to the problems of curriculum design and organization.

Need for Planning and Developing the Curriculum in Learning Situations

Among the many problems of planning and developing the curriculum
in learning situations to which we have called attention are the following:

 1. Failure to use the organized life of the school and the class-
    room group to develop democratic processes

2. Neglect of individual differences in learning situations
3. The restricted nature of learning activities in many situations
4. Ineffective teaching of skills
5. Lack of pupil-teacher planning to promote more effective learning
6. Reliance on ineffective procedures such as the recitation and meaningless drill
7. Poor use and inadequate provision of resources for learning

Part 4 is devoted to the problem "How Shall the Curriculum Be Developed in Learning Situations?" Chapter 12 describes effective uses of resource units and unit plans, and Chapter 13 deals directly with the cooperative work of teacher and pupils in developing learning experiences. Chapter 14 is concerned with the selection and use of resources for learning, and Chapter 15 with classroom research and experimentation.

Need to Organize for and Evaluate Curriculum Planning

In general, all of the problems we have enumerated relate to the need for school personnel and others concerned to participate in curriculum planning and to carry on continuous evaluation of their curriculum planning processes. We have also noted such specific problems for school organization as the lack of exchange of information about learners among teachers, the pressure on the curriculum of administrative factors such as schedules, the restrictions placed on the proper use of resources, and the need of well-organized programs of in-service education. Specific attention is given to these matters in Chapter 11, Part 4. Chapter 16 defines means of cooperative participation in curriculum planning; and Chapter 17, steps and devices for evaluating curriculum planning.

The Interrelatedness of Curriculum Problems

As just shown, we have attempted to develop a logical organization of this book which would help educational workers in finding solutions to their problems of curriculum planning. We should make it clear, however, that curriculum problems are so interrelated that the steps in curriculum planning may not be nearly so discrete and logical as this outline indicates. That is, one may not be able to first study such a factor in curriculum planning as learning, then plan a curriculum framework to facilitate learning, then develop appropriate learning experiences in the classroom, and, lastly, evaluate the soundness and results of these plans. Actually one may have to study the factor of learning as one plans and evaluates learning experiences. In other words, curriculum problems are not solved in a piecemeal or mechanical fashion. Since curriculum problems bear very close relationships to each other, curriculum workers, that is, school personnel, need as complete an understanding of all these problems as possible. The total process of curriculum planning needs to be viewed in all the relationships we are trying to develop logically in this book. Those of us who work in schools must continue the study of curriculum problems throughout our educational careers, improving our curriculum planning as the result both of systematic study of curriculum planning and of experience with a variety of curriculum plans.

The interrelatedness of curriculum problems is shown further in Chapter 2 in its analysis of basic issues which must be constantly faced in studying and doing curriculum planning.

For Further Study

Alexander, William M., and J. Galen Saylor, *Secondary Education: Basic Principles and Practices.* New York: Rinehart & Company, Inc., 1950.

Chapters XI-XII describe general characteristics, and Chapters XIII-XX specific phases, of the high school curriculum.

American Association of School Administrators, *American School Curriculum.* Thirty-first Yearbook. Washington, D.C.: The Association, 1953.

See Chapters V and VI for a survey of curriculum practices in elementary and secondary schools.

Association for Supervision and Curriculum Development, National Education Association, *Action for Curriculum Improvement.* 1951 Yearbook. Washington, D.C.: The Association, 1951.

See Chapter II, "Conditions Compelling Curriculum Change."

————, *Creating a Good Environment for Learning.* 1954 Yearbook. Washington, D.C.: The Association, 1954.

See for many illustrations of good curriculum practice.

Caswell, Hollis L. (ed.), *The American High School.* Eighth Yearbook of the John Dewey Society. New York: Harper & Brothers, 1946.

Critical analysis of the high school curriculum, with proposals for the future.

Cook, Walter W., "Individual Differences and Curriculum Practice," *Journal of Educational Psychology,* 39:141–48 (March), 1948.

Critical analysis of the relationship of curriculum practice to psychological knowledge concerning individual differences.

Cooperative Study in Elementary Education, Southern Association of Colleges and Secondary Schools, *Promising Practices in Elementary Schools.* Atlanta, Ga.: The Association, 1952.

An excellent collection of photographs, annotated to illustrate promising practices in the instructional program of elementary schools.

Douglass, Harl R. (ed.), *The High School Curriculum.* New York: The Ronald Press Company, 1947.

Thirty-one chapters by various authors describe the status and problems of the subject fields included in the high school curriculum.

Educational Policies Commission, *Education for All American Children*. Washington, D.C.: National Education Association, 1948.

Part I describes hypothetical schools and school systems hoped for by the Commission in 1958. Part II decribes excellent practices observed in selected elementary schools. See Chapter 3 for descriptions of actual curriculum practices considered outstanding.

———, *Education for All American Youth: A Further Look*. Washington, D.C.: National Education Association, 1952.

A 1952 revision of the popular 1944 edition, which proposed a postwar program for American secondary education. See especially Chapters 1, 2, and 10 on current problems and practices.

Grim, Paul, and Vernon Anderson, "Is the American High School Serving Today's Youth?" *Educational Leadership*, 6:338–349 (March), 1949.

Reports of a study of a sample of high school students as to their opinion on the title question and a parallel study of opinions of specialists in secondary education.

Gruhn, William T., and Harl R. Douglass, *The Modern Junior High School*. New York: The Ronald Press Company, 1947.

Chapters 5 to 7 deal with the development and present status of the curriculum of junior high schools.

Hand, Harold C., *Prospectus of the Local Area Consensus Studies*. Circular Series A, No. 51, Illinois Secondary School Curriculum Program, Bulletin No. 15. Springfield, Ill.: Superintendent of Public Instruction, State of Illinois, March, 1951.

Plan for conducting studies of opinion regarding the effectiveness of the secondary school curriculum in local communities, with a report of previous studies in Illinois.

Lee, J. Murray, and Dorris May Lee, *The Child and His Curriculum*. 2d ed.; New York: Appleton-Century-Crofts, Inc., 1950.

Comprehensive treatment of present and emerging practices in the elementary school curriculum, including analyses in each major field.

Leonard, J. Paul, *Developing the Secondary School Curriculum*. Rev. ed.; New York: Rinehart & Company, Inc., 1953.

Comprehensive treatment of the modern secondary school curriculum.

McNerney, Chester T., *The Curriculum*. New York: McGraw-Hill Book Company, Inc., 1953.

Nine of the fourteen chapters of this book deal with curriculum practices in the various curriculum areas: language, social development, arithmetic and science, art and music, home and industrial education, and physical, health and safety education.

National Society for the Study of Education, *Adapting the Secondary-School Program to the Needs of Youth*. Part I, Fifty-second Yearbook. Chicago: The University of Chicago Press, 1953.

Comprehensive treatment of secondary school curriculum needs. See especially in relation to appraisal of current practice, Chapters IV and XVI.

Shane, Harold G., and E. T. McSwain, *Evaluation and the Elementary Curriculum*. New York: Henry Holt and Company, Inc., 1951.

Chapter 2 describes values to be sought in the elementary school; Chapters 6–11 give specific criteria for evaluating various phases of the elementary school curriculum.

United States Office of Education, *Offerings and Enrollments in High School Subjects, 1948–49*. Chap. 5, Biennial Survey of Education, 1948–50; Washington, D.C.: Government Printing Office, 1951.

Data on curriculum offerings and enrollments in high schools, 1948–1949; first such survey since a 1934 report.

chapter 2

Basic Issues of Curriculum Planning

All curriculum planning is based on choice. School officials and staffs
choose, for example, to offer French rather than Latin; to offer driver
education rather than advanced algebra; to organize a student council; to
provide physical education for boys but not for girls; to set up separate,
short periods for the teaching of spelling, writing, and reading rather
than a long period for the teaching of all communicative skills on an
integrated basis; to teach young children to recognize words rather than
single letters of the alphabet; to promote children from grade to grade
with their age and social group rather than on the basis of standards of
achievement, or vice versa; not to permit competitive athletics in the
junior high schools; and so on for a multitude of choices that determine
the real curriculum of pupils as was described in Chapter 1.

These choices which curriculum workers make—and it should be
emphasized that everyone who makes decisions relative to the kinds of
educational experiences boys and girls will have in school is a curriculum
worker—represent a point of view as to what constitute appropriate educational experiences for boys and girls. The person or persons making
such decisions may not fully analyze at the time the concepts involved in
such actions, but it is nevertheless true that choices of this type and all
choices made relative to possible procedures and practices in the schools
are based on assumptions as to the purposes, function, and nature of education in our society. Basic to sound decision making, then, are the formulation and clarification of basic points of view on significant issues which
will arise in curriculum planning.

Our purpose in this chapter is to review certain significant issues in
curriculum planning and then to resolve these issues by a statement of
our own point of view on the desirable characteristics of curriculum planning. We are analyzing the issues which are decided so differently by curriculum workers as to be responsible for the great diversity and problems
of curriculum planning discussed in Chapter 1. Hence we feel that these

39

issues constitute needs for better curriculum planning and also that better curriculum planning must resolve them.

DOES CURRICULUM PLANNING AT PRESENT MAKE ADEQUATE PROVISIONS FOR ALL CHILDREN AND YOUTH?

Obviously, the American people believe that all children within certain defined age limits should have an opportunity to be educated at public expense. We have even passed compulsory attendance laws, so that they are compelled to attend school within these prescribed limits. Yet curriculum workers, upon serious reflection, know that schools are not universally providing adequate educational opportunities for many youngsters in this nation of ours. As we plan a curriculum for children and youth we must face squarely the issue of whether provisions for an appropriate educational program are to be made available to all.

Inadequate Provisions for Some Children

Among groups of children who need special consideration, often not now provided, are the following:

1. Exceptional children. Many school systems, particularly the smaller ones, do not provide programs, or certainly not adequate ones, for many children who deviate markedly from the normal. Included in such groups are children who have physical infirmities, such as the crippled, those suffering from cerebral palsy, the blind or partially seeing, and the hard of hearing; children with physical deficiencies such as the cardiopathic, the epileptic, and the speech defective; children with extreme mental deviations, such as the mentally retarded and the gifted; and children with serious emotional disturbances.

Citizens, as well as educators, have become increasingly aware of the needs of these deviates, and within the last decade or two, many school systems have developed programs designed to serve the special requirements of such groups.[1] However, curriculum planning has often not kept apace with even the provision of physical facilities (where needed) and rich experiences appropriate to the special needs of such groups have not been developed. Particularly, many educators and parents feel that the schools have not always challenged the very gifted pupil to the extent desirable.

2. Children of migratory workers. The neglect of the children of migratory workers has been sharply called to the attention of educa-

[1] Arthur S. Hill, "Extending Special Education through State Legislation," *School Life,* 35:140–142 (June), 1953.

tors;[2] yet the problem has not been solved. They comprise a group of youngsters who must be properly educated if they are to be the best citizens possible and are to enjoy the privileges of a democratic society, but schools in affected areas have not met the problem satisfactorily. Curriculum planning needs to give attention to this problem.[3]

3. Inhabitants of sparsely settled areas. Children who live in remote or isolated areas frequently have very limited opportunities for securing an education. While this group is relatively small, we do have in this country a large number of children who live in rural areas in which the only school available is very small, both at the elementary and secondary levels, with the result that the curriculum is extremely limited, opportunities for social development are hampered by lack of age mates, school activities are greatly restricted in choice, and teaching resources and facilities are apt to be meager.

4. Bilingual children. Some school districts have large numbers of parents who speak only a foreign language and their children grow up in a bilingual environment. Especially in the early years of their attendance in American schools, the language problem is a serious handicap, and some attention must be given to it in curriculum planning.

5. Children with lower-class backgrounds. Sociologists have pointed out that the school curriculum is usually based on the concepts, meanings, value patterns, and cultural backgrounds familiar to middle- and upper-class children, and that hence the children from the lower classes are handicapped in terms of experiential and conceptual backgrounds. Curriculum planners are urged to develop experiences that utilize the backgrounds of these children, too. Davis charges that "the most important inference to be made from the studies briefly reported in this paper, dealing with the socialization and mental activities of children, is that most of our efforts to revise the curricula of the public schools have been superficial." [4]

[2] President's Commission on Migratory Labor, *Migratory Labor in American Agriculture* (Washington, D.C.: Government Printing Office, 1951).

[3] See Walter H. Gaumintz, "Educating Migrant Children—Some Proposed Solutions," *School Life,* 29:11–12 (December), 1946, and "Problem of School Organization Resulting from Migration," in National Society for the Study of Education, *American Education in the Postwar Period* (Forty-fourth Yearbook, Part II; Chicago: The University of Chicago Press, 1945), pp. 43–55.

[4] Allison Davis, *Social Class Influences upon Learning* (Cambridge, Mass.: Harvard University Press, 1951), p. 99.

Planning for Children and Youth outside the Limits of Compulsory Attendance

In some school systems curriculum planning encompasses programs for the very young who may have the privilege of attending kindergarten, or even nursery school, and in most communities it includes training for those beyond the upper limit of compulsory attendance, since most pupils do not complete the secondary school by the end of the required period of attendance.

TABLE 4

Enrollment of Children and Youth in School, 1950

AGE AND GRADE GROUP	TOTAL POPULATION IN AGE GROUP	ENROLLED IN SCHOOL	PER CENT ENROLLED
Elementary School			
Age 5—Kindergarten	2,720,795	933,125	34.3
Age 6—First Grade	2,774,070	2,130,530	76.8
Age 7—Second Grade	2,830,180	2,670,295	94.4
Age 8—Third Grade	2,560,165	2,448,490	95.6
Age 9—Fourth Grade	2,349,465	2,257,985	96.1
Age 10—Fifth Grade	2,321,085	2,228,955	96.0
Age 11—Sixth Grade	2,229,155	2,145,630	96.3
Junior High School			
Age 12—Seventh Grade	2,298,150	2,204,840	95.9
Age 13—Eighth Grade	2,189,720	2,099,085	95.9
Age 14—Ninth Grade	2,137,390	2,025,730	94.8
Senior High School			
Age 15—Tenth Grade	2,130,005	1,945,790	91.4
Age 16—Eleventh Grade	2,079,990	1,682,200	80.9
Age 17—Twelfth Grade	2,093,745	1,426,930	68.2
Higher Education			
Age 18 ⎤	2,182,290	867,695	39.8
Age 19 ⎟ College or Other	2,159,195	533,025	24.7
Age 20 ⎟ Institutions	2,187,885	392,160	17.9
Ages 21–24 ⎦	9,249,420	1,088,270	11.8

Source: U.S. Department of Commerce, Bureau of the Census, *United States Census of Population: 1950* (Washington, D.C.: Government Printing Office, 1953), Vol. II, Pt. I, Tables 109, 110.

Enrollment at various age levels. Table 4 gives us an insight into the situation as it existed in 1950. It shows the percentage of children and youth of each age group who were enrolled in school. Enrollment in nursery schools is not included; neither is enrollment in vocational, trade, or business schools unless such schools were graded and considered a part of a regular school system. However, enrollment in "regular" schools could be full time or part time. The census figures simply indicate the number and percentage of children enrolled in school at any level; the assignment of grade levels in the table was done by us and follows usual practice.

Actually only about one third of the children five years of age are enrolled in school, and even a fourth of the six-year-olds are not yet attending. The biennial survey of education for 1949–1950 shows that 1,680 school systems of the 3,141 reporting from urban areas, or only about one half, made provision for children below the formal first grade.[5]

At the upper end of the scale, Table 4 shows that enrollment drops off rapidly after age 15. Table 5 shows the percentage of youth of various

TABLE 5

Percentage of Youth of Selected Age Groups Who Had Completed High School, 1950

AGE GROUP IN YEARS	PER CENT WHO HAD COMPLETED HIGH SCHOOL
16	1.2
17	8.2
18	37.3
19	52.7
20	54.2
21–24	52.0

Source: U.S. Department of Commerce, *op. cit.,* Table 114.

ages who have already completed high school. Combining the two figures we see that 76.4 per cent of the seventeen-year-olds are still in school or have already finished high school. Table 5 reveals that just slightly more than half of our young adults have graduated from high school. The median year of school completed is actually 12.1.

Implications for curriculum planning. The implications of these data for curriculum planning seem clear. For the younger age groups—

[5] U.S. Office of Education, "Statistics of City School Systems, 1949–50," Chapter 3 in *Biennial Survey of Education in the United States, 1948–50* (Washington, D.C.: Government Printing Office, 1953). p. 19.

the five- and six-year-olds—curriculum workers should exert every effort to obtain adequate educational opportunities for them. Certainly, kindergartens should become universal in establishment, and nursery schools are desirable and should be developed wherever resources permit. We would hope that all children might enjoy the rich experiences that the young tots depicted in Plate 3 are having. When such facilities are pro-

PLATE 3. EDUCATIONAL PROGRAMS FOR YOUNG CHILDREN CONTRIBUTE GREATLY TO SOUND GROWTH AND DEVELOPMENT. *These children are more fortunate than many, for they may attend a kindergarten. (Courtesy of Bancroft School, Teachers College, University of Nebraska)*

vided, obviously, curriculum planning must include a consideration of the kinds of educational experiences that are most appropriate for young children in terms of their needs, their maturation, and their social development and in terms of what experiences may best be deferred until later grades.

It is the facts relating to school attendance by older youth that are particularly dismaying to curriculum workers. One looks aghast at figures presented in Tables 4 and 5; even though we have a fairly universal acceptance of the principle that educational opportunities at elementary and secondary school levels should be provided at public expense for all children and youth, actually only about half of the youth of our nation take full advantage of these opportunities. The American concept of education for all youth certainly falls short of realization in actual practice.

Why do these boys and girls fail to take advantage of the opportunities that the American people provide them? What can curriculum workers do to bring practice more in conformity with the ideal? These may be appropriate recommendations:

1. Throughout the nation, secondary schools must be developed that will serve effectively and efficiently all of the proper educational needs of all youth. Curriculums must be functional, in the broadest sense, providing rich and meaningful learning experiences for all youth—the academic-minded, the gifted, the nonacademic type of pupils, and so on for the whole gamut of the adolescent population. It is our aim to present in ensuing chapters plans for the development of such a program of education.

2. All young adolescents, prior to the time they reach the end of the period of compulsory school attendance, should have a sound understanding of the purposes it serves and the values to be gained from continuation in school until the completion of the usual twelve-year program. Moreover, since the evidence clearly indicates a direct relationship between continuation in secondary school until graduation and the socio-economic status of the family, attention should also be given to the development of a broader understanding on the part of many parents concerning the contributions which formal education can make to the lives of their own children.

3. The educational structure should be improved so that adequate secondary school opportunities are readily available to all youth.

4. Boards of education and school administrators should remove obstacles that now prevent some youth from continuing in secondary schools. In some situations blocks to the regular progression of pupils from the elementary school to the secondary school still exist.

5. Opportunities for youth to obtain education at the secondary level in part-time and evening schools should be extended and broadened. Curriculum workers and administrators should give much more attention and consideration to these programs than has heretofore been the case. In most curriculum improvement programs, these aspects of the school's educational program have largely been ignored. Consequently, the work in part-time and evening classes is too often planned on the basis of the

instructors that might be available to teach a class on a volunteer basis, and often instruction is based on a trade training manual developed by a trade union or an occupational training group.

6. Teaching methods should conform more fully to modern concepts of the nature of learning. A major concern of all curriculum workers is to plan and organize classroom experiences in terms of the basic motivational patterns of our pupils and to organize learning activity in conformity with our knowledge of how learning takes place. We think this aspect of the improvement of the curriculum to be so important that we have devoted Chapter 6 and all four chapters in Part 4 of this book to it.

WHAT SHOULD BE THE PHILOSOPHICAL BASIS FOR CURRICULUM PLANNING?

Education has purposes. It is unthinkable that a social group would establish and operate schools, as the American people do, without having in mind basic purposes that they should serve. Ask any citizen why that community has a school, or what functions a school should serve and he undoubtedly could give a sensible answer.

If the purposes of the school are stated in very broad, general terms, such as the development of the powers of critical thinking, the cultivation of loyalty to America, or the development of basic skills essential for effective living, probably little disagreement would exist among the citizens of this country on the proper role of the school in our democratic society. It is when we attempt to break down these broad objectives into the specific outcomes we seek and particularly when we attempt to formulate a program that will achieve these basic objectives, that disagreements appear among citizens as well as among educators. We should examine, then, more fully the whole issue of how to determine goals in curriculum planning.

Basic Concepts of Education

Essentially, goals for education are derived from two basic sources: (1) sources of authority external to the stream of social experience of the individuals themselves, such as divine authority or eternal truths; and (2) the stream of social experience of mankind itself. Five basic points of view have been formulated in terms of these two sources of authority for educational objectives. These schools of educational thought have been more or less commonly identified under these titles: (1) Catholicism, (2) perennialism, (3) essentialism, (4) experimentalism, and (5) reconstructionism.[6]

While there are many areas of agreement among these five points of view, particularly when the basic theory is translated into actual school practice, yet basically there is a different conception in each philosophy as to the pervading over-all functions of education in a modern society. Undoubtedly a great many curriculum workers and teachers do not deliberately and overtly identify many of their practices, or even their beliefs about education, with any particular school of educational philosophy. Yet it is our contention that in making the innumerable choices as to what should be done in classrooms and in the school, teachers and other curriculum workers inevitably reflect a point of view about education and its proper role in modern society. Day-by-day decisions of teachers on what to teach and how to teach it in the classroom and what activities and experiences to provide children outside of the organized classroom stem from some basic concept of what constitutes a desirable education for children and youth. Curriculum workers should deliberately examine the choices they make and evaluate these choices in terms of the philosophy of education exemplified.

Philosophies and School Policies

Actually, if one were to visit five schools, each one of which consistently followed a different philosophy of education, he would probably observe many common practices and a great deal of similarity in the kinds of learning activities going on. However, there would be important variations in program and method that resulted from differences in the five points of view. He would note, for example, that in schools which consistently applied the Catholic point of view considerable attention is being given to the study of religious doctrine, to the practice of religious ceremonies, to the study of the scriptures and religious creed, and to a religious interpretation of many of man's activities and institutions.

A school that subscribed wholeheartedly to the perennial point of view would devote considerable time to a study of the so-called classics or great books written by the great scholars of all time. Considerable

---

[6] For more complete delineation of these points of view see the following: Theodore Brameld, *Patterns of Educational Philosophy* (Yonkers, N.Y.: World Book Company, 1950); Sidney Hook, *Education for Modern Man* (New York: The Dial Press, 1946); James N. Brown, *Educational Implications of Four Conceptions of Human Nature* (Washington, D.C.: The Catholic University of America Press, 1940); Glen Johnson, *Some Implications of a Naturalistic Philosophy of Education* (New York: Bureau of Publications, Teachers College, Columbia University, 1947); John L. Childs, *Education and the Philosophy of Experimentalism* (New York: Appleton-Century-Crofts, Irc., 1931).

attention would be given to a logical analysis of principles and concepts and to a consideration of basic principles enunciated by them. Pupils would be expected to acquire an understanding of the principles that have withstood the test of time as well as an understanding of the meth- ods used by these intellectual giants in establishing these truths. The observer would note that very little consideration would be given to current social and economic problems or to the study of current affairs and happenings in the world today.

In a school subscribing to the essentialist's point of view, our ob- server would notice a great deal of emphasis on the study of logically organized subjects. In classwork, pupils would be expected to master a considerable body of knowledge and of facts about the world as it had developed up to the present time. Formalized recitations in which the pupils were tested on their acquisition of these knowledges and facts would dominate the methods used. The curriculum, particularly in the secondary school, would be a systematic study of an irreducible body of knowledge plus the development of skills deemed essential for an edu- cated person. Stress would be placed upon an adequate mastery of con- tent and adherence to rigorous standards of scholastic attainment.[7]

The most striking thing our observer would see when he visited a school implementing the concepts of experimentalism, in contrast to the previous three types of schools, would be the widespread participation of the pupils in a variety of types of learning experiences. Instead of seeing pupils seated at fixed desks reciting the facts and information which they had previously studied in preparation for the recitation, or engaging in practice on skills, he would note them moving about the room, working together in small groups, conferring together as indi- viduals or as groups, using reference materials or going to the library for information and help on problems, participating in committee dis- cussions, presenting a report before the class, or undertaking similar sorts of learning experiences. As he listened to what was occurring in the oom, he would probably note that the pupils were discussing some prob- em which they had set for themselves, under the guidance of their teacher. Thus in a progressive school he would observe the predominance of pupil-centered activities, and the attention given to significant prob- lems of concern to the pupils themselves. He would note the absence of rigid schedules and the limited time spent in formal recitations.

The reconstructionist has not yet had much opportunity to demon-

---

[7] A popular plea for essentialism and a caustic indictment of the experimentalist's point of view by laymen are contained in Albert Lynd, *Quackery in the Public Schools* (Boston: Little, Brown & Company, 1953) and Mortimer B. Smith, *And Madly Teach* (Chicago: Henry Regnery Co., 1949).

strate his theories in actual school practice, but, if we understand his concepts properly, a school adhering to this point of view would at first glance resemble rather closely a progressive school. Pupils would be engaged in a variety of activities in which they were assuming responsibilities for obtaining facts, developing concepts, and the like. The essential difference between this kind of school and the progressive school would be in the content studied, particularly in the secondary school. While in the progressive school problems of concern to the pupils themselves as they live in a social group would be major areas for organizing the curriculum, the reconstructionist would orient the curriculum much more to the problems arising from the social crises in which people find themselves. Not only would they study these problems; presumably they would formulate possible solutions and, working with the adults of the community, seek to carry out these solutions in order that a better society for all concerned might be established.

Our Own Position

Essentially, we are experimentalists. We subscribe fundamentally to the basic concepts enunciated by Dewey, Kilpatrick, Childs, and other leaders in the experimentalist movement. We believe in the unity of the individual—that the intellect and the body are aspects of a total integrated organism. We believe that when an individual engages in an activity he engages in it as a total organism, calling both on his intellectual powers and on his bodily functions in facing the situation and in carrying on the activity.

The activities in which an individual engages and the ways in which he participates in these activities, and consequently his learnings, are determined by his basic motivational pattern. These basic motivational forces represent an integration of his physiological needs, his ego needs, and his social needs. Drives for engaging in activity and the purposes of such activity are personal; they are determined by the individual himself in terms of these basic wants and needs. Learning results from activities in which he engages with purpose. These purposes determine the nature of the learning which will take place for the individual concerned. Purpose is fundamental to all learning. The purposes of an individual will be the product of his physiological and social needs, but the particular form which they will take and the nature of the satisfaction of these needs will be determined by the social environment in which the individual has lived and in which he is now living.

What the person values will be what he believes will contribute most to his own immediate and future happiness, satisfaction, and well-being as well as that of the entire social group with which his own interests are inextricably identified. Thus the basic purpose of education is to help the individual lead a good life both for himself and for others. What the good life means in modern democratic America in terms of particular goals for the school will be discussed more fully in Chapter 7. Suffice it to say here that what constitutes the good life is predicated not only on the basic physiological and integrative needs of the individual but on the racial experience of the social group with which the individual is associated. At this point in history the good life for a youngster growing up in Russia or in Samoa is not the same as the good life for a youngster growing up in democratic America. Life's basic values for each youngster are derived from the cultural meanings which the social group has developed, and while we believe that our system of values is the best yet refined from human experience and that the young should learn them, they are not accepted as universal values by all people of the world.

Since the future is unpredictable, schools can best help children and youth meet this uncertain future by guiding them in the development of a valid system of values and in the acquisition of the methods of rational thinking and the habits of scientific thought so that they can reach the most valid decisions on questions that confront them in the years ahead. Man is best able to face the future if he has developed the basic abilities necessary to think rationally in applying his values and knowledge to new sets of conditions. One of the basic elements which any person should take into account in thinking rationally about any problem which he faces in the future is the past experience of mankind in meeting similar situations. Consideration of the values which man as an intellectual being has winnowed from his previous experience will be one of the primary factors to be taken into account in thinking rationally about any new problem. Hence the accumulated heritage of the race, with the value patterns which man has formulated on the basis of this racial experience, will be the major element in arriving at decisions on problems in the future.

Education, therefore, will obviously need to fortify the individual with a thorough understanding of these values and of the cultural experience of the social group. Mere knowledge of this heritage or past experience, however, will not in itself result in the achievement of the good life in any unforeseen circumstances in the future. These values must be built into character so that the individual acts and behaves in terms of basic concepts that have proved successful in meeting situations in the past. However, the individual must be free to evaluate his value patterns, to see in what respects new situations differ from the old, to weigh alternative courses of action, and, on the basis of intelligent action, to formulate new ways of meeting situations if these should be called for. Education would aim at the improvement of behavior, the ways in which individuals live together with their fellow men. Mere knowledge of what man should do is not enough; such knowledge must be coupled with action that carries into effect the values that have accumulated from the previous experience of the social group. These things, fundamental to curriculum planning, we believe.

WHAT KINDS OF EDUCATIONAL EXPERIENCES SHOULD BE PROVIDED BY THE SCHOOL?

Closely related to the issue of the philosophical concepts that are accepted as a basis for curriculum planning is the issue of the kinds of educational experiences that should be provided pupils to achieve the overall ends of education. Even in terms of any one basic philosophical approach, curriculum choices still must be made and decisions must be reached on what constitutes the best education possible in terms of our basic concepts. However, it is apparent that the types of learning experiences planned for children will be basically dependent on the primary concepts of education held by the curriculum workers doing the planning. So in that sense this issue is an elaboration of the former issue.

Should the Curriculum Be Organized Primarily in Terms of the Organized Cultural Heritage or of Functional Units of Work?

The cultural heritage approach. Many educators and lay citizens believe that the fundamental purpose of the school is to facilitate the acquisition of the cultural heritage of the race. This concept of curriculum planning holds that the major, if not exclusive, efforts of the school should be concentrated on providing pupils with a mastery of basic skills and a knowledge of the most significant aspects of our cultural heritage. Educational experiences would be selected so that pupils would have opportunity to develop the skills that not only are necessary in carrying on our daily activities but make life rich and enjoyable, and to master the subject matter that best contributes to a basic understanding of man, his institutions, and his place in the world.

In terms of this point of view pupils should become acquainted with and understand the great literature of the world; they should know the history of mankind, particularly with reference to the development of our own country; they should know the basic principles and facts of science; they should have competence in mathematical skills and in the use of mathematical symbols; they should understand the structure and principles of constitutional government; and similarly with regard to other important organized bodies of knowledge.

The functional approach. On the other hand, many educators and citizens believe that the program of the school should be primarily functional in nature. Its job, so they maintain, is to provide experiences that serve the important life needs of the pupils themselves. The major criteria for selecting educational experiences in this approach are usefulness and significance, both now and in the future, to the pupils concerned. While the school would accept responsibility for providing breadth of experience so that pupils would acquire skill and knowledge useful to them in dealing with the broad scope of life's activities, it nevertheless would not attempt systematically to acquaint pupils with many aspects of the cultural heritage, nor would it seek to inculcate knowledge sheerly for the sake of knowledge.

Contrast in the two positions. To contrast these two positions, we will illustrate from the field of mathematics. Application of the point of view that children should acquire an understanding of the cultural heritage would result very likely in the establishment at the secondary school level of systematic courses in mathematics, which would be required of all pupils. Such courses traditionally would be algebra and geometry, and possibly solid geometry and trigonometry. Thus in such a program students would be expected to acquire a knowledge of such things as factoring, the use of positive and negative numbers, the binomial theorem, the main theorems on the congruence of triangles, tests for parallelism of lines, and many similar concepts.

Under the functional use theory, mathematics would probably be organized into courses which have commonly been called applied mathematics or general mathematics. The subject matter of such courses is usually centered around practical, everyday problems that involve the use of mathematical skills. Pupils learn how to calculate our income taxes, how to use percentages in numerous practical, everyday situations, how to figure interest and charges in installment buying, how to keep household budgets, and how to use mathematics in dealing with situations that presumably he would encounter in his day-by-day living. Under this latter type of program they may never study the binomial theorem or the conditions that determine the congruence of triangles.

Deciding the issue. In trying to decide this issue educators are faced on one hand with the possibility that youngsters schooled on the basis of the acquisition of the cultural heritage may not be well prepared to face practical life situations and may have few if any opportunities to use their knowledge in real day-by-day living now or later. What use, it might be asked, does a truck driver, a housewife, or a dentist have for the binomial theorem or for the names of the generals who led armies in the Civil War? Knowledge of this kind may not in and of itself help them face squarely and confidently some of the most important problems that citizens confront daily.[8] On the other hand, if the school uses the functional approach to the selection of school experiences, youngsters may not acquire the information and knowledge they will need later on or become acquainted with parts of the cultural heritage that on some future occasion would be of considerable value to them or would serve them well in deciding problems they meet. However, as Benjamin Franklin said when he faced a decision on what to include in the curriculum of his academy, "But art is long and their time is short."

In actual practice curriculum workers usually strike some kind of compromise between these two approaches to the selection of school experience. Schools include a considerable portion of learning activities that involve the acquisition of knowledge and the development of an understanding of the cultural heritage without much reference to functional use in the foreseeable future. On the other hand, practically all modern schools try to help children in every way possible with the important problems they will face in day-by-day living. Plate 4 illustrates such a procedure. The primary aim of the school is to help youngsters live more effective and satisfying lives not only as they grow up but as adult citizens.

Of course, on this issue we see the same cleavage in point of view that we have already noted in discussing philosophies of education, for the selection of learning experiences is in terms of one's concepts of the purposes of education. Those who believe that the curriculum should be largely devoted to a systematic acquisition of the culture accept, in the main, the point of view that knowledge is power and that the best kind of education is one that disciplines the mind and develops the intellect of the individual so that he may use his mental powers in facing life's problems. Those who favor the functional approach quite largely accept the point of view of the experimentalists as to the nature of education. They believe that the best preparation for the here and now as well as for the future is to give pupils experiences in solving problems that are significant to them now. In the future, as they face problems about which they may lack some essential knowledge, they will at least know how to use the scientific approach and how to obtain the data necessary to reach a sound decision. Supporting this position, of course, is the large amount of research on forgetting, which shows that pupils, often within a short time and certainly over a period of time, forget many, many of the facts that

[8] William F. Russell, "The Caravan Goes On," *Teachers College Record*, 54:6–7 (October), 1952.

were taught in school. The knowledge, which the one school of thought believes to be so essential, actually is not retained by pupils; hence it can be of little direct help in solving life's problems.

PLATE 4. KNOWLEDGE CAN BE ACQUIRED THROUGH A STUDY OF MEANINGFUL TOPICS. *These pupils are increasing their vocabulary and learning to read as well as learning about democratic processes through use of topics on a presidential election. (Courtesy of the Lincoln, Nebraska, Public Schools)*

What Should Be the Relative Emphasis Given to General and to Specialized Education?

There is some variance in the point of view of educators relative to the amount of time that the school should devote to a common program of general education for all pupils and the time that it should devote to the development of specialized interests, including vocational education. Certainly a wide variation in practice also exists.

Common learnings. As one formulates basic purposes for the educational program as it extends from the kindergarten through the common school, such as we present in Chapter 7, it is evident that there is a large body of skills, knowledge, attitudes, appreciations, ways of working, and ways of behaving that should be learned in common by all pupils as they participate in the curriculum experiences of the school. For example, most everyone would agree that children should learn the ways of living that are essential to good health and should develop an attitude of wanting to protect their health and physical well-being. Likewise, most everyone would agree that all pupils should possess the skills necessary to communicate reasonably well with other people through spoken and written language. Such desired outcomes of the educational program and many more like them should be achieved by all pupils within the limits of their capacities. This phase of the educational program is designated as "general education," or "common learnings." However, the term "common learnings" does not imply that every pupil in all the schools throughout the country should have common educational experiences; it is the broad desired outcomes that are common to all programs of education, not identical experiences. In this connection it must be recognized that any particular broad outcome sought through the educational program may be achieved through a variety of learning experiences. Thus in teaching pupils to communicate effectively with each other in spoken and written language it is not to be assumed that children in California would write themes about the same things as children in Maine, or that during their conversational periods children would talk about the same happenings or discuss the same problems in Texas schools as they would in North Dakota schools.

Specialized interests. Children differ in capacities, abilities, interests, home backgrounds, and needs. This fact has been proven exhaustively by psychological research. Similarly, not all children in the United States will, as adult citizens, do the same things or engage in the same activities or vocations. The question then becomes one of the extent to which the school should take account of these individual variabilities, interests, and needs and should differentiate its program in terms of them. The issue becomes particularly sharp at the secondary school level in determining the extent to which the secondary school should provide vocational education and opportunity to engage in specialized programs of study.

Since this issue involves the whole question of the structure and scope and sequence of the curriculum, we will defer further consideration until this aspect of curriculum planning is explored in Chapter 11. Recog-'

nition is given here to the fact that it is an important issue in curriculum planning, and that educators must come to grips with the problem.

How Far Should the School Go in Providing Occupational Training?

Another issue that arises in connection with the character of the educational experiences to be provided pupils in our common schools is the extent to which specific occupational preparation should be given in the secondary school. Should its program be limited to a broad basic training that would be useful in a cluster of occupations, or should the school give pupils specific job training so that they would be able to take positions in a particular occupation upon leaving the school? Or should the school seek to do both of these things?

Many curriculum workers believe that the primary function of vocational training in the secondary school is to offer a broad type of work experience, so that those enrolled will obtain fundamental skills that will enable them to be successful workers in any occupation which they may later choose to enter. This does not refer to the general education program, which, of course, should provide educational experience that will enable all pupils to live more effective lives. Rather, we are considering the vocational educational program itself; its primary purpose, in the view of many educators, is to give pupils participating in it significant experiences in work, in occupational orientation, and in job selection that will enable them to hold with success whatever jobs they choose to enter and to advance in their chosen occupational group.

But, in addition to these basic skills, knowledges, and understandings, many authorities believe that the schools should provide basic, specific introductory training in a particular occupation or in closely related groups of occupations. Acquisition of such job skills will enable the individual to obtain a job and to undertake further apprentice training or advanced training on the job so that he may become skilled in his occupation. Few educators hold that it is the responsibility of the school to provide such specific and intensive occupational training that the individual, upon leaving the school, would be able to enter a job as a finished worker in a particular occupation. Such intensive training would rob the pupil of the time needed to acquire the broad vocational orientation just described as well as his general education.

TO WHAT EXTENT SHOULD THE SCHOOL ACCEPT RESPONSIBILITY FOR THE EDUCATION OF THE WHOLE CHILD?

The extent to which the school should take responsibility for guiding the total growth of pupils is an important issue that must be faced in curriculum planning, even though it is closely related to one's concept of the purposes of education.

Intellectual Development

To those who believe that the chief purpose of education is to discipline the mind and to provide learners with a wider range of knowledge and basic skills, the school's function becomes primarily one of fostering the intellectual development of the child. Thus Van Doren says:

> Elementary education can do nothing better for a child than store his memory with things deserving to be there. He will be grateful for them when he grows up, even if he kicks now. They should be good things; indeed, they should be the best things, and all children should possess them. . . .
>
> There should be no school in which the young mind fails to receive, like seeds destined to germinate in later years, a full sowing of sentences great men have spoken—poems or parts of poems, and passages of prose—along with pieces of powerful music, glimpses of powerful painting, classical formulas in mathematics, chemistry, and physics, and the patterns of certain instruments without which science is helpless. We take it for granted that the multiplication tables must be learned, but these other things are no less necessary to the mind.[9]

In terms of this point of view the job of the school is to prepare the young for the future. The school is to take little or no account of the here and now in the life of the child as he grows and develops. It is not to concern itself with his problems, his frustrations, his desires, his physical, emotional, and social needs, or the physiological problems of simply growing up. The school's responsibility is primarily to train a mind—a mind that for all practical purposes is considered to be something set apart from the rest of the human organism itself. The attitudes the child develops, the ways he works, the ways he behaves, the appreciations he acquires, and the adjustments he makes to his playmates and classmates and to his parents and the adults in his home and community life are not to be a concern of the school.

The school, under such a concept, is not directly concerned with character or personality development. Rather, the mind is thought of as a blank tablet on which are to be entered, under the stern discipline of the teacher, the important knowledges and facts which the youngster may, perchance, need later in life. Such concepts dominated the old classical school described in histories of education as the kind of school that

[9] Mark Van Doren, *Liberal Education* (New York: Henry Holt and Company, Inc., 1943), pp. 94–96. Reprinted by permission of Henry Holt and Company, Inc.

typified most educational practice here and in foreign countries up until
well into the nineteenth century. It is this type of school that has set the
tradition for even considerable segments of educational practice today.

Development of Total Personality

On the other side of this issue are those who hold that the school has a
basic responsibility of guiding the total development of its pupils, physically, emotionally, and socially as well as intellectually. Kilpatrick states
this position thus:

> *Education must primarily seek character and behavior, all-round
> character of a kind to lead to proper behavior.* An essential aspect
> of this character, underlying in fact all the rest, is the well-adjusted
> personality. With this and beyond this we wish a vigorous and effec-
> tive character which acts after thinking and out of warm human
> values, which feels and acts with appropriate reference to self and
> others and the world.[10]

Those who subscribe to this point of view—and most present-day
educators do to a greater or lesser degree—believe that the school must
be concerned with the development of a total personality. Behavior, attitudes, character, value patterns, and human relations become important concerns of the school. As is illustrated by Plate 5, this responsibility
in fact permeates the entire program and life of the school. The school,
however, is but a part of the total culture that impinges on character
and personality development. As the one institution primarily intrusted
by society to guide the growth of all children, it has a primary obligation, however, to round out, correlate, and supplement learnings provided by other social agencies, as well as to develop many important
learnings that are its unique function, so that total development is
sound.[11]

WHO SHOULD PLAN THE CURRICULUM?

This issue of the responsibility for curriculum planning is very important in curriculum making and one on which there is a wide divergence
in points of view and actual school practice. Full consideration is given

[10] William H. Kilpatrick, *Philosophy of Education* (New York: The Macmillan
Company, 1951), p. 226. Reprinted by permission of The Macmillan Company, publishers.

[11] James L. Hymes, Jr., makes a significant contribution on this subject in his
chapter, "Better Humans, Better Citizens," in *The American Elementary School* (Thirteenth Yearbook of the John Dewey Society, Harold G. Shane, editor; New York:
Harper & Brothers, 1953).

in Parts 4 and 5 of this book to the role of pupils, parents, school personnel, and others in curriculum planning. Here we shall merely define the problems and state briefly our point of view. On this issue, one extreme position is the view that all concerned in the process, but primarily learners themselves, should participate in curriculum planning; on

PLATE 5. THE MODERN SCHOOL TAKES RESPONSIBILITY FOR THE DEVELOPMENT OF THE TOTAL PERSONALITY. *A happy, congenial, friendly social climate is conducive to personality development. (Courtesy of the Des Moines Public Schools)*

the other hand is the opposing view that holds that this is a highly technical matter and should be the responsibility of experts working within the framework of broad policy formulated by lay citizens. Thus Hopkins states:

> Pupils of all ages take an active part in determining what needs shall be studied in school. They aid in isolating and investigating their incipient needs to see which are profitable for study. They help to shape continuity and relevance in any need which is being studied. They purpose, they plan, they contribute leads, they gather mate-

rials, they make anecdotal records, they judge the quality and value of results.[12]

As an opposing view Briggs states:

> I have proposed the development of a hierarchy of committees of representative citizens, extending from a central group of the highest ability down to those in the lowliest villages. These representative citizens will be informed of the need for a new curriculum, will agree on the objectives that should be sought, and will approve the few fundamental, directive principles. . . . Sharing with the lay committees on the setting of objectives and the understanding of directive principles and working up of raw materials into teaching-learning units will provide all the opportunity and the freedom that even the best of the educational profession can desire.[13]

It is apparent that some of these differences in points of view stem from the definition given to the term "curriculum." But even though we all accept the broader concept of the term—the experiences that pupils have under the direction and guidance of the school—we still are faced with the issue of who shall determine what kinds of experiences the school will choose to guide and develop for and with its pupils. Should this be solely the prerogative of educators? of parents and lay citizens? of both groups working in close liaison? of a class of pupils and their teacher? or of all these parties, cooperatively? If the last, what is the appropriate role for each group?

The Role of the Layman

In broad, general terms the entire program of the school, as will be shown in Chapter 4, is a reflection of the culture and the value patterns, traditions, and beliefs of the citizens that maintain and support the school, but here we are concerned with the responsibilities that laymen might well assume in overt planning of the curriculum. Views on this matter vary from one that parents and citizens are not competent to participate in—and, moreover, are not interested in participating in —direct curriculum planning to the view that such groups have a great deal to contribute to the process and should participate fully.

In deciding the proper area of responsibility of parents and citizens and of educators it should be kept in mind that the process of curriculum

---

[12] L. Thomas Hopkins, *Interaction: The Democratic Process* (Boston: D. C. Heath & Company, 1941), p. 334. Reprinted by permission of D. C. Heath & Company, publishers.

[13] Thomas H. Briggs, "The Secondary School Curriculum: Yesterday, Today, and Tomorrow," *Teachers College Record*, 52:447–448 (April), 1951. Reprinted by permission of the Bureau of Publications, Teachers College, Columbia University.

development involves four major tasks: (1) a definition of the kinds of outcomes desired from school experience, (2) the selection of the learning experiences and the subject matter content as a part of such experiences which will contribute maximally to the attainment of these desired outcomes, (3) the guidance and development of such learning experiences in the school effectively and skillfully so that the desired learning may be achieved, and (4) the evaluation of behavior in terms of the desired outcomes, so that subsequent experiences may be planned more efficiently.

It is our own belief that parents and citizens can make significant contributions to the process of curriculum making in the first and fourth aspects of planning and guiding learning that are listed above, and that curriculum workers should utilize them directly and fully in these phases of the process. Would not parents and citizens be highly competent to advise with members of the school staff on the kinds of behavior that is considered by the social group to be desirable and essential for effective citizenship in our modern democratic society? This is simply another way of saying that parents and citizens should help define the objectives of education or the desired outcomes of the educational program. Furthermore, who could make more effective evaluations of the attainment of these desired goals by pupils than their own parents or citizens generally in the community? They are the ones who see the pupils in action in many more ways than the teacher does.

We believe that little is to be gained by asking parents to help teachers select learning experiences for the attainment of our desired outcomes or to advise the teacher on how to develop these experiences with pupils. That does seem to be a highly professional job, and one for which the educator is trained. This is not to say that parents and citizens could not make worth-while contributions, but rather to suggest that their time and efforts could better be devoted to the job of helping the professional educator define objectives and evaluate the school experiences in terms of the attainment of these objectives than they could in the detailed process of planning the day-by-day learning experiences of the school.[14]

Role of Pupils

Uppermost in reaching a decision on the proper role of pupils in curriculum planning should be a recognition of the fact that the most effective learning results when the experience is meaningful, purposeful, and significant to the learner himself. Utilizing this fundamental principle, the advocates of the extreme child-centered type of school hold, therefore, that the most meaningful and significant learning experiences

[14] Mrs. John E. Hayes, "A Fence along the Right-of-Way," *NEA Journal*, 40:265–267 (April), 1951.

for pupils are those that they themselves select, plan, carry forward, and evaluate. On the other hand, those who believe that the primary function of the school is to discipline the mind and to provide the learner with a basic stock of information and knowledge and the necessary skills for living assume that pupils are not competent to make decisions on what knowledge and skills are of most worth. Moreover, they contend that pupil selection of learning activities in terms of likes and interests leads to a namby-pamby, watered-down set of experiences that fail to discipline the mind. They therefore believe that the school curriculum should be planned by adults in order that it may best serve the basic purposes of education.

Many curriculum workers reject both of these extreme positions; they believe that the major purposes and desired outcomes of the educational program and the broad areas of experience or aspects of the program should, in the final analysis, be determined by adults. However, within these broad objectives and areas of instruction, they hold that the pupils of a particular class or group, working under the leadership of a competent teacher, can assume a large measure of responsibility for actually planning and carrying forward the particular learning experiences that they will undertake from day to day. It is primarily the obligation of the teacher, but also of the pupils, to evaluate constantly to make certain that these day-by-day experiences contribute as maximally as possible to the attainment of the desired outcomes and basic objectives set by adults for the school. Dewey states this responsibility of teachers in these terms:

> It is then the business of the educator to see in what direction an experience is heading. There is no point in his being more mature if, instead of using his greater insight to help organize the conditions of the experience of the immature, he throws away his insight. Failure to take the moving force of an experience into account so as to judge and direct it on the ground of what it is moving into means disloyalty to the principle of experience itself.[15]

Thus, to spell out this point of view, let us consider that a major outcome desired in the elementary school program—one that is accepted by teachers, curriculum planners, and adults generally—is the development of the ability to read effectively. It is the responsibility of the entire school staff to see that provisions are made in the school program for learning experiences that will contribute to this objective, and the responsibility of the individual teachers to guide learning experiences that

[15] John Dewey, *Experience and Education* (New York: The Macmillan Company, 1938), p. 32. Reprinted by permission of The Macmillan Company, publishers.

will enable each child to develop this ability as effectively as possible. Selecting, planning, and developing the particular classroom experiences in which the pupils engage day after day in order to develop reading ability, however, may very well remain the prerogative of the group of pupils themselves, working with the teacher as a guide and counselor.

The Role of Teachers

Teachers are the key persons in curriculum planning. In the final analysis they will determine in a large measure the actual learning experiences that will go on in the classrooms, halls, and cafeterias and on the playgrounds of our schools. Some school systems may try to circumscribe greatly the range of choices that teachers may make in curriculum planning by insisting that they follow rigidly prescribed courses of study, follow adopted textbooks, or teach according to plans made by supervisory personnel. On the other hand, officials in other schools openly ackowledge the importance of teachers in curriculum planning and administer the school so that individual teachers and building staffs have a large measure of freedom in planning educational experience for pupils.

Much of this book is devoted to a consideration of the responsibilities of the teacher in the role of curriculum planner; hence no further effort will be made here to define that role. In brief, our own position is this: of necessity teachers have and always will have very important responsibilities for actually determining the nature of the educational experiences that are developed in the school. The best approach to curriculum planning is to start with this basic principle and proceed along lines that will aid teachers to make the best choices possible of the kinds of experiences that they plan and develop with pupils. Issuance of courses of study and curriculum bulletins, adoption of approved textbooks, consultation with the supervisory staff, development of in-service education programs, and organization of curriculum development programs for teachers should all be directed to this end.

WHAT ARE THE DESIRABLE CHARACTERISTICS OF GOOD CURRICULUM PLANNING?

We have indicated our own point of view regarding the various issues of curriculum planning presented in this chapter. In this final section our position is summarized in a statement of the four major characteristics that we believe better curriculum planning should have. Attention is given first to a definition of the nature of the curriculum planning process itself.

The Nature of Curriculum Planning

One's interpretation of curriculum planning is determined by one's concept of the curriculum. If the curriculum is considered to be the list of subjects offered or the content of these subjects, then curriculum planning involves merely the listing of subjects or content of subjects. This, unfortunately, has been a rather general practice in the past. If, on the other hand, it is recognized to be the school's total program to effect desired learnings, every phase of that program should be included in curriculum planning. And the program includes not only physical facilities, learning activities, and subject classes but also the interactions of learners with teachers and other adults and with each other. Considering the curriculum as "those experiences for which the school has some responsibility and which it has some opportunity of affecting," Miel, in her penetrating analysis of the process, describes curriculum change as being

> something much more subtle than revising statements written down on paper. To change the curriculum of the school is to change the factors interacting to shape that curriculum. In each instance this means bringing about changes in people—in their desires, beliefs, and attitudes, in their knowledge and skill. Even changes in the physical environment, to the extent that they can be made at all, are dependent upon changes in the persons who have some control over the environment. In short, the nature of curriculum change should be seen for what it really is—a type of social change, change in people, not mere change on paper.[16]

In our discussion of curriculum planning we have been and will be guided by the implications of the broad concept of the curriculum. These implications may be summarized as follows:

1. All phases of the school's program must be included in curriculum planning—all experiences and all factors which determine those experiences.

2. The interrelationship of the many factors influencing the curriculum and its various phases must be considered, since it is the impact of the *total* program (that is, all effects) with which we are basically concerned.

3. Since the function of the curriculum is to achieve "desired learnings," the purpose of curriculum planning is to identify the learnings desired and find ways and means of attaining them. Thus planning

[16] Alice Miel, *Changing the Curriculum* (New York: Appleton-Century-Crofts, Inc., 1946), p. 10. Reprinted by permission of Appleton-Century-Crofts, Inc., publishers.

always includes both goals and procedures. To the extent that curriculum planning is effectively directed toward improved goals or improved procedures or both, curriculum planning and curriculum improvement are virtually synonymous.

Curriculum Planning Should Improve Educational Opportunities

Many facts document the existence of unequal educational opportunity in the United States. As noted in this chapter, some groups are not served adequately at present. Large numbers of youth drop out of school before completion of the twelfth grade. Great differences exist among the states in respect to educational expenditures for each child, and differences within many states in regard to the expenditures of local districts are as great. Socioeconomic status of the family has been found to be significantly related to the extent of formal schooling that children have. Wide differences exist between large and small and wealthy and poor schools as to the facilities provided. An equally critical fact in regard to curriculum planning is the frequent confusion of *identical* and *equal* educational opportunities. We believe that identical educational programs in different communities or for different individuals in the same group may actually constitute unequal educational opportunities. If educational programs should be adapted to the needs of local communities in accordance with American traditions and if educational opportunities should be provided each individual to fit his varying needs and abilities, identical opportunities are undesirable. Yet certain facts indicate the existence of considerable uniformity.

We have been conscious of the principle of improved educational opportunity as we have written each chapter of this book. We hope the procedures of curriculum planning dealt with in Parts 3, 4, and 5 will help to equalize, extend, and improve educational opportunity. We particularly invite the reader's attention to the factors analyzed in Part 2 which affect the provision of educational experiences and opportunity, and therefore curriculum planning.

Curriculum Planning Should Be Comprehensive

All of the factors cited in Chapter 1 and the positions we have taken on the issues dealt with in this chapter add up to the need for comprehensive curriculum planning in every school situation.

Although the curriculum movement in American education has established many curriculum needs and procedures, certain deficiencies should be noted. In the first place, a systematic study of curriculum problems and planning procedures has been inadequately provided for in the education of most teachers. An understanding of these aspects of a teacher's responsibility should be a part of the training of all teachers, so that throughout their teaching career their participation in curriculum planning is an accepted and understood part of the job. In the second place, curriculum planning has been too frequently regarded only as a task that involves a few committees which are given an assignment of writing courses of study or curriculum bulletins; then curriculum planning ends until, a few years later, another committee is appointed to revise the old bulletin. Curriculum planning, we believe, must go much further than this.

In the third place, a typical approach has been to begin curriculum study with some particular problem, such as improving spelling or introducing intercultural relations units, without undertaking a fundamental examination of the relation of this problem to the entire curriculum. It is feasible to begin with specific problems, but they can be examined effectively only in relation to the total framework of a sound comprehensive curriculum plan. In the fourth place, the chief outcomes of many curriculum studies have been the addition of new subjects and the production of new courses of study. Neither result is likely to solve many of the most serious curriculum problems that we have described, although both new subjects and new courses of study might, in combination with other devices, make such changes.

Finally, too much of our curriculum planning has been done on city-wide, county-wide, and state-wide levels. Although these types of planning are desirable, the major responsibility for improving the learning experiences of children rests with the curriculum workers, parents, and pupils of each individual school, and especially with the pupils and teacher of individual learning groups. This is the level at which curriculum improvement in terms of children's learning will occur. We are concerned with curriculum planning which gets results for learners. Such planning must be comprehensive, not piecemeal or on paper only, and is the kind discussed in Parts 2, 3, 4, and 5 of this book.

Curriculum Planning Should Be Continuous

The school's program to effect desired learnings must be planned in accordance with the planners' interpretation of "desired learnings." This interpretation, as we have shown in this chapter, is a product of one's point of view on certain basic issues. A major factor in our own philosophy is the recognition that social conditions and individuals and their interactions are constantly changing. We believe that there must be a dynamic curriculum, sensitive to changing social and individual needs. The desired learnings change with social and individual conditions and needs; hence curriculum planning must be a continuous process.

For example, recent social changes have had at least two fundamental effects on the curriculum. In the first place, these conditions create new social problems with which pupils must deal now and later. How can modern methods of production, transportation, and communication be used to improve living? How can citizens participate more effectively in the changing political and economic systems? How can family life be improved and stabilized? How can the new leisure time be used constructively? How can war and depression be avoided? crime and mental illness? In the second place, to deal with these new conditions and problems, there is a vast new body of subject matter. The science of 1900 is not adequate to interpret the environment in the 1950's, nor the social studies to explain the new social problems.

Furthermore, it is neither desirable nor possible to wait fifty years or even one year to deal with these changes; they are occurring continually, sometimes dramatically and sometimes gradually, and our pupils' lives are being affected. The teacher who objects to dealing with current developments because of inadequate information ignores the fact that the pupils are being affected, regardless of the accuracy and adequacy of information.

The curriculum must also be dynamic because no group of children in our school today is identical with last year's pupils. The learnings we desire for our present group must be planned with respect to their maturities, needs, and interests, and the experiences through which we hope the learning will develop cannot therefore be identical with those used in another group. In addition to the differences between children of the same age and grade groupings, we must remember, too, that the range of individuals attending school should constantly widen. As we noted, nursery schools and kindergartens are needed, as are various types of adult education and college programs and programs for handicapped children. All these new groups in school will require new curriculum plans.

The interrelationship of the curriculum with social aims and with the individual is fully analyzed in Part 2. The point to be made here is that the school's program is continuously being affected by a changing society and by changing individuals. We can make the same curriculum provisions year after year and for group after group and so fail to achieve desirable adjustments of individuals to their times, or we can keep the curriculum dynamic. The former alternative is a denial of the school's inherent responsibility for improving living; the latter, our obligation.

Curriculum Planning Should Be Cooperative

We have already stated our position on the issue of who should plan the curriculum. We believe that a curriculum is more likely to possess the desirable characteristics set forth in Chapter 1 if there is participation from the community in defining social aims; from parents and children in defining goals of personal development; from the public, parents, pupils, and school staff in planning for comprehensiveness and continuity; from the pupils and staff in checking on balance; from the pupils in securing flexibility in the selection of alternative procedures as well as purposes; and from the school administration in securing adequate resources. The extent and nature of such participation has to be worked out for each situation, but the development of maximally effective cooperation is desirable. Cooperation, it should be noted, is desirable in each stage of planning. Techniques of cooperative planning are described throughout this book, but Part 5 gives particular attention to this aspect of the organization and evaluation of curriculum planning.

For Further Study

Alberty, Harold, "Bridging the Gap between General and Vocational Education in the High School," *Educational Forum*, 13:211–217 (January), 1949.

A significant statement on this important issue.

Alexander, William M., and Galen Saylor, *Secondary Education: Basic Principles and Practices*. New York: Rinehart & Company, Inc., 1950.

Chapter X presents evidence of the extent to which youth attend secondary school and factors related to attendance.

American Association of School Administrators, *The Expanding Role of Education*. Twenty-sixth Yearbook. Washington, D.C.: The Association, 1948.

Chapters II, IV, and V deal respectively with educational provisions for young children, adults, and exceptional children.

Association for Supervision and Curriculum Development, *Action for Curriculum Improvement*. 1951 Yearbook. Washington, D.C.: National Education Association, 1951.

See especially Chapter II, "Conditions Compelling Curriculum Change," and Chapter III, "Initiating Curriculum Change."

Brameld, Theodore, *Patterns of Educational Philosophy*. Yonkers, N.Y.: World Book Company, 1950.

Analyzes and critically evaluates, from his point of view, three philosophies of education, and then discusses at length his own theory, which he calls reconstructionism.

Briggs, Thomas H., J. Paul Leonard, and Joseph Justman, *Secondary Education* Rev. Ed.; New York: The Macmillan Company, 1950.

Chapter 18 discusses some of the major problems and issues facing secondary education.

Caswell, Hollis L. (ed.), *The American High School*. Eighth Yearbook of the John Dewey Society. New York: Harper & Brothers, 1946.

Chapter IX considers the place of vocational education in the whole program of the secondary school.

————, "Significant Curriculum Issues," *Educational Leadership,* 9:207–214 (January), 1952.

Discusses a number of curriculum issues raised in this chapter.

————, and associates, *Curriculum Improvement in Public School Systems*. New York: Bureau of Publications, Teachers College, Columbia University, 1950.

Chapters 1–5 deal with background materials for evaluating programs of curriculum development.

Childs, John L., *Education and the Philosophy of Experimentalism*. New York: Appleton-Century-Crofts, Inc., 1931.

A systematic discussion of the experimentalist's point of view on education.

Demiashkevich, Michael, *An Introduction to the Philosophy of Education*. New York: American Book Company, 1935.

A philosopher educated in Europe looks with favor on the old classical school, and states the position of the essentialist on educational aims and procedures.

Dewey, John, *Democracy and Education*. New York: The Macmillan Company, 1931.

A basic book on Dewey's philosophy of experimentalism. Considers the role of education in a democratic society and the source of educational aims and purposes.

————, *Experience and Education*. New York: The Macmillan Company, 1938.

Dewey, even though he emphasizes the role of experience in learning and the relationship of interest to education, maintains that the quality of the experience and the direction of growth is of paramount importance.

Edwards, Newton, and Herman G. Richey, *The School in the American Social Order*. Boston: Houghton Mifflin Company, 1947.

Chapter 16 presents extensive data on school attendance and factors related to nonenrollment.

Hutchins, Robert M., *The Conflict in Education in a Democratic Society*. New York: Harper & Brothers, 1953.

One of Hutchins's basic statements on his concept of education, referred to in this book as perennialism.

Kilpatrick, William H., *Philosophy of Education*. New York: The Macmillan Company, 1951.

One of Dewey's leading interpreters presents a basic statement on the philosophy of experimentalism. Various aspects of curriculum planning and teaching are discussed.

Mays, Arthur B., "The Relationship between General and Vocational Education," *Journal of General Education*, 2:156–160 (January), 1948.

A penetrating discussion of this issue.

Miel, Alice, *Changing the Curriculum*. New York: Appleton-Century-Crofts, Inc., 1946.

An excellent analysis of curriculum planning as a process of social change.

National Society for the Study of Education, *American Education in the Postwar Period: Structural Reorganization*. Part II, Forty-fourth Yearbook. Chicago: The University of Chicago Press, 1945.

Chapter II considers problems relative to the provision of educational opportunities for special groups of pupils, such as the exceptional child, children of migratory workers, and the like.

———, *Early Childhood Education*. Part II, Forty-sixth Yearbook. Chicago: The University of Chicago Press, 1947.

Chapter IV presents data on the extent that provisions are made for young children in nursery schools and kindergartens.

———, *The Education of Exceptional Children*. Part I, Forty-ninth Yearbook. Chicago: The University of Chicago Press, 1950.

Chapter I discusses the need for provisions for exceptional children and some evidence on the extent of such provisions at present.

Storen, Helen F., *Laymen Help Plan the Curriculum*. Washington, D.C.: Association for Supervision and Curriculum Development, 1946.

A discussion of the role of parents and other citizens in curriculum planning.

United States Office of Education, *Schools for Children under Six*. Bulletin 1947, No. 5. Washington, D.C.: Government Printing Office, 1947.

A study of educational opportunities for young children.

part 2

WHAT MAJOR FACTORS MUST BE CONSIDERED IN CURRICULUM PLANNING?

Everything a teacher, a coordinator, a supervisor, a principal, or an administrator does in providing educational experiences for pupils is an aspect of curriculum planning. Such planning can be thorough and systematic, taking account of the pertinent factors in the situation and being directed to a preconceived goal, or it can be helter-skelter, opportunistic, chaotic, and inconsistent. In Part 1 we noted that too often curriculum planning in the past has been deficient, with the result that the curriculum has fallen short of the best we know how to provide. In concluding that discussion we stated the desirable characteristics of a sound procedure for curriculum planning.

The five chapters comprising Part 2 begin the application of these characteristics by considering the factors that must be taken into account by all curriculum workers if curriculum planning is to be comprehensive and is to improve educational opportunities. We first consider in Chapter 3 some of the forces that influence curriculum planning. In the next two chapters attention is given to the two basic elements in the educative process. Chapter 4 will discuss the society as a factor in curriculum planning, emphasizing that schools must seek approved cultural values if they are to fulfill their function. Values, however, are attained only in the lives of individuals; hence Chapter 5 will consider the pupil as a factor in the educative process, pointing out the necessity of gearing learning experiences to the developmental level of the learner. How to plan school experiences that will be psychologically sound is discussed in Chapter 6.

Finally, all of these factors and elements that affect curriculum planning must be brought to focus in the definition of the basic purposes and functions of the school. Chapter 7, therefore, presents goals for education that may well guide the final selection of curriculum experiences.

chapter 3

Forces That Influence Curriculum Planning

On the opening day of school a class of, say, twenty to thirty-five pupils presents itself to the teacher. He is responsible in a large measure for the educational experiences that these boys and girls will have in his classroom during the year. What will he do? What kinds of activities will he have them engage in? As was stated in introducing the previous chapter, many choices can and must be made as educators plan a curriculum for boys and girls. Some issues that arise in curriculum planning were discussed in that chapter. In this chapter we shall consider important forces that influence curriculum workers as they make decisions, and consider the extent to which they may be circumscribed in their choices.

FACTORS ARE INTERRELATED

Before we begin our analysis it must be pointed out that these influences are interrelated. It is virtually impossible to establish a direct causal relationship between a present-day curriculum practice and a particular factor or force in American life. As has been pointed out, curriculum planning is a matter of making choices, and many pressures may affect the decisions that are made. In most schools, for example, children are taught to read in the first grade. Is that practice due to research findings on the growth and development of children, to tradition, to parental pressure, to theories of the role of education in a society, to pupil desires? Or is it due in some measure to each of these things and possibly to many others? Why have secondary schools added instruction in automobile driving to the curriculum in recent years? Because of research findings, pressure groups, pupil interests, parental demands, desire to keep up with other schools, state law, educators' views on what constitutes the proper function of the school, or because of a number of these factors taken together? With this caution to avoid any one-to-one relationship between a particular factor and a curriculum practice, let us analyze some of the forces that have shaped the curriculum.

HISTORICAL PRECEDENT AND TRADITION

Almost all of us as teachers, supervisors, or administrators accept positions in going school systems. The school will have been in operation and have had a program in previous years. This program has become more or less institutionalized, that is, it is an established plan of education that is usually continued as a matter of course until positive action is taken to change it. Teachers, for example, are assigned to teach the fifth grade in the Park School or English in Central High School. They will likely find in existence courses of study to guide their planning and sets of textbooks to be used in carrying on the work of the grade or class. Administrators and supervisors assume that the teacher, in general, will follow an instructional plan that has been in use in the system in previous years. While it is taken for granted, and most schools will encourage the practice, that the teacher will use his own ingenuity in planning his methods of teaching and classroom procedures, it is generally assumed that the subject matter to be covered will conform in a large measure to what has traditionally been taught in that particular grade or course. Curriculum improvement usually represents a change in accepted practice, a planned departure from what has been done in the past. Thus we see that precedent and tradition become a major factor in determining what experiences any particular group of pupils will have during a school year.

This statement does not imply that the American school does not change. Anyone familiar with education in this country knows that changes in the curriculum are constantly being made, and that our whole pattern of education represents an evolution of a distinctive American school system. Innovations, experimentation, the development of new procedures, and the introduction of new courses and new subjects characterize educational practice. But these developments are worked out within the framework of an existing structure. Traditional programs and practices continue in use until plans are deliberately formulated to change the existing curriculum. If these new practices prove meritorious in the opinions of the educators and citizens concerned, they remain a part of the program, to become in turn institutionalized, to be accepted by those who come on the scene later. It is this adherence to traditional practices that gives stability and continuity to the school program. It provides a base so that the work of the school may continue while we are developing better practices and are experimenting with new methods and new ways of doing things. On the other hand, we should not continue the traditional just because it is customary. The times demand that the curriculum change, and educators need constantly to analyze and evaluate all aspects of the program of the school to see if it is the best program that can be devised for the particular boys and girls being educated at that particular time and place.

American Schools Break with Historical Antecedents

The earliest schools established in America were modeled on European schools. It is quite understandable that the colonists would establish in the New World the same kinds of schools that they had known in their mother countries. This means that the antecedents of the American school system in its organization and program are in the main English with some transplantings from Holland and Germany. But even though the colonists at first imitated the mother countries, they gradually evolved a unique system that was more indigenous to the American culture with its emphasis on democracy, equal rights, and opportunity for all. Today our plan of education is quite unlike that in any other country and represents an ideal for democratically minded people everywhere. As this unparalleled program of education has evolved over the past three centuries, it has clearly become differentiated from its antecedents and its earlier form in these major respects:

1. Development of a unitary plan of education for all pupils. As was true in the seventeenth century, European education to this day has adhered to a two-track plan—one kind of education for the masses and another kind for the elite classes. The education of children of the common people is restricted quite largely to the three R's, music, drawing, and religion, topped off by vocational training, often in part-time or apprentice programs. The children of the more privileged classes attend selective institutions whose curriculum trains for admission to technical and professional occupations or college.

As everyone knows, in this country we have a unitary system of schools in which children progress naturally from one grade to another and from one level of schooling to the next without artificial barriers or restrictive standards of admission being applied. This unitary plan of education for all children is probably the unique contribution of the American people to educational thought and practice throughout the world.

2. Development of a system of free schools under public control. Closely related to the unitary plan of American education is the provision of a system of free public schools extending from the kindergarten or first grade through the secondary school, which may even include the thirteenth and fourteenth grades. These two practices must go hand in hand, for we could not maintain a unitary program if a barrier were erected at some point and only children whose parents could afford to pay a tuition charge were permitted to go beyond that point or enter a particular type of school.

3. *Adaptation of the curriculum to the basic needs and developmental growth patterns of pupils.* The curriculums of the old Latin Grammar School and that of the European secondary schools on which it was patterned were primarily humanistic. Latin constituted the main subject of study, comprising about three fourths to nine tenths of the curriculum. Some Greek was introduced after the pupils had mastered Latin. European secondary schools have largely retained this humanistic tradition. The German *Gymnasium* and *Realschule,* the French *lycée,* and the English "public" schools all stress even today the mastery of languages. Some mathematics, history, and science have been introduced, but heavy emphasis is placed on the traditional humanistic learning.

In America, although the Latin Grammar School persisted until late in the eighteenth century, it declined rapidly in importance. Its curriculum was appropriate only for a small number of youth who desired to enter college. The people, particularly the new commercial classes, demanded a more functional education. This gave rise to the development of private instruction in bookkeeping, astronomy, surveying, English, navigation, geography, geometry, and the like. From this foundation, the distinctive American academy developed. Its original purpose was to provide instruction in these more practical subjects needed by the people to carry on the trade and industry of the day. As they developed, the academies took on the task of preparing youth for college, and while they retained much of the practical curriculum, they also taught the traditional subjects. The academies were not public institutions, and tuition was usually charged. Such institutions served as the forerunner of the American high school—a distinctly American contribution to educational practice.

Boston established the first high school to serve children who were not interested in attending the traditional Latin Grammar School but who wanted a more complete education than that furnished by the elementary schools of the day, yet did not want to pay the fees demanded by the academies or private schools. The popularity of this unique institution is apparent, for today it is found in every American community, and at least 90 per cent of the young people enroll in it, half of them remaining to graduate. No other country in the world has such a school, and in no other country, except in Canada and in England since 1944, can any child look forward to twelve years of continuous full-time schooling at public expense.

This popular American high school has been particularly sensitive to the needs and wishes of the people. Educators, in response to public demand or with popular approval and support, have continuously modified the program of the school through an expansion of its offerings and its services, through more democratic teaching procedures, through reorganization of the curriculum pattern, and through revision of the content included in traditional courses. Even the high school of seventy-five years ago would bear little resemblance to a modern comprehensive high school. Basic training for a number of vocations is provided in many of our high schools; health and physical conditioning are emphasized; in numerous courses and activities current affairs and pressing problems of American life are considered; courses in homemaking and family living are provided; outstanding opportunities in music and art are available; and the pupils participate in a wide variety of activities outside the classroom. Such programs and educational experiences are a far cry from the Latin Grammar Schools of colonial days or the academies of the early national period; they certainly represent a radical departure from the strict humanistic education that still characterizes secondary education in most European countries.

As is illustrated in Plate 6, the curriculum of the present-day elementary school in turn is as different from that of the old reading and writing schools known to the colonists, as the high school is different from the Latin Grammar School. The most revolutionary changes have been in the methods of teaching and in the attitude toward children. The harsh discipline and stern treatment of the colonial schools have been replaced by a new concept of education as guided growth and development. Rote learning and excessive drill on what was often meaningless material have been superseded by purposeful activities of interest to the learner. A variety of learning resources are used in place of a very limited number of formal textbooks. A child draws on his life outside the school to add meaning and significance to the activities sponsored by the school. Group activities have often replaced highly competitive recitations. The formal offerings of the school have also expanded. Science, art, music, handicrafts, health, community civics, and similar subjects have been added to the curriculum of the elementary school.

No, the curriculum of the American elementary and secondary school has not been a static thing, continuing generation after generation in the same vein and following the same pattern. Once the basic principle that change is necessary to meet the changing needs of each new generation has been accepted, the concept of change itself becomes institutionalized and carries forward the momentum that engenders still further adaptations and modifications from year to year.

4. School objectives emphasize behavior and effective citizenship. Teachers, parents, and everyone concerned with curriculum planning for the schools in this country place great emphasis on the necessity of the school's giving direction to the actions of its pupils—their behavior, their relations to others, their attitudes, their concern for their own welfare and for that of their fellow men. We believe that the school has a

PLATE 6. GONE ARE THE HARSH DISCIPLINE AND STERN TREATMENT OF THE OLD SCHOOL. *These young pupils enjoy a school that is aware of their growth needs. (Courtesy of the Des Moines Public Schools)*

primary responsibility for developing good citizens who are competent to direct their own individual actions to the end of attaining the good life for all.

While all schools of all times have been concerned with the development of character and with the inculcation of the values prized by society, the modern American school, accepting the concept that the pupil must learn through his experiences, has developed a whole educational program that is designed to provide experiences in being a good person and hence an effective, conscientious citizen. The traditional school stressed knowledge and acquisition of information, accepting the doctrine that knowledge would result in desirable action. But empirical evidence as well as research has demonstrated that to know is not necessarily to do. So the modern school places emphasis on action with knowledge. Action without knowledge is blind; knowledge without action is sterile.

Any statement of basic objectives for the modern school stresses citizenship, worthy home membership, ethical character, the use of critical judgment, healthful living, self-discipline, and the like in addition to the acquisition of knowledge. In contrast to the stern, harsh treatment of children and the *memoriter* methods of the old school, the ways of working with children and the very life and climate of the modern school also reflect this concern for the development of personality and character.

5. *Responsibility of the local community for education.* Another important difference between European systems of education and the American system is the degree of control vested in the people of the local community. Control of the school systems of France, Germany, and other countries of the Continent is primarily a function of the state or national government. The ministries of education largely determine the curriculum, select the teachers, choose the textbooks, and regulate the conduct of the school. In England, the local school boards organized in the latter part of the nineteenth century have impoitant responsibilities over education, although the national government still exercises much greater control than does the government in this country.

Here responsibility for the establishment and control of schools has largely rested in local communities. This was the result of pioneer conditions in our early history, but it rapidly became the accepted practice because it conformed to democratic beliefs. As each new state was organized, the state government provided for the organization of local school districts, which were given considerable autonomy over the schools. The district board of education is a legal body created by state law, and it exercises its authority within a framework of state legislation. It is an accepted principle in all states that this local school board should have major responsibilities for the establishment of the schools needed in the district, the determination of the curriculum, the appointment of the teachers, and the control over the schools.

This large measure of local control over the education of children places a great obligation on teachers and administrators. Each one must be an expert in curriculum development, for he will have a part to play in determining what the curriculum for pupils will be. The school staff will need to make many important decisions relative to the kinds of experiences to provide children in the way of formal course offerings, the methods to be used in the classroom, the treatment to be accorded children, the activities outside of classrooms that will be made available to pupils, and many similar important curriculum matters. If these decisions, which greatly affect the development of boys and girls, are to be sound and the best that can be made, each teacher has an important obligation to decide curriculum matters on the basis of a thorough understanding of what constitutes a good education for boys and girls.

Tradition Should Be Respected but Not Revered

Tradition and precedent give stability to the educational program and enable us to carry on while continuously evaluating what we are doing and thinking through better ways of educating pupils. The American school system, however, has never been a slave of custom and tradition. From our earliest colonial days, we have modified traditional practice and have adapted practices and ideas from other countries to our own unique purposes and conditions. In fact, we have developed a tradition of change and progress. The whole American pattern of thought is geared to change, to improving what now exists. This attitude is apparent in our approach to education. We have evolved new institutions as other institutions have become outmoded; we have introduced new curriculum offerings as the conditions of daily life changed and as the needs of those attending the school shifted; we have modified teaching procedures and methods to conform to new concepts of child growth and development and the psychology of learning.

In curriculum development we must start with a basic concept of what constitutes a good educational program; we should then evaluate carefully what has evolved as the educational program, retaining what has proven to be good and sound education, but being ready to work for modification and change if that is clearly indicated.

CULTURAL PATTERNS AND SOCIAL AIMS AS CURRICULUM DETERMINANTS

Undoubtedly, the most important influence in shaping the curriculum of any school is the cultural pattern and value system of the society that establishes and supports the school. The impact of the culture on the curriculum of the school and the school's obligations to the social groups are such important matters that the next chapter (Chapter 4) will be devoted to these topics. However, since the present chapter considers factors that shape the curriculum, brief attention should also be given here to the impact of cultural values on the curriculum.

Why do the educational programs of Germany, Japan, England, France, Mexico, and, in fact, of all other countries differ markedly from that of the United States? The nature of learning and the physiological and mental development of boys and girls do not vary in basic respects from nation to nation. What does vary markedly, however, is the social setting in which education takes place, and this is what accounts in the main for the major variations in educational programs around the world.

Schools are powerful instruments for the realization of social policies and aspirations. It is indeed to be expected, then, that our educational program will be planned in terms of what we as a people believe to be good and what we seek to perpetuate through each succeeding generation. No nation would establish and support a system of schools unless its citizens believed that they should guide the development of their young in an organized fashion, that they should seek to make boys and girls something they would not become naturally. These goals or aims which permeate the program of deliberate education are but expressions of the social values and modes of living which the society favors, or at least those members of the society who are in a position to make their views effective.

Teachers, administrators, and boards of education are constantly making decisions which affect the nature of the educational program. Each person involved in such decision making approaches an issue with a set of values, with concepts of what comprise proper educational experiences for boys and girls. If the decisions made are at cross purposes with the dominant values of the social group that controls and maintains the schools, conflict and dissension arise. Legislation may be imposed, oaths may be required, board members may be attacked or defeated in elections, administrators are criticized and their decisions reversed, and teachers are overruled or dismissed.

Teachers and other curriculum workers obviously, then, will plan an educational program that they feel is acceptable to the social group. The school will reflect their ideals and values. In recognizing this influence on curriculum development it becomes apparent that teachers and all educators should (1) understand thoroughly the basic social aims and values which the American people accept, (2) assume an active role in helping citizens themselves more thoroughly analyze and understand these values, and (3) seek a broad base of decision making in school matters so that minority opinion and the views of pressure groups or vested interest groups are not mistakenly assumed to be the voice of the people.

INFLUENCE OF EDUCATIONAL PHILOSOPHY, RESEARCH, AND
EXPERIMENTATION ON CURRICULUM DEVELOPMENT

If we accept as a fact that tradition and custom are important forces in
determining what we do in the school day after day, we still have not
answered the question of why these things became traditional or accepted
practices. If we agree that the educational program will inevitably reflect the social values and beliefs of the cultural group that maintains the
schools, many matters that must be decided in the actual planning of
the program of the school are still to be resolved. On what basis do we
make such decisions? The insights that educators gain from a study of
philosophical concepts and from research and experimentation have important bearings on these decisions, and we should examine these influences on educational practice.

The Role of Philosophy in Educational Planning

Curriculum decisions are philosophical decisions—they represent
a choice of values. Ever since early man first planned formal procedures
for the education of the youth, decisions have been made as to the nature of the educational program. If the choice was a good one and resulted in better accomplishment of the goals sought, the tendency would
be, of course, to follow these practices in the future. Thus tradition comes
to be established and practices come to be institutionalized. It is only as
venturesome souls point out defects in the established procedure in terms
of accomplishments, new conditions, or new ends to be sought, and propose new courses of action which they or other practitioners try out, that
traditional practices are changed. In turn these better procedures again
become tradition.

These individuals who propound new ways of doing things, who
question established practice, and who point out new elements in the
present situation have had tremendous influence on the development of
education. The history of education is replete with the records of great
thinkers who have challenged established practice and who have provided
educators with new insights and new understandings as to the nature of
the educational process. Socrates, Ignatius, Comenius, Pestalozzi, Herbart, Froebel, Spencer, Rousseau, Montessori, and Dewey are some of the
educational philosophers who have given curriculum makers invaluable
help in the development of better programs of education.

All curriculum workers, of course, have a philosophy of education
—a conception of what the purposes, goals, and methods of education
should be. As they plan learning experiences for pupils, these concepts
will be a major factor in arriving at important curriculum decisions. Un·

doubtedly the key factor in curriculum planning is the points of view held by teachers. The development of a philosophy of education is a complex process. Study, the analysis of research, empirical evidence, experimentation, discussion, knowledge, the points of view held by professors, educational leaders, and laymen, reports of professional committees and groups, temperament, and many other influences of this type affect the evolvement of a philosophy of education. It is the purpose of this book, for example, to analyze the processes of curriculum planning and to present concepts about the curriculum that will influence the points of view of curriculum workers.

Use of Educational Research in Curriculum Planning

The scientific movement in education has had a profound effect on curriculum development in this country. Yet the use of scientific methods in studying educational problems and the developmental patterns of youngsters dates back less than seventy-five years. One needs only to compare the educational practices and teaching methods at the turn of the century with those of today to find ample evidence of the influence of research on curriculum planning. Research has found its way into curriculum practice as it became the basis for the formulation of philosophical concepts and eventually for decision making of all who plan instructional programs for children.[1] Chapter 15 discusses the role of research and experimentation in further improvement of the curriculum. Here we shall consider briefly some areas in which research has made important contributions.

Nature of learning. The most significant research related to curriculum planning has been in the nature of learning. The old doctrine of formal discipline was discredited by the research of Thorndike, Woodworth, and others. This has resulted in the elimination from the school subjects of much of the absurd, unrealistic, and artificial subject matter that had no functional value to the learner but had been retained on the grounds that it trained the mind. Other research has provided ample evidence of the totality of learning and of the importance of understanding for effective learning. The role of motives in determining the nature and quality of learning has also become established by such studies.

[1] A penetrating analysis of the methods and contributions of educational research to elementary school practices is contained in Walter J. Moore and Celia B. Stendler, "Some Research Studies in Education and in Related Disciplines Which Suggest Good Elementary-School Practices," in the Thirteenth Yearbook of the John Dewey Society, *The American Elementary School* (Harold G. Shane, editor; New York: Harper & Brothers, 1953), Chap. XII.

Human growth and development. Research in human growth and development has provided educators with an understanding of the developmental needs of boys and girls and has given us an insight into the types of experiences that contribute significantly to the emotional, social, physical, and mental development of pupils. The harshness, stern discipline, and formalism of the old school have given way to self-discipline and freedom with responsibility. Also, learning experiences that are more meaningful and purposeful to the pupils and are better adapted to their maturing capacities and interests have replaced the rote memorization and formal drill of the old school. Chapter 5 considers in detail the implications of research findings for this aspect of curriculum planning.

Functional curriculum experiences. A more functional curriculum has resulted from the extensive research that has been done within the past forty years on the activities of both children and adults. For example, the famous Thorndike Word List and subsequent lists of this type have been used to keep school readers and spelling books within conceptual patterns of youngsters. Topics included in science courses are based on tested interests of pupils; mathematics is for use, not computational manipulation; geography emphasizes group living of people and their relationships to their environment, rather than memorization of capitals, rivers, and the like. Every subject field has been markedly affected by research on the functional use people make in their day-by-day living of concepts, principles, and knowledge. Once the theory of mental discipline and faculty psychology was discredited, the primary purpose of all educational experiences became one of contributing maximally to the development of boys and girls in accordance with approved goals, rather than one of exercising the mind.

Individual capacities, abilities, and achievements. Curriculum development in this country has been profoundly affected by the use of scientifically developed tests and similar instruments for measuring capacity, abilities, achievements, interests, and the like. During the past half century Thorndike, Courtis, Judd, Freeman, Haggerty, Terman, Lindquist, and many other scientific workers have applied the statistical procedures of the biometricians to the measurement of pupil traits as well as various elements in the educational program. Teachers of today are well aware of the vast array of standardized tests that are available for measuring achievement. These are extensively used throughout the nation to ascertain how well pupils are achieving in terms of a so-called normal group of pupils. Courses of study, school offerings, and teaching methods are often revised or modified in the light of the results revealed by such tests.

While the testing movement has spurred teachers and other curriculum planners to undertake a critical examination of the work of the school, this approach to educational planning has not been without its drawbacks. The most serious question that may be raised about such tests is the extent to which their use distorts or overemphasizes certain aspects of the educational program. The second shortcoming of such tests is that the standards for achievement are not set in terms of what may be desirable for particular pupils but rather in terms of what may have been achieved by some selected group of pupils who are used as the population for determining the norms.

In recent years major strides have been made in broadening the base for evaluating the educational program as will be shown in Chapter 17. Through a variety of methods, used as scientifically as possible, teachers, administrators, parents, and the pupils themselves seek information on how well the outcomes desired from the school are being attained. The evidence used for making such judgments is not limited to pupils' scores on a test, or the deviation of these scores from norms. Teacher observation, parent observation, behavior journals, anecdotal records, conference reports, and numerous other devices are used to obtain evidence on the accomplishment and development of pupils. Test makers are also developing other types of tests that endeavor to give measures or information on other factors used in curriculum planning; tests of personality development, interest finders, tests of problem-solving ability, tests of rational thinking, attitude tests, social-distance scales, aptitude tests, and many others.

Methods of working with pupils. In keeping with our increasing concern for wholesome development of pupils in all phases of growth, considerable research in recent years has been directed to a study of methods of working with children. The programs of cooperative action research now being carried out by school systems and colleges, which are discussed in Chapter 15, are primarily organized to study what happens to pupils in classroom and home situations and the effects that such events have on children. The whole field of group dynamics, which has in a large measure evolved since the middle 1930's, is developing a body of very important research findings in the area of human relationships, group action, group status, leadership, and the like. Undoubtedly educational practice will be greatly affected by the findings of research workers in such areas.

Experimentation Influences Curriculum Development

The proposals of educational philosophers and leaders and the findings of research become significant only as they are translated into action and someone actually develops educational programs that try out the ideas proposed or the changes suggested by the findings. Hence experimentation and the trying out of promising practices, as is pointed out in Chapter 15, are essential aspects of curriculum development. Willingness to try out new practices has been a distinguishing characteristic of American schools in past decades. The problem is not so much one of getting serious proposals tried out as it is to evaluate the new practice to see if it really merits retention in the educational program, and to get practices that have been proven sound in experimental situations spread to schools generally throughout the country.

Much of our experimentation consists of such unpretentious things as introducing new courses into the educational offerings, reorganizing the content of existing courses, changing the grade level at which certain topics or skills are formally introduced into the curriculum, using new methods of teaching, and the like. Sometimes the introduction of such innovations is a move in the wrong direction. The educators who undertake the modifications lack sufficient insight or understanding of the basic factors involved in the educational process and make erroneous guesses on sound educational procedure. For example, the idea may spread that instruction in phonics is not desirable in teaching reading in the elementary grades. Teachers and administrators may unchallengingly accept this idea and drop all instruction in the phonic sounds, only to discover later that their pupils lack proper methods for attacking new words they encounter in reading; or teachers may decide that an exercise workbook is a good method of drilling pupils in language usage, not recognizing that language usage is best learned by actually using language in meaningful situations.

This is not to say that teachers should not experiment; certainly progress comes through trying out new ideas and new practices. Before such practices are tried out, however, they should be subjected to the most careful scrutiny in terms of the known facts about learning, child growth and development, and teaching methods, and in terms of the outcomes really sought through the educational program of the school. Parallel to any such experimentation should be the most careful evaluation of the practice so that as soon as is feasible a judgment may be made about the soundness of the plan.

TEXTBOOKS AS CURRICULUM DETERMINANTS

It is difficult to assay the extent to which textbooks determine the curriculum of the school. That teachers in American schools make extensive use of the textbook is not to be questioned. But is this to say that the textbook determines the curriculum? that it determines the nature of the experiences which children have in school? Unquestionably, whatever the influence of the textbook has been in the past, it is much less in the modern school. Its value as a teaching resource is unquestioned, however, and we have considered its proper use in Chapter 14. In this chapter we shall consider the textbook as an influence on curriculum planning.

Influence of the Textbook on the Elementary School Curriculum

Reflect on the experiences which pupils have in a modern elementary school: the learning experiences they have on the playground, in the school lunchroom, in the auditorium, in the halls, and in the excursions they take around the school grounds or to places of interest in the community are not determined to any appreciable extent by the textbooks used in the school. Neither does the textbook have much influence on some of the learnings that take place within the classroom itself. Experiences in keeping the room livable and neat, in putting work materials away at the appropriate time, in caring for pets or flowers in the room, in playing with the numerous manipulative materials available in a modern school, in singing and playing musical instruments, in expressing creative impulses with art or handicraft materials, and many others are surely not dictated by or dependent to any important extent on a textbook.

In the organized, systematic classwork of the school, such as in arithmetic, reading, language arts, social studies, and science classes, textbooks are used extensively. It would be easy to say that in such areas of instruction they do determine in a large measure the curriculum. But is that necessarily true? Pupils working in even such formal classes have many learning experiences other than acquiring subject matter or developing skills from the use of the textbook. They are learning to work as members of a group, to develop an interest in reading, to respect the opinions of other pupils, to share ideas, to express thoughts and opinions, to take pride in success and to be depressed over failure, and to develop many other types of behavior that are not dictated by textbooks. It is in the subject matter used, the skills acquired, and the methods by which the teacher teaches such content that the textbook most significantly shapes the curriculum.

Unquestionably in most elementary schools the textbooks for the academic areas of instruction do in a large measure determine the scope and sequence of the curriculum and the nature of the learning experiences. Nevertheless, as has been stated, even in these areas the teacher and the pupils still exercise important responsibilities for determining curriculum experiences of various types.

The Influence of the Textbook on the High School Curriculum

Unquestionably, the textbook is a much greater determiner of the curriculum of the high school than it is of the elementary school. Here much greater emphasis is placed on the acquisition of knowledge as such, and the textbook is often a major factor in determining what subject matter is studied and what concepts are developed. The program of studies itself is often circumscribed by the textbooks that can be made available to carry on instruction.

In the academic subjects, the common practice is to follow a text in the development of the course. Far too many teachers use few or no additional teaching resources. Moreover, the teaching method used in these areas is frequently a sterile textbook procedure—a question-and-answer period in which pupils are called upon to recall from memory what the book said on a particular matter. It is even not too difficult to find teaching going on in the secondary school in which pupils read in rotation from the assigned lesson. The sole objective of the teacher appears to be one of imparting a limited amount of information to pupils.

On the other hand, great numbers of teachers of the academic subjects in secondary schools are no more slaves to the textbook than are our best primary grade teachers. To these master teachers, it becomes simply a convenient tool for use as appropriate in developing the attitudes, concepts, and points of view and in acquiring the knowledge which they, and possibly the members of the class themselves, consider worth while in attaining the desired outcomes of education. For such teachers, the textbook is not an inexorable tyrant that prescribes curriculum experiences. Rather, as is shown in Plate 7, textbooks, as well as other reference works, are valuable aids in achieving predetermined objectives.

In the newer subjects of the high school curriculum the textbook never has been as significant a factor as it has been in the academic areas. Teachers of music and art, for example, seldom follow a textbook. In the practical arts and vocational fields, textbooks are usually used as guides to aid in carrying on some practical project planned by the pupil and the instructor. Textbooks are seldom used in physical education classes, except for instruction in health, hygiene, and first aid. We could similarly canvass the situation in all areas of the curriculum, but that hardly seems necessary for this discussion.

In conclusion, it is fair to say that the textbook exerts less influence than was formerly true. Textbooks are more important curriculum determiners in the high schools and the upper grades of the elementary school and in the academic areas than they are in the lower grades of the school and in the so-called practical subjects.

PLATE 7. TEXTBOOKS AND REFERENCE WORKS ARE TOOLS FOR LEARNING, NOT CURRICULUM GUIDES. *When a high school has a good library, there is less tendency to rely on a textbook as a basis for curriculum planning. (Courtesy of the Westinghouse High School, Pittsburgh)*

CURRICULUM CONTROLS EXERCISED BY EXTERNAL AGENCIES

The curriculum must be planned within an administrative structure and within limits blocked out by legal authority as well as in conformity with agencies that are in a position to make demands on the school. In this section the impact of such control on curriculum planning will be considered, and we shall see further limitations placed on the area of discretion that teachers and other curriculum workers have in planning the curriculum.

Influence of Colleges

The colleges and universities of this country have had marked influence on the development of the curriculum of our schools, particularly of the secondary school. In fact, historically the secondary school has been primarily a college preparatory institution. Until well into the twentieth century a large proportion of the youngsters going to secondary schools continued on into college. It was to be expected that the curriculum of the secondary school in those days would be planned to help the college-bound student.

This strangle hold of the colleges on the curriculum of the secondary schools held tight until recent years, and even yet it has been only slightly relaxed in some situations. However, as a more heterogeneous population came into the secondary schools in the second quarter of the twentieth century, many colleges, usually at the insistence of secondary school educators, have modified to a considerable extent their entrance requirements. As a result, only a portion of the course program of even college preparatory pupils is now prescribed. More and more the colleges and universities are demanding less and less in the form of specified subjects and are permitting their enrollees to present a much more varied pattern of work than was formerly the case. The best example of such modifications is the Michigan Secondary School College Agreement, developed cooperatively by the colleges and universities and the secondary schools of that state:

> The college agrees to disregard the pattern of subjects pursued in considering for admission the graduates of selected accredited high schools, provided they are recommended by the school from among the more able students in the graduating class. This Agreement does not imply that students must be admitted to certain college courses or curricula for which they cannot give evidence of adequate preparation.[2]

On their part the high schools permitted to join in the agreement promise to initiate and develop a plan for obtaining adequate personal data about each pupil and to submit a summary of such data to the college, a basic study of the curriculum and an evaluation of the purposes and program of the high school, a plan for making follow-up studies of former pupils, and a program in occupational orientation and information.

In addition to setting entrance requirements, domination of the curriculum of the secondary school by colleges and universities has been far-reaching because of the prestige that has subsequently been developed

---

[2] Leon S. Waskin, "The Michigan Secondary School-College Agreement," *Bulletin,* National Association of Secondary School Principals, No. 159, 33:51 (January), 1949.

for the college preparatory subjects, with the resultant prominence given them in the curriculum. Thus colleges have been primarily responsible for the development of a tradition that the "solid" parts of the high school curriculum are the subjects in the five fields of English, foreign languages, mathematics, science, and social studies. Most general requirements for graduation from high school are stated in terms of these academic fields, although many forward-looking schools in recent years are including requirements in physical education, the arts, homemaking, or industrial arts.

Control through Accreditation

Another type of control over the secondary school curriculum by the colleges has come about through the practice of accrediting high schools. In direct recognition of the fact that the high school was a preparatory institution for the college, these higher institutions developed lists of "accredited" high schools whose graduates would be admitted to the college without examination. Since accreditation was initiated by the University of Michigan in 1871 the practice has boomed so that now not only universities accredit high schools, but powerful regional accrediting associations and state departments of education also exercise the right to approve or accredit secondary schools. Accreditation came about in the early days because of the great variation that existed in secondary school facilities, offerings, schedules, and quality of instruction. The colleges wanted to recognize superior schools and give their graduates a preferred status. By doing so they of course encouraged other high schools to adopt these approved practices and thereby gain the prestige of such recognition. The regional accrediting associations developed in order to facilitate acceptance of graduates from out-of-state high schools.

Standards for approving a high school have often been stated in terms of objective, quantitative factors: the length of the class period, academic preparation of the teachers, number of volumes in the school library, equipment available for laboratory work in science, class size, teacher load, and so forth. These quantitative standards have had considerable impact on the curriculum. For example, schools might not offer work in a science unless they were reasonably certain that their laboratory facilities and equipment would meet accreditation standards. Certain practical courses, such as typing or shop, had to be scheduled for two forty-minute periods to meet the standards, thus limiting the number of other subjects that pupils could take.

No one would deny that the practice of accreditation did much in the earlier days of the development of the American high school to bring about a more desirable and more uniform administrative pattern for secondary education. It served to bring system out of chaos and to assure minimum physical facilities and equipment for carrying on an educational program. However, by setting such uniform patterns for the administration of the school and for its educational program, experimentation and eventual development of even better practices on the part of the more forward-looking schools may have been stifled. Accreditation procedures raise the old dilemma in educational administration of whether it is desirable to try to bring all schools up to a desirable minimum through prescribed standards while running the risk of endangering fruitful and promising experimentation on the part of able and alert educational leaders. In some states universities and colleges have abandoned accreditation in recent years and rely on the state list for admission purposes. This type of control will be considered in the next section.

Curriculum Determination by State Departments of Education

Since by constitutional authority education is a responsibility of the states, it follows that the state is the controlling authority in curriculum matters, as it is in all other matters relating to the provisions for education. Obviously, if it chooses to do so, the state has the authority to determine the formally organized curriculum experiences of boys and girls. It is equally apparent, however, that no such rigid control over the curriculum is exercised by any state.

To carry out its responsibilities for education, each state has established a system of school districts. These districts are created by law, and hence are subject to whatever control the legislature wishes to establish. However, the states have wisely granted the local school districts a great deal of autonomy in organizing, planning, and carrying forward the educational program for children, but subject to general control and supervision by a state department of education. The authority of the state department of education over curriculum matters varies considerably from state to state but it is usually exercised through the following means:

1. Issuance of state courses of study and curriculum guides. The state usually has the authority to require observance of its curriculum recommendations, and in past decades many states demanded rather strict adherence to the plans presented. More recently, however, most states regard their materials as suggestive, to be used in such ways as the local school officials deem wise. Yet it is understandable that local school staffs should feel that they are expected to conform to the wishes of the state, on whom they rely for support and legal status. It therefore behooves the state department, because of its official standing, to lay the best foundation possible for good curriculum practices in the school, suggesting desirable types of learning experiences, but at the same time encouraging the local school staff to use its own initiative in planning an instructional program appropriate for local needs and conditions. Efforts of this type are discussed more fully in Chapter 16.

2. *Supervision and inspection.* Considerable control over the curriculum is exercised by state departments through their supervisory and inspectorial functions. Such control is often informal in nature but nevertheless can be of major signficance. When professional staff members visit schools in the state they often advise local school officials on curriculum matters. They may recommend that certain courses or subjects be dropped, new ones be added, grade placement be changed, or subject matter content be modified. They may make suggestions on methods of teaching, on appropriate teaching materials, and on many similar matters that influence the learning experiences of the children. Even though such recommendations and suggestions are given as advice and not as commands, the official position of state department representatives invariably means that local school staffs will give great weight to them. In some states, the state department expects its official recommendations to be carried out; failure to do so may subject the school to reprimand or to denial of certain privileges or even of support. Everyone who has worked in the curriculum field has repeatedly heard such statements as, "The state department of education requires this," or "The state department recommends that we do it this way," or "The state regulations specify such a course for the school," or "The state department says that we can't do that."

3. *Issuance of regulations.* As has already been implied, state departments exercise control over the curriculum through the issuance of official regulations. These may state the requirements for graduation from high school, the textbooks approved for use, the requirements to be met for special subsidies, the standards to be attained for accreditation or approval, as well as a myriad of other matters which the state seeks to control. All have curriculum implications.

4. *Accreditation.* Curriculum control through accreditation procedures has been discussed earlier in this chapter. Here it should be listed as a means used by the state department to exercise control. In the hands of the state agency officially responsible for the educational program of the state it becomes a powerful tool. State accreditation is also now being more generally applied to elementary schools. One aspect of accredita-

tion is the fact that special phases of the school program often need special approval if they are to be eligible for state funds. For example, a number of states provide special subsidies for the education of the physically and mentally handicapped. To receive such grants the local school must meet special standards set by the state. General state support is also dependent in most states on approval or accreditation, in terms of requirements set by law or the state department pursuant to law. In reality, accreditation, approval, supervision, inspection, conformity to state regulations, and adherence to state courses of study and curriculum guides are simply aspects of the general control exercised by the state departments and are seldom applied singly in any situation.

5. *State examinations.* Some states use a state examination system as a means of curriculum control. The Regents' examinations in New York State are the most famous example. There has been considerable relaxation in the rigidity of this examining system, but these tests still exert a strong influence over some of the offerings of the secondary schools in that state. In a few states voluntary, state-wide testing programs have been developed. Frequently, such programs have a bearing on the curriculum. If the tests used are the usual type of achievement tests, the pressure on individual teachers to make a good showing is apparent. Considerable attention is given in the instructional program to drill for these examinations. A poor showing may result in upheavals in the school and ill-advised curriculum changes. On the other hand, a good showing in the particular tests used may lead to a smug attitude that stifles curriculum improvement. Those interested in genuine curriculum improvement, planned and carried forward by the local school staff under the general leadership of the state department, should vigorously oppose any efforts to foist a state-wide testing program on the schools.

6. *Leadership.* The most important method by which state departments of education influence curriculum development is through the exercise of their leadership function. While it is difficult to disassociate leadership from the procedures previously discussed in this section, there is still the intangible influence of the staff of the state department in guiding curriculum planning.[3]

The role of the state department of education is to assist teachers, in whatever ways are proper, to provide the best educational experiences

[3] The leadership function of the state department of education has been analyzed in William M. Alexander, *State Leadership in Improving Instruction* (Contributions to Education No. 820; New York: Bureau of Publications, Teachers College. Columbia University, 1941).

possible for the children of the state. This means that the staff of the state department should develop programs which are pointed to the improvement of the teachers themselves—their professional understanding and skill, their conceptualizations of the purposes and functions of education in a democracy, their understanding of the culture and the basic values of our society, their knowledge of the cultural heritage of America, and their comprehension of how children grow, develop, and learn. The state department should also provide classroom teachers and administrators with materials of various types that will aid them in planning a good curriculum for boys and girls. These may take the form of curriculum guides, resource teaching materials, lists of teaching aids, guides for the study of pupils, summaries of research findings and investigations that have implications for curriculum planning, guides for the study of community needs and value patterns, accounts of good learning activities being carried on in school, and similar printed materials of the types described in Chapter 11.[4]

Curriculum Making by Legislative Action

State constitutions and laws are significant determiners of some aspects of the curriculum, since such provisions are of course binding on the schools. Constitutional or legislative action on curriculum matters is in theory an expression of the wishes of the citizens. In actuality, special-interest groups may be able to force through curriculum legislation of no major concern to citizens generally.

The phases of education that have been most subject to legislative prescription are citizenship education, character development, and health and physical education. For example, the teaching of American history in either the elementary or the high school or both is required by law in thirty-seven of the states.[5] All of the states but two require that instruction in civics or government be given. A number of the states require the observance of specified patriotic days, such as Washington's and Lincoln's birthdays. The teaching of state history is also required in some of the states.

Generally speaking, curriculum workers believe that prescription of the curriculum by legislative enactment is not the best approach to

[4] For descriptions of three forward-looking state curriculum programs see Hollis L. Caswell and associates, *Curriculum Improvement in Public School Systems* (New York: Bureau of Publications, Teachers College, Columbia University, 1950), Chaps. 13–14, and Harland A. Ladd, "Down East Experiences in Curriculum Change," *Educational Leadership*, 8:203–207 (January), 1951.

[5] Ward W. Keesecker, *Education for Freedom as Provided by State Laws* (U.S. Office of Education Bulletin 1948, No. 11; Washington, D.C.: Government Printing Office, 1948).

sound planning. This is especially true when the law specifies the content to be covered, the time to be allocated to the area, or the grade level at which it is to be offered. Such laws circumscribe the freedom of the local school staff in developing curriculum experiences that are most appropriate for a particular group of children at a particular level of development. Nevertheless educators must recognize that such laws indicate that the public deems some things of such great importance in the education of children and youth that they are not to be neglected in the schools. Citizens want to be sure that the schools will not slight such instruction or they may feel that schools have been derelict in not providing some essential elements of a good program of education. Recent laws relating to the education of physically and mentally handicapped children are undoubtedly of the latter type.

Closely related to legislation requiring certain types of instruction are laws providing state or even federal subsidies for specified phases of the educational program. The best examples of such an approach to curriculum development are the subsidies granted to schools for offering approved work in agriculture, homemaking, trades and industries, and distributive education under the Smith-Hughes and George-Barden acts of the federal Congress. Many states also make special grants for vocational education and for the education of exceptional children. Certainly such grants affect curriculum development. Schools previously unable to offer such programs may find it possible with the subsidies to add one or more of them to their curriculum offerings. In any case, the granting of such aid is a stimulus to schools to move ahead in such areas.

Even though we recognize the desirability of providing instruction in such areas, the granting of state and federal subsidies for particular phases of the curriculum may easily have deleterious effects on the curriculum in general. Schools may neglect other essential phases of a sound program so that they can meet requirements for special aid. Other schools, unable to qualify for such aid, neglect to do anything at all since such grants engender an attitude that schools simply don't offer work in these areas unless they take on the subsidized program. Moreover, as a basis for approving grants, considerable control over these particular aspects of the curriculum is usually exercised by the state or the federal government. Many decisions on curriculum matters are removed from the jurisdiction of local school officials. Although this may result in the attainment of minimum prescribed standards, it also inhibits local experimentation and adaptation to community situations and individual pupil needs. Most curriculum workers feel that a better curriculum in terms of individual boys and girls will result if general financial aid is given the schools, and if leadership on the part of state and even federal officials is used to stimulate local initiative in the development of appropriate all-round programs.

Organized Pressure Groups

Invidious but potent forces in curriculum determination in American education are organized pressure groups that have as their avowed purpose the development of educational programs that suit their particular interests, beliefs, or dogma. The operation and influence of such groups are difficult to analyze but we do know that because of their activities in some communities, teachers and administrators are forced out of their jobs; others become incensed, bitter, and discouraged (the hope of some of the pressure groups); many submit to demands in the face of public sentiment aroused by these groups; others kowtow so as to avoid an open fight over school matters; and many other educators, fearful of repercussions in their communities, abandon plans or practices that may arouse a local pressure faction.

In analyzing such situations in a community it is difficult to distinguish the activities and protestations of a minority group, guided by self-interest and a misconception of the role of education in a democracy, from genuine public concern and demands for the improvement of the educational program. We must recognize that the schools do belong to the people, but to all of the people, the reactionary, the radical, the wealthy, the poor, the educated, the uneducated, the religious, the irreligious, the self-centered, the public-spirited, and so on ad infinitum. When demands are made on curriculum workers by organized groups or even by individuals they will need to determine whether such pressures represent the views of only a small, self-centered faction of the community or the views of a substantial number of citizens who may be unselfish in the matter and genuinely concerned about the education of boys and girls, but for whom the organized group leading the attack happens to be a spokesman.

Pressure groups may seek to control the curriculum of the school through any one or more of these avenues: the passage of laws compelling schools to do certain things or restraining them from doing others; pressure on the board of education to adopt certain policies or actions that serve their ends; public statements, news releases, and statements made at board of education meetings to intimidate administrators and teachers so that they will kowtow to the wishes of the group in carrying on the educational program; attempts to discredit the schools in the eyes of the citizens so that they will refuse to support bond issues, millage increase levies, and the like; insistence that the schools do not use certain textbooks or reference works that do not conform to their point of view.[6]

The major points of attack of pernicious pressure groups are usually directed at textbooks, which they feel are slanted to ends inimical to their own interests (and therefore presumably inimical to the best interests of the entire nation), and so-called progressive education. They demand a "return" to the three R's and to the old fundamentals in education, which they assert are being neglected in the modern school.[7]

Other types of pressure groups that indirectly affect the curriculum are the organized antitax groups, such as taxpayers' leagues, property-owners' groups, and the like. We often have such groups among our citizenry, for the amount of money to be spent on any public enterprise is always a debatable question. Such groups usually seek to reduce taxes or to keep expenditures for school purposes as low as possible, thus curtailing the educational program. They often work for the elimination of the "frills" from the educational program, advocating a simple, inexpensive type of curriculum.

In view of the activities of these various types of pressure groups, what should curriculum workers and educators do? Four interwoven approaches are suggested. First, educators should themselves subject their own policies, points of view, and plans and proposals to careful scrutiny. Second, the professional educator must use every means possible to develop sound understanding of the purposes and methods of modern education among *all* people. Third, we need to evaluate carefully and comprehensively what we are doing in the schools so that we may have assurance that our programs are contributing as fully as possible to the achievement of our goals. Fourth, we need to turn the spotlight on the demands of pressure groups, showing who is making these demands, what it is they demand, and the possible reasons for them. We also need to show what the consequences of acting on the basis of these demands

---

[6] Analyses of such pressure groups and their methods of attack are made in the following: David Hulburd, *This Happened in Pasadena* (New York: The Macmillan Company, 1951); Robert A. Skaife, "They Want Tailored Schools," *Nation's Schools,* 47:35–37 (May), 1951; Frank Buchanan, "Lobbying and Its Influence on the Public Schools," *Nation's Schools,* 48:23–27 (July), 1951; David K. Berninghausen, "On Keeping Our Reading Free," *Educational Leadership,* 6:104–108 (November), 1948; Kimball Wiles, "Building America: A Case in Point," *Educational Leadership,* 6:108–114 (November), 1948; John Bainbridge, "Save Our Schools" and "Danger's Ahead in the Public Schools," *McCall's Magazine,* 79, No. 6, 45 and 80, No. 1, 56 (September and October), 1952; Association for Supervision and Curriculum Development, *Forces Affecting American Education* (Washington, D.C.: National Education Association, 1953); Robert A. Skaife, "The Conflict Continues," *Nation's Schools,* 53:44–49 (March), 1954.

[7] Two excellent rebuttals to attacks on modern education are William F. Russell, "The Caravan Goes On," and Hollis L. Caswell, "The Great Reappraisal of Public Education," *Teachers College Record,* 54:1–11 and 12–22 (October), 1952.

would mean in terms of school practice and the development of a good program of education for boys and girls.

If, then, educators can develop an informed public opinion about schools, their purposes, and their goals; can give reliable evidence of what the schools are now accomplishing in terms of these goals; and can point out in a penetrating manner to such an informed citizenry what the consequences of various proposed courses of action would probably be if followed in the educational program, we do not need to fear self-interest pressure groups.[8] When self-seeking groups interested only in serving their own ends seek to control the program of the school, educators should relentlessly challenge such groups, pointedly asking their motives and what it is they want in education, and should try to bring out for public scrutiny the individuals backing such demands and the sources of their control and support. We should counter the demands of such groups with the demands of the public-spirited citizens of the community for a sound educational program true to democratic traditions. Congressman Frank Buchanan points out the danger in letting minority self-interest groups control the program of the school: "It is no longer education when curriculums and course content are tailored to meet the special demands of whatever private groups happen to be most vocal in the community." [9]

INFLUENCE OF THE ADMINISTRATIVE STRUCTURE AND ORGANIZATION ON CURRICULUM PLANNING

Schools are organized and administered so that the education of boys and girls may proceed expeditiously. The nature of the school organization and the type of administrative structure in which the program is carried on will influence markedly the kinds of educational experiences that the school may provide boys and girls. In this section we shall consider some of these factors that have a bearing on curriculum planning.

Grade Organization of the School

The graded school itself represents a type of school organization that has an important bearing on curriculum planning. On the one hand, it means that over-all planning is in terms of a systematic scheme that indicates in at least general terms the nature of the learning experiences to be provided children at each grade level. On the other hand, since

[8] Some attempts to work along these lines are described in Illinois Survey Associates, *A Look at Springfield Schools: A Report of the Survey of the Public Schools of Springfield, Missouri* (Springfield, Mo.: Board of Education, 1948) and subsequent feature stories in the *Springfield Leader and Press.*

[9] Quoted in Skaife, "They Want Tailored Schools," *op. cit.,* p. 35.

children vary greatly in their rates of development, capacities, aptitudes, and previous educational experiences, the grade method of organization means that children enrolled in any particular grade will nevertheless differ considerably in their stages of development. So even though a grade organization makes possible the orderly progression of children through the school program, curriculum workers still find that experiences provided at any particular grade level need to be adapted to a wide range of interests, the past achievements, and the abilities of the children enrolled in that particular grade or class. In view of the millions of children who are now enrolled in school, it would be difficult to provide an educational program without some systematic grouping of children, so it is quite apparent that our planning must take account of any limitations as well as benefits imposed by grade organization and must be adjusted accordingly.

Organization into School Units

The division of our instructional program among elementary, secondary, and higher schools represents another type of administrative arrangement that influences curriculum development. In the first place, the particular functions and purposes of each type of school must be formulated and the methods by which instruction can most appropriately be provided at each school level need to be determined. In the second place, the problem of planning a unified program that provides for the continuous and all-round development of each pupil is intensified by the breaks that occur between school levels. It is quite desirable and necessary that teachers and other curriculum workers give adequate consideration in planning to the learnings which the youngsters have acquired earlier and those which may best be postponed until a later period.

This problem of providing continuity, breadth, and scope in the total educational life of boys and girls as they progress from the nursery school or kindergarten through the college is one of the most difficult problems in all curriculum planning. Certainly it has not been solved in American education, for there is needless duplication as pupils progress through the program.[10] More serious, however, are the gaps that occur because of the assumption of one school unit that the other may well take care of a particular aspect.

Organization of the educational program into grades and of grades into school units thus raises some important questions that curriculum planners need to consider: (1) How do the interests, developmental

---

[10] Faculties of Andover, Exeter, Lawrenceville, Harvard, Princeton, and Yale, *General Education in School and College; A Committee Report* (Cambridge, Mass.: Harvard University Press, 1952).

characteristics, and needs of children vary from grade to grade and what implications does this progressive development have for curriculum planning? (2) In what ways may the work of each grade level best contribute to the achievement of the total objectives of education? (3) On what basis should the educational program be planned so as to provide a satisfactory sequence of educational experiences as children progress from grade to grade? (4) Should arbitrary standards of achievement in terms of skills, knowledges, understandings, and appreciations be expected of each child at a particular grade level before he is permitted to undertake the work of the next grade? (5) What unique educational opportunities should be provided by each unit of school organization? (6) What steps can be taken to be sure that each child, as he progresses from grade to grade and from school to school, will have the best education possible up to that point, so that, if he is unable to continue, his needs will have best been served?

School District Organization

The type of school district organization found in the state also influences curriculum planning. In some situations a single board of education is responsible for planning and administering the educational program for the entire period of public school education from entrance to kindergarten or first grade until graduation from high school or community college. However, in other states one board of education administers the elementary school, another board controls the secondary school, and still a third board of education operates the community college for that area. In many states a rural youngster goes to a school that is under the control of a rural school board but when he enters high school he goes to a school that is under the control of a town board of education and in which rural residents have no voice. It is quite obvious that the best kind of planning can be done in situations in which the total schooling of the youngster is under the control of a single administrative board.

In recent years there has been a marked trend in some states to reorganize schools, both as to size and control, so that larger districts, in which the entire program of common school education is under one board, have been created.

Size of School and Class

The size of a school and the size of a school district in which it is located constitute important controls over the curriculum. For example, the educational program provided in an eight-grade, one-room rural school is likely to be quite different from that of an elementary school in a large city system. Similarly, a small high school of fifty to seventy-five pupils will have a different program of offerings from that of a high school in a metropolitan city that enrolls two thousand students. Curriculum planning must take account of these different situations.

About 36 per cent of the approximately twenty-four thousand public high schools in the United States in 1946 enrolled less than one hundred pupils. On the other hand, only slightly more than 6 per cent of these high schools enrolled one thousand or more pupils. However, half of the pupils attended a high school which enrolled five hundred or more pupils.[11]

Obviously, the program offered by the ninety-five hundred high schools that enroll less than one hundred pupils will differ materially from the program offered by the large high schools. However, the question of whether the curriculum of the larger school is a better one or not must be judged in terms of what the objectives of education are and what the school does to attain them. It should not be assumed that there is a direct correlation between the quality of the curriculum provided and the size of the school. As a matter of fact, it may be possible that the larger schools do not provide as vital curriculum experiences as do schools of more moderate size. The research on this point is not at all comprehensive or conclusive.[12] Officials of the United States Office of Education, in presenting their study on size, made the following statement:

> There seems to be some recognition that the very large high schools tend to a mass production type of education which is undesirable. No clear minimum or maximum size of high school has been established as the result of research, but definite ideas are emerging to suggest that high schools ranging in enrollment from 300 to 1,200 tend to include the optimum. The exact center of this emerging optimum cannot be definitely fixed. It is probably somewhat different for various communities and types of high schools.[13]

[11] U.S. Office of Education, *How Large Are Our Public High Schools?* (Circular No. 304; Washington, D.C.: Government Printing Office, 1949), p. 19.

[12] Some introductory studies on this question are the following:

Carol M. Larson, *School Size as a Factor in the Adjustment of High School Seniors* (Bulletin No. 511; Pullman, Wash.: The State College of Washington, 1949).

Lillian Portenier, "Does Classification of High Schools Differentiate Seniors Being Graduated from the Schools?" *Bulletin,* National Association of Secondary Principals, No. 179, 35:69–73 (May), 1951.

Arthur J. Nebelsick, "Educational Factors Associated with the Size of Secondary Schools" (unpublished doctoral dissertation; Lincoln, Neb.: University of Nebraska, 1950).

Erwin H. Goldenstein, "Relationships between Some Aspects of Social Competence and Pupil Background Factors" (unpublished doctoral dissertation; Lincoln, Neb.: University of Nebraska, 1950).

[13] *How Large Are Our Public High Schools?* pp. 2–3.

Thus on one hand probably many high schools existing in America today are too small to provide the kind of educational program needed for present-day living, but on the other hand some are so large that probably their effectiveness in meeting the individual needs of the boys and girls enrolled is hampered by sheer size.

About the same situation prevails in the elementary school. In 1950, for example, 59,700 of the 128,200 public elementary schools, or about 47 per cent, were one-teacher, one-room schools.[14] Other elementary schools vary from two-teacher schools to schools with as many as fifty teachers and over a thousand pupils. Again, there is no reliable evidence as to what constitutes an optimum-sized elementary school. However, the National Commission on School District Reorganization has established a guide for the reorganization of school districts. It states that an elementary school should bring together enough pupils so that at least one teacher may be provided for each grade. This means that in a six-year elementary school, three hundred or more pupils are desirable. The Commission also maintains that the school should be located in a district in which there are at least twelve hundred pupils between the ages of six and eighteen. Such a district can provide supervisory and administrative services that will enable the school to serve better the needs of its pupils.[15]

The size of the class group is also an important influence on the educational experiences that are provided boys and girls. Here again research is not conclusive, but the judgment of teachers themselves probably constitutes a valid basis on which to proceed. Many educators feel that the optimum class size in the elementary school is from twenty-two to thirty pupils. Smaller classes are probably unnecessarily expensive and if they are too small, as they often are in the small rural schools, social experiences for children will be restricted greatly. On the other hand, classes as large as forty, forty-five, or fifty pupils militate against the development of educational experiences that best meet the varying needs of all the pupils. As our educational objectives have come to stress the all-round growth and development of the child, attention to class size has become an important consideration in curriculum planning.

The same point of view prevails in the secondary school. In general, classes in the secondary school have been smaller than in the elementary school, but unfortunately there seems to be a tendency in recent years for the size of these classes to increase. The extent to which teachers in the

---

[14] U.S. Office of Education, "Statistics of State School Systems, 1949–1950," Chapter 2 in *Biennial Survey of Education in the United States, 1949–1950* (Washington, D.C.: Government Printing Office, 1952), p. 60.

[15] National Commission on School District Reorganization, *A Key to Better Education* (Washington, D.C.: National Education Association, 1947), pp. 10–11.

secondary school can give pupils individual opportunities to participate in various kinds of learning experiences—presentation of a report to the class, working with a committee of class members, participation in panel discussions, planning together, and the like—is severely curtailed if the class becomes extremely large. On the other hand, in the extremely small high school of thirty-five to fifty pupils in which there are only six to fifteen pupils in a grade, the types of learning experiences may likewise be quite limited because of the small number of pupils involved. Teachers themselves feel that a class of less than eleven to thirteen pupils is too small, that a class of thirty-two to thirty-three or more pupils is too large for efficient instruction, and that a class of twenty-five pupils is ideal as to size.[16]

Those concerned with curriculum development in our schools must necessarily, then, be concerned not only with the size of the school itself but with the size of the classes in which teachers will work. On the one hand, curriculum workers should strive to achieve optimum-sized schools and optimum-sized classes within the schools. On the other hand, curriculum workers must take account of conditions as they exist, and if they work in situations involving small schools, they should seek to develop the most meaningful type of educational experiences possible for the boys and girls enrolled. It is quite apparent to anyone familiar with practices in small elementary and high schools that teachers in these situations have failed quite generally to capitalize on unique opportunities existing in such schools. Too often these teachers attempt to ape the large school, with the result that they do a poor job of imitating their big neighbors and at the same time fail to make use of the opportunities peculiar to the small school situation. Similarly, curriculum workers concerned with large schools and large class situations should strive constantly to develop techniques and procedures that will take the fullest account of the individual needs of each boy and girl and give each one security and a feeling that he belongs and counts for something.

Financial Support of the Educational Program

Another important determinant of the curriculum is the relative amount of money available to spend on the educational program. It would be foolhardy to maintain that a direct correlation exists between the level of expenditure for education and the quality of the program; however, it is quite obvious that within broad limits the level of expenditure will have an important influence on the kind of the curriculum provided. Mort and Vincent, who have done extensive research on the rela-

[16] U.S. Office of Education, *What Teachers Say about Class Size* (Circular No. 311; Washington, D.C.: Government Printing Office, 1949), p. 38.

tionship between the quality of education and numerous administrative factors, have this to say:

> Three hundred factors have been studied for their effect on schools and of all of them, the amount of money which a school district has to spend for teachers, for supplies, equipment, apparatus, books is the most favorable single factor. Although this single factor, where lacking, may at times be offset by a combination of other favorable circumstances to produce a good school, the modern adaptable school is for the most part found in those communities which support their schools at the level of $180 [1946 dollars] or more per pupil per year. This is a minimum; $250 is a safer minimum. The 1900-model school was always a cheap school, for the services it performs can be managed by almost anybody with a little training; and provision of a handful of subjects taught from a handful of books does not require much equipment, apparatus, or up-to-date sources of information. The 1900-model school today is a school trying to get along on $75 or less per pupil per year.[17]

The relative level of financial support of the educational program affects the curriculum in four important ways. In the first place, the quality of teaching service is a more or less direct reflection of the level of salaries that are paid teachers. The correlation here is not direct, of course, but in the long run, school systems which maintain relatively high salary schedules will attract to their systems better teachers than will schools with low salary schedules. Moreover, the entire level of salaries paid teachers will be a factor in determining the kinds of young people who will be attracted to the profession.

Second, the relative level of financial support influences curriculum planning in terms of the scope and breadth of the curriculum itself. For example, a high school of one hundred and fifty pupils which employs ten teachers cannot offer as varied and rich a program as can a high school of the same size which employs twelve or thirteen teachers. Also, the relative amount of money available will determine whether a school can offer a number of vocational courses, a broad program of electives to meet special interests, or opportunities in art, music, and the like. The length of the school year will also be determined in part by the finances available to pay teachers and in part by the operating costs of the school. Some schools operate for as few as thirty-two weeks, while others remain in session for as long as forty weeks. Also, because of their high level of financial support, some schools are able to offer educational opportunities in the summer months, such as camping experiences, a summer rec-

[17] Paul R. Mort and William S. Vincent, *A Look at Our Schools* (New York: Cattell and Company, 1946), p. 89.

reational program, summer leisure-time reading programs, and even regular academic or remedial instruction.

Financial support of the schools is reflected, third, in the kinds of facilities and equipment made available to carry on the educational program. As Plate 8 so clearly demonstrates, the kind of building in which

PLATE 8. A FINE, MODERN BUILDING ENABLES THE SCHOOL STAFF TO PROVIDE RICHER EDUCATIONAL EXPERIENCES. *Curriculum planning is facilitated by excellent equipment and buildings. (Courtesy of the Des Moines Public Schools)*

the school program is housed is obviously a reflection of the level of financial support. Relative level of expenditures for schools is shown in the provision or absence of such facilities as a library, an auditorium, a gymnasium, a swimming pool, a shop, an activity room, and the like. These facilities control important aspects of the curriculum. Availability of teaching resources, such as books and reference works, art materials, school supplies, audio-visual materials, science equipment, shop equipment, and the like, also reflects the level of financial expenditures.

The level of financial expenditures is shown in a fourth way in the kinds of services which a school may provide for its pupils. These may include services in the areas of health, guidance, vocational placement, psychiatry, counseling, nutritional needs, and the like. Also, special programs for exceptional children, including the home-bound, and numerous other services which better schools today perform in order to meet the particular needs of each individual child may be organized. Schools which spend relatively small amounts of money on their educational program shortchange pupils because such services are meagerly provided if they are offered at all.

CURRICULUM PLANNING IN TERMS OF THESE INFLUENCES

As a social institution the school is subject to powerful forces in society that seek to shape its program. Primarily, it must function within a framework of ideals, traditions, values, and concepts of the good life that prevail in the social group which establishes and maintains the school. In a democracy these guides to social action are not laid down by a supreme authority; hence there is still a broad area of decision making relative to the specific nature of the educational program that is subject to the influence of various forces, agencies, groups, and individuals that give direction to the school curriculum. In this chapter, some of these major influences on curriculum planning have been described.

Influences on Curriculum Planning

By way of summary, Figure 1 illustrates major forces that influence curriculum planning, and the nature of the factors that tend to move the schools in the direction of a better educational program for pupils and those that tend to maintain the *status quo* or even to push education backward. As was stated early in this presentation, these forces do not act singly, and the pattern of interrelationship is complex. Neither do these factors act with equal force on the curriculum. In general, however, we regard the factors listed in the left-hand column as forces that tend, by and large, to move the schools forward, to facilitate the development of a better curriculum, and those listed in the right-hand column as forces that retard curriculum improvement.

The dynamics of curriculum making are exceedingly complex, but, in general, as the forces listed in the left-hand column are strengthened and given greater weight or as forces listed in the right-hand column are lessened or conditions are ameliorated, curriculum improvement will result. Undoubtedly, other forces impinge on curriculum planning in the schools, but the factors listed comprise major influences that must be taken into account as we seek to improve the programs of our schools. Teachers and other curriculum workers are not free to create *de novo* the kind of curriculum that they may consider best for the boys and girls en-

FACTORS THAT FACILITATE OR IMPEDE DEVELOPMENT
OF A GOOD CURRICULUM FOR PUPILS

Factors That Interrelatedly Facilitate or Promote the Development of a Good Curriculum	Factors That Interrelatedly Tend to Impede or Restrict the Development of a Good Curriculum
Towards a Better Curriculum → *The Curriculum* ← Maintain *Status Quo* or Regress	
Experimentation and trial of promising practices →	Adherence to tradition and precedent ←
Research; study of children; study of societal needs →	Legislation specifying curriculum experiences and practices ←
Reports, recommendations and activities of national professional groups and committees that take account of total situation →	Reports, recommendations, and activities of professional groups that are guided by self-interest and narrow concepts ←
Textbooks and teaching resources that contribute to attainment of outcomes sought on basis of sound planning →	Textbooks and teaching resources that prescribe the nature and quality of learning experiences ←
Evaluative methods that are used to ascertain extent to which educational objectives are being achieved →	Standardized tests that are used as basis for determining nature of educational experiences ←
State departments of education and accrediting agencies that help curriculum workers gain better understanding of good curriculum practices and skill in planning better curriculums and that aid in maintaining a minimum administrative structure for carrying on a good program →	State departments of education and accrediting agencies that require conformance to rigid standards and regulations and that prescribe nature and quality of pupils' experiences ←
Administrative arrangements that facilitate all-round development of pupils in uninterrupted manner →	Unnecessary administrative impediments and organizational arrangements that interfere with continuous, orderly development of pupils ←
School systems of sufficient size to provide both a broad program and adequate leadership for curriculum planning →	School systems too small to provide broad program to meet individual needs or to provide adequate leadership for curriculum planning ←
Class groups of a size that permit teachers to know intimately each child and to use cooperative group techniques, yet large enough to provide rich social environment →	Class groups too large to permit desirable attention to individual needs or so small that group socialization and stimulation are lacking ←
Financial support adequate for the development of a good program →	Meager, insufficient financial support ←

FIG. 1. FORCES INFLUENCING CURRICULUM PLANNING

Parent and community groups interested in well-being of all children	Organized, selfish pressure groups
———————————————————→	←———————————————————
High quality of leadership; high level of staff morale; high resolve of staff to seek perfection	Inertia; lack of coordinated drive on part of staff; weak leadership
———————————————————→	←———————————————————
Professional climate favorable to change; security in change; pervasion of experimental attitude	Professional climate of "standpattism"; staff resistance to change; smugness; hold the line
———————————————————→	←———————————————————
Curriculum workers, including teachers, that conceive of education as the total development of the child along socially approved lines and that hold to a sound philosophy of education	Curriculum workers that conceive of education as the mastery of prescribed bodies of subject matter and skills and that fail to view education in broad perspective
———————————————————→	←———————————————————
Cooperative action by high schools and colleges to provide for the best continuous development of youth	Domination of the colleges and rigid college entrance patterns of prescribed subjects
———————————————————→	←———————————————————

FIG. 1. *continued*

trusted to their care. It will be necessary for them to plan a curriculum in the light of the forces which bear on the educational program. In most cases curriculum workers will find themselves in ongoing situations. The school has been established for many years and through its program it has been serving the community in a more or less acceptable manner. Educational experiences of some type are being provided boys and girls; a curriculum is in operation. Hence curriculum improvement comes about by bringing about a change in what is going on in the schools at present. Diminishing the force of the items listed in the right-hand column or increasing the effect of the items listed in the left-hand column will create a condition conducive to curriculum change.

Teachers Have Major Responsibilities

In the final analysis, however, curriculum change takes place as teachers themselves develop educational experiences of higher quality with pupils in the classrooms. Inasmuch as the curriculum consists of all the experiences that children have under the direction of the school, teachers have a great deal of responsibility for the determination of the curriculum. The acts of legislatures, the policies of boards of education, the issuance of state curriculum guides, the publication of new textbooks, the relaxation of college entrance requirements, the reorganization of school districts, the adoption of bigger budgets, and similar actions considered in this chapter, while they have an important bearing on the curriculum, in the final analysis have a relatively minor influence compared to the influence of teachers themselves. The most important way to bring about change in the curriculum, therefore, is to bring about a change in the ways in which teachers work with boys and girls and in the kinds of educational experiences they provide for pupils. To help teachers make these changes is the primary purpose of this book.

For Further Study

Alexander, William M., *State Leadership in Improving Instruction.* Contributions to Education No. 820. New York: Bureau of Publications, Teachers College, Columbia University, 1941.

Describes services rendered by state departments of education in curriculum improvement and establishes criteria for judging the adequacy of such services.

American Textbook Publishers Institute, *Textbooks in Education.* New York: The Institute, 1949.

An excellent treatment of the place of the textbook in education and the history of development of textbooks in this country.

Association for Supervision and Curriculum Development, *Forces Affecting American Education.* 1953 Yearbook. Washington, D.C.: National Education Association, 1953.

Discusses pressures that are brought to bear on education, and lists organizations that seek to control or direct education.

Brubacher, John S., *A History of the Problems of Education.* New York: McGraw-Hill Book Company, Inc., 1947.

Chapters VII through X show the impact of tradition on the curriculum and how America has evolved new approaches to education.

Brumbaugh, A. J., "The Significance of Accreditation," *Annals of the American Academy of Political and Social Science,* 265:61–68 (September), 1949.

Traces the history of college accreditation, considers some of the objections, and suggests procedures for improvement.

Carter, Mary, "The Modern Secondary School Looks at College Admission," *College and University,* 26:349–361 (April), 1951.

Surveys new trends in college admission practices and suggests improved procedures.

Edwards, Newton, and Herman G. Richey, *The School in the American Social Order.* Boston: Houghton Mifflin Company, 1947.

An excellent book on the evolution of the American school system, showing the efforts of the people to develop a unique program suited to their own needs.

Gwynn, J. Minor, *Curriculum Principles and Social Trends.* New York: The Macmillan Company, 1950.

Chapter VIII considers the influence of the textbook on curriculum planning and presents charts to show the extent to which selected series of textbooks keep pace with changing curriculum concepts.

Hullfish, H. Gordon, *Educational Freedom in an Age of Anxiety.* Twelfth Yearbook of the John Dewey Society. New York: Harper & Brothers, 1953.

Considers the whole problem of educational freedom and discusses some of the threats to schools.

Knight, Edgar W., *Fifty Years of American Education.* New York: The Ronald Press Company, 1952.

Chapters 2 and 3 trace very well the evolution of a distinctive American school.

Leonard, J. Paul, *Developing the Secondary School Curriculum.* Rev. ed.; New York: Rinehart & Company, Inc., 1953.

An excellent historical account of the development of the curriculum. Shows the influence of movements and committees on curriculum planning.

Melby, Ernest O., and Morton Pruner (eds.), *Freedom and Public Education.* New York: F. A. Praeger, 1953.

A series of papers on the nature of recent attacks on education and the nature of freedom in public education.

Mort, Paul R., and William S. Vincent, *A Look at Our Schools.* New York: Cattell and Company, 1946.

A popular presentation of some problems relating to the provision of good schools.

National Society for the Study of Education, *American Education in the Postwar Period: Structural Reorganization.* Part II, Forty-fourth Yearbook. Chicago: The University of Chicago Press, 1945.

The place of research in developing improved programs of education is discussed.

————, *Changing Conceptions in Educational Administration.* Part II, Forty-fifth Yearbook. Chicago: The University of Chicago Press, 1946.

Chapter II discusses the role of the state department of education in curriculum improvements; Chapter VII considers various aspects of school building planning.

————, *Education in Rural Communities.* Part II, Fifty-first Yearbook. Chicago: The University of Chicago Press, 1952.

An excellent discussion of the entire problem of providing good programs of education in rural areas. Chapter IV presents data on size of schools, nature of administrative units, and the like. Chapter VI suggests procedures for improving rural education.

————, *The Foundations and Techniques of Curriculum Construction.* Part I, Twenty-sixth Yearbook. Chicago: The University of Chicago Press, 1926.

Section I is an excellent treatment of the historical development of the curriculum and of educational forces that have shaped it.

————, *The Scientific Movement in Education*. Part II, Thirty-seventh Yearbook. Chicago: The University of Chicago Press, 1938.

Exhaustive analysis of the development of educational research in this country and its contributions to practice.

Noble, Stuart G., *A History of American Education*. Rev. ed.; New York: Rinehart & Company, Inc., 1954.

Discusses the religious, economic, political, and cultural forces that have created our educational systems.

Otto, Henry J., *Elementary School Organization and Administration*. Rev. ed.; New York: Appleton-Century-Crofts, Inc., 1944.

Chapters 2 and 4 consider some aspects of grade organization and effects of organization on curriculum.

Scott, C. Winfield and Clyde M. Hill, *Public Education under Criticism*. New York: Prentice-Hall, Inc., 1954.

Analyzes current attacks on public education.

"Services of State Departments of Education," *School Executive*, 66:43–52 (July), 1947.

This special section discusses a number of services of state departments.

Shane, Harold G. (ed.), *The American Elementary School*. Thirteenth Yearbook of the John Dewey Society. New York: Harper & Brothers, 1953.

Chapters V, VIII, IX, and XII are pertinent to topics discussed in this chapter.

Sturgis, Horace W., "Trends and Problems in College Admissions," *College and University*, 28:5–16 (October), 1952.

Discusses briefly the history of college admission practices and considers problems relating to admission today.

chapter 4

Social Aims as a Factor in Curriculum Planning

The first half of the twentieth century has certainly been a rich and fruit-ful period in the development of educational theory and practice. John Dewey, who has been a guiding genius in the formulation of modern educational theory, set the pattern in the opening years of the century for the new education when he wrote:

> The fundamental factors in the educative process are an immature, undeveloped being; and certain social aims, meanings, values incarnate in the matured experience of the adult. The educative process is the due interaction of these forces. Such a conception of each in relation to the other as facilitates completest and freest interaction is the essence of educational theory.[1]

It is this insistence by modern educators on a complete and thorough consideration of each of these three elements in the educative process—the child, the society, and the interaction of the two—that characterizes the new approach to curriculum planning in recent decades. Most of our educational research and the writings of educational leaders have been devoted to an exploration and estimation of the respective contributions of each of these three factors to the educational program and the ways in which the school curriculum can best serve children and society to the mutual advantage of both.

Goals for American education are derived philosophically from a broad and penetrating analysis of social life, institutions, cultural values, and social aspirations on the one hand, and an analysis of the nature of the developing, immature child on the other. Curriculum planners must bring their basic understandings of each of these elements together to formulate an adequate conception of an educational program that will be best for the maturing individual in the American culture. Educational

[1] John Dewey, *The Child and the Curriculum* (Chicago: The University of Chicago Press, 1902), pp. 7–8. Reprinted by permission of The University of Chicago Press, publishers.

113

experiences occur in a social setting; the context and substance of the experiences themselves are social in nature. What the individual learns from them, however, is a matter that he himself must decide; it is specific for him and is determined by what he brings to the social experience and what he takes from it. The interactive process of the individual and the social group determines what he as a person will value, what, on the basis of his experiencing, he considers important.

Curriculum workers, therefore, need to understand thoroughly the nature of the individual, the nature of society, and the nature of the interactive process if curriculum planning is to be basically sound. Hence in this chapter we shall explore rather fully the social factor as a basis for educational planning. In the following chapter, consideration will be given to pupils as factors in curriculum planning, and in subsequent chapters these two basic factors in the educative process will be brought together into a statement on the theory and practice of education that we believe indicates the kind of educational program needed if we in America are to realize to the utmost the social potentialities of democracy as a way of life and if we are to develop the individual to the fullest extent compatible with these social ideals.

THE SCHOOL IS A SOCIAL INSTITUTION

Schools for the education of the young are established by a social group so that it may maintain and perpetuate itself as a society, as well as strive to improve the quality of group and individual living in terms of what the social group prizes and values as best for itself. The school is one of the chief instrumentalities by which a society seeks to ensure the acceptance by children and youth of the ways of living as individuals and as members of the society that the group deems to be best. Hence as a social agency the school must always seek to develop in its pupils the skills, knowledges, understandings, attitudes, value patterns, and ways of behaving and living that those in control of the schools believe to be most conducive to living the good life in that society. Both the end goals and the means used in the school to achieve them must inevitably reflect the dominant social belief of those who control the school. Otherwise the social group will repudiate the school and either abolish it and turn to other means of achieving social aims or reconstruct the program of the school in terms of the social ideals that the group feels must be perpetuated.

In Chapter 2 differences in points of view relative to educational purposes and procedures were considered. It should be pointed out, however, that in America there is no disagreement as to the primary function of the school—it is to develop citizens who will carry on the basic values and modes of individual and group life that we all accept as the essence of our democratic society. We may disagree on what constitutes the highest type of citizenship or, principally, on how the school can best develop good citizens, but we are unanimous in insisting that the school do all it can to help youngsters live effectively and happily in our society. It is incumbent on curriculum workers, then, to analyze shrewdly and skill-

PLATE 9. THE SCHOOL MUST INCULCATE SOCIAL VALUES. *Americans prize their right to vote and the school is expected to provide pupils with the understanding and knowledge necessary for discharging their responsibility. (Courtesy of the Lincoln, Nebraska, Public Schools)*

fully the basic value patterns of democratic living and to ascertain the fundamental characteristics of our society so that, in spite of disagreements on methods and procedures, they may be able to plan the best educational program possible for perpetuating these democratic values. Plate 9 illustrates such an effort by the school; in this case children are learning the processes by which citizens exercise their right to vote in a democracy.

The Teacher Is an Interpreter of Social Ideals

The educational experiences that children have under the direction of the school represent innumerable choices. Teachers, acting in terms of the forces that impinge on them in the planning of the curriculum, as described in Chapter 3, inevitably make choices that determine the kinds of experiences pupils will have. On what grounds do curriculum planners make such choices? Obviously, they make them on the basis of their conception of the purposes of education and of the outcomes desired from school experiences. The teachers' conceptions of the goals of the school and the outcomes desired on the part of pupils, however, must inevitably reflect the dominant social view of the group that establishes and maintains the school. Otherwise these teachers will not long remain in charge of educational planning and the guidance of the learning experiences of pupils in that community. To illustrate, at a patriotic exercise early in the school year in one community, high school pupils and teachers were asked to pledge allegiance to the flag. A teacher new to the community stood with folded arms and failed to recite the pledge of allegiance. At the conclusion of the patriotic exercise the principal asked the teacher why he did not salute the flag. The teacher responded that it was against his beliefs to do so. Right then and there the principal requested the teacher to write out a resignation and to terminate his services in the school immediately. The teacher did so. During the noon hour a delegation of citizens of the community, hearing of the incident through pupils, called on the principal to protest the action of the teacher. When he showed them the signed resignation of the teacher everyone was satisfied and a new teacher was later employed to fill the position. Social control of the curriculum of the school may not be as clearly evident in all cases as in this one, but nevertheless it is equally effective. Yes, teachers make choices relative to the educational experiences of the pupils, but these choices must conform to the broad social views held by those that govern and control the school.

Education is a social act. The choices made by those in control of the schools—teachers, administrators, boards of education, and citizens generally—represent social choices. Education is not timeless or placeless; it inevitably takes place in a social order at a particular stage of its development. The program of the school, the experiences which the school will provide its pupils, must inevitably reflect this particular cultural pattern. These choices of curriculum experiences indicate a preference for certain goals or for the realization of certain cultural values. The school fosters certain kinds of behavior and certain kinds of learnings among pupils—their skills, their knowledges, their understandings, their attitudes, their ways of working, their appreciations, and all the other outcomes of the learning process—as opposed to other outcomes which might be achieved through the educational program. The very life of the school commends, fosters, and encourages certain kinds of behavior on the part of its pupils. The question becomes one, then, not of ignoring social values and social goals but rather one of determining what goals and what values are to be fostered by the school and how the school can best aid in the development of these ways of behaving and these socially approved learnings.

Schools as Instruments for National Self-Realization

The use of the school to achieve the social ideals of those in control may best be understood by a brief analysis of the relationship in certain nations of the educational programs to social philosophy.

The educational system of Germany. An examination of the school system of Germany will illustrate very well the social orientation of the schools. Throughout modern times the basic pattern of German education has been the provision of a rather complete and comprehensive educational program for an elite group whose members were destined for positions of authority and leadership in the state, and a rudimentary education for the vast majority of ordinary citizens. This is true of education under the old empire of the kaisers, the Weimar Republic, and Hitler's national socialistic regime. This type of program conforms closely to the Germans' conception of leadership and authority and the aristocratic or autocratic nature of the government. The roles of leadership have been vested in a small elite class who control the government from top to bottom, rule the business enterprises, and constitute the professional people of Germany. In government, for example, the prevailing practice has long been that decisions are made by a small coterie of people who occupy positions of authority, such decisions being then handed down to the people. Even such minor jobs as mayors of villages and similar positions quite largely remain in the hands of a small number of families from one generation to the next even though elections are held. The common ordinary citizen has few opportunities for participating in decision making with respect to social institutions and political agencies; his function is to be a good follower and be obedient to the authority of those of the upper class.

Thus through the years German education has been organized and planned to single out an elite group and provide it with what those in control felt was an appropriate education so that these selected members of the young generation could in turn assume their rightful places as members of a ruling and socially distinctive class. In the days of the German Empire children were segregated at the outset of schooling into the privileged group and the masses. Education for the masses was provided in a common *Volksschule* for eight years. In more recent years a compulsory period of vocational education has been added to the elementary school, but in many cases this program is quite meager and relatively insignificant. The children of the elite, on the other hand, were educated in different schools that extended through a thirteen-year program. Beginning with the Weimar Republic, a common program of schooling for the first four years was established so that all children attended this basic school through Grade 4. Selection took place at that point, and the children destined for the intellectual and elite classes were then transferred to the secondary school. The secondary school program began with the fifth grade and continued for eight or nine years. At the most, not over 15 per cent of the German children entered the secondary school. Selection was based on rigid examinations given to those who applied for admission to the school. Only a small percentage of the parents applied for admittance of their children to the school, since it was a tuition school and many parents could not afford to send their children even if they could pass the tests. Secondary education was thus restricted to children of the wealthier parents who had acceptable levels of intellectual capacity. If a child of an upper-class family was not too bright, prestige might help him to gain admission; otherwise, private secondary schools would take him.

Although some minor reforms were made, this differentiation of education into one program for the masses and another for the elite continued through the periods of the Weimar Republic and Hitler's regime. In fact, this concept is still so thoroughly engrained in the German social structure that the powers which occupied western Germany following World War II found it quite difficult, if not impossible, to bring about a modification of the German conception of public education.

Use of schools in Mexico to achieve revolutionary aims. The most vivid examples of the manner in which schools are used to carry out the social ideals and values held by those in control of social institutions are to be found in countries in which revolutions bring about drastic social change. Probably one of the most striking of such uses of education is to be found in the case of the Mexican republic. The educational system itself has been a handmaiden of the Revolutionary party in Mexico during the past quarter of a century as a new social structure has been developed. It will not be feasible here to discuss all aspects of this use of the school as an agency for social reform, but it has been well stated in other sources.[2]

[2] George I. Sanchez, *Mexico: A Revolution by Education* (New York: The Viking Press, 1936).

George C. Booth, *Mexico's School-Made Society* (Stanford University, Calif.: Stanford University Press, 1941).

George F. Kneller, *The Education of the Mexican Nation* (New York: Columbia University Press, 1951).

Suffice it to point out that the National Revolutionary party in 1933 amended the Constitution of Mexico relative to education to read as follows:

> Article 3. The education imparted by the State shall be a socialistic one and, in addition to excluding all religious doctrine, shall combat fanaticism and prejudices by organizing its instruction and activities in a way that shall permit the creation in youth of an exact and rational concept of the universe and of social life.[3]

Under the socialistic revolution in Mexico, education is conceived as primarily an instrumentality to be devoted to the furtherance of the revolution. The structure, organization, administration, and curriculum of the Mexican schools have been drastically and basically altered to conform to the principles of the revolutionary party. Thus Sanchez says:

> It is a school that wants Mexico for Mexicans and that seeks to stimulate an appreciation of the value of Mexican ideals, Mexican institutions, Mexican accomplishments, and Mexican culture. It seeks to accentuate those aspects of Mexican life that give Mexico individuality and character as a nation. In short, it insists that Mexico is no longer a colonial province to be exploited at will by foreign nations and ideas, but rather that Mexico is a sovereign power with cultural attributes worthy of recognition.[4]

Educational reform in Great Britain. In Great Britain, a country with a long tradition of aristocracy and class distinction, we see an example of the reform of the structure of education in the upsurge of social change. Barnard[5] traces in considerable detail the evolution of an educational system that reinforced and contributed to the maintenance of the aristocratic traditions of that country. Prior to World War II, under this system of education only 10 to 15 per cent of the children of the United Kingdom entered the secondary school, at about the age of eleven or twelve. The remaining 85 to 90 per cent continued in a type of higher elementary school, which they left when they reached the legal minimum age of fourteen.[6]

Recognizing the importance of education in a democratic country, the contributions of the common people to the very existence and continuation of the country during the period of World War II, and the

---

[3] Sanchez, *op. cit.,* p. 102.

[4] *Ibid.,* p. 104. Reprinted by permission of The Viking Press, publishers.

[5] H. C. Barnard, *A Short History of English Education* (London: University of London Press, 1947).

[6] Mervyn W. Pritchard, "The Challenge of Secondary Education in Postwar England," *Bulletin,* National Association of Secondary School Principals, No. 162, 33:67–73 (April), 1949.

need for subsequent redirection of social and economic policies for the good of the common people, Great Britain dramatically and strikingly reorganized its basic educational structure in the famous Education Act of 1944. Under this sweeping reform all children enter the secondary school when they reach the age of eleven or twelve. It is the obligation of the local education authorities to provide satisfactory free secondary schools for all children, and attendance is compulsory. The new program of secondary education is designed to serve the needs of all children; hence some differentiation is made in the program in terms of future plans and expectations of each pupil.[7] Greenough and Crofts state this new point of view of British education:

> In the new social order, "the people" are not only required to elect their representatives, but more and more to take into their hands direct control and power. . . . If democracy in the modern age is to work, we need a people not only skilled in the three R's, and not only having a wider knowledge, but a people able to exercise judgment, capable of thinking for themselves, ready to accept responsibilities with privilege, willing to undertake duties commensurate with their powers of control; that is, our people must be physically fit, mentally alert, and emotionally mature.
>
> If our children, now growing up, are to be able to exercise their responsibilities commensurate with the powers of control which will be in their hands, the new Secondary Schools must play an important part in preparing them for it.[8]

Use of schools to further social ends. The use of the schools by those in power as instruments of social realization is dramatically illustrated by the experience of a German girl who attended schools in Germany under the Nazis and later under the Russian occupation authorities. She later served as a secretary in the American occupation headquarters and related her experiences to one of us. She had grown up in Leipzig and had entered secondary school shortly before the outbreak of the war. During the years under the Nazis, the old textbooks were gradually replaced by books sponsored and approved by the Nazi authorities. Particularly was this true of such subjects as history and geography. The textbook material and the lessons she and her fellow students studied were heavily loaded with Nazi doctrines of race superiority, the superiority of the German people, and their destiny in the world. At the school assemblies or

[7] *Ibid.*

[8] A. Greenough and F. A. Crofts, *Theory and Practice in the New Secondary Schools* (London: University of London Press, 1949), pp. 35–36. Reprinted by permission of the University of London Press, Ltd., publishers.

convocations held several times weekly the principal of the school would engage in long and violent harangues in praise of Nazism, while bitterly attacking the United States, Great Britain, France, and, following 1941, Russia. The glories of the fatherland were reiterated over and over again, and standard techniques of propagandization were used to indoctrinate the pupils in the theories of the National Socialist party.

After the hostilities were over in 1945 and Russia occupied Leipzig, the schools were quickly reoriented to policies acceptable to the Communist authorities. The principal found it expedient to switch masters completely. Although he continued to hold school assemblies, his harangues lauded communism and Russia as the great savior of the human race. The same bitter tirades against England, France, and the United States continued. As fast as they could be replaced, the old textbooks were eliminated and new ones emphasizing the role of Russia in world affairs and interpreting life in Russia under communism were introduced into the German schools in Leipzig. Where it had not yet been possible to publish new books favorable to the conquerors, the pupils were required to cut out or black out with ink the sections in their old German textbooks not consistent with communist doctrine. On the basis of all the evidence that has been gathered we can assume that Russia is rather completely remaking the schools of Eastern Germany so that their program, organization, and instruction conform to the Russian concepts of social organization and cultural values. It is difficult for us to understand the emotional difficulties of East German students who were indoctrinated as adolescents by the violent Nazi regime and then were suddenly required to switch loyalties to an equally authoritarian but opposite doctrine.

While the direct relationship of the educational structure and program of a country to its dominant social philosophy is perhaps most dramatically seen in countries that have undergone violent change in government, it is nonetheless as true in more stable countries, such as the United States, that over a period of years the program of the school has evolved gradually in response to social change. As new ideals gradually appear and as new values gain acceptance by the social group, the schools inevitably reflect these evolutionary changes even though a dramatic and violent revision in their structure and program is not evidenced in the history of these countries. However, even a more stable country such as England does at times take major steps to reform education as shown by the enactment of the Education Act of 1944. The reforms brought about by this law undoubtedly represented views that had been building up for many years and are reflected in other social reforms.

Implications

The point of these examples and discussions is again to emphasize that education is certainly not timeless or placeless. It operates within a structure of social values and cultural aims, and inevitably the school must be an agency that contributes to the realization of these aims and the achievement of these values or it will be displaced.

Since we have established the principle that the school is a social agency, it is necessary, in considering the nature of the curriculum in schools established by a democratic society, that we analyze rather carefully some of the dominant social values which characterize our society and that, therefore, must be foundational to the program of the school. Let us, then, consider what the democratic values are that characterize an effective and participating citizen in a democratic society.

HOW DOES A PERSON BEHAVE WHEN HE ACTS DEMOCRATICALLY?

On the one hand the citizens of a democracy are primarily concerned with the way an individual behaves and acts in his own personal life and in his relations to his fellow men and to the agencies and institutions of the social group; and on the other hand the school exists to bring about changes in the individual—changes in his stock of knowledges, in his skills, in his attitudes, in his appreciations, in his ways of working, in his understandings, and in his behavior. Hence we shall consider in this section the basic values and characteristics of a democratic society from the point of view of how a person who truly acts democratically does behave. This will give us the proper foundation on which to build an educational program in terms of the social responsibility of the school.

1. HE TREATS OTHERS WITH DIGNITY AND RESPECT, ACCEPTING EACH IN-DIVIDUAL IN TERMS OF HIS OWN INTRINSIC WORTH AND NEITHER DEGRADING ANY PERSON NOR TREATING HIM PRIMARILY AS A MEANS OF ACHIEVING HIS OWN ENDS. This type of behavior in a society stems from the underlying belief of democratic people in the dignity and worth of the individual. This is the fundamental and basic value of a democratic society, for it permeates all other values and aspects of democratic living. Individual personality is of utmost worth. The individual is supreme. All political, social, and economic structures and institutions exist for the purpose of preserving and enhancing the dignity and worth of the individual. The individual is an end in himself, not a means to an end to be used by social agencies or other individuals to promote and foster their ends without regard for the welfare and development of the individual himself.

Corollary to this basic value of democratic society is a belief in the perfectibility of man. Democratic societies believe that man can improve his own life and can bring himself to a higher state of human existence and attainment of the good life. People who believe in democracy seek and support methods whereby all individuals may improve their status and their own ways of behaving. They foster opportunities for the development of all individuals and help to bring about a social structure in which each individual may seek to improve his personality and stature not only in his own eyes but in the eyes of his fellow men.

2. HE DOES NOT DENY TO OTHERS THE RIGHT TO LIVE THEIR OWN LIVES, SO LONG AS THEIR ACTIONS ARE NOT DETRIMENTAL TO THE COMMON GOOD OF ALL. The democratic citizen does not try to dictate personal choices of other people or to deny them the right to make choices relative to their own actions, so long as these actions do not militate against the common good as determined by society. In fact, the democratic citizen not only does not interfere with the right of each individual to lead his own life, he encourages other individuals to develop their own talents and capacities, to enjoy the things they appreciate, to do the things they like, to engage in the kinds of work and avocational activities that they enjoy, and in other ways to live full and rich lives without interference from other people. Moreover, the democratic citizen speaks out against others who try to interfere in the lives of people and who would deny to any citizen the right to live his own life within the structure of social values and institutions. He opposes those individuals who use their offices or high position to castigate and belittle other people who differ in their points of view or in their opinions. He opposes attempts to pass laws that interfere unnecessarily and beyond the minimum requirements of the common good with the rights of other individuals to speak, think, worship, and do as they please.

3. HE PERMITS AND ENCOURAGES OTHERS TO ENJOY THE SAME FREEDOMS, RIGHTS, PRIVILEGES, AND LIBERTIES THAT HE ENJOYS. A democratic citizen believes in as large a measure of freedom and liberty as possible, consistent with the social objectives of the group. In his demands for his own rights, freedoms, and liberties he does not deny to any other citizen an equal measure of freedom, liberty, and rights. He opposes legislation or official acts that would deny to individuals because of their social status, race, religion, or color the same privileges and opportunities he enjoys.

4. HE DOES NOT SEEK FOR HIMSELF OR EXERCISE SPECIAL PRIVILEGES UNDER THE LAW AND UNDER OUR SOCIAL INSTITUTIONS THAT HE WOULD DENY TO OTHERS. He believes in equality before the law and works to see that all citizens have equal protection of the law and equal opportunity to share in the benefits of our social institutions and social gains.

5. HE WORKS CONSTANTLY TO BROADEN AND IMPROVE OPPORTUNITIES FOR ALL CITIZENS TO LIVE FULLER, RICHER, AND MORE COMPLETE LIVES AS MEMBERS OF THE SOCIAL GROUP. The democratic citizen seeks to remove artificial barriers that prevent or hinder any individual from achieving his own full measure of worth, within, of course, the framework of the common good for all. Rather than seek to block or hinder the development and growth of other persons, he fosters opportunities whereby each individual may grow and develop to the limits of his capacity and talents and may have free opportunity of self-expression and self-realization within the social structure. He seeks to elevate to positions of leadership at appropriate times those who have special capacities and abilities to carry on the functions of leadership for the particular project or activity.

6. HE SEEKS TO DEVELOP HIS OWN PERSONALITY TO THE FULLEST WITHIN AN ACTION PATTERN THAT ENABLES OTHERS TO DO LIKEWISE. The democratic citizen welcomes opportunities to broaden his own understandings and knowledges and he seeks to obtain information important in meeting problems which he faces. He seeks to develop a broad pattern of interests and to develop avocational activities that fit his own personality and make him an interesting individual with whom to be associated.

7. HE EXERCISES A MAXIMUM OF INDIVIDUAL SELF-DIRECTION. A democratic citizen accepts responsibilities and seeks to discharge them to the fullest. He exercises initiative and self-control in the accomplishment of desirable goals for himself and for the social group. He believes in a minimum of compulsion and favors its use only as a means of protecting the best interests of the social group. His behavior is characterized by self-discipline and self-control.

8. HE USES HIS CAPACITY FOR INTELLIGENT ACTION AND RATIONAL THINKING TO ANALYZE PROBLEMS AND SITUATIONS WHICH HE FACES, TO OBTAIN PERTINENT FACTS AND INFORMATION ABOUT SUCH PROBLEMS, AND TO DECIDE ON A COURSE OF ACTION THAT PROMISES THE MOST FOR HIS OWN WELFARE AND FOR THE WELFARE OF OTHERS AFFECTED BY HIS ACTIONS. Man is a rational being; he can use his intellectual capacities to think through his courses of action and to guide his behavior. The use of creative intelligence in facing and solving problems is one of the prime requisites of citizenship in a democratic society.

9. HE SEEKS TO BROADEN PARTICIPATION IN DECISION MAKING, SO THAT THOSE WHO CARRY OUT PLANS AND POLICIES, OR ARE DIRECTLY AFFECTED BY THEM, MAY PARTICIPATE, INSOFAR AS THEY ARE CAPABLE OF DOING SO, IN THE FORMULATION OF SUCH DECISIONS, PLANS, AND POLICIES. This attribute of democratic behavior is difficult to spell out in specific detail, but basi-

cally the democratic citizen will seek to involve in decision making, policy formulation, and planning as many persons who are directly affected by such acts as it is feasible to do. The more crucial and fundamental the decisions, the more important it is that participation be as widespread and as thorough as possible. It is not assumed that every minute act of management as people work together on a common enterprise will need to be the subject of discussion by all of those directly affected; nevertheless, determination of policy and plans should be a cooperative venture.

Participation of the citizens in the formulation of policy and in decision making through elected representatives or through direct participation in a town meeting type of local organization has long been an essential aspect of political life in a democracy. One of the ever-present problems of a democratic government is to find ways of utilizing fully the judgment and will of the people in reaching decisions on matters of primary importance to them. No one would assume that our political institutions are perfect in this respect, but certainly the democratic citizen seeks to improve the mechanics and procedures by which the will of the people is expressed in basic governmental decisions. In our social and economic organizations and institutions, the participation in decision making of those directly concerned is particularly difficult to implement in practice. But even in these areas of human affairs a democratic citizen will seek to develop better techniques and better approaches to participation in such matters. Not only does such widespread participation utilize the creative intelligence of those concerned, but it results in the formulation of better plans and policies for the group in terms of the interests and needs of those involved. It is axiomatic in a democracy that insight into the problems facing citizens in human affairs is not restricted to an elite group.

Participation in decision making carries with it the obligation of those participating to use intelligence. If citizens are to share in decision making they must be willing to use the processes of rational thinking and creative intelligence to arrive at such decisions. Decision making cannot be at a high level if prejudice and self-interest constitute the bases upon which those participating reach such conclusions. Concern for the common welfare is essential to sound planning and policy making.

10. HE PARTICIPATES FULLY AND ON HIS OWN INITIATIVE IN ACTS NECESSARY AND DESIRABLE FOR THE ACHIEVEMENT OF GOVERNMENT OF THE PEOPLE, BY THE PEOPLE, AND FOR THE PEOPLE. This is the essence of democratic government. The democratic citizen participates in acts of government and in the manner prescribed by laws of his own making; he votes for repre-

sentatives to carry out the responsibilities of government; he votes on issues submitted to the people for decision; he makes his views on public issues known to his chosen representatives; he carries out the responsibilities specified by law as duties and responsibilities of a citizen.

Not only does the democratic citizen carry out his own obligations and responsibilities for political action; he does not deny to other citizens similar rights and responsibilities. He seeks to improve the processes of democratic government so that the will of the people may secure expression in the laws and acts of government. He seeks to arrive at a basis of common consent, insofar as possible, on public issues rather than to impose the will of the majority over the minority.

11. HE OBEYS THE LAWS OF THE LAND, WORKING THROUGH LEGAL PROCESSES TO CHANGE THOSE HE BELIEVES TO BE UNSOUND. The democratic citizen must be law-abiding if the rights of all are to be safeguarded, and he seeks to bring about changes in the laws through the legal methods established by the Constitution and the laws of the country.

12. HE USES LEGAL METHODS PROVIDED BY SOCIETY TO SETTLE CONTROVERSIES AND DISPUTES WITH HIS FELLOW MEN OR WITH SOCIAL AGENCIES AND INSTITUTIONS. Democracy rules out the use of arbitrary and illegal force to compel someone to submit to the will of another individual or to agents of political or social institutions. The use of arbitrary force by one individual against another, by agencies of the government against citizens, by employers against employees, by employees against employers, and by citizens generally against other citizens is abhorrent to a democratic people.

13. HE OPPOSES ANY STEPS THAT WOULD MAKE COURTS OF JUSTICE SUBSERVIENT TO THE WILL OF AN AGENT OR AGENCY OF THE GOVERNMENT, OF A PARTICULAR SOCIAL GROUP, OR OF AN INDIVIDUAL. All citizens must be equal before the law; they must share equal rights to the protection of the court and obtain the same equal measure of justice. One of the prime steps taken by a dictatorship is to make courts of justice subject to its will.

14. HE DISCUSSES FREELY AND OPENLY HIS VIEWS ON ISSUES, POLICIES, ACTIONS, AND CONDITIONS AND HE DOES NOT INTERFERE WITH THE RIGHTS OF OTHERS TO ENJOY THIS SAME PRIVILEGE. The right of free speech is a sacred right to a democratic citizen. Of course, he must use this right judiciously, and not bring injury and harm to other citizens through his utterances.

15. HE WORKS FOR THE ORDERLY IMPROVEMENT OF POLITICAL, SOCIAL, AND ECONOMIC INSTITUTIONS AND CONDITIONS SO THAT THE WELFARE OF ALL CITIZENS MAY BE ENHANCED. A democracy offers the means whereby the citi-

zen may work to improve his own life. A democratic citizen, therefore, uses the democratic processes to work for an improvement in the structures and agencies of the social group so that he himself may enjoy a richer and fuller life and so that his fellow citizens may also enjoy the same improved conditions.

16. HE WORKS FOR THE ADVANCEMENT OF KNOWLEDGE AND FOR THE IM-PROVEMENT OF THE OPPORTUNITIES FOR ALL CITIZENS TO GAIN KNOWLEDGE, INSIGHT, AND UNDERSTANDING ESSENTIAL FOR INTELLIGENT DECISION MAKING AND CREATIVE LIVING. Knowledge and understanding are essential for effective citizenship in a democratic society; hence the democratic citizen not only seeks to increase his own understanding and insight about conditions in his nation and the world but also seeks to provide adequate opportunities for other citizens to do likewise.

17. HE WORKS FOR THE ESTABLISHMENT AND DEVELOPMENT OF GOVERN-MENTAL AND SOCIAL AGENCIES AND INSTITUTIONS THAT CAN CARRY OUT EFFI-CIENTLY AND ADEQUATELY THE MANDATES OF THE PEOPLE. Government in a democracy must be responsive to the will of the people, and it must be efficient and effective in carrying out that will through appropriate agencies. Likewise, social institutions established and developed in addition to the agencies of government should also serve the people in promoting their own welfare.

This list of behavior traits of a democratic citizen is, obviously, not complete, but we believe that it encompasses the most important characteristics of adequate citizenship. A citizen who exercises to the best of his ability the seventeen traits listed would certainly be deemed an effective member of a democratic social group. As a basis for planning the school curriculum, this list of behavior traits should give adequate guidance to the process. The curriculum planner may utilize it or one which he himself may wish to develop as a basis for considering the responsibilities of the school in planning learning experiences for its pupils. It gives us clues as to the kinds of experiences that the school should provide if it is to educate for effective democratic citizenship.

THE ROLE OF EDUCATION IN IMPROVING SOCIETY

In considering the social responsibilities of the school in a democratic society one of the most difficult questions concerns the role of the school in promoting social change. Should the school primarily attempt to transmit the cultural heritage and inculcate in the young the values and modes of living approved by the group, or should it seek to change patterns of behavior, values, and even social structures and institutions? Even if it sought to do so, can the school really change the behavior and personality of its pupils beyond the patterns generally approved and accepted by the community or by the social group as a whole? After all is said and done, is the school really just an efficient agency for transmitting the accumulated knowledge and skills of the race and its culture patterns, values, and modes of living or is it an agency that should foster social improvement in its manifold aspects? Our own position on these questions is closely related, of course, to our whole concept of the function of education in a democracy.

Can the School Bring About Change in Behavior Patterns?

Most educators would agree that schools can contribute to the reconstruction of society as well as to its perpetuation. We have faith that education can change and modify the behavior patterns of its pupils in spite of the tremendous impact of the culture on the young. Yet the evidence is not overwhelming or even substantial. The school functions in a cultural milieu that exerts great influence on its pupils. They are subject to many pressures. The effect of these cultural and environmental forces on the young in terms of these behavior patterns is well stated by the Gluecks in their comprehensive analysis of the factors involved in juvenile delinquency:

> Modern culture, especially in crowded urban centers, is highly complex, and it is ill-defined because of conflicting values. The demands upon the growing human organism by every vehicle of today's culture are numerous, often subtle, and sometimes inconsistent. This is true of the home, the school, the neighborhood, and the general, all-pervasive culture of the times. Against insistence that he be honest, nonaggressive, self-controlled, and the like, the child soon finds vivid contradicting attitudes, values, and behavior all about him in an environment that in large measure rewards selfishness, aggression, a predatory attitude, and success by any means. Thus, the demands made upon the growing child at every level at which he is called upon to adapt his natural inclinations to the taboos, laws, and other prohibitions are neither simple nor well defined. They require a great deal of adaptive power, self-control, and self-management, the ability to choose among alternative values and to postpone immediate satisfactions for future ones—all this in a cultural milieu in which fixed points are increasingly difficult to discern and to hold to. This means that during the earliest years, when the difficult task of internalization of ideals and symbols of authority is in process, desirable attitudes and behavior standards are not clearly enough defined, or are

inconsistent, leaving a confused residue in the delicate structure of personality and character.[9]

In view of the cultural forces in the home and the community generally, the school does face a real challenge in seeking to change value patterns or even modify behavior. Harold F. Clark, who directed a series of experiments for the Alfred P. Sloan Foundation designed to improve living standards, poses these questions:

> What proof is there that education can improve the quality of living in communities? For a hundred years educators have believed that schools made for better living. If you asked for the evidence, what did you get? Usually pious statements and reaffirmations of faith.
>
> Reasonable proof could be offered that the schools teach most of the children to read and to write. Some knowledge of spelling and of the facts of history and geography could be taught. Were the children healthier because they went to school? Were they better citizens? Did they use their leisure time more wisely? Were home and family affairs conducted more intelligently? What was the proof that the schools had changed anything in the community? [10]

Evidence of Change

Clark believes that the Sloan experiments prove that the school can improve living conditions through the introduction of appropriate learning experiences into the curriculum.[11] He answers his own questions in these terms:

> Schools can improve the quality of housing, of food, and of clothing in a community.
>
> Schools may become powerful instruments for the improvement of living in the immediate community, and in the larger world community, if teachers understand how this can be done.[12]

A number of other investigations and experiments designed to secure answers to this question have been conducted in recent years. One of the most important was the Miami Experiment in Democratic, Action-Centered Education conducted by Charles C. Peters. On the basis of his experiments Peters concludes:

---

[9] Reprinted with permission of The Commonwealth Fund and the publishers from Sheldon and Eleanor Glueck's *Unraveling Juvenile Delinquency* (Cambridge, Mass.: Harvard University Press), 1950, pp. 278–279.

[10] Harold F. Clark, Introductory Statement to a Special Series of Articles on the Sloan Experiment in Applied Economics, *NEA Journal*, 36:14 (January), 1947. This and the following excerpt are reprinted by permission of the *NEA Journal*.

[11] For a description of the Sloan experiments see Clara M. Olson and Norman D. Fletcher, *Live and Learn* (New York: Alfred P. Sloan Foundation, Inc., 1946).

[12] Clark, *loc. cit.*

1. Social behaviors can be changed by purposeful instruction.

2. Teaching for such changes in behaviors to be effective, how-ever, must have specific objectives in terms of the many particularized behaviors which make up citizenship. Instruction not planned according to such specific objectives but hoping to achieve them "incidentally" as by-products is usually abortive.

3. The changes effected even by purposeful instruction tend to be small.[13]

Leonard and Eurich have brought together in one volume summaries of a large number of investigations of educational practice. On the basis of this analysis they conclude:

> Enough research has been done to prove that schools are not justi-fied in assuming that desirable social attitudes will be developed as by-products of ordinary school instruction. However, by means of care-fully planned activities and discussions, with an emphasis upon prob-lems that are real and meaningful to young people, it has been shown that it is possible to modify attitudes and prejudices and to help students develop a sound philosophy of life and a value pattern that will enable them to take their place in the world as intelligent, mature citizens. . . .

> Schools that are concerned about education for the defense of de-mocracy need to define their objectives more clearly in terms of the specific behaviors which they hope to develop. Only as teachers know what they mean by competent citizenship, desirable social at-titudes, social sensitivity, and the like can they direct the educational experiences of their students to develop these behaviors.[14]

Changing Basic Cultural Values

These conclusions of Clark, Peters, and Leonard and Eurich largely re-late to changes in overt behavior patterns that bring about desirable im-provements in food habits, hygiene, personal relations, participation in civic affairs, and the like. These are areas in which our culture permits considerable leeway in behavior and a range of behavior patterns. Cer-tainly, these are important changes, for the school should do all it can to develop patterns of action and behavior that exemplify the best stand-ards of society. It is in helping the young attain the best and richest life possible in terms of the finest of our democratic traditions and highest cultural values and standards that schools can perform an outstanding

[13] Charles C. Peters, *Teaching High School History and Social Studies for Citizen-ship Training* (Coral Gables, Fla.: The University of Miami, 1948), p. 138. Reprinted by permission of Charles C. Peters.

[14] J. Paul Leonard and Alvin Eurich, *An Evaluation of Modern Education* (New York. Appleton-Century-Crofts, Inc., 1942), pp. 145–148. Reprinted by permission of Appleton-Century-Crofts, Inc., publishers.

service. It is adherence to these highest ethical values and richly rewarding patterns of behavior that the school should seek to develop in its
pupils. The hallmarks of democratic education, discussed in the following section, point the way at least in part to such an educational program.

The possibility that schools can change the basic value patterns of
the culture itself is more questionable. Values are built from the refinement of innumerable experiences, and the school is only one cultural
agency that impinges on the immature. Value patterns do change—of
that we are certain. The school, if it should deliberately seek to change
value systems, probably can bring about such a change, but the task is
difficult and complex, especially if the new values find little practical acceptance by the adult society. Yet we see that dictators, such as were
Hitler and Stalin, rely on the schools as one of the principal agencies for
obtaining converts to a new social order. Unquestionably, however, other
aspects of the culture have provided a congenial climate for the new patterns of behavior, and the school, even in revolutionary countries, more
or less follows cultural change rather than leads it.

Perhaps Linton well states the situation relative to basic cultural
change:

> Under existing circumstances it seems highly improbable that the
> educator can bring about any great or revolutionary changes in our
> culture, at least as it concerns the generation with which he has to
> deal. His hope of changing and directing future developments must
> rest upon two things, a series of minor but intelligently directed
> changes in existing culture patterns and the inculcation of values
> whose general acceptance would make for a better society. . . .
>
> On the side of the inculcation of values the task of the educator is
> a more difficult one. Values are tenuous things and most of them lie
> below the level of consciousness but for these very reasons they are
> less susceptible to attack than the behavior patterns which reflect
> them. Once established in the personality they are exceedingly diffi-
> cult to uproot. . . . If the educator can establish a particular value
> system in his pupils he can control the future of his society not in
> detail but in gross.[15]

THE HALLMARKS OF DEMOCRATIC EDUCATION

In the light of the concepts presented in this chapter, consideration
should now be given to the essential elements of an educational program

[15] Ralph Linton, "Potential Contributions of Cultural Anthropology to Teacher
Education," in *Culture and Personality* (Washington, D.C.: American Council on
Education, 1941), pp. 15–16. Reprinted by permission of the Council.

that is designed to develop citizens who will exemplify the highest type of democratic behavior. To accomplish this function the program of the school must be deliberately focused on social realization and a curriculum must be planned that will seek not only to perpetuate the best of our traditions of group living and the finest elements of our value patterns, but will also provide the basis for the improvement of society.

A program of education that will contribute to the development of the kinds of citizens who best exemplify the characteristics of democratic behavior in their day-by-day living should

1. DEVELOP IN THE YOUNG THE ATTITUDE OF RATIONAL ACTION AND THE ABILITY TO USE SCIENTIFIC METHODS OF DECISION MAKING IN DETERMINING COURSES OF ACTION. Since we learn what we live, this hallmark states that the program of the school should provide all pupils with ample opportunity to exercise rational thinking in the school, to make decisions based on intelligent consideration of the facts and conditions involved, to act on such decisions, and to evaluate the consequences. The pupil should have opportunity to apply methods of scientific inquiry to matters of concern to him in his daily living in the school and in the outside world. This, of course, presupposes that the level of decision making will be within the maturity level of the youngster himself. Young children in the early elementary grades will make judgments about matters of immediate concern to them. As the pupil matures, the level of decision making and the comprehensiveness of his methods of inquiry will progressively advance so that the experiences in rational thinking will be as appropriate as possible to the levels of ability of the pupils.

2. PROVIDE PUPILS WITH A STOCK OF ESSENTIAL KNOWLEDGE THAT WILL ENABLE THEM TO TAKE INTELLIGENT ACTION ON PROBLEMS AND SITUATIONS THAT CONFRONT THEM. Intelligent action must be based on a knowledge of the facts pertinent to the situation. Through the school program pupils need to acquire a fund of information and knowledge that will be most helpful to them in facing the most common concerns of life. Moreover, they should acquire the ability to locate and find facts pertinent to a problem and to organize and marshal such data in usable form in arriving at rational actions on the matter.

The school will need to determine what are the essential facts and knowledges that pupils should possess. Obviously, pupils cannot acquire a mastery of all the cultural heritage; selection will necessarily need to be made, and the school should choose those things considered most useful to pupils in their lives here and now and in the future. This matter of the selection of information and knowledge to be learned is a paramount one, and the school must use great care in making the choices. It is easy for the curriculum to become cluttered with information and knowledge that in itself has merit but is not the most useful information that pupils could acquire. Curriculum workers need to use great foresight and draw on a keen understanding of social conditions and social trends to determine what knowledge is of most worth. But along with the knowledge which is acquired by pupils through the school program must also come the ability to find new information and to know how and where to obtain necessary data on problems that may arise.

3. AID PUPILS IN DEVELOPING AN UNDERSTANDING OF DEMOCRATIC VALUES, TRADITIONS, AND INSTITUTIONS AND THE TRAITS THAT CHARACTERIZE DEMOCRATIC CITIZENS. In discharging its responsibilities for perpetuating the democratic way of life, the school must develop within each youngster an understanding of what these democratic values are and what constitutes the basic democratic traditions of our society. He needs to know what these concepts mean in terms of group living and how the citizen best exemplifies these principles in his own behavior. These democratic values need to become a part of the behavior pattern of each individual, so that he is continuously guided by them. Knowledge of these basic principles of democracy is essential in developing such behavior. Such an understanding may be gained in part through contrasting democratic concepts with the concepts that permeate other social orders and modes of living.

Pupils also should have an understanding of the development of the democratic tradition in America. They should, for example, understand the struggle of the American people to achieve democracy, the efforts of mankind to gain freedom and liberty for the individual, the struggle against tyrants and the autocratic control of people's lives, and the enslavement of mankind that results from totalitarianism, fascism, or communism. They should become familiar with the workings of our democratic institutions; they should gain an understanding of what constitutes democratic action in our relationships with other persons. They should know the great traditions of America and be familiar with the efforts of our people to perfect and improve our democratic society. When they have acquired such knowledge, they will understand why democracy is the highest order of group living.

4. PROVIDE PUPILS AN OPPORTUNITY TO LIVE TOGETHER DEMOCRATICALLY. To learn democracy, pupils must live democratically. The program and life of the school should be so planned that pupils at their various maturity levels will have ample opportunities to exemplify in their group living in school the best democratic values. The instructional program and the group life of the school should give pupils opportunities to arrive

at decisions through rational action, to respect the other person, to work for the perfectibility of each individual, to make group decisions, to acquire self-discipline in terms of acceptable patterns of group behavior, and to behave democratically in group relationships. The school, obviously, cannot do the entire job of developing character in harmony with

PLATE 10. A STUDENT COUNCIL PROVIDES RICH OPPORTUNITIES TO LIVE TOGETHER AS A DEMO-
CRATIC GROUP. *When pupils can reach decisions on matters that affect their group
living, they are learning democracy. (Courtesy of the Pittsburgh Public Schools)*

democratic values; the home, the social institutions of the community, the church, and other agencies also have great responsibilities in this respect. However, the school should certainly be a shining example of the ways in which pupils can live together as a group democratically. Thus an active, representative student council, such as is pictured in Plate 10, provides excellent opportunities for pupils to implement democracy in action.

5. EXEMPLIFY THE BEST TRADITIONS OF DEMOCRACY IN ITS OWN LIFE AND WORK. This hallmark is a direct corollary of the one just discussed, but here emphasis is placed on the life and fabric of the school itself. In all aspects the school should be as democratic as it is possible to make it.

Children learn through experience and by imitation of the behavior patterns of persons whom they respect and admire. In their work with pupils and in their work together as a staff, teachers should exemplify the best traditions of democracy. The very organization and control of the school and its government should be consistent with democratic concepts. It is difficult for pupils to learn to live democratically if they are constantly subjected to the most authoritarian practices in the school, in the home, and in other social agencies with which they come in contact. As they work with pupils teachers and administrators should respect the integrity and worth of the individual; they should allow a maximum of self-discipline consistent with group welfare; they should provide pupils with opportunities to make decisions, to work together, to accept responsibility, to cope with meaningful problems, and to do similar things that set high examples of democratic living.

6. DEVELOP ON THE PART OF ITS PUPILS A SENSITIVITY TO THE PROBLEMS OF GROUP LIVING AND AN AWARENESS OF THE PROBLEMS THAT FACE CITIZENS AS THEY SEEK TO PERFECT OUR SOCIAL ORDER. It is the school's responsibility in part to develop within pupils an attitude of concern for the welfare of the group and for the welfare of each member of the group. As pupils mature and become adult citizens themselves, democracy can be improved and perfected if each citizen assumes his just share of responsibility in seeking to improve the conditions of group life. We cannot be certain what problems of group living will face citizens in the future, but the school can develop concern on the part of pupils about the stresses and strains of the social order and a desire to work cooperatively in solving problems that face each generation as it matures into adult life. The school should develop pupils who will oppose efforts to stifle and curtail democratic privileges and rights when such attempts arise in the future, and who will resist efforts to subvert democratic institutions or to curtail the implementation of our best democratic concepts.

These hallmarks of democratic education are not prescriptions for the curriculum as such. Rather they are guides by which we should constantly evaluate the curriculum and the life of the school to see that its educative experiences do provide the opportunities for the pupils to learn the essence of democratic living and to work for the perfection of our group life.

For Further Study

Becker, Carl L., *Modern Democracy*. New Haven: Yale University Press, 1941.
  Considers the democratic ideal in modern society and its achievement.

Childs, John L., *Education and Morals*. New York: Appleton-Century-Crofts, Inc., 1950.

A definitive statement of the relationship between education and social aims and values, showing how the society uses education to achieve its goals.

————, "Should the School Seek Actively to Reconstruct Society?" *Annals of the American Academy of Political and Social Science*, 182:1–9 (November), 1935.

Discusses the role of the school in seeking to promote social change.

————, "A Student of Public Affairs Views the Problem of Curriculum Development," *Teachers College Record*, 50:232–240 (January), 1949.

An excellent statement on the social basis of curriculum planning.

Counts, George, *Dare the School Build a New Social Order?* New York: The John Day Company, Inc., 1932.

Suggests that the school actively seek to build a new society. A contrasting point of view from his *Education and American Civilization*.

————, *Education and American Civilization*. New York: Bureau of Publications, Teachers College, Columbia University, 1952.

An analysis of the evolution of the American culture. The characteristics of a program of education needed in our democratic society are stated.

————, "The End of a Myth about Education and Democracy," *Vital Speeches of the Day*, 15:266–269 (February 15), 1949.

Points out that dictatorships also use education to achieve their social ends, and that democracy needs an educational program geared particularly to its needs.

Educational Policies Commission, *The Education of Free Men in American Democracy*. Washington, D.C.: National Education Association, 1941.

A penetrating analysis of democracy and the loyalties of free men. Presents basic platform for education for democratic citizenship.

————, *Learning the Ways of Democracy*. Washington, D.C.: National Education Association, 1940.

Chapter I lists hallmarks of democratic education. The remainder of the book describes school practices that educate for democracy.

————, *The Unique Function of Education in American Democracy*. Washington, D.C.: National Education Association, 1937.

Traces the historic relationship between education and the evolution of democracy in this country and states the function of education in our democracy today.

Jones, Galen, "The Role of the American High School in Developing Social Responsibility," *Bulletin,* National Association of Secondary School Principals, No. 134, 31:7–15 (February), 1947.

Suggests curriculum practices through which the high school may aid in perpetuating our democratic society.

Kilpatrick, William H., "Better Education for Citizenship," *The Educational Forum*, 15:419–426 (May), 1951.

Suggests that if pupils are to learn to live democratically they must live democratically in the school.

King, Bernice, *Russia Goes to School: A Guide to Soviet Education*. London: William Heinemann, Ltd., 1948.

A detailed account of Soviet education, illustrating relationship of education to social patterns.

Kneller, George F., *The Education of the Mexican Nation*. New York: Columbia University Press, 1951.

Traces early educational developments in Mexico and shows how the school was reformed as part of the national revolutionary movement.

———, *The Educational Philosophy of National Socialism*. New Haven, Conn.: Yale University Press, 1941.

A comprehensive analysis of the role of the schools in achieving national socialism under Hitler in prewar Germany.

Linton, Ralph, *The Cultural Background of Personality*. New York: Appleton-Century-Crofts, Inc., 1945.

Some attention is given to the fundamental question of whether schools can change the basic value patterns which the individual acquires from the social group.

Meier, Arnold, Florence Cleary, and Alice Davis, *A Curriculum for Citizenship*. A Report of the Citizenship Education Study. Detroit: Wayne University Press, 1952.

A report on a comprehensive program of citizenship education carried on in the Detroit Public Schools. Suggests a program of education for democracy.

Merriam, Charles, *The New Democracy and the New Despotism*. New York: McGraw-Hill Book Company, Inc., 1939.

States four basic assumptions of democracy and presents the validation of each assumption.

National Society for the Study of Education, *Citizen Cooperation for Better Public Schools*. Part I, Fifty-third Yearbook. Chicago: The University of Chicago Press, 1954.

A comprehensive treatment of methods that may be used to obtain direct participation of citizens in the development of school policies and programs.

Peters, Charles C., *Teaching High School History and Social Studies for Citizenship Training*. Coral Gables, Fla.: The University of Miami, 1948.

A report of the Miami Experiment in Democratic, Action-Centered Education.

Pflieger, Elmer, and Grace L. Weston, *Emotional Adjustment: A Key to Good Citizenship*. A Report of the Citizenship Education Study. Detroit: Wayne University Press, 1953.

Conclusions drawn from a five-year study of practices designed to promote good citizenship.

Sanchez, George I., *Mexico: A Revolution by Education*. New York: The Viking Press, 1936.

An authoritative analysis of the national orientation of education in Mexico to new social structures.

Stanley, William O., *Education and Social Integration*. New York: Bureau of Publications, Teachers College, Columbia University, 1953.

Chapters 6–10 are pertinent to a consideration of the social obligations of the school and the role of the school in a democracy.

Ziemer, Gregor, *Education for Death: The Making of the Nazi*. New York: Oxford University Press, 1941.

Describes schools and educational programs under the Nazis. Based on first-hand observation and study of official documents.

chapter 5

The Pupil as a Factor in Curriculum Planning

Every aspect of an educational program represents choices that have been made by the participants in these activities. On what basis are these choices made? At the outset of Chapter 4 we stated that three basic factors are involved in the educative process—the social group that organizes, plans, and directs the educational program; the pupils who participate in the educative experiences and learn from these experiences; and the interactive process of pupils with a particular culture. Choices, then, are made in terms of these basic elements in curriculum planning. The relationship of the social group to the educational program has already been considered. That chapter also stated the kinds of basic decisions and choices that need to be made in the planning and carrying forward of the educational program so that the ideals, values, and essential cultural heritage of the group may be perpetuated and improved. In this chapter consideration will be given to the individual as a factor in the educative process. We shall consider the kinds of choices that should be made so that the needs of the learners may be adequately cared for in the program of the school.

THE PUPIL AND THE EDUCATIVE PROCESS

Obviously, all organized educational programs have taken account of the learners involved in the educative process. The important consideration is the status assigned them. On one hand, as was too true of the older conceptions of education, the child is regarded primarily as a passive agent to be dutifully prepared for life in the future—a life that conformed to the goals established by the adult society. At the other extreme, some theorists have considered the individual as the paramount factor in the educative process and have sought to establish an educational program designed primarily to develop the potentialities and capacities of the individual and to cater to his individual needs and demands. Neither conception takes adequate account of all three factors in the educational process. Education must be concerned with the development of an intelligent, self-directive, self-disciplined, rational individual who, as a result of his educative experiences, is best able to achieve the ends sought by the social group of which he himself is a member.

Importance of the Individual in Democratic Society

In any adequate conception of education there are two important reasons why primary consideration must be given to pupils as one element in the process. In the first place, a democratic society such as the American culture elevates the individual to a position of pre-eminence in that society. The fundamental concepts of democracy are based on respect for the individual. It is the perfectibility of the individual that is sought through all social institutions and agencies, and the people of a democracy, rightly, evaluate social institutions and modes of living in terms of the contribution they make to the full realization of the potentialities of the individual, consistent with the total welfare of the entire group. Since we as American people believe in the right and ability of man to make decisions affecting his personal and collective welfare, in the right of an individual to develop his potentialities and capacities, and in the freedom of the individual to lead his own life consistent with commonly accepted social ideals, the school, as a social institution, must be designed to assist the individual to achieve these objectives.

It is not the role of the school in a democratic society to "train" a pupil for a role of subservience to external authority over which he has no control, but rather to aid in the development of an individual who is competent to play his proper role in the direction of his own and the group's general welfare. It is upon the development of each person that the hope of democracy rests. Certainly much of our conception of a democratic society is summarized in Jefferson's statement: "Nothing is unchangeable but inherent and unalienable rights of man." One of the basic functions of a school in a democracy, then, must be that of helping man to achieve these unalienable rights. Education in this country is inevitably concerned with the individual—his interests, his capabilities, his potentialities, his problems, his aspirations, his values, and his mode of living as a member of the social group.

Necessity of Gearing the Curriculum to the Development of Learners

Curriculum workers should, in the second place, give primary consideration to the individual because an educational program can be maximally effective and worth while only if it is properly geared to the develop-

PLATE 11. THE CURRICULUM SHOULD BE GEARED TO THE DEVELOPMENTAL AGE OF THE CHILD. *Sometimes a nap is the best experience the school could provide for a tired youngster. (Courtesy of the Des Moines Public Schools)*

mental level and needs of the individual learner. Plate 11 illustrates in an appealing manner the fact that human needs are basic, and that the school must be aware of them. Maximum educational results are obtained in the school if the educational experiences provided for children are planned in terms of the mental, emotional, social, and physical growth and development of the pupils. Furthermore, educational experiences will be most meaningful and significant to the pupil if they are related to the evolving interest pattern of the learner and are closely correlated with his past experiential pattern. Motive and purpose are central to rich, rewarding educational experiences; a youngster does not readily find meaning and purpose in educational experiences that lie beyond his developmental capacity or are foreign to his present stock of understandings and concepts.

Maier has shown that frustration may be developed in animals by setting tasks or conditions that are too involved for the animal or that are beyond his capacity to cope with in terms of past learnings. Hence he concludes that the human personality is also frustrated through the assignment of tasks and duties or through the requirements of situations that are beyond the developmental capacity of the individual.[1]

Why Study Pupils?

If we accept as guiding principles that the school should strive for the perfectibility of the individual and that the best choices of educational experiences for pupils in school are those in harmony with the emotional, social, physical, and intellectual development of the child, then obviously all curriculum workers need to know how to obtain reliable information about the potentialities of pupils and their developmental characteristics and the factors that affect motivation and behavior.

PROCEDURES HELPFUL IN GAINING AN UNDERSTANDING OF PUPILS

At least two procedures are available by which curriculum workers may gain insight into the developmental characteristics, needs, concerns, and interests of children and youth. School faculties that wish to do a fundamental job of curriculum planning will undoubtedly want to utilize both of these procedures.

Analysis of Research Studies

A substantial number of important research studies have been made and are continuing to be made in the area of human growth and development by various agencies and by specialists in the field. Teachers will want to consult these studies, or at least summaries of their findings and implications, as a basis for sound planning. Among the various sources of such investigations are the following:

[1] Norman Maier, *Frustration: The Study of Behavior without a Goal* (New York: McGraw-Hill Book Company, Inc., 1949), Chap. 4.

1. Institutes for research in human growth and development. Much of the work of these agencies is highly technical, and to be most useful to curriculum workers the findings need to be correlated and integrated in terms of a common conceptual pattern of growth.

2. Governmental agencies. The United States Office of Education and the United States Children's Bureau perform a useful service in publishing reports on growth and development and summarizing research studies performed by other workers. The White House Conferences on Children and Youth, held once each decade since 1910, have made important contributions to the literature on this subject and on the facts relating to the status of the young.

3. Professional organizations for the promotion of child study. A number of national professional groups are quite active in promoting specific research projects, in publishing research studies, and in fostering the use of improved methods in carrying on such studies.

4. Public school research bureaus. Research bureaus in public school systems have made important contributions, more particularly in studies on achievement, levels of intelligence, the nature of the school population, and the like, to our body of knowledge.

5. Individual research workers. The child study movement has enlisted the long and continuing efforts of some outstanding research workers. Usually they are associated with major universities, but some work independently, or at child guidance clinics and the like. Certainly their work, often published in the form of books, monographs, and articles, should be familiar to curriculum planners.

Cooperative Study by School Faculties

A second method by which school staffs may gain an understanding of pupils is organized study, either cooperatively in a group or individually. Generalized information about human growth and development as found in the literature does not provide a teacher with intimate knowledge about the specialized and particularized needs and growth patterns of each individual child in that teacher's own classroom. Any group of children or adolescents in a normal classroom situation will be composed of pupils of all types, with various rates of maturation, various characteristics of development, and various needs and interests. So within the framework of our general knowledge about human growth and development, a teacher still needs to make studies, at least within a limited scope, of physical, emotional, social, and intellectual growth, as well as studies of maturity patterns and needs of particular pupils. Learning experiences will not be the most appropriate for any particular group of children unless the individual children themselves are studied and their needs understood by those responsible for planning their experiences.

Moreover, carrying on studies of individual children is a highly desirable professional activity for teachers because it enables them to clarify their concepts of the individual and to understand better the need for adapting educational experiences to the individuals concerned. A teacher who participates in a study of pupils will almost invariably have a better conception of the individual as one of the basic factors in the educational process.

The child study movement among teachers and school staffs has made tremendous headway in recent years. Three approaches are currently being used:

1. Group and individual study of children. Cooperative faculty study of children attained a great deal of popularity beginning in the early part of the 1940's through the efforts of the Commission on Teacher Education of the American Council on Education. This procedure has proved to be most helpful to teachers in the ensuing years and has become a widely accepted approach to child study.[2]

2. Cooperative action research. This procedure brings together school staffs and staff members of organized institutes of research and experimentation in a cooperative study of children in actual school situations.[3] Such a program stimulates classroom teachers to undertake rather penetrating investigations of children's developmental traits with the guidance and help of specialists in planning the study and analyzing the data. The movement seems destined to expand and develop in the years ahead, and holds considerable promise for improved understanding.

3. Staff study of school population. Many school systems, particularly the secondary schools, have made rather extensive studies of adolescent youth, both those in school and those that have left school either after graduation or by dropping out. Often these are follow-up studies, but they are also designed to obtain data on the characteristics of the group attending school, particularly with relation to socioeconomic sta-

[2] American Council on Education, Commission on Teacher Education, *Helping Teachers Understand Children* (Washington, D.C.: The Council, 1945).

[3] As an example of the procedure see Ruth Cunningham and associates, *Understanding Group Behavior of Boys and Girls* (New York: Bureau of Publications, Teachers College, Columbia University, 1951). See also Chapter 16 of this book.

tus. Investigations are also made of pupil interests, problems, out-of-school activities, leisure-time habits and activities, and the like. Some state departments of education have issued guides for conducting such investigations.[4]

METHODS OF STUDYING PUPILS

For sound and comprehensive curriculum planning, teachers must of necessity continuously study children and youth in many ways. It is not the function of this book on curriculum planning to provide exhaustive help for teachers in carrying on such studies but we shall indicate briefly some of the major areas of growth and development that should be investigated and some sources useful in defining procedures for making them. It is not presumed that every curriculum worker will or should become a specialist in the study of human growth and development, but certainly he should be able to carry on individually or cooperatively with other staff members basic studies that will provide him with essential understandings of the pupils with whom he works.

Comprehensive Methods of Study

Excellent guides and reference works are available that discuss a number of methods useful in studying children or that present a comprehensive procedure of study. Among these sources the following are particularly appropriate:

William W. Greulich and others, *A Handbook of Methods for the Study of Adolescent Children* (Washington, D.C.: Society for Research in Child Development, 1938).

Gertrude Driscoll, *How to Study the Behavior of Children* (New York: Bureau of Publications, Teachers College, Columbia University, 1947).

Ruth Cunningham and associates, *Understanding Group Behavior of Boys and Girls* (New York: Bureau of Publications, Teachers College, Columbia University, 1951), especially Chap. XI.

Willard C. Olson, *Child Development* (Boston: D. C. Heath & Company, 1949).

Hilda Taba and others, *Diagnosing Human Relations Needs* (Washington, D.C.: American Council on Education, 1951).

American Council on Education, Commission on Teacher Education, *Helping Teachers Understand Children* (Washington, D.C.: The Council, 1945).

[4] Illinois State Department of Public Instruction, *How to Conduct the Follow-up Study* (Springfield, Ill.: The Department, 1950).

New York State Department of Education, *Improvement of Holding Power through a Continuous Study of Youth in School* (Albany: The Department, 1952).

Association for Supervision and Curriculum Development, *Fostering Mental Health in Our Schools* (Washington, D.C.: National Education Association, 1950), Part III.

Eugene Lerner and Lois B. Murphy, *Methods for the Study of Personality in Young Children* (Washington, D.C.: Society for Research in Child Development, 1941).

Ruth Strang, *An Introduction to Child Study* (New York: The Macmillan Company, 1951), Chaps. 8, 13, 17, and 21.

Studying the Physical Development of Boys and Girls

Since modern educational practice takes account of the whole child it is important that curriculum workers have some insight into the physical growth and development of pupils. Numerous studies have shown the close interrelationship between physical development and mental, social, and emotional development;[5] moreover, the school would be unable to plan adequately for the development of the child unless it knew at least some elementary things about his physical condition and his growth problems.

The most important method by which teachers may obtain insight into the physical status of pupils is careful analysis of the health and physical development records regularly maintained by the health department. Considerable information may also be gained through direct observation and interviews. Some schools have had success in using a type of parent report to the school on the sleeping, eating, and play habits and similar facts about the child as observed by the parents. In evaluating the physical growth and development of pupils, the Wetzel grid technique has also been found to be most useful.[6]

Studying the Intellectual Development of Pupils

Standardized tests of mental ability or intelligence are usually employed to study the mental development of young persons. These tests and their uses are quite familiar to all educational workers. The most reliable are those that are administered individually and that minimize reading on the part of the person being tested. Group tests that rely heavily on the reading of directions and the test items themselves may not be highly re-

[5] Bernice Neugarten, "Body Processes Help to Determine Behavior and Development," in *Fostering Mental Health in Our Schools* (1950 Yearbook of the Association for Supervision and Curriculum Development; Washington, D.C.: National Education Association, 1950), pp. 52–63.

[6] Norman G. Wetzel, *The Treatment of Growth Failure in Children* (Cleveland, O.: NEA Service, Inc., 1948).

"Growth Measurement," *What's New* (North Chicago, Ill.: Abbott Laboratories, November, 1946).

liable for individual diagnosis. However, these group tests, when given at rather frequent intervals over a considerable period of time, do pro-vide useful results for teachers.

In addition to tests of general intelligence extensive efforts have been made within recent years to test the specialized abilities of young people. Results from such tests made available by guidance and school psycholog-ical departments may be particularly helpful to teachers in adapting edu-cational experiences to the particular needs of individual students.

Studying the Personal-Social Development of Boys and Girls

Up to the present time definitive methods for studying the personal-social development of youngsters have not been developed as fully as have those for studying physical and mental growth. Hence many of the methods listed in this section are devices for securing rather crude data or for securing bits of evidence here and there that must, after all, be fitted together into a pattern before dependable conclusions may be formulated. Many of the procedures and methods of study used or de-scribed by Cunningham and her associates are particularly appropriate for the study of personal-social development.[7]

Direct observation and personal conferences. Direct observation and personal conferences with pupils are, without doubt, two of the most im-portant methods that classroom teachers may use to study the personality status and the social development of their pupils.[8] In using these proce-dures teachers must learn to divorce their own personal reactions to par-ticular children and their own feelings from the behavior being observed and to consider the behavior in terms of the children involved and their motives rather than in terms of subjective interpretations of such behav-ior at the time it is being observed.

The second principle to be followed in making observations or re-porting conferences is to make as specific and definitive a record of be-havior or of problems and tensions revealed as is possible. Such records are usually known as anecdotal records and there is much help for teach-ers in the literature on procedures for making such anecdotal records valid and useful.[9]

[7] Cunningham and associates, *op. cit.,* pp. 340–393.

[8] Excellent discussions of the use of observation and the analysis of such observa-tions in gaining an understanding of children are contained in Gertrude Driscoll, *How to Study the Behavior of Children* (New York: Bureau of Publications, Teachers College, Columbia University, 1947), and American Council on Education, *op. cit.*

[9] See, especially, American Council on Education, *op. cit.* and Helen Bieker, "Using Anecdotal Records to Know the Child," in *Fostering Mental Health in Our Schools.* cited above.

Pupil-prepared records. Another method for gaining information about pupils is to use the records made by the pupils themselves. Such records may include autobiographies, logs of daily activities, records of use of time, and written responses to set questions. Jersild has made an exhaustive study of pupils' analyses of themselves as indicated in essays written on the subjects "What I Like about Myself" and "What I Dislike about Myself." [10] Taba and her group discuss the use of diaries, participation schedules, and logs of class procedures.[11] Some clues may also be obtained from time to time through the creative activities of pupils, such as their drawings, their roles in dramatization, or their music and rhythmic activities. Teachers of young children often obtain valuable bits of information in free discussion periods.[12]

Parent conferences. Parents may provide very useful information about the personal-social development of their own children. Many school systems have already developed methods for systematically holding teacher-parent conferences and some obtain written reactions from parents on appropriate report forms. These efforts need to be expanded and extended if proper understanding of pupils is to result. Some behavioral acts of children that prove most troublesome in school are more readily understood after conferences with parents about home situations and conditions.[13]

Tests and inventories of social-personal development. Quite a variety of published tests are available for use in studying and analyzing personality and social and emotional development, but no attempt will be made here to list all of them.

Special mention, however, should be made of the California Test of Personality, since it is particularly useful in the study of the personality of pupils.[14]

In addition to tests of personality and social development and adjustment, a number of inventories and check lists have been published

[10] Arthur T. Jersild, *In Search of Self* (New York: Bureau of Publications, Teachers College, Columbia University, 1952).

[11] Hilda Taba and others, *Diagnosing Human Relations Needs* (Washington, D.C.: American Council on Education, 1951), Chaps. 2, 4, and 7.

[12] Gladys Willcutt, "Informal Talks with Children and Parents," in *Fostering Mental Health in Our Schools*, pp. 226–241.

[13] Katherine D. Evelyn, *Individual Parent-Teacher Conferences* (New York: Bureau of Publications, Teachers College, Columbia University, 1945); Taba and others, *op. cit.*, Chap. 3.

[14] California Test Bureau, *California Test of Personality: A Profile of Personality and Social Adjustment* (Los Angeles: California Test Bureau, 1939–1943).

which seek to survey problems that children feel they face, as well as their interests, wishes, and the like. Two lists designed to give pupils, particularly of adolescent age, an opportunity to check problems that concern them are the Mooney Problems Check List[15] and the SRA Youth Inventory.[16]

Several studies have also been made of children's interests, and the check lists or scales used in these studies may also be helpful to teachers. The Springfield Interest Finder,[17] the Wishing Well,[18] and Doane's inventory[19] are all useful devices. Essays and autobiographies written by pupils and class discussions often reveal some insight into their individual interests, hobbies, and likes and dislikes.

Projective methods of studying children. Within recent years considerable use has been made of projective techniques in studying the emotional and social status of young persons. The Rorschach Test is one of the most famous of these projective devices, but it should be used only by people highly skilled in its administration and interpretation. The Horace Mann–Lincoln Institute of School Experimentation has done some experimentation with the use of pictures and unfinished stories as projective techniques.[20] The principal difficulty in the use of such techniques, however, is the interpretation of the reactions or responses of pupils. A considerable body of evidence needs to be developed before we can categorize pupil responses to such situations.

Many teachers have found sociodrama or role playing a worth-while projective technique to help them understand their pupils.[21]

Various devices with which to study social acceptance or rejection have also been used. The best-known methods are the sociometric test and the sociogram. This technique has been widely discussed in the lit-

---

[15] Ross L. Mooney, *Problems Check List* (New York: The Psychological Corporation, 1950).

[16] Herman H. Remmers and Berymann Shimberg, *SRA Youth Inventory* (Chicago: Science Research Associates, 1948).

[17] Arthur T. Jersild and Ruth Tasch, *Children's Interests and What They Suggest for Educators* (New York: Bureau of Publications, Teachers College, Columbia University, 1949).

[18] Louis Raths, *The Wishing Well* (Columbus, Ohio: Bureau of Educational Research, The Ohio State University, 1940).

[19] Donald Doane, *The Needs of Youth* (New York: Bureau of Publications, Teachers College, Columbia University, 1942).

[20] Cunningham and associates, *op. cit.,* pp. 361–363.

[21] A discussion of sociodrama as an educative technique may be found in Helen Hall Jennings, "Sociodrama as Educative Process," in *Fostering Mental Health in Our Schools,* pp. 260–285; Robert B. Haas (ed.), *Psychodrama and Sociodrama in American Education* (New York: Beacon House, 1949).

erature and many teachers have used it in at least a simplified form.[22] Cunningham and her associates have formulated a method of translating sociometric reactions into numerical scores in terms of a socio-distance scale.[23]

CHART SUMMARIZING DEVELOPMENTAL CHARACTERISTICS OF PUPILS

Since the pupil is a basic factor in the educational process, teachers and other curriculum workers cannot develop sound educational objectives, envisage desirable outcomes for the educational process, or plan and develop educational experiences wisely unless they have an understanding of the nature of the growth and development of children and youth and their developmental characteristics and needs. Consideration has already been given to sources of help in developing such insights and methods useful in studying boys and girls. We realize, however, that many curriculum workers do not have access to much of the literature or the time to digest it. Therefore we have attempted to bring together in succinct and summary form for the convenience of curriculum workers the more important facts about child and adolescent growth and development. Obviously, the following chart or outline in Table 6 is a summary, since the literature and research studies on this subject are voluminous and are growing apace. However, we believe that the chart presents the major facts known to date about growth and development that are of most significance to educators.

Growth is a continuous process and is not marked by discrete periods of development. Nevertheless, for purposes of convenience we must organize our information into some type of schematic form; hence the chart is presented in three basic parts. Some of the most pertinent developmental characteristics of children at the approximate age of entrance to school are stated; growth developments during the period of attendance at the elementary school are presented next; and finally the chart summarizes development during the adolescent period, or roughly the period of attendance at secondary school. It should be emphasized

[22] For a more complete discussion of the use of sociometric devices see Helen Hall Jennings, "Sociometric Grouping in Relation to Child Development," in *Fostering Mental Health in Our Schools,* pp. 203–225; Cunningham and associates, *op. cit.,* pp. 154–204; American Council on Education, Staff of Inter-Group Education in Cooperating Schools, *Sociometry in Group Relations* (Washington, D.C.: The Council, 1948); Horace Mann—Lincoln Institute of School Experimentation, *How to Construct a Sociogram* (New York: Bureau of Publications, Teachers College, Columbia University, 1948).

[23] Cunningham and associates, *op. cit.,* pp. 401–406.

again that these are not discrete periods of development, but rather base points useful in describing growth and development.

The chart describes growth and development in general terms. While most children follow the same general developmental patterns and go through pretty much the same growth cycles, it must constantly be kept in mind that each child grows and develops in his own individual way. Consequently, general statements and averages may not apply to a particular developmental pattern or to the particular arrangement in which growth in each aspect of development takes place. Comparison with norms or group averages is not the best way to assess the growth and development of an individual child; it is much more important to study his development in terms of his own individual growth pattern. However, comparisons with norms and common tendencies are helpful in understanding the developmental needs of the child, particularly in relation to any frustrations or anxieties which may develop as a result of sharply deviating developments. With these cautions, we present the chart summarizing the growth and development of children and adolescents.

TABLE 6

Patterns and Characteristics of the Growth and Development of Children and Youth

I. *Physical Development*

A. Bodily Growth

AT ENTRANCE TO SCHOOL

Growth has slowed down a great deal from period of infancy. Period of relatively slow structural growth. Postural defects, if any, are often established by this time. Starts losing his "baby" teeth and permanent teeth begin to appear. Bones are relatively soft, thus avoiding fractures in many falls and blows. Six-year molars appear between five and six years of age; important that they be cared for, since they help set jaw and alignment of other teeth. Various parts of body develop at differing rates with resultant awkwardness at times, different appearance from that of adults, etc.

A child has a basic growth and maturation pattern and efforts to force growth are strongly resisted; an optimum nurture for his individual pattern is most desirable, rather than any effort to force or speed up or slow down the process. There is marked resistance to interference with his growth patterns, either through excessive deprivation or stimulation; when such conditions are overcome or removed individual largely returns to his basic growth

TABLE 6 *continued*

pattern. Because of this basic pattern of growth, efforts to develop
a skill or attainment before child is ready developmentally usually
results in much wasted effort, thwarting, and unnecessary stress
and tension.

THE ELEMENTARY SCHOOL YEARS

Period of rather stable, regular growth; adds from three to five
pounds yearly; no rapid spurts until adolescence; growth is slower
than in preschool or early adolescent period. Develops permanent
teeth. Very active; sitting still is an effort. May have nervous habits
as nailbiting, tongue sucking, etc. Rapid increase in weight and
height may begin in girls at about age eleven; a few girls may begin menstruation by age twelve; girls are fully a year ahead of
boys in physical maturity and development. Children's muscles
develop rapidly during school years. Posture is important, since
bones are developing and hardening.

Must judge growth in childhood not in terms of other children
of his age, but in terms of his own build and that of his parents.
Comparison in growth should be to his own status at an earlier
period, rather than to group age averages. Parts of body do not
grow evenly; each organ or part has its own growth pattern. This
accounts for awkwardness. Growth process of each individual is
characterized by his own pattern of regularity and rhythm; little
we can do to change basic time pattern and growth cycle.

THE SECONDARY SCHOOL YEARS

Pubescence results in rapid increase in growth and rates of
growth. Timing is the great factor in understanding rates. Individual's physical development, status, and pattern of growth
can be understood best through study of relationships of various
parts of body. Rate of growth correlates with degree of sexual
maturity. Year of most rapid growth for girls is, on the average,
a little more than two years earlier than for boys. Girls, on average, start period of accelerated growth at about age nine or ten;
within two or three years rate of growth slows down. Full growth
is usually attained at about age seventeen for girls and age nineteen for boys.

Internal bodily changes proceed at different rates; neural development, as far as weight but not function is concerned, is
about complete at approximately age six; lymphoid tissue over-
develops in a rapid growth period from about ages eight to ten;
then shrinks. Genital tissue develops little until about age ten;
then develops rapidly in adolescent period. Endocrine balance
changes; pituitary glands are very active just prior to pubescent

TABLE 6 *continued*

growth cycle; then secretion of sex hormones increases greatly. Metabolic rate increases just before puberty; then declines to adult level in later adolescence. Other bodily developments show some prepubescent spurt as is revealed in height and weight.

Late-maturing boys tend to have broader shoulders and narrower hips, while early-maturing boys have narrower shoulders and broader hips. Children who are tall tend to enter the adolescent period of rapid growth earlier than short children. Correlation is about o.75 between relative height at about ages nine to twelve and adult height, but individual variation must be considered.

No reliable correlation between body build as such and temperament. The time puberty occurs may have important social-emotional consequences for those who mature early as well as late sexually and may produce maladjustments and behavior problems of a serious nature if not properly understood. Also, growth and physical conditions have important social and emotional consequences, especially for the adolescent who deviates markedly; strong, well-built boys and attractive small girls gain social acceptance easier. A sudden growth spurt may occur without corollary changes in behavior or acceptance of a more mature role so that adults criticize the adolescent for not "acting his age."

Menstruation may be quite irregular in early years. Menarche in girls appears at an average of from thirteen to thirteen and a half years, although there is great individual variation, varying from ages ten to sixteen. Two thirds reach puberty between twelve and fourteen years of age. No specific act in boys indicates puberty, but evidence shows it is about two years later than for girls. Secondary sex developments also occur at this time—growth of pubic hair, change of voice in boys, change in body contour, etc. Occasionally, girls and women develop conspicuous growth of fine hair on upper lip or on sides of face; there is no evidence that such growth itself indicates masculinity. The concept of maturity status is regarded by some as a more useful frame of reference than chronological age; the best measure of this is anatomic age as revealed by skeletal development.

B. Motor Development

AT ENTRANCE TO SCHOOL

In view of the fact that a human being has over six hundred muscles and forty million muscle fibers, it is understandable that it takes him about twenty years to organize this system. Control over large muscles is much better than control over small ones. Gross motor control is well developed, but control of fingers and

TABLE 6 *continued*

hands is far from being complete. Skill in use of arms, legs, and trunk precedes skill in use of hands and fingers.

By age of five, handedness is usually definitely established; 90 per cent are right-handed. Evidence now indicates that changing left-handed child to right-handedness does not affect motor development; danger may come in emotional pressure and tension.

Motor skills unevenly developed. Sex differences in muscular control can be seen in throwing a ball. Likes to climb onto chairs and tables and to jump off. Development of motor control and skills affects social and emotional life—builds self-confidence, aids in social ability and growth in advancing independence, affects kinds of activities engaged in and play. Maturation is major factor in development of skills; practice in advance of suitable maturity is largely wasted. Motor growth follows an orderly maturation pattern just as do other aspects of growth.

THE ELEMENTARY SCHOOL YEARS

Muscular development improves. General form of motor activity varies with age and with inborn ability rather than with type and nature of exercise per se. All children tend to go through same sequence of motor development but rate varies greatly. Efforts to force it are quite unsuccessful. Maturity is fundamental in determining nature of motor traits of growing children.

Young child is always in motion, but in later years settles down for longer periods. Activity of young child is often clumsy. Often has a "run" on an activity, and may stay at one thing until about exhausted. By age of nine reveals his psychomotor make-up. Individuality expressed in postural and physiognomic factors. In later years shows great interest in his own strength. Small muscles and eye-hand coordination sufficiently developed by age eight to enable child to do work involving manual dexterity. Elementary children take great pride in physical performance. Proper motor development and appropriate level of skill give child security and social acceptance.

THE SECONDARY SCHOOL YEAR

There is no generalized motor ability; different functions mature at different rates and reach maturity at different ages. Rate of development of strength is closely related to advent of pubescence. Some studies tend to show that young adolescent is not necessarily more awkward physically, except for youngster who had an unusual early growth spurt; observable "awkwardness" may have social basis in lack of social adequacy. Sex differences in motor ability are probably not as great as is commonly as-

TABLE 6 *continued*

sumed; boys have greater gross strength, but girls may be practically as good on precision skills and motor agility. Period of most rapid growth in manual strength is between ages twelve and thirteen for girls and fifteen and sixteen for boys; at age eleven boy is twice as strong as at six, and by sixteen his strength has doubled again. Volume of bodily activities declines in later adolescent years.

C. Health Status; Disease; Somatic Conditions

AT ENTRANCE TO SCHOOL

Very susceptible to infectious diseases. Preponderance of respiratory diseases in winter and spring and alimentary tract ailments in summer and fall. Bones more subject to septic infection. Not much concern about health in general unless they themselves are sick. Can be taught personal cleanliness. Body chemistry changes with age, as indicated by susceptibility to diseases and to allergies. Organ systems have own rates of development; hence irregularities of child development. Tensional behavior is at low ebb at age five. Health relatively good except for contagious diseases.

THE ELEMENTARY SCHOOL YEARS

Very susceptible to infectious diseases at younger ages. Membrane of throat, bronchial tubes, and ears especially vulnerable. In early grades, children subject to stomach aches and nausea. Muscular pain in younger age groups. In later years general improvement in health status; fewer illnesses, but some may have prolonged illness. By age ten most are past period of contagious childhood diseases, but tuberculosis is serious threat. Accidents are leading cause of death; much higher for boys. Automobile, bicycle, street accidents, and burns most common causes. Child of six to eight is in most careless age—in a hurry, lack of caution. Needs much supervision to reduce risk. Admonition not too effective. Tensional activity increases sharply upon entrance to school— speech tensions, nail biting, chewing, biting lips, hand-to-face gestures. In middle years much tension—jiggles legs, fidgets, grimaces, smacks lips. Some quieting down in later years. Beginning in the first grade child can assume some responsibility for his own health, care of teeth, dressing properly, etc.

THE SECONDARY SCHOOL YEARS

Illness and death rates are at the lowest point during the period of the teens. However, there are some illnesses and physical ailments, particularly skin diseases, tonsil infection, and glandular imbalance or malfunctioning. Visual defects may occur in 20 to

TABLE 6 *continued*

30 per cent of the population; hearing loss to point of being a handicap in 5 to 10 per cent. Defects have important social, emotional, and intellectual consequences; hence parents and teachers should look for visual and auditory defects in cases of slow learning and maladjusted children. Accidents are the single greatest cause of death, especially in age group from fifteen to nineteen. In physical education programs and sports be careful to avoid irreparable damage to tendons, cartilage, terminal parts of bones, etc. Rapid growth of this period makes attention to nutrition essential; adequate diet necessary for proper development. In these days smoking may become established by middle or late adolescent period, and in very active boys may have some effect on the heart.

D. Eating Habits; Nutrition

AT ENTRANCE TO SCHOOL

Usually eats same foods as rest of family. Well able to feed self, but has "terrible" manners. Child can readily acquire liking for most wholesome foods. Parental anxiety and compulsion may cause blocks in eating habits and food selection.

THE ELEMENTARY SCHOOL YEARS

Usually has excellent appetite although some may be serious exceptions. Likes to eat lots between meals; bolts food. May have decided dislikes in food, but gradually overcomes these. Parents scold considerably about manners, giving rise to tensions and serious interference with pleasant meal experiences. Not truly ill-mannered—just growing up. Often demands in decorum are out of proportion to skill or maturity. Friendly atmosphere, maturity, and example are best means to good manners. Usually will balance his own diet quite well if given opportunity; hence should not try to overcome honest aversions to certain foods.

THE SECONDARY SCHOOL YEARS

Big appetite during this period, but apt to become finicky about food. Girls will begin to curb eating or go on special diets to avoid too much gain in weight. Much eating between meals, especially of sweets. Food selection often has social basis.

E. Fatigue; Rest; Sleep

AT ENTRANCE TO SCHOOL

Child normally sleeps soundly throughout the night. Sleep should be from ten to twelve hours. Naps for kindergarteners often desirable. Fatigue is shown by restlessness and crossness rather

TABLE 6 *continued*

than by lying down or resting. Habits of regular hours for sleep should be established. Process of going to sleep may be period of anxiety; may have apprehensions, imaginings, and clinging behavior. Seeks reassurance; wants companionship. Has dreams and often nightmares.

THE ELEMENTARY SCHOOL YEARS

Sleeps from ten to twelve hours in earlier years; most sleep through night, although some waken for toilet or from dreams. May have trouble going back to sleep and wants reassurance— often mother sharing bed or coming to child's bed. As he grows older tries to postpone going to bed; dillydallies. Rebellion may be as much against parent domination as against sleep. Younger child fatigues, but refuses to give up.

THE SECONDARY SCHOOL YEARS

Rest needs are similar to those of adults, with about eight to eight and a half hours of sleep necessary. But many resist rest and fail to get as much sleep as is desirable.

F. Toilet Habits; Elimination

AT ENTRANCE TO SCHOOL

Should be well established and child able to care for himself. Few children will wet the bed at night; if they do, probably has a psychological basis. Regard use of toilet as natural, accepted thing. May put off going to toilet and needs to be reminded. Only occasional toilet accidents.

THE ELEMENTARY SCHOOL YEARS

May need reminder in early grades to go to toilet. Occasional accident that causes embarrassment. Bowel movements, especially of lower-grade children, usually occur at home. Toilet practices and arrangements at school need careful examination, so that child faced with urgent situation may be accommodated.

THE SECONDARY SCHOOL YEARS

Adult status established.

G. Personal Dress; Clothes; Cleanliness

AT ENTRANCE TO SCHOOL

Child should be able to manage his own clothes at toilet and put on outer clothing. Child should be taught self-reliance in properly dressing self and putting on outdoor clothing, galoshes, etc. Needs help with bath. Necessary to remind about washing.

TABLE 6 *continued*

THE ELEMENTARY SCHOOL YEARS

Can dress self, but needs help on selection of clothes to be worn. Dawdles in dressing. In early years often needs assistance in dressing. Drops clothes about own room; careless about clothes. Usually girls are sensitive to appearance and neatness; many boys sloppy and careless. Must dress like other children. Can bathe self, but often has to be reminded about bath and to wash before meals. Marked increase in responsibility from age eight on in selection of clothes, care of clothes and their adaptation to occasion. In later years boys quite indifferent to cleanliness and appearance; girls very conscious of appearance.

THE SECONDARY SCHOOL YEARS

With increased interest in opposite sex, adolescent becomes greatly concerned about personal appearance, neatness, and appropriateness of clothes. Adolescent often becomes concerned about physical condition and facial blemishes that may militate against desirable appearance; may even avoid peer groups if condition is not corrected or overcome. Body odor and cleanliness are important matters to adolescents, who are very prone to reject individuals whose body odors are noticeable; much use of perfumes, etc., to creat artificial odors. Cleanliness, in contrast to childhood period, becomes decided virtue, especially for acceptance by opposite sex.

II. *Personal-Social Development*

A. Emotional Development

AT ENTRANCE TO SCHOOL

Emotions are structures which grow like any other human process or behavior; are structured modes of behavior. Have basis in instinctive behavior of individual. The child likes supervision. Is friendly, affectionate, helpful, curious, enjoys humor, likes to talk. Has temper tantrums, calls names, threatens.

Fear is an important factor in child behavior. Fears of the child should be taken seriously by adult and respected. Outstanding fear is that of being deprived of his mother. Fears change with age and maturity. Fear arises from insecurity or threat of it. Close personal relationship to mother. Is aware of death, though not emotional problem.

Concept of self is evolving. Interested in own origin, babyhood, and the like. Likes to have experiences of earlier childhood revived for him. Likes little responsibilities and duties which he

TABLE 6 *continued*

can do well. Everything considered, five-year-old is in excellent equilibrium; self-contained; poised. He is quite at home in his world. Is consolidating growth of earlier years prior to tempestuous period of six-year-olds. He takes life as it comes; but he is beginning to assert his independence; resists parents' demands or contradicts them. If there is a lack of affection in the home, conflicts, misunderstandings, and displays of anger are usually more frequent. Emotional behavior greatly affected by emotional atmosphere of the home. He is still highly dependent on adults.

While personality is not "frozen," foundation is laid prior to entrance to school, and school will have to build on what the child brings with him in terms of emotional development, traits, etc. One of his basic needs is to establish feeling of belongingness; in early years this is largely furnished by family, but the child gradually needs to broaden his relationships and gain acceptance in peer groups. He also needs to develop a close, confidential, intimate relationship with a few individuals—at first it is his mother, but later he needs to develop this relationship with agemates. Treatment in home—attitude toward aggressive behavior, frustrations, acceptance, etc.—has highly significant influence on child's behavioral patterns in school groups and among playmates. Emotional development does not seem to have the same relationship to maturation as physical, social, or mental growth.

THE ELEMENTARY SCHOOL YEARS

In early years is highly emotional: is boastful, easily hurt, shows evidences of temper, is noisy, excitable, calls names, is jealous, anxious to please, worries about acceptance, given to tantrums, cries at anything, threatens, contradicts, fights, is explosive, assertive.

In later years, there is some disequilibrium between self and others; demanding; bossy. Gets mad at parents. Curious about personal activities. Raises voice when angry or tired. Develops more responsibility. Enjoys competition, likes to exceed other fellow, sensitive to ridicule and loss of prestige, loyal to friend, cries when emotions are overtaxed, develops group loyalty. There is fighting among boys.

Fears shift more to personal nature—fear of being lost, of dark, of being left alone; later increase in fear of supernatural—witches, ghosts, hidden criminal. In later years, concern and worry over school failure, competitive situation, trouble at home. Likes to frighten others, brags about being frightened. Fears more complex and need more skillful management by parents and teachers than anger. Emotional response to death. In early years worries

TABLE 6 *continued*

that mother may die; curious about death of animals, etc. Later accepts idea that he will some day die.

Selfhood becomes firmly established. Understands his own development from babyhood. He consolidates the past; orients self to future. Gradually establishes own independence; resents being treated as a child. Puts up bold front; in middle and upper grades wants to make decisions.

In middle and upper grades hero worship common. Needs to belong—to be member of a group, club, or clique. Group or peers set standards for dress, activities, and interests. Wants privacy—place to call his own, to hide possessions. Feelings of inferiority may develop in those whose physical development is retarded.

Emotions will be aroused if child is bored, if he is defeated or thwarted by things that overtax him, or if he cannot fulfill his interests or aspirations that have developed. Often the immediate manifestation of emotional disturbance may not be cause or basis at all; child attempts to conceal real basis of emotional disturbance. Evidences of emotional maladjustment appear upon entrance to school; too often these children remain maladjusted, even into adult life. As child grows older he will have loyalties outside the home; these need to be encouraged and developed. Need to belong to peer group and to develop close intimate relationships with a few friends is very strong. Emotional conflict, serious repressions, and frustrations in home often lead to social difficulties, emotional disturbances, and delinquency in child.

THE SECONDARY SCHOOL YEARS

Status of physical growth and development may have significant effects on emotional equilibrium; those who deviate markedly from the averages, especially those whose physical growth is retarded, may develop strong tensions, become emotionally disturbed, and be rejected by peers. Boys particularly who deviate markedly may lose peer status and face extreme social handicaps, with emotional repercussions. Acne and other physical defects, also, may adversely affect social acceptance and peer status and hence lead to worry, anxiety, and emotional stress. On the other hand, the strong, well-built adolescent boy and the small, attractive, well-shaped girl gain social acceptance and roles of leadership more readily. For the great majority of young people, however, adolescence does not seem to be a period of undue emotional stress or maladjustment.

Adolescence does present its own particular problems of adjustment that should be understood by adults and by youth themselves. In general, problems of adjustment revolve around (1)

TABLE 6 *continued*

establishing adequate heterosexual relationships, (2) handling biological sex drives, (3) achieving independence and status and acceptance as an adult, (4) establishing vocational sufficiency and economic independence, (5) developing an adequate set of adult values and a behavior code, and (6) developing mature abstract concepts and generalizations about the modern world and society.

During adolescence, there are an increasing awareness of self and the development of self-ideals, and a drive for self-assurance and acceptance. Since the adolescent is forced into a subordinate role, this role may become so much a habit and accepted type of behavior that some may be reluctant to give it up. Two basic factors characterize parent-child relationships in terms of his emotional development—dominance vs. submission and acceptance vs. rejection. Domination and rejection have far-reaching effects. Fantasy and daydreams substitute for reality when it is not satisfying but they are not serious unless they come to replace genuine effort and experience.

Much of the socialization of the adolescent is based on a socially derived anxiety that drives the individual to attain status and prestige and to avoid the failure to attain reward and acceptance through behavior or acts not acceptable to one's group, class, or clique. Thus adolescents of lower-class families tend to display adaptive forms of behavior which give them status and prestige in their groups or classes; similarly, middle-class youngsters are more or less driven to behavior in ways that will give them status and acceptance in middle-class circles. Teachers and other adults may fail to recognize the group patterns and prestige systems of children from lower classes and thus be unprepared to help these children form anxiety drives that will motivate them to attain a more acceptable type of behavior approved by middle and upper classes.

Major areas of frustration in adolescence lie in inadequacy of childish habits and behavior in meeting more mature demands and needs. Adolescence seems to be a period of greater anxiety for girls than for boys because of culture pressures. Mobility of adolescents in our modern culture brings them face to face with many of our cultural inconsistencies, thus adding to their conflicts and insecurity. American culture operates to thwart two major drives of the adolescent—for independence and for sexual satisfaction. His period of irresponsibility is further extended by modern technological culture.

The major fact about interests of adolescents is their sexual-social orientation; there is also a decline of interest in simple activities involving physical activity. Particular interests do not

TABLE 6 *continued*

develop until there is the prerequisite development of physical and mental abilities; within these limits environmental facilities and cultural conceptions greatly influence the nature of interests.

B. Interpersonal Relations; Family Relations

AT ENTRANCE TO SCHOOL

Fluctuations in child's attitude toward parents. Mother is center of child's world; likes to be with mother and help her. Relations with father usually pleasant and smooth. Proud of father. Enjoys family group. Obeys mother readily. Generally, a good adjustment within himself and to others. Relationships are personal in nature. Gets along rather well with younger siblings. Engages only in small group relationships—two or three. Mostly concerned with parents and in winning their approval.

Does not share possessions readily. Much of small group behavior is parallel behavior—doing much the same thing as other children, but not really group activity. But give-and-take and cooperation are developing. Must learn techniques of give-and-take, of getting along; too much adult interference may stifle his development of socially approved methods. Has developed ideas of competition.

THE ELEMENTARY SCHOOL YEARS

Parent-child relationship is highly flexible; marked variation in child's attitude. Child's developing concept of family life is dependent on his own home experiences. Maladjustments in home may have serious effects on child. Comes to resist domination by mother; argues more; very sensitive to moods and acts of mother; sensitive to praise or blame of mother. Child trying to achieve some independence, yet needs adult approval and affection. It is trying period for parents. Some quarreling.

In later years, sharp resistance to mother's demands. Relations with father may be smoother, less intense. May worship father; accepts punishment or correction by him more gracefully. Often teases and quarrels with brothers and sisters; wants to boss younger siblings; may be embarrassed by actions of group siblings; doesn't want them to tag along or mix in play with own age group. But can be very protective and considerate of younger siblings. Likes family group and activities, but in later years may want to be more on his own.

In early years, gradual shift from individual to group activity; in later years, intense group feeling; formation of clubs. Membership in clubs and groups becomes important at about age 11. In earlier years, choice of friends not based on social or economic

TABLE 6 *continued*

status; later becomes selective. No strong racial antipathies develop naturally; if they develop, are outgrowth of contacts with adults. In upper grades choice of friends influenced by similarity of interests. Approval of peer group very important; it sets standards for behavior, activities, interests, etc. Likes to "shine" in some activity prized by the group. Cooperation and teamwork can be learned, but child needs practice in these traits. In later years of childhood, rejection of adult standards and control becomes apparent; much of behavior seems to be characterized by friction with adults, and much problem behavior grows out of conflict in home.

THE SECONDARY SCHOOL YEARS

Social consciousness and concern over social matters are very high in the adolescent period, partly because of the school environment, the pressure to belong, to be accepted by a group. Peer culture is very important in determining conduct, dress, interests, and the like. Conformity to peer culture is paramount. The role of the adolescent in the group is major factor in determining his present and future social adjustment. Group role enables adolescent to boost his ego. Domination of the group is strongest in the middle phase of adolescence; hence this is also the period of greatest resistance to domination by parents and other adults. The prestige factors and group preferred type of behavior shift from late childhood through early adolescence to middle and late adolescence. Hence the difficulties which a youngster faces in adjusting to the demands of the group as the individuals mature are apparent; what is prized at age ten is decidedly out of place at age fifteen.

Social backgrounds of parents and class and caste lines begin to be important factors in determining friendships and groupings in junior high school period; size, motor ability, and age are also important factors among boys. A junior or senior high school pupil who deviates sharply from accepted patterns of the group very likely loses status with the group unless he already has established prestige, in which case he may set a new pattern. Physical prowess and athletic ability are very important factors in social acceptance and status of adolescent boys, although some gain status through other strongly compensating factors. A youngster who is unable to play an accepted part in physical activities of his peer group because of illness, late development, physical defects, or other factors may lose acceptance unless, with the help of his teachers, parents, and advisers, he may gain acceptance through other attainments. Ease in social situations involving the opposite

TABLE 6 *continued*

sex makes for social acceptance by both sexes. Girls may have more difficulty in social adjustment because characteristics that make them popular with boys do not always endear them to other girls. The late-maturing adolescent may be at a disadvantage in heterosexual relations, since he or she lacks social skill while others have already often established satisfactory relations. In later years of adolescence there is less emphasis on larger group activities, as in early adolescence; the tendency is to form small groups, except for large, impersonal organizations.

Dating between members of different social classes is often frowned upon by both peer groups and parents. Dating often starts in large group setting. Crushes on a member of own sex or on older person are quite common among girls. The establishment of adequate social heterosexual relationships is aided by group activities and opportunities for young adolescents of both sexes to work and play together. Relationship of adolescent to his peer group and his acceptance by group is one of the most important factors in his life. Good adjustment before marriage is related to proper adjustment in marriage.

Cliques play an important part in the life of the adolescent; often formed after age twelve, they involve youth of same general social classes and emotional attachments and are an influential factor in adolescent behavior. Informal activities of the clique take a much greater portion of an adolescent's leisure time than do organized school or community clubs and character-building groups. High school sports events are very popular, not just for the game, but for the opportunity to be away from home, to be with the group, and perchance to have a date. A large proportion of girls but smaller proportion of boys visit frequently in friends' homes, although there is less of this in lower-class families. Gangs are much closer-knit groups, usually growing out of conflict or the possibility of it; they often lead to delinquency, and result from the need of the individual to find ego-satisfaction, to identify himself with something, to attain group solidarity. Bias toward racial and minority groups becomes more general in high school group.

Home relationships and family background are extremely important factors in the personal-social development of the child. The relative cultural and economic position of the home in the society at large will be extremely important in determining not only the nature of parent-child relationships in the home, but the status of the child in his out-of-home life and the problems he encounters there. Conflicts with parents increase as the child moves into adolescence; especially is this true for girls because of

TABLE 6 *continued*

efforts at closer supervision. Although these conflicts tend to sub-side as the adolescent matures, they are most pronounced over the relationships of the child with his peer group. Parents tend to resist development of independence and self-reliance on the part of their children, and they thus play a crucial role in the degree to which full independence is achieved. In childhood and early adolescence, preference is shown for mother, but by late adolescence there is no marked general preference for either parent.

C. School Relationship

AT ENTRANCE TO SCHOOL

Period of tension, but early adjustment will depend on emotional maturity. If school situation is too much to cope with, may have upsets, physically and emotionally. But on whole, school goes quite smoothly. Not too talkative about school at home.

THE ELEMENTARY SCHOOL YEARS

Likes to please teacher and to be commended. Wants approval; teacher's opinions very important. In first years reacts more to program and activities; in later years relationship is more personal—adjustment is to teacher as a person. May be very demanding of teacher in early grades. Likes to take things to school to show, and from school to parents to see. Wants to help teacher. First-grader works in spurts and short shifts, in constant activity. Likes group oral work. Second-grader wants to be correct; likes to overdo practice or activity. Third-graders like to work together as a group; this is an expansive period of development. In fourth and fifth grades, advance in critical thinking; wants to perfect skill; more self-reliance and independence.

Maturity traits and individual growth pattern determine general nature of adjustment to demands of school; should not be too concerned over seeming deficiency in a skill or ability at a particular time. Teachers need a developmental point of view. Cannot set arbitrary standards for a grade in learnings involving motor skills. Must recognize individual rates of development. School needs to deal realistically with assets and liabilities of each child as indicators of his make-up and maturity status. Child's behavior in elementary school increasingly becomes oriented to what peer group favors, rather than to home influences.

THE SECONDARY SCHOOL YEARS

One of the great problems in high school centers around the extremely wide range in the intellectual ability and achievement

TABLE 6 *continued*

levels of the pupils enrolled. Studies show that teachers are highly inconsistent in their treatment of pupils, so that for some the classroom is a hostile environment. Pupils who are consistently treated in a negative manner by teachers do not do as well as they could. Maladjusted teachers tend to create instability in pupils. Circumstances of home and family are of primary importance in the selection of vocational careers; the cultural prestige of certain occupations, parental advice, ability, hobby experience, and special circumstances are all important factors in vocational preferences.

D. Sex Interest, Habits, and Relations

AT ENTRANCE TO SCHOOL

Familiar with differences between sexes. Not much sex play. Interest in own origin and in birth processes. Little sex consciousness in play.

THE ELEMENTARY SCHOOL YEARS

Some sex play. Begins to be interested in marriage and papa-mamma relationships. By age seven will understand physical differentiation of sexes; interested in birth processes; sex modesty begins. By age nine or ten, boys and girls play apart; intolerant of other sex. Interest in own marriage and future. Interest in opposite sex in upper grades shown by teasing, hitting, chasing; interest in own bodies.

THE SECONDARY SCHOOL YEARS

Adolescence, of course, marks the beginning of interest in the opposite sex, sex desires, and romantic and love interests. Adolescents want to attract the opposite sex. About 60 to 90 per cent of the men and slightly more than one half of the women admit masturbation, which is often begun about the time pubescence is reached. Some young adolescents shrink from situations that may reveal prominent sex developments, such as breasts in girls, while others tend to accentuate such maturity. Boys easily aroused sexually may avoid situations which might reveal erection. Adolescent sex desires and activities often lead to emotional disturbances and guilt reactions. There is a great deal of sex activity of one type or another in late adolescence among boys, such as masturbation and nocturnal emissions. Social restrictions and inhibitions regarding these sexual manifestations create severe problems.

TABLE 6 *continued*

E. Play and Interest Choices

AT ENTRANCE TO SCHOOL

Play is major activity of all children; has instinctive basis, but culture directs it. Adults may structure play too much. Development and maturity has much to do with type of play activity. Child should be free to develop own spontaneous play activities. Much imitative play. Enjoys cutting out things. Likes to make houses out of blocks or chairs. Much interest in babies or dolls. Activities are those that involve whole body and large-muscle activity. Parents often push child into play activities or give them toys for which they are not ready. Love to play in water and mud. Much solitary or parallel play rather than group play.

THE ELEMENTARY SCHOOL YEARS

Danger of too much structuring of play of children; need plenty of opportunity for unregimented play, for simple, unsophisticated play life. Movies, television, radio, comics may contribute to his induction into adult world and to development of imagination, etc., but should not replace some basic, simple play growing out of initiative and resourcefulness of child. At young ages may concentrate on one or a few play activities for long periods. Likes to dress up and imitate adults; plays cops and robbers and Indians. At younger ages play is in small groups; boys and girls play together; play involves whole body—climbing, running, jumping.

Beginning at about age eight sexes separate for play activities. Differences in play interests become apparent; girls like to dramatize, to "dress up"; boys like rough and tumble games but also show increasing interest in games requiring coordination of small muscles and games that involve mind and memory. Ceaseless activity. Collect anything and everything. The eight- and nine-year-olds have greater variety of play interests than any other group. As they approach teens more interested in group games and team play; begin to develop special interests in play. Interest in social dancing may develop in upper grades; imaginative play largely disappears. Children in early grades show preference for games involving running, chasing, handling a large ball, climbing.

THE SECONDARY SCHOOL YEARS

There is a sharp drop of interest in "secret gang" activities as youngsters move from childhood into middle adolescence. The older adolescent shows more interest in the affairs of the world and in current happenings. Studies have repeatedly shown great interest on the part of adolescents in later years in vocations and

TABLE 6 *continued*

in their vocational future. Practically all adolescents attend movies to some extent. Girls begin to show much greater interest in romantic pictures; boys like adventure, comedy, historical, and sports pictures. Radio listening and television viewing, where available, are extensive. Girls show most interest in dance music and dramatic plays; boys, in dance music, comedy skits, and mystery plays. The major development in the interests of adolescents is in activities that bring sexes together socially—dancing, "coking," spectator sport events, congregating in the corner hangout, etc. There is a big decline in activities involving considerable physical vigor or participation.

F. Moral and Ethical Sense

AT ENTRANCE TO SCHOOL

Concept of good and bad quite specific—largely on basis of being allowed or forbidden by parents. Conforms to parents rulings quite well. Usually denies own guilt if questioned. Very poor at taking care of things. Recognizes ownership.

THE ELEMENTARY SCHOOL YEARS

At first, sense of goodness or badness is specific—in terms of things to do or not do; gradually evolves a generalized notion of goodness or badness. Begins to set standards of conduct for self and others. Wants to be "good," and is disturbed about being "bad." In earlier years, usually denies own guilt if accused; or if confronted with wrongdoing, alibis, blames it on others. Often directly accuses others of wrongdoing. Most children have experience of taking things that don't belong to them. Delays carrying out requests or tasks. Has difficulty making up his mind, waivers; once he decides, doesn't like to change.

In later years develops sense of right and wrong; judges behavior of himself and others by group standards. Usually some basis in fact if he accuses others. Will listen to reason and change his mind; aware of moral codes. If surroundings are unfavorable, juvenile delinquency may occur in middle grade level. In upper grades great interest in earning money; desire for money may lead to difficulties in family and to undesirable activities. Development of moral character is part of total process of growing up. Is influenced by home, associates, and peer group. Character traits are specific in nature.

THE SECONDARY SCHOOL YEARS

By the time they reach adolescence, youth's concepts of right and wrong agree quite closely with adult standards. Peer groups

TABLE 6 *continued*

and parents have an important influence on attitudes. High school students, according to a number of studies, reveal an inadequate understanding of social issues and have little disposition to be concerned about them or to accept personal responsibility for civic action. Research tends to show that youngsters who have had actual experience in democratic living, self-government, and civic action have better attitudes and understandings and better exemplify democratic principles of behavior than youth whose learning is verbal.

The great majority of adolescents live well within restrictions legally placed on citizens. There is no evidence of a spurt in delinquency at adolescence in spite of popular opinion; most delinquents showed delinquent tendencies prior to adolescence, although arrests are more numerous in teens and early twenties than before. Boys have a higher rate of delinquency than girls. Delinquents tend to come from neighborhoods of marked social deterioration, but the majority of children even in such circumstances grow to maturity without a delinquency record; two conflicting social codes vie for control in such areas, while children in better neighborhoods seldom witness crime or hear first-hand reports of it. Delinquents tend to come from families in which insecurity, stress, and conflict are commonplace; escape from this bad home situation throws youngster with companions who breed delinquency in area hangouts.

Delinquents are in general duller than the general population, show more physical defects and ill-health, are retarded educationally, show much more insecurity, are under stress and in conflict, and reveal more evidence of aggressive behavior. In children, moral behavior is more specific in terms of learning in actual situations; in adolescents, it becomes more generalized, with abstract concepts being developed. Adolescents have a number of problems relative to religion and want help on them; yet church attendance tends to decline in the adolescent period. But religion is a matter of great importance to these youngsters; about half, on the average, are members of a church and more than half tend to accept rather than reject religious beliefs. Religion is a powerful cultural factor and may help youth to establish their value patterns.

TABLE 6 *continued*

III. *Intellectual Development*

A. General

AT ENTRANCE TO SCHOOL

Great intellectual curiosity; asks innumerable questions; wants to examine things, open packages, and go places. Attention span is closely related to motivation. Experiences success and failure. Make-believe is very strong. In general, preschool children ordinarily will sustain attention on a task or activity from seven to twenty minutes. By age five, most will understand time concepts of short span, such as "yesterday" or "tomorrow."

THE ELEMENTARY SCHOOL YEARS

In lower grades, child is chiefly concerned with his own immediate personal affairs and matters related to his own day-by-day living. Later, child, while still preoccupied with himself, encompasses concern for future and for others, and persons and matters outside his own experience. Younger children have difficulty joining in a common group intellectual experience—mostly individualistic—while older children can and do carry on group intellectual discussions and activities. It is not until the upper elementary grades that children have much concept of time in historical relationship.

There is some evidence that many pupils in elementary school do not grasp many of the concepts or understandings the school seeks to teach; this may be due in part to ineffective teaching and failure to develop instruction in terms of concerns, purposes, and interests of pupils, but probably in considerable part to immaturity of pupils—their lack of intellectual development sufficient to understand concepts and ideas. As child matures he is willing and able to stay at one task or activity for longer period; develops perseverance; but this will vary greatly with individuals and with interest in task. "Big, but dumb" is not true, since there is a correlation, although not high, between physical size and intelligence.

Particular levels of maturity are necessary for various types of learning. Must judge development and achievement in terms of each child's own pattern of growth, not in terms of arbitrary standards. Principle of pacing is important—there is a proper time in the development of each individual for introducing new skills and learning experiences; to try to develop them before child is ready is wasteful and inefficient and may lead to tensions

TABLE 6 *continued*

and frustrations. When child is ready he should have plenty of opportunity for practice and stimulating learning experiences. Development of skills appropriate to child's maturity leads to personal security and poise.

Recent studies emphasize two-cycle nature of mental growth—growth in preadolescent period and growth in adolescent period. Each has its own aspects of acceleration, leading to a maximum in late adolescence. Rather than be too concerned about the constancy of the I.Q., we need to take account of child's individual growth pattern and his maturation in terms of his potentialities through a stimulating environment. The evidence seems to be quite strong that school achievement when properly nurtured is a function of the total growth of the child. Standards need to be set in terms of growth pattern of individual child rather than in group averages.

THE SECONDARY SCHOOL YEARS

Intellectual ability is function of neural growth. During adolescence, a youth will increase his sheer intellectual power vertically, but will develop "horizontally" in added knowledge, skills, understandings, and ability to use his intellectual talents to reason, to draw on meanings, to make decisions, to foresee, to evaluate actions, and the like. The adolescent reaches the peak of his intellectual growth by eighteen to twenty years of age or at best will show only a slight increase thereafter. Thus, in general, a high school student has the *power* to learn, but may lack previous learnings essential to carry on the activity. However, we should consider that, just as in physical maturation, some adolescents are slower to mature than other children, so some adolescents may mature late intellectually. Hence a youth who had trouble with abstract learnings as a freshman may be better able to learn such things as a senior, not only because of greater intellectual maturation but because of greater breadth of related knowledge.

There is no reliable evidence of basic differences in intelligence due to racial origin, nationality, or sex; reported differences are probably due to lack of learning experiences, the composition of tests, etc. Children from families of upper socioeconomic levels average higher than children from families of lower levels—socioeconomic status is probably a reflection of superior intelligence of parents. In view of the variations due to individual growth rates, to physical condition at the time of the test, to chance errors, and the like, it is unwise in making critical decisions to judge intelligence on one test, especially a group test. Intellectual ability is related to hereditary factors; correlations are from 0.88 to 0.97

TABLE 6 *continued*

between identical twins, 0.45 to 0.55 between parent and child, 0.53 to 0.70 between nonidentical twins, and 0.45 to 0.55 between siblings in the same home. The correlation between height and weight and mental ability, as measured by tests, is low. The evidence on rate of intellectual growth is not too conclusive, but the rate seems to be fairly constant from childhood until near the point of maturity. It is doubtful if there is noticeable spurt near the onset of puberty or early in pubescence as is true of physical growth, but there may be a small relationship between physical maturity and intelligence.

B. Reasoning

AT ENTRANCE TO SCHOOL

Able to comprehend ideas; can accept reason for things and give his own reasons; can grasp notion of cause and effect. Is not logical or rational in his approach to many things.

THE ELEMENTARY SCHOOL YEARS

In early grades reasoning is based on direct observation and concrete situations. By about age ten, child is able to discuss problems, to see different sides of a question. Capacity for thought and reason increases markedly after that age. Understands abstract ideas in upper grades; can look ahead and may postpone satisfactions. Best able to solve problems involving concrete situations within own experience. In upper grades can talk out group problems and draw conclusions from scanty data.

THE SECONDARY SCHOOL YEARS

Test results tend to show that high school boys are slightly superior to girls in reasoning power. Girls have tested somewhat higher in memory. Ability to reason is closely related to intelligence; hence facts relative to growth of intelligence are pertinent here. However, the use of reason in situations confronting an adolescent is also a function of experience and practice in reasoning in similar situations and in understanding the processes of reasoning.

C. Language Development; Reading

AT ENTRANCE TO SCHOOL

Likes to be read to; enjoys stories about animals that act like persons and daily happenings of children. Environmental, in-

TABLE 6 *continued*

cluding socioeconomic, factors greatly influence development of speech. Language development tied up with opportunities in home and neighborhood; child who has much opportunity to talk with adults and older children has advantage; hence great variability among children at entrance to school. May need to unlearn much that was acquired prior to school entrance. Except in unusual cases, preschool child is not ready for reading, but "prereading" activities are desirable. Speech is highly egocentric.

THE ELEMENTARY SCHOOL YEARS

In early years commonly uses up to 2,500 words; increases rapidly, going to 7,500 by age eight and 14,000 by end of this period. Takes delight in learning to read. Stories of the past and fairy tales are of interest to eight- and nine-year-olds. Differences in reading interests of boys and girls begin to appear at about fourth grade. Fine-muscle work still difficult and taxing by age eight or nine, so ability to write smoothly is just developing. Range in reading ability widens and is often four or five years in upper grades. Reading disabilities may influence development of entire personality. Lots of interest in leisure reading by age nine. In upper grades stories should be relatively true to life.

Development of ability in reading and in other school subjects is just one aspect of total development. Retardation in these areas may be only one phase of general immaturity. Language used is important clue to level of maturity. Considerable diversity in visual ability in kindergarten and first grade because of eye control; child needs this control before reading begins; must be able to recognize differences in word forms.

THE SECONDARY SCHOOL YEARS

The extent of the vocabulary of high school students varies in different studies. One study shows the average vocabulary of basic and derived words to be as high as 80,000 for seniors, but most studies show a much lower count of basic words—about 25,000. Girls, on the average, seem to have a larger vocabulary than do boys. Tests show that girls in high school are generally superior to boys in language ability. Basic skills and habits of reading and writing are fairly well established by the time children reach junior high school. Reading interests shift from fiction and adventure stories to more factual realistic material, although girls show considerable interest in glamour stories and accounts, and boys in westerns and detective stories. Most adolescents read the newspaper; they also report spending a considerable amount of leisure time in reading books.

TABLE 6 *continued*

D. Mathematics

AT ENTRANCE TO SCHOOL

Likes to play simple number games. Enjoys counting objects. Usually has some concept and knowledge of numerical quantities and concepts.

THE ELEMENTARY SCHOOL YEARS

Is interested in numbers and number concepts by time of entrance. Can grasp processes of multiplication and division about age nine and ten.

THE SECONDARY SCHOOL YEARS

Test results tend to show boys somewhat superior to girls in mathematical ability. Studies show that mathematics ranks both as a subject most liked and as a subject least liked; that is, those with ability in mathematics and who have had success in it express interest in it as a subject, whereas others do not.

E. Science

THE ELEMENTARY SCHOOL YEARS

In middle grades great interest in facts, in things—what things are made of, how they work.

THE SECONDARY SCHOOL YEARS

Expressed interests in science as a field of study is discouragingly low; many pupils have little interest in science or in taking science subjects. On the other hand, a small proportion of the pupils express keen interest in the field, an interest often reflected in their hobbies and leisure-time activities.

F. Art

AT ENTRANCE TO SCHOOL

Will engage spontaneously in many art activities if given opportunity. Imagination enters into art activities; imaginative play is at peak at school entrance age. Will dance, march to music, and sing. Child will respond with enthusiasm to new possibilities in the arts if given help in succeeding with what he enjoys doing. Adults should not set too difficult standards or dictate activities.

THE ELEMENTARY SCHOOL YEARS

Creative ability can be developed and improved in practically all children. Maturity level is an important factor in stage of

TABLE 6 *continued*

development. Young children try to reproduce what they see; later they develop some sense of relationships and want pictures to look real. Most children have desire to create. In early grades, interest in large-muscle activities—broad, sweeping lines, large, unrestrained movements. With much greater control over small muscles in middle and upper grades, child can give greater attention to detail and design; techniques can be developed. Child needs ample opportunity for creative expression if good growth is to result. Should be interwoven in total program of child, not restricted to separate period for "art."

THE SECONDARY SCHOOL YEARS

Art should emphasize originality, creative design, and opportunity for expressing oneself. There is a considerable interest in music; studies show an increasing interest in opera and serious music, although most enjoy and like popular and dance music.

G. Leisure Interests

THE ELEMENTARY SCHOOL YEARS

Radio listening and television viewing appeal to basic interests of children for fantasy, make-believe, and vicarious experiences. Extent is matter of competing interests. If there are other well-developed interests that can be satisfied, as in the summer time, less time is spent on these passive activities.

PRINCIPLES OF GROWTH AND DEVELOPMENT BASIC TO
CURRICULUM PLANNING

Even the summary chart shows the scope and breadth of our present knowledge about growth and development. While this information is basic to an adequate understanding of pupils, the teacher will feel overwhelmed by the great mass of data collected from research studies and other literature on growth. In organizing such information, the curriculum worker will gradually recast it into basic concepts that are essential generalizations for curriculum planning. It is these principles, drawn from the mass of available data, that give direction to curriculum planning. The actual planning of educational experiences will, of course, necessitate an understanding in detail of the particular children involved, but for general planning by school staffs or individual teachers, principles are pertinent. In this section we shall present some principles, derived from what is known about child growth and development, that are basic to curriculum planning.

PRINCIPLE NO. 1. GROWTH AND DEVELOPMENT ARE CONTINUOUS PROC-
ESSES. Although for convenience of study we mark off stages in the growth
and development of human beings, such as infancy, childhood, adolescence,
and adulthood, actually growth and development are continuous processes proceeding from conception to death. There are no sharp breaks or
sudden changes in the pattern; certain types of changes in behavior and
development may become most marked, however, during a particular period of growth if judged by the contrast between behavior or development at the beginning of the period and during or at its end. Change
from one year to the next is developmental and more or less continuous
rather than sporadic and sharply differentiated.

Because of the continuous nature of growth it is highly important
that teachers know the total developmental pattern of each child if they
are to understand adequately his stage of development at any particular
point. The present is built upon the past, just as surely as the present
becomes the foundation for the future. The types of adjustments he
makes to situations, the relationships he has to other individuals, and the
characteristics of his own personality are the outgrowth of the developmental pattern he exhibited in his earlier period, the kinds of adjustments he made at that time, and the personality traits he exhibited then.
Similarly, his present patterns become a basis for understanding his developmental characteristics at a future date.

PRINCIPLE NO. 2. GROWTH IS HIGHLY INDIVIDUALIZED. Every curriculum
worker is well aware of the fact that no two children are alike. This
concept of individuality is basic to an understanding of the maturation
of individuals and to adequate planning of educational programs in the
school. From the standpoint of growing up, individuals differ in (1) rate
of growth, (2) the pattern of growth and consequently the level of development at any one stage, and (3) the maximum level of development attained. All status studies as well as longitudinal studies confirm
these basic differences among individuals.

Differences in rates of growth among boys and girls become quite
apparent when measures of growth are charted on a graph. Some children exhibit a rather smooth growth curve, at least in some characteristics, while others show a great variability in the rate of growth at
different periods. The rate of growth at different stages may vary for
children who nevertheless require approximately the same time to reach
about the same maximum level of maturity; on the other hand, some children take longer periods of time to attain a similar ultimate level. Plate
12 depicts this situation very well, for all of the youngsters pictured are
of the same chronological age and in the same grade in school; yet their

physical maturation, obviously, varies considerably. Some children may show sudden spurts at particular stages of development, while other children will proceed with their growth in a more regular and orderly fashion. These differences in rates of growth indicate that two children who may appear to be alike at a particular point actually differ considerably in their rates of growth. For example, in the fourth grade child A

PLATE 12. CHILDREN HAVE DIFFERENT RATES OF MATURATION. *These pupils are all of the same chronological age and are in the same school grade, yet they show wide variations in physical maturation. (Courtesy of National City Junior High School, San Diego County, California)*

and child B may exhibit the same level of development in reading, yet actually child B may have been considerably below child A at an earlier period and has simply caught up at the point at which the children are tested in the fourth grade. Thereafter, child B may develop much more rapidly and be considerably superior to child A at a later period of testing.

Total growth patterns also show a great deal of individuality, so that the study of the particular growth pattern of each child is essential. When charted on a graph, the growth curves of many children follow a rather uniform rate in many phases of growth, although there may be some minor variations. On the other hand, some children may show great variation in particular aspects of growth so that the pattern of total growth presents quite a different picture from that of other children. Thus it is possible that a youngster who shows a sudden spurt in physical growth may not show a comparable growth in reading, with the result that his developmental age in that area is considerably below his maturation age in height even though it was comparable at a base point. However, there is considerable similarity in growth characteristics; many children show a rather consistent pattern in many areas of development. This means, also, that the total growth pattern of a particular child may show an early rate of maturation, while the growth pattern of another child may show a late pattern; consequently, a child who may be judged to be dull in school achievement at one point in his schooling in relation to other children may actually make a late spurt and come out at about the same level as the children who were considered much superior to him at an earlier age.

However, we must, of course, recognize that children do differ in the maximum levels of growth attained. Just as not all of us are the same height or the same weight or can run a hundred yards in the same time, so not all of us have the same maximum level of ability in reading, reasoning, or other human traits. In spite of the discomfort it may cause parents and others, it is an inescapable fact that each individual seeks his own maximum level of development, provided the environmental conditions do not seriously interfere with this growth toward the maximum. Nevertheless, we must be extremely cautious in assuming that a child who is still growing up is inevitably doomed to a lower maximum of maturity in some respects than is another child who may be superior in attainments during the maturing process. It is the end level of development that is the most important thing in considering capacity and ability, since the rate at which this maximum level is achieved will vary for individual children. Moreover, suitable environmental conditions should exist if the individual is to mature to his maximum attainable level. The evidence is not yet clear as to the effect of deprivation in the environment on the total growth pattern. Certainly, we should not run the risk of stunting an individual's development because of a grossly inadequate or poor environment for the nurture of such growth.

PRINCIPLE NO. 3. GROWTH IS A UNITARY PROCESS. Even though growth is a highly individualized matter, the child tends to exhibit a unitary pattern in his total growth and development. Child study specialists have used several methods of showing the interrelationships existing in the growth traits of the individual. One of the most popular of these methods is the concept of organismic age formulated by Olson.[24] These graphic methods of portraying growth not only show in a clear-cut manner its totality, but also show its unitary nature as well as the sharp deviations from the common growth pattern that may occur in particular traits in certain individuals. Of course, there are many exceptions, as has been indicated in the preceding discussion; nevertheless there is already available sufficient evidence to indicate that the total growth pattern of an individual is a relatively safe prediction of the maturation rate of individual aspects of the person's development. Thus school achievement in the traditional skill areas is much more likely to be a function of the total growth pattern of the individual, provided a normal, stimulating environment is maintained, than a function of particular teaching techniques, devices, or drill. We must hasten to point out, however, that this is a very broad and somewhat tentative conclusion, and in view of our concept of the individuality of growth it is still incumbent on the curriculum planner and the teacher to consider the individual needs of each child and seek to assure him a satisfactory learning environment in terms of his individual growth patterns.

Also, it should be pointed out that growth in mental activities of the type emphasized in school is modifiable; nevertheless, some recent studies have tended to confirm the observation that intensive drill and so-called remedial procedures have not been particularly effective in permanent or long-term results if the child was not ready for such types of learning activities at his particular maturity level. In other words, forcing a child to undertake a type of growth for which he is not ready—physically, mentally, or socially—may represent considerable waste of effort as well as lead to some emotional and social maladjustments.

PRINCIPLE NO. 4. GROWTH IS CYCLIC IN NATURE. The cyclic nature of physical growth is quite apparent and is substantiated by an extensive body of research. The evidence on the cyclic nature of mental growth is not as substantial, but there seems to be some evidence that it, too, is of a cyclic nature. Thus growth is characterized by a series of accelerations and decelerations as the individual develops from conception to maturity. There are at least two major cycles, and possibly some additional minor cycles, during this period of growth.

In view of the interrelation of all growth, discussed previously, it is important that curriculum workers recognize the cyclic nature of growth so that educational experiences may be more appropriately

[24] Willard C. Olson, *Child Development* (Boston: D. C. Heath & Company, 1949). Chap. 7.

planned in terms of the growth pattern pertinent to the particular school
level.

PRINCIPLE NO. 5. HUMAN BEHAVIOR IS EXCEEDINGLY COMPLEX. Our
outline on growth and development (Table 6) indicates the complexity
and scope of human behavior. We, as teachers and curriculum workers,
would be extremely foolish if we attempted to judge the behavior and
maturity level of a youngster on the basis of quite introductory information of a casual type, or if we tried to generalize about anyone at all on
the basis of limited knowledge about that person. In any behavior situation there are an acting individual and an interacting environment. The
individual brings to the situation numerous predispositions, inherited
capacities and abilities, a particular level of general maturity as well as
maturity in particular traits utilized in the situation, personal motivational forces, and previous learnings acquired from earlier experiences.
Nor is the environmental situation simple, for the situation is whatever
it becomes for the individual reacting to it. He brings to the situation his
own interpretation of the environment, his own meanings and values,
and his own purposes and desires.

In view of this complexity, we must dig deeply, analyze carefully,
and search widely if we really want to try to gain an understanding of
the behavior of an individual. Moreover, we can make some decidedly
erroneous judgments about a child if we rely extensively on simple comparisons with other children in terms of the status of attainment at a
particular time.

To illustrate, one child, on the basis of the usual measures, may be
quite inferior to another child in reading achievement in the third grade.
The teacher might hastily judge this child to be retarded in development
or inferior in capacity to the other child, when actually the first child
might be quite superior to the second child in a number of other abilities and attainments. Moreover, the first child might have a quite different cycle of development, so that although he is inferior in reading
at the third-grade level, his cycle of growth may begin late but accelerate
very rapidly so that actually he ends at a level of reading ability superior
to the child who tested higher at the third-grade level. Obviously, we cannot hold out such hope for all such slow achievers, for our study of individuality shows that children will vary greatly not only in the cycle of
growth but in the maximum levels attained at maturity.

Shuttleworth well states this fact of the complexity of growth in the
single area of physical development in summarizing his data on twenty-
two dimensions of physical growth as measured in the Harvard Growth
Study:

In brief, our theory is that the patterns of physical growth shown by different dimensions and different groups from conception to maturity are the resultant of a progressive balancing of endocrine factors, of the timing of endocrine stimulation, of factors peculiar to each dimension, of factors determining mature size, and of factors associated with sex. Each of these five factors represents an exceedingly complex set of forces some of which operate persistently throughout the growth span while others operate for only limited intervals and at different ages. None acts independently. All are inextricably entangled by their mutual action and interaction in a single continuous process. An observed growth pattern is the external manifestation of the constantly shifting balance of such underlying forces.[25]

PRINCIPLE NO. 6. MATURATION TAKES PLACE IN A SOCIAL SITUATION. While growth itself is largely based on innate factors, maturation occurs in a social setting which also makes demands on the individual and shapes his development, particularly in the personal-social phases.

This social environment consists of innumerable factors that impinge on the individual as he grows up. Among the more important of these elements are the demands made upon him by his parents, his brothers and sisters, his playmates, his teachers and classmates at school, the social groups of his community, and organized social and political agencies to grow up to be the kind of person they think he ought to be. He is also greatly affected by the values and mores held by these individuals and groups. In other words, social forces in general bear in on the individual to shape his personal-social development. They profoundly affect his maturing process.

These social groups inevitably set certain learnings, adjustments, achievements, and evidences of maturation which the individual must manifest if he is to enjoy a normal, satisfactory existence in the social group of which he is a part. Failure to accomplish these *required learnings* will result in maladjustment, discontent, tension, and blocking of the desirable social maturation of the individual. Developmental tasks, then, constitute the required learnings in the area of personal-social development that an individual must achieve at appropriate levels of maturity if he is to find a full measure of satisfaction, happiness, acceptance, and security in the social group. They result from the interaction of pressures in the social environment with pressures from within the maturing individual. Research workers have prepared statements of what they believe constitute these requirements, and curriculum planners will

[25] Frank K. Shuttleworth, *The Physical and Mental Growth of Girls and Boys Age Six to Nineteen in Relation to Age at Maximum Growth* (Washington, D.C.: Society for Research in Child Development, 1939), p. 216. Reprinted by permission of the Society.

find them useful in bringing together concepts of growth in the personal-social area.[26] We believe that Corey's list is a useful and succinct one, so it is presented here in its entirety.

Early Childhood:

1. To handle, chew, swallow, and like solid foods.
2. To get himself from one place to another; eventually by walking.
3. To understand the general idea of verbal symbolism and eventually to use it and respond to it intelligently.
4. To control the elimination of body wastes so as not to violate numerous amenities.
5. To behave modestly sexually.
6. To behave in consistency with certain fundamental concepts of the physical world.
7. To make simple judgments regarding right and wrong.
8. To behave appropriately in his relationships with brothers and sisters, parents and relatives.

Later Childhood:

1. To care for his person in the sense that he can dress himself and keep himself reasonably clean.
2. To use his body as an instrument of his will; that is, to co-ordinate his movements so that his behavior becomes more effective.
3. To assume a sex role appropriate to little boys or girls.
4. To get along reasonably well with his age mates.
5. To use the fundamental intellectual skills that are necessary for everyday life, such as reading, writing, and computing.
6. To develop a sharper sense of right and wrong and the ability to behave consistently with some acceptable scale of values.
7. To behave consistently with certain conventional attitudes toward social groups and institutions such as race, religion, school, and the family.
8. To inhibit, to some degree at least, his emotional impulses.

Adolescence:

1. Coming to terms with their own bodies.
2. Learning new relationships to their age mates.
3. Achieving independence from their parents.

[26] Stephen M. Corey, "The Developmental Tasks of Youth," in *The American High School: Its Responsibility and Opportunity* (Eighth Yearbook of the John Dewey Society, Hollis L. Caswell, editor; New York: Harper & Brothers, 1946), pp. 70–99.

Caroline Tryon and Jesse W. Lilienthal III, "Developmental Tasks," in *Fostering Mental Health in Our Schools*, pp. 77–128.

Robert J. Havighurst, *Human Development and Education* (New York: Longmans, Green & Co., 1953).

4. Achieving adult social and economic status.

5. Acquiring self-confidence and a system of values.[27]

PRINCIPLE NO. 7. LEARNING IS A FUNCTION OF GROWTH. The interrelationship of learning and the physical, mental, social, and emotional maturation of the individual is quite generally recognized. For example, we do not ordinarily attempt to teach long division to a six-year-old child; neither do we have a unit on marriage and family relations in the fifth grade. Learning is dependent on maturation. Just as it would be unwise to attempt to teach a child two years old to ride a bicycle, so it is unwise to attempt to teach a child to read before he is developmentally ready to read. Thus the total growth pattern of the individual—his particular level of maturation in terms of his growth cycle as well as his growth in a particular phase of development—are all major factors in learning. Particular types of learning will occur most readily when the child has reached a satisfactory maturity status for learnings of that particular type. This principle of learning is fully developed in the following chapter, which deals with the implications of what is known about learning for curriculum planning. Indeed, several subsequent chapters (see especially Chapters 11 and 13) present principles and practices of curriculum planning which are based on the facts of individual growth and development presented here.

For Further Study

American Council on Education, Commission on Teacher Education, *Helping Teachers Understand Children*. Washington, D.C.: The Council, 1945.

A detailed report on methods used in a school system to carry on a cooperative study of growth and development.

Association for Supervision and Curriculum Development, *Fostering Mental Health in Our Schools*. 1950 Yearbook. Washington, D.C.: National Education Association, 1950.

A valuable guide to child study.

Cunningham, Ruth, and associates, *Understanding Group Behavior of Boys and Girls*. New York: Bureau of Publications, Teachers College, Columbia University, 1951.

A comprehensive treatment of various methods that may be used to study children in group situations.

Driscoll, Gertrude, *How to Study the Behavior of Children*. New York: Bureau of Publications, Teachers College, Columbia University, 1947.

Discusses methods that may be used in studying children.

[27] Corey, *op. cit.*, pp. 72, 73, and 98. Reprinted by permission of Harper & Brothers, publishers.

Faculty of the University School, The Ohio State University, *How Children Develop*. Columbus, Ohio: The University, 1946.

An excellent summary of the facts about growth and development of children and adolescents.

Garrison, Karl C., *Growth and Development*. New York: Longmans, Green & Company, 1952.

Summarizes what we know about growth and development of children.

Gesell, Arnold, and Frances L. Ilg, *The Child from Five to Ten*. New York: Harper & Brothers, 1946.

Based on exhaustive studies of children; a standard reference on the subject.

Glueck, Sheldon, and Eleanor Glueck, *Unraveling Juvenile Delinquency*. Harvard Law School Studies in Criminology. Cambridge, Mass.: Harvard University Press, 1950.

A report of a comprehensive investigation of the factors associated with juvenile delinquency. Considers basic needs of youth.

Greulich, William W., and others, *A Handbook of Methods for the Study of Adolescent Children*. Monograph, Vol. 3, No. 2, Serial No. 15; Washington, D.C.: Society for Research in Child Development, 1938.

An exhaustive discussion of methods and techniques that may be used in studying adolescents.

Havighurst, Robert J., *Human Development and Education*. New York: Longmans, Green & Company, 1953.

A detailed discussion of the developmental tasks and the implications of each task for curriculum planning.

————, and Hilda Taba, *Adolescent Character and Personality*. New York: John Wiley & Sons, Inc., 1949.

The first four parts of the book present studies and draw some conclusions on character formation in adolescents; Part 5 discusses methods useful in studying character and personality.

Horrocks, John E., *The Psychology of Adolescence*. Boston: Houghton Mifflin Company, 1951.

A comprehensive treatment of the adolescent period of development.

Jersild, Arthur T., *Child Development and the Curriculum*. New York: Bureau of Publications, Teachers College, Columbia University, 1946.

An excellent discussion of the significant facts about development and their implications for curriculum planning.

Kuhlen, Raymond G., *The Psychology of Adolescent Development*. New York: Harper & Brothers, 1952.

An outstanding textbook in this field. It is comprehensive and effective in interpretations.

Lerner, Eugene, and Lois B. Murphy, *Methods for the Study of Personality in Young Children*. Monograph, Vol. 6, No. 4, Serial No. 30; Washington, D.C.: Society for Research in Child Development, 1941.

Discusses many tests and techniques that may be used in studying personality development.

Millard, Cecil V., *Child Growth and Development in the Elementary School Years*. Boston: D. C. Heath & Company, 1951.

Excellent textbook on growth and development.

National Society for the Study of Education, *Adapting the Secondary-School Program to the Needs of Youth*. Part I, Fifty-second Yearbook. Chicago: The University of Chicago Press, 1953.

The first three chapters explore the needs concept and suggest methods of determining the needs of adolescents.

————, *Adolescence*. Part I, Forty-third Yearbook. Chicago: The University of Chicago Press, 1944.

A detailed summary of studies on the growth and development of adolescents.

Olson, Willard C., *Child Development*. Boston: D. C. Heath & Company, 1949.

A widely used textbook on growth and development. Gives special emphasis to interrelationships and to the individual nature of growth.

Shuttleworth, Frank K., *The Adolescent Period: A Graphic and Pictorial Atlas*. Monograph, Vol. 3, No. 3, Serial No. 16; Washington, D.C.: Society for Research in Child Development, 1938.

Presents 458 charts, graphs, and pictures summarizing numerous studies of adolescents.

Strang, Ruth, *An Introduction to Child Study*. 3d ed.; New York: The Macmillan Company, 1951.

Suggests methods useful in studying children and summarizes significant facts about development.

Taba, Hilda, and others, *Diagnosing Human Relations Needs*. Washington, D.C.: American Council on Education, 1951.

Describes six methods that may be used in studying pupils.

Wisconsin State Department of Public Instruction, *Guides to Curriculum Building: The Junior High School Level*. Bulletin No. 8, Wisconsin Cooperative Educational Planning Program; Madison, Wisc.: The Department, 1950.

Presents in chart form the growth characteristics of junior high school youth and their meaning for curriculum planning.

chapter 6

The Learning Process and Curriculum Planning

We consider knowledge of the learning process essential to all phases of curriculum planning. Unless the curriculum plan is based on such understandings of learners and learning as are presented in our Chapters 5 and 6, it is doomed to failure regardless of how carefully all other factors have been considered. In the final analysis, the goodness of the curriculum is determined by the learning that takes place. This chapter is therefore devoted to a description of the learning process with emphasis on its chief implications for curriculum planning. Appropriate references to certain materials on which our interpretation of the psychology of learning is based are given in the bibliography at the end of the chapter. Our intent is to present only those major aspects of the dominant theory of learning which are considered essential to effective curriculum planning.

CONCEPTS OF LEARNING

At least three general concepts of learning have had great influence in curriculum planning and teaching. Two of these have been discredited by research, but we still find school practices which appear to be based on these concepts. For that reason it seems worth while to describe each briefly.

Learning as Memorization

An early theory of learning conceived the mind as a storehouse for knowledge which, once learned (memorized), was stored and later used as needed. Learning, under this concept, was storing. In order to store information, the learner had to memorize. Once fully memorized, material was "learned" and thereafter ready when needed.

This interpretation of learning, erroneous as it now seems, has dominated teaching far longer than any other. That it still dominates at some points is revealed by observation of the kinds of learning exercises that pupils are frequently given. "Learn the rules (tables, classifications, dates, and the like)" is an assignment to memorize. Note taking, cramming, and similar activities even of college students are generally exercises in memorization.

The orderly arrangement of knowledge into subjects is intimately related to the storehouse-memorization theory of learning. The steps of curriculum planning and teaching are clear enough: (1) classify the knowledge into subjects; (2) determine the subjects to be taught; (3) select the phases of the subjects to be taught at different grade levels; (4) assign these phases (lessons, exercises, and so on) to pupils to learn (memorize); (5) test pupils' retention of materials assigned for memorization. This kind of planning is relatively simple, is aided by logically organized textbooks, and makes easy the preparation of tests of mastery (memorization). But when such tests are given after the period of cramming is well over, the learner is found to have retained very little (after two years, as little as 20 per cent) of what he "learned"!

The "learning as memorization" concept, though practiced more widely than we might hope would be true, has been discredited on several bases. In the first place, the forgetting which follows memorization is greater than can be explained away by the principles of use and disuse. Studies of forgetting and retention and learning factors have established the fallacy of the storehouse concept of mind. In the second place, other more plausible concepts of learning have come into existence. In general, these concepts recognize the importance of understanding, as contrasted with rote memorization, in learning. It is realized that people must and do remember; and sound teaching practices encourage the use of memory in learning. But modern teaching places emphasis on understanding first and remembering later so that what is remembered may be of use.

Learning as Mental Discipline

Another concept, not quite as old but also widely held even after being discredited, is that learning consists of disciplining or exercising the so-called mental faculties or functions. Thus, one was supposed to cultivate the faculty of reasoning through its exercise in any way; that of memory through miscellaneous memorizing; that of imagination through imagining (anything); and so forth.

This concept gave authority for citing the importance of various subjects for their effectiveness in exercising or disciplining the mental faculties. Mathematics and languages particularly were cited for their power as exercises to strengthen certain faculties. If one could get sufficient exercise in mathematical reasoning, it was argued, he could reason about anything. If he could memorize enough language forms, he would be trained to remember all things.

Curriculum planning in terms of the mental discipline concept followed a somewhat different pattern from that inspired by the mental storehouse idea. Exercise of the mind rather than its cramming became important. The criterion for selecting subjects became their usefulness in training the mind. The object in assigning tasks to pupils was to give mental exercise. However, sharp distinctions between the two quite different concepts were sometimes lost, and pupils might be assigned memory work, for example, because "you may need to know this some time; besides, it will train your mind."

Research studies have rather completely denied the theory of mental faculties and their discipline, although there is evidence of limited transfer of training in learning. But, in spite of the research, the values of certain subjects for training the mind are still argued and difficult, impractical tasks to exercise mental faculties are still assigned.

Learning as Experience

Modern education accepts the concept that learning occurs through experience. This concept is basic in the philosophy of experimentalism which was developed by John Dewey and others and has profoundly influenced American education of this century. Various psychological theories assigning increased significance to the cognitive (knowing) factors in learning place emphasis on intellectual processes rather than on the earlier, mechanical concepts of learning.[1] Thus teaching and curriculum planning become more difficult but also more challenging. It is more satisfying to guide problem-solving activities and see boys and girls solve their problems than to spend one's days giving directions and tests to the robot kind of learner envisaged by earlier theories.

The concept of learning through experience may be defined more fully as follows: *Learning consists of the changes in an individual—his knowledge, skills, attitudes, ways of his own behaving—that result from his experience.* Several emphases in this definition should be noted. First, all possible types of *changes* in all aspects of behavior—physical, emotional, mental—are involved. Second, learning is an *individual* matter for it results from goal-seeking activity, and goal-seeking activities of individuals can never be identical because, as we noted fully in Chapter 5,

---

[1] See Ernest R. Hilgard, *Theories of Learning* (New York: Appleton-Century-Crofts, Inc., 1948), for an analysis of ten systems of learning theory. The final chapter (12) emphasizes the trend toward recognition of the factors mentioned above. Also see as a basic reference on learning systems: Boyd Henry Bode, *How We Learn* (Boston: D. C. Heath & Company, 1940).

individuals differ in goals, maturities, and other factors. Third, changes in the individual result from his *experience*. To effect changes in pupils, teachers must therefore provide or stimulate the experiences of these learners in appropriate ways. Memorizing and mental exercising are types of experiences, but whether or not these are appropriate ways depends on the kinds of changes to be effected in boys and girls. Thus the ultimate purpose of curriculum planning is the kind of changes de-

PLATE 13. CHILDREN LEARN THROUGH EXPERIENCE. *Arithmetic is learned through a lifelike grocery store. (Courtesy of the Bristol, Tennessee, Public Schools)*

sired in learners. To effect these desired changes (goals, aims, outcomes, learnings), there must be developed learning experiences which will stimulate goal-seeking activities that result in the outcomes sought.

In the remainder of this chapter we shall be dealing with the experience concept of learning. The preceding treatment of this and two other concepts should help eliminate from consideration principles of learning which are based on concepts of learning as memorization and as mental discipline. At the same time we should note that acceptance of the concept of learning as experience in no way eliminates the proper use of memorization as a learning experience or of appropriate learning situations containing elements that may be found in other, different situations to which the same learning process may be applied. That is, good teaching utilizes all possible types of experiences to secure desired outcomes rather than trusting only one type. Attention is now turned to a more detailed analysis of the learning process.

THE LEARNING PROCESS

The curriculum worker finds *Learning and Instruction,* the 1950 Yearbook (Part I) of the National Society for the Study of Education, an excellent source on the interrelationship of the learning process and curriculum and teaching.[2] This volume is a most significant effort to relate the theory of learning to instruction by synthesis of the findings of psychological research. It contains the following description and illustration of the learning process:

> The essential elements in a learning situation are shown in Figure 1. [See Figure 2]: environmental stimulation of a living, motivated organism; incentives which when attained will lead to satisfaction of the motives; and at least a temporary blocking or inability of the learner to respond in ways that will enable him to gain the incentive. Motivation is assumed to be an inner state of need and is a necessary condition if the learner is to engage in learning activity. Needs, wants, and interests and set are terms which are used to refer to motivating conditions. Satisfaction of a motive may be blocked by the learner's inability to attain the incentives which could satisfy the need.
>
> When satisfaction of a motive is blocked, the learner, under appropriate stimulation, makes a series of responses. These responses may or may not be approximations of successful goal behavior. They are "provisional try's" [*sic*] In Figure 1 the responses are labelled R_1 R_2 R_3 and R_4. At first, this behavior is variable; the responses may be extraneous or irrelevant, confused or inefficient. As learning proceeds, some responses are eliminated, and appropriate responses are selected. These successful responses are ultimatly stabilized as variability is reduced. This reduction in variability is characterized by the processes of differentiation, integration, and generalization. The attainment of the incentive, which frequently involves seeing the relation between means and end, with the consequent satisfaction of

---

[2] Also see the following comprehensive treatments of the teaching-learning process: Nathaniel Cantor, *The Teaching-Learning Process* (New York: The Dryden Press, 1953); and Ray H. Simpson, *Improving Teaching-Learning Processes* (New York: Longmans, Green & Co., 1953). Other helpful sources are listed at the end of this chapter.

the motive is the condition that determines which responses will be retained (learned) and which will be eliminated.[3]

This process may be clarified by an illustration of a teaching-learning situation and also by definition of its essential elements: situation, motives, response, incentive, mental processes. Let us imagine a fourth-grade classroom in which the teacher is just introducing children to the use of the dictionary. A list of words which various children did not understand in an earlier discussion of a map of the United States, is on

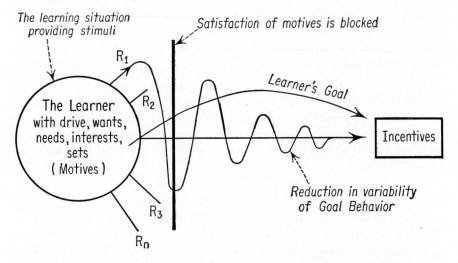

R_1, R_2, R_3, R_n ...... *Responses which are not relevant, hence eliminated*

FIG. 2. ESSENTIAL ELEMENTS IN A LEARNING SITUATION. *(From* Learning and Instruction, *National Society for the Study of Education, 1950, p. 17)*

the blackboard. The map is displayed from a rack. Each child has at his desk a small dictionary. The teacher asks the children to look up the meaning of the first word in the list and pauses until most have found it. Some children are observed to do considerable thumbing through the pages, others to find the place almost immediately, others to have to ask the page number. The teacher repeats the procedure for a second, a third, and a fourth word. Observing that several children seem to have difficulty with each word, she asks these children to work with her at a table and

[3] G. Lester Anderson and Arthur I. Gates, "The General Nature of Learning," Chapter I in *Learning and Instruction* (Part I, Forty-ninth Yearbook of the National Society for the Study of Education; Chicago: The University of Chicago Press, 1950), pp. 16–17. Figure 1 referred to in the quotation is reproduced in the accompanying Figure 2. This passage is quoted by permission of the Society.

tells the others to continue work at their seats, looking up any words they wish. At the table she first has each child write out the alphabet in order, then works with them in finding in the dictionary short and later longer words. After about a half hour of this drill the small group rejoins the other children, and the teacher continues with the words on the board. When the end of the list is reached, she raises these questions for discussion: "When do you use the dictionary?" "What do you learn about each word?" "How do you find words in a dictionary?" Then she asks the children to keep a list of all the words they look up in the dictionary during the rest of the day, and to write an original sentence using each word correctly.

Elements of the Process

It should be noted that the foregoing description has been of a total teaching-learning situation. The actual process of learning on the part of individual children is not indicated. However, we may further clarify the process by describing its elements with reference to two hypthetical learners: John, who was in the small group drilled by the teacher, and Mary, who was not.

Learning situation. John's and Mary's external learning environments (the situation) are identical, except for the period in which John is working with the teacher and the small group. This environment for each includes all the other children and the teacher, the room and its furniture, the words on the board, the map, and the desk dictionaries. The ways in which John and Mary react are different, however, despite the fact that certain stimuli have been used by the teacher: the word list, the map, and the questions and directions. These differences are due to the unique characteristics of each child, including his or her relations with the other children and the teacher. Thus we may imagine that Mary is quite conscious of her status with the group and anxious that certain girls see how quickly she finds the words. John rarely gets his hand up first, but perhaps he likes the teacher very much and wants to have her notice him kindly.

Motives. Both John and Mary have several basic drives, wants, needs, and interests, which constitute motives. Although all human beings have certain primary needs, such as hunger, in common, the effect of these needs upon an individual is modified somewhat by experience and social acceptance. Many acquired motives arise from one's experience. Whatever their origin, motives are the fundamental needs of a person which cause him to engage in his goal-seeking activities. The need for approval or recognition may be assumed to be basic motives for John's and Mary's activities in this situation. Basic to the reaction of each are these motives of being accepted and approved. Many other motives might be important, of course, to different learners: the desire to succeed, a compulsion to do what is expected, and an interest in learning something new, and so forth.

Incentives. John and Mary do not deliberately plan their actions to secure approval or acceptance of an abstract type. But the teacher supplied an incentive by asking the children to look up a word, raising their hands when they had found it. We may imagine that both children were eager to have their hands go up along with the others. Actually, there is some difference between the incentive set by the teacher—finding the words—and the goal of the children—having their hands seen up. Thus the goal is intimately related to the underlying motives of behavior. John experiences still another incentive when his group withdraws, that of finding the words more quickly than during his previous difficulties. This incentive, too, relates to his basic desires for approval and acceptance, for he wants the teacher to approve his activity.

Goal-seeking activity. The reactions of John and Mary to the stimuli (the words, the map, the teacher's directions, interpersonal relations) constitute their responses in goal-seeking activity. This activity as observed is the overt element of the learning experience. We may imagine that Mary, having understood very well previous instructions about and experiences with the dictionary, turned very quickly to the "L's," and located the "lat's" at once, and then down the page to "latitude," for example. With her, the only block is that of knowing the meaning of "latitude," and as she raises her hand to show she has found the word she is reading the definition and looking at the map to grasp the meaning. Thus, her behavior with respect to the original stimuli is with a minimum of irrelevant or "try" responses and she is developing a new goal.

John, on the other hand, finds himself blocked at several points. He has forgotten whether "L" precedes or follows "K" and has to thumb the pages to locate the "L's." Then he has difficulty finding the "lat's" and still hasn't located the word when the teacher gives the second word. In the group which works apart, John finds that he can respond to the word better after he has drilled with the teacher on the alphabet and on shorter, more familiar words. He is made happy when the teacher says, "that's better, John." When the group reassembles his responses are so much less variable that he has found most words by the time other children have.

Mental processes. We may also note certain mental processes at work with the learners. Mary's responses to stimuli involving the location of words in the dictionary have become *differentiated;* that is, she differentiates between correct and incorrect alphabetical relationships. Mary's responses are moving toward *integration,* too: not only does she find the word quickly but she goes on to the next step of learning its meaning and to do so consults the map to understand the relationship of latitude and longitude. Integration is the process of relating and organizing elements of a complex response. Mary has also acquired *efficiency*—location of the word without incorrect responses. The teacher's questions at the end give both Mary and John an opportunity to make *generalizations*—to reason that one uses the dictionary to learn the meanings of words, that one finds words by determining their alphabetical relationships, and so forth.

This relatively simple illustration contains the basic elements of the learning process, regardless of the complexity of stimuli and responses. Always there is a learning situation containing stimuli, basic motives of the individual, an incentive which will satisfy the motive, and difficulty in reaching the incentive, which causes goal-seeking activity or responses that, when sufficiently organized and stabilized, attain the incentive. Thus the learning is the pattern of successful responses, that is, the behavior which attained the incentive. Some factors probably involved but not fully revealed by the example include the maturity of Mary and John, their previous experiences, the emotional phases of the interpersonal relations of the classroom, and others. The general relationship of some of these factors to learning is discussed in the following sections.

Maturity and Learning

Maturity is essentially the result of learning and maturation. The contrasting nature of learning and maturation is illustrated by Olson's statement that "in a strict sense, learning may be thought of as a modification of the pattern of the organism in response to specific stimuli present in the external environment, while maturation might be defined as the development of the organism in response to internal stimuli impelling it toward growth." [4] However, it is impossible to determine the relative influence of either process (or of the underlying factors of heredity and environment), and as difficult to plan for further learning without consideration of their total influence. A distinction of more significance for the curriculum worker is that of maturity, defined by Olson as "a child's

[4] Willard C. Olson, *Child Development* (Boston: D. C. Heath & Company, 1949), p. 6.

total stage of readiness for an activity under discussion." [5] Maturity is always relative when used in this sense; that is, one is mature in relation to a particular activity such as reading or swimming. A "mature" swimmer, for example, is one who can be expected to swim with due regard for his own safety.

Maturity and learning are somewhat interdependent. That is, the level of maturity determines readiness to learn, but the influence of previous learning is a factor in determining the extent of maturity. In addition to learning and maturation, physical development influences maturity. Reading readiness may be used as an illustration of the interrelationship of these factors. At the age of about six and one half years most children are interested in and able to begin reading. As a result of their maturation, these children have sufficient visual coordination, auditory discrimination, and verbal intelligence to begin reading. They have developed a vocabulary so that they can identify by words many objects in the environment. Their physical development is such that they are healthy individuals with normal interests in play and in association with other children. For such children it is a natural step to learn by sight the words with which they associate a meaning, and then to read and write these words in meaningful combinations. That is, they are sufficiently mature, or ready, as a result of their maturation, development, and learning, to read. Other children will be at this stage of maturity later, and some were ready earlier.

Similarly, the maturity of an individual is an important determinant of learning of all types. In our example of learning to use the dictionary, it is quite probable that some children were not ready to use the dictionary because as yet they had not developed any real interest in learning new words. Others may not have developed sufficient maturity in reading. Mary, by contrast, had probably been using a dictionary for some time. Similarly, wide variations in maturity will be found in letter writing, arithmetic skills, map use, mechanical operations, competitive sports, and so forth. One of the most challenging tasks of the teacher is to determine the maturity of each pupil in relation to the learnings desired. The failure to determine this maturity and to adjust learning experiences accordingly is a major source of difficulty for teachers and pupils alike.

The Role of Experience in Learning

The learning process and experience are identical. That is, we learn as we experience, or as our organisms interact with the environment. John and Mary were experiencing as they saw the words on the board, as they

[5] *Ibid.*, p. 4.

listened to their teacher, as they thumbed their dictionaries, and as they did these things, they were learning. Without the teacher's direction, however, they might have been having less purposeful experiences with less effective learning. All experience involves learning, but we should note certain principles of significance about the nature of this relationship.

In the first place, it is possible to affect the quality of learning by the planning of experience. In fact, this is the basic justification of formal education. The child will learn whether or not he attends school, but our hope is that his learning will be of more benefit to himself and to society if it is of the kind anticipated by the experiences planned by the school. The role of curriculum planning is to develop experiences calculated to result in behavior patterns or learnings considered desirable. Teachers could attempt to achieve almost any kind of learning in school but they should attempt only those kinds which contribute to educational goals. Accordingly, instead of experiences in pickpocketing, which is not a goal considered appropriate, schools provide experiences in group discussion, which is.

In the second place, maturity is determined in part by previous experience. Hence teachers seek maximum information about pupils' previous experiences through such means as are available: conferences with pupils, parents, and previous teachers; and pupil records, personal histories, autobiographies, and case studies. Furthermore, experiences are planned in sequences that seem related to maturity at different levels in terms of previous experience.

In the third place, we attach much significance to the fact that experience is an individual matter, that is, an interaction of an individual with his environment. Thus, no two individuals have identical experiences in the same environment presenting the same stimuli. McSwain has developed the point that "each pupil attends and interacts with the 'private' classroom that he creates daily out of his accepted purposes, ideas, and feelings," and further that "the child that a teacher sees and interacts with is a psychological creation that exists only in the mind of the teacher." [6] The teacher in planning and directing learning is confronted with the need to arrange as many experiences as there are learners, although this may frequently be done by a single situation in which it is recognized and even desired that individual learners will experience differently.

[6] E. T. McSwain, "What Child Do You See?" *Educational Leadership*, 7:540 (May), 1950.

Motivation and Learning

In Chapter 1 some attention was given to the gap between what is known and what is practiced in motivation. Here we should cite some of the principal things that are known. First, we should emphasize the dual relationship of motivation and learning. As pointed out in our discussion of the learning process, the response of children to environmental stimuli is determined by their personal drives and by immediate incentives which will satisfy such drives. The teacher then must seek to understand the pupil's own motives, and to provide appropriate incentives to satisfy them. The teacher must also seek to direct the formation of desirable motives, for they can be acquired as a result of experience or learning.

Problems of motivation are intimately related to the interests of learners. Research of Jersild and Tasch regarding interests supports the importance of interest-developing activities in the school program. The conclusions of this research point out that these activities are not merely to "utilize the interests a child happens to have acquired as a guide to what and how to teach" but to help the learner discover and realize "the resources of his nature":

> This view of the role of interests underscores the importance of making provision in the educational program for a variety of interests in order to take account of the fact that children differ so markedly in their make-up. Only by this means can the diversities of human nature come into their own and only then can the individual youngster, with abilities that may be of high or low degree, learn to make the most satisfactory use of his talents, whether these are equally proportioned or whether his greatest strength happens to be in mental tasks or in a form of manual dexterity, in a creative art, or in some other endeavor. Variety of opportunity is needed not only to enable children to develop interests in keeping with the kinds and levels of their abilities, but also to enable them to pursue such interests at a pace and with an intensity suited to their temperament.[7]

Three issues in particular exist with respect to motivation, which we may define as the state of need which results in goal-seeking behavior or learning activity. First, there is the issue of whether motives are internal or external drives. That is, can an individual be motivated by factors outside himself? This issue is reconciled by acceptance of both types of motives. According to Olson, motivation "has an internal aspect in which

[7] Arthur T. Jersild and Ruth J. Tasch, *Children's Interests* (New York: Bureau of Publications, Teachers College, Columbia University, 1949), p. 86. Reprinted by permission of the publisher.

growth, psychological state, and past experience are influential, and it also has an external aspect in which the total situation and specific incentives are observable." [8]

A second issue is whether intrinsic or extrinsic rewards should be relied upon for learning. Intrinsic motivation is that in which the learning activity carries its own reward; extrinsic, that in which it does not. Thus the writing of a letter for the pleasure the child gets in writing a friend is intrinsically motivated. If the motive is to receive a satisfactory mark in school, the reward is extrinsic. In practice, both types of rewards may operate in motivational behavior. According to Hilgard and Russell, "all relations which become effective become to some extent intrinsic . . . any effective incentive must communicate in some way with a motive which is real for the learner." [9] However, these authors agree with the general objection to two types of external motivation: (1) the authority of the teacher—that is, behavior because "the teacher said to"; and (2) competition in which only one person wins. Behavior forced by authority is not likely to carry over into other situations. When only one person wins, frustration may occur to many losers. However, we feel that there may have to be such situations and that the solution in these cases is to have various types of competition so that different pupils may experience the important satisfaction of winning.

A third issue arises in connection with teachers' and pupils' motives. That is, should they be the same? The foregoing discussion should make clear the fact that they are not the same since individuals are driven in terms of their unique personalities. The teacher's responsibility is to identify the motives of pupils, to give these an opportunity of achievement appropriate to educational purposes, and, further, to encourage the development of modified, improved motives. Thus it is not a problem of reconciling conflicting aims of teacher and pupils so much as it is one of utilizing and developing individuals' own drives for achieving the educational results recognized by the teacher. For example, an important goal for most learners is acceptance by their peers. This can be used by teachers to influence the pupil's participation in group activity in general.

Some Learning Problems

The foregoing brief analysis of the learning process suggests several other questions which arise in curriculum planning. Some of those which occur most frequently are discussed briefly in the following paragraphs.

[8] Olson, *op. cit.,* p. 339.
[9] Ernest R. Hilgard and David H. Russell, *"Motivation in School Learning,"* Chapter II in *Learning and Instruction,* pp. 45–46.

Forgetting and retention. Anderson and Gates hold that retroactive inhibition or interference—with old by new learning—is the most important explanation of forgetting. According to this explanation, the conditions which will prevent interference of old by new learnings are those essential to promoting retention and minimizing forgetting. These authors suggest the following principles:

1. Things learned are best retained, i.e., are subject to least interference, when they are well-structured or organized . . . when material is seen in all its interrelatedness with other material and when it is learned and used as a part of an organized body of material it is best remembered . . . meaningful material is easiest learned and best retained.
2. When material is thoroughly learned it is less subject to interference. . . . We err at all levels of education in providing too many concepts to be understood with too little time for thorough learning of them.[10]

That is, curriculum planning must make for learnings which are interrelated, built upon one another, understood in reference to previous learning. It must also provide for complete or thorough understanding. Learners will quickly forget the wording of the amendments to the Constitution, for example, but an understanding of the process of making amendments and its relation to our democratic processes can be a persistent learning related to many developments, including specific amendments, in our national history. This principle will also be understood and remembered best when it is studied thoroughly in relation to the development of the Constitution rather than as one of many provisions to be memorized.

Transfer of learning. Whether learning can be transferred from one situation to another has been a frequent subject of discussion and research in education. Under the concept of learning as mental discipline, many subjects and activities in the curriculum have been justified on the basis that their values would transfer to other situations. As already pointed out, the arguments that certain subjects "train the mind" have been effectively denied by evidence to the contrary. It is now generally accepted that transfer does take place, but only as there are common features recognized as such in old learning and new problems. Thus the technique of reading a graph, once learned, may be applied to various sets of data. But this is a quite different type of transfer from that assumed by the argument that exercises in reading graphs train certain mental func-

[10] Anderson and Gates, *op. cit.*, p. 33. Quoted by permission of the National Society for the Study of Education.

tions so that a person thinks more systematically. Education's highest achievement is to effect transfer of identical elements, that is, to develop behavior learned in one situation which will be utilized in another. According to Anderson and Gates, such transfer occurs most readily "when learning is so directed that experiences are meaningful, result in the formulating and understanding of principles, lead to a comprehension of the rational basis of skill (e.g., understand the 'why' of a particular form in athletic performances), or otherwise lead to an insightful structure or organization." [11]

Learning products and processes. The products of the learning process are quite varied. They are classified in *Learning and Instruction* as motor activities; concepts, meanings, and generalizations; motives, interests, and attitudes; social and emotional controls; aesthetic type of behavior; and the technique of problem solving. The last-named, it should be noted, is also a learning process; that is, a way of learning may also be a product of learning. In fact, a major purpose of the curriculum is to develop processes of learning of the highest levels possible. Thus, the mature person is able to make increasing use of the problem-solving process instead of trial-and-error procedure. When he is confronted by a new situation his trial responses to the blocks it contains are chosen on the bases of intellectual activity rather than at random. The pupil who has been given guidance in developing problem-solving techniques weighs the feasibility of solutions to his problem before attempting any solution. Thus he is learning through a problem-solving approach.

Success and failure. The role of success in learning is obvious from the analysis presented of goal-seeking behavior. That is, learning is success in reaching goals. Although learning involves failure and new responses, always its accomplishment (the attainment of the goal) is a success. Each success is a step toward maturity and an aid to further learning. Uniform goals cannot be achieved by different learners, but progress through success at their respective levels toward some general goal can be expected. "Failing" grades, nonpromotion, and related practices based on uniform goal expectations attempt to force the accomplishment of the impossible rather than to set goals so that success can be attained by individual learners. Psychological research is conclusive as to the relative merits of success in motivation as compared to failure. Similarly, rewards are more effective than punishment.

Teaching method. A great deal of research and literature in education has been devoted to the aim of finding the "best method" of teach-

[11] *Ibid.*, p. 29.

ing. Although some techniques that teachers use are more directly related to the learning process as described than are others, there is no single pattern of techniques—that is, a "method"—which will be better for encouraging all learners, with their varying traits, to engage in the most effective learning. The problem of teaching is primarily that of influencing and guiding the goal-seeking behavior of learners. Since individuals vary so widely, no one device will influence them all equally well. The teacher has to make some provisional tries, too, in working with each group to find the best combination of techniques in order to motivate the best learning behavior of the optimum number of learners. Some of the principles and techniques of effective teaching which are implied by the process of learning and which should influence his tries are described in subsequent sections of this chapter and in following chapters.

The place of drill. It is not to be implied from previous emphasis on the acquisition of understanding and from criticisms of meaningless drill and memorization that practice has no place in learning. The criticisms are leveled at teaching practices which assume that learning will come from drill or memorization alone. As pointed out in Chapter 1, three steps are necessary in the effective acquisition of any skill:

1. The individual must recognize some incentive for acquiring the skill—that is, he must want to learn it. This is the step most frequently overlooked in the teaching of skills.

2. He must understand how to perform this skill. Here his maturity as well as the quality of the explanation or demonstration and of his own tries is involved. In any group situation some individuals will probably not be able to understand the skill when it is first introduced. These persons need more time, more maturity, or more help. Because they frequently get none of these, their drill is meaningless.

3. He will become more efficient in the skill through adequate practice, the amount depending on the nature of the skill and his progress. Practice is essential, but only after there is desire to learn, and understanding. In some learning situations, drill is assigned with virtually no attention to the prior steps. This practice results not only in poor learning but in the frequent distaste of both pupils and teachers for drill activities.

RELATION OF THE LEARNING PROCESS TO THE CURRICULUM

The function of the school's program to effect desired learnings is readily identified by review of the elements of the learning process. We should note, first, that there is in effect a curriculum *planned* for the total group of learners with whatever provisions are included for individual learners, and that there is also a curriculum as actually *had* (experienced) by each learner. For example, the teacher plans for a period of total group activity in discussing some questions related to the instructional unit on which the group is working, but it is inevitable that the extent of participation of learners in the discussion will vary widely. In general, to

PLATE 14. DEFINITE PLANS AND MATERIALS MAKE BETTER LEARNING. *Plans, pieces of creative work, and reports on the blackboard help. (Courtesy of the Cooperative Study in Elementary Education, Southern Association of Colleges and Secondary Schools)*

the extent that the curriculum planned and the curriculum had coincide, the planning was flexible and comprehensive and therefore effective. We believe that coincidence for these reasons is desirable and that a planned curriculum is desirable. A group discussion related to a unit which has been selected for group work is likely to be more effective than a group discussion on just any topic of the moment. Furthermore, we believe it will be a more effective discussion if the questions discussed have been identified in advance, preferably by group planning. Both the unit plan and the questions for discussion are parts of the curriculum *planned.*

The principal relation of the curriculum plan to the learning process is in the situations it provides for learning to occur. Returning to our earlier illustration of the learning process, the curriculum planner for this group of fourth-graders anticipated the experience of using the dictionary. Accordingly, a list of words of which pupils had asked the meaning had been maintained, a map had been used and kept available for reference, dictionaries had been provided. The curriculum plan also anticipated a procedure of working with a small group of pupils needing special dictionary drill. Thus observation of children's responses was necessary. Moreover, the plan had to assume some motive and provide an incentive; a motive known to the teacher was the pupils' desire for approval, so the hand-raising technique was used as an incentive. The teacher also felt a responsibility to stimulate higher mental processes, and the curriculum as planned included questions which might lead to generalizations. The teacher felt practice in the skill was desirable, and so the curriculum plan included the maintenance of a list of words that pupils looked up in the dictionary. In order that the practice might be in meaningful situations the words were to be those encountered by the pupils and were to be used in original sentences.

Thus the curriculum provides situations in which stimuli are planned to arouse pupils to goal-seeking behavior. The curriculum also provides incentives related to pupils' motives or utilizes their own incentives. It further provides means of observing or otherwise evaluating the goal-seeking behavior, of modifying the stimuli when different patterns of behavior are indicated, and of practicing and generalizing when these are desirable. In other words, *the curriculum plan is the force for stimulating, guiding, and evaluating effective learning processes; and the curriculum is what is actually experienced by those for whom the plan is made, as the planned (and unplanned) experiences take place.* The plan constitutes the difference between a learning experience that has structure and purpose and one that just happens. For example, a group of children happening to play ball together are having an experience that will result in some learning outcomes for most or all involved. The same group led by a skilled instructor through a series (the plan, as modified) of drills and scrimmages, including games of ball, will have experiences that result in much greater learning outcomes for all. The plan makes a difference! Curriculum plans are the *dynamics* of instruction.

The function of curriculum planning is to develop the kind of curriculum just described. Note, however, what is involved in this process: there must be consideration of the kinds of learning situations most appropriate to the curriculum purposes and the pupils concerned, frequently involving the planning of a variety of such situations. The basic drives of the learners must be understood, incentives related to these motives provided or anticipated, and stimuli planned to produce behavior seeking these incentives. For example, the teacher of a particular group of boys and girls needs to answer such questions as these: (1) What are the important drives or motives of these learners which call for or relate to desirable outcomes? (2) What incentives can be used for particular learning efforts which satisfy these motives? (3) What questions, statements, materials, and situations can start off efforts to attain these incentives?

Planning must anticipate the various responses learners may make to the stimuli and have alternative procedures ready when responses seem inadequate and unsuccessful. Planning must envisage the entire group of learners, the possibilities of stimulating the fundamental mental processes, and the provision of practice opportunities. It must also relate one set of experiences to another so that skills and understandings will be developed as pupils are ready for them, and so that there will be maximum meaning developed in all learning.

IMPLICATION OF PRINCIPLES OF LEARNING FOR CURRICULUM PLANNING

The process of learning and its underlying principles have many implications for curriculum planning and improvement. Certain implications pertaining to the following problems of curriculum planning are discussed in this section: goal setting, the learning environment, individual differences, interpersonal relations, the organization and quality of experiences, and the process of learning.

Planning for Goal Setting

The nature of goal setting in learning suggests two implications of major importance in curriculum planning. The learner, we may recall, learns in relation to his own goals, although immediate incentives may be provided by the teacher. The following distinction is helpful:

> The goal of the learner is the end-state which gives direction to motivated behavior. It must always be defined according to the aroused motives of the learner. Because the acceptability and satisfying consequences of an incentive depend in part upon the goal-expectations of the learner, the incentive and the learner's goals have to be distinguished. The goal is what the learner is seeking rather than the incentive that the teacher is providing. They may have much or little in common.[12]

[12] Hilgard and Russell, *loc. cit.*, p. 39. Quoted by permission of the National Society for the Study of Education.

But learners' goals and incentives may have "more in common" by co-operative goal setting. When boys and girls participate in defining purposes of their activities, several values accrue. There is close identification of group and individual goals. The goals recognized by individuals may differ somewhat from the group's statement but not as much as in reference to an assignment by the teacher. The experience of seeking the goal is more meaningful to the pupil because he has had a hand in its definition. Therefore the quality and permanence of the learning are improved. There is lacking the conflict between pupil desires and teacher directions which frequently results in rebellious or uncooperative behavior vastly different from that anticipated by the teacher.

This implication that curriculum planning should provide for cooperative goal setting does not mean that preplanning is undesirable.[13] For illustration, we may assume that a social studies teacher in a junior high school believes that both the community and the pupils expect to have some experiences included at this level in the organization and services of community government. Several alternatives are possible. The teacher might assign certain reading in a civics textbook, and perhaps arrange for the mayor to come speak to the class. On the other hand, the pupils might be told that they are to study community government and asked what they wish to study. The latter procedure might well terminate in the same experiences as suggested in the first alternative, since pupils would have little basis for answering such a question adequately. A sounder procedure would be to survey the class members to find out what questions they have about their community government and services, to discuss means of securing answers to these questions, and then to arrive at procedures for reaching these goals (that is, information to answer learners' questions). Note that neither of the first two alternatives involves any real preplanning, but that the last procedure—the sounder one because it begins with pupils' questions—involves the teacher's previous analysis of the unit so as to anticipate possible questions and experiences which would bring about learnings regarding these questions. That is, the teacher's curriculum planning for cooperative goal setting must serve as a guide in the formulation of appropriate goals and the selection of related experiences. The nature of cooperative planning and its relation to the teacher's pre-planning is discussed more fully in Chapter 13. We should note here that both cooperative planning with pupils and advance planning on the part of teachers, as well as planning by curriculum

[13] See for illustrations of cooperative planning of curriculum experiences, Chapter V, "Planning Studies," in Alice Miel and associates, *Cooperative Procedures in Learning* (New York: Bureau of Publications, Teachers College, Columbia University, 1952).

committees, are included in our general concept of curriculum planning.

A second implication of knowledge about the role of goals in learning is that curriculum planning must provide for progressive goal setting. Children and youth, we know, are generally concerned with immediate goals, although the motivation of deferred values increases with maturity. Curriculum plans must recognize that children and youth will work best toward the attainment of incentives that are near at hand. They must also recognize that immediate learnings may influence the development of more remote goals. Experiences with one goal, if appropriately chosen in terms of possible later goals and if successfully attained, lead to others. By the same reasoning, the child who experiences difficulty in reading too advanced material may become frustrated and avoid further reading. In short, curriculum planning must provide incentives which are attainable and which are related to larger and more remote goals.

Planning the Environment

The learning environment contains the factors which stimulate learning. These stimuli may be in the physical environment or in the interpersonal relations of individuals with one another or in both. Here we are concerned with the first. Since the physical environment may influence learning, its optimum arrangement for that purpose is a problem of curriculum planning. The relation of environment to learning is quite obvious when one observes young children, or even older children and adults, in a new environment. Young children finger and poke experimentally; older ones ask questions of a great variety. In the new setting adults forget their preoccupations and seek to find out about all the new things and people they see. The classroom is a very limited environment. Ideally, children would be going from one new environment, when understood, to another; practically, teachers must be resourceful in introducing new materials into the environment when new curiosities need stimulating.

In their discussion of "the school as a learning laboratory" Anderson, Whipple, and Gilchrist describe a desirable physical environment and contrast it with an undesirable one in the following paragraphs:

> In a learning laboratory the environment arouses the child's curiosity and starts him on a search for new understanding. A bulletin board calls attention to items of interest. A supply of attractive pictures reflects the season or the units of study underway or suggests stimulating questions that lead to thoughtful work. The classroom contains a variety of attractive, illuminating reading materials chosen in the light of the goals to be achieved. Current magazines and pamph-

lets are available for finding answers to many questions as the children, singly or in groups, try to broaden their background on a topic. Photographs, slides, motion pictures, and the phonograph or radio are available in either the classroom or the school for the use of pupils as needed. Also, movable desks and worktables are arranged in a variety of ways according to the activities underway at the time.

In contrast to this type of room is the one in which few pictures and exhibits are displayed and these are mostly prepared by the teacher. Moreover, they are seldom changed during the term as learning activities change. If movable desks are provided, they are kept in straight rows.[14]

The implications for curriculum planning are clear. Items for the bulletin boards, pictures, reading materials, and other physical supplies and equipment must be selected in terms of their potentialities in arousing interests related to the experiences in view by the teacher, or in terms of their pertinence to goals already planned by the group. When a new venture is being planned, the environment is arranged to supply stimuli for the planning of this venture; when it is underway, the environment must include materials which will help learning directly and also those that will aid the setting of new, related goals.

Planning for Interpersonal Relations

The arrangement of desks, tables, and chairs is planned to facilitate good interpersonal relations in the group of learners. The arrangement of desks in straight rows creates a difficult situation for discussion, since children cannot see the others' faces. It further focuses attention on the teacher facing the group, and underlines an authoritarian relationship. Small groups at work need tables around which to gather. Individuals with specific jobs to do need space for their accomplishment which will not deprive other children of proceeding with their activities. Thus the physical environment and the social environment are intimately related.

As already indicated, modern theories of learning place great importance on the role of interpersonal relationships in motivational behavior. The teacher's way of working with pupils and their ways of working with each other directly influence the quality and strength of goals and learning behaviors. Experiences which create optimum interpersonal relationships are characterized by a natural atmosphere in which strain

[14] G. Lester Anderson, Gertrude Whipple, and Robert Gilchrist, *"The School as a Learning Laboratory,"* Chapter XIII in *Learning and Instruction*, p. 345. Quoted by permission of the National Society for the Study of Education. Also see for illustrations of good learning environments: Association for Supervision and Curriculum Development, *Creating a Good Environment for Learning* (1954 Yearbook; Washington, D.C.: The Association, 1954).

and pressure are absent. Considerable freedom of movement is allowed, but at the same time regard for the rights of other people is expected. Differences of opinion are expected to arise but opportunities are provided for their resolution. Learners stimulate each other to friendly discussion of their ideas, and to cooperative evaluation of progress. Small groups are organized as needed for drill at their level, for committee investigations, or for specific jobs because better interpersonal relations are possible within small groups.

The teacher is particularly concerned with planning his own relations with pupils. How can he establish himself as a guide rather than a dictator, since the former relationship results in more effective goal seeking? How can he maintain informality and ease without sacrificing good work habits? How can he secure pupils' confidences sufficiently well to get insights into individual behavior patterns? How can he give help when needed to individuals without creating insecurity and dependence for them? How can he give recognition without appearing to be playing favorites? How can he be friendly without having "pets"? Such questions indicate that the scope of curriculum planning includes rigorous analysis of self and of personal relations as well as the more customary matters.

Planning Learning Experiences

Part 4 of this book deals with learning experiences in detail. Here we shall merely summarize some of the implications of three major principles for the improvement of the experiences of the curriculum: (1) learning is an individual matter of experiencing; (2) experiences should be meaningful; and (3) learning should be well organized.

Planning for individuals. It is obviously impossible for curriculum planning in general to identify a specific experience for each child concerned. The central curriculum committee may be planning for thousands of children; the building faculty, for hundreds. The individual teacher in a departmentalized program may be teaching a hundred and fifty to two hundred children a day. Hence the plans must generally provide for maximally effective experiencing of individuals by methods other than that of labeling alternative experiences by names of children, although the elementary school teacher of twenty-five or thirty or so children may frequently have definite children in mind as plans are made. Various such methods are described in Part 4.

Planning for meaningful experience. Frequently we have referred to the importance of experience being meaningful. Perhaps a better statement of the principles is that the most effective learning results from experiences the understanding of which would approximate the true meaning. That is, every experience means something to the individual, but the meaning may be quite different from that which we would usually attach. Thus, children who learn rules of grammar or arithmetic without first understanding the problems to which the rules apply may understand merely that these were to be learned and have been memorized, however unpleasant the process and temporary the association. Those who understood the need for and use of the rules may be guided by their meaning in future related problems. In the one case, memorization meant something but not the thing memorized; in the second there was meaning with or without memorization.

Curriculum plans to utilize experiences which have approximately true meanings to pupils must give great consideration to the readiness factor in learning. Group planning may help both to identify and to develop readiness. It may also provide a basis for planning different experiences for groups at closely related levels of readiness. Plans will also anticipate a maximum number of situations in which children's needs will be revealed so as to lead to meaningful experiences. Of major importance in planning is the practice of relating school activities to those outside.

Possibly the chief significance of the principle of meaningful experience is its relation to planning for the acquisition of skills. The curriculum organization must provide situations in which skills are developed by use. Maximum opportunity is provided, for example, for the use of language in speech rather than for busywork in filling out blanks in workbooks on grammar. Although practice periods will be provided, these, too, will be in connection with use so far as possible.

Planning for well-organized learnings. In general, learnings which are well organized are meaningful. However, there are qualities of experience other than meaning which seem related to the achievement of transfer and retention and to effective learning processes in general. The curriculum plan must anticipate a series of experiences having related elements which will lead to principles and generalizations. This implication leads to the organization of "units" or other major divisions of the curriculum. The goal of the curriculum planner is to develop an organization of experiences which will facilitate the development of behaviors that will persist in the area of experience involved.

Planning for Learning Skills

The fact that learning is not mechanical and automatic suggests another important task for curriculum planning: the provision of experiences which will increase a learner's skill in attacking learning situations. Certain learnings can be so developed as to lead to further ones. The example described earlier of using the dictionary is such a learning. So is learning the use of encyclopedias, tables of contents and indexes of books, maps and graphs, and similar tools.

This principle applies particularly to the problem-solving method of learning. We agree with Anderson and Gates that "this experimental way of going about things is probably a more important educational objective than is the attainment of a given knowledge content or set of technical skills." [15] In planning with learners, teachers who emphasize the problem-solving method ask: What problems do we have in connection with this idea, experience, or unit? What possible ways of solving these problems may be investigated? How can we get facts to show us what way is best? In view of the facts, what can we decide? What other facts do we now need?

In an extended analysis of children's learning of problem solving, Robert L. Thorndike concludes that "there is no single pattern or routine of problem-solving which can be isolated and taught in the schools as a simple unitary skill" but that the school should try to develop "a wide range of interests and experiences, an organized and functional stock of background information, perseverance yet flexibility in attacking problem situations, a willingness to suspend judgment until the evidence is in, habits of testing critically any proposed solutions, attitudes of critical appraisal of the reliability and bias of sources, skill in 'if-then' thinking." [16] Effective curriculum planning will attempt to develop such qualities.

Planning, we should note, is itself a form of problem solving. Curriculum planning on a cooperative basis in the classroom may bring about better-motivated behavior and in addition help to develop skill in attacking problems and finding solutions. But for these results to be attained, both preplanning by the teacher and cooperative planning in the classroom must consciously identify the processes being followed: purpose, plan of attack, action, results. There is concern not only for the immediate goal, but for how we reach goals. The factor of goals or outcomes of learning experiences is considered in the next chapter.

For Further Study

Anderson, G. Lester, "Theories of Behavior and Some Curriculum Issues," *Journal of Educational Psychology,* 39:133–139 (March), 1948.

[15] Anderson and Gates, *loc. cit.,* p. 27.
[16] Robert L. Thorndike, "How Children Learn the Principles and Techniques of Problem-Solving," Chapter VIII in *Learning and Instruction,* p. 215.

States implications of psychological theories of behavior for various curriculum issues.

Association for Childhood Education, *Helping Children Live and Learn.* Washington, D.C.: The Association, 1952.

Describes, defines, and shows through illustrations, good learning experiences in school of children 7–12 years old.

Association for Supervision and Curriculum Development, National Education Association, *Creating a Good Environment for Learning.* 1954 Yearbook. Washington, D.C.: The Association, 1954.

Many helpful illustrations of environmental factors in curriculum and teaching.

Blair, Glenn Myers, "How Learning Theory Is Related to Curriculum Organization," *Journal of Educational Psychology,* 39:161–166 (March), 1948.

Draws implications for curriculum planning from the following areas of learning theory and research: readiness, motivation, organization in learning, and transfer of training.

Bode, Boyd Henry, *How We Learn.* Boston: D. C. Heath & Company, 1940.
Basic theory of learning from the standpoint of an eminent educational philosopher.

Cantor, Nathaniel, *Learning through Discussion.* Buffalo: Human Relations for Industry, 1951.

Helpful and interesting analysis of the operation of learning processes in group situations.

————, *The Teaching-Learning Process.* New York: The Dryden Press, 1953.

Excellent material on the learning process.

Cole, Luella, *Psychology of Adolescence.* 4th ed.; New York: Rinehart & Company, Inc., 1953.

A standard, comprehensive reference on adolescence, with extended consideration to learning processes and problems.

Cook, Walter W., "Individual Differences and Curriculum Practice," *Journal of Educational Psychology,* 39:141–148 (March), 1948.

Analyzes the implications of modern knowledge about individual differences for practices in teaching and curriculum planning.

Hilgard, Ernest R., *Theories of Learning.* New York: Appleton-Century-Crofts, Inc., 1948.

Analysis of ten systems of learning theory, with a final chapter summarizing points of agreement and trends.

Jersild, Arthur T., and Ruth J. Tasch, *Children's Interests.* New York: Bureau of Publications, Teachers College, Columbia University, 1949.

Report of a cooperative study of children's interests in Springfield, Missouri.

Kingsley, Howard L., *The Nature and Conditions of Learning.* New York: Prentice-Hall, Inc., 1946.

Comprehensive analysis of the nature, principles, conditions, and problems of learning, with careful documentation of basic research and experimentation.

Miel, Alice, and associates, *Cooperative Procedures in Learning*. New York: Bureau of Publications, Teachers College, Columbia University, 1952.

Comprehensive report of research studies carried forward by the Horace Mann–Lincoln Institute and associated school systems, dealing with cooperative procedures used in school organization and classroom work.

Millard, Cecil V., *Child Growth and Development in the Elementary School Years*. Boston: D. C. Heath & Company, 1951.

Review of the theory and research regarding the growth and development of the elementary school child.

McSwain, E. T., "What Child Do You See?" *Educational Leadership*, 7:540–544 (May), 1950.

Advances the idea that each child interacts with his "private classroom," and that the teacher sees each child as a psychological creation.

National Society for the Study of Education, *Learning and Instruction*. Part I, Forty-ninth Yearbook of the Society. Chicago: The University of Chicago Press, 1950.

An interpretation of the learning process and its implications for curriculum and teaching. A very helpful synthesis of research findings for the curriculum worker.

Olson, Willard C., *Child Development*. Boston: D. C. Heath & Company, 1949.

Interprets a considerable amount of research by the author and others, and relates basic principles of child development to problems of learning and teaching.

Simpson, Ray H., *Improving Teaching-Learning Processes*. New York: Longmans, Green & Co., 1953.

Emphasizes the problem-solving nature of learning and deals with the teacher's role in aiding learners' problem-solving processes.

Sugerman, Myrtle F. (ed.), *Effective Learning for Use in Junior High Schools*. Denver: The Public Schools, 1949.

Treats problems of learning in terms of a hypothetical discussion reported as held by a group of teachers in a workshop. Illustrated and well written.

Wright, Hubert F., "How the Psychology of Motivation Is Related to Curriculum Development," *Journal of Educational Psychology*. 39:149–166 (March), 1948.

Analyzes implications of the psychology of motivation for curriculum planning.

chapter 7

Outcomes Desired from School Experiences

Now that we have considered some of the current issues in curriculum planning (Chapter 2), some of the important factors that influence curriculum development (Chapter 3), the impact of the culture on curriculum planning (Chapter 4), the necessity of relating the curriculum to the growth and development of pupils (Chapter 5), and principles of learning applicable to teaching (Chapter 6), we are ready to bring all of these considerations together into a comprehensive plan for education in the schools. In this final chapter of Part 2 we shall present basic goals for education in a democracy; then in Part 3 we shall consider the over-all organization or design of the curriculum and how we may determine what constitutes an adequate scope and sequence for learning experiences.

THE NATURE OF CURRICULUM GOALS

Since all educational experiences provided by the school involve choices, curriculum workers must, obviously, have some grounds on which to make such decisions. Fundamentally such judgments will be based on the teacher's conception of the underlying purposes and goals of education in our society. So the most important process in curriculum planning is the formulation of some generalizations about the aims of education and the purposes for which the school exists.

Goals, Aims, and Objectives

In discussing the fundamental concepts that constitute a basis for guiding choice, the meaning of several terms should be clarified. Some of the terms encountered include these: goals, aims, objectives, desired outcomes, purposes, needs, interests, desires, wishes, aspirations, goal-set, and expectations. How are these terms used and which one more properly designates the basis for selecting experiences?

A little reflection would indicate that all of these terms might be used to describe the motivational forces of an individual. They may describe conditions internal to an individual who is experiencing—conditions that impel him to engage in an experience or guide its nature. Obviously, from the point of view of the person doing the experiencing, the terms have varying qualities, degrees of intensity, and directional power. These terms may also be used, however, to designate the kind of experiences one individual thinks another person should have. They might be used by teachers to describe the elements that should unify educational experiences and give direction to them. They could be terms that designate the criteria for selecting educational experiences.

Thus it is apparent that such terms as "goals," "aims," and "objectives" may have two important connotations: (1) as statements of the factors that are motivating an individual to behave in a particular way; (2) as statements of what an individual thinks should be the kinds of experiences in which another person ought to engage. This distinction is made for one reason only: to emphasize the fact that as teachers guide the educational experiences of children the objectives that the teacher has in mind for an experience may or may not be the objectives that motivate the pupils engaging in it. The objectives of the teacher are not automatically the objectives of the pupils.

The Concept of Desired Outcomes

Because the terms "goals," "aims," "objectives," and "purposes" may be used to describe the motivational force of the individual who is engaging in the experience as well as the products of the experience desired by the teacher, we shall use the term "desired outcomes" to designate the results of learning desired by the teacher who is guiding the experience. We feel that this term better conveys the idea of the goals or objectives the teacher has in mind in planning and directing learning experiences for children. We have no serious objection to the use of the other terms; in fact, we have used them throughout this book to designate the outcomes sought from learning experiences, but for purposes of formally defining the major over-all objectives of the educational program, we prefer to designate the values sought as desired outcomes.

One further point should be considered in discussing objectives of educational experiences. In planning and carrying forward learning activities the teacher will be an actor in the situation and will be motivationally oriented to the experience situation, that is, will be himself motivated as a participant in terms of his own goals or objectives. His motivations will probably be in terms of personal satisfactions that accrue to him as a teacher. Thus as a learning experience moves forward in the school, three sets of goals or purposes really exist: (1) the purposes and objectives of the pupils as they participate in the learning experience; (2) the pupil outcomes sought by the teacher as he guides and directs and also participates in the learning situation; and (3) the personal goals and objectives of the teacher.

To illustrate, let us analyze a learning experience going on in the school in the second grade involving the addition of simple numbers. Possibly some of the objectives may be as follows:

A. *Objectives of pupils*
1. To learn to add simple numbers
2. To please the teacher and secure her approval
3. To get a good mark
4. To do as well as or excel classmates
5. To be able to write the problems neatly on the paper
6. To do what the teacher demands so as to avoid punishment or criticism

B. *Pupil outcomes desired by the teacher*
1. To learn to add simple numbers correctly
2. To learn to place problems neatly on the paper
3. To achieve a feeling of success on assigned responsibilities
4. To work diligently on assigned tasks
5. To add to the pupils' skill and stock of knowledge

C. *The teacher's purposes and objectives*
1. To provide a learning experience that will contribute significantly to the growth and development of second-grade pupils
2. To comply with the prescribed course of study
3. To win the approval of supervisory and administrative officials
4. To be a success as a teacher
5. To contribute to the realization of the over-all purposes and objectives of the school

It is not our purpose in this chapter to discuss the teacher's personal motivations and objectives in planning, guiding, and participating in learning experiences in the school. Nevertheless, curriculum workers should be cognizant of them and should recognize that their own personal motivations will be important considerations as they seek to develop and improve the learning experiences of children.

METHODS OF DETERMINING CURRICULUM GOALS

Curriculum goals or the outcomes desired from educational experiences are derived from three sources:

1. The learners
2. The society
3. The interaction of the two as a basis for formulating concepts of the good life for individuals living in such a society

Thus in formulating goals for educational experiences we must again take account of the three basic factors in the educative process—pupils, society, and the interaction of the two. The outcomes desired may be primarily oriented to the individual—his psychobiological needs, his ongoing purposes, his developmental needs, his interests, his past patterns of experience, and the like. On the other hand, outcomes may be primarily oriented to the society—the cultural heritage to be passed on from one generation to the next, the values held by the social group, the mores of the social group, the requirements set by adults for successful participation in the social group, the traditions and customs of the society, and similar aspects of a culture. Yet a third approach seeks to formulate objectives that provide for the maximum development of the individual within the value patterns and mores of a culture. Obviously, the educational outcomes sought by those who share in planning the school program will represent their conceptualization of the good life for the social group that maintains the school. The question becomes one, then, of deciding what kinds of educational experiences promise to contribute most to the realization of the good life for all persons. Major methods of determining goals in terms of these three factors will be discussed briefly.

Formulation of Educational Goals by Philosophers

While all statements of educational goals represent a formulation made by someone or by a group on the basis of critical judgment and definition of point of view, nonetheless attention will be given here to the formulation of objectives by some of the great philosophers of the past. Such men as Socrates, Plato, Aristotle, Aquinas, Rousseau, Locke, Herbart, Spencer, Pestalozzi, and Dewey quickly come to mind. Their influence on educational planning has been tremendous.

Philosophers in general have used two bases for defining objectives for education: (1) a priori, deductive methods, and (2) naturalistic methods. The former is sometimes referred to as the Aristotelian method,[1] and the latter as the experimental method. Socrates, Plato, Aristotle, Aquinas, and Locke might typify the former; Rousseau, Herbart, Spencer, Pestalozzi, and Dewey, the latter.

Essentially, the a priori method of determining educational objec-

---

[1] William H. Kilpatrick, *Philosophy of Education* (New York: The Macmillan Company, 1951), pp. 62ff.

tives utilizes the deductive approach. Attention must first be given to the determination of the eternal verities, truths, or ideals that should be exemplified in the lives of men. Once this concept of the nature of things and of the nature of man is determined on a philosophical basis, one can deduce what educational objectives should be sought through the program of the school. The job of the school becomes one of helping the individual to accept these eternal verities and to so order his life that he will live in accordance with these truths.

The Age of Enlightenment in the latter part of the eighteenth century and the early part of the nineteenth century brought a violent reaction, at least in philosophical circles, against the Aristotelian approach of defining man's place in the scheme of things. The upsurge of concern for the common man and for equality, fraternity, and liberty as inalienable rights of the individual, as typified in the political and social realms by the American and French revolutions, inevitably had its parallel movement in the field of education. A number of eminent philosophers applied these ideals of individual liberty and equality to the problems of education and educational planning. Morley contrasts these two positions in these terms:

> Faith in a divine power, devout obedience to its supposed will, hope of ecstatic, unspeakable reward, these were the springs of the old movement. Undivided love of our fellows, steadfast faith in human nature, steadfast search after justice, firm aspiration toward improvement, and generous contentment in the hope that others may reap whatever reward may be, these are the springs of the new.[2]

The works and writings of such educational philosophers as Rousseau, Pestalozzi, Herbart, Spencer, and Dewey embody these new concerns. They all make the child the center of educational endeavor and of their pedagogical theories. They regard education as the development of the individual. All of these men and others of their contemporaries, such as Thomas Jefferson in this country, talked about the natural state of man and his inalienable rights. Educational programs were to be attuned to the development of the individual child. The aim was to foster his own inherent growth, and the development of the individual in terms of his innate capacities and potentialities was a paramount aim. Their method of education was to follow the natural tendencies and interests of the child. They regarded firsthand experience as an important base for educational practice.

These naturalistic philosophers laid the foundation for a considerable part of our modern educational theory. In fact, many of the present

[2] John Morley, *Rousseau* (London: Macmillan and Co., Ltd., 1891), I, 2.

schools of educational philosophy have their roots in the naturalism of
the nineteenth century.

Formulation of Educational Objectives by Committees and Professional Groups

While some attention was given to the general, over-all purposes of education in the early days of American education, little effort was made by
school people to define detailed aims and objectives for the school. The
elementary schools were primarily established as schools for teaching
reading, writing, and arithmetic, and the secondary schools were designed
to prepare the students for admission to college. It was not until about
the beginning of the present century that extensive efforts were made to
spell out in some detail the purposes and objectives that the school should
seek to achieve.

A great upsurge of interest in the problems of education on the part
of a new professional group—the educators—in the last part of the nineteenth century and the early part of the twentieth century resulted in the
establishment of a number of national committees to study educational
problems. They exerted tremendous influence on the organization and
curriculum of the school.[3] Inevitably, these committees had to come to
grips with the question of what constituted an adequate and sound program of education; in other words, What are to be the objectives of the
educational program? Also, these professional educators were vigorously
debating the ideas of Spencer, Herbart, Froebel, and, later, Dewey. The
National Herbart Society was formed in 1895 and the first two yearbooks
of that society, published in 1895 and 1896, were important theoretical
discussions of educational issues.

The Committee of Ten formulated objectives. The first of these influential national committees was the Committee of Ten. Although the
committee itself was concerned primarily with a consideration of the organization of the curriculum, with time allotments for the various subjects, with grade placement, and with the scope and sequence of the curriculum, the committee organized nine conferences that dealt with
various subjects of the secondary school curriculum. Most of these nine
conferences gave consideration to objectives of instruction for their particular area. For example, the conference on the study of English includes
in its report this statement of the objectives for the teaching of English:

[3] The activities and influence of such groups are comprehensively treated in the
Thirteenth Yearbook of the John Dewey Society, *The American Elementary School*
(Harold G. Shane, editor; New York: Harper & Brothers, 1953), Chapters 8 and 9.

The main direct objects of the teaching of English in schools seem to be two: (1) to enable the pupil to understand the expressed thoughts of others and to give expressions to thoughts of his own; and (2) to cultivate a taste for reading, to give the pupil some acquaintance with good literature, and to furnish him with the means of extending that acquaintance.[4]

The conference on the teaching of history, civil government, and political economy felt these to be the main purposes of the study of history:

> The principal end of all education is training. In this respect history has a value different from, but in no way inferior to, that of language, mathematics, and science. . . . history properly taught offers the first opportunity for a growth of discriminative judgment; it should train the pupil to throw away the unimportant or unessential, and to select the paramount and cogent. It may be so taught, also, as to lead him in some degree to compare and weigh evidence; that is, through history a child should be taught to exercise these qualities of common-sense comparison, and plain, everyday judgment which he needs for the conduct of his own life.[5]

Similarly, the Committee of Fifteen had much to say about the program of elementary education and in rather broad, sweeping terms set up objectives for the various aspects of the elementary school.

Seven Cardinal Principles of Secondary Education. Primarily, it was the Commission on the Reorganization of Secondary Education that undertook a major responsibility for defining objectives for the secondary school as a totality and for various subject fields taught in the secondary school. The commission itself formulated the now-famous Seven Cardinal Principles of Secondary Education. These were enunciated in 1918 and have been widely quoted and extensively used since that time as a basic statement of the purposes and objectives of secondary education. The commission defines the goal of education in a democracy in the following terms:

> The purpose of democracy is so to organize society that each member may develop his personality primarily through activities designed for the well-being of his fellow members and of society as a whole. . . .
> Consequently, education in a democracy, both within and without the school, should develop in each individual the knowledge, interests,

[4] The National Educational Association, *Report of the Committee of Ten on Secondary School Studies* (New York: American Book Company, 1894), p. 86.

[5] *Ibid.,* pp. 168–169.

ideals, habits, and powers whereby he will find his place and use that place to shape both himself and society toward even nobler ends.[6]

In formulating objectives to achieve this goal of education in America, the commission states that it is necessary to analyze the activities of the individual. On the basis of such an analysis the commission proposed these Seven Cardinal Principles as the basic objectives of secondary education:

1. Health
2. Command of fundamental processes
3. Worthy home-membership
4. Vocation
5. Citizenship
6. Worthy use of leisure
7. Ethical character.[7]

The commission recognized that since it is individuals who are involved in the educational process, these objectives do not imply separate fields of instruction. It maintained that the pupil is indivisible and that therefore the educational program should be an integrated, correlated effort to achieve these objectives.

Statements of objectives by Educational Policies Commission. Other committees of national influence have also made pronouncements about the objectives of education and have formulated aims and objectives for particular subjects or particular aspects of the school curriculum. The most meaningful efforts in recent years of a national policy-making group to set purposes for the educational program are the pronouncements of the Educational Policies Commission. In a report called "The Purposes of Education in American Democracy" the commission enunciated a set of objectives for education in this country. These goals have been organized around four broad objectives. The statement is as follows:

THE OBJECTIVES OF SELF-REALIZATION

The Inquiring Mind. The educated person has an appetite for learning.

Speech. The educated person can speak the mother tongue clearly.

Reading. The educated person reads the mother tongue effectively.

[6] Commission on the Reorganization of Secondary Education, *Cardinal Principles of Secondary Education* (Bureau of Education, Bulletin 1918, No. 35; Washington, D.C.: Government Printing Office, 1918), p. 9.

[7] *Ibid.*, pp. 10–11.

Writing. The educated person writes the mother tongue efficiently.

Number. The educated person solves his problems of counting and calculating.

Sight and Hearing. The educated person is skilled in listening and observing.

Health Knowledge. The educated person understands the basic facts concerning health and disease.

Health Habits. The educated person protects his own health and that of his dependents.

Public Health. The educated person works to improve the health of the community.

Recreation. The educated person is participant and spectator in many sports and other pastimes.

Intellectual Interests. The educated person has mental resources for the use of leisure.

Esthetic Interests. The educated person appreciates beauty.

Character. The educated person gives responsible direction to his own life.

THE OBJECTIVES OF HUMAN RELATIONSHIP

Respect for Humanity. The educated person puts human relationships first.

Friendships. The educated person enjoys a rich, sincere, and varied social life.

Cooperation. The educated person can work and play with others.

Courtesy. The educated person observes the amenities of social behavior.

Appreciation of the Home. The educated person appreciates the family as a social institution.

Conservation of the Home. The educated person conserves family ideals.

Homemaking. The educated person is skilled in homemaking.

Democracy in the Home. The educated person maintains democratic family relationships.

THE OBJECTIVES OF ECONOMIC EFFICIENCY

Work. The educated producer knows the satisfaction of good workmanship.

Occupational Information. The educated producer understands the requirements and opportunities for various jobs.

Occupational Choice. The educated producer has *selected* his occupation.

Occupational Efficiency. The educated producer succeeds in his chosen vocation.

Occupational Adjustment. The educated producer maintains and improves his efficiency.

Occupational Appreciation. The educated producer appreciates the social value of his work.

Personal Economics. The educated consumer plans the economics of his own life.

Consumer Judgment. The educated consumer develops standards for guiding his expenditures.

Efficiency in Buying. The educated consumer is an informed and skillful buyer.

Consumer Protection. The educated consumer takes appropriate measures to safeguard his interests.

THE OBJECTIVES OF CIVIC RESPONSIBILITY

Social Justice. The educated citizen is sensitive to the disparities of human circumstance.

Social Activity. The educated citizen acts to correct unsatisfactory conditions.

Social Understanding. The educated citizen seeks to understand social structures and social processes.

Critical Judgment. The educated citizen has defenses against propaganda.

Tolerance. The educated citizen respects honest differences of opinion.

Conservation. The educated citizen has a regard for the nation's resources.

Social Applications of Science. The educated citizen measures scientific advance by its contribution to the general welfare.

World Citizenship. The educated citizen is a cooperating member of the world community.

Law Observance. The educated citizen respects the law.

Economic Literacy. The educated citizen is economically literate.

Political Citizenship. The educated citizen accepts his civic duties.

Devotion to Democracy. The educated citizen acts upon an unswerving loyalty to democratic ideals.[8]

In addition to this set of general objectives for education, the commission in later statements formulated lists of particularized objectives for both elementary and secondary education. These sets of purposes have been widely used by teacher committees and individual teachers in planning curriculum experiences for pupils. Because of their outstanding merit and widespread acceptance, we are presenting the lists here for the convenience of curriculum workers.

The statement of purposes for the elementary school is as follows:

VALUES IN THE GOOD ELEMENTARY SCHOOL

Independence and Initiative must be developed in each child by means of thorough mastery of many kinds of learnings:

knowledge and practiced skill in health—to protect himself and others;

skill in reading—so that he can understand others;

skill in writing and speaking—so that others can understand him;

accuracy and understanding in the use of numbers and measurements—so that he can deal with things in quantity;

practice in understanding and weighing the opinions of others—so that he may make good judgments;

practice in critical thinking—so that he will be in the habit of examining his own motives and the purposes of others.

Skills of Communication and Understanding Ought to Be Stressed in the Elementary School

The Humane and Constructive Talents of each child should be stimulated to full development. Each child ought to learn to feel:

concern for the general welfare;

kinship with others;

respect for each person as an individual;

respect for laws and social institutions.

Self-Respect and Respect for Others Must Be Taught and Practiced in the Good Elementary School

Social Responsibility and Cooperative Skills must be learned and practiced by every child through:

sharing in the gathering of data—so that the best evidence may be obtained;

[8] Educational Policies Commission, *The Purposes of Education in American Democracy* (Washington, D.C.: National Education Association, 1938), pp. 50, 72, 92, and 108. Reprinted by permission of the Commission.

sharing in the forming of group decisions—so that the decisions may
reflect the opinions of all;

planning changes and improvements of institutions—so that progress
may be made;

practicing the use of reason rather than force—so that the rights of
minorities may be respected.

*Habits of Responsible Citizenship Should Begin in the Elementary
School* [9]

PLATE 15. THE HUMANE AND CONSTRUCTIVE TALENTS OF EACH CHILD SHOULD BE STIMULATED
TO FULL DEVELOPMENT. *These pupils are learning to work with others as well as developing their creative talents. (Courtesy of the Dallas Public Schools)*

The statement of purposes or objectives for the secondary school is
known as the Ten Imperative Educational Needs of Youth. The statement retains the basic Seven Cardinal Principles of Secondary Education,
so famous among educators, but restates them in more usable form and
extends these principles to cover several desirable aspects of a program of

[9] Educational Policies Commission and Department of Elementary School Principals, *Teach Them All in Elementary Schools* (Washington, D.C.: National Education
Association, 1948), pp. 12–13. Reprinted by permission of the Commission.

secondary education. This list of imperative needs is widely used in curriculum planning, and curriculum committees working in the field of secondary education in recent years have generally used the statement as a base point of reference for curriculum planning. The list is as follows:

IMPERATIVE EDUCATIONAL NEEDS OF YOUTH

1. All youth need to develop salable skills and those understandings and attitudes that make the worker an intelligent and productive participant in economic life. To this end, most youth need supervised work experience as well as education in the skills and knowledge of their occupations.

2. All youth need to develop and maintain good health and physical fitness.

3. All youth need to understand the rights and duties of the citizens of a democratic society, and to be diligent and competent in the performance of their obligations as members of the community and citizens of the state and nation.

4. All youth need to understand the significance of the family for the individual and society and the conditions conducive to successful family life.

5. All youth need to know how to purchase and use goods and services intelligently, understanding both the values received by the consumer and the economic consequences of their acts.

6. All youth need to understand the methods of science, the influence of science on human life, and the main scientific facts concerning the nature of the world and of man.

7. All youth need opportunities to develop their capacities to appreciate beauty in literature, art, music, and nature.

8. All youth need to be able to use their leisure time well and to budget it wisely, balancing activities that yield satisfactions to the individual with those that are socially useful.

9. All youth need to develop respect for other persons, to grow in their insight into ethical values and principles, and to be able to live and work cooperatively with others.

10. All youth need to grow in their ability to think rationally, to express their thoughts clearly, and to read and listen with understanding.[10]

Formulation of Objectives by Teacher Committees

In the meantime a period of intensive activity in the preparation of courses of study and curriculum bulletins was under way in American education, and another approach to the formulation of educational ob-

---

[10] Educational Policies Commission, *Education for All American Youth: A Further Look* (Washington, D.C.: National Education Association, 1952), p. 216. Reprinted by permission of the Commission.

jectives was being used. In general, this period of intensive course-of-study preparation extended from the late 1920's to World War II. As this movement took shape, the preparation of curriculum guides was quite largely carried out by committees of teachers. Sometimes specialists from college faculties would serve as consultants. These committees were set up both by local school systems and by state departments of education.[11]

The usual starting point of these teachers' committees in the preparation of courses of study was the formulation of objectives or aims. These statements were often quite exhaustive and worked out in great detail. Usually, such committees would first develop aims for the whole subject field with which they were concerned; next would come aims for each particular subject encompassed within the field; and these in turn were even further subdivided into aims for particular units in the course. This process of formulating objectives was quite largely a deductive process, starting from general aims and deducing more specific aims until one got to the aims or objectives for even each day's work in the classroom. Considerable attention was often given to making fine distinctions between aims and objectives or between general aims, specific aims, and the like.[12] During this period, the scientific movement was flowering in American education, and many of these committees relied heavily on the so-called scientific derivation of educational objectives. It was this desire to be "scientific" that often lead to involved and lengthy statements of objectives and their breakdown into related categories, sub-objectives, and the like.

The Determination of Educational Objectives by Scientific Analyses

Quantitative scientific methods began to be applied to the study of educational problems in the second decade of this century. Scientific method seized the imagination of educators and almost everyone tried to be "scientific." The methods of science were to be a boon to the pedagogue, and most educational problems were to be readily solved by their application to planning and practices. This is the period that marks the development of intelligence tests and standardized achievement tests, the formulation of norms, the use of biometrics in the analysis of educational data, the development of the age-grade tables, and many similar efforts to reduce educational problems and educational procedures to quantitative

[11] Galen Saylor, *Factors Associated with Participation in Cooperative Programs of Curriculum Development* (New York: Bureau of Publications, Teachers College, Columbia University, 1941), Chap. 1.

[12] See L. Thomas Hopkins, *Curriculum Principles and Practices* (New York: Benjamin H. Sanborn and Company, 1930).

studies. It was inevitable that curriculum planning would also be subjected to the new methods of science, so efforts were made to determine educational objectives scientifically.

For the purposes of this brief discussion, the methods used to determine educational objectives scientifically will be grouped into five categories:[13]

1. Analyses of pupil interests, activities, deficiencies, and skills. This method of determining educational objectives and school experiences involved tabulation after tabulation of the habits, interests, and activities of children and of the skills they used in their day-by-day living.[14] Perhaps the technique is best illustrated by Thorndike's determination of the ten thousand basic words needed by elementary school children.[15] He tabulated over 4,565,000 words from forty-one sources, including materials read by children.

2. Analyses of adult activities, interests, and deficiencies. These studies quite closely parallel the types of investigations made of children. The primary purpose was to ascertain the activities pupils would be likely to engage in and the skills they would probably use in adult life, so that they could be properly taught these things during their school days. The school curriculum at that time was unquestionably cluttered up with a lot of useless and meaningless information, drill, and activities that represented tremendous waste in educational effort, and these investigations undoubtedly did help to get some of this senseless content eliminated.

An illustration of the attempt to analyze scientifically adult activities is from the field of arithmetic. Charters made an analysis of the arithmetic used by salesclerks in making out sales slips in department stores.[16] Through school children, Wilson collected a list of arithmetical computations used by parents during the day. He obtained 14,583 problems con-

[13] For a fuller discussion of the scientific approach to the determination of educational objectives, read Edgar M. Draper, *Principles and Techniques of Curriculum Making* (New York: Appleton-Century-Crofts, Inc., 1936); Henry Harap, *The Technique of Curriculum Making* (New York: The Macmillan Company, 1928), pp. 37–150; Harold Rugg, "Curriculum-Making and the Scientific Study of Education Since 1910," in *Foundations and Technique of Curriculum-Construction* (Part I, Twenty-sixth Yearbook, National Society for the Study of Education; Chicago: The University of Chicago Press, 1926), Chap. 4.

[14] National Education Association, Department of Superintendence, *Research in Constructing the Elementary School Curriculum* (Third Yearbook; Washington, D.C.: The Association, 1925).

[15] Edward L. Thorndike, *The Teacher's Word Book* (New York: Bureau of Publications, Teachers College, Columbia University, 1921).

[16] W. W. Charters, *Curriculum Construction* (New York: The Macmillan Company, 1923), pp. 231–236.

tributed by 4,068 different persons representing 155 different occupational groups.[17]

3. Analyses of skills used in an occupation. Analyses of the skills and activities involved in carrying on particular occupations or performing certain jobs have been used extensively as a basis for formulating objectives and developing curriculum content in the field of vocational education. Much of our vocational program today is based on the job analysis approach. Essentially this method consists of studying closely and intensively the activities of workers in a particular job or cluster of jobs. These analyses are then used as a basis for setting up particularized objectives and learning activities in the teaching of the trade. The nature of the studies made and the techniques used are well described by Charters.[18]

4. Survey of competent opinion. The formulation of educational objectives on the basis of the opinions of presumably competent persons has also been widely practiced. Essentially, this method consists of presenting a jury of persons, or a sampling of individuals selected on the basis of some criteria, with a list of possible objectives, or units of instruction in a particular subject or subject field, and asking them to rate or rank these statements on the basis of what they consider to be their importance for curriculum planning. A variation of the technique consists of simply asking such experts or a cross section of the population to list freely what they regard to be the major objectives to be attained by pupils in the subject field, or to list what they consider to be important knowledges, skills, or attitudes that people should possess in this area of learning. The use of this method is illustrated by Craig in his study of the formulation of objectives for science instruction. He presented 188 laymen with a list of possible objectives of such instruction and asked each person to rank the objectives in terms of what he considered to be their importance.[19]

5. Analysis of curriculum materials. A fifth type of analysis used in determining educational objectives consists of a survey of existing courses of study, textbooks used in the school, and other pertinent material of this type. In this procedure objectives that are now sought through exist-

[17] Guy M. Wilson, *A Survey of the Social and Business Usage of Arithmetic* (New York: Bureau of Publications, Teachers College, Columbia University, 1919).

[18] Charters, *op. cit.,* pp. 273–307.

[19] Gerald S. Craig, *Certain Techniques Used in Developing a Course of Study in Science for the Horace Mann Elementary School* (New York: Bureau of Publications, Teachers College, Columbia University, 1927).

ing courses of study or textbooks are tabulated. A good example of such technique is Schorling's efforts to obtain "valid" objectives for courses in junior high school mathematics. He tabulated the objectives listed in twenty-nine "scientific" investigations, seven texts commonly used in junior high school mathematics, and thirty courses of study in this field.[20] Hockett developed a list of 396 major social problems by analyzing the contents of books recommended by experts in this field and by critically examining news summaries in 312 issues of the *Literary Digest*.[21]

Determining Educational Objectives on the Basis of Children's Interests, Developmental Characteristics, and Motivations

With the development of a new psychology and new concepts of motivation, a more thorough understanding of the psychology of learning, and a more general understanding and acceptance of Dewey's emphasis on experience as a basis for learning, violent reaction against both the subject domination of the curriculum of the old school and the mechanistic approaches of the so-called scientific method began to develop. The committee which formulated the statement of the philosophy of progressive education states its objections to this new method of defining purposes in these terms:

> The deadening subordination of the individual, characteristic of mass methods, stirred educational leaders to seek ways to escape procedures which threatened to perpetuate an emerging scheme for the regimentation of minds. . . . Their protests were directed against the standardization of education which the wide adoption of the methods of business for determining educational efficiency was tending to foster. The protests were made the more vigorous by the fact that this seeming efficiency was at the time supported by a developing educational science which fostered a mechanistic attitude in teaching and in administration.[22]

This protest movement, as is apparent, is the basis for the so-called progressive education movement and for the organization of the experimental, progressive schools of the 1920's and 1930's. In its most extreme expression, reaction against the subject domination of the curriculum and the rigid, formal methods of the traditional school took the form of child-

[20] Raleigh Schorling, *A Tentative List of Objectives in the Teaching of Junior High School Mathematics* (Ann Arbor, Mich.: George Ware Publishing Company, 1925).
[21] John A. Hockett, *A Determination of the Major Social Problems of American Life* (New York: Bureau of Publications, Teachers College, Columbia University, 1927).
[22] Progressive Education Association, Committee on Philosophy, "Progressive Education—Its Philosophy and Challenge," *Progressive Education*, No. 5, Supplement 18:3 (May), 1941. Reprinted by permission of *Progressive Education*.

centered schools. In this version of the progressive school, educational objectives as guides to the instructional program were not to be set in advance at all by the teacher, the staff, or any adult external to the situation. The purposes of the activities of pupils and the very activities in which they engaged were to emerge out of the ongoing interests and activities of the children themselves.[23] Under this concept of curriculum planning, purposes of educational activities and the nature of the activities were to be the products of a consensus of expressed interests of the children themselves, somewhat guided and managed by the teacher in charge of the group.

Needless to say, very few schools actually carried this concept completely into practice, although some experimental schools did attempt, in developing educational experiences, to utilize to a very large extent the interests and desires of pupils. While the foundation for this approach to curriculum planning lies in Dewey's concept of experience, Dewey himself felt constrained in his later years to repudiate this extreme version of experience as a basis for planning the educational program.[24] He pointed out that a variety of experiences could feasibly be developed by the school and that selection has to be made. He felt that it was encumbent on the teacher and the educator to guide the selection of educational experiences in terms of socially approved objectives and goals. Nonetheless, the work of child-centered schools and the enthusiastic efforts of its proponents to promote this approach to educational planning did have considerable influence on curriculum development in this country and undoubtedly were important factors in awakening a new interest in the pupil as a basic element in the educative process.

The most significant efforts to take account of the pupil as a factor in the determination of educational objectives and in planning the curriculum of the school have resulted from the new child study movement, which has already been fully described in Chapter 5. We are just now in the evolutionary stages of this movement, and efforts to translate the things we are learning about the growth and development of children into objectives and plans for the educational program have really just begun. Basically this approach subscribes to the idea that the educational experiences of the school should be geared to the developmental characteristics and maturity levels of the children concerned.

Specialists in child study do not propose, however, that we simply

[23] This type of school is described in Harold Rugg and Ann Shumaker, *The Child-Centered School* (Yonkers, N.Y.: World Book Company, 1928); and the basic philosophy of such a school is stated in L. Thomas Hopkins, *Interaction: The Democratic Process* (Boston: D. C. Heath & Company, 1941).

[24] John Dewey, *Experience and Education* (New York: The Macmillan Company, 1938).

take expressed interests or observable desires and motivations of children as a basis for planning the educational program; rather they hold that the activities in which children do engage should be appropriate to their developmental needs and maturity levels. The nature of the educational experiences to be fostered by the school is still a matter to be determined on the basis of other criteria as well. Facts that we learn from the study of children themselves will enable curriculum workers to plan the types of educational experiences that will be of most value to pupils and that in totality will contribute maximally to the full growth and development of the child in all of his potentialities. Bode states the situation well:

> If we may trust the findings of modern psychology and the social sciences, it is just as impossible to find educational objectives by inspecting the individual child as it is by looking for them in a transcendental realm. The most that the study of childhood can reveal is the nature of the raw material with which we have to work. If we expect such study to produce an educational program, then, no matter how excellent our intentions may be, the interests of democracy are bound to suffer.
>   . . . It [progressive education] has nurtured the pathetic hope that it could find out how to educate by relying on such notions as interests, needs, growth, and freedom. The futility of this is reflected in the excrescences that have grown up about the movement.[25]

Determining Educational Objectives on the Basis of Developmental Needs of Pupils Growing Up in a Changing Culture

Since the three basic factors in the educative process are learners, a society, and the interaction of the two, educational objectives, to be valid, must be oriented to all three of these factors. It is the situation of an individual growing up in a culture which is constantly changing that determines the nature of educational objectives. In formulating educational objectives for the school it is vital that all who participate in this process must take into account the learner, the social situation in which learning takes place, and the interactive process. Dewey points out this requirement in strong terms:

> The immediate and direct concern of an educator is then with the situations in which interaction takes place. The individual, who enters as a factor into it, is what he is at a given time. It is the other factor, that of objective conditions, which lies to some extent within the possibility of regulation by the educator. . . .
>   When it is said that the objective conditions are those which are

[25] Boyd H. Bode, *Progressive Education at the Crossroads* (New York: Newsom & Co., 1938), pp. 39–40. Reprinted by permission of Newsom & Co., publishers.

within the power of the educator to regulate, it is meant, of course, that his ability to influence directly the experience of others and thereby the education they obtain places upon him the duty of determining that environment which will interact with the existing capacities and needs of those taught to create a worth-while experience. The trouble with traditional education was not that educators took upon themselves the responsibility for providing an environment. The trouble was that they did not consider the other factor in creating an experience; namely, the powers and purposes of those taught.[26]

Thus in setting desired outcomes for educational experiences to be provided in the school and in selecting and guiding the development of learning experiences, the curriculum worker must gain his clues from two sources: the developmental requirements, interests, psychobiological needs, past experiences, and motivations of the learner involved; and the cultural values, the mores, the cultural heritage, and the concepts of the good life held by those who establish and control the schools. These, then, become the bases upon which curriculum workers determine educational objectives. We shall seek in the next section of this chapter to develop statements of desired outcomes based on this approach.

OUTCOMES DESIRED FROM EDUCATIONAL EXPERIENCES IN THE SCHOOL

Now that attention has been given to the sources used in formulating desired outcomes for the educational experience provided by the school, it would be appropriate to give consideration to what comprises some of the most important outcomes that should be sought through school experience.

Who Should Determine What Constitute Desirable Outcomes?

Consistent with the concepts discussed throughout this book it is apparent that ultimately the teacher and the pupils who participate together in educational experiences in the school must determine what outcomes are to be sought from these learning activities. No one can formulate purposes and goals for other persons; one can only suggest what might constitute desirable purposes or goals that may well guide their experiences. Purposing, however, is the prerogative of the individual who is engaging in the experience. Any formal statement of desirable educational outcomes, then, is only a suggestion of what might be used by teachers and pupils as a basis for determining their own goals. This is the point of

[26] John Dewey, *Experience and Education* (New York: The Macmillan Company, 1938), pp. 43–44. Reprinted by permission of the Macmillan Company, publishers.

view we have taken in presenting in this section our conception of what constitute some important outcomes that should be sought through school experience. Teachers and other curriculum workers may wish to use this statement as source material in working cooperatively with pupils and other members of the staff in the formulation of the consuming purposes that shall guide the selection, evolvement, and development of the experiences themselves.

Desirable Outcomes for School Experiences

In thinking through for themselves what constitute desirable outcomes for the school, curriculum workers doubtless will want to examine various statements of educational objectives that have received widespread recognition and acceptance. We have already quoted in a previous section some lists formulated by competent authority. We consider the most important of these statements—all prepared by the Educational Policies Commission—to be these:

"The Purposes of Education in American Democracy"
"The Imperative Educational Needs of Youth"
"Values in the Good Elementary School"

These are indeed valid statements, prepared by groups of outstanding educators, and they constitute essential materials for study by curriculum workers engaged in the process of thinking through desired outcomes for learning activities. In addition to recommending these lists highly, we wish to present a statement of what we consider to be desirable outcomes that may well guide teachers and pupils in selecting and developing learning experiences. Our list of desired outcomes is presented on pages 234-239.

In formulating our own statement, we have been guided by the point of view that educational objectives are most serviceable when they are stated in terms of outcomes that should be sought through the curriculum. We believe that when teachers and pupils plan and develop learning activities in terms of what is expected from the experience, learning will carry over into the behavior patterns of the participants more completely and effectively. These desirable outcomes comprise (1) skills and abilities developed by the learner; (2) enjoyments and aesthetic satisfactions of the learner; (3) ways of thinking and arriving at solutions of his problems; (4) ways of working and living in his own personal behavior and in his relations to others; (5) attitudes that characterize his behavior and modes of living; and (6) generalizations, concepts, knowledges, and understandings that the learner possesses.

Obviously, many, many learnings that would inevitably result from educational experiences have not been listed. Our statement has been confined to broader, more general outcomes, each of which would include a cluster of many closely related, particularized outcomes. Even then, the list may seem long, but learning experiences sponsored by and carried on in the school are extensive, broad, and comprehensive. It should be emphasized again that these outcomes are not discrete, each being sought

PLATE 16. THE SCHOOL MUST DEVELOP THE ABILITY TO USE CORRECT ENGLISH IN ORAL AND WRITTEN COMMUNICATION. *These secondary school pupils are acquiring English skills in meaningful situations. (Courtesy of the Pasadena City Schools)*

separately through particular learning experiences. Rather, they are interwoven and, indeed, often results of the same experience. Any worthy curriculum experience will make a primary contribution to one or more of the outcomes, but concomitantly it will contribute significantly to many others.

OUTCOMES DESIRED FROM EDUCATIONAL EXPERIENCES

Skills and Abilities

As outcomes of educational experiences in school and out of school the individual, at a level appropriate to his own maturity, should be able and willing to

1. Read English readily, effectively, and with meaning so that what is read is understood and enjoyed.

2. Broaden his stock of words and concepts and use them with understanding.

3. Speak clearly and concisely, in good grammatical form and so as to convey meaning accurately.

4. Write English in acceptable grammatical form and with clarity, good organization, and appropriate style.

5. Listen to the speech of others of importance to the individual so as to understand what thoughts, concepts, and meanings are being presented.

6. Use accurately and efficiently computational methods appropriate for his activities as a citizen and as a worker.

7. Gather and interpret information, data, and concepts needed in carrying on his work and personal activities and use sources for obtaining such data.

8. Follow established practices and procedures basic to maintenance of good health, physical stamina, and physical well-being.

9. Care for his own physical needs and his bodily functions.

10. Engage in personal and group activities that provide relaxation, enjoyment, and socially approved pleasure.

11. Recognize, develop, and utilize his unusually strong talents and abilities that may be used to make a distinctive contribution to his own well-being and to society's welfare.

12. Develop increasingly, as he approaches and enters adulthood, vocational skill appropriate to his interests, capabilities, and well-being.

13. Participate effectively as a member of a group—with the family, with occupational associates, with fellow members of social, civic, religious, and political groups.

14. Use wisely and efficiently material resources, such as income, land, and natural resources.

15. Use the process of arriving democratically at shared decisions.

16. Observe the amenities of social behavior.

17. Study effectively and acquire desirable information and concepts from printed materials.

18. Understand and use appropriate methods of presenting data and information—maps, graphs, charts, pictorial material, and so on.

Enjoyments

As outcomes of educational experiences in school and out of school the individual, at a level appropriate to his own maturity, should obtain personal enjoyment and satisfaction from

1. Listening to music, both to that of real merit indigenous to the culture and to the great works of all time.

2. Participating in the performance of music.

3. Viewing works of art of both modern and classic conception.

4. Reading literature, both the works of modern authors and the writings of outstanding authors of all time.

5. Seeing natural beauty wherever it exists.

6. Viewing man-made structures of appealing design and conception.

7. Creating objects of beauty himself.

8. Engaging in leisure-time activities that enrich life.

9. Making his own surroundings in home and in places of work appealing and pleasing to one's sense of beauty and attractiveness.

10. Carrying out his tasks and responsibilities satisfactorily so that they reflect credit on his integrity and capabilities.

Ways of Thinking

As outcomes of educational experiences in school and out of school the individual, at a level appropriate to his own maturity, should be able to

1. Use rational methods in reaching decisions, solving problems, and exploring issues.

2. Understand the techniques and use of the scientific method of inquiry.

3. Obtain data and information pertinent to matters of concern to him and to evaluate its significance and meaning.

4. Analyze the points of view and generalizations of others in terms of their validity and meaning.

5. Face new and novel situations with confidence in his ability to deal with them realistically.

Ways of Working and Behaving

As outcomes of educational experiences in school and out of school the individual, at a level appropriate to his own maturity, should be able and willing in his own personal behavior and in his relations with others to

1. Accept and carry out to the satisfaction of himself and others directly concerned assigned or personally assumed responsibilities, tasks, and duties.

2. Discipline himself in organizing his energies and activities in terms of accepted and approved purposes of a group or morally legitimate purposes of his own, and carry through to a satisfactory termination enterprises that contribute to the achievement of these purposes.

3. Work in harmony with associates and group members on activities mutually acceptable and of common purpose.

4. Select for his activities those that are morally acceptable, consistent with social ideals and moral values, promise most for his personal satisfactions, and promote the good of those directly concerned.

5. Reject for his activities those that tend to degrade or compromise his own personal integrity and that of others.

6. Make sound and morally appropriate decisions for himself as a basis for action.

7. Grant to others the same socially accepted opportunities, rights, and privileges which he wants for himself.

8. Support and work for the full implementation in our society of the basic moral values and principles of a true democratic society.

9. Contribute effectively to the happiness, contentment, and security of his family group.

10. Seek and enjoy the companionship of his own peers of both sexes.

11. Direct his own efforts and energies in terms of personally and socially significant purposes, but when there is conflict between personal desires and interests and those of others directly concerned, act in terms of what promises most for the best interests of all.

12. Maintain personal poise and integrity in meeting situations that challenge his principles or threaten his security and welfare.

13. Take reverses and disappointments in stride, without letting them destroy equilibrium or principle.

14. Do his best in carrying on his daily activities; give sustained effort to what is worth while.

15. Respect constituted authority, so long as it is based on the will of the people.

16. Respect the rights of others to hold opinions different from his own and to live their own lives so long as they adhere to socially approved standards of conduct.

17. Expand his knowledge, skill, and range and depth of interests and grow intellectually.

Attitudes

As outcomes of educational experiences in school and out of school the individual should give evidence by his actions that he believes in the

1. Dignity of man.

2. Ability of the citizens to govern themselves.

3. Equality for mankind in the process of law, in responsibility for governing themselves, and in fulfillment of one's potentialities.

4. Freedoms defined in our basic constitutional law.

5. Peaceful settlement of individual, group, and national disputes.

6. Democratic principles and ideals that have evolved from the experience of mankind.

7. Moral values that pervade American life.

8. Due processes of law.

9. Desirability of alleviating social conditions that contribute to disease, crime, and human degradation.

10. Desirability of planning his expenditures in terms of wise use of his resources.

11. Obedience of laws ordained by the citizens.

12. Perfectibility of mankind.

13. Orderly processes of attaining social ends.

14. Conservation and wise use of human and material resources.

Generalizations, Concepts, Knowledges, and Understandings

As outcomes of educational experiences in school and out of school the individual should understand, at levels appropriate to his own maturity, these things in addition to the knowledges, concepts, and generalizations necessary to achieve the outcomes stated previously:

1. The important facts about the development of the American nation: its achievements and accomplishments and its shortcomings.

2. The basic values of our democratic society.

3. The role of government in protecting the welfare of the citizens.

4. The machinery of government and his part in it.

5. The interdependence of the peoples of the world as individuals and groups.

6. The social structures and processes of local, national, and international significance.

7. The changing nature of all social institutions and conditions of life.

8. The important facts about health and disease and the relation of health to individual and group well-being.

9. The incentive and organizational genius of mankind which makes possible in ever-increasing abundance the material comforts of life.

10. The fact that the welfare of all would be improved if the material resources of the world were used effectively.

11. The efforts of our citizens to achieve political liberty and the struggle to achieve it in other parts of the world.

12. The influence of man's physical environment on his customs, modes of living, and behavior patterns.

13. Man's ability to control nature through his discovery of cause and effect.

14. The natural laws that explain common and useful natural phenomena.

15. The sources and nature of our cultural and moral values.

16. The necessity of adapting social, political, and economic institutions and processes to changed conditions.

17. The dependence of man's accomplishments on his control and use of natural forces.

18. The impact of natural science on ways of living, thinking, and working.

19. The long efforts of man to free himself from arbitrary domination and subjection by the few.

20. The quality of the relationships of person to person as a key to the realization of democratic values.

21. The operation of economic factors in our society.

22. The importance of the family as a social unit.

23. The meaning of democracy and the privileges, rights, and responsibilities of the individual in a democracy.

24. The role of education in the achievement of democratic principles.

25. The advantages of a democratic form of government, and the status of individuals in a society that adheres to democratic types of social organization.

USE OF A STATEMENT OF GOALS IN CURRICULUM PLANNING

Everyone recognizes the necessity of setting goals for the educational program as a basis for curriculum planning; yet three pitfalls beset the curriculum worker in the process of formulating educational objectives. There is danger that (1) the goals will be so general and broad as to be relatively meaningless in the process of actually planning educational experiences, (2) the goals will become in fact the basis for planning units of work, and (3) teacher energy and enthusiasm may be dissipated in the efforts to formulate statements of goals.[27] Let us then consider appropriate uses that may be made of a statement of educational objectives.

In view of the totality of learning and the necessity of avoiding a piecemeal and fragmentary approach to the planning of curriculum ex-

[27] Difficulties inherent in formulating educational objectives are discussed by President Taylor in relation to college instruction in "Clarification of Program and Course Objectives," in *Improving College Instruction* (American Council on Education, Study Series One, No. 48, 1950; Washington, D.C.: The Council, 1951), pp. 47–59.

periences, statements of educational goals and objectives should be regarded, not as organizing centers for educational experiences, but rather as guide lines to be used by curriculum workers in maintaining a sense of direction in selecting, planning, developing, and evaluating educational experiences. Statements of objectives or the outcomes desired from educational experiences should serve the following purposes in curriculum planning:

1. Bases for making curriculum decisions. What choices promise to contribute most to the realization of the outcomes desired?

2. Guides for the development of pupil purposes. Have the pupils formulated purposes that conform with the fundamental purposes of education so that they will gain maximally from the activity?

3. Criteria for judging the adequacy and appropriateness of the total program of education. Are all of the important outcomes which the school should seek being provided for in the experiences of pupils?

4. Criteria for evaluating pupil growth and development. Do pupils attain the outcomes desired?

It has been our point of view in this chapter that all curriculum workers must formulate for themselves a clear and understandable conception of what constitute desirable goals for education. We have emphasized the necessity of conceiving of these curriculum goals in terms of the growth and development of pupils as well as in terms of the social demands of the group that supports and establishes the school. Part 3 of this book will consider methods and procedures for establishing the total framework of the curriculum so that it will contribute most significantly to the realization of acceptable goals.

For Further Study

Barton, George, Jr., "The Derivation and Clarification of Objectives," *Journal of Educational Research,* 41:624–639 (April), 1948.

Discusses methods used by educational authorities to define objectives for education.

Bode, Boyd H., *Progressive Education at the Crossroads.* New York: Newsom & Company, 1938.

A critical analysis of the concept of curriculum building that is based on pupil needs and interests, and a plea for social orientation of the curriculum.

Charters, W. W., *Curriculum Construction.* New York: The Macmillan Company, 1923.

The leader of the activity analysis approach to curriculum planning presents his method of defining objectives.

Commager, Henry Steele, "Our Schools Have Kept Us Free," *Life,* No. 16, 29:46–47, (October 16), 1950. (Also reprinted in *NEA Journal,* 40:18–20 (January), 1951.

An excellent statement on the role of education in a democracy.

Dewey, John, *Democracy and Education.* New York: The Macmillan Company, 1925.

A classic discussion of the nature of education, with particular reference to the definition of aims. Chapter VIII is especially pertinent.

——, *Experience and Education.* New York: The Macmillan Company, 1938.

Everyone interested in defining goals for American education should critically weigh Dewey's position as presented in this statement.

Draper, Edgar M., *Principles and Techniques of Curriculum Making.* New York: Appleton-Century-Crofts, Inc., 1936.

Part II discusses various methods utilized to determine educational objectives by analytical methods.

Educational Policies Commission, *The Purposes of Education in American Democracy.* Washington, D.C.: National Education Association, 1938.

A basic statement of purposes that should guide American education.

Jensen, Gale E., "The Establishment of Valid Aims for American Education," *Educational Administration and Supervision,* 37:129–152 (March), 1951.

An excellent statement of the bases necessary to the determination of goals.

Kearney, Nolan C., *Elementary School Objectives.* New York: Russell Sage Foundation, 1953.

In this report, prepared for the Mid-Century Committee on Outcomes in Elementary Education, recommended goals for the elementary school are presented in Part II.

Kilpatrick, William H., *Philosophy of Education.* New York: The Macmillan Company, 1951.

A discussion of educational goals and objectives from the point of view of an experimentalist.

National Society for the Study of Education, *The Foundations and Technique of Curriculum Construction.* Part I, Twenty-sixth Yearbook. Chicago: The University of Chicago Press, 1926.

Section I by Harold Rugg traces methods used in curriculum making for American schools in the past century.

Progressive Education Association, Committee on Philosophy, "Progressive Education—Its Philosophy and Challenge," *Progressive Education,* Vol. 18, No. 5, Supplement (May), 1941.

A significant statement by an organization that has done much to promote child-centered education.

Quillen, I. James, and Lavone A. Hanna, *Education for Social Competence*. Chicago: Scott, Foresman and Company, 1948.

Chapter 3 discusses methods of stating educational objectives and lists a number of such statements.

Smith, B. Othaniel, William O. Stanley, and J. Harlan Shores, *Fundamentals of Curriculum Development*. Yonkers, N.Y.: World Book Company, 1950.

Chapter 11 sets up criteria for judging the validity of educational objectives.

Spencer, Herbert, *Education*. New York: Appleton-Century-Crofts, Inc., 1860, (1912 printing).

Spencer defines an educational program based on an analysis of life activities.

Wolman, Benjamin, "Scientific Study of Educational Aims," *Teachers College Record*, 50:471–481 (April), 1949.

An analysis of statements of educational aims formulated by great philosophers.

part 3

HOW SHALL THE CURRICULUM
FRAMEWORK BE ORGANIZED?

In the preceding section of this book, we presented a concept of the basic purposes of education, a concept based on the factors and forces that must be considered in curriculum planning. We are now ready to utilize these concepts in actually planning the curriculum. The first step in a comprehensive approach to curriculum planning is to determine a framework or structure that will guide curriculum workers in selecting, planning, and developing learning experiences with pupils. Part 3 analyzes various aspects of this whole problem.

Chapters 8 and 9 consider matters of design, scope, and sequence, and discuss four major methods used to define the structure of the curriculum. Chapter 8 explores the traditional subject matter types of organization and Chapter 9 describes some newer approaches that have been used by some schools. Chapter 10 considers the whole core curriculum movement, one of the significant and widely discussed developments in education during the past two decades. Once the basic framework or structure of the curriculum has been determined, curriculum workers still need to set up guides for balancing the types of experiences that will be included in the school experiences of children. Some other aspects of educational administration also bear on curriculum planning. So these matters will be discussed in Chapter 11.

chapter 8

The Subjects and Broad Fields
as Bases for Organizing the Curriculum

It is readily apparent that the program of a school must be planned and organized on some basis; it would be highly wasteful of the capacities, energy, time, and effort of pupils if teachers and school officials simply permitted them to carry on educational experiences willy-nilly or on a hit-and-miss basis. Moreover, if basic curriculum goals such as those stated in the previous chapter are to be achieved, there must necessarily be some planned procedure for seeking these goals through learning experiences. It is essential that these experiences be selected, planned, and carried forward on the basis of some pattern of organization that will give continuity, meaning, and significance to the educational program. The organization of the curriculum brings to a direct focus, then, the entire question of how we shall achieve the basic purposes and outcomes desired from the educational program. It is one of the most pivotal concerns in the whole area of curriculum planning.

THE DESIGN OR ORGANIZATION OF THE CURRICULUM

What Is Meant by Curriculum Design?

By curriculum design we mean the pattern or framework or structural organization used in selecting, planning, and carrying forward educational experiences in the school. Design is thus the plan that teachers follow in providing learning activities. Obviously, the term comes from art and architecture. One architect may use building materials in such a manner that he comes out with a home of colonial style, another might use building materials in such a way that he has a ranch type of house, another decides to build a house that is designed as a French provincial home, or still another architect builds a house in the adobe style. Yet they are all homes and intended to provide shelter, comfort, and living accommodations for a family. So we may organize the educational experiences of pupils in a school in a pattern known as a subject organization, or we may organize them in such a way that we have a curriculum organization built around major areas of social living, or we may utilize the needs and interests of pupils as a basis for selecting and developing experiences and thus have a problems type of organization.

For example, one of the desired educational outcomes in the whole general area of the development of communicative skill is the ability to spell words in common usage. How shall this skill be attained? The teacher, and other curriculum workers who affect decisions relative to the selection of educational experiences, could decide to have formal class instruction in spelling. A time in the daily schedule, say fifteen or twenty minutes, could be set aside for drill on English words in common usage, the children being required to memorize the spelling of these words. The lists of words that would comprise the daily or weekly allotment could be selected from one of the standard word lists or from a spelling book.

On the other hand, the teacher might decide to develop the skill of spelling through giving attention to words used in day-by-day activities in the school. That is, in working with the children in various types of learning experiences the teacher could list on the board or on paper words that the children use in conversation and in written work and then see if the children know how to spell the words. If not, some exercise in spelling the words could be undertaken right then and there or perhaps at some other time during the day. However, the teacher might decide that neither of these methods is a good approach. If the teacher assumes that the children will sooner or later learn to spell properly, and as a matter of course, the words they use in written or oral communication, there may be no formal instruction in spelling at all. Instead, the teacher will emphasize the need for good spelling, point out misspelled words in written work, and teach the children how to find the correct spelling of a word in the dictionary.

The Importance of Curriculum Design

The design of the curriculum is closely related to the basic goals or purposes of the school, just as the design or structure of a building is closely related to the uses to which it may efficiently and appropriately be put. It would be difficult to make a warehouse into an efficient and comfortable home or an office building into a school. It is just as difficult to achieve some of the avowed purposes of the school through some types of curriculum organization. As a matter of fact, the pattern of the curriculum organization may in a considerable measure determine

the nature of the outcomes that will be achieved by the school. Just as
a good architect starts the planning of a building with a clear and definite understanding of the purposes and functions which the building is
to serve, so the curriculum worker should start with an understanding
of the purposes and goals of the school and the major outcomes to be
sought from school experiences as the basis for designing the pattern of
the educational program. To determine the form of curriculum organization and the pattern of the educational program first and then to see
what outcomes might be expected would be as foolhardy as for an
architect simply to build a building and then decide about the uses to
which it might possibly be put.

The relationship of the curriculum pattern or design to the achievement of the desired goals of the school is stated quite bluntly by Caswell:

> It is true that improved teaching always results in better education,
> but the conventional curriculum framework is the greatest single
> obstacle to the development of a program in the high school which
> provides the necessary assistance to youth in achieving in actual liv-
> ing the various developmental tasks which our society demands.[1]

The designing of the curriculum, by which is meant the process of
selecting, organizing, and guiding the learning experiences to be provided by the school, gives reality to all our theories, concepts, and points
of view about the curriculum. The design of the curriculum indicates
the bases upon which decisions are made as to the types of experiences
that may appropriately be included in the educational program and
those that are beyond the province of the school, or that are not appropriate for the school to sponsor. While the design itself does not determine the criteria for selecting and guiding educational experiences,
it indicates the nature of the decisions on these points that already have
been made.

To illustrate, if a decision has been made that the school will not
permit pupils to make excursions beyond the school grounds, then the
teacher does not even weigh the possibility of taking children on a trip
to a nearby farm, to a factory, or to a police station in the neighborhood. Likewise in the secondary school, if the teacher has been handed a
course of study or a syllabus and told in effect that it outlines the content of a course he is teaching, and that he is expected to cover that content, he undoubtedly will reject suggestions from students or any ideas
he may have about the introduction of a discussion of some current social

[1] Hollis L. Caswell, "Curriculum Proposals for the Future" in *The American High
School* (Eighth Yearbook of the John Dewey Society, H. L. Caswell, editor; New York:
Harper & Brothers, 1946), p. 140. Reprinted by permission of Harper & Brothers,
publishers.

or political problems that arise during the course of the semester, but which were not provided for in the prepared syllabus.

In summary, then, the design of the curriculum is a very important aspect of curriculum planning because it (1) indicates the elements that should receive attention in the matter of planning the curriculum and the interrelationship of these elements in the process of curriculum development, (2) serves as a method for determining the selection and organization of the learning experiences provided by the school, and (3) indicates the role of teachers, children, and others concerned in the process of curriculum planning.

Determining the Scope and Sequence of the Curriculum

One important phase of the designing of the curriculum is to determine its scope and sequence. Obviously, this is a necessary step in formulating a total structure for the curriculum of the school, since we must know the types of educational experiences that may appropriately be included in the curriculum in terms of our basic planning of structure, and the time at which it is proper to develop particular experiences encompassed within the total program. To continue our analogy from architecture, determining scope in curriculum designing would be comparable to determining the number and types of rooms, offices, and other accommodations to be included in a building, such as deciding if a building designed as a school is to have a teachers' lounge, a faculty conference room, a cafeteria, a library, or a multipurpose room. Also, how many floors are to be included in the building? Sequence is not analogous to any aspect of architecture; it is easily understood in relation to curriculum planning, however.

Defining scope and sequence. By scope is meant the breadth, variety, and types of educational experiences that are to be provided pupils as they progress through the school program. Scope represents the latitudinal axis for selecting curriculum experiences. It may be thought of as the "what" of the curriculum, the types of educational experiences that are believed by curriculum planners to be appropriate for the education of pupils at particular stages of development so that educational objectives are realized. For example, the determination of scope involves decisions on such matters as these: Is sex education to be offered in the school? Are pupils to be permitted to investigate current social and political problems of a controversial nature? Are vocational training courses to be offered in the junior high school? Are all pupils required to study a foreign language? Is physical education to be taught in the elementary school? Is a study of the United Nations organization to be included in the social studies? These are questions relating to scope.

By sequence is meant the order in which educational experiences are developed with pupils. Sequence refers to the "when" in curriculum planning. Determination of the sequence of educational experiences is a decision as to the most propitious time in which to develop those educational experiences suggested by the scope. If we think of scope as the latitudinal aspect of curriculum planning, sequence becomes the longitudinal axis.

It is quite apparent to anyone that it would be more appropriate to provide educational experiences in a sequence or an orderly arrangement than on a helter-skelter basis. This order becomes the sequence aspect of curriculum planning, and all preplanning of the curriculum obviously deals with the matter of sequence or orderly development of educational experiences. Thus sequence involves such questions as, When should long division be taught? typewriting for personal use? the geography of the United States? American history? a unit on marriage and family relations? foreign languages? science?

Design and scope and sequence. As we discuss the four principal methods of formulating a design for the curriculum in this and the following chapter and the practices used to design the core part of a curriculum in Chapter 10, procedures used in determining the scope and sequence of the curriculum under each type of design will become clear. Methods of setting scope and sequence are inextricably a part of design and will be treated as such in this book. Each type of design has its own procedure for defining scope and sequence, as will be evident from a study of these three chapters.

Principles for Designing the Curriculum

Since curriculum designing is so important and does bring to a focus our entire conception of the educational process and the objectives and goals of the school, curriculum workers should be guided by fundamental principles in the formulation of a design, which includes the determination of the scope and sequence of educational experiences to be provided boys and girls. The check list for appraising a school's curriculum included as Table 3 in Chapter 1 would be an appropriate guide to follow in this process, but largely for purposes of emphasis and to restate these guides more specifically as criteria for determining design and scope and sequence they are given here in that form.

1. The design of the curriculum should facilitate and encourage the selection and development of all types of learning experiences essential for the achievement of the desired outcomes sought by the school.

2. From among all the learning experiences that might contribute significantly to the realization of educational objectives, the design should enable teachers to develop those that are most meaningful to the particular group of pupils working with a teacher.

3. The design should permit teachers to utilize sound principles of learning in selecting and guiding the development of learning activities in the school.

4. The design should enable teachers to adapt the experiences to the developmental needs, capacities, and maturity levels of pupils.

5. The design should encourage teachers to take account of the learning experiences which children have outside the school and relate these to activities carried on within it.

6. The design should provide a continuity in learning experiences so that the learning activities in which pupils are engaged at any one time build on and fully develop learnings gained from earlier experiences and lead on to further experiences of maximum worth.

7. The curriculum should be so designed that it will assist pupils in building into character, personality, and their stock of knowledges the basic democratic values that characterize our culture.

8. The design of the curriculum should be realistic, feasible, and acceptable.

Types of Curriculum Design

Consideration will now be given in the remainder of this chapter and the following one to important methods that may be used to organize or design the curriculum. These types of curriculum organization are (1) the school subjects, (2) the broad fields of subject matter, (3) the major social functions of living, and (4) the interests, needs, and problems of learners. Attention will be given to the bases for the organization of each of these four types of curriculum design, the merits and shortcomings of these methods will be analyzed, and an estimate of their uses in modern curriculum planning will be presented. Some may wonder why the core type of program is not listed here as a method of designing the curriculum, but we regard it as a different aspect of curriculum planning and consider it separately in Chapter 10.

The curriculum worker should keep in mind that in actual school practice several methods of organizing curriculum experiences may be found in the same school, or certainly in the same school system extending from the kindergarten through the twelfth or fourteenth grades. More will be said on this point later.

USING THE SCHOOL SUBJECTS AS A BASIS FOR CURRICULUM DESIGN

The School Subjects as a Method of Organizing the Curriculum

The subject-organized curriculum is by far the most widely used method of organizing educational experiences today and has a long tradition of centuries behind it. In this type of design the subjects become the primary method of organizing and carrying on learning experiences, and mastery of the subject matter becomes a basis through which the educational objectives of a school are in a large measure to be attained. In the most formal type of organization, a child in the first grade starts studying such subjects as reading, arithmetic, music, art, hygiene, spelling, penmanship, and the like, and works his way during the succeeding eleven years of his school career through an array of similar subjects until he completes the prescribed program of the school in terms of passing subjects or attaining units of credit until he has enough to be graduated. Plate 17 illustrates a scene familiar to all teachers—secondary school pupils studying a school subject. Chemistry is one of the most specialized of all of our fields of knowledge and is usually taught on a highly abstract and logical basis of organization.

The school subject is a logical and convenient organization of the cultural heritage of the race. The inherent logic of racial experience becomes the primary method of organizing the subject, and this is usually done by a specialist who is a scholar in the particular field and who has a keen understanding of the interrelationships of the concepts, facts, principles, and the like, that constitute a logical system of knowledge. New discovery and new knowledge can thus be easily fitted into existing bodies of knowledge, so that the subject is reorganized in terms of these new findings and discoveries, or the subject field is extended and expanded accordingly.

The school has taken over these systematic bodies of subject matter as a basis for organizing learning experiences. The selected body of subject matter becomes the material to be learned by the pupil, and one of the primary functions of the teacher is to guide the pupil in learning it. Minimum essentials or standards may be set in terms of the amount of subject matter that must be mastered by the child before he can be considered successful in his learning experiences. To aid those who have difficulty in acquiring this mastery, remedial classes or remedial techniques are often employed and various devices are used so that the child will more readily want to learn the subject matter selected and will be able to learn it more readily. The textbook, representing the selected portion of this organized body of subject matter, becomes the chief type of teaching material and the main source for learning experiences.

PLATE 17. USE OF THE SUBJECT DESIGN IN CURRICULUM PLANNING. *The study of chemistry in the secondary school illustrates the use of the subject framework in planning the curriculum. (Courtesy of the Pasadena City Schools)*

In the subject-centered curriculum, the primary responsibility in curriculum planning is to determine the particular subjects to be offered by the school and the body of knowledge to be encompassed within each subject. Thus most of the efforts of curriculum workers, such as teachers, curriculum directors, and curriculum committees, consist of evaluating the merits and worth-whileness of various subjects already included or that might be included in the curriculum, and in selecting the facts, information, principles, generalizations, and the like, that should be acquired by the pupils. Suitable attention may also be given to methods that may be used by the teacher to promote the acquisition of such bodies of subject matter by the pupils. A further concern of curriculum workers in this type of organization is to devise ways of evaluating pupil mastery of subject matter, through formal tests, problem-solving situations, and the like.

Arguments Advanced in Favor of the Subject-Centered Curriculum

1. The subjects constitute a logical and effective method of organizing learning and of interpreting and systematizing new knowledge and facts. Everyone, of course, assembles his learnings into a more or less organized system. New learnings are used, as appropriate, to rebuild our systematic body of knowledge, skills, attitudes, behavior patterns, and the like, to add to our existing stock of learnings, or to round out and develop new concepts and principles. Thus a child learns computational skills in arithmetic, and as they are developed organizes the skills into some kind of systematic approach to the ability to compute. He is able to use a number of processes of computation that he has learned as more or less discrete items and also to bring them to bear in proper relationship on the solution of a problem that may involve a number of these skills. New knowledge and new skill are built into the existing pattern of computational ability and understanding of computational processes. This organized body of knowledge helps the pupil to interpret and better understand new learnings as they are experienced.

On the basis of this premise it is felt by many educators and by many lay citizens that the school subjects represent a desirable basis of organizing experiences in the school. It is maintained that the systematic study of human knowledge through the organized bodies of subject matter enables the learner to build more efficiently and adequately his stock of understandings, concepts, information, principles, and generalizations; also the subjects serve as a desirable method of building new learnings into experience by relating them to knowledge already acquired. As a learner proceeds through a school curriculum it is assumed, then, that he acquires a considerable amount of information and knowledge available to him in the form of organized bodies of racial experience. He is able to bring this organized body of knowledge and understanding to focus on a problem or situation that he faces in life more effectively because it is schematically organized around basic unifying principles or concepts.

2. The subject curriculum is most appropriate for developing the intellectual powers of the individual. Many citizens and educators maintain that the full intellectual powers of the individual can best be developed through the study of logically organized subject matter.

This point of view is, of course, strongly supported by those who still cling to the old traditional doctrine of mental discipline, believing as they do that we can train the faculties of the mind by disciplining it and using it for abstract thinking, memorizing, and acquiring abstract meanings. In terms of this concept the more abstract and more difficult the subject matter to be learned the better it is for training and disciplining the mind.

Many other conscientious citizens who recognize the error in the theories of formal discipline nevertheless feel that the study of subject matter provides the most feasible method for developing abilities to do logical thinking, to deal with abstract concepts and principles, and in general to develop the qualities that characterize high-level intellectual activities of educated people. This point of view holds that mathematics, science, history, geography, and similar subjects offer the best opportunities to develop the ability to think and to deal realistically with problems, particularly on the abstract level. It is through doing abstract thinking in the field of mathematics, in developing basic principles and laws in the field of science, in coming to grips with abstract ideas in literature, in learning the rules of grammar, and the like, that the individual can best develop his powers of abstract reasoning and logical thinking, as well as basic habits of intellectual thought and concern for ideas and principles that control actions.

It is held by the advocates of the subject curriculum that it is primarily through the systematic study of knowledge, especially with the emphasis on generalizations and abstract principles, that we can adequately challenge the intellectual powers of the individual. Not to provide him with these opportunities is to shortchange the pupil, particularly the intellectually capable pupil, and is to leave him without the real substance of an education. It is felt that any other approach is cheating the good pupil and giving him a thin gloss of practical and functional information that does not educate him sufficiently to use his intellectual abilities in dealing with life situations, in expanding the frontiers of knowledge, and in applying such knowledge to the uses and enjoyments of mankind.

3. The subject type of curriculum organization is consistent with certain basic concepts of the educational process. The subject type of curriculum organization is a logical consequence of some of the basic points of view about the educational process that are accepted by many educators and citizens generally. Those who subscribe to the educational concepts of perennialism and essentialism naturally accept school subjects as the most feasible and practical method of organizing the curriculum in conformity with these premises about education.[2] These groups regard knowledge as power, and knowledge may best be obtained through a systematic study of the major disciplines of human knowledge; hence the soundness of the subject approach.

4. *The subject curriculum best utilizes the accumulated heritage of a race.* Many would maintain that the subject type of curriculum organization makes the most effective use of the accumulated cultural heritage of the race. It enables pupils to acquire rapidly and efficiently the basic concepts, understandings, principles, and knowledge developed by the race over centuries of experience. The young are then best able to utilize racial experience and move forward into new areas of achievement, make new discoveries, and improve the quality of human living. Progress becomes more feasible if the individual has such knowledge as a starting point in his own experience.

5. *The subject curriculum is backed by long tradition and is widely accepted.* The subject type of curriculum organization has centuries of tradition behind it. Such extensive use of this method has, of course, resulted in its general acceptance by citizens, teachers, pupils, and school officials generally. It is the going method of curriculum organization, and any other method proposed faces the initial handicap of having to overcome tradition and the prestige that attaches to the subject approach. The assumption of almost everyone is that children go to school to study their "subjects." To make other provisions represents a radical departure, and involves all the problems inherent in changing from accepted modes of thinking and behavior. Consequently, the school can maintain a traditional subject type of organization without raising serious question on the part of most parents or having to engage in extensive efforts to inform and obtain the approval of patrons of the school necessitated by the use of any new approach.

Moreover, the present system of college admission requirements reinforces the subject design, since admission to most colleges is based on accumulating credits or passing examinations in the traditional school subjects. Some colleges tend to perpetuate the traditional subject pattern, furthermore, by questioning credits earned in new types of curriculum organization.

6. *The subject design is more readily used by present-day teachers.* It is of course true that the great majority of teachers have themselves been educated in the subject type of curriculum and that their professional training has been based on the subject organization. Particularly

[2] See Chapter 2.

is the latter true of teachers of the secondary schools. Inevitably, it becomes much easier for such teachers to work in a curriculum that is organized on the subject basis than it is to work with other types of curriculum design, and schools find it much easier to go ahead with the traditional type of subject curriculum than to re-educate teachers to work with a new type of design. In fact, it often has proved quite difficult for many teachers, especially at the secondary level, to change to a new method of organizing educational experiences. They flounder, are insecure, and exhibit considerable difficulty in adjusting to a new approach. Consequently, some curriculum planners feel that it is better to maintain the traditional type of curriculum organization than go to the trouble of developing a staff that can work with a different type of design.

7. Curriculum planning is simpler and easier in the subject-centered curriculum. At the present time it is admittedly easier to carry on curriculum planning efforts within the subject organization than it is in other types of design. This is due in part to the fact that much of our know-how and our curriculum planning in the past have largely been based on the subject approach and in part to the fact that curriculum revision under this plan largely becomes a matter of dropping certain subjects, adding new subjects, or reorganizing the content of existing subjects or making it psychologically more teachable. Efforts of curriculum committees and teachers are directed to the reorganization of the program of studies and the content of the subjects rather than to thinking through the problems of a new design for learning experiences. Moreover, most of our national professional organizations devote their energies to the reorganization and improvement of the subject design rather than to the development of entirely new designs and organizations. Teachers may obtain a great deal of help in reorganizing their subject curriculum from such professional groups and from subject specialists at the teacher education institutions.

The questions of scope and sequence also become easier in the subject type of design. Scope simply becomes a question of what subjects a school should offer, including such matters as which ones should be required, which ones should be taught for single periods and which ones for double periods, and the like; questions of sequence become questions of the order in which the subject matter should be presented in the various grade levels or in the sequence of the secondary schools.

8. Evaluation of the educational program is readily carried on in the subject type of curriculum. The subject curriculum lends itself easily to evaluation, for evaluation consists primarily of testing the acquisition of subject matter and the development of skills and abilities. Standardized and teacher-made tests based on recalling the facts covered in the prescribed course are easily formulated and used. Much of our efforts in the field of evaluation have been devoted to just this sort of thing. Some states even foster state-wide testing programs that set quite uniform methods of evaluating the curriculum in terms of subjects, and consequently perpetuate the existing subject basis of organization.

Shortcomings of Subject-Centered Curriculum

In spite of the arguments advanced in favor of the subject type of curriculum organization, many educators believe that it has some serious shortcomings.[3] Many of the advantages claimed for other types of curriculum design, discussed in subsequent sections, represent the positive side of the objections raised here against the subject curriculum. Nevertheless, we shall present in rather systematic fashion some of the most serious weaknesses charged to this type of organization. Everyone, of course, recognizes that what are listed as advantages or shortcomings of particular types of curriculum design depend entirely on one's point of view as to the basic nature of the educational process and the function that a school should serve in a democratic society. Hence the points made here will be in terms of the curriculum concepts that we ourselves hold and elaborate throughout this book.

1. Logical, systematic organization of subject matter is not an appropriate psychological organization. In view of what is known about the growth and development of children and the psychology of learning, the subject basis for organizing learning experiences leaves a great deal to be desired in terms of its psychological soundness. Particularly is this true for children in elementary schools and for many pupils in secondary schools. Since learning consists purely and simply of what the learner chooses to build into his stock of learnings out of an experience, the motives and purposes of the learner are of paramount importance. If he participates in an experience in order to solve a real problem that faces him, to achieve something that he desires, to carry on an interest that he has, or to satisfy a basic need that shapes his motives, the individual undertakes it with purposes that will more surely result in genuine learning—additions to his useful stock of understandings, knowledges, abilities, attitudes, enjoyments, and ways of behaving.

[3] For a challenging answer to the charges made against the use of the subject organization in the secondary school, see William B. Featherstone, *A Functional Curriculum for Youth* (New York: American Book Company, 1950), pp. 93–112.

Unfortunately, too many pupils, especially younger pupils, do not find significant purpose in the study of logically organized subject matter set out to be learned. However, educators should recognize that many children, particularly as they mature and come into the secondary schools, do find meaning in the systematic study of subject matter, and that such an arrangement suits their purposes, psychologically. Such purposes are present if the pupil accepts the subject matter as serving some useful and desirable function in his own life, be it preparing for college, learning a great deal about an aspect of knowledge in which he is interested, improving his skill and ability in a particular area, or simply gaining prestige that may accrue from knowing a great deal about some area of knowledge or being able to think accurately in the concepts of this field. However, many children have difficulty in setting up purposes of these kinds and often do not see meaning in subject matter as such; the same is true of a considerable portion of older pupils. For them the principal purposes in mastering subject matter may become those of pleasing the teacher, making a passing grade, avoiding criticism or punishment, or similar low-level motives. Unfortunately, since the mastery of subject matter does not seem worth while in terms of their personal interests or well-being, much of the subject matter learned is soon forgotten.

Also, if pupils do not have an adequate background of experience for interpreting and understanding the material studied, much of the meaning is lost and the effort becomes futile. The teacher may require that subject matter be memorized or learned without regard for the development of meaning or the ability to generalize.

It is only fair to recognize that the psychological unsoundness of the subject approach quite frequently lies in the methods used to teach the subject rather than inherently in the subject design itself. This is particularly true at the secondary school level. Outstanding teachers may use the subject design with great effectiveness with many pupils, provided that the pupils understand the purposes and significance of what is studied, that learning activities are related to past experience, and that concrete material and firsthand experiences are introduced insofar as possible as a basis from which to deduct principles and concepts. Nevertheless, it seems that the subject type of organization does lend itself very readily to the rote type of learning, memorization, meaningless regurgitation of facts, and the like.

2. *The subject design of the curriculum limits the school in the attainment of its desired outcomes.* Probably the most serious shortcoming of the subject method of organizing curricular experiences is the fact

that it is very difficult to encompass a worth-while set of desired outcomes for pupils within the subject type of design. This is especially true if the entire curriculum is organized on a subject basis. If we carefully compare a widely accepted statement of the outcomes desired from educational experiences provided by the school, such as those presented in Chapter 7, with the types of educational experiences usually provided through a subject curriculum, it becomes apparent that the subject organization does not lend itself to a realization of a number of these desirable outcomes.

In fact, one of the major criticisms of the traditional school—which certainly is subject-organized—listed in Chapter 1 is that it neglects many desirable aspects of pupil growth and development, particularly in the areas of physical growth, social development, and emotional maturation. The subject curriculum concentrates almost altogether on intellectual development. While, of course, intellectual development is a primary function of the school, a modern conception of education recognizes the responsibility of the school to provide experiences that will foster the desirable growth of children in other aspects of personality.[4] In fact, many authorities in the field of mental health maintain that forcing children into a rigid, logically organized subject type of school curriculum may have serious effects on wholesome personality development, since it places many children in situations with which they are not mature enough to cope or forces them to undertake activities and experiences that are frustrating and meaningless to them.[5]

No doubt the rigid subject curriculum that is imposed on them in the secondary school is in considerable measure responsible for pupils dropping out of school prior to completion of a program of secondary education. A study of the required school subjects becomes more or less meaningless to them, they see little relationship between such study and their life needs, and so they lose interest and drop out of school.

Many of the outcomes desired from a modern program of education could, perhaps, be realized through the subject organization of the curriculum but the very traditions of the subject organization militate against the development of experiences designed to obtain broader outcomes. When a teacher teaches geometry and students study geometry, they naturally expect that a primary if not exclusive emphasis is to be placed on the acquisition of geometric facts and principles and learning methods of geometric proof in relation to geometric theorems. If

[4] Harvard University, Committee on the Objectives of a General Education in a Free Society, *General Education in a Free Society* (Cambridge, Mass.: Harvard University Press, 1945), pp. 73–78.

[5] For further discussion of this point see William C. Menninger, "Mental Health in Our Schools," *Educational Leadership*, 7:510–523 (May), 1950.

pupils study spelling, they naturally assume that the outcome desired is to learn to spell the assigned words, not some of the other objectives usually set up for the educational program. Under the subject type of organization it is easy and natural for teachers to assume that the primary objective is the mastery of the subject matter itself and the subjects are looked upon as the ends in themselves. Even though we recognize that this does not have to be the case in a subject organization, unfortunately this is the situation that usually prevails.

3. Subjects per se do not train the mind. While no one should make the error of assuming that all of those who favor the subject design believe in formal discipline, it is nevertheless true that those who believe in formal discipline almost invariably accept the subject design as the essential organization for the school curriculum. If subjects are justified on that basis, we are forced to reject this argument, since research in psychology and research in learning have disproved the old traditional doctrine of formal discipline.[6] There is no authoritative evidence that subjects of an abstract and verbal nature, that deal with abstract ideas and concepts, or that require extensive memorization and mastery of rules and principles have any particular merit as such for training the mind. As human beings we learn what we experience; if we build into experience the techniques, methods, and attitudes of logical thinking, however, from, say, the study of geometry, it is because we have experienced logical thinking and have built it into our own learnings. The methods of logical thinking might equally well or even better be experienced in a class in problems of democracy, agriculture, home economics, or mechanics, or in any number of other areas of learning.

As a matter of fact, the best way to learn logical thinking is by thinking logically about problems that are pertinent and meaningful to us as we face them in our day-by-day living. However, methods of logical thinking will not be built into learning unless attention is given in the experience to the process of logical thinking itself.[7] We need insight with experience. What the modern curriculum worker does is to start with the basic outcomes desired from educational experience and then devise learning activities that will best provide these kinds of outcomes. That is a more logical fashion of building a curriculum than to start with subject matter as such and then attribute a whole gamut of outcomes to

[6] An analysis of the doctrine of formal discipline and the evidence against such a theory are well presented in Boyd H. Bode, *How We Learn* (Boston: D. C. Heath & Company, 1940), Chap. 1–8.

[7] See Harold Fawcett, *The Nature of Proof* (Thirteenth Yearbook, National Council of Teachers of Mathematics; New York: Bureau of Publication, Teachers College, Columbia University, 1938).

it. Learning inheres in experience, not in subject matter in and of itself. It is the quality of the experience the pupil has that is important in determining the outcomes.

4. The subject organization fractionates learning. One of the most serious objections made to the subject type of curriculum organization is that it artificially segments learning experiences, drawing arbitrary lines that seldom exist in actuality. As an individual faces a life situation, he grapples with it as a whole and not on the basis of segments or fractions of knowledge. He must utilize whatever knowledge and understanding is pertinent to the problem or the situation, regardless of the logical divisions of such subject matter that may have been developed by the specialist. The subject curriculum, therefore, sets up an artificial condition that is not lifelike and is not consistent with the way individuals themselves behave as total personalities. In the subject curriculum the learner often sees little relationship between the subjects studied as separate entities, and often fails to organize his learning into a systematic whole in relation to life problems. Even an adult who is a highly trained specialist faces situations as a totality that necessitates the use of knowledge cutting across a number of subject fields.

The noted English philosopher Alfred North Whitehead pointed out the deficiencies of our typical subject curriculum in these terms:

> The result of teaching small parts of a large number of subjects is the passive reception of disconnected ideas, not illumined with any spark of vitality. Let the main ideas which are introduced into a child's education be few and important, and let them be thrown into every combination possible. . . .
>
> The solution which I am urging is to eradicate the fatal disconnection of subjects which kills the vitality of our modern curriculum. There is only one subject-matter for education, and that is Life in all its manifestations.[8]

5. The subject curriculum is not based on a functional use of knowledge. Knowledge does not automatically translate itself into action.[9] The important questions in curriculum planning are these: Knowledge for what? What uses are made of the knowledge that citizens possess? The subject type of curriculum organization in and of itself does not provide the answers to these questions.

Evidence gathered in the famous New York Regents' Inquiry into

[8] Alfred North Whitehead, *The Aims of Education and Other Essays* (New York: The Macmillan Company, 1929), pp. 2–3, 10.

[9] For a further statement on this subject, see William F. Russell, "The Caravan Goes On," *Teachers College Record*, 54:6–7 (October), 1952.

the character and cost of public education in the state of New York brings out sharply the shortcomings of the traditional subject-centered curriculum of the secondary school in carrying over functionally into the life situations faced by pupils after they leave the school. The conclusion was reached that

> *a major reason for young people's lack of success in meeting out-of-school problems is that the secondary schools give them insufficient chance to master important abilities which the out-of-school world will require of them.* What the schools actually teach they teach with reasonable effectiveness, but they fail entirely to teach many significant things which boys and girls are quite unlikely to learn except as the schools do teach them. . . .
>
> If schools in general are to add effectively to their pupils' social competence, it is clear also that they must give much closer attention than most high schools now give to pupils' out-of-school needs. The usual academic curriculum is only remotely related to the pressing out-of-school concerns of the great majority of boys and girls. The subject matter which it includes has been selected because of tradition, or because educated people a generation ago were familiar with that subject matter, or because a few young people will find use for it in college courses. The academic curriculum as a whole rests its claim to general value on faith that it will be effective, and not on any pragmatic testing of its outcomes.[10]

Probably the most serious weakness in the traditional conception of education, and the point most vigorously challenged by modern educators, is the idea that a person who is "educated" in terms of mastering a systematic body of subject matter in various pertinent disciplines of knowledge is therefore an educated person who is able to deal effectively with the problems of living in a democratic country in the present. Empirical evidence seems to indicate that there is in and of itself no close relationship between the mastery of systematic bodies of subject matter represented by the traditional academic or classical curriculum, or by concepts involved in "the great-books approach" in education, and behavior that characterizes the best qualities of democratic citizenship.

This, of course, is not to say that knowledge of subject matter is not essential, for the effective citizen cannot act without adequate knowledge about the situation being faced, and, of course, specialized knowledge is necessary to carry on specialized jobs. It is only to say that the claims made in the past for the traditional subject curriculum, to the effect that a mastery of systematic bodies of subject matter was the best method

---

[10] By permission from *High School and Life*, pp. 149, 155, by Francis T. Spaulding. Copyright 1938. McGraw-Hill Book Company, Inc.

of developing good citizens, are not sound claims in terms of our knowledge of human behavior and the evidence gained from evaluating behavior. Again, it should be kept in mind that the individual learns what he experiences; therefore if he only experiences the understanding of subject matter in systematically organized bodies, that is what he learns. Inevitably, there will be many unplanned learnings, but another error of traditional education was to ignore these concomitant learnings and to place almost sole emphasis and evaluation on the mastery of the subject matter itself. If the individual is to develop an attitude of cooperativeness and mutual helpfulness, he must experience cooperativeness and build it into his personality. Of course, he could experience cooperativeness in working with students in his class in the mastery of subject matter, but he will build such a learning into character only if he recognizes the fact that he is developing cooperativeness and experiencing cooperativeness, not because he just accidentally cooperates with other children in learning algebra. Dewey touches on this point in his statement:

> . . . . no prescribed and ready-made scheme can possibly determine the exact subject-matter that will best promote the educative growth of every individual young person. . . . There is nothing more blindly obtuse than the convention which supposes that the matter actually contained in textbooks of arithmetic, history, geography, etc., is just what will further the educational development of all children.[11]

6. The subject curriculum is seriously limited in the range of the subject matter covered. One of the serious limitations of the traditional subject curriculum lies in the limited range of subject matter that can be encompassed in the typical school program. In the typical subject organization whole areas of knowledge are not treated at all, and many other areas are considered in only an introductory and sketchy fashion. For example, consider the program of high school pupils in the subject type of curriculum. Any one pupil will take from a minimum of fifteen to a maximum of twenty one-year courses in a four-year secondary school program. If some of the courses are offered for only a semester, the number of separate courses taken would increase slightly, but most high school courses are offered as a one-year subject. Since a typical pupil may take two, three, or even four years of course work in one particular field of study, such as English, we see how drastically limited is a student's opportunity to enroll in courses in other fields. This situation is not altered for pupils in large high schools, for even though the school

[11] John Dewey, "The Need for a Philosophy of Education," *New Era*, 15:211–214 (November), 1934.

itself may offer as many as two hundred separate courses of various types, any one student will take only from fifteen to twenty one-year courses. The difference between the large and the small school lies in the choice the student has of subjects to be studied, not in the amount of subject matter that he could take in a four-year program.

This shortcoming of the subject curriculum might be illustrated in the field of science. A secondary school pupil may take the course known as general science, which gives him a brief and sketchy introduction to the disciplines in the science area. He may follow this course with a one-year course in general biological science, and perhaps a one-year course in chemistry and a one-year course in physics. Ordinarily this would comprise the extent of offerings available to the pupil in even the large secondary school. An analysis of these opportunities shows that the pupil has only a very limited knowledge of scientific subject matter. He has had little or no acquaintance with such organized bodies of knowledge as geology, astronomy, bacteriology, botany, zoology, earth science, meteorology, and so on through the field of science. However, unless they are majoring in science, few pupils take more than two courses offered by the school. This means, then, that they will have slight information if any about vast bodies of knowledge in the science field.

The Place of Subjects in Curriculum Designing

A common-sense appraisal of the situation indicates that the subject method of designing the curriculum will continue to be a dominant method of organizing the educational experiences to be provided pupils in the secondary schools. Undoubtedly, for at least a part of the secondary school curriculum, this is as it should be. As pupils mature and develop a broader experiential background, it is highly desirable, and in fact necessary, that they organize their knowledge, understandings, and concepts on some systematic basis so that they will be able to apply these concepts and knowledges to new situations, to see the inner relationships that exist among concepts, principles, and generalizations, and to interpret and understand new knowledge as it is encountered in the future.

The farmer, for example, organizes his knowledge about stock raising into some systematic pattern, so that he is able to apply the things he knows about stock raising to the practical problems he faces in fattening his cattle for market, in increasing milk production, or in trying to develop a more profitable breed of swine. Out of all the things he has learned from practical, firsthand experience, from reading, from conversations, from lectures, and the like, he organizes a body of practical knowledge that helps him handle the day-by-day situations that confront him or helps him make plans for the future. Also, his organized body of knowledge aids him in interpreting and making use of new information or new research that he comes across from time to time; so he constantly rebuilds his knowledge of stock raising through new discoveries of his own, new material he reads, and experiences shared by other stock raisers and by agricultural experiment workers.

Similarly, the pupil, as he matures and broadens his stock of learnings about a matter of importance to him, will need to organize them into some systematic understanding of that particular area of human activity. Certainly the very youngest child begins to organize his knowledge and learnings from the very earliest of his learning experiences, and as the child matures into an adolescent the need for opportunities to organize his knowledge in terms of broad areas of human experiences increases. Contrary to the position assigned him by critics, Dewey also saw the need for systematically organizing our knowledge: "The next step [in learning] is the progressive development of what is already experienced into a fuller and richer and also more organized form, a form that gradually approximates that in which subject-matter is presented to the skilled, mature person." [12]

Even though the desirability, yes even the necessity, of organizing subject matter for functional use at the upper school level is granted, we must hasten to say that this does not argue for (1) the retention of the same list of subjects traditionally offered in the secondary school, or (2) the use of the subject type of curriculum design for the entire school life of the secondary school pupil. Furthermore, the desirability of using rigid subject organization for younger and less mature pupils in the elementary school is particularly questionable.

THE BROAD FIELD TYPE OF CURRICULUM DESIGN

The Nature of the Broad Field Approach

The broad field type of curriculum organization represents a modification of the traditional subject design. This type of design constitutes the least break with the traditional subject organization; yet it seeks to eliminate some of the difficulties or shortcomings of this latter approach. The broad field design eliminates the sharp demarcations that exist in the traditional subjects; it seeks rather to bring together into a broad organization of the subject matter the knowledge and understandings pertinent to a whole area of study. It represents an effort to "fuse" and "integrate" (two terms that have been used in curriculum planning) the

[12] John Dewey, *Experience and Education* (New York: The Macmillan Company, 1938), p. 87. Reprinted by permission of The Macmillan Company, publishers.

subject matter of closely related disciplines or school subjects. Strictly speaking, it is a subject approach, but one in which the basis of selecting and organizing subject matter is different from that used in the traditional subjects.

The broad field approach may best be illustrated by citing the course in biology now commonly taught in many secondary schools. This recently developed course represents an effort to bring together into one instructional unit the knowledge, concepts, and principles from the highly specialized disciplines of botany, physiology, zoology, anatomy, bacteriology, and similar closely related subject matter areas. Likewise, courses designated as general science, advanced science, or physical science represent efforts to bring together important subject matter from such disciplines as physics, chemistry, anthropology, geology, astronomy, and the like. In the field of the social studies, efforts have been made to amalgamate the highly specialized disciplines of political science, sociology, cultural anthropology, history, geography, and the like into broad courses simply designated as social science, problems of democracy, or a similar title.

Efforts to build broad field courses of this type have been particularly extensive at the college level. Many colleges have developed a so-called survey type of course or a general education course that represents efforts to bring together the essential understandings and knowledges of a whole area of subject matter. The work required in general education in such institutions as the University of Chicago, Harvard University, Michigan State College, Columbia University, University of Iowa, and a large number of other institutions is centered in such integrated or survey type of broad field courses.[13]

Use of Broad Fields in Elementary Schools

The broad field type of design has been used rather widely in the elementary school, particularly in recent years. The plan used in the elementary school is not strictly the same as that used in the colleges or in the secondary schools; yet it utilizes the same techniques. Thus, in the elementary school the individual subjects of reading, spelling, and writing have been replaced by a broader subject area designated as the language arts or the communicative arts. Similarly, the separate subjects of history, geography, and civics have been replaced by a broad subject field simply designated as the social studies. Science, which is gaining great headway in the elementary school, has never been broken

[13] For a more complete discussion of this approach see *General Education in a Free Society,* cited above.

up into the specialized subjects taught in secondary schools and colleges, but the old subject of nature study has been replaced by a broad approach to the development of science understandings through a course simply designated as science. Some schools have also offered a general arts course for the development of creative experiences rather than providing separate courses in music, drawing, handicraft, and the like.

In fact, the movement to change to a broader basis of curriculum organization in the elementary school has been so extensive that very few modern schools still adhere to the rigid, strict subject schedule that characterized elementary schools of a quarter of a century or more ago. In the schools of that day it was quite common for the school day to be broken up into short ten- to twenty-minute periods, depending on the number of grades assigned to any one teacher, in which the children recited on the various subjects that made up the curriculum. The modern elementary school often uses quite long periods of time in which instruction is offered in terms of the broad fields of the language arts, the social sciences, the general arts, science, arithmetic, and physical education, health, and recreation.

Broad Field Courses in the Secondary School

Within the last thirty years or so a number of courses that we might designate as the broad field type of course have been developed in the secondary schools of this country. Biology, general science, and advanced science have already been cited. Likewise, many schools are using the problem type of course in the field of social studies, such as problems of democracy, American institutions, and similar courses to integrate the social sciences. Also, new courses have been developed in the area of family living or problems of marriage that often represent an integration of subject matter from the fields of home economics, psychology, and sociology. Some schools have developed new types of courses in the communicative arts. These schools usually organize into a common course what was previously taught in separate courses in English, speech, and even dramatics. The course designated as general mathematics has had a rather wide acceptance in the secondary school. This course represents an effort to bring together for general students basic mathematical skills and understandings from the fields of arithmetic, algebra, geometry, and perhaps simple trigonometry. Some efforts have also been made to develop a general language course, although this has not had widespread acceptance.

It is probably quite accurate to say that many of the subjects now taught in the secondary school have been considerably modified, if not completely reorganized, as a result of the impact of the broad field approach to curriculum design. Even subjects that might still be designated by the traditional subject names have been broadened in scope. For example, the course in American history often draws on geography, political science, and even economics to a much greater extent than was true a quarter of a century ago. The same thing could be said of separate subjects in the field of science, such as chemistry, physics, and anatomy. More effort is made to draw on subject matter that is, strictly speaking, a part of closely allied disciplines. A number of schools, particularly junior high schools, have indicated their swing to the broad field approach by eliminating specific course titles for subjects offered; instead, they designate their courses by such titles as Science I, Science II, and Science III, or Social Studies I, Social Studies II, and Social Studies III. The content of the course is then developed by the teachers on the basis of previous planning by faculty committees and by the use of staff-prepared curriculum guides rather than on the basis of textbooks prepared by specialists.

Basis for Organizing Broad Field Courses

To organize a broad field type of course is not easy. Since the development of these courses is relatively a recent venture, curriculum workers have not had as extensive a body of experience in organizing them as they have for the traditional subject organization. Needless to say, the body of experience is growing and better methods for organizing broad field courses are constantly being developed. In the early efforts to broaden the narrow subject organization, the content of the new course largely consisted of a selection of the most essential subject matter from each of the separate subjects to be included in the new broad field course. Curriculum workers and textbook writers who understood the necessity of broadening the traditional subject curriculum were not content with this early approach to the broad field organization, and considerable attention was devoted to the problem of developing a more satisfactory organization for such new courses. The bases commonly adopted were broad generalizations or principles, real life problems, or aspects of social living pertinent to the field of knowledge. The fields of science and social studies best illustrate the use of these methods of synthesizing knowledge. In fact, the greatest advances in developing the broad field type of course for the elementary and secondary schools have been in these two areas of study. Specialists in each of these fields have devoted tireless efforts and a great deal of research study to the evolvement of new and better methods for organizing and integrating the content of the science and the social studies fields into broader, integrated types of courses. It is not necessary here to cite all of these research studies and the numerous pronouncements that have been made by specialists about the bases of organizing the content in their respective fields.

By way of illustration, in the field of science the usual approach is to organize the broad field courses around the most important scientific principles that underlie the whole area of science. Sometimes these principles or generalizations are stated in terms of the problems that man faces in living in the modern natural world. These new strands of organization may be illustrated by citing the titles of units included in a modern secondary school text in the field of biological sciences.

Unit 1: Problems and Characteristics of Living Things
Unit 2: Using Our Biological Resources Wisely
Unit 3: The World's Food Supply
Unit 4: Food and Life
Unit 5: The Conquest of Disease
Unit 6: The Behaviors of Living Things
Unit 7: Life Continues from Age to Age
Unit 8: Kinds of Life[14]

Integration of the traditional disciplines of the social sciences into broad field courses has been extensive. Rugg did some of the pioneering efforts in this movement, and his work has received widespread attention. It was his contention, and it is the point of view of many other workers in this field, that the whole area of the social sciences should be reorganized at the elementary and secondary school levels. He stated his point of view thus: "We must invent a new synthesis of knowledge and make it the basis of the entire school curriculum. The conventional barriers between the existing subjects must be ignored in curriculum-making. The *starting point* shall be the social institution, or the political and economic problem,—not the subject." [15]

Arguments Advanced in Favor of the Broad Field Type of Curriculum Organization

Since the broad field approach is a variant of the subject type of design, much of the discussion in that section relative to the merits and faults of the subject design are pertinent to the analysis of the broad field type of organization. Hence only brief attention will be given here to several additional factors.

[14] Francis B. Curtis and John Urban, *Biology in Daily Life* (Boston: Ginn and Company, 1949), pp. x–xi.
[15] Harold Rugg, "A Preface to the Reconstruction of the American School Curriculum," *Teachers College Record*, 27:607 (March), 1926. Reprinted by permission of the Bureau of Publications, Teachers College, Columbia University.

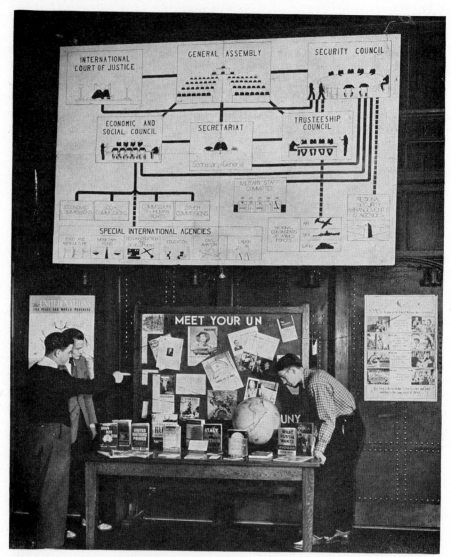

PLATE 18. A STUDY OF THE UNITED NATIONS ORGANIZATION UTILIZES VARIOUS FIELDS OF KNOWLEDGE. *In studying such topics as the United Nations' organization, pupils integrate knowledge from a number of specialized disciplines. (Courtesy of the Baltimore Public Schools)*

1. Integration of subject matter is facilitated by the broad field approach. Obviously, the one thing that distinguishes the broad field approach from the subject organization is the effort made to integrate a number of disciplines into one area of study. This has the decided advantage of bringing together for the pupil bodies of closely related knowledge, so that interrelationships are more easily understood and so that a broader approach to the understanding of society and the problems of living and to the application of knowledge to present-day affairs are more easily attained. In fact, the primary purpose of the broad field approach is to bring about what many educators consider to be a needed integration of subject matter into a broader organization that is more meaningful to the learner.

The broad field approach represents an effort to tear down the walls that have separated classrooms in the past, so that instead of the youngster's studying history for forty minutes, then studying geography or civics for forty minutes, or studying them separately in consecutive years, the pupil considers these two closely related bodies of information at the same time. Thus, in the study of the United Nations Organization, such as is illustrated in Plate 18, pupils may bring together knowledge from closely related disciplines in discussing problems that face us as citizens. Similarly, it is much better for youngsters to consider facts and principles about living organisms growing up in a natural environment than it is to study plants in a separate course of botany, man as an organism in a course of physiology, and other animals as organisms in a course in zoology. The subject matter becomes much more meaningful to the typical immature pupil when it is organized into a coherent body of knowledge that more closely parallels actual conditions of living in the natural world.

2. *The broad field type of organization provides for a more functional organization of knowledge.* As most broad field type of courses have developed in the elementary and secondary school, a more functional organization of knowledge has usually resulted. Of course, the merit of this argument depends entirely on the method used to organize the courses, but the whole trend is to organize the subject matter on a much more meaningful basis in terms of the ongoing concerns and the actual life situations faced by learners. Particularly is this true of broad field courses developed in the elementary grades and in the junior high school. Senior high school and college level courses are often still quite abstract.

3. *The broad field organization enables the school to encompass more subject matter and to provide a broader understanding of modern affairs.* It has already been noted that one of the shortcomings of the subject type of organization is the fact that a pupil can study only a limited number of subjects. The broad field organization overcomes this

criticism to some extent in that it integrates a number of closely allied subjects so that the pupil will be able to gain at least a general understanding of more extensive areas of knowledge. It enables him to have at least a greater awareness of the whole gamut of human knowledge than is possible in the usual subject type of organization. This is perhaps the chief contribution of this modification of the traditional subject curriculum.

4. The broad field courses place emphasis on basic principles and generalizations, rather than on information and facts. This approach probably places less emphasis on the mastery of detailed information, dates, and facts, all of which may soon be forgotten, than the subject type of curriculum entails. By putting the emphasis on basic principles and concepts, it is felt that the learner will have a better working knowledge of the field than he would have if he simply acquired a mass of facts and data which he himself must often synthesize into some workable scheme of knowledge.

Shortcomings of the Broad Field Approach

As has already been stated, the broad field design is a modification of the subject approach, so most of the shortcomings charged against the latter apply with equal weight to the former. However, the broad field approach has several additional shortcomings of its own.

1. The broad field approach provides only a sketchy knowledge of a subject area. In view of the nature of broad field courses, particularly at the secondary school level, it is claimed by some critics that the pupil is given only a smattering of information about a number of subjects, and that he does not have an opportunity to gain any real knowledge of any one area. It is maintained that he merely gets a very general introduction to areas of knowledge and that because of the necessity of introducing many topics and aspects of the field into this type of course the pupil does not really penetrate deeply into the subject matter of any area. The result is that he may become acquainted with quite a mass of information and knowledge about a broad field, but will not have much of a body of working knowledge or information about any one subject.

The broad field approach prevents the learner from specializing in a subject matter field or acquiring basic skills and abilities which characterize people who are educated in the subject type of curriculum. Thus it is felt that he has a smattering of knowledge, but is not really a scholar.

2. The broad field approach may result in an abstract, academic type of course that is beyond the grasp of many students. In contrast to the usual argument for this approach it is charged by some critics that the principles, generalizations, or problems used as a basis for synthesizing knowledge are too abstract for ready apprehension by the typical school pupil. It is maintained that the illustrative and explanatory materials that do much to enable the average learner to understand a subject and to give him a basis for interpreting principles and generalizing on his own are squeezed out of the subject when it is amalgamated into a fused type of broad field course. It is claimed that because of the interest in covering as many essential principles and basic generalizations as possible, these are strung together one after the other, with the minimum of discussion, explanation, and illustrative material. The average pupil—in fact, most pupils at the immature adolescent level—is rather overwhelmed with abstract learning of this kind and loses interest in the subject or fails to grasp the real meaning of much of the subject matter. The subject has become more abstract and more difficult than it ever was under the traditional subject organization.

3. *The broad field type of course does not enable the learner to grasp the inherent logic of subject matter.* One charge made against the broad field approach is that by attempting to integrate what are logically developed disciplines the unitary discipline of a subject field is eliminated in favor of a new method of organization. This prevents the learner from grasping and gaining an understanding of the inherent logic of a subject field. He does not obtain experience in the methods of analyzing and synthesizing knowledge in terms of an inherent logic or basic principles that formulate the organizing strands of a particular body of subject matter.

For example, it is maintained that general mathematics is just a smattering of introductory concepts in several fields of mathematics and does not present a logically organized system of symbolic thinking and abstraction that characterizes study of a specific field of mathematics, such as algebra, geometry, trigonometry, and the like. Similarly, it is maintained that the broad field type of social studies course flounders around in introductory concepts and interesting material about human affairs and human institutions, but does not really come to grips with the systematic analysis and subsequent synthesis of generalizations or principles basic to any particular area of human behavior or of human institutions.

The Place of the Broad Fields in Curriculum Design

Even a casual observer of curriculum development in our elementary and secondary schools recognizes that the broad field approach for organizing at least a part of the curriculum of a school is well established and accepted. Certainly there is no indication that curriculum workers in the elementary school who use this method will want to abandon it to return to the old subjects. Those who have used a longer period for the teaching of communicative arts as a field, for example, will seldom if ever want to return to short individual periods for spelling, penmanship, reading, and literature. Similarly, in the secondary school there is no indication that such courses as general science, biology, and advanced science will decline in importance. In fact, the whole trend in the secondary school is to plan course offerings in terms of a broader approach.

The fields of social studies and science have already been used as illustrations. Homemaking courses are tending more and more to be organized on an integrated basis around problems and phases of home and family living rather than around the specialized areas of cooking, sewing, and the like. In the field of business education, courses in general business and office practice have become quite accepted in secondary schools. General shop courses and arts and crafts programs also illustrate the trend. In the various subject fields of the secondary school curriculum other examples may be cited of the tendency to develop broader, more integrated types of courses in contrast to the highly specialized, narrow type of subjects that characterized the curriculum a quarter of a century ago. No doubt the emphasis placed on general education in recent years has stimulated this effort.

The main problem facing curriculum workers in utilizing this type of organization is to find the most satisfactory bases or methods for organizing the subject matter in terms of the integrated approach. Without question, some of the broad field types of courses that have been developed in recent years have not always used satisfactory procedures for organizing the subject matter of the field. But it must be recognized that these are initiatory efforts. A number of promising approaches in the organization of the subject matter of the broad fields should be tried. It will be necessary, also, in using the broad field approach, to overcome some of the shortcomings listed above. It is difficult to cover the vast body of subject matter encompassed in a broad field within acceptable limits of grade and secondary school courses of study and yet on the one hand to develop an understanding of basic principles and concepts in that field, and on the other to make the subject interesting, meaningful, and understandable to pupils. It is difficult to strike a proper balance between abstractions and interesting and worth-while information that clarifies principles.

We need to see the broad field type of organization in relation to other methods of curriculum design before we can propose an over-all pattern for curriculum organization. Hence we make no commitment to the broad field plan at this point. In Chapter 9 other methods of organizing the curriculum will be examined, and in Chapter 10 considerable attention will be given to the development of core curriculum programs in the schools of this country. The reader will then have a broader view of the whole problem of curriculum organization.

For Further Study

Alberty, Harold, *Reorganizing the High-School Curriculum.* Rev. ed.; New York: The Macmillan Company, 1953.

Chapter V discusses the subject type of curriculum organization.

Bathurst, Effie, Paul E. Blackwood, Helen K. MacIntosh, and Elsa Schneider, *The Place of Subjects in the Curriculum.* U.S. Office of Education Bulletin 1949, No. 12. Washington, D.C.: Government Printing Office, 1949.

Discusses the subject design with special reference to the elementary school.

Dewey, John, *Experience and Education.* New York: The Macmillan Company, 1938.

A very important statement on some of the basic problems of designing the curriculum. Pleads for continuity of experience and recognizes the need for organizing experience.

Featherstone, William B., *A Functional Curriculum for Youth.* New York: American Book Company, 1950.

Discusses various approaches to designing the secondary school curriculum, but presents a strong case for the subject and broad field approaches.

Hand, Harold C., "The Whip Socket Stereotype," *Educational Leadership,* 5:117–118 (November), 1947.

A pointed comment on the design of the curriculum.

Harvard University, The Committee on the Objectives of a General Education in a Free Society, *General Education in a Free Society.* Cambridge, Mass.: Harvard University Press, 1945.

A defense of the subject framework for the curriculum, with a presentation of the broad aspects of the subject fields that should comprise the curriculum.

Herrick, Virgil, and Ralph Tyler (comps.), *Toward Improved Curriculum Theory.* Chicago: The University of Chicago Press, 1950.

Section II presents three papers on the organization of the curriculum.

Hopkins, L. Thomas, *Interaction: The Democratic Process.* Boston: D. C. Heath & Company, 1941.

Chapter IX presents a particular point of view on curriculum designing; Chapters I and II discuss various approaches to curriculum design.

Lee, J. Murray, and Dorris M. Lee, *The Child and His Curriculum.* 2d ed.; New York: Appleton-Century-Crofts, Inc., 1950.

Chapter 6 presents criteria for judging the adequacy of curriculum experiences and other aspects of curriculum organization; Chapter 7 discusses the unit of work approach to design in the elementary school.

Leonard, J. Paul, *Developing the Secondary School Curriculum*. Rev. ed.; New York: Rinehart & Company, Inc., 1953.

A general consideration of problems of designing the curriculum with several chapters considering the subject design.

Mackenzie, Gordon N., "Curriculum Patterns for the Modern Secondary School," *Bulletin*, National Association of Secondary School Principals, No. 162, 33:124–133 (April), 1949.

An excellent discussion of problems of designing the curriculum and of the development of school subjects as a basis for design.

Mosier, Richard D., "A Logical Analysis of Subject Matter," *Journal of Educational Research*, 44:373–379 (January), 1951.

Discusses a basis for organizing subject matter.

Otto, Henry J., *Principles of Elementary Education*. Rinehart & Company, Inc., 1949.

Chapters 5 through 8 present a basic plan for the elementary school curriculum that is largely subject-centered.

Rugg, Harold (ed.), *Democracy and the Curriculum*. Third Yearbook of the John Dewey Society. New York: Appleton-Century-Crofts, Inc., 1939.

Chapter XV is one of the early discussions of curriculum planning in which the term "design" is used.

Smith, B. Othaniel, W. O. Stanley, and J. H. Shores, *Fundamentals of Curriculum Development*. Yonkers, N.Y.: World Book Company, 1950.

Chapters 12, 16, and 17 are pertinent to a study of the subject approach to curriculum organization.

chapter 9

Newer Approaches to Curriculum Design

In the previous chapter attention was given to the organization of the curriculum, and the traditional subject type of design and a modification of it were discussed. It was stated that design is the basis used to select, organize, and carry forward learning experience. The two approaches analyzed are primarily oriented to the culture. In this chapter consideration will be given to two additional possibilities for organizing curriculum experiences. These approaches take greater account of the individual and his needs and concerns as factors in the educative process.

THE SOCIAL FUNCTIONS METHOD OF ORGANIZING THE CURRICULUM

The Nature of the Social Functions Approach

The method of organizing curriculum experiences through the social functions approach is of relatively recent origin, although it might easily be claimed that its roots extend back to Herbert Spencer's five categories of the significant types of activities that constitute human life. The advocates of this approach believe that curriculum workers should organize learning experiences in terms of the major activities of mankind as he lives in his culture. Since education has as its primary function the aiding of the individual to live the good life of his social group it is felt that pupils should be given experiences that will best enable them to carry on these basic life activities in the most acceptable manner. Thus it is maintained that a curriculum based on an analysis of life activities will have maximum value and significance to the pupil in his day-by-day activities as well as later enable him to participate most effectively in adult life.

Consequently, those who use the major social functions of living approach to curriculum designing draw heavily on cultural anthropology and sociology to obtain a penetrating analysis of the major life activities of mankind. The organizing centers for this type of design become what the curriculum worker generalizes as the major concerns or activities of groups living together as a society. Both primitive and modern social groups are analyzed to determine what these major social functions of living seem to be. We may think of them as the important types of activities about which the work, leisure, and family activities of people as individuals and as members of a group seem to cluster. This approach assumes that learning activities in school should have a direct and functional relationship to these activities of social groups.

Aspects of Life's Activities

Obviously, one of the major tasks facing curriculum workers in utilizing this basis for designing the curriculum is to define the major social functions of living. Probably one of the first modern efforts to classify man's aspects of living was that made by Herbert Spencer, who listed these five major types of activities as constituting human life:

1. Those activities which directly minister to self-preservation
2. Those activities which, by securing necessaries of life, indirectly minister to self-preservation
3. Those activities which have for their end the rearing and discipline of offspring
4. Those activities which are involved in the maintenance of proper social and political relations
5. Those miscellaneous activities which make up the leisure part of life, devoted to the gratification of the tastes and feelings[1]

The first organized efforts to apply the major social functions of living concept to the organization of the curriculum or at least a portion of it was made in a number of states whose curriculum committees worked under the direction of Hollis L. Caswell at George Peabody College for Teachers. Many state and city school systems were actively engaged in efforts to reorganize and improve the curriculum of the schools in the 1930's. Educational officials in a number of these states sought counsel from the Division of Field Studies of George Peabody College. Caswell was appointed to serve as the consultant to these state committees. The social functions method of organizing the curriculum was first formulated and used in the Virginia State Curriculum Program, for it was there that committees, working under his direction, developed a scope and sequence chart for the curriculum and formulated curriculum guides for teachers which utilized this approach. The over-all state committee set out eleven

---

[1] Herbert Spencer, *Education* (New York: Appleton-Century-Crofts, Inc., 1860), pp. 13–14.

major functions of social life as the broad aspects around which the core part of the curriculum should be developed:

1. Protection and conservation of life, property, and natural resources
2. Production of goods and services and distribution of the returns of production
3. Consumption of goods and services
4. Communication and transportation of goods and people
5. Recreation
6. Expression of aesthetic impulses
7. Expression of religious impulses
8. Education
9. Extension of freedom
10. Integration of the individuals
11. Exploration[2]

Other states that later utilized the same approach included Mississippi, Georgia, Arkansas, Florida, and Kansas.

Following this initial attempt to define the major areas of living, some analysis of pronouncement by authorities and of research in appropriate areas produced a statement defining the major social functions of the living:

1. Protecting life and health
2. Getting a living
3. Making a home
4. Expressing religious impulses
5. Satisfying the desire for beauty
6. Securing education
7. Cooperating in social and civic action
8. Engaging in recreation
9. Improving material conditions[3]

These nine areas of living were used as a basis for curriculum organization in most of the other states that prepared curriculum guides embodying this approach. Table 7, which is a portion of the scope and sequence chart developed for the Mississippi state program, illustrates this approach.

One of the most recent efforts to design a curriculum based on the major activities of man is the work of Stratemeyer, Forkner, and McKim. In developing a comprehensive plan for designing a modern

[2] Virginia State Board of Education, *Tentative Course of Study for Virginia Elementary Schools* (Richmond, Va.: State Board of Education, 1934), p. 16.

[3] O. I. Frederick and Lucille Farquear, "Areas of Human Activity," *Journal of Educational Research,* 30:672–679 (May), 1937.

TABLE 7

Relation of Suggestive Units to the Curriculum Framework, Mississippi Program for the Improvement of Instruction

(Grade and center of interest)

Major Phases of Life	Grade IV—Life in Markedly Different Physical Environments	Grade V—Influences of Discoveries and Travel upon Living	Grade VI—Development of Inventions, Agencies, and Tools of Civilization
I. Protecting Life and Health	Seasons in Our Country Safety	Preventing Disease Making Our Community Healthy	Preventing and Controlling Floods
II. Making a Home	A Trip up the Congo River Where Did My Breakfast Come From? How We Get Our Automobile Tires How We Protect Our Wild Life Kinds of Farms in Mississippi Frogs and Toads	Homes in a City	Modernizing Our Homes
III. Conserving and Improving Material Conditions	How the People Live in Switzerland How People Live in Holland Market Day in France Living in a Large City	Improving Plant Life Getting Fuels (how we use and obtain fuels) Securing Materials for Shelter (how we use and obtain building material)	Conserving Our Forests The Factories at Work in Our Community Canning Our Food Products How the Race Has Recorded Its Progress
IV. Cooperating in Social and Civic Action	Uses of Our Domestic Animals Growing and Using Grain in Mississippi Fishing in Mississippi	How We Control Malaria	Improving Our Methods of Communication How We Can Help Prevent Crime How We Send Messages The School Bank
V. Getting a Living	Going to School in Japan	Trucking and Gardening in Mississippi Use of Cars, Buses, and Trucks	Dairying in Mississippi Growing and Using Cotton Developing and Using Our Electricity

Courtesy of Mississippi State Department of Education, *Curriculum Reorganization in the Elementary School* (Jackson, Miss.: The Department, 1939), p. 31.

TABLE 7 *continued*

Major Phases of Life	Grade IV—Life in Markedly Different Physical Environments	Grade V—Influences of Discoveries and Travel upon Living	Grade VI—Development of Inventions, Agencies, and Tools of Civilization
VI. Securing an Education	Holidays and Festivals in Other Lands	Traveling in the United States Interesting Places in Mississippi Latin American Neighbors	School Newspaper
VII. Expressing Religious Impulses	Christmas (toys from other lands)	Religious Denominations in Mississippi	Going to Church in Mississippi Giving a Religious Pageant
VIII. Expressing Aesthetic Impulses	An International Fair	Puppet Show	Giving Life to the Dramatic Instinct
IX. Engaging in Recreation	A Trip up the Congo River A Winter in Norway	Participation in and Choosing Recreation (picture shows, radios, reading, hobbies) Recognizing and Protecting Our Birds	Making a School Museum What Clubs Should I Join in School and Community?

school curriculum, these workers utilized the concept of persistent life situations which learners face.[4] In presenting their proposal these authors state:

> The learner and the society of which he is a part are brought into relationship and the needed synthesis achieved when the situations of everyday living which children and youth are facing are seen as aspects of persistent life situations with which all members of society must be able to deal.
>
> . . . The scope of the curriculum lies in the range of the persistent life situations with which every individual deals in some measure; its sequence and continuity, in the changing aspects of these persisting situations as the learner moves from childhood into the

[4] Florence B. Stratemeyer, Hamden L. Forkner, and Margaret McKim, *Developing a Curriculum for Modern Living* (New York: Bureau of Publications, Teachers College, Columbia University, 1947).

full responsibilities of adulthood; its contribution, in widening horizons and in relating individual needs and those of society. [5]

Stratemeyer, Forkner, and McKim list these persistent life situations as follows:

I. *Situations calling for growth in individual capacities*
    A. Health
        1. Satisfying physiological needs
        2. Satisfying emotional and social needs
        3. Avoiding and caring for illness and injury
    B. Intellectual power
        1. Making ideas clear
        2. Understanding the ideas of others
        3. Dealing with quantitative relationships
        4. Using effective methods of work
    C. Responsibility for moral choices
        1. Determining the nature and extent of individual freedom
        2. Determining responsibility to self and others
    D. Aesthetic expression and appreciation
        1. Finding sources of aesthetic satisfactions in oneself
        2. Achieving aesthetic satisfactions through the environment

II. *Situations calling for growth in social participation*
    A. Person-to-person relationships
        1. Establishing effective social relations with others
        2. Establishing effective working relations with others
    B. Group membership
        1. Deciding when to join a group
        2. Participating as a group member
        3. Taking leadership responsibilities
    C. Intergroup relationships
        1. Working with racial and religious groups
        2. Working with socio-economic groups
        3. Dealing with groups organized for specific action

III. *Situations calling for growth in ability to deal with environmental factors and forces*
    A. Natural phenomena
        1. Dealing with physical phenomena

[5] *Ibid.*, pp. 73–74. Reprinted by permission of the Bureau of Publications, Teachers College, Columbia University.

    2. Dealing with plant, animal, and insect life
    3. Using physical and chemical forces
  B. Technological resources
    1. Using technological resources
    2. Contributing to technological advance
  C. Economic-social-political structures and forces
    1. Earning a living
    2. Securing goods and services
    3. Providing for social welfare
    4. Molding public opinion
    5. Participating in local and national government[6]

Further subdivisions are made of each of these major types of activity. A comprehensive chart, extending for 170 closely printed pages, is presented in which suggestions are made for types of learning experiences that might appropriately be used to help youngsters develop needed knowledge, attitudes, ways of working, and the like, in dealing with these persistent life problems.

Arguments Advanced in Favor of the Major Social Functions of Living Approach to Curriculum Design

1. The major social functions of living approach provides for learning experiences that are closely related to the life activities of learners. Since the learning experiences selected and organized by the school are based on major areas of living, the pupil, obviously, will see the direct relationship of these experiences to his day-by-day activities and the day-by-day activities of adults. While a pupil may have difficulty in seeing the relationship between the study of American history, or chemistry, or the reading of a literary selection and his day-by-day activities outside the school or even the activities of his parents, this difficulty is obviated in the functions of living approach. Moreover, he acquires an understanding of the social situations and problems he faces as an individual and will be confronted with as a mature citizen of our society.

For example, if some of the pupil's curriculum experiences are organized around the major social activity of "getting a living," the youngster will probably obtain information about various kinds of work in which people engage, opportunities for employment, procedures for obtaining a job, purposes and functions of labor unions, problems of management involved in carrying on a business, governmental requirements and agencies designed to assist or protect both workers and management, interdependence of people, qualities that make for success in jobs, and

---

[6] *Ibid.*, pp. 106–118. Reprinted by permission of the Bureau of Publications, Teachers College, Columbia University.

many other things of this kind. It is maintained that this approach to curriculum design does not leave to chance a direct application of what is learned in school to the life activities of the individual. What he learns in a subject curriculum may not always be utilized in practical, workaday situations because the pupil does not see the relationship of school learning to his life outside the school. The functions approach is an effort to bridge the gap between academic learning in school and its application to life.

2. Learning experiences under the major social functions of living design are more significant and meaningful to the learner. This claimed advantage of the major social functions of living approach has been alluded to in the previous section, but it should be listed separately. As has already been indicated, if this method of selecting and organizing learning experiences is fully utilized, the activities in which the youngster engages in school will be more meaningful to him and he will see a real purpose in them. It is more likely that under such a type of curriculum design the school would utilize a great deal of real experience, providing a wide variety of learning activities outside the school itself. Trips to community institutions, agencies, places of business, and other points of interest are more likely to take place in such a program than in the traditional subject curriculum, since the functions of living plan would be difficult to carry on without such firsthand experience, study, and observation. Presumably, under a program of this kind the pupils will be much more likely to develop worthy purposes and motives and will have much more interest in carrying forward learning activities, since they have meaning and significance to the pupils themselves.

3. The major social functions of living approach contributes directly to the social obligations of the school. Since the school has a primary responsibility to perpetuate the basic social values held by the society, the advocates of the major social functions of living approach feel that it best enables the school to discharge this obligation. If pupils study the major aspects of group life, it is believed that they will more properly be prepared to live in the society and to participate effectively in its improvement. They will be aware of the major phases of living that concern members of the social group, they will have a better understanding of each of these important aspects of living as it relates to their own lives, and they will be in a position to help bring about improvement in the various life activities of mankind.

4. The major social functions of living approach provides for better integration of learning experiences. This approach to curriculum design can very well provide for a better integration of the school experiences of the youngster than does the subject curriculum. It has already been noted that one criticism of this latter approach is the discrete nature of learning experiences as they are organized around units of subject matter. It is maintained that the core part of the curriculum organized under the social functions of living plan provides a better integration of learning experiences since such units of experience would utilize whatever specialized aspects of subject matter might be pertinent to the problem under consideration.

Shortcomings of the Major Social Functions of Living Approach

In spite of the favorable aspects of this method of organizing the curriculum, it has some shortcomings; moreover, there are some practical difficulties involved in its use.

1. The major social functions of living approach may result in an artificial organization of learning activities. In spite of the statement above that the social functions approach may bring about better integration of the curriculum, it must also be recognized that a program as highly fragmented as the subject curriculum may result. On the very basis of dividing up life's activities into various functions, the curriculum design itself suggests artificial divisions. If the units of work are organized as more or less discrete bits of experience devoted to the various areas of living in rotation, the lines of demarcation might become as sharp as they are under the traditional procedure.

In the early use of this plan, as in the Virginia state course of study, such compartmentalization was indicated in the over-all guide to scope and sequence. In later applications, as in the Mississippi and Kansas programs, this weakness was corrected to a large extent by the use of the various aspects of social living as bases for guiding the selection of learning units, rather than as organizing centers for the units themselves. When used in this way, the plan would be less apt to result in an unnatural breakdown of experience.

However, it should be pointed out that any curriculum must be organized on some basis, and that a division among learning experiences included in the program is necessary. If the major social functions of living type of design is used as a basis for evaluating the breadth and scope of the program and for selecting broad types of learning activities that aid pupils with the problems of living, it can serve a most useful purpose in curriculum planning.

2. The major areas of social living are adult rationalizations and not genuine life activities. Critics of this plan of curriculum organization maintain that the schemes presented to date represent adult rationalizations about life activities rather than statements of life activities of people themselves. It is maintained that the activities of human beings do not fall discretely into nine or eleven or any number of areas which can be so carefully analyzed and classified. Life's activities frequently cut across any number or even all of the so-called areas of social living that have been defined by curriculum workers. While at one particular time an adult may be primarily concerned in getting a living, he may at the same time be engaged in carrying on many other of the so-called life activities proposed by curriculum workers, such as cooperating in social and civic action, improving material conditions, protecting life and health, or similar aspects. Even a simple act of living cannot be strictly classified into one and only one of these categories; certainly more complex activities of human beings would be more difficult to so classify.

Again, in relation to this criticism of the plan, it must be pointed out that the social areas of living categories are best used as criteria or bases for judging the adequacy of the curriculum and for guiding the selection and planning of the learning experiences rather than as themselves constituting elements for organizing specific learning activities.

3. The major social functions of living approach may slight some highly desirable outcomes of the educational program. It is of course apparent that some of the chief advantages of the subject type of organization, as presented in the previous chapter, very well represent shortcomings of any other type of curriculum organization. So in this case those that see much merit in the subject type of organization would criticize the major social functions approach as minimizing the systematic study of various bodies of human knowledge with the result that the learner does not acquire important insights, understandings, and generalizations that he should possess, and presumably would gain from a curriculum organization of the subject type.

These same critics assert that the social functions of living approach puts too much emphasis on the here and now and on what might often prove to be quite temporary and ephemeral aspects of living, neglecting to help pupils attain basic information and understanding that would be useful as long as they live. Moreover, these critics would maintain that this type of design does not lend itself to a proper organization of learning, so that the learner has not been helped in systematizing his knowledge and in developing generalizations, principles, and concepts such as he would have attained in a study of logically organized subject matter itself.

The answer to this criticism is largely contained in the objections made to the traditional subject type of design as presented earlier. The proponents of the major social functions of living approach claim that knowledge is organized for pupils when their method is followed, and, moreover, that it is organized on a much more functional and meaningful basis than it is in the system of traditional subjects. Moreover, they assert that much of the subject matter learned in the subject curriculum is forgotten because it is not meaningful to the youngsters; hence it is much better to use subject matter that is functional to them with the likelihood that it will be remembered and used much more effectively. Also, in this plan of organization a large amount of subject matter is used, probably as much as in the traditional curriculum, even though it is selected and organized in a different manner.

4. The major social functions of living approach presents a practical difficulty in utilizing this method in present-day schools. Even schools that wish to use the major social functions of living approach for at least a core part of a program find difficulty in fully implementing this type of organization because of a lack of teachers trained and prepared to use it and because of the lack of suitable books and resource materials. Consequently, schools utilizing this approach have to spend a great deal of time and effort in practically training teachers on the job as well as in developing their own learning materials or in selecting suitable sections from a variety of books and texts. These are very real difficulties, but certainly not insurmountable since a number of schools have been able to utilize the areas of living approach in core programs and in problem courses.

Place of the Major Social Functions of Living Approach in Curriculum Planning

It is difficult in such a complex matter as curriculum planning to maintain that a direct one-to-one relationship exists between some particular theories or concepts of curriculum development and present programs in the school; nevertheless it seems quite clear that the major areas of living approach has had great impact on much of the experimentation and many of the new developments that have taken place in curriculum planning in the last two decades. In this connection, it should be pointed out that this plan of curriculum organization blends so imperceptibly into the next approach to be discussed—the needs and concerns of learners themselves—that it is difficult to draw a sharp distinction between the two in some aspects of curriculum development. As a matter of fact, there may be considerable justification for maintaining that the present emphasis on pupil problems, concerns, and needs as organizing centers for curriculum experiences grew out of these earlier efforts to organize the curriculum in terms of social functions of living. It seems accurate to state that many of the new developments in curriculum planning stem from these two closely related approaches to the curriculum design. It is well that educators understand these approaches and their application to present-day curriculum planning in forward-looking school situations.

Use in elementary school. This approach to curriculum design is closely related to the activity movement in elementary schools. We have not set up the activity movement or the so-called "activity curriculum" as a separate type of curriculum design, since it represents more a method of organizing instruction than a method of selecting and organizing learning experiences themselves. Even in the activity curriculum it still becomes necessary to determine what will be the basis for selecting desirable activities or learning units in which children might engage. Moreover, all types of curriculum organization utilize activities, so this is not truly an accurate descriptive term for a type of design. Nevertheless, we should recognize that the emphasis on the development of meaningful activities for children in the elementary school as part of the activity movement is closely related to the use of the social functions of living and the problems and needs of learners as bases for curriculum design. These educational developments are all attempts to carry into practice the more modern concepts of learning expounded by the experimentalists, particularly by John Dewey and his close associates. Consequently, these efforts really represent different approaches or different aspects of the whole effort to make education functional and to select learning experiences in terms of the developmental needs and characteristics of learners.

In selecting teaching units for the activity curriculum in the elementary school major aspects of the activities of people as members of social groups have been widely used so that the social functions of living approach has been utilized to a considerable extent in many of the more modern elementary schools of the present day. Units of work may be organized around the problems of protecting life and health, feeding and clothing people, life in the home, cooperating in social and civic action, governing ourselves, and the other areas that have been designated as major social functions of living.

Use in the secondary school. In the secondary school this approach to curriculum organization has often been used as a method of organizing the core program, which will be discussed in the following chapter, and also as a method of selecting the learning experiences in certain problem type of course. These courses—social living, family relationships, American problems, consumer education, functional science, and the like, are examples—often use areas of living as a basis for selecting the units of work to be developed by pupils. Some of these courses themselves represent efforts to give attention to the major facets of living, such as some of the newer courses concerned with marriage and family relations, social

PLATE 19. MAKING A HOME IS ONE OF LIFE'S MAJOR ACTIVITIES. *As a part of the work in homemaking classes, girls learn the best methods of child care and rearing. (Courtesy of Allegheny High School, Pittsburgh)*

problems, and consumer problems. For example, Plate 19 illustrates the type of problems now being included in courses in homemaking in many of our modern high schools. Girls, and in some cases boys, too, obtain experience in caring for babies and young children and learn the essential facts about child growth and development and the role of the parents in properly guiding the development of their children.

In addition to its use in the selection of learning experiences to be included in core programs and problem courses, the major areas of living approach has often affected the selection and organization of learning experiences in the traditional subjects themselves. For example, professional groups and specialists in the various subject fields are constantly trying to make their respective subjects in the secondary school more functional and meaningful to learners. Often they utilize areas of living or problems of living as a basis for selecting the subject matter units to be included in the courses.

It seems safe to say that much of the curriculum development of the next few years will certainly involve the use of the major areas of living and the needs and concerns of learners as these may blend into one approach as a basic method for developing new types of core programs and problems courses in the junior and senior high schools and in the lower divisions of the college.

ORGANIZING THE CURRICULUM ON THE BASIS OF THE INTERESTS, NEEDS, AND PROBLEMS OF LEARNERS

The fourth and last method of curriculum design to be considered is one that provides for the selection and organization of learning experiences in the school on the basis of the interests, needs, or problems of learners. While there might be some minor differences in the kind of curriculum that would evolve, depending upon whether interests, needs, or problems are utilized, these bases for selecting learning experiences are so similar in theory and concept that they will all be considered together. This approach to curriculum planning is sometimes called the "experience" type of curriculum design, but we choose to avoid that terminology, since it is quite clear that, in any curriculum, learning experiences of some type are used. To avoid using a more awkward expression, this procedure will be designated here as the needs approach.

Needs as a Basis for Curriculum Design

In the needs type of curriculum design the needs, problems, and interests of the learners are used as bases for selecting, guiding, and evaluating the learning experiences of pupils. These motivational forces were discussed in some detail in Chapter 5; the concepts of learning developed in Chapter 6 are also pertinent here, for this school of thought holds that the needs approach is really a sincere and thoroughgoing effort to plan learning experiences that are psychologically sound and most meaningful and purposeful to the pupil. All learning, so it is maintained, is what we build into behavior from an experience; we learn best those things that help us solve a problem, meet a situation, attain a desire, satisfy a want, or fulfill an interest. Thus the most vital curriculum will be one that provides pupils with experiences that grow out of their needs, broadly conceived.

This approach to curriculum design seeks to bring into school experience the methods which an effective citizen uses in solving his problems, pursuing his interests, or meeting his needs. A person who is confronted with a problem should utilize his intelligence to think it through rationally, drawing on the learnings he has acquired from his past experiences, and making use of whatever new data and new information he can obtain to reach an intelligent decision on the problem. But the individual needs experience of the most appropriate kind if he is to deal with his problems realistically and in an intelligent and sound fashion, such as this procedure implies. In brief, he should have experience in solving problems, acting rationally, gathering data, and the like. The school that uses the needs approach is making a genuine effort to provide pupils with such experiences so that outside the school and later as mature adults they will have the ability to deal with the situations of daily living in an intelligent and rational manner. The rationale of this method of curriculum design has been well stated by one of its strongest advocates.

The experience must begin with and continue to grow out of the real felt needs of pupils. A need represents any disturbance which an individual feels so keenly about that he wants to resolve it in order to achieve a new equilibrium. A movement toward the restoration of equilibrium is search and exploration. The recovery is fulfillment or satisfaction. From this statement some leads seem to be obvious: (a) An individual must work on his own disturbance, not that of some other person. . . . (b) The movement toward the resolution of a need can become intelligent search and exploration only when the persons feeling the need set up the purposes, the method of achievement, and their evaluation, for they are inherent in intelligent behavior. A child cannot work intelligently on purposes set out by others, for he will have no adequate means of testing them in action. (c) The recovery of fulfillment or satisfaction cannot be adequately achieved by an individual unless he is working for the fulfillment of his own need. . . . (d) An individual must work on his own needs in order to achieve other aspects of experience such as continuity, unity, sociality, and creativeness. (e) The school curriculum should then represent a series of experiences based upon the needs of the children at the various ages. (f) The life curriculum of individuals is such a series of experiences based upon such needs. The curriculum for children in the school should be no less effective than the curriculum which they are meeting in life outside of the school.[7]

---

[7] L. Thomas Hopkins, *Interaction: The Democratic Process* (Boston: D. C. Heath & Company, 1941), p. 219. Reprinted by permission of D. C. Heath & Company, publishers

Comparison of social functions and needs approaches. As was stated earlier in this chapter, the social functions of living approach and the needs approach to curriculum design are closely related, the one blending into the other without any sharp lines of demarcation. However, we might distinguish between the two methods by saying that the areas of living approach considers primarily the responsibilities of the learner as an adult citizen, giving a great deal of attention in the school to the problems he will face and the activities he will engage in as a member of the social group, both now and in the future. The needs approach places greater emphasis on the present, giving primary consideration to the problems that learners face here and now or, in some plans, to the interests which the learners express at the present time.

Obviously, it would be an error to assume that it is an either-or distinction, since the major areas of living approach also utilizes ongoing concerns and present problems of learners as organizing centers for many of the learning experiences, while the needs approach, at least in its present-day uses, is certainly not indifferent to the future. In their extreme forms it is easy to point out considerable differences between approaches. The formal chart used in the early Virginia program obviously provides for a curriculum that is quite different from the extreme child-centered curriculum that has no blocked-out areas for organizing curriculum experiences in advance of the actual participation of the learners in them. On the other hand, the major areas of living used in the Kansas program and the preplanned design prepared by the state committee for schools in that program are similar to the statements of needs proposed by the Commission on Secondary School Curriculum of the Progressive Educational Association and that of Prescott.[8]

The child-centered school. If the extreme approach to the needs organization, as formulated by its advocates, were followed, there would be no preplanned selection or organization of learning experiences. According to this position, if the curriculum is to be based on the interests, needs, and problems of children, obviously it would vary from one group of children to another and it would be impossible to block out in advance the learning experiences that should be developed by the school. The only way we could examine such a curriculum would be to analyze the kinds of learning experiences in which the children had engaged in that

[8] V. T. Thayer, Caroline B. Zachry, and Ruth Kotinsky, *Reorganizing Secondary Education* (prepared for the Commission on Secondary School Curriculum of the Progressive Education Association; New York: Appleton-Century-Crofts, Inc., 1939), Chap. II.

Daniel A. Prescott, *Emotion and the Educative Process* (Washington, D.C.: American Council on Education, 1938), Chap. VI.

particular school situation. The curriculum would be an emerging thing that would be developed by the teacher and pupils as they worked together in the school environment.

Although a few experimental schools have tried out this type of designing, actually it has seldom been used in the schools. The child-centered school, described by Rugg and Schumaker,[9] probably proceeded as far as any school program described in the literature in implementing this extreme version of the experience curriculum. Even this account, however, indicates considerable direction and guidance on the part of teachers in the selection of the broad learning units in which children participated. Moreover, to provide continuity from one year to the next, there is evidence that these teachers together planned, at least in broad outline, the general nature of the learning experiences that might be appropriate for each succeeding group of children as they progressed through the school.

In the early days of these efforts to utilize a needs approach there was little literature on the subject, and only a few reliable studies of the interests, needs, and problems of children and youth had been conducted. However, since then an extensive number of researches and investigations of various types have been carried on in an attempt to ascertain what constitute the basic psychobiological needs of children and adolescents, their consuming interests, and their important problems and concerns. At the present time, we have a considerable body of literature that does bring together for the curriculum worker what psychologists, psychiatrists, students of child growth and development, and other workers of this type consider to be the most important of these needs, interests, and problems. Reference was made in Chapter 5 to a number of these studies, but Doane and Featherstone[10] have provided us with two excellent reviews of some of the studies most pertinent to curriculum planning in terms of the needs concepts.

More structured designs. With such research and pronouncements available and because of shifts in points of view, recent efforts to formulate a curriculum based on needs have taken a more definite form. In fact, the early unstructured plans have largely been discarded by curriculum workers in favor of designs in which the broad scope and general nature of the learning experiences are planned in advance. It is in this

[9] Harold Rugg and Ann Shumaker, *The Child-Centered School* (Yonkers, N.Y.: World Book Company, 1928).

[10] Donald Doane, *The Needs of Youth* (New York: Bureau of Publications, Teachers College, Columbia University, 1942), Chap. II.

William B. Featherstone, *A Functional Curriculum for Youth* (New York: American Book Company, 1950), Chap. IV.

newer, more structured approach that the needs design most closely approximates the major social functions approach. One of the most extensive efforts in recent years to draw up a curriculum design based on this concept is that developed by the Commission on Secondary School Curriculum of the Progressive Education Association. This commission, seeking a better basis for organizing the curriculum of the modern secondary school, presented an extensive statement of needs that may well be used as a basis for selecting and organizing curriculum experiences. These needs are based on what the commission states to be research studies and studies of the personal-social development of young people. Needs in this statement are classified into four broad areas:

I. *Area of personal living*

    A. The need for personal health

    B. The need for self-assurance

    C. The need for a satisfying world picture and a workable philosophy of life

    D. The need for a range of personal interests

    E. The need for aesthetic satisfactions

II. *Immediate personal-social relationships*

    A. The need for increasingly mature relationships in home and family life, and with adults outside the family

    B. The need for successful and increasingly mature relationships with age mates of both sexes

III. *Social-civic relationships*

    A. The need for responsible participation in socially significant activities

    B. The need for social recognition

IV. *Economic relationships*

    A. The need for emotional assurance of progress toward adult status

    B. The need for guidance in choosing an occupation and for vocational preparation

    C. The need for wise selection and use of goods and services

    D. The need for effective action in solving basic economic problems[11]

[11] Progressive Education Association, Commission on Secondary School Curriculum, *Science in General Education* (New York: Appleton-Century-Crofts, Inc., 1938), pp. 64, 144, 188, 241.

To implement this concept of needs as a basis for curriculum planning, the commission then sponsored the preparation of a number of books which were designed to show how this method could be used even with the traditional subject organization.

Present use of needs approach. At the present time the use of the needs approach in curriculum planning follows these lines of development: (1) Some core programs in both elementary and secondary schools have utilized at least some aspects of the needs organization as a basis for planning that part of the curriculum. (2) The new type of problems courses, particularly in the secondary school, is using pupil needs as a basis for developing units of work. We have already indicated that a number of secondary schools have developed problems courses of various types. Oftentimes, the pupils themselves take a large part of the responsibility for actually selecting the learning units to be studied in such problems courses. (3) The needs and problems of learners are used as a basis for revising existing subject courses. While it might be difficult to see the relationship between the needs approach and the traditional subject method of designing the curriculum, it is fair to say that the needs approach has had considerable influence on the organization and content of the traditional subjects offered in the school. This approach is well illustrated by the work of the Commission on Secondary School Curriculum of the Progressive Education Association, already described. Many present-day courses in the secondary school now try to give attention to the problems of learners as they grow up in a society.

Arguments in Favor of the Needs Approach to Curriculum Design

Those who advocate the needs approach to curriculum organization maintain that it possesses these advantages:

1. The needs approach to curriculum organization is psychologically sound. The proponents of this approach believe that it constitutes the most psychologically sound method of selecting and organizing curriculum experiences for at least the core part of the program. They maintain that this method of design is the most complete and satisfactory implementation of the experimentalists' concepts. The psychological basis of the needs approach lies in the fact that it gives primary emphasis to pupils' purposes, interests, and needs—all basic motivational factors. Motivation is the primary factor in determining the kinds of experiences in which the individual will engage with meaning and purpose, the kinds of learnings that will result from these experiences, and the extent to which these learnings will really be built into the individual's behavior so that he has them available for future use. If a pupil engages in learning experiences in the school which are based on his interests, needs, problems, and ongoing concerns, the pupil will of course engage in them with enthusiasm and energy and with purposes of his own that ensure a high level of participation in the experience and resulting efficiency in learning. In terms of curriculum design the important question is whether learning experiences that are based on the interests of the learners, on their psychobiological needs, or on problems that they face in their daily living or anticipate in their future living are the only types of learning experiences that provide this high type of motivation.

2. *The needs approach provides functional learnings that are directly related to the life experience of the individual.* A curriculum based on the needs approach is highly functional, provided, of course, that the needs are genuine ones and the learning experiences have been properly selected. There is no need to worry about transfer, or training the mind, or similar generalized bases for justifying the traditional curriculum; the needs type of curriculum is directly functional since it deals with the very real life situations facing the youngsters themselves. Learnings resulting from such activities in school should have direct application to the things the pupil does, both in school and out of school, and should provide a set of learnings that will be highly useful as he grows and matures into adult life.

3. *The needs approach contributes to the attainment of many of the desired outcomes of the school program.* The needs approach has possibilities of contributing to a large number of the outcomes desired from a good educational program. Since this method of curriculum organization encourages extensive activity on the part of the pupils in planning and carrying forward their own learning experiences under the guidance of the teacher, and, moreover, since it usually calls for a different method of working in the school from that required by the traditional subject curriculum, it enables the school to achieve many of the educational objectives that might not be attained in other types of curriculum organization. This is particularly true when we consider the desired outcomes in terms of ways of working and the attainment of democratic values, attitudes, appreciations, and the like. Attainment of some of these desirable outcomes of learning, however, does not inhere in the approach itself, but rather in the way in which learning activities are carried on in the school when it is used.

4. The needs approach to curriculum design places the emphasis primarily on the growth and development of learners. By the very nature of this kind of curriculum organization the emphasis of the school is placed on the growth and development of pupils rather than on the imparting of subject matter. In the needs approach, attention is given to the physical, emotional, social, and intellectual needs of children so that the school is more likely to give concern to the over-all problems of growth and development rather than only to intellectual development.

5. The needs approach best emphasizes the mental hygiene concept of guiding development. Since the pupil is working on meaningful activities and these activities are concerned with his problems and needs, the school is more likely to aid pupils in finding security, developing poise, and achieving stability than may be true in other curriculum designs that often result in considerable frustration, insecurity, and failure on the part of many pupils.

6. The needs approach provides for better integration of learning activities in the school. As has already been pointed out in the social functions of living approach, these new curriculum designs provide for much better integration of subject matter in the school. Subject matter is selected in terms of meaningful life situations or problems and is put to use in working on and solving these problems. Subject matter is not broken down into discrete units as in the subject curriculum, but any subject matter appropriate for use in the learning activities under way is utilized. Thus it becomes functional and is more readily learned in terms of use than it is when set up as a body of subject matter to be mastered.

Shortcomings and Difficulties of the Needs Approach to Curriculum Design

The needs approach to curriculum design has some shortcomings; moreover, some difficulties inhere in putting this plan into practice. These will be considered briefly.

1. It is difficult to determine genuine interests, needs, and problems. One of the most difficult aspects of the needs approach is to determine authoritatively and with assurance the genuine needs, problems, or even interests of the group with which the teacher is working. If the problems, interests, or needs used as a basis for selecting and organizing curriculum experiences are to be those of the pupils engaging in the experience itself, the teacher will find it difficult to ascertain just what these may be. Without a great deal of practice in this area, it is entirely possible that t'.ᵣ teacher may accept as a basis for planning needs that are not genuine, but just fleeting interests or, in fact, the teacher's own spur-of-the-moment hunches about the needs or problems of pupils. Moreover, if the teacher lets the needs emerge from the group, what assurance is there that they are the most essential needs facing that group of youngsters? Are youngsters even willing to state their most deeply felt needs as problems for the group to work on? Do pupils themselves recognize their own basic needs and the problems that in actuality are most critical for them?

Unquestionably, some schools that have used the needs basis for organizing core programs have permitted groups of pupils to engage in learning experiences that proved to be quite trivial and of little real significance to the pupils themselves. If, on the other hand, a teacher relies on expert authority, such as psychologists and students of child growth and development, to ascertain what the needs are—or should be—he may be disregarding some genuine ones of the pupils who are participating in that particular learning activity. A closely related problem is one of determining how universal a felt need should be before a group of children should use it as a basis for organizing learning experiences. Should a majority of the class feel the need for the experience or should it be almost unanimously a need of the entire class before it is used as a basis for planning learning activities? Might not a pupil who has a unique need, even though it is not a felt need of any other member of the group, have as much right to work on his need as do other members in the group? Perhaps to this pupil his need is the most serious problem facing him and the one with which he most needs the help of the school; yet because it is not a felt need of other members of the group, the school is very likely to neglect it.

Personally, we feel that these difficulties may in a large measure be overcome by the exercise of high-level professional skill on the part of the curriculum worker. He should be thoroughly familiar with the best and most reliable studies of the interests, needs, and problems of children and adolescents and should use these as basic points of reference in utilizing the needs approach. At the same time he should be sensitive to any particularized needs, interests, or concerns of his own group of pupils. By utilizing his skill in studying children he should be able to discover any specialized needs and concerns of individual pupils.

Even Dewey himself, a number of years after the so-called progressive education movement had gotten well under way in this country, felt constrained to call to account some of the extreme proponents of the child-centered school and point out that just not any kind of experience would be appropriate for the school to sponsor for learners. He states his position in these terms:

Traditional education tended to ignore the importance of personal impulse and desire as moving springs. But this is no reason why progressive education should identify impulse and desire with purpose and thereby pass lightly over the need for careful observation, for wide range of information, and for judgment if students are to share in the formation of the purposes which activate them. In an *educational* scheme, the occurrence of a desire and impulse is not the final end.

. . . That the conditions found in present experience should be used as sources of problems is a characteristic which differentiates education based upon experience from traditional education . . . it is part of the educator's responsibility to see equally to two things: First, that the problem grows out of the conditions of the experience being had in the present, and that it is within the range of the capacity of students; and, secondly, that it is such that it arouses in the learner an active quest for information and for production of new ideas.[12]

2. The needs approach may minimize the social responsibility of the school. One of the major charges made against the needs approach and against the so-called progressive education movement of several decades ago was that the child-centered school and the needs approach to curriculum organization minimized the social responsibility of the school. By placing great emphasis on the child himself and on his needs and problems, the school probably did neglect the development of an understanding of the society in which the youngster lived or the social institutions with which he dealt, or the development of an over-all consuming desire to be concerned about the welfare of his fellow men. The needs approach, at least in its extreme form, may have placed too much emphasis on the growth and development of the child without recognizing the necessity of giving the individual a sense of social direction and of social responsibility in his life and relationships with other members of the group. Many responsible educators in past years have leveled strong charges against the progressive school on this very ground. The needs concept places great emphasis on the pupil as a factor in the educative process, but too often minimizes the society as the other indispensable factor, just as the subject approach makes the same mistake in reverse.

3. The needs approach does not provide for an adequate mastery of subject matter. As was pointed out in discussing the shortcomings of the social functions of living design, the needs approach is also criticized on the grounds that it fails to organize knowledge for the individual in a

[12] John Dewey, *Experience and Education* (New York: The Macmillan Company, 1938), pp. 83, 96–97. Reprinted by permission of The Macmillan Company, publishers.

sequential manner or in terms of basic generalizations and principles that will be useful to him in many situations in the future and that the major areas of knowledge are not studied systematically; hence serious gaps in his understandings and knowledges may occur. It is maintained that pupils who work in the experience type of curriculum do not have ample opportunity to generalize and grasp the significance of what is studied and learned in relation to many broad aspects of living. Learning may be in terms of immediate and specific things rather than in terms of broad applications to many situations.

4. The needs approach may ignore to too great an extent the past and the future. Some critics of the needs approach feel that by placing so much emphasis on the problems and concerns of the learners themselves, the accumulated cultural heritage of a race is too much ignored and pupils do not learn to probe to the roots of problems so that they may profit from the previous experience of the race in meeting somewhat similar situations. Likewise, it is maintained that in dealing with the here and now in terms of present concerns, the individual does not look ahead enough and to the problems that will face him in the future. Again, Dewey felt constrained to take some of the most extreme interpreters of the experience concept to task by making this point:

> Just as the individual has to draw in memory upon his own past to understand the conditions in which he individually finds himself, so the issues and problems of present *social* life are in such intimate and direct connection with the past that students cannot be prepared to understand either these problems or the best way of dealing with them without delving into their roots in the past. In other words, the sound principle that the objectives of learning are in the future and its immediate materials are in present experience can be carried into effect only in the degree that present experience is stretched, as it were, backward. It can expand into the future only as it is also enlarged to take in the past.[13]

5. The needs approach to curriculum organization presents serious difficulties in developing an organized educational program. If the needs approach to curriculum organization is strictly followed according to theory, it becomes quite difficult to organize systematic programs of education, such as must prevail in present-day schools. If the school bases the educational experiences of children on their needs and concerns, there may be little preplanning or organized development of the educational program itself. This presents a number of practical difficulties in terms of providing desirable sequence to the educational program for

[13] *Ibid.*, p. 93. Reprinted by permission of The Macmillan Company, publishers.

children in various age groups, in making books and other teaching resources available, and in providing for the sequential growth of youngsters.

The needs approach to curriculum organization presents practical difficulties for planning the curriculum for each successive grade level. If school officials did not know what learning experiences would be developed in any grade or secondary group until the children themselves determine them with the help of the teacher, it would be difficult for the teacher who worked with the children to make any preliminary plans or prepare for the year's work. Administrative problems would be multiplied a great deal under this type of curriculum organization. Transfer of pupils, for example, would present much more of a problem than it does under other types of curriculum organization. In actual practice, few if any teachers use an extreme version of the needs approach; rather, they rely on their knowledge of the problems, needs, and concerns of pupils in general to determine cooperatively with other staff members the general scope and sequence of the learning experiences that would be likely to serve as a basis for much of the curriculum, making provision for the spending of some time on personal interests and needs.

6. *The needs approach to curriculum organization may result in serious gaps in the child's educational experiences.* It is highly conceivable that if the needs approach to curriculum organization is fully utilized, serious gaps in the child's education might occur. If the theory is fully accepted, no predetermined statement of aims of education or of desired outcomes would be an acceptable basis for planning the curriculum, except the one general aim of helping pupils with their problems. Since the curriculum would be based on the felt needs of the youngsters themselves, if they did not feel the need for particular types of learning experiences, presumably they would have no school experience in those phases of living, regardless of how essential the adult might think them to be. Therefore, it is conceivable that they could come through the school without having had some essential and necessary types of learning activities in terms of what adults do and the uses they make of knowledge and skills.

7. *The needs approach is not feasible in many present-day schools.* It is quite apparent that the use of the needs approach to curriculum planning represents quite a radical departure from traditional practices in the schools of today. There are certain practical difficulties in utilizing this method of curriculum design. In the first place, few teachers are adequately trained to make full-fledged use of the needs approach. Most of our teachers, particularly those educated for the secondary school, are

well versed in the methods of the traditional subject curriculum and in methods of teaching in this curriculum. Many of them, certainly if the change were quite abrupt, would be ill at ease and confused if they were plunged into the needs type of curriculum organization. Needless to say, there are numerous teachers, both inexperienced and experienced, who know how to work with boys and girls and who know how to use the more informal methods of teaching that could be adapted very readily to the needs method of curriculum planning. However, this lack of teachers is a severe handicap to the use of this type of organization in our schools to-day.

Moreover, the problem of obtaining community support for such a type of curriculum is indeed a major one. Without doubt, many school staffs could obtain the support and cooperation of parents in implementing such a concept if they planned the whole program cooperatively with them and helped them develop a thorough understanding of the rationale and methods of the new program. However, in many communities this task of obtaining parental support offers a considerable obstacle to the development of such a curriculum organization.

If the concept is fully carried out, there would be little in the way of curriculum bulletins or teachers' guides for use by teachers in planning learning experiences. Curriculum guides which offered suggestions for using the method would, of course, be pertinent, but teachers would largely have to proceed in terms of their own initiative and ingenuity in actually setting up and planning learning experiences with the group. This absence of pertinent curriculum guides might prove to be a severe handicap to many teachers in giving proper direction and scope to the actual learning experiences of pupils.

The Place of the Needs Approach in Curriculum Planning

We believe that in its extreme form of the child-centered school, in which the curriculum, presumably, would be developed from the felt interests, problems, and needs of youngsters, this method of curriculum design has little real place in curriculum planning at the present time. The difficulties discussed above, and particularly the fact that it neglects to too great an extent the social responsibilities of the school, make it unwise and unsound in our opinion to use this approach to curriculum designing.

On the other hand, if a more moderate interpretation of the needs approach is followed, so that curriculum design is based on what highly trained specialists in the field of child growth and development consider to be the genuine needs of youth growing up in a modern culture, we believe that we have a much sounder basis for selecting and organizing curriculum experiences, at least in the core part of the program. This latter concept of the needs approach closely approximates the major social functions of living organization, which we favorably considered in the previous section. If curriculum workers utilize the research of specialists in child growth and development, cultural anthropology, sociology, mental hygiene, and closely related disciplines to ascertain what seem to be the most important needs, problems, and developmental tasks facing youngsters, we have valid guides for the selection and organization of curriculum experiences.

In terms of this position, then, we believe that curriculum workers should utilize the needs and interests of youngsters as determined by competent people, including the teacher, as one basis for selecting experiences which the school should provide. When used along with other basic factors that must be considered in the educational process, particularly the demands of the culture in which the individual lives, we have appropriate bases for designing the curriculum. For example, Plate 20 illustrates how one school utilizes children's interests in camping to develop an

PLATE 20. SCHOOL-OPERATED CAMPS PROVIDE EXCELLENT LEARNING EXPERIENCES. *During their stay at the school camp these pupils are studying conservation. (Courtesy of the Superintendent of Schools, San Diego County, California)*

understanding of nature as well as the need for conservation. Feather-stone states this point well in these terms:

> The needs of youth are not only valid but also necessary guides to practical action in developing a suitable curriculum. They are sources of criteria and standards for judging the suitability and adequacy of any teaching and learning enterprise. They are both the beginning and the end of education. But basing the curriculum on the needs of youth is by no means so easy as it seems to a great many persons who speak with conviction about the desirability of doing so. It requires extraordinary clarity and depth of insight into human behavior and into the cultural context in which men live to discern youth's needs.[14]

The needs of youth, as determined by competent experts in the field, may also be used as a basis for selecting some of the content of traditional subjects which may constitute other parts of the curriculum, particularly in the secondary school. Moreover, acceptance of the needs concept of curriculum design to the extent indicated here may very well call for the development of new types of problems courses in the junior and senior high school and the community college. Thus we believe that new types of courses in such areas as marriage and family relations, problems of the consumer, social problems, problems of living, problems of democracy, and the like may well utilize to a considerable extent the basic needs of learners as organizing centers for the educational experiences to be provided.

For Further Study

Alberty, Harold, *Reorganizing the High-School Curriculum*. Rev. ed.; New York: The Macmillan Company, 1953.

Chapter 5 discusses these newer approaches to curriculum organization and contrasts them with subject design.

———, "Should the Modern Secondary-School Curriculum Be Experience Centered?" *Bulletin*, National Association of Secondary School Principals, No. 162, 33:115–124 (April), 1949.

Pleads for the development of the experience type of curriculum in the secondary school and suggests problem centers.

"Areas of Neglect in the Secondary School Curriculum," *Progressive Education*, 28:37–67 (November), 1950.

This series of articles discusses five aspects of education that the authors believe to be neglected at the secondary school level and then presents two approaches for correcting the deficiency.

[14] William B. Featherstone, *A Functional Curriculum for Youth* (New York: American Book Company, 1950), p. 89. Reprinted by permission of American Book Company, publishers.

"Bases for Selecting School Programs," *School Executive,* 70:61–74 (May), 1951.

A series of articles on five methods of designing the curriculum and a critique of each plan.

Caswell, Hollis, and Doak S. Campbell. *Curriculum Development.* New York: American Book Company, 1935.

A thorough analysis of the social functions approach is made in this basic book.

Gilchrist, Robert S., "Education for Youth in These Times," *Bulletin,* National Association of Secondary School Principals, No. 146, 31:162–174 (April), 1947.

Believes that the secondary school should organize its curriculum on the basis of life needs, and suggests the nature of such a design.

Grim, Paul R., "Designs for Curriculum Improvement," *Journal of Educational Research,* 42:18–29 (September), 1948.

Reviews historically the bases used for designing the curriculum.

Herrick, Virgil E., "Planned and Unplanned Curriculums," *Elementary School Journal,* 47:563–570 (June), 1947.

Considers planning in the experience type of curriculum design.

Hopkins, L. Thomas, *Interaction: The Democratic Process.* Boston: D. C. Heath & Company, 1941.

An advocate of the "experience" type of curriculum planning discusses at length this whole approach. Contrasts experience and subject design.

————, "Needs or Interests: A Sufficient Basis for the Elementary School Curriculum," in University of Pennsylvania Bulletin, *Viewpoints on Educational Issues and Problems.* Proceedings of the Thirty-ninth Annual Schoolmen's Week. Philadelphia: University of Pennsylvania Press, 1952, pp. 104–111.

Maintains that needs are the only basis on which to design a curriculum.

Leonard, J. Paul, *Developing the Secondary School Curriculum.* Rev. ed.; New York: Rinehart & Company, Inc., 1953.

Chapters 9 and 10 discuss newer approaches to curriculum organization.

Shane, Harold (ed.), *The American Elementary School.* Thirteenth Yearbook of the John Dewey Society. New York: Harper & Brothers, 1953.

Chapters 6 and 13 are especially pertinent to a discussion of curriculum designing in the elementary school.

Smith, B. Othaniel, William O. Stanley, and J. Harlan Shores, *Fundamentals of Curriculum Development.* Yonkers, N.Y.: World Book Company, 1950.

All of Part IV considers methods of designing the curriculum.

chapter **10**

The Core Curriculum Plan

In a consideration of the design and organization of the curriculum, special attention should be given to the new types of programs generally designated by the title "core curriculum" and occasionally by the terms "general education" and "common learnings." Curriculum workers have given a great deal of thought to the core type of organization in recent years, and a number of schools have done considerable experimental work in organizing and developing various types of core and general education programs.

While the term "core curriculum" has been used to describe more particularly types of instructional organization used in junior and senior high schools, the basic characteristics of core programs apply equally well to elementary schools. In fact, the core plan is quite largely an effort to carry over some of the best features of instructional organization in elementary schools to secondary schools. Few elementary schools designate their curriculum organization as a core program; yet they may more truly adhere to the characteristics that we will develop for core progams than do many secondary schools. Nevertheless, it should be recognized that the term is used in curriculum planning primarily to describe a type of curriculum organization used in junior and senior high schools rather than a special type of curriculum organization used in the elementary school. The same general approach in the elementary school is often designated by the term "activity curriculum."

CHARACTERISTICS OF THE CORE PLAN OF
CURRICULUM ORGANIZATION

Some of the newer terms that have been introduced into curriculum terminology in recent years—"the core curriculum," "general education," and "common learnings"—have been used in a variety of ways by different curriculum workers. Consequently, these terms do not always mean the same things to the educators who use them. It seems desirable at the outset, therefore, to develop our ideas of what these terms mean.

What Is Meant by General Education and Common Learnings?

The basic and underlying concept in these newer approaches to curriculum planning is general education. The theory and practice of general education pervades all of our recent efforts to develop a more functional and more significant curriculum for youth. General education is the phase of the total educational program that is provided each pupil to help him attain the basic and essential outcomes necessary to be an effective, useful, and well-adjusted member of the social group and to live the good life of the group. It is through the general education program that we seek to attain the broad outcomes of education that should be the common possession of all persons. It is a generic term.

Paralleling general education is specialized education, which is designed to develop the individual potentialities, capacities, and abilities that characterize the pupil as an individual. To illustrate, every member of the social group should be able to communicate effectively with other members of the group; this desired outcome then becomes a primary objective of general education. On the other hand, not every member of a social group needs to be able to type, to speak a foreign language, to trace the electric circuit of a television set, or to know how to solve a quadratic equation for an unknown. These, then, become aspects of specialized education.

The term "common learnings" is of recent origin. While there may have been some limited use of the term earlier, it was first used as a concept in curriculum planning by the Educational Policies Commission.[1] In coining this expression, the commission defines it in these terms: "What does this title, 'Common Learnings,' mean? It means that this course consists of learning experiences which *everyone* needs to have, regardless of what occupation he may expect to follow or where he may happen to live." [2]

From this definition and the fuller description of the course and its objectives as presented in the pronouncement of the commission, we ourselves believe that this term is synonymous with "general education," as that term is used in curriculum planning at the secondary school level. Because of the fact that the term "general education" has already come to have several usages in the secondary schools and is also widely used at the college level to denote a variety of programs, the commission prob-

[1] Educational Policies Commission, *Education for All American Youth: A Further Look* (Washington, D.C.: National Education Association, 1952), pp. 218–229, 237–254.
[2] *Ibid.*, p. 241.

ably believed that its new term "common learnings" would connote a more precise concept of the basic program of general education at the secondary level. It would certainly distinguish the secondary program from the college program and would help to free the secondary schools from domination by the colleges in the development of a program of general education. In any case, we regard the two terms at the secondary level as synonymous and will use them as such in this book.

Before we leave this discussion, it would be well to point out that several secondary schools in the country have used the term "general education" to designate their own particular programs or offerings. Such a use of the term has also tended to confuse the issue, for people familiar with such programs may think of general education in terms of particular offerings of a school system rather than as a generic term that designates the basic educational experiences that should be provided all youth. We use the term "general education" in the broad sense and not as a designation of a new type of course or as a title of a new type of core program.

What Is the Core Curriculum?

The term "core curriculum" designates a plan for organizing and scheduling a major portion of the program of general education in a school. This is the sense in which we shall use the term in this book. In reality the plan should appropriately be called a core curriculum plan. In practice the term has many meanings and is used in a variety of ways; some curriculum workers do not even attempt to define it, but rather describe or characterize the sort of educational plan they mean by use of the term. However, we believe that the best use of this term is to use it in the manner indicated—as a designation of a plan for providing some aspects of general education in the school.

Some writers use "core curriculum" synonymously with "general education." Thus Faunce and Bossing define the term as follows: "The 'core curriculum' designates those learning experiences that are fundamental for all learners because they derive from (1) our common, individual drives or needs, and (2) our civic and social needs as participating members of a democratic society." [3] To our way of thinking it is better to designate those learning experiences which are fundamental for all learners as "general education" and to use "core curriculum" to designate one plan for providing them.

Alberty recognizes the confusion that exists in the use of the term

[3] Roland C. Faunce and Nelson L. Bossing, *Developing the Core Curriculum* (copyright, 1951, by Prentice-Hall, Inc., New York), p. 4. Reprinted by permission of the publisher.

but maintains that it is always used in one way or another to designate all or part of the program of general education. He then categorizes six types of general education programs which he labels as core programs. This means, in effect, that Alberty regards any type of general education program as a core program, even though it be a strict subject plan.[4] On the basis of such a definition of the term, every school and college has a core curriculum plan, even though it may be simply a list of required subjects of the traditional type.

A number of school systems use the term much as we define it: that is, to designate a particular type of plan for offering and scheduling essential parts of the general education program. Thus, The University School of The Ohio State University takes this position:

> The secondary school is responsible to help all young people define the major problems of our society and arrive at generalizations and conclusions which will make it possible for the democratic way of living to thrive. To this end, a program of general education, consisting of common learnings required of all students, is an integral part of the secondary program. These common learnings and experiences are cared for in the core class.[5]

The New York City Schools use the term in a somewhat similar manner:

> First, it means a class which meets two or more periods per day with a teacher who also acts as a guidance counselor for the group. Secondly, it means a class which deals with the problems that are selected by teachers and pupils cooperatively and that cut across traditional subject-matter lines.[6]

The Philadelphia Public Schools similarly use the term, stating that they define "core curriculum" thus:

> A total school program within which time is provided for pupils to spend more than one period per day with one teacher. This may be one, two, or three periods plus home room time.[7]

[4] Harold Alberty, "Designing Programs to Meet the Common Needs of Youth," in *Adapting the Secondary-School Program to the Needs of Youth* (Part I, Fifty-second Yearbook, National Society for the Study of Education; Chicago: The University of Chicago Press, 1953), Chap. VII; and his *Reorganizing the High-School Curriculum* (Rev. ed.; New York: The Macmillan Company, 1953), Chap. VI.

[5] The University School, The Ohio State University, *A Description of Curriculum Experiences: The Upper School* (Columbus, Ohio: The University School, 1952), p. 10. Mimeographed. Reprinted by permission of the University School.

[6] Board of Education of the City of New York, *Suggestions to Teachers of Experimental Core Classes* (Curriculum Bulletin, 1950–1951 Series, No. 2; New York: The Board, 1951), pp. 4–5.

[7] Philadelphia Public Schools, *Core Curriculum in Philadelphia* (Philadelphia: The Schools, 1949), p. 3. Mimeographed.

Core curriculum is a relatively new concept in curriculum planning, having evolved in the last quarter of a century as a part of the efforts of forward-looking educators to develop a more functional and significant program of general education for all youth. Schools that do not utilize the core curriculum plan do have programs of general education. Traditionally, general education has been provided through a system of required subjects or courses. The core curriculum plan is another method of providing at least a major part of the general education program. Thus, there are today three basic plans for providing general education in the secondary school: (1) the subjects and courses required of all students; (2) the core curriculum plan; and (3) a combination of required subjects and a core curriculum program.

It seems desirable, therefore, for the sake of clarity to avoid the use of "core curriculum" as a synonymous term for "general education," and instead to restrict it to designate one plan for providing major phases of general education. It is evident that core curriculum plans are always of a general education nature, but not all general education is core curriculum. It should also be noted that since core curriculum plans in a few communities have been subjected to severe criticism by lay groups, some school systems have developed programs that exhibit all of the essential characteristics of a core program, but have not designated them as core programs in order to avoid a predisposition on the part of some parents to attack such programs regardless of merit. Essentially, then, what we are examining in this chapter is a method of providing general education under a particular type of organization, regardless of the name; however, curriculum workers quite generally designate such approaches as core curriculum plans.

Characteristics of Core Curriculum Plans

Since the core curriculum idea is relatively new, schools have experimented with various approaches to this method of providing general education. Consequently, a core curriculum plan does not follow the same pattern in every school system in which it is used. Yet at the present time most programs exhibit certain characteristics, and these have been generally accepted by curriculum workers as essential features of core plans. These six characteristics will serve as a set of criteria to ascertain whether a particular program is a true core curriculum plan or not.

1. The core curriculum program always provides general education, and the objectives of the program are as broad as the basic outcomes sought through the general education program. All of the educational experiences carried forward by a core class are planned to contribute as fully as possible to the realization of the outcomes desired for general education.

2. The core class is scheduled for two or more of the usual class periods. So that it may more adequately attain the objectives sought, a core class is usually scheduled for a minimum of two of the traditional class periods, and often a third to a half of the school day is devoted to the core program. The core period also usually replaces the traditional home room period when such a period is used to provide group guidance, to assist pupils in registration, and the like. The long period is considered essential so that the group may have enough time to work cooperatively on the solution of problems, to take trips and excursions, to undertake group activities of considerable breadth and scope, to engage in research and study activities in the library, and the like.

3. The learning experiences of the core group are usually organized on the basis of broad units of work and are not delimited by the traditional subject matter divisions. Good core curriculum programs utilize broad units of work for organizing learning activities and generally avoid the traditional recitation methods used so widely in the typical subject type of organization. Strict subject matter lines are disregarded, and any subject matter that is pertinent to the development of a unit or problem is utilized in carrying forward the learning activities of the core group. It is this use of broad units for organizing learning experiences, usually around problems meaningful to the student, that primarily distinguishes the core curriculum approach from the traditional subject method of providing general education.

4. The core teacher utilizes much more flexible and freer instructional methods and cooperative group procedures in planning and carrying forward the learning activities of the core group. Since the core group generally uses the unit method of organizing instruction, it is easy and natural for the teacher and pupils to work cooperatively in organizing and planning the activities of the core group. While it is, of course, possible to use cooperative group methods in the subject type of curriculum, all of the features of the core curriculum plan are conducive to and facilitate the use of much more informal and democratic prodecures in carrying forward learning experiences. In the best core programs, the pupils participate with the teacher in setting goals for the group, planning the learning activities, organizing the group for carrying forward learning activities, sharing experiences and dividing responsibilities and areas for investigation, arriving at conclusions or achieving the goals set, evaluating the learning activities that have been carried on, and managing the group activities. As is illustrated in Plate 21, learning in a good core program becomes a vital and exciting experience in group living for the members of the class.

PLATE 21. A CORE CLASS USES COOPERATIVE GROUP PROCEDURES IN CARRYING ON LEARNING ACTIVITIES. *Research, committee activities, and group discussions are being used in core class. (Courtesy of the Whittier Junior High School, Lincoln, Nebraska)*

5. *A variety of learning experiences is used in the core curriculum program.* In contrast to the typical recitation method that characterizes many subject classes, core groups use a wide variety of experiences in developing their units of work and in carrying forward activities designed to solve their problems: making excursions into the community, carrying on research activities, engaging in panel and group discussions, presenting reports and findings, summarizing the results of investigations and conclusions reached, reading a variety of materials in the classroom and library, conducting interviews, preparing exhibits and displays, listening to guest speakers and specialists who can contribute to the problem being studied, utilizing the creative arts for expressing ideas or

presenting concepts and information, using dramatic sketches or recordings to present material and findings or to bring out vital aspects of the unit, and carrying on many other such types of learning activities. Again, it must be emphasized that these methods might also be used in carrying forward the learning activities of a traditional class; nevertheless, the core curriculum plan facilitates and encourages the use of a variety of procedures as pupils and teacher work together cooperatively.

6. Guidance of the best sort is an essential part of the activities of the core teacher. The core group should constitute the basic group for guidance purposes. The core teacher usually accepts responsibility for helping each pupil plan his educational program, his participation in activities outside the classroom, and his future when he leaves the school. He also helps pupils with their problems and needs, and guides their growth and development. Real guidance is possible only as a teacher or a counselor has an opportunity to work and talk freely with pupils who have confidence in him and whom he understands and knows well. The core curriculum plan provides just such an opportunity for teachers.

THE DESIGN OF CORE CURRICULUM PROGRAMS

While the core plan usually implies a problem-centered organization, there is no one type of curriculum design that is common to all core programs. They may utilize a number of the methods of designing or organizing learning experiences that were described in Chapters 8 and 9. As a matter of fact, some of these types of design require a core plan as a basis for using that particular type of instructional organization. Obviously, this is not true of the school subject or broad field types of curriculum design, since the core curriculum stands in contrast to the subject type of curriculum organization.

It is appropriate at this point to summarize briefly the various methods used to organize learning experiences in core programs.

The Unified Studies Approach

In core curriculum plans that use the unified studies type of organization, learning activities usually are organized around units of subject matter taken from the fields of social studies and English. Occasionally science may provide the basic units, with English integrated with the science units. Thus the core curriculum class, extending for a minimum of two periods, replaces required subjects in these areas. Broad instructional units, selected and organized on the basis of the social studies or science content usually taught at that grade level, are used as the basis for organizing the learning experiences of the core group. English is correlated with the learning activities. Communicative skills are strengthened through reports to the class, written reports and summaries of research activities, group discussions, small committee presentations, and in other ways in which communication is used. Literature is, of course, used in carrying forward the learning activities of each unit selected for study. Thus the literature that the pupils read is chosen in terms of its contributions to the unit of study.

An illustration of the unified studies approach is found in the Vallejo (California) Junior High School. In this school a two-period core program called "Social Living" is used in the seventh and eighth grades. The class combines English and social studies. In developing the new program the school staff states:

> . . . it was found that English and Social Studies could be easily correlated. Many English skills were considerably improved because they were made functional in the Social Studies classes. Before this new program started students had great difficulty in their English course in writing compositions and in giving oral reports, because they did not have sufficient materials at their disposal. Under the new system they can call on the experiences which they have obtained and the subject matter which they have mastered in the Social Studies class to provide them with materials for use in oral and written work.[8]

The units included in the social living courses are as follows:

Seventh Grade
  1. Our country
  2. Nations beyond the sea

Eighth Grade
  1. From the old world to the new
  2. Colonial times in America
  3. Westward expansion
  4. Industrial north vs. the cotton south states
  5. The emergence of modern America.[9]

The Decatur (Illinois) High School uses a two-hour core plan that combines instruction in English and American history:

---

[8] Vallejo Junior High School, *Social Living Course of Study for Seventh Grade* (Vallejo, Calif.: The School, no date), p. 1. Mimeographed.

[9] *Ibid.*, p. 3, and Vallejo Junior High School, *Social Living Course of Study for Eighth Grade* (Vallejo, Calif.: The School, 1949). p. 3. Mimeographed.

By combining these two traditional subject areas, it is believed that the historical phase of the course will be enriched by the readings from our literary masterpieces and that the literature phase will be made more satisfying and meaningful by emphasizing the social implications of the selections and relating them to the culture in which they developed. The two-hour block also permits more student-teacher planning, offers greater flexibility in organization, procedure, and materials, and affords more opportunity for effective guidance in dealing with individual differences.

As the course is now organized, the work is centered around problems rather than topics so that the students will be more likely to see purpose in their activities; thus, interest will be heightened and real motivation furnished. The problems were formulated by student-teacher discussions regarding the myriad issues confronting the American people.[10]

On the basis of such teacher-pupil planning five broad problem areas have been identified as the main units to be included in the year's course:

1. What people make up America and how can they better live together?
2. How can we resolve the problems brought about by our great technological advance?
3. How can we improve and perpetuate democracy?
4. How can we live the good life?
5. What is to be the role of the United States in world affairs? [11]

A few schools have experimented with the unification of science with the social studies–English type of core. In such cases, the core usually extends for three regular class periods. If science is included, some of the units developed during the year draw heavily on science content. If social implications are apparent in the science topic, the social studies are also correlated in such a unit. However, few schools use a unified studies core of this type to replace the traditional science courses.

The unified studies organization is undoubtedly the one most commonly used in core programs at the present time. This is easy to understand since this type of organization represents less of a break with the traditional curriculum than do other types of core design. Many teachers who are experienced in the usual subject curriculum may take over the unified studies type of core more readily than they could radically different types of organization. The unified studies approach retains much of

[10] Illinois State Department of Public Instruction, *The Story in Nineteen Schools* (Circular Series A, No. 51; Springfield, Ill.: The Department, 1950), p. 74. Reprinted by permission of The Department.

[11] *Ibid.*, pp. 74–75.

the basic subject matter that has been taught in the school at each particular grade level, so that both pupils and parents are on familiar ground and there are likely to be fewer difficulties involved in obtaining parental support. Moreover, it is easier to develop units of instruction on the basis of the traditional social studies than it is to develop entirely new units utilizing some other types of approach. Teaching resources, textbooks, teaching aids, and other help are readily available to the teachers in planning and organizing instruction along these lines.

The Major Social Functions of Living Organization of the Core Course

Chapter 9 discussed in some detail this approach to the organization of learning experiences in the school. Needless to say, this approach requires a core type of organization to implement the concept fully.

An illustration of a core plan that utilizes this method of organizing learning experiences is the program at the Folwell Junior High School of Minneapolis. The suggested units of instruction for the core program are as follows:

Seventh Grade

1. Orientation to my school
2. Knowing my community
3. Making the most of ourselves
4. Living with my family
5. Conserving our natural resources
6. World outlook
7. Making a living

Eighth Grade

1. Knowing my community
2. Making the most of ourselves
3. Conserving our natural resources
4. Preservation and extension of democracy
5. World outlook
6. Making a living

Ninth Grade

1. Knowing my community
2. Making the most of ourselves
3. Living with my family
4. Conserving our natural resources
5. World outlook

6. Driver education
7. Making a living [12]

The Harford County (Maryland) Schools do not prescribe a fixed set of units for core classes that have been organized in the junior high schools of that county. Rather, teachers are urged to develop units that are significant to the particular groups of children with whom they work. However, the county school officials recognize that many teachers desire and need help in defining a scope and sequence for the core class. Consequently, without in any way rigidly prescribing the program, the county school system has suggested a number of units that teachers may wish to develop with their pupils in the three junior high school grades. The suggested units are as follows:

Seventh Grade

1. Living in the junior high school
2. Exploring my educational opportunities
3. Knowing Harford County
4. Discovering Maryland as America in miniature
5. The finest machine
6. Keeping physically fit
7. Preventing accident and disease

Eighth Grade

1. Relating our land and our resources to our history
2. Conservation of our natural resources
3. Finding fellowship with Americans north and south
4. Our physical environment shaping our living

Ninth Grade

1. Appreciating the contributions of other cultures
2. Our shrinking world
3. How science and technology affect our lives
4. Finding one's place in the world of work [13]

As is often true, the units suggested for both Folwell and the Harford county schools represent a combination of the unified studies approach, the major social functions of living approach, and even the adolescent problems approach. Such a combination of units within the core program is quite common, since social studies units are often used

[12] Malcolm Keck, "A Personalized Program to Improve Instruction and Human Relations" (a mimeographed circular available from Folwell Junior High School, Minneapolis, Minn., no date).

[13] Dorothy Mudd, *A Core Program Grows* (Bel Air, Md.: Board of Education of Harford County, 1949), pp. 23–24.

as the basic organizing material for the core program, with other units on personal-social problems being introduced as may seem appropriate at respective grade levels. This is illustrated by the program at Murphy High School, Mobile, Alabama. Plate 22 shows that the group is studying the problems of the consumer, even though the core organization is built around the required subjects of the curriculum.

PLATE 22. A CORE CLASS STUDIES THE PROBLEMS OF THE CONSUMER. *One of the important areas usually studied by a core class using the areas of living approach is the role of the consumer. (Courtesy of Murphy High School, Mobile, Alabama)*

One of the best known of all core courses has actually never been developed in a high school. It is the core plan formulated by the Educational Policies Commission for its hypothetical school in American City. The commission recommends that educational experiences in the core course in American City Senior High School, known as the common learnings course, be developed in the following six areas:

1. Civic responsibility and competence
2. Understanding of the operation of the economic system and of the human relations involved therein

3. Family relationships
4. Intelligent action as consumers
5. Appreciation of beauty
6. Proficiency in the use of language[14]

Organization of the Core Program around the Problems of Living

The learning experiences of pupils in core curriculum classes are often organized around problems of living. These problems may vary from strictly personal concerns to broad social problems of society. The type of curriculum design listed by some writers as the adolescent needs approach is also encompassed within this type of core organization. As was pointed out in Chapter 9, the line of demarcation between the social functions of living and the problems of living approaches is not sharp, and the two methods of design often blend gradually in actual practice.

The broad problem areas around which learning experiences in the core group are organized are usually selected by the faculty of the school offering the core program. To this extent there is considerable preplanning of the whole core area; however, a great deal of flexibility within a broad problem area is provided so that teachers and pupils cooperatively as groups may determine particular aspects of the area to be developed, goals to be set for the study, types of learning activities to be undertaken, and the like. Most curriculum specialists who have been strong advocates of the core type of organization favor the problems of living approach. Although they differ as to the types of problems that are appropriate for core groups to develop, all favor the selection of units for study that are meaningful and significant to learners.

One of the best illustrations of a core plan that utilizes the problems of living approach is the program at the University School of The Ohio State University, described in the next section of this chapter. Another illustration of this approach is to be found in the core program of McKinley High School of Honolulu, which replaces required subjects in English and social studies. It is centered around seven problem areas:

1. Vocational problems
2. Citizenship problems
3. Problems of home membership
4. Problems of health
5. How to use leisure time
6. How to live a better life
7. Improvement of written and oral English[15]

---

[14] *Education for All American Youth: A Further Look*, p. 238.

[15] Miles E. Carey, "Learning Comes through Living," *Educational Leadership*, 4:491-495 (May), 1947.

Pupil Interests and Experience as a Basis for Organizing Core Activities

In Chapter 9 the "experience" method of organizing curriculum experiences was considered briefly. The experience type of organization would necessitate a core plan. In such a program there would be no prescribed list of learning units or problems that the core group should study. The whole concept of the experience curriculum is that the learning activities of the class are planned cooperatively by the group itself on the basis of the interests, concerns, and felt needs of the participants. Hence a core program that utilized fully this type of curriculum design could not be described in advance in terms of learning units that might be studied by the group. To get an idea of what a core class would do under such a type of curriculum organization, we would have to examine the learning activities that had been undertaken by the group after it had completed its year's work in the core class.

In actual practice no schools are known that utilize completely the experience type of curriculum design, but a number draw heavily on this approach. Moreover, the experience concept is utilized to some extent in many core plans. Even though the basic organization may be formulated in terms of unified studies, the social functions of living, problems of living, or adolescent needs, most core plans allow the individual class and teacher considerable freedom to select and develop cooperatively particular learning units which the class may work out within the broad basic plan predetermined by the faculty of the school or by other appropriate school officials. Frequently, in the early stages of developing a core plan, schools throughout the country did considerable experimentation with the experience approach, but in time most schools have given it greater structure by moving to the problems of living, social functions, or even the unified studies approach. By experimentation with the experience types of approaches, however, school staffs have gained much knowledge about pupils' problems, interests, and concerns that have later been used as a basis for preplanning by teachers in more formal types of core organization.

Of core programs known to us, the core groups at Denby High School, Detroit, Michigan, make the most use of the experience approach. This high school organized an experimental core group within the large student body of the school. At the present time there are eight core classes organized in the four grades of nine through twelve; five teachers are involved. The classes meet for double periods in the ninth and eleventh grades, with the core program replacing social studies and English. In the tenth and twelfth grades the core groups meet for only one period a day and this class replaces English as a subject. Except for very limited restrictions, the core group, under the direction of its teacher, is free to develop any unit in which it is interested. In the ninth grade two units are required—an orientation unit and a unit on democracy. In the tenth grade a unit on English grammar is required; the whole core area of the eleventh grade is limited to American history; the twelfth grade is free to select the problems and units on which it wishes to work, with the exceptions of a unit on grammar and a unit on selection of a college, which is also required of pupils planning to attend college. The problem areas most frequently selected for study in the lower grades of the high school are those of a personal type, while those selected for study in the twelfth grade frequently deal with vocations and human relations.[16]

Relationship of Core Curriculum Plan to Curriculum Design

We are now in a better position to summarize the relationship of the core curriculum plan to the whole matter of design. From what has been stated so far in this chapter it is clear that the core curriculum plan itself is not a method of designing the curriculum in the sense that it indicates the basis used for selecting, organizing, and carrying forward the learning experiences of children. Rather, the core curriculum plan is an administrative method for scheduling and offering major aspects of the program of general education. It is apparent, however, that only certain types of curriculum design are appropriate for use in core plans. The traditional subject organization, for example, is inconsistent with the core concept. Moreover, core usually implies that certain types of approaches and methods are used in organizing and developing the learning experiences of pupils, such as the broad unit of work, cooperative group procedures, meaningful problem situations, and the like. Yet the core curriculum plan itself does not specify the kinds of learning experience that might be carried on in the core group; hence, strictly speaking, it is not a type of design.

Perhaps these distinctions are rather finely drawn for most teachers and curriculum workers, yet the important point to be made is that once a school faculty decides to use a core curriculum plan, it still needs to make further decisions as to the method to be used for determining the kinds of learning experience to be selected and carried forward by the core class and the type of work methods to be used in developing the learning experiences. These are important decisions involving questions of design and scope and sequence.

[16] Based on mimeographed material distributed by Denby High School to a group of visitors in February, 1951.

TYPES OF CORE PROGRAMS

Core developments in secondary schools throughout the country could be analyzed in several different ways. One method is based on the plan used for organizing learning experiences in the core group. This method has been followed in the previous section, where brief descriptions were given of types of curriculum organization used in a number of core programs. In this section, however, a more extensive description of several core programs or modified types of programs will be given. They will be classified according to the following four types of development of core programs in this country:

1. Core curriculum plans in junior high schools
2. Core curriculum plans in experimental high schools
3. Core curriculum plans in public high schools
4. Modified core curriculum plans in secondary schools

Since the core curriculum is quite new and many curriculum workers have not had firsthand contact with such programs, these longer descriptions, in which time schedules are illustrated and other points about the organization of the core program are discussed, should be an aid to understanding the basic concepts as well as the procedures used in such programs.

Core Curriculum Plans in the Junior High School

The core curriculum movement is expanding rapidly among the junior high schools of the nation. While no figures are available that are based on any sort of nation-wide survey, it is quite apparent to anyone who studies curriculum development that many junior high schools in all parts of the nation have adopted core programs of some type. Practically all of the junior high schools in Baltimore, as well as those throughout the state of Maryland, have core programs. The core plan is being widely used by junior high schools throughout Florida. Core programs are known to exist in the junior high schools of such city schools systems as Minneapolis, Denver, Tulsa, Oklahoma City, Kansas City and Springfield (Missouri), Newton (Massachusetts), Lincoln (Nebraska), Schenectady (New York), Battle Creek, Grand Rapids, and Flint (Michigan), and New York. California reports that 175 junior high schools offer a basic or core course.[17] Unquestionably, many, many other junior high school systems throughout the country have core programs. It should be pointed out that for one reason or another, not all schools label developments of this kind as core curriculum programs. However, many such programs

---

[17] U.S. Office of Education, *Core Curriculum Development: Problems and Practices* (Bulletin 1952, No. 5; Washington, D.C.: Government Printing Office, 1952).

conform to most, if not all, of the principal characteristics of core programs, regardless of the name.

The rapid development of core programs in the junior high school, as contrasted with the situation in four-year or senior high schools, is readily understandable. In the first place, the whole college admission problem does not weigh as heavily on the junior high schools. Second, the junior high school is a transitional institution between the elementary and the senior high school and is in a position to emulate the good practices of both institutions. Thus the development of the activity program in the elementary school has had its impact on the junior high school. Also, educators have come to believe that it is unwise to place a young seventh-grade pupil abruptly into the formal, rigid pattern of the typical secondary school program. Hence a core plan that enables one teacher to work with a group of pupils for two or more hours a day on a more informal basis, being responsible not only for important areas of learning but for the guidance, counseling, and all-round development of the child represents a sound compromise with the usual secondary school procedures.

Finally, the junior high school, as a newer educational institution, has not established long traditions of a formalized program, and undoubtedly this fact has encouraged faculties to experiment and to develop promising practices that represent a break with the traditional structure of secondary education.

The core class in English–Social Studies at Whittier Junior High School, Lincoln, Nebraska. As an illustration of the core program at the junior high school level, we shall describe the program of the Whittier Junior High School in Lincoln, Nebraska. The program in this school seems to be typical of many core programs in junior high schools throughout the country. Whittier Junior High School has an enrollment of approximately 600 pupils.[18]

As is shown by the daily schedule, excerpts of which are given in Table 8, the core classes in this school extend for three periods—two hours and ten minutes for some groups and up to two hours and thirty-five minutes for other groups. The course, designated as English–Social Studies, replaces separate courses formerly required in English and social studies and a home room period. Guidance activities and out-of-class and student activities such as are usually carried on in home rooms are taken care of in the core classes.

[18] This report is based on materials furnished by Mr. Emory Priefert, Principal, Mr. Henry Ross, Assistant Principal, and Miss Nora Veerhusen, Coordinator, and on transcriptions of wire recordings of planning sessions of core teachers, of classroom activities, and of discussions with core teachers, supplied by Dr. Will Leeds.

TABLE 8
Whittier Junior High School
(Second Semester 1953–54)

Emory Priefert—Principal   *Henry Ross—Ass't Principal*

TEACHER	ROOM	PER. 1	PER. 2	PER. 3	PER. 4	PER. 5	PER. 6	PER. 7
A	108	Plan	Elect. Home Ec.	7th Home Ec.	7th Home Ec.	7th Home Ec.	Elect. Home Ec.	8th Home Ec.
B	100	Type 2	Type 1	Type 1	Type 1	Plan	Type 1	Type 1
C	316	——7th Eng. & Soc. St.——			Plan	——7th Eng. & Soc. St.——		
D	207		——8th Eng. & Soc. St.——			——8th Eng. & Soc. St.——		
E	110 220	8th Home Ec.	8th Home Ec.	Plan	Cafe.	——7th Eng. & Soc. St.——		
F	312	8th Science	Dancing	Plan	8th Science	8th Science	8th Science	8th Science
G	320	——7th Eng. & Soc. St.——				——7th Eng. & Soc. St.——		
H	307	8th Arith.	8th Arith.	8th Arith.	Plan	——9th Eng. & Soc. St.——		
I	203	7th Arith.	7th Arith.	7th Arith.	Plan	——9th Eng. & Soc. St.——		
J	102	7th Arith.	——9th Eng. & Soc. St.——			Plan	7th Arith.	7th Arith.
K	303	8th Arith.	——9th Eng. & Soc. St.——			8th Arith.	Plan	8th Arith.
L	112	Plan	——8th Eng. & Soc. St.——			——8th Eng. & Soc. St.——		
M	222	——7th Eng. & Soc. St.——			Plan	——7th Eng. & Soc. St.——		
N	209	——9th Eng. & Soc. St.——			Applied Math.	Applied Math.	Plan	Applied Math.
O	212	Plan	Algebra	Algebra	Algebra	——9th Eng. & Soc. St.——		
P	113 106	——9th Eng. & Soc. St.——			7th Phys. Ed.	7th Phys. Ed.	8th Phys. Ed.	Plan
Q	305		——8th Eng. & Soc. St.——			——8th Eng. & Soc. St.——		
R	205	——9th Eng. & Soc. St.——			Plan	——9th Eng. & Soc. St.——		
S	210	——7th Eng. & Soc. St.——				——7th Eng. & Soc. St.——		
T	115 310	Plan	7th Science	8th Phys. Ed.	7th Science	7th Phys. Ed.	7th Science	7th Science
U	318	8th Arith.	Applied Math.	Applied Math.	8th Arith.	Applied Math.	Applied Math.	Plan
V	308	9th Science	7th Science	Plan	9th Science	7th Science	9th Science	9th Science

Period 1— 8:40– 9:33   Period 5— 1:05–1:45
Period 2— 9:37–10:22   Period 6— 1:50–2:30
Period 3—10:26–11:11   Period 7— 2:35–3:15
Period 4—11:15–12:00

NOTE: Excerpts only; sections not pertinent to this illustration are not included.

A better picture of the core program may be obtained by examining the class schedule. The schedule has been arranged so that usually the multiple-period teachers of any one grade level are free at the same time. This enables them to hold group planning sessions. This schedule illustrates one of the striking advantages of the core plan. For example, note that teachers C, D, G, L, M, Q, R, and S work with only two groups of pupils during the entire school day, or a total of 55 to 60 pupils in contrast to the 180 to 190 pupils in the classes of such teachers as A, B, F, T, U, and V. Likewise, the pupils work with not more than four different teachers during the school day, while under the conventional program a single youngster may have had as many as six different teachers and yet another teacher for his home room teacher.

In terms of the organization of learning experiences in the core program the Whittier plan may be identified as a unified studies approach. The faculty of the school follows in general the city-wide courses of study in social studies and English for the junior high school grades. Learning units are organized around social studies material, with English skills and literature being closely integrated in the development of the social studies unit. However, as is illustrated in Plate 23, ample opportunity

PLATE 23. THE CORE GROUP AT WHITTIER PLANS A STUDY OF TIMELY TOPICS OF THE DAY. *The flexibility of the core plan permits a class to give attention to current problems and events. (Courtesy of the Whittier Junior High School, Lincoln, Nebraska)*

is available for the development of units on subjects of current interest. A résumé of units of work and subject matter covered by the core classes as reported by core teachers to the coordinator follows:

Seventh Grade

1. Social studies area

    Geography and history of the Old World with emphasis on cultural backgrounds. Reports of core teachers show that they have developed units on Russia and its satellite countries, Spain, Germany, the Scandinavian countries, the islands of the Pacific, China and India, and the Union of South Africa. The countries studied and the order in which they were studied varied somewhat from group to group, but in general the units are organized around European and Asiatic countries and their peoples.

2. English

    a. Sentence building
    b. Punctuation
    c. Paragraph building
    d. Parts of speech
    e. Parts of sentences
    f. Use of library and reference material
    g. Free reading period
    h. Assigned readings for comprehension and appreciation
    i. Oral discussion and report
    j. Spelling

Eighth Grade

1. Social studies area

    American history and geography: Teacher reports show that most of the units developed in the eighth grade include the usual units included in American history and geography at this level. Attention is given to the colonization of America, the struggle for independence, the development of a new nation, the struggle over slavery, the development of the West, the emergence of the United States as a world power, and similar units.

2. English

    a. Parts of speech
    b. Subjects and predicates
    c. Direct and indirect objects
    d. Business letters
    e. Sentences and sentence structure
    f. Paragraphing

g. Spelling and vocabulary
h. Form
i. Outlining
j. Capitalization
k. Oral discussions and reports

Ninth Grade

1. Social studies area

   Community and world living: Teacher reports indicate that units were developed on the community, the state, the national government, international affairs, conservation, responsibilities of citizenship, and preparation for senior high school. Each of the ninth-grade core groups has charge of an issue of the school paper, so at the appropriate time each home room develops a unit revolving around the preparation and publication of the paper.

2. English

   a. Sentence structure and use
   b. Punctuation
   c. Parts of speech
   d. Phrases and clauses
   e. Use of correct oral English
   f. Principles of oral discussion
   g. Development of writing techniques
   h. Use of oral and written presentations, such as panels, speeches, and the like
   i. Development of listening skills
   j. Choral readings and poetry
   k. Reports on books

As is true of all good core programs, many of the vital educational experiences of children in the core class are not revealed through a simple listing of the units studied or the skills developed in English. Such a list does not reveal, for example, the experiences that children have in group living, in cooperative planning, in the development of the units, in the planning of excursions and trips, and in the planning of presentations of materials and findings, or the experiences in group relations gained through room parties, student activities, folk and social dancing, and the like. Neither does a listing of units indicate the extent to which genuine guidance goes on in the group, with the teacher helping pupils with their problems and counseling them on their future. Reports of Whittier teachers and transcriptions of teacher planning sessions reveal that the teachers themselves feel that important values of the core program are found in the greatly improved morale of both pupils and teachers, in the interests developed on the part of pupils in the activities of the core group, and in the opportunities this approach provides for the all-round growth and development of children. Many examples are cited where shy children or children with personality difficulties were aided in overcoming these difficulties through participation in group activities of the core class.

Core Curriculum Plans in Experimental High Schools

The term "experimental school" is used here to designate those laboratory and demonstration schools established by colleges of education in connection with teacher education programs. A number of these secondary schools have done considerable experimentation with core programs and consequently have contributed a great deal to our present know-how in developing and organizing such plans. Foremost among these schools were the Horace Mann School and the Lincoln School of Teachers College, Columbia University, until their disbandment a few years ago in favor of a program of action research in public school systems. The University School of The Ohio State University has also been very active in the movement. A number of other schools have contributed significantly to the development of our concepts and understandings about core programs but no effort will be made here to single them out. We have selected as illustrative of core curriculum developments in these experimental schools the program of the upper division of The University School of The Ohio State University.[19]

The secondary school of The University School includes Grades 7 through 12. Approximately 240 pupils are enrolled in these six grades. The societal needs of young people are analyzed by the staff as a basis for building the core program. The core program primarily provides for the general education of pupils; opportunities are offered for the development of special interests through a program of elective subjects. The core program is scheduled for three hours each day in Grades 7, 8, and 9 and for one and one half hours daily in Grades 10, 11, and 12, plus an additional period on Mondays. However, in the seventh, eighth, and ninth grades music is scheduled during the core periods, and on Wednesdays forty-five minutes of core time is used for meetings of school organizations.

Pupils in the junior high school grades take three subjects in addition to core: physical education, mathematics, and an arts course. The

[19] This report is based primarily on The University School, The Ohio State University, *A Description of Curricular Experiences: The Upper School* (Columbus. O.: The School, 1952).

arts elective includes related arts, home arts, music, typing, and science. Pupils in the upper three grades include three elective subjects in their schedule, thus permitting them to take a total of nine elective subjects during the three years. In addition, senior high school pupils elect each year from the following: orchestra, band, instrumental ensemble, chorus, dramatics, or school service in the art area. These groups meet during a forty-five minute period only. It will be noted that in Grades 7, 8, and 9 separate classes in social studies and English are not offered. Since these subjects are usually offered in the subject curriculum, it is apparent that the core replaces these traditional subjects. In Grades 10, 11, and 12 subject offerings in social studies, English, and science are available in the elective program so that the core as such does not replace specialized studies in these three areas.

In the secondary program at The University School the core classes

1. Are required of all students.
2. Are scheduled for a longer period of time than are other classes (approximately three hours—Grades seven, eight, and nine; one and one half hours—Grades ten, eleven, and twelve).
3. Are responsible for a major part of the common learnings which are defined as the learning activities that are thought to be basic to the education of all students.
4. Provide learning activities which cut across conventional subject matter lines.
5. Provide learning activities and experiences which are in harmony with adolescent interests, needs, and concerns.
6. Function in such a way as to care for individual differences in a learning climate conducive to personal and class guidance.

The core classes also carry responsibilities for

1. The continuous experiences as stated in the *Philosophy and Purposes.*
2. Activities related to student government and school organizations.
3. Immediate problems of group living (planning class dances, class money-making projects, participation in Red Cross drives, etc.).
4. Individual reading and writing programs.
5. Free choice experiences in other areas (science, arts, physical education, social sciences, and mathematics) to the extent that it is feasible.[20]

[20] *Ibid.,* p. 10.

As a result of extended planning by the school staff the following problem areas have been selected as bases for organizing core learning units in the various grades. However, considerable flexibility exists as is indicated in the statement of the staff:

The list of problem areas is not final and all-inclusive. In the process of selecting a learning unit, pupils and teacher will occasionally find their major interest to be in a problem not included in the list. When this occurs the teacher will present the matter at a grade staff meeting for the purpose of obtaining permission for the group to study the topic. Seldom, if ever, is permission denied when the proposed topic appears promising to pupils and teacher who have expressed desire in studying the topic.[21]

Problem Areas for Grades Seven, Eight, and Nine

   A. Personal living (problems related to growing up)
1. Understanding my body
2. Beliefs and superstitions
3. Hobbies
4. Managing my personal affairs

   B. Personal-social living (problems related to living with others)
1. Sports and recreation
2. Living in the University Schools
3. Living in the home
4. Living in the neighborhood
5. Personality and appearance

   C. Social-civic-economic living (problems of living in and understanding society)
1. Earning a living
2. Housing
3. Natural resources
4. Community agencies and services
5. Communication
6. Living in Columbus
7. Living in Ohio
8. Living in another country or in other countries

[21] *Ibid.,* p. 12.

Problem Areas for Grades Ten, Eleven, and Twelve

A. Tenth grade

 1. Problems of healthful living
 2. Problems of living in an urban society
 3. Problems of the family as a basic social unit
 4. Development of the American scene

B. Eleventh grade

 1. Problems of living in the atomic age
 2. The problems of establishing beliefs
 3. The problems of making a living (exploring vocations)
 4. Current world problems

C. Twelfth grade

 1. Problems of producer-consumer economics
 2. Implications of scientific advancement
 3. Major conflicting ideologies
 4. The bases for determining values by which to live

Core Curriculum Programs in Public High Schools

True core programs that conform to the characteristics established earlier in this chapter have not been developed extensively by the four-year or senior high schools of this country. No definitive survey of the status of such programs has been made, although the United States Office of Education did endeavor to obtain information on the situation.[22] The difficulty in obtaining accurate data lies in the definition of the core, for what some schools call core is not a true core program at all. Moreover, a number of schools that report core programs use it only on an experimental basis with but a small part of the student body participating, such as is the case at the Denby High School, whose program was described earlier in this chapter.

As a result of our extensive visits to secondary schools in all parts of the country and conferences with a large number of officials in state departments of education and with curriculum directors, we believe that the core program at Murphy High School, Mobile, Alabama, will serve very well to illustrate the movement as it has developed in those high

[22] U.S. Office of Education, *Core Curriculum in Public High Schools* (Bulletin 1950, No. 5,) and *Core Curriculum Development: Problems and Practices* (Bulletin 1952, No. 5; Washington, D.C.: Government Printing Office, 1950, 1952).

schools that are making extensive use of the core organization.[23] Murphy High School is a large four-year high school, with a normal enrollment of about four thousand pupils. Approximately one half of the student body is enrolled in the core program, and the principal states that considerably more would be in the program if more trained teachers were available. Enrollment in the core program is entirely voluntary. With such a fine group of young people as the one pictured in Plate 24, it is

PLATE 24. A CORE GROUP IN A PLANNING SESSION AT MURPHY HIGH SCHOOL, MOBILE, ALABAMA. *Group planning under student leadership is an important aspect of a good core program. (Courtesy of the Murphy High School, Mobile, Alabama)*

readily understandable why the core program is so effective. Even though Murphy has fourteen buildings on the school campus, the faculty has resisted any suggestions that the core groups be clustered together in one or two of the buildings. This procedure results in a more normal situation, without singling out the core as an experimental or separate phase of the school's program. As is shown in Table 9, the core program extends for a minimum of two one-hour periods, and in some cases also includes the home room period. This schedule shows the complete assignments for teachers working in the program; single-period classes listed are assignments outside the core program. A teacher remains with the same core group throughout the four years, but he may utilize teachers in the specialized areas as resource persons as the need arises.

[23] This account of the core program at Murphy is based on personal observation by one of us and on information supplied by Dr. Raymond G. Wilson, Principal.

TABLE 9

Daily Class Schedule for the Core Program, Murphy High School, Mobile, Alabama

TEACHER	H. ROOM	PER. 1	PER. 2	PER. 3	PER. 4	PER. 5	PER. 6
A	8-113	Eng. 8 and Hist. 8			Stu. Coun.	Eng. 2 and G.S. 2	
B	8-171	Eng. 2 and G.S. 2		Eng. 8 and Hist. 8			Eng. 2
C	2-222	Eng. 6		Eng. 6	Eng. 6	Eng. 2 and G.S. 2	
D	6-220	Eng. 2 and G.S. 2		Eng. 8 and Hist. 8		Counsel. Testing	Eng. 2
E	6-226	Eng. 6 & Pro. Liv. 6		Eng. 6 & Pro. Liv. 6		Eng. 2 and G.S. 2	
F	8-161	Eng. 8 and Hist. 8		Eng. 2 and G.S. 2		Eng. 2 and G.S. 2	
G	2-120	Journalism	Eng. 2	Hi Times	Eng. 2 and G.S. 2		Hi Times
H	2-305	Eng. 2 and G.S. 2		Eng. 2 and G.S. 2			
I	2-212	Eng. 4 and C. 4		Eng. 8	Eng. 8	Eng. 5	
J	8-123	Eng. 8 and Hist. 8		Eng. 2 and G.S. 2			Eng. 2
K	8-170	Eng. 8 and Hist. 8		Eng. 8 and Hist. 8		Span. 2	
L	6-181	Eng. 8 and Hist. 8		Eng. 8 and Hist. 8		Eng. 6 & Pro. Liv. 6	
M	2-110	Eng. 2 and G.S. 2			Eng. 2 and G.S. 2		Eng. 5
N	6-224	Eng. 6 & Pro. Liv. 6		Eng. 2		Eng. 6 & Pro. Liv. 6	
O	8-252	Eng. 6 & Pro. Liv. 6		Eng. 6 & Pro. Liv. 6			Math. 2
P	6-161A	Eng. 6 & Pro. Liv. 6			Eng. 3	Eng. 6 & Pro. Liv. 6	
Q	2-218	Eng. 2 and G.S. 2		Eng. 2 and G.S. 2			Speech 3
R	2-250	Eng. 6 & Pro. Liv. 6		Psych. 8	Psych. 8	Psych. 8	
S	4-122	Eng. 4 and C. 4		Eng. 1	Stu. Coun.	Eng. 2 and G.S. 2	

G.S.—General Science; C.—Civics; Pro. Liv.—Problems of Living; Eng.—English; Hist.—History; Psych.—Psychology; Span.—Spanish; Stu. Coun.—Student Council; Counsel.—Counseling.

Note: Single period subjects are teacher assignments outside the core program; the complete school schedule is not given here.

The traditional subject requirements, still required for those not electing the core program at Murphy, are:

Ninth Grade

English
General science
Physical education

Tenth Grade

English
Civics
Physical education

Eleventh Grade

English

Twelfth Grade

English
United States history

Except for physical education, the core program replaces these required subjects, and pupils enrolled in core are given credit in them. In addition, since the core includes two periods, pupils in the eleventh grade are given credit in problems of living.

The faculty of the school has suggested a tentative list of units for development in the core program. In general, this constitutes the scope and sequence of the core program, but it is subject to change if the teach' ers so decide.

SUGGESTED SCOPE AND SEQUENCE PLAN
Core Program, Murphy High School, 1952–1953

Ninth Grade

Orientation to

a. School
b. Core
c. Being an adolescent
d. Abilities, talents
e. Community membership
f. Literature
g. Vocational possibilities
h. Geography
i. Nature

Tenth Grade

Tolerance and understanding through

a. Citizenship
b. Law and justice
c. Peace and war
d. Recreation
e. Current affairs
f. Culture of other peoples
g. Appreciation of fine arts

Eleventh Grade

American life and culture
a. Literature
b. History
c. Economic system
d. Government
e. People
f. Conservation
g. Civil defense

Twelfth Grade

Life adjustment to
a. Literature
b. Family life
c. Consumer education
d. College or job
e. Mental health
f. World affairs (United Nations)
g. World religions
h. History, political parties

While the core program at Murphy draws heavily on the unified studies approach, it certainly contains important elements of the functions of living and problems of living approaches, too.

Modified Types of Core Programs in Secondary Schools

A large number of secondary educators throughout the country see a great deal of merit in the core curriculum plan, believing that it represents a significant effort to develop a more functional and meaningful program for adolescents in our schools. Yet faculties of many of these schools have felt that it is not appropriate to develop a full-fledged core program at this time. In an effort to gain as many of the advantages of the core plan as possible and yet not encounter some of the serious obstacles inherent in developing such a plan in a public high school, many high schools have developed various types of functional courses that have most of the characteristics of a true core program, except that they are scheduled for only single periods. Although problems courses of various types are not new in American secondary schools, the movement has developed by leaps and bounds within the last decade. The important characteristics of these new types of courses are these:

1. Learning experiences are organized principally around units that deal with the needs, problems, and concerns of the pupils themselves.

2. Subject matter from any appropriate field is used. However, most of the courses draw heavily on the social studies field, although content from the biological sciences, health, psychology, and family life education is also used rather extensively.

3. Instruction is organized around large units of work.

4. Cooperative group methods are used in carrying forward the learning units, and often in selecting at least some of the units to be developed.

5. These classes give considerable attention, and often primary attention, to guidance and counseling.

6. The problems class usually does not replace the traditional required courses in English, American history, civics or government, or world history.

A comparison of this statement of characteristics with those of core programs, given earlier in this chapter, shows that these new types of problems courses are quite similar to core courses, with the exception that they are scheduled for only single periods and do not attempt to replace any traditional academic subjects usually required of pupils. Often these problems courses are required. A great variety of titles are used throughout the country to designate them, such as Social Studies I, IX, or other appropriate numeral designations, Freshman (or Sophomore, Junior, or Senior) Goals, Social Living, Basic Living, General Education, Family Living, Human Relations, and the like. Obviously, the units developed in such courses vary, yet basically they all represent an effort to deal with the important personal and social problems that concern adolescents in today's world. Many of the courses have evolved as a result of the guidance movement in the American secondary school, and represent efforts to provide group and individual guidance in scheduled class situations. In these classes in which the guidance function looms large, the class often serves as a place for carrying on the testing program, obtaining personal data about each pupil, developing cumulative and other guidance records, and carrying on the functions of educational planning.

Descriptions of literally scores of such courses, drawn from educational literature and from our own personal knowledge, could be given, but we will limit our descriptions here to a brief résumé of some of the courses that illustrate this new approach to curriculum planning in the secondary school. The Canton (Illinois) High School has developed two such courses, one at the freshman level and one at the senior level. The freshman course, which is required, is called Social Studies 9. This course is divided into four major areas, each of which extends for a period of nine weeks. These areas are personality and etiquette, guidance and vocations, family living, and health and safety. The senior course, designated as Social Studies 12, comprises three areas, each scheduled for a twelve-week period. The three units are family living, educational guidance, and psychology.[24]

The Champaign (Illinois) Junior High School has recently added to the school offerings a new one-semester course called personal-social living. Separate sections of the course are offered for boys and girls. The primary objective of the course is to help youngsters with the five developmental tasks listed by Corey.[25] The senior high school in the same school system has a one-semester course for senior girls called personal relations. On the basis of teacher-pupil planning it has been decided to include five broad units of work in the course: dating, social adjustment, courtship and engagement, marriage, and relationships within the family.[26]

The Oakwood Township High School, Oakwood, Illinois, offers a senior course in social problems. The required units of study in this course include family life and marriage problems, consumer buying, war —its causes and costs, securing action for community improvements, current national problems, how the culture affects the individual, achieving intercultural understanding, selecting a college, choosing a vocation, post-school recreation, and developing your personality.[27]

The Lincoln Senior High School, Lincoln, Nebraska, has developed a group guidance course that is required of all students throughout the six semesters. These classes meet for two single periods a week. This

[24] Illinois State Department of Public Instruction, *The Story in Nineteen Schools*, (Springfield, Ill.: The Department, 1950), pp. 17–20.

[25] See Chapter 5.

[26] Illinois State Department of Public Instruction, *op. cit.*, pp. 48–52.

[27] *Ibid.*, p. 232.

program encompasses the group counseling and guidance program, with attention being focused on problems involving guidance situations. These classes are taught by the boys' and girls' counselors for each of the three senior high school grades.[28]

This résumé should give curriculum workers some understanding of the development of the problems type of courses in high schools throughout the country. Illustrations could be multiplied many times over, for many educators have had considerable firsthand experience with such courses in schools with which they have been associated.

THE PLACE OF CORE PROGRAMS IN CURRICULUM PLANNING

We shall analyze the core plan in general on the basis of the principles and points of view presented throughout this book. In various places we have stated our views on the educational process, on the nature of learning, and on desirable characteristics of a good educational program. Anyone who starts with different ideas about the educational program and the nature of learning may have a different attitude toward the core plan.

Merits of the Core Curriculum Plan

In our opinion, the chief merits of the core curriculum plan, when such a plan is properly organized and soundly developed, are as follows:

1. The core curriculum plan encourages the use of learning experiences that are meaningful and significant to pupils. In core curriculum plans that genuinely adhere to the criteria previously listed for a true core program, more purposeful units of work should result. The core plan itself signifies that pupils participate cooperatively in the planning of learning exeriences, at least within broad, designated areas of study. In selecting, planning, and developing such units the needs, concerns, interests, and problems of pupils will be important considerations. This should make for better learning activities.

2. The core curriculum organization facilitates the attainment of broad outcomes desired in the educational program. We have already presented in Chapter 7 statements of basic outcomes desired from the educational program. A critical comparison of the core curriculum plan as it has been organized and carried out in some of our schools and the traditional subject organization indicates that these broad and basic objectives of education may more readily be realized through the former than through the latter. The subject organization places emphasis on the

[28] Based on personal conferences with Mr. William Bogar, Principal.

mastery of subject matter and the acquisition of skills. While these are essential outcomes and it is true that many of the other basic outcomes may be attained under such a curriculum organization, it nevertheless is evident that the core plan will facilitate the attainment of a number of important outcomes not so readily achieved in the usual subject approach, such as problem solving, cooperative action, self-discipline, and many other values of this type. The core curriculum procedure places an emphasis on democratic social living in the school group.

3. The core curriculum plan, by utilizing broad units of work and encouraging the cooperative planning of such units, is psychologically sound. If the pupils play important roles in determining the type of learning experiences in which they will engage and if the learning unit itself is planned on a broad scope, the pupils see meaning and purpose in what they do in the school, with the result that learning is at a higher level of efficiency and pupils have a strong motivation for undertaking the activities that have been cooperatively planned.

4. The core curriculum plan promotes the use of problem-solving methods and the techniques of critical thinking. Learning activities in the core are usually organized around meaningful problems, and the pupils participate in widespread activities of a problem-solving nature. They are concerned with finding solutions to problems which are important to them. They are encouraged to use the methods of reason, such as collecting and organizing data, synthesizing, weighing evidence, proposing solutions, testing conclusions, and the like. Since ability to face squarely our problems and to deal with them efficiently and adequately is a desirable and basic purpose of education, the core curriculum program contributes significantly to the attainment of this objective.

5. The core curriculum aids in the development of relationships among the various fields of knowledge and provides for the use of knowledge in meaningful situations. The true core curriculum program organizes learning experiences around broad problems or areas, and consequently subject matter from any field is used that will contribute to the solution of the problem or to the development of the area of study. Thus pupils learn to integrate subject matter and to see interrelationships between various subject fields. Also, the core curriculum plan encourages the use of knowledge in functional situations.

6. Many skills and abilities are developed in meaningful situations and are used to further ongoing activities. One of the most important characteristics of the core approach is that English skills and, to a limited extent, computational skills are utilized to carry forward learning activities of importance to the pupil. Thus, skills are developed in a functional situation, not in an academic, unrealistic recitation procedure, as is too frequently true in the subject curriculum.

7. *A functional program of guidance that endeavors to help pupils with their problems and concerns is more readily developed in the core group.* On one of the basic characteristics of a good core program is that functional guidance is carried on by the teacher. Learning experiences and guidance activities are integrated in the core. Moreover, the core teacher, by working with the pupils in his core group for longer periods of time, comes to know the pupils better and is in a better position to help them with their problems.

8. *The core curriculum plan facilitates the adaptation of learning experiences to the individual needs and capacities of the pupils.* It is easier to adapt learning experiences to the individual abilities and capacities of pupils and also to their interests and needs in the broad types of learning units developed in good core programs. Through cooperative group planning and the development of a variety of learning activities, each pupil finds something of importance to do in carrying forward the units of work, and he may readily work at a task within his capacity and level of attainment.

9. *The core curriculum plan encourages the use of broad, flexible methods of teaching.* In the core program teachers usually make greater use of cooperative group methods and utilize a variety of activities in developing units of work. This provides a rich and stimulating environment for learning.

We would not be so foolhardy as to maintain that all core programs exhibit these advantages in a high degree or that classes organized under the traditional subject curriculum do not achieve any of them. Obviously, such a position would be absurd. Rather, we feel that a critical comparison of educational experiences provided under the core approach and those provided under other methods of curriculum design indicates that, by and large, core programs do exemplify to a greater degree the characteristics of good curriculum listed in Chapter 1.

Difficulties in Using the Core Plan

If the core curriculum plan promises so much in providing rich and meaningful educational experiences for pupils, why is it not used more at present in the schools of the United States? A number of difficulties militate against its widespread use at the present time. These will be considered briefly.

1. There is an inevitable lag between theory and practice in human affairs. Everyone, of course, is well aware of the fact that we never put immediately into practice what has been developed on a theoretical and experimental basis, even though the early testing out of the theory indicates its soundness. In the first place, it takes time for theory to spread; the matter under consideration must be widely discussed and the people who work in the field must have ample opportunity to explore its assumptions, to become thoroughly familiar with the things proposed, and to examine the operation of the practice in experimental operation. Second, it is not to be supposed that all the people concerned readily accept the theory or are impressed by experimental practice, new developments, or new inventions in human affairs. And third, there is the matter of sheer inertia; many people are much more content to carry on in the traditional ways or to do things as they have been done before, even though they might be convinced that the newer methods are sounder or offer promise for improved practice. It is a difficult thing for people to give up old ways, to explore new approaches, and to develop new methods of work.

Mort, on the basis of rather extensive research in the area of school adaptation to new practices, estimates that there is a lag of approximately fifty years between the time that a new educational practice is accepted in theory and proved meritorious in experimental practice and the time that it is adopted quite generally by the schools of the country.[29]

2. Lack of adequate curriculum guides and teaching materials makes it difficult to develop the core program. One of the most serious deterrents to the use of the core organization in many schools is the lack of adequate curriculum guides for teachers and of well-developed and useful teaching materials, such as textbooks, source materials, and the like, for use in such programs. Too frequently core teachers have been left pretty much on their own, without adequate guides and without even any experience to help them in carrying forward the core type of program. Sometimes this has resulted in a hodgepodge of classroom activities and a lack of organization that laid the school open to criticism by both parents and teachers. In some instances the types of units developed in the core program by individual teachers in the absence of systematic

[29] Paul Mort, *Principles of School Administration* (New York: McGraw-Hill Book Company, Inc., 1946), p. 200.

planning by the faculty and parents have discredited the core program and led to its abandonment or modification.

Teachers are familiar with the subject organization and feel secure in this approach. Very likely their own school experiences and certainly most of their college work were organized in terms of the subject fields. Most of our city and state school systems have developed over a long period of years curriculum guides and courses of study of various types to help the teacher in planning instruction in the common subjects. But seldom have schools prepared comprehensive guides for use by teachers in planning core programs. Before school systems can undertake the sound development of core programs, they will need to have appropriate members of their staff spend a great deal of time in preparing guides and other types of materials for teachers who will work in the core program.

3. Teachers are not adequately prepared to teach in core programs. Another serious obstacle to the development of core programs is the lack of trained teachers. At the present time it is difficult to find many teachers who have had special preparation for teaching in core programs. They have not studied the theory of core programs, nor have they had the opportunity to observe good core programs in action in demonstration schools or in public schools. Few have had any opportunity to do student teaching in such programs. Consequently a school system that seeks to develop a core organization is faced with the necessity of training its teachers on the job. While this may be very effective training, it places an additional responsibility on the school that it is often not in a position to assume. The result is that schools are reluctant to undertake the development of core programs, since it means that the in-service education of teachers in core methods must parallel the development of the core itself. For schools that do develop such programs this lack of trained teachers often creates a great many difficulties until the teachers have gained adequate experience on the job.

4. Often parents and the public generally are not ready to accept the core plan of curriculum organization. In some communities it is difficult to obtain the widespread support of parents for core programs. This failure is due to two factors: the reluctance of many parents to approve new practices in general in the school, and the disfavor with which the core concept is regarded by many parents in many communities. For example, many parents are very critical of what they regard as progressive education. Since to them core programs represent the epitome of progressive education, it is likely that they will at the outset be quite hostile to their development in the schools. Also, reactionary groups of citizens who do not favor the investigation of social conditions and controversial social issues by young adolescents may oppose any programs that encourage such study.

On the other hand, a number of schools have worked closely with parents in exploring the basic concepts of the core program and in formulating plans for the development of the program; such schools have obtained enthusiastic support for the core plan and have benefited from the counsel of parents. It should be apparent to any thoughtful curriculum worker that it is quite unwise to develop a core type of organization without the full cooperation and understanding of the parents of the school children involved.

5. College entrance requirements have often militated against core programs. The extent to which college entrance requirements throttle curriculum improvement in the secondary school has been discussed previously. Suffice it to say here that the usual pattern of college entrance requirements is not conducive to the development of core programs. These requirements are often stated in terms of specific subjects and no adjustments are made for the core type of program. Pupils who take core may be deficient in entrance requirements unless the college applies credits in core to the requirements in English and social studies. Some colleges even refuse to accept credit in the newer type of problems courses. However, many schools that have developed core programs have found it possible to work out arrangements so that pupils who desire to go to college are not handicapped thereby in gaining admission.

6. The demands for specialization in a field of knowledge hinder the development of core programs. Many pupils, as well as their parents, feel that their desires to specialize in certain areas of work will be curtailed under a core plan. They fear that it may be difficult to obtain the amount of specialization they would like or to elect subjects in certain fields if they are forced to participate in a core program that extends for longer periods of time. For example, pupils in vocational schools, or in vocational courses in the comprehensive type of school, may find it difficult to take all the work they want in their field of specialization if they spend two periods a day in a core program. Similarly, pupils who are college-bound, and want to build up a knowledge of particular subject fields, feel that they will be unable to elect enough specialized courses in the field if they must spend time in the core programs. This demand for specialization and the feeling that a person is not educated unless he has taken work in certain academically respectable fields are serious deterrents to the development of the core program in the senior high school.

Use of the Core Organization in Curriculum Planning

From what has been stated in this chapter, the reader will logically conclude that we ourselves feel that the core plan represents a desirable procedure for organizing part of the educational experiences of pupils in the junior and the senior high schools. Obviously it is not a panacea for all the ills of education; yet it holds considerable promise for improving curriculum organization at these levels. However, to constitute an adequate basis for curriculum organization, the core program must be soundly planned and carefully developed by curriculum workers who are thoroughly familiar with the psychology of learning, the basis for human motivation, and the outcomes desired from the educational experiences provided by the school.

In view of the difficulties inherent in developing a core program, we would be quite reluctant to urge schools to rush pell-mell into the adoption of such procedures. The core must be developed on a sound base or it will be doomed to failure; moreover, it should not be established until the staff of the school, the parents, and the pupils themselves thoroughly understand the core idea and generally approve the use of this approach. As a matter of fact, it may be desirable for many schools, particularly four-year or senior high schools, to utilize some intermediate types of programs before attempting to develop a full-fledged core program. As is indicated in an earlier section, the use of problems courses represents a desirable stage in the development of the core program. Most high schools are already offering some courses of this type, and they provide the school staff with valuable experience in developing units of work with boys and girls based on significant social and personal problems, as well as opportunities to gain experience in cooperative planning with pupils. Moreover, through such courses parents come to recognize the contribution which the school can make to the education of boys and girls through the organization of instruction around problems of significance to the pupils themselves.

Another approach to the development of a core curriculum plan is through the unified studies approach. This type of curriculum organization has been discussed as one type of core program. Many schools are finding that this is a desirable type of instructional organization to use in moving toward a core program based on a more functional approach. Also, it provides more security for many teachers, since they can teach on the basis of subject areas; moreover, parents feel that the traditional subjects are still being emphasized.

Throughout this discussion the emphasis has been placed on junior and senior high schools. This is proper, not because we do not feel that the whole core idea does not have merit for the elementary school, but because we recognize that the program in good elementary schools has long since exemplified the best characteristics of core programs, and that it is from the elementary schools that the main concept of the core plan has developed. We confine the discussion to junior and senior high schools because the term "core curriculum" is usually used to designate a plan of curriculum organization at that level. Nevertheless, we should acknowledge that many good elementary schools are already following these same basic concepts in curriculum planning.

Although we believe that the core curriculum plan holds much promise for the formulation of a richer and more functional educational program for the secondary school, we do not wish to minimize the fact that a great deal of improvement in the curriculum of the secondary school may be brought about without its adoption. We do not wish to imply that progress is not possible unless a school is willing to go all-out for a core program. Actually, very promising improvements in the secondary school can be brought about without the formal adoption of a core curriculum plan as such.

As for the development of a core program in the secondary school, we believe that in the four-year high school or the senior high school the educational experiences in the core should be organized around the significant personal-social problems which concern adolescents. At the junior high school level, some attention should be given to the important personal concerns of young adolescents, and help should be given them in the core program in adjusting to secondary schools. It should be emphasized that the core group becomes the guidance group also, so that the core teachers should be concerned at all levels with the personal problems of their groups and should use time in the core classes to help these young adolescents with their major problems of growing up.

A number of educators and members of school staffs are giving increasing attention to the bases for organizing educational experiences in core programs. While no one would presume that school systems throughout the country should adopt a uniform set of problems to be developed in core programs, the results of the thinking of various specialists and committees that have given considerable attention to the matter should be helpful to curriculum workers in planning core programs. Harold Alberty of The Ohio State University, among others, has proposed a set of problem areas that may be suggestive to core workers:

1. Orientation to the school
2. Home and family life
3. Community life
4. Contemporary cultures

5. Contemporary America among the nations
6. Competing political, social, and economic ideologies
7. Personal value systems
8. World religions
9. Communication
10. Resource development, conservation, and use
11. Human relations
12. Physical and mental health
13. Planning
14. Science and technology
15. Vocational orientation
16. Hobbies and interests
17. Public opinion
18. Education
19. War and peace[30]

For Further Study

Alberty, Harold, "Developing a Curriculum That Meets the Needs of Junior High School Youth," *Bulletin,* National Association of Secondary School Principals, No. 146, 31:69–81 (April), 1947.

Considers the core curriculum and describes various types of core programs. Explains the use of the resource unit in core teaching.

--------, "A Proposal for Reorganizing the High-School Curriculum on the Basis of a Core Program," *Progressive Education,* 28:57–61 (November), 1950.

Presents basic principles of curriculum planning at the secondary school level, and gives a list of problem areas that are appropriate for core organization.

--------, *Reorganizing the High-School Curriculum.* Rev. ed.; New York: The Macmillan Company, 1953.

Chapter VI discusses core programs.

Board of Education of the City of New York, *Suggestions to Teachers of Experimental Core Classes.* Curriculum Bulletin, 1950–1951 Series, No. 2. New York: The Board, 1951.

A guide for developing the core program in the ninth and tenth grades, based on three years' experience with the XG program in that city.

Bostwick, Prudence, and Chandos Reid, *A Functional High-School Program.* New York: Hinds, Hayden & Eldredge, Inc., 1947.

Discusses the core curriculum and suggests problems suitable for study in such programs.

Burnett, Will, and Bernice Burnett, "Core Program in Action," *Education,* Vol. 73, No. 5 (January), 1953.

[30] Alberty, "Designing Programs to Meet the Common Needs of Youth," *lcc. cit.*

This special issue describes several core programs in considerable detail. Recordings of core class sessions are given and procedures are analyzed.

Caswell, Hollis L. (ed), *The American High School*. Eighth Yearbook of the John Dewey Society. New York: Harper & Brothers, 1946.

In Chapter 8 Caswell proposes a curriculum plan for the secondary school that includes a personal-social problems type of core program.

Educational Policies Commission, *Education for All American Youth: A Further Look*. Washington, D.C.: National Educational Association, 1952.

The common learnings program of a core type of organization in this hypothetical high school in described on pages 218–229 and 237–254.

Faunce, Roland, and Nelson Bossing, *Developing the Core Curriculum*. New York: Prentice-Hall, Inc., 1951.

A thorough discussion of core programs, including examples of actual programs in operation.

Harap, Henry, *Social Living in the Curriculum*. Nashville, Tenn.: George Peabody College, Division of Surveys and Field Services, 1952.

Reports the author's observations of a core type of class at each grade level in the school.

Illinois State Department of Public Instruction, *The Story in Nineteen Schools*. Circular Series A, No. 51, Illinois Secondary School Curriculum Program, Bulletin No. 10. Springfield, Ill.: The Department, 1950.

Describes newer types of programs in certain Illinois secondary schools.

Krug, Edward, and others, *Multiple-Period Curricular Organization in Wisconsin Secondary Schools*. Madison, Wis.: School of Education, University of Wisconsin, 1952.

A survey of the extent of multiple-period types of curriculum organization and practices followed in the various schools.

Leonard, J. Paul, *Developing the Secondary School Curriculum*. Rev. ed.; New York: Rinehart & Company, Inc., 1953.

Chapter 14 discusses the core curriculum; the entire book provides background information.

MacConnell, Charles M., Ernest Melby, C. O. Arndt, and Leslee Bishop, *New Schools for a New Culture*. Rev. ed.; New York: Harper & Brothers, 1953.

Describes the core program and its development at Evanston Township High School.

Mudd, Dorothy, *A Core Program Grows*. Bel Air, Md.: Board of Education of Harford County, 1949.

An extensive description of the core programs in the junior high schools of Harford County.

National Society for the Study of Education, *Adapting the Secondary-School Program to the Needs of Youth*. Part I, Fifty-second Yearbook. Chicago: The University of Chicago Press, 1953.

Chapter VII, by Harold Alberty, classifies core programs according to types, and discusses the strengths and weaknesses of each type.

Noar, Gertrude, *The Junior High School*. New York: Prentice-Hall, Inc., 1953.

Chapters 6, 9, and 10 discuss the core curriculum plan, with illustrations from practices followed in Gillespie Junior High School in Philadelphia.

Ovsiew, Leon, *Making the Core Work*. New York: Metropolitan School Study Council, 1951.

A discussion of the core program in the junior high schools of Elizabeth, N.J.

Pierce, Paul R., "Shaping the Curriculum of Youth," *North Central Association Quarterly*, 23:339–344 (April), 1949.

Describes the core program at Wells High School, Chicago.

Spears, Harold, *The High School for Today*. New York: American Book Company, 1950.

Chapter 7 presents the characteristics of core programs and illustrates with an account of the development of a core program in a high school.

Tyler, Ralph, "The Core Curriculum," *NEA Journal*, 42:563–565 (December), 1953.

An excellent summary of the current situation and evaluation of possibilities.

The University School, The Ohio State University, *A Description of Curricular Experiences: The Upper School*. Columbus, O.: The School, 1952.

An excellent discussion of the purposes and methods of the core plan and a description of the program in this particular school.

Van Til, William, "Credo in Action," *Peabody Journal of Education*, 29:212–228 (January), 1952.

An excellent description of what the members of a core class in the University School of Ohio State University studied, and of how they worked.

Wright, Grace S., *Core Curriculum in Public High Schools: An Inquiry into Practices, 1949*. U.S. Office of Education Bulletin 1950, No. 5. Washington, D.C.: Government Printing Office, 1950.

Reports a survey of practices in the United States in the use of core curriculum plans.

————, *Core Curriculum Development: Problems and Practices*. U.S. Office of Education Bulletin 1952, No. 5. Washington, D.C.: Government Printing Office, 1952.

Classifies core programs according to types, and illustrates practices in each type.

chapter 11

Administrative Considerations in Curriculum Planning

In concluding our consideration of the organization of the total educational program of the school, which has been the subject matter of Part 3 of this book, we shall discuss certain administrative considerations of importance in curriculum planning. A total plan of education for boys and girls must be envisaged if the entire program is to serve most effectively the needs of youngsters growing up in a culture. So here attention will be directed to some aspects of curriculum planning that must receive the consideration of the entire school organization as a basis for action.

ASPECTS OF THE EDUCATIONAL PROGRAM

As curriculum planning moves toward its final and ultimate phase—the development of experiences with pupils in the school—one further step in the formulation of a structure for the curriculum is desirable. This is the determination of the basic aspects that will constitute the curriculum of the school. This is an intermediate step between the determination of the structural organization of the curriculum and the selection of the learning activities themselves. It is a phase of planning the scope of the curriculum, for it helps to set the over-all pattern of experiences to be provided by the school. This step in developing an educational program will become clearer as we discuss the aspects of the program at both the secondary and elementary levels.

Major Aspects of Secondary Education

An adequate and sound curriculum for secondary school pupils should encompass the following broad types of educational experiences or opportunities:

I. *A general education program:* The program planned to provide experiences that will aid all pupils attain in the fullest measure possible those broad, basic outcomes that everyone should possess so that he may be the finest citizen possible and live the good life to the fullest. There are two broad phases of this aspect of the program:
   a. The common studies
   b. The program of physical education, recreation, and health instruction
II. *The specialized studies:* The program that provides experience that will aid all pupils attain outcomes of an individualized character, such as the development of individual interests and capacities, preparation for an occupation or for further study in college, and opportunities to explore various specialized fields of activity. Major phases of this program include:
   a. Elective courses
   b. Vocational education courses
   c. Exploratory courses
III. *The organized student life of the school:* Informal activities of the school, group social activities, and the traditional out-of-class activities that contribute to both the general education program and the specialized studies.
IV. *Special services for pupils:* Certain types of health services, counseling services, services for exceptional children who need them, and services for children with serious adjustment problems.

Somewhat similar divisions of the curriculum have been proposed by Caswell, Featherstone, and the Educational Policies Commission. Curriculum workers may also wish to consider their proposals for the development of the secondary school curriculum.[1]

Obviously the delineation of these broad aspects of an adequate program of secondary education still does not suggest in any detail the kinds of learning experiences that should actually be provided adolescents. Moreover, we do not propose to blueprint the curriculum to that extent here. Such an effort would be contrary to one of the basic concepts of curriculum planning, namely, that curriculum workers should be granted a great deal of flexibility in planning and developing learning experiences. Secondly, throughout this book we have discussed basic principles that may well guide curriculum workers in determining the actual

[1] Hollis L. Caswell, "Curriculum Proposals for the Future," in *The American High School*, Hollis L. Caswell, editor (Eighth Yearbook of the John Dewey Society; New York: Harper & Brothers, 1946), pp. 135–157.

William B. Featherstone, *A Functional Curriculum for Youth* (New York: American Book Company, 1950), pp. 133–163.

Educational Policies Commission, *Education for All American Youth: A Further Look* (Washington, D.C.: National Education Association, 1952), pp. 147–153; 218–234.

types of educational experience that may be provided in each of these aspects of the program. However, brief, general comments will be made here to explain the over-all nature of each aspect of the secondary school program.

The general education program. The general education program of the secondary school, already considered briefly in Chapter 10, is those phases of the learning experiences provided by the school that are designed to help each pupil achieve the common desired outcomes all pupils should possess. Thus the program of general education is the program that is common to all pupils and that provides the basic, integrating, educational experiences planned to help all pupils be good citizens and happy, well-adjusted individuals, exemplifying to the highest degree possible the good life as envisaged by the cultural group.

In most school programs there are two phases of the general education program: the program of common studies, and the program of physical education, recreation, and health instruction. It should be emphasized that all aspects of the educational program will have some general education values. Certainly, the program of specialized studies, as discussed later, has much to contribute to the outcomes sought in the educational program. Also, the student life of the school and the specialized services provided for pupils all have contributions to make to the realization of the general outcomes. Nevertheless, the primary emphasis in the program of specialized studies is to develop individual interests and capacities rather than to emphasize the attainment of common goals.

The program of common studies may be organized on the basis of a core program or in terms of school subjects. The core approach to general education in the secondary school was discussed in some detail in Chapter 10. If the school does not use the core program, it undoubtedly follows the school subject approach to general education. It is quite clear from our definition that the general education program in a subject type of curriculum consists of the subjects that are required of all pupils. Since these required subjects become the common integrating experiences, they necessarily constitute the school's definition of its general education program. Practically all secondary schools do require certain subjects that they consider basic to the achievement of the school's objectives. Even in those schools that use the core design, some subjects in addition to the core are usually required, particularly science and mathematics. This total prescribed program becomes the program of general education.

One of the most important curriculum decisions which a school staff makes is the decision as to what subjects shall be required of all pupils.

This decision should be made only on the basis of very careful study and a highly penetrating analysis of what contributions each required subject can make to the attainment of the objectives of general education. It is easy for a school faculty to decide to require a particular subject, just because it is traditional, it sounds good, or there seems to be an apparent demand for it. This is hardly an adequate basis on which to determine the program of the general education. The subjects to be required should be determined on the basis of what they can contribute to the objectives of general education of the school.

The second phase of the general education program is the provisions for physical education, recreation, and health instruction. In core programs this aspect of general education is usually given outside that program. In most schools it constitutes a subject offered for credit. Since this is a part of the general education program, such learning activities should be so planned that they will correlate closely with the experiences provided in the program of common studies or core so that together both programs will contribute maximally to the realization of desired outcomes.

The specialized studies. The program of specialized studies is designed to develop individual interests, enable children to explore various areas of learning and various types of learning experiences, provide at least initial training for an occupation, or prepare pupils to pursue a program of studies in higher institutions. Again, some very important, basic decisions are involved in planning the program of special studies. In practically all secondary schools these studies are organized on the subject basis, although many phases of vocational preparation are provided through some type of cooperative work experience program and shop apprenticeships.

What are the bases a school staff should use in determining the subjects to be provided to meet specialized interests? Two principles are pertinent: (1) whatever studies and experiences are offered by the school to meet individual interests and needs should contribute to the over-all objectives of the school; and (2) since choices must be made, they should be in terms of the needs, interests, and aspirations of the particular group of children served, so long as the program conforms to the over-all goals. Few, if any, schools could offer work that meets the individual interests of all children, so the principal approach to the determination of the program of specialized studies is to ascertain through highly analytical studies of pupil interests, aspirations, and plans for the future, and through comprehensive surveys of the kinds of occupations that pupils may enter after leaving school, the subjects that will serve most significantly the largest number of pupils. The smaller the school, the more it will have to limit its program to simply a few specialized studies that serve the needs of the most pupils; the larger the school, the more diversified the program it can offer. Again, schools can be criticized for retaining in the curriculum subjects that have a long tradition and have been offered by the school for decades, rather than exploring periodically what constitute the basic needs of its pupils for offerings of a specialized nature.

The student life of the school. In all modern secondary schools many learning experiences take place outside formally organized class situations. These include such things as school assemblies, pep rallies, sports events, school parties and dances, special-interest groups and clubs, noon-hour activities, and the like. These are all part of the curriculum, and the school staff should accept responsibility for seeing that the rich potential of these activities is used to attain the educational goals of the school. It is through these activities that some of the important outcomes desired from the educational program may best be achieved.

Since these activities constitute an important part of the school's program, they should be given commensurate attention in planning so that educational potentialities are realized as fully as possible. Too many sponsors of such activities consider them an imposition and a drudgery so that they fail to plan carefully for the achievement of desirable outcomes. Such teachers merely tolerate the activities and do little to make them meaningful and significant to pupils. Unless the school is willing to take full responsibility for such activities and unless it clearly recognizes them as an essential part of the educational program, it would probably be better if it did not sponsor them at all. On the other hand, they constitute but one aspect of the school's program for pupils; hence they should not be permitted to overshadow other parts of the educational program. Important choices must be made as to what types of activities will be sponsored and their relationship to the rest of the educational program. These choices, like all curriculum choices, must be made in terms of the basic criteria for judging the appropriateness of educational experiences.

The specialized services of the school. The modern secondary school provides a number of important specialized services for its pupils. These include health services, counseling and guidance services, and special provisions for the exceptional child. These services have important curriculum implications, since all of them are designed better to guide the growth and development of boys and girls. If the school uses a core program, the major aspects of guidance are taken care of by the core teacher. If the school follows the subject type of organization, this responsibility is often assigned to a home room teacher as counselor. In any case, teachers need the help and assistance of a specialist in counseling and guidance, particularly on problems of maladjustment, serious behavioral offenses, and the choice of an occupation. Again, curriculum workers should recognize the important part that services of this type play in the realization of the school's over-all objectives, and the contributions that these services can make to the growth and development of youth should be clearly recognized by all teachers.

Maintaining Balance in the Curriculum of the Secondary School

In establishing a framework for the curriculum and in determining scope and sequence, one of the most important problems facing curriculum workers is the maintenance of balance in the educational program. The classification of the various aspects of the curriculum into the major categories listed above is useful in establishing balance and developing proper scope for the secondary school curriculum. Utilizing this division of the curriculum, Table 10 presents a suggested division of pupils' educational activities in terms of these major categories. This chart allocates the time that pupils spend in school or the work load they carry for a school year among the three aspects of the curriculum. Since the special services and general out-of-class activities of the school should be closely coordinated with the program of common studies, and the specialized activities, such as clubs and special-interest groups, should be closely coordinated with the specialized studies, no separate time allotment has been established for these phases of the program. Moreover, no sharp distinction is made among the three aspects of the specialized studies for purposes of maintaining balance in the program. At the time a pupil takes a class, it is difficult to say whether it is for the purpose of exploring that area of activity, developing an individual interest, or laying the foundation for an occupational career. An illustration would be typewriting. A pupil may take it for his own personal use but he may find that he likes typewriting and decides to prepare himself for a secretarial job. In that case the course becomes in fact a basic course in preparation for a vocation.

In the junior high school Table 10 uses 1,200 class periods a year as the basis for establishing balance in the program. This assumes that pupils will be engaged in organized activities or classes for six class periods a day, five days a week, for forty weeks of the year. The school may have even seven periods, or six periods and a home room, but the assumption

TABLE 10

Suggested Time Division in Secondary Schools

	General Education		Specialized Studies	Total
	Common Studies, including special services and common activities.	Physical Education, Recreation, and Health.	Occupational preparation, college preparatory courses, exploratory courses, and individual interests.	

Junior High School		*Class Periods a Year*		
Grade 7	800	200	200	1200
Grade 8	700–800	200	200–300	1200
Grade 9	600–700	100	400–500	1200

(A class meeting 1 period a day, 5 days a week for the 40 weeks of the school year would constitute 200 class periods. In this table, the pupil is assumed to be in 6 classes each day, 5 days a week for 40 weeks.)

Senior High School		*Semester Hours a Year*		
Grade 10	25	5	20	50
Grade 11	25	5	20	50
Grade 12	20	5	25	50

(A class meeting 1 period a day, 5 days a week for a semester of 18 to 20 weeks constitutes 5 semester hours' credit. This table assumes that a senior high school pupil will be enrolled in classes or activities carrying full credit for an average of 5 periods a day each semester throughout the senior high school.)

Community College				
Grade 13	10	5	20	35
Grade 14	10	5	20	35

(This part of the table is based on the traditional semester hour of college credit.)

here is that the pupil will be participating in six periods of activity a day. It is highly desirable that we avoid more formal methods of establishing units of credit and the like at the junior high school level, such as prevail in the senior high school. For schools that do not have this many class periods a week, or forty weeks in the school year, the chart may be easily adapted by changing the figures to fractions or percentages and applying these to the total number of periods in which pupils engage in learning activities a year.

We have used the semester-hour basis for computing time spent in the senior high school. The semester-hour provides a better unit for quantitative measurement of the educational program than do the old units of credit. However, if a school still uses the Carnegie unit, the table can easily be converted into these units by dividing by ten. A semester-hour of credit is granted for class participation for one period a day, five days a week, for a semester of eighteen to twenty weeks. This table indicates that the pupil, on the average for the three years of senior high school, would be in five organized classes or activities for credit each day. This may be somewhat greater than the amount of time pupils in many high schools now spend in organized educational activities for credit. However, the trend in many modern high schools is to increase the number of classes and activities in which children participate each week over the old traditional program of a quarter of a century ago that called for four classes and four study halls a day. In many high schools at present the pupil is scheduled for organized classwork and activity for from twenty-two to even the full thirty periods a week in schools that schedule six periods a day, five days a week. In fact, some schools have modified their graduation requirements so that the pupils must average twenty-two to twenty-seven periods a week in credit activities for the six semesters of senior high school to graduate.[2]

We have included in the table a suggested time allotment for Grades 13 and 14, which may be organized separately in a community college. This allocation is based upon the traditional semester-hour basis. The figures for the semester-hour used for the senior high school and community college may be readily changed to the basis used for the junior high school—periods a year—by multiplying the figure by 20.

This is only a suggested division of the year's organized activities among the three major categories. Such an allocation leaves many unanswered questions and fails to take account of some aspects of the school's program. For example, the informal educational experiences that take place in the school, such as the learning activities that occur in the halls, in the cafeteria, at sporting events, at school dances in the evening, during the noon hour, and the like, obviously are not listed in this table. However, we feel that such a table is useful for directing attention to the problem of maintaining balance in the program. Moreover, it provides one way of analyzing the programs of individual pupils. In fact, it would be wise for school staffs to take a number of sample student programs and calculate the balance in terms of time units along some such line as is presented in this table.

[2] Lincoln Senior High School of Lincoln, Nebraska, recently increased its graduation requirements to 150 semester hours of credit for the senior high school, or an average for the entire six semesters of 25 periods a week out of the 30 weekly class periods. California high schools require a minimum of 190 semester hours in a four-year program.

Major Aspects of the Elementary School Curriculum

The development of a basic framework for the curriculum of the elementary school presents much the same problem as it does for the secondary school, since the curriculum at both school levels should conform to the same general principles of curriculum planning. However, the process may not be quite as complex as it is in the secondary school, since the elementary school is primarily a school for the development of common understandings and for guiding the growth and development of pupils toward common goals. Interests and goals of children are not as specialized and differentiated in the elementary school as they often are in the secondary school. Nevertheless, for analytical and planning purposes the curriculum may be classified into the following major aspects:

I. *The common integrating studies*
  1. Communication arts: speech, language usage, reading, writing, listening, discussing, and spelling
  2. Computational skills and quantitative thinking: arithmetic, reasoning, and problem solving
  3. Social and group living: history, geography, government, community living, human relations, citizenship, value building, character building, and sensitivity to problems of group living
  4. Science: understanding of scientific phenomena and natural law, the use of methods of science in problem solving, understanding the world
  5. Aesthetic development: music, art, and handicrafts
  6. Health: knowledge of the body, nutrition, health habits

II. *Recreation, play, physical education, and handicrafts*

III. *School activities*

IV. *Camps and summer programs*

It must be emphasized again that these are not discrete items of the elementary curriculum, but simply phases or aspects of a total program designed for the proper development of boys and girls.

The common, integrating studies. This constitutes the basic part of the elementary school program. In many modern elementary schools, these common studies are integrated into a broad core or activity program, without any sharp distinction existing among the six aspects of the program. In other schools, the program is organized on the basis of a broad fields approach to each of the areas. Seldom would schools schedule short periods for reading, spelling, writing, arithmetic, geography, history, music, and the like. Instead, the schedule would call for a long period or several shorter periods devoted to the communicative arts, and similarly for the other phases of the common studies program. However, it is recognized that some schools still favor a curriculum pattern in which each subject is scheduled individually and short periods of time are devoted to a variety of offerings.

In our own judgment, one of the most important implications of the principles of learning for the organization of the school is the need for large blocks of time. It is most difficult to carry on significant pupil-teacher planning, for example, in the short period assigned by some schedules to each of many subjects. In general, large blocks of time are more difficult to secure in departmentalized than in nondepartmentalized programs. However, when the day in the elementary school is broken into many periods the same limitation exists even if there is only one teacher for the group.

It is possible to have large blocks of time and still vary the experiences included in accordance with learners' attention spans. That is, the designation of one or two hours for language arts in a primary grade does not mean that the children must work as one group throughout the period. Instead, as illustrated by the second-grade program cited in Chapter 13, there may be a period for individual writing, a period for reading and other activities in small groups, a period for spelling, and a period for storytelling or reporting. But in view of the related skills involved, it seems preferable to have these periods within the same block of the day rather than scattered. In this way there can be flexibility in shifting from one skill to another. Another advantage of the large blocks of time is illustrated by Plate 25. Pupils have ample opportunity to carry out meaningful projects and to do research on a topic.

Recreation, play, physical education, and handicrafts. This is not really a distinct phase of the elementary school program but rather simply one aspect of an integrated program. Nevertheless, it is usually scheduled separately from the program of common studies. Most elementary schools make provisions for play, recreation, and programs of physical education and handicrafts in the regular school day, but in addition to these educational experiences, many schools provide such opportunities for children in afterschool hours and during the summer. The modern school recognizes not only that experiences in these areas are essential to sound growth and development, but that many children will not have even adequate—and certainly not rich—opportunities for these activities outside the regular school hours unless the school provides them. Need for such a program is particularly pressing in cities, but children in small towns and rural areas can profit a great deal from opportunities to play together and to engage in various types of handicraft activities under proper supervision. In many cities opportunities of this type in after-school hours are developed cooperatively by the school system and a city recreation agency of some type.

PLATE 25. THE MODERN ELEMENTARY SCHOOL PROVIDES AMPLE OPPORTUNITY FOR PUPILS TO ENGAGE IN MEANINGFUL PROJECTS. *These children, as a part of their studies in the social living area, are carrying on a study that correlates history and geography. (Courtesy of the Dallas Public Schools)*

School activities. The modern elementary school provides a number of highly valuable learning experiences in activities that fall outside the more formal class program. These include such things as the all-school pupil council, school assembly programs, school safety patrol, school paper, special-interest clubs, school garden program, special campaigns, lunchroom activities, and assistance in the library and the halls. These activities, if properly organized and directed, may make valuable contribution to the attainment of desired outcomes. Similarly, as in the case of secondary schools, these activities will not make their fullest contribution to the educational program unless proper planning is carried on and the activities are developed in terms of the contributions they can make to the realization of the objectives of the school.

Camping and summer activities. An increasing number of school systems now provide highly valuable educational experiences for children during the months usually set aside for the vacation period. These programs take a variety of forms. A number of school systems are able to provide camping experiences for children of the community; some of these comprise day camps carried on within the facilities of the community itself, but a few fortunate school systems have regular campsites, fully equipped for extended stays in the camp. If the school controls a camping site, it is frequently used during the school year to provide camping experiences for children as a part of the school program. Other school systems provide various types of recreational and developmental activities during the summer months. These may include supervised playground activities, handicraft programs, musical programs, supervised leisure reading, or even opportunities for children to obtain special help in such basic skills as reading. Some school systems cannot directly provide such opportunities, but cooperate with city recreation boards, voluntary child service agencies, and other organizations of this type in providing rich educational experiences for children during the vacation period.

Maintaining Balance in the Elementary School Program

Because of the integrated nature of a good elementary school program, it is not appropriate to present a suggested time division of the school year among the various aspects of the elementary curriculum such as we did in the case of the secondary school program. In the elementary school the pupils remain together with the same teacher during the year for all or almost all of their educational experiences. It is highly desirable that the teacher be given a great deal of freedom to plan learning activities in terms of the needs of the particular group of children. Suggested arbitrary time divisions are not in keeping with this philosophy. In the lower elementary grades, for example, much more emphasis may be placed on the communicative arts, social living, and the arts than on science and computational skills, while in the upper elementary grades greater emphasis is given to science experiences and problem solving and quantitative thinking. Moreover, the time devoted to various aspects of the curriculum will vary as the basic needs of pupils vary. One group of children may possibly devote more time to the strengthening of skills in reading than will another group of children at the same grade level.

Specific guides for developing a balanced program have to be determined in the light of the physical needs and general maturities of the learners, the facilities of school and community, and the school level involved. Certain common-sense principles should be followed, however. First of all, school organization must recognize the need of learners for play, work, and rest. Any program that ignores the need for play and rest as well as work runs into so-called "behavior" problems. Although the proportion of time which can be devoted to work increases with maturity and the need for rest decreases, some alternation of work and leisure activities is always desirable. Balance between more or less passive and active experiences is rarely as well provided for in the departmentalized program, although the hourly movement of classes does provide a periodic break and physical activity. Even adults do not sit quietly reading and studying for extended periods without breaks, and it cannot be expected that growing boys and girls will do so. In the second place, a balance of out-of-school activities should be facilitated by school guidance. Assignments of homework in some situations add up to many hours of reading and writing—more than is done by most children, and rightfully so. More reasonable attitudes toward homework mean that learners who need the challenge or the special practice of outside work are given this help but without uniform assignments for all learners. Also, pupils who carry work loads or home responsibilities are identified and special care is taken so that they do not accept other unduly heavy responsibilities.

A Balanced Program for Teachers

Teachers, too, need a balanced program. In addition to time for direct work with children, their working day should include time for conferring with other teachers, parents, and pupils; time for planning learning experiences; time for paper work; and time for relaxation. Unfortunately, the traditional concept that the job of teaching consists only of work with children has tended to push all other responsibilities of teachers outside the formal school day. As a result, most planning, paper work, and conferences must be attended to after the children are gone. However, a planning period is frequently provided the teacher in a departmentalized program, and sometimes arrangements for a daily break are made for the teacher of the self-contained classroom unit. Some schools are initiating the practice of scheduling a short break during the forenoon for both teachers and pupils, but although it provides a moment of relaxation it does not enable the teacher to carry out other responsibilities.

Inasmuch as the teaching day is relatively continuous, such suggestions as the following may help to maintain a balance of activities for the teacher:

1. Varied activities within the classroom are as sound for the teacher's mental health as for the learner's. Probably as exhausting a day as could be spent is one in front of successive classes devoted solely to question-answer recitation.

2. If no planning period is provided within the school day, the teacher should have an afterschool period free of other duties. Some schools set a work schedule for teachers which designates the hour after children leave as the planning period.

3. Whether the planning period occurs during or after school hours, there should be a suitable place for the teacher to work, where he can have privacy when needed, and in which he can also hold conferences.

4. When teachers are expected to hold conferences at school they should have a suitable place for conferences and be relieved of teaching and other responsibilities at the time.

5. The maintenance of a pleasant, relaxed atmosphere throughout the school helps relieve strain and pressure.

6. Interruptions of classroom activities for announcements, messages, and so forth, should be held to an absolute minimum.

7. Rotation in such extra duties as supervision of lunchrooms and special activities provides a maximum break at these times.

8. Principals and other nonteaching personnel can help in emergency situations involving temporary absences. Children frequently assume responsibility for their own direction at such times.

GROUPING AND PROMOTING PUPILS

An important problem of school administration in relation to the curriculum is the organization of pupils in groups and the regulation of pupil progress. Among the issues involved are those relating to grouping for instruction and for all-school activities, admission, marking systems, reports to parents, and promotion and graduation. The intent here is to state the issues and the positions indicated by the curriculum principles we have presented rather than to describe and analyze prevailing practices.

Grouping for Classroom Instruction

The graded system of American public schools has established the basic pattern of grouping for instructional purposes and, to a considerable extent, has controlled many curriculum practices such as grade standards, basic textbooks, and promotion. That is, pupils are grouped together by grades, and traditional practice has stipulated the kinds of materials to use in each grade, the standards for promotion to the next grade, and so forth. Modern curriculum planning has eliminated to some extent many of the practices associated with the graded system, but the system itself remains. Although some attempts have been made to classify pupils as six-year-olds, seven-year-olds, and so forth, by and large the pupils still progress by grades from the first through the twelfth.

The major issue in connection with the grouping of pupils for instructional purposes arises in situations where there is more than one group in a grade, for example, two third-grade groups, or three ninth-grade English classes. How shall the groups be divided? A common, though far from universal practice, has been to organize the groups according to ability. That is, the top half of fifty third-grade pupils as measured by intelligence tests would be placed in one group and the bottom half in the second group. Caswell and Foshay analyze the philosophical issue involved as follows:

> The position one takes on ability grouping depends largely on certain basic conceptions of the nature of the individual and of the purposes of education. If one views the curriculum as pretty much predetermined, with an accepted common expectation from which adjustments may be made, then he will be predisposed to plans of ability grouping. If, on the other hand, he holds that each curriculum developed by a given group of pupils and a teacher is in many respects unique, that it is a result of the potentialities of that particular situation, he will be disposed not to accept such a plan. If one holds that uniformity of ability and achievement within an instructional group is a desirable condition for education and a goal for further activities, he will support ability grouping. If, in contrast, he believes that diversity and uniqueness are essentials of stimulating educational experiences and that differences are fostered by education, he will consider ability grouping unsound. If one views the democratic process as one which permits the able to rise through their individual efforts to positions of power and leadership and which conditions the less able to acceptance of such leadership, he will support ability grouping. However, if the democratic process is considered one in which real respect for the personality of every person is basic, with leadership resting on the participation of all and shifting from situation to situation, ability grouping will not be accepted. A social philosophy as well as a view of the ways and means of educational organization is involved.[3]

[3] Hollis L. Caswell and A. Wellesley Foshay, *Education in the Elementary School* (2d ed.; New York: American Book Company, 1950), pp. 319–320. Reprinted by permission of the American Book Company, publishers.

Furthermore, even if the social and educational implications of ability groupings are waived, there is evidence that ability grouping does not reduce heterogeneity very substantially because of variations in individual abilities, and also that ability grouping does not increase achievement.[4]

Another type of grouping practiced in schools, particularly secondary schools, is made on the basis of achievement. This is a form of ability grouping and at the elementary school level largely results in such a basis of selection since it is impractical to shift pupils from class to class on the basis of achievement in particular subjects. However, grouping by levels of achievement in the secondary school is quite common. For example, if a high school has five sections of tenth-grade English, pupils may be assigned to the respective sections according to scores on an English achievement test, previous marks in the subject, or both. For world history, the pupils are reassigned to sections on the basis of reading ability, test scores in history, previous marks in social studies, or a combination of these.

In the secondary school, the system of required and elective subjects constitutes another basis of grouping. If electives are chosen on the basis of interest and need, the grouping is a natural one. Unfortunately, pupils are sometimes guided into subjects on the basis of ability, so that a type of ability grouping results. Thus the pupils of higher intellectual ability may be guided into mathematics, and those of lower ability into shop or homemaking. Such a practice violates the basic principle of planning a curriculum for each individual in terms of his needs and interests.

Grouping is certainly one of the most vexatious problems in curriculum planning and no pat solution can be offered. Each faculty will have to decide the matter in terms of what is known about the developmental characteristics of pupils, of what is conceived to be the functions of the school in a democratic society, and of what promises to contribute best to the attainment of the goals of education. Shane has described a new approach to the problem in the elementary school[5] that offers much promise for schools prepared to implement it. In the secondary school undoubtedly several procedures will be used throughout the total program. It seems apparent that during the course of their school careers pupils should be placed in a class situation in which they (1) will be able to carry on the work of the group with a reasonable degree of success and satisfaction to themselves, (2) will be challenged and stimulated by the

[4] See Willard C. Olson, *Child Development* (Boston: D. C. Heath & Company, 1949), pp. 361–363.

[5] Harold G. Shane, "The Promotion Policy Dilemma," *NEA Journal*, 42:411–412 (October), 1953.

activities of the class, and (3) will have the opportunity to work with other pupils of varying backgrounds of experience, ability, interests, needs, and competences.

Class Size

Another problem in the grouping of pupils for classroom instruction is that of determining class size. In general, there is no objective formula available to answer in absolute terms the question of desirable class size. The factors involved are so variable as to make a uniform answer impossible for all school situations or even for a particular school. The quality of learning experiences is affected by such matters as the attractiveness of the environment, the facilities afforded by the classroom and the school for various types of activities, the capacities of the teacher, the interpersonal relations of teacher and pupils and pupils with each other, and the availability of appropriate materials. Class size is important as it relates to these factors.

The class size and the physical facilities are closely interrelated. The limiting factor is not necessarily the number of individuals but may be the inadequacy of space for these individuals to do effective work. The learning of an individual might even be facilitated by the presence of a larger number of other individuals if space and facilities are adequate. Unfortunately, most classrooms are much too small for free movement and for work in small groups; this is true of even the class of twenty-five to thirty pupils fairly commonly regarded as a desirable size. As long as classrooms are so limited in size and so inflexible in arrangement the number of pupils occupying them should be held to a minimum.

Another consideration suggests that the number should be held small regardless of physical facilities. The quality of pupils' interpersonal relationships with the teacher and with each other is affected by the number of individuals; the greater the number of individuals the less intimate the comradeship. What the optimum number of individuals is for desirable relationships probably cannot be objectively determined because of the variations in personalities of pupils and teachers, as well as in the amount of time provided in the plan of organization. It is obvious, however, that there is some minimum number below which, in general, interrelationships are too limited for a desirable breadth of social experiences as well as some maximum number beyond which, in general, interrelationships become too numerous for adequate intimacy. In the lack of a better standard perhaps the common one of twenty-five to thirty is satisfactory—at least it is in the right direction of decreased class size.

Still another factor should be considered—teacher load. Each additional child increases the number of personalities to be understood, the number of pupil and parent conferences to be held, the number of individuals to whom consideration should be given in planning, guiding, and evaluating experiences. When the teacher works in accordance with accepted principles of learning rather than as a director of group drill and recitation, each individual added to the load is significant. Again, the optimum number of individuals depends upon variations in the maturities and personalities of learners and the adaptability of the teacher. In general, we may again conclude from the inadequate consideration given individual differences in most classrooms that a reduction in class size would help. However, the number of classes is also important. The elementary school teacher can deal much more adequately with 35 children five hours a day than can the secondary school teacher with 175 pupils a day. Thus a part of the solution may be to increase the length of time with individual pupils through core curriculum plans as well as to decrease the size of classes.

In general, school organization should resolve the problems of optimum class size through consideration of these factors:

1. The class should be small enough that the facilities provided will conform to acceptable standards for good working conditions.

2. The class should be of such size as to provide for desirable interpersonal relations of pupils with the teacher and with each other.

3. The number and length of pupil contacts should be such as to create a reasonable load for the teacher in carrying on a program of learning experiences for each child.

It is recognized that financial considerations generally play a large part in determining class size. From a curriculum standpoint, however, we believe that the foregoing considerations so far as possible should determine financial need regardless of whether the existing budget is adequate or whether the school organization must ask for more funds to operate on these bases. Perhaps schools would be more successful in securing additional funds by demonstrating more frequently that a program for better teaching of individual children can be done with smaller classes.

Admission Policies

The major issue with respect to school admission has to do with the age at which children are admitted to the beginning grade, kindergarten, or the first grade. The problem is of some importance since most schools, in accordance with the traditions of the graded system, have certain expectations as to the readiness of pupils for school. In view of the great variations among children on individual traits, the common criterion of chronological age is probably the best. If the school regards as its chief purpose that of promoting academic achievement, perhaps a more economical procedure would be to determine the readiness of children for achievement in the skills, let them enter school according to some standard of readiness, and proceed as rapidly as possible. Actually, this practice is approached by a flexible entrance age combined with an intelligence test to determine readiness and practices of acceleration thereafter. The frequently resulting social maladjustment of children so pushed along is reason enough to adhere to the relatively inflexible policy of admission on the basis of chronological age.

If the school program is based on the recognition of individual differences and attempts to take each child where he is, probably the best basis for determining whether or not to admit a child would be his social maturity in relation to the group. This criterion, however, is very difficult to apply and even more difficult to interpret to parents. Hence adherence to a criterion of chronological age is most simple and common.

Another problem in relation to admission concerns the transfer child. Shall he be admitted to the grade to which he was or would have been assigned in the previous school or to some other grade? Although the best available criterion is his probable adjustment to the possible groups, the usual practice is to place the child in the grade to which he would have been assigned in the previous school. When a question does exist as to the placement of a child, he is frequently put in the lower of the two possible grades and his adjustment observed there to determine if he might be moved to the higher.

A very important function of school organization in relation to the admission of new children is their proper orientation to school. The nature of the adjustment to the new environment is of significance in determining the quality of learning. Various policies are followed to aid the transition from home to school or from one school to another. Reception of incoming pupils in small groups, parent-teacher initial conferences, orientation materials for parents and for pupils moving to a new school, visits of pupils to the next school (that is, from one level to another), and orientation tours of the building are among the devices used to ease the transition.

Marking System

The traditional marking system is a device used both to motivate learning and to evaluate and regulate pupil progress. In regard to the regulation of progress, marks may be and are used as a basis for determining promotion, classification, and assignment in cases of transfer. Their use for this purpose is directly related to a philosophy of curriculum planning that holds to the establishment of minimum essentials for each grade and subject, to an emphasis on intellectual achievement alone, and to an expectation of relatively uniform learning. The inconsistency of this use of marks with what is known about learning is obvious. Furthermore, standards of marking systems are generally based on a comparison of the individual with the group, whereas a democratic philosophy of education demands the maximum development of an individual with reference to his own potentialities. The practical difficulties of determining individual potentialities and of evaluating on this basis do not deny the fallacies of marking systems based on comparative achievement.

There is also evidence that marking systems are injurious to the mental hygiene of children and therefore incompatible with the curriculum goal of developing well-balanced personalities. Olson points out, among other criticisms of the mental hygiene aspects of marks, that "the marking system may be emphasized to the extent that it constitutes a major frustration in the lives of many children," that "competitive marks have been found to promote dishonesty and other undesirable traits in children," and that "marks have undesirable effects on children of high achievement as well as those who achieve poorly." [6]

The question arises, then, as to what substitute the school organization may use for determining promotion and classification. The real question, in our own judgment, is whether promotion and classification should be based on academic achievement alone. As indicated earlier, modern principles of learning and curriculum suggest that grouping on ability (or achievement) alone is undesirable. As shown later in the section, achievement is not considered an adequate basis for determining promotion. The only valid argument for marks seems to be their general requirement for high school pupils' records for college admission and for employers. Although new school-college agreements place increased emphasis on criteria other than marks, and employers generally want broader information, the necessity for records of marks is still so common as to require some system of record keeping in high school. Probably there is no alternative but to keep them for this purpose, but this purpose does not necessitate the use of marks deliberately as motivating devices and almost as the sole such devices, or as a basis for reports to parents and pupils. Once made and filed, they may be used in individual cases as needed for guidance.

Reports to Parents

A major use of the marking system is to report pupils' progress to parents. The purpose is both to inform parents and to motivate learning,

[6] See Olson, *op. cit.*, pp. 312–315, for a full statement on this subject.

and underlying the entire system is the general assumption that unsatisfactory marks mean children may suffer in promotion, classification, and assignment. As just indicated, marks seem undesirable as motivators and regulators of progress. There remains, however, the important need of informing parents of their children's progress and, indeed, of school and home cooperation in developing an effective curriculum for learners. How, then, can this need be met without marks?

Various methods of evaluating pupil progress are described in Chapter 17. So far as possible, progress should be reported to parents in terms of the better of these methods. Thus pupils' own evaluations, teachers' records of pupils' behavior, summaries of experiences, and individual participation provide data which should be used in reports to parents. However, the limitations of communication are very real, and such material cannot be handled as easily as the simple report card. Two general types of reporting systems are used more and more frequently to obviate the shortcomings of the typical report card and to recognize the problem of teacher-parent communication.

One type of newer reporting system utilizes written reports but of a different kind. These may be individual letters, check lists, or written summaries according to some classification of learners' progress. In all these kinds of reports the emphasis is on the individual child's progress without reference to marks or comparative factors. These reports point to specific accomplishments and difficulties instead of assigning a mark which means only that the child's progress in the particular subject was judged to be at a level designated by the mark. Also the new type of reports generally provide for reporting progress in areas other than, or at least in addition to, the conventional subjects.

Another newer system substitutes teacher-parent conferences for the written report. In some instances a combination of written report and conference is employed. The conference provides an opportunity for the teacher to interpret progress and for the teacher and parent to share in planning for the child's further progress. Its advantages for reporting progess are summarized by Olson as follows:

> (1) The growth of the individual child may be stressed rather than a comparison with other children. The incongruity between the modern knowledge of growth and the traditional competitive and comparative systems resting on a philosophy of selection is thus avoided. (2) The teacher and school maintain a systematic contact and an educational process with the parent instead of attempting to solve problems on an individual, incidental, or complaint basis. (3) A series of interviews supplies the teacher with the corrective of parent values, enables him to adjust the treatment of both the group and individual

children in terms of these values, and lets him introduce other objectives for consideration. (4) The method has a maximum of flexibility and individuality. (5) Teachers are relieved of the busywork involved in much marking, posting of marks, and reporting. (6) The teacher receives the tonic of contact with parents who are highly pleased to offset those who are disgruntled and who, through their greater initiative, may distort the picture.[7]

The conference method involves a number of problems for school organization. There must be sufficient understanding and desire for the use of conferences on the part of teachers and parents to justify their introduction. Teachers need to do considerable advance planning and need some skill in conducting conferences. Suitable times must be scheduled and appointments arranged with parents. Some schools arrange for the dismissal of children or for their care in a particular room while the conferences are being held. A plan for reaching the parents with whom conferences cannot be scheduled is needed. Some type of uniform record of conferences is desirable for the information of subsequent teachers, guidance personnel, and others. These problems would appear surmountable in a school organization whose staff is sincerely interested in relating organization to basic curriculum principles.

Use of the new types of reporting has generally been confined to elementary and junior high schools because of the hold of formal marks at the senior high level. However, the new types of reports which inform parents about pupil participation and progress in areas other than the subjects are used in some high schools. Conferences with parents are held in connection with reports of marks and may tend to dissipate some of the poor effects if the conferences are devoted to understanding and promoting pupils' total development rather than merely to reporting failing marks.

Promotion and Graduation Policies

The real test of school organization, in terms of its relation to the learning of individual children, comes at the point of determining whether a learner moves along the graded system year by year or is held back from promotion or graduation because of his failure to achieve whatever standard is held. Wherever grade standards (or standards for graduation) in terms of subject matter achievement are held to, it follows that pupils who fail to attain these standards are retained. If, however, the curriculum is based on the principles of a sound philosophy of education and psychology of learning, there are no group standards. Such a curriculum recognizes the individual differences of learners and the individ-

[7] *Ibid.*, p. 320. Reprinted by permission of D. C. Heath & Company, publishers.

uality of learning and does not attempt to force uniformity and stand-ardization. In short, the issue becomes this: Should the curriculum be adjusted to learners or the learners to the curriculum? The former posi-tion seems the only one tenable and rules out nonpromotion for failure to meet academic standards. By the same reasoning, graduation means merely the completion of the last grade of the school system and not the achievement of uniform standards. And graduation from the elementary school to the secondary school in the sense of qualifying for the latter is eliminated by the theory and practice of universal secondary education.

A considerable body of research and literature on promotion prac-tices rejects nonpromotion on other than theoretical bases. Caswell and Foshay reviewed a large number of studies in their 1950 publication to show that the following assumptions, widely used to justify nonpromo-tion, were *not* valid:

1. Nonpromotion maintains high achievement standards.
2. Nonpromotion makes instruction easy by having all the children in a class approximately equal in achievement.
3. Nonpromotion makes pupils work harder and achieve more than they otherwise would.
4. Nonpromotion protects society from individuals who are sup-posed to be educated, but are not.[8]

It is not to be implied that 100 per cent promotion and graduation should be the policy of school organization. Rather, the policy of school organization should be to provide for each pupil a learning situation in which he can learn with maximum effectiveness. Under optimum cur-riculum conditions 100 per cent regular movement or promotion would occur. Since optimum conditions do not prevail and since many factors operate to create individual maladjustments within groups, it is neces-sary to make occasional adjustments. In these cases the real objective of placement is to put the pupil in the best situation for his learning, not to punish or reward him for achievement in subject matter.[9] Probably the first problem of school organization is that of developing the concept that the curriculum serves individual learners, in contrast to the concept that the learners must achieve essentials of the curriculum. When the staff accepts and implements the former concept, the issues of promotion and graduation and other aspects of pupil progress described in this section begin to disappear.

However, it is recognized that in dealing with the more mature pu-pils of the secondary school special situations arise that tax the ingenuity

[8] See Caswell and Foshay, *op. cit.*, pp. 354–378.
[9] Harold G. Shane describes very well this procedure. See Shane. "The Promotion Policy Dilemma," *loc. cit.*

and judgment of teachers. In spite of the best efforts of sincere, conscientious teachers to develop learning experiences that are meaningful and purposeful to all pupils concerned, occasionally some pupils still do not respond, and so fail to attain proper and legitimate goals in terms of their capacities, abilities, and needs. They may be lazy, indifferent, indolent, or simply content to "get by"—perhaps the product of overindulgent parents. Modern teachers who use good methods of group work, such as are described in Chapter 13, in which the group participates in setting goals and standards of accomplishment, in planning activities, and in evaluating results, may do much to stimulate all pupils to do their best. But if some few pupils still fail to work at a level that is reasonable in terms of their capacities and abilities, failure in the subject is probably warranted. Certainly the school should not encourage shoddy work, meager efforts, indolence, and the attainment of goals without commensurate effort. The school's guidance department may be of great assistance in locating the problems of such pupils and aiding in their solution.

PLANNING FOR EXCEPTIONAL CHILDREN

All curriculum workers recognize that some children deviate so much from the great majority of children that some of their most urgent needs cannot be taken care of in normal group situations. In educational practice we have come to designate these boys and girls as exceptional children, and modern curriculum planning is making strenuous efforts to provide special programs for these markedly different children insofar as is possible and feasible. Obviously, if we believe that the school should provide educational experiences that contribute maximally to the growth and development of each child and that are consistent with the over-all objectives of the school, provisions for these exceptional children must be made in the school program.

Types of Exceptional Children

Exceptional children deviate from the normal group in one or more major respects. They may be classified into the following groups:

I. *Children with physical handicaps*
   1. The orthopedically handicapped: those with deformities resulting from poliomyelitis, cerebral palsy, and congenital causes; those with other orthopedic handicaps; children with cardiac difficulties
   2. Defective in hearing: the congenitally deaf, the adventitiously deaf, and the hard of hearing
   3. Defective in vision: the blind and the partially seeing

   4. Defective in speech
   5. Other physical handicaps: those with tubercular, epileptic, or en-
      docrine disorders

II. *Children with mental deviations*

   1. The mentally retarded: the feeble-minded and those less seriously
      defective in intellectual development
   2. The mentally gifted: those with special talents, and those superior
      in general intelligence

III. *Children with emotional or social maladjustments:* serious behavior
disorders and emotional imbalance

Careful surveys of children throughout the United States indicate
that these groups of exceptional children comprise approximately 10 to
12 per cent of all children. Certainly this is a large enough group of
children to challenge our best efforts to provide an optimum educational
program for each of them, and most modern schools, like that shown in
Plate 26, are making such provisions.

Guiding Principles for Developing Educational Programs for Exceptional Children

In developing a curriculum for exceptional children, certain guiding principles should be observed. Among the most important are the
following:[10]

   *1. The educational objectives for exceptional children are the same
as for other pupils.* Obviously, the basic objectives that apply to the
total educational program of the school are equally appropriate for planning special programs for exceptional children. The objectives remain
the same; it is only that the types of educational experience planned to
achieve these objectives differ in some important respects for the exceptional child.

   *2. Except in relation to their particular handicap, exceptional
children follow the same basic growth patterns as other children.* For example, the child who is hard of hearing basically has the same needs, interests, wants, and aspirations as other children. Undoubtedly his physical growth patterns, his personal-social development, and his intellectual
development follow much the same patterns as those of normal children.

[10] Many of these principles are adapted from the National Society for the Study of
Education, *The Education of Exceptional Children* (Part II, Forty-ninth Yearbook;
Chicago: The University of Chicago Press, 1950), Chap. I.

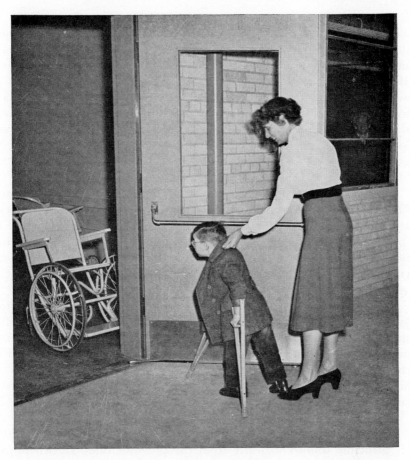

PLATE 26. THE MODERN SCHOOL MAKES ADEQUATE PROVISION FOR EXCEPTIONAL CHILDREN. *Exceptional children have special needs which must receive individual attention in the school. (Courtesy of the Dallas Public Schools)*

3. The school should provide special services for all types of exceptional children. If at all possible, the school should make provisions for all types of exceptional children; none should be neglected. Practically, it is recognized that it is sometimes difficult for school systems, particularly small school systems, to provide special programs for only a few individuals with particular types of handicaps. If the school itself does not have the facilities or the staff to provide special programs, arrangements should be made if at all possible to take care of the special needs of these children in some centralized facilities.

4. Provisions for exceptional children should be made at all school levels. The needs of exceptional children often persist through the secondary school period. Hence school systems should provide special programs insofar as they are needed at the secondary school level as well as at the elementary school level. It may also be necessary for the school to provide certain types of special facilities even beyond the secondary school so that exceptional pupils may be given types of vocational preparation and assistance with their developmental problems that will enable them to take their places as self-respecting, fully participating citizens.

5. Educational experiences for exceptional children must be individualized. It is quite apparent from the nature of exceptional children that in some aspects of the program educational experiences will need to be particularized. Some of the needs of such a child are peculiar to him; hence obviously in these areas his educational experiences must be especially planned for him.

6. Exceptional children should be placed in educational activities with normal children insofar as possible. This principle is not in conflict with the previous principle; rather, if the exceptional child can profit from experiences with groups of normal children, he should be placed in such situations. But some exceptional children cannot possibly be accommodated with normal class groups and will be unable to participate at any time in their educational activities.

7. The class placement of exceptional children should be flexible. This principle follows logically from the previous ones. If rich opportunities are to be provided the exceptional child, class arrangements will need to be most flexible.

8. Guidance for exceptional children is essential. Guidance is a necessary part of all phases of the educational program, but it must be emphasized that it is even more important in developing programs for exceptional children. The exceptional child, by definition, is one who has special problems and special needs; hence a good guidance program is essential to help him meet those needs and to guide him in the richest possible types of educational experiences.

9. In programs for exceptional children there must be close cooperation between the home and the school. The exceptional child has unusual needs, and efforts to guide his growth and development properly must be continuous. Because the home has an exceedingly important role to play in the development of the exceptional child, one of the first prerequisites of a good program is the development of close cooperation between school and home.

No attempt will be made here to block out in detail the various aspects of an appropriate program for each type of exceptional child. This is a quite technical matter and curriculum workers who are concerned with this phase of the program should be specialists in it. Nevertheless, it is important to emphasize again that all curriculum workers, as they plan the framework of the educational program, must be aware of the needs of exceptional children and must make provisions in all their curriculum plans for serving this group of pupils.

MAKING THE SCHOOL A COMMUNITY SCHOOL

In recent years curriculum workers have heard a great deal about the development of community schools. Some educators believe that the community school concept is the most promising educational development of recent decades. Since the plan for the community school has significant curriculum implications, it is quite appropriate that we consider this movement here.

What Is a Community School?

In Chapter 4 it was pointed out all schools are instrumentalities of society to achieve ends sought by the social group. All schools, in a sense, are community schools because they exist to perpetuate the value sought by the people of the community. The real test of a community school, as that concept is used in curriculum planning today, therefore lies in the types of educational experience that it utilizes to achieve these social ends and in the extent to which it really serves as an agency for the fulfillment of ends sought by the group of people who comprise a community.

A community school exists only in a relative sense. On the one hand, a school in a community may seek to perpetuate the basic social values sought by the entire society of which the people of the community are a part; yet the learning experiences which it develops with children may not necessarily be directly related at all to the life of the community. On the other hand, a school may seek the same basic social values and over-all outcomes but may develop learning experiences with children in seeking to attain these values that are indigenous to that community and could be provided only in that particular locality. It is this latter type of school that we designate as a community school.

We may think of a community school in terms of the extent to which its program is so inextricably interwoven with the life of the community that it would be impossible for the school to carry on its program without the community, and it would be impossible for the people of the community to enjoy the type of life they have without the particular school and its program.

Characteristics of a Community School

We can best gain an understanding of the community school by listing some of the essential characteristics of such a school. To be truly a community school, the school should exhibit to a marked degree the characteristics listed below:

1. Many of the educational experiences provided by the school grow out of and are developed in terms of life in the community. In a community school many of the educational experiences are real, firsthand experiences that children have as a part of their community living. Moreover, as units of work are developed in the school, many of the activities relate closely to life in that particular community, or to the experiences of the children as they grow up in the community group.

2. Pupils participate fully in the activities of community living, studying the life of the community and taking part as organized groups in community activities. One of the primary characteristics of a community school is that the school concerns itself with the life of the community. In the school program pupils have ample opportunity to learn about the community and to study its life and problems. Children can learn about the resources of the community, its economic activities, the work of its people, its traditions as a community, its value patterns, and the problems which face the social group. Plate 27 illustrates a study of the resources and industries of a community, such as we would expect to find in a community school program. Moreover, the community school provides organized opportunity for its pupils to participate in the activities of the community. For example, the pupils may develop and carry on a recreational program for young people in afterschool hours; at appropriate times they may participate in campaigns of various kinds, such as get-out-the-vote or clean-up campaigns; they may have appropriate parts in community festivals and affairs of various kinds.

3. The people of the community play a significant role in the determination of the program and policies of the school. One of the most important characteristics of the community school is that the people of the community have a very close relationship to the school, participating in the planning of the educational program of the school and in the determination of the policies of the school. While the basic policies and broad aspects of the program of all schools are determined to a greater or lesser degree by the social group that supports the school, in a community school every citizen feels a close and direct relationship to the school. Chapter 16 discusses procedures for such participation in co-operative curriculum planning in detail.

PLATE 27. IN A COMMUNITY SCHOOL PROGRAM THE LIFE AND RESOURCES OF THE COMMUNITY ARE STUDIED. *By making a model of the port and industrial section of the city, these pupils learn a great deal about the life of the community. (Courtesy of the Baltimore Public Schools)*

4. *The school is an important part of a total program of community living.* The staff of the community school recognizes that other organized agencies in the community are concerned with the improvement of community life and with the guidance of the growth and development of youngsters. Consequently, the school is constantly seeking to tie in its program with the activities of other agencies and groups in the community so that the total program of service and activities is coordinated, and, most important of all, so that it is developed on such a broad front that it encompasses all of the desirable activities for organized group living. It is usually desirable for the school, as the one central public agency in the community, to take the lead in coordinating all desirable activi-

ties of this kind in the community. Frequently, some type of community council or over-all agency formulates the total community program.

5. *The facilities of the school are used by the people of the community to carry on desirable aspects of community living.* In a community school, the school is so planned that its facilities are available for the use of all groups of the community that are furthering worthwhile activities. Of course, the activities of adult groups and activities not directly a part of the regular educational program of the school should not be permitted to interfere unduly with the school program, but it is obvious that the people of the community could use the school plant and its facilities in afterschool hours and during the months when the school is not in session without any interference with the regular program of the school. In fact, many of the facilities may be used during the school day by small groups without disturbing the school program. The facilities of the school may be used to provide services for the people of the community that would otherwise not be available. For example, adult education programs are desirable aspects of a community school program. Leisure time and recreational activities may best be carried on within the school facilities in many communities. The school may provide day nurseries for mothers who work, library services for the people in the community, and many services of this type.[11]

6. *In developing its educational experiences, the school utilizes fully resources in the community that will contribute significantly to the learning activities.* If the educational experiences of the school are to be concerned with the life of the community, it is apparent that the school will utilize resources in the community in developing these learning experiences. The true community school makes widespread use of these resources. It might be well to point out here that many schools have placed great emphasis on this characteristic as a base for developing a community school. While it is important, certainly the mere use of various resources in the community to carry on the learning activities of the school is not the basic factor in making a school a community school. It is primarily the type of learning activities that are carried on in the school itself, plus the close integration of the school with the activities of the community and the life of the people, that really makes a school a community school. Nevertheless, the desirability of drawing on peo-

[11] The Holtville school in Alabama provides an extensive group of services for the people of its rural community. For further details see Whilden Wallace, James Chrietzberg, and Verner Sims, *The Story of Holtville* (Deatsville, Ala.: The Holtville School, 1944).

ple and resources of the community in developing curricular experiences is evident.

7. *The school staff concerns itself with the activities of pupils outside the school so that life may be rich and may also be coordinated with the pupil's life in the school.* This characteristic of a community school has been suggested previously, but it should be pointed out again that the community school concerns itself with the total development of boys and girls and recognizes that this takes place outside the school as well as within it. Consequently, the school seeks to provide as lush an environment as possible for the desirable growth of boys and girls whether it be in the school or in the community at large. Once the school becomes concerned about the activities and learning experiences of children outside the school, it will naturally coordinate the program in the school with these activities so that needless duplication of effort may be avoided, but primarily so that the child will have a well-rounded growth and development and that no aspect of his development will be neglected in the total community approach to education.

Why a Community School?

Now that the characteristics of a community school have been delineated, it is appropriate to raise the question of why the development of community schools has been emphasized in modern curriculum planning.

An effective educational program. A community school provides a rich, significant program of education for its pupils. The characteristics described above indicate that any school that does a good job in all seven of these aspects will unquestionably have a more effective program of education for its pupils than a school that does not interweave to any appreciable degree its program with the life of the community. Educational experiences in the school have more meaning to the children because many of them are rooted in the life of the community itself.

Rich community life. The community school provides a lush environment for the growth and development of boys and girls. Since there is a total community approach to guiding the development of boys and girls, the environment in which children live is rich and inclusive. Moreover, it is quite apparent that a community school cannot exist without a total community approach to group living. This makes for a rich community life for all members of the community.

Improved community life. We need community schools so that communities may improve the quality of living for their members. It is through the community school approach, involving as it does the coordination of related activities, that communities can bring about improvement in the character of community life. In fact, as indicated previously, one of the primary characteristics of the community school is its interest in improving the quality of living for all citizens of the community.[12] The Holtville community in Alabama is a much better place in which to live because of the activities of its community school and other agencies in the community over the past quarter of a century.[13]

The Development of a Community School Program

The development of a community school and a community approach to a total program of education has important implications for the determination of the design of the curriculum of the school. Actually, it would be quite unlikely that curriculum workers could develop a good community school program within the traditional program of a subject-centered school.

Since the community school idea pervades the whole life and program of the school, there are implications of this concept for all aspects of the curriculum. Within the usual subject offerings of the school, units of work may be developed that consider various aspects of community life. For example, in the American history class pupils may do original research on the history and development of the community. Young children may take trips to historical sites and write their own original stories about incidents in the early history of the community. There are many ways in which aspects of the physical environment of the community would be used in the study of geography. Science classes would draw extensively on the community for rich learning activities.

In the development of the usual units of work in the traditional subjects many learning activities would grow out of community situations. For example, in studying world history, the class might want to invite natives of different countries to discuss conditions as they knew them or discuss problems facing their homelands. In creative art work, pupils may wish to use local scenes with which they are familiar. Classes in geometry may wish to visit various structures in the community to study design and the use of various principles of geometry in construction. There is literally no end to the things pupils may do in regular classwork in utilizing real life experiences in the community.

Most community schools, however, go far beyond these procedures

[12] Baker Brownell discusses the important part which the community should play in the lives of the citizens and the part the school may well take in the development of such communities. See Baker Brownell, *The Human Community* (New York: Harper & Brothers, 1950).

[13] See Wallace, Chrietzberg, and Sims, *op. cit.*

and develop aspects of their programs that will enable the school to play a vital role in the life and development of the community. In schools with core types of programs, considerable attention is usually given in the core to community life and problems. In fact, in some core programs much of the work for a year or a semester is centered in a study of the community.

THE PREPARATION OF GUIDES FOR CURRICULUM PLANNING

An important administrative concern in curriculum planning is the development of plans whereby the efforts of teachers and all other curriculum workers in the system will be stimulated, coordinated, and directed toward proper ends. In Chapter 16 we discuss procedures that may be followed in organizing a staff and the citizens of a community for curriculum planning, but here we shall give attention to use that may be made administratively of various types of curriculum guides in promoting curriculum planning.

Types of Curriculum Guides

A brief description of the various types of curriculum guides that are currently being prepared by school systems and other agencies may be helpful to curriculum workers in planning their own resource materials.

General guides to over-all curriculum concepts. At one time or another some school systems and other agencies concerned with curriculum planning find it desirable to publish a statement of their philosophy of education or an over-all statement of the objectives of the school or the outcomes desired from educational experiences provided by the school.

General guides to design and scope and sequence. Some state and local school systems prepare curriculum bulletins that describe or outline a general design for the curriculum and define the bases for determining scope and sequence, with possibly charts or outlines of suggested scope and sequence plans.

Guides to the development of learning experiences in various areas or at different maturity levels. Most of the curriculum guides published by state and local school systems fall in this general category. Such publications present suggestions for the development of actual day-by-day learning experiences in the school. Instructional guides of this sort are of many types and the material is presented in many forms, but some general classification has been attempted here.

INCLUSIVE GUIDES FOR THE ELEMENTARY AND SECONDARY SCHOOLS. A number of state departments of education and a few local school systems publish a large comprehensive curriculum guide for the planning of the entire instructional program in the elementary school, the junior high school, or the senior high school. Such publications, however, are usually restricted to the elementary school.

CURRICULUM GUIDES FOR THE SUBJECT AREAS. Most curriculum guides published by state and local school systems contain suggestions for the planning of instruction in the various subject areas usually included in the school program. Some school systems develop curriculum guides for subject areas that include all grade levels, thus presenting curriculum suggestions for Grade 1 through Grade 12. However, most of these guides are planned for particular levels of the school system, such as the elementary school, the secondary school, or even individual grades or small groupings of grades such as Grades 4, 5, and 6.

GUIDES FOR THE DEVELOPMENT OF CORE PROGRAMS. In the discussion of core programs in Chapter 10 it was indicated that school systems often prepare guides of some type for the use of teachers in developing the core program. Usually guides for the development of core programs are quite similar to the guides for the development of instruction in the subject areas. They give consideration to the nature of core programs, suggest scope and sequence for the core program, and contain suggested units of work and procedures for developing them.

GUIDES TO THE DEVELOPMENT OF SPECIAL ASPECTS OF THE EDUCATIONAL PROGRAM. In addition to guides to the development of learning experiences in the subject and core types of organization, a number of state and local school systems issue curriculum guides on certain specialized aspects of the educational program that cut across various subject areas or grade levels, such as bulletins on teaching safety, citizenship, and the like.

Resource units and local teaching materials. A number of state and local school systems, as well as organized professional groups, prepare resource units for the use of teachers in planning instruction. Chapter 12 discusses resource units; many school systems have found them to be especially helpful to teachers as guides in developing such units.

Descriptions of practice. Another type of curriculum publication is the bulletin that describes practice or explains some particular aspect of the school program. These vary greatly in type and content, many of them being designed primarily for the interpretation of the school program to the parents and to the public. However, they certainly constitute an important type of curriculum material, since teachers themselves, not only in preparing the pamphlets but in referring to them later and using them with parent groups, are developing concepts that should guide the formulation of the educational experiences of the school.

Guides to curriculum planning. Some state and local school systems issue general guides to curriculum planning, including suggestions for the organization and development of instruction, the evaluation of learning experiences, and various materials of this type.

Principles for the Preparation of Curriculum Guides

We ourselves believe that the preparation and publication of good curriculum guides of the right kind is a highly desirable aspect of sound curriculum planning. When the educational millennium did not arrive following the issuance of a plethora of courses of study and curriculum guides in the 1930's and early 1940's, many curriculum directors and specialists became quite skeptical about such materials and took the position that the results obtained in improved curriculum practice were not commensurate with the time and effort involved in their preparation. In recent years, the pendulum has partially swung back again and an increasing number of state and local school systems are now issuing curriculum guides of the types described.

It is quite apparent to any curriculum worker that curriculum improvement will not result automatically from the mere issuance of a new course of study or a curriculum guide of some type. The curriculum is improved, as has been pointed out repeatedly in this book, only as teachers develop better learning experiences with children in classrooms. However, teachers who are interested in providing better educational experiences for their pupils can get help and guidance from appropriate curriculum publications. This point of view is necessarily based on the position that such curriculum guides will be of the right kind and will meet certain basic criteria that should characterize curriculum materials.

The following principles are desirable guides to the preparation of good curriculum bulletins for teachers:

1. Curriculum guides should stimulate and help teachers develop all types of educational experiences for pupils that promise to contribute most to their growth and development in terms of the outcomes desired from the educational program. Obviously, curriculum bulletins have one primary and basic function: to help teachers provide better experiences for children. Curriculum bulletins should offer help in attaining all of the desired outcomes of the educational program, not just limited phases of it. Hence a wide variety of publications of the types described above is desirable.

2. Curriculum bulletins should provide teachers with a guide to the broad framework of the curriculum so that appropriate scope and sequence and continuity may be maintained in the entire educational program. If the growth and development of pupils are to be consecutive and maximum, teachers at all levels and in all aspects of the program should have some guide to the basic framework for determining the types of educational experiences that are appropriate to the maturity level of their pupils and that encompass proper breadth for the all-round growth of the children.

3. Curriculum guides should broaden the insights and deepen the understandings of teachers and stimulate and direct their professional growth. The key to curriculum improvement is the teacher, so it is only as the teacher plans better educational experiences for children that curriculum improvement takes place. Therefore, one of the primary functions of all curriculum guides is to develop better understanding on the part of teachers as to what constitutes good educational experiences for children and how they can best develop learning experiences consistent with these understandings.

4. Curriculum guides should serve to free the teacher rather than impose uniformity. Throughout this book we have emphasized the necessity of planning educational experiences in terms of the interests, capacities, needs, and concerns of the particular group of learners engaging in the experience. To be consistent with this concept, all curriculum guides should give the teacher a great deal of freedom and flexibility, so that he may plan instruction on such a basis. Courses of study that dictate the exact nature of the curriculum experiences or content to be covered are inconsistent with a modern concept of curriculum planning.

5. Curriculum guides should provide a wealth of suggestions for developing educational experiences. As has already been suggested, not only do curriculum guides need to allow the teacher a great deal of freedom in planning instruction; they will be of little value unless they provide a wealth of suggestions for the planning of educational experiences. A curriculum guide should become a very valuable resource for the teacher in developing plans for selecting, organizing, and carrying forward learning experiences with pupils.

In terms of these criteria, many of the types of curriculum publications listed previously in this section would have a place in a modern curriculum improvement program. In determining the appropriateness and soundness of curriculum publications, those responsible for the preparation of such bulletins should ascertain carefully the purposes to be served by a guide, the procedures or techniques to be used in achieving these purposes, and then weigh these plans carefully against the basic criteria to make certain that the guides are properly planned. It is often easy for committees of teachers and others to undertake the preparation of a curriculum guide without seriously considering the purpose to be served by the guide and whether the approaches to be used are consistent with a sound philosophy of education.

In the light of this discussion, it would seem highly desirable for school systems sooner or later to prepare curriculum guides and materials of the following types: (1) a statement of the philosophy of the school, including a statement of the broad objectives or outcomes desired from the educational program; (2) a basic statement on the scope and sequence of the curriculum and the general framework of the educational program; (3) guides to planning instruction at the various grade levels and in the subject or core areas, including a wealth of suggestions for developing learning experiences with children; (4) suggested resource units, unless these can be included in the general guides to the planning of instruction; (5) miscellaneous guides for teachers, such as guides to the study of children, suggestions for evaluating pupil growth and development, suggestions for planning and organizing instruction, suggestions for meeting individual needs of children in group situations, suggestions for cooperative group planning, and the like.

For Further Study

American Association of School Administrators, *The Expanding Role of Education.* Twenty-sixth Yearbook. Washington, D.C.: The Association, 1948.

Chapter V deals with the problem of the exceptional child.

Baker, Harry J., *Introduction to Exceptional Children.* Rev. ed.; New York: The Macmillan Company, 1953.

A standard textbook in the field of the exceptional child.

Board of Education, City of New York, *Helping the Physically Limited Child.* Curriculum Bulletin, 1952–1953 Series, No. 7. New York: The Board, 1953.

An excellent guide to the development of educational experiences for the physically handicapped child.

Caswell, Hollis L. (ed.), *The American High School.* Eighth Yearbook of the John Dewey Society. New York: Harper & Brothers, 1946.

Chapter VIII discusses the various aspects of secondary education.

Caswell, Hollis L., and A. Wellesley Foshay, *Education in the Elementary School* 2d ed.; New York: American Book Company, 1950.

An excellent treatment of the various phases and elements in a good elementary school program.

Educational Policies Commission, *Education for All American Youth: A Further Look*. Washington, D.C.: National Education Association, 1952.

Chapter 8 considers the various aspects of secondary education and proposes a division of school time among the various parts.

Elsbree, Willard S., and Harold J. McNally, *Elementary School Administration and Supervision*. New York: American Book Company, 1951.

Comprehensive treatment of problems of elementary school organization.

Evelyn, Katherine D., *Individual Parent-Teacher Conferences*. New York: Bureau of Publications, Teachers College, Columbia University, 1945.

Suggestions and help in planning a method of reporting that involves conferences with parents.

French, Will, J. Dan Hull, and B. L. Dodds, *American High School Administration: Policy and Practice*. New York: Rinehart & Company, Inc., 1951.

Chapter 19 considers problems of admission, progress, and graduation in high school.

Harris, Fred E., *Three Persistent Educational Problems: Grading, Promoting, and Reporting to Parents*. Bulletin of the Bureau of School Service, College of Education, University of Kentucky, Vol. 26, No. 1 (September), 1953.

A discussion of issues, practices, and new developments in these three aspects of planning.

Kirk, Samuel A. (chm.), "The Education of Exceptional Children," *Review of Educational Research,* Vol. 23, No. 5 (December), 1953.

An excellent review of new developments in the education of the exceptional child, and an extensive bibliography on the subject.

National Society for the Study of Education, *The Community School*. Part II, Fifty-second Yearbook. Chicago: The University of Chicago Press, 1953.

A comprehensive and significant yearbook on the community school in all of its aspects. A detailed treatment of this new emphasis in curriculum planning.

————, *The Education of Exceptional Children*. Part I, Forty-ninth Yearbook. Chicago: The University of Chicago Press, 1950.

A basic reference on the subject of the exceptional child.

Olson, Edward G. (ed.), *The Modern Community School*. New York: Appleton-Century-Crofts, Inc., 1953.

This publication of the Association for Supervision and Curriculum Development presents examples of the development of community schools as well as an exploration of the basic concepts.

Olson, Willard C., *Child Development*. Boston: D. C. Heath & Company, 1949.

See Chapter XIII, "Concepts of Child Development in the Organization and Administration of Schools."

Otto, Henry J., *Elementary School Organization and Administration*. 2d ed.; Appleton-Century-Crofts, Inc., 1944.

Chapters II and III discuss promotion, grouping, and kindred problems.

Research Division, National Education Association, *Teaching Load in 1950*. Research Bulletin, Vol. 39, No. 1. Washington, D.C.: The Association, February, 1951.

Research study of the facts of teachers' loads and of conditions which are considered to make the job of teachers pleasant and unpleasant.

"School and Community Improvement," *School Executive* (Special Issue), Vol. 72, No. 5 (January), 1953.

An extensive consideration of various aspects of the community school.

Shane, Harold G., "The Promotion Policy Dilemma," *NEA Journal*, 42:411–412 (October), 1953.

Presents five principles that should characterize promotion policies.

————, and E. T. McSwain, *Evaluation and the Elementary Curriculum*. New York: Henry Holt and Company, 1951.

Chapter 12 is an excellent treatment of problems relating to grouping and related matters in the elementary school.

Southern Association of Colleges and Secondary Schools, Cooperative Study in Elementary Education, *Promising Practice in Elementary Schools*. Atlanta, Ga.: The Association, 1952.

A popular and pictorial presentation of various aspects of a good program of elementary education.

Strang, Ruth, *Reporting to Parents*. New York: Bureau of Publications, Teachers College, Columbia University, 1947.

A review of new trends and developments in reporting pupil progress to parents.

Theman, Viola, *A Good School Day*. New York: Bureau of Publications, Teachers College, Columbia University, 1950.

Contains many helpful suggestions, including illustrative daily programs, for a good school day for elementary school children.

Yauch, Wilbur A., *Improving Human Relations in School Administration*. New York: Harper & Brothers, 1949.

Suggestions for elementary school principals on the use of good techniques of human relations.

Yeager, William A., *Administration and the Pupil*. New York: Harper & Brothers, 1949.

Comprehensive analysis of current practices in the administration of pupil personnel.

HOW SHALL WE PLAN THE CURRICULUM FOR BETTER TEACHING?

In Part 3 we considered the various problems of organizing or reorganizing the general framework of the curriculum. In Part 4 we turn our attention to the basic curriculum problem of planning and developing learning experiences—the curriculum—for and with particular learning groups and learners. We realize that curriculum planning would logically begin with the general framework and then proceed with planning for and with learning groups but that in practice this logical order (see Table 11) is not necessarily followed. Very frequently, the one step possible is for the individual teacher to provide better learning experiences within the established framework. Although more basic reorganization might be desirable, we believe that every important improvement is to be encouraged and hope that the following chapters will aid teachers desiring to make changes on their own. We further believe that their changes will be made more advisedly if the factors and plans described in Parts 1, 2, and 3 are considered, and also that change in the general framework (Part 3) is fruitless without eventual changes in learning situations.

Part 4 contains the following chapters:

Using Resource Units and Unit Plans

Curriculum planning for particular learning groups involves both the teacher's preplanning of learning experiences, and the cooperative pupil-teacher selection and development of appropriate experiences. The teacher's preplanning activities, particularly in reference to the preparation and use of resource units and unit plans, are dealt with in this chapter. Since this planning is primarily that of designing, selecting, and organizing learning experiences for the group (s) concerned, we should first identify the characteristics of desirable learning experiences which are sought through resource units, unit plans, and other preplanning activities.

CHARACTERISTICS OF DESIRABLE LEARNING EXPERIENCES

The characteristics of desirable learning experiences may be inferred from the principles of learning which were cited in Chapter 6. It should be emphasized again that experiences *planned* and experiences *had* are not necessarily the same since the precise nature of each learner's experience depends upon his unique characteristics. This fact does not make planning for groups undesirable but does mean that plans should be sufficiently broad and flexible to provide for a range of individual differences.

Directly Related to Goals

That experiences of learners should be related to curriculum goals seems obvious, but the relationship in practice is not nearly so clear. For example, a commonly stated goal of curriculum plans for history classes is "to interpret the present in the light of the past," but examination of the activities listed in many plans and especially those occurring in classrooms indicates that the experiences relate only to "the light of the past" which apparently is never "shone" on the present! Such conflicts arise from an erroneous procedure in the planning of experiences for learners: the experiences are planned in advance of stating goals or without reference to the latter.

In personal living we relate experiences to goals very readily. If, for example, an individual desires to buy a new suit because his wardrobe is inadequate for his social and business obligations, the procedures are clear-cut. He finds a store selling suits, examines those available in terms of his wants and perhaps his financial abilities, weighs the facts, and buys what seems the best for him. Relating our curriculum experiences to goals can be almost as direct. If the teacher's knowledge of the members of the class indicates that their ability to participate in group discussion is less than society (perhaps the school) demands, the teacher simply canvasses the possibilities of developing that ability. The teacher considers the opportunities for discussion in the total learning group, in small groups, and perhaps in all-school activities. Since no one situation will fit each child any more than one suit would fit each of thirty men at random, many opportunities, all related to the goal of increased ability to participate in group discussion, are planned. Having identified these opportunities, the teacher must also determine just how and when each might best be utilized: What group? What problems? What leaders? What length? That is, the planning process in accordance with this criterion is:

1. Select a goal or goals which apply for the group concerned.

2. Make an inventory of the types of opportunities which can be provided by the teacher's initiative with the help of the group, and which fit the goals.

3. Develop possible ways and means of utilizing each such opportunity.

4. Recheck the full but tentative list of experiences as to whether they have adequate possibilities for achieving the goal or goals.

Meaningful to Learners

We have already explained the importance of meaningful experiences for retention of learning, development of problem-solving techniques, and other purposes. The present question is how to plan experiences which have maximum meaningfulness. Plate 28 shows such an experience.

Meaningful experiences are planned through selecting situations which are sufficiently related to the previous experience of the learners as to be accurately understood. In selecting such situations these questions must be asked: Have the pupils had sufficient previous acquaint-

PLATE 28. LEARNING EXPERIENCES SHOULD BE MEANINGFUL. *Geography is made more meaningful by airport "props." (Courtesy of the Denver Public Schools)*

ance with the central idea or object involved in this experience to behave as anticipated? Will the meaning of the idea or object be clear enough so that behavior will be purposeful rather than guesswork or mechanical?

Appropriate to Maturity of Learners

Experiences may have meaning to pupils and still be inappropriate to their maturities. Thus experiences which are meaningful to fourth-graders are likely to be just as meaningful to eighth-graders but inappropriate to the maturity of the latter. Experiences which are appropriate psychologically—that is, are adapted to children's intellectual readiness —may be completely inappropriate to their social and emotional development. For example, teachers cannot assume that all junior high school children have become sufficiently mature to be interested in discussions of boy-and-girl relationships. The fact that girls become adolescent considerably in advance of boys creates a very difficult problem in the selection of experiences related to the maturities of children from about eleven to fourteen years of age. The physical maturity of the learner sets a relatively obvious limitation on experience. All such factors as the foregoing challenge teachers to consider carefully the maturities of the boys and girls they teach. The chart of developmental characteristics presented in Chapter 5 may be a helpful guide in evaluating the maturity status of a particular individual or group.

Satisfying to Learners

The concomitant result of much of the rote learning that children do in school is a feeling of dissatisfaction and, indeed, dislike for the material memorized. The element of satisfaction is closely bound to the nature of motivation employed. As explained in Chapter 6, success in goal attainment and satisfaction in learning are synonymous. Experiences are satisfying when they result in the ends desired by the learner. If the goal involved is an artificially engendered one that is sought in order to escape punishment and failure, the result is satisfying only in that he goes free. When the pupil attaches significance to an experience in terms of values he holds important, success in that experience is satisfying.

To be satisfying, experiences must also have an element of challenge. Bored boys and girls generally are those for whom the experiences of the classroom introduce little that is new and even less that is interesting. The quality of challenge is affected by the factor of difficulty. That is, experiences for which ready-made responses are available, such as recitation of multiplication facts, involve no new goal and no new pattern of behavior for children who know these facts. But opportunities to take cost inventories in the school store are new situations in which the facts may be applied. The learner who can marshal his facts sufficiently well to take the inventory finds this a satisfying task, but the one who does not already understand the relation of multiplication facts to dollars-and-cents problems may be frustrated. In other words, the first learner finds the task sufficiently difficult to be challenging and sufficiently successful to be satisfying, while the second finds it both too difficult and unsuccessful.

Application of this criterion in advance of the learning situation is difficult. At best the teacher can only estimate the satisfaction of a particular experience by consideration of the desires and maturities of the learners. Careful observation and evaluation of the experiences help in planning subsequent modifications and different experiences.

Flexible in Development

Remembering that there will be as many experiences as there are learners, the wise teacher anticipates a maximum number of modifications by learners of the general type of experience planned. Accordingly, the plan includes a minimum of uniform assignments and a variety of suggestions related to possible interests of the class. For example, two contrasting types of experiences might be planned in relation to the curriculum goal of increased acceptance of responsibility for care of school property. One approach would be for the teacher to present pupils with a list of suggestions as to how they might assume more responsibility for the care of the classroom, and thereafter to appoint a pupil committee to check on how these suggestions operate. Another type of experience would be a class planning period in which common problems in caring for the room and school property in general are identified, suggestions are made as to how the children might work on these problems, and, finally, jobs are divided among the group. Preplanning of this experience might very well include some problems and jobs, but if the discussion is guided democratically, the final list might be quite different from the teacher's preliminary plan. That is, in the second instance a plan was developed which charted a process of problem solving, rather than a "telling" experience. This process has flexibility and opportunities for individual participation in accordance with maturity, whereas the "telling" experience does not.

Flexibility as a characteristic of desirable learning experiences has two implications. First, the plan itself should be flexible. The teacher of the preceding example had merely planned some questions for discussion. Furthermore, the teacher should turn to some other question suggested in the discussion if the procedure seems better at that time. Second, the plan should provide for varying experiences of individuals. Discussion permits individuals to participate in terms of their readiness, whereas formal recitation procedures assume uniform readiness and penalize pupils who give incorrect answers. Also, the plan described proposed that learners would accept certain responsibilities on a voluntary basis.

Related to Other Experiences

Several implications of the principles of learning analyzed in Chapter 6 point to the necessity of selecting learning experiences which are related to each other. In order to be meaningful and therefore promote effective learning products and processes, a learning experience must be built on the readiness which develops in part from previous related experiences. Learning is greatly affected by interpersonal relationships, and planning must recognize the effects on boys and girls of their previous relations with each other and anticipate means of improving these relationships through satisfactory group activities. Experiences planned to develop skills must anticipate other situations in which these skills will be used. Thus in a subject organization, plans for reading and writing need correlation with those for social studies and science. However, it is not to be inferred that all learning activities must be related to some unit topic. A great many valuable learning experiences occur without direct relationship to others. Other things being equal, an activity closely related to some previous experience would be chosen, but frequently things are not equal, and an interesting and valuable experience is preferable to a sequential but relatively ineffective one. A section of the next chapter deals with learning experiences not organized in units.

Particularly important in connection with the present characteristic is the principle that the most effective, best retained, and most significant learnings are well organized. The idea of a unitary organization of experiences is based on this principle, and is one of two closely related procedures for planning experiences with desirable relationships to one another. The other procedure is that of the over-all framework of the curriculum, with which we dealt in Part 3. We turn now to the unitary organization of learning experiences.

THE UNITARY ORGANIZATION OF LEARNING EXPERIENCES

The first problem the teacher must solve as he prepares curriculum plans for his learning group (s) is that of the organization of learning experiences. As noted in connection with the discussion of the broad curriculum framework (Part 3), several alternatives are possible. Shall there be some logical organization as that of the textbook or course of study, shall there be "units" of some other type, or shall there be no particular pattern of organization of learning experiences? Although both the first and the third alternatives are found in operation, the unit organization is widely accepted. However, as already pointed out, not all desirable learning experiences can or should be fitted into unitary organization. For example, a high school assembly program may be a very fine learning activity but one which cannot possibly be related to the units on which all learning groups in the school may be working. The wide usefulness of unitary organization, however, makes essential the teacher's understanding of this concept and related principles and procedures.

What Is a Unit?

One of the terms that has persisted in the educational terminology of the twentieth century is "unit." Although defined in various and conflicting ways, the term itself is definitely in common professional usage and has at least a limited common meaning, namely, an organization of related learning experiences. Because of the many additional and conflicting meanings, we ourselves prefer to deal with the concept as that of a unitary organization of experiences. We should note that a frequent distinction is made between "units of experience" and "units of subject matter." Since subject matter is recorded experience and is also a major source of learning experience, we do not consider the distinction a real one.

The concept of an organization of learning experiences around some source of unity is not new in education, but there has been considerable change in the sources of unity recognized. The traditional unitary organization was a series of "lessons" relating to some "topic." Being in need of a term to describe a somewhat larger organization of learning experiences than lessons or series of lessons, curriculum workers have used the term "unit" or, frequently, "unit of work." At least the following meanings are rather commonly associated with the term: (1) a unit is an organization of more experiences than a lesson or period or activity or similar somewhat arbitrary division of experience; (2) a unit is organized in relation to some one of many possible sources of unity (see Chapters 8 and 9)—logical divisions of subject matter or social problems or children's needs or others; and (3) a unit involves both a unitary organization in planning the curriculum and in its classroom development.

It should be emphasized that the foregoing meanings are merely those which are generally accepted. Persons who accept these meanings still can and do differ as to formal definitions, the source of unity, the kind of plan, and the kind of classroom program related to the concept. These differences stem in part from at least two major but conflicting influences which have popularized the general concept of unitary organization. The first influence is that of the "unit method" first described in Morrison's *The Practice of Teaching in the Secondary School,* published in 1926. Morrison's idea of the learning unit as "a comprehensive and significant aspect of the environment, of an organized science, of an art, or of conduct, which being learned results in adaptation of personality," [1] and his exposition of the five steps of the unit method (exploration, presentation, assimilation, organization, recitation) have had great influence

---

[1] H. C. Morrison, *The Practice of Teaching in the Secondary School* (Chicago: The University of Chicago Press, 1926), pp. 24–25.

on the organization of curriculum materials and, perhaps to a lesser extent, on classroom instruction in secondary schools. Probably the chief result of Morrison's work was a much more rigorous evaluation of the subject matter and its organization included in secondary school classes.

A second movement which has made wide use of the term "unit," although with quite different interpretations, is a series of curriculum studies and practices we might group together because of their generally greater concern for the needs and interests of learners than for subject matter. Included in this movement are such significant developments as the pioneer work of the Lincoln School of Teachers College, Columbia University, in preparing various curriculum materials, including units of work; the various efforts to break down an emphasis on subject matter which are frequently grouped as "the activity movement"; the curriculum studies and publications of the Progressive Education Association; and the more recent studies relating child development and the curriculum and those having to do with "life adjustment education" in secondary schools. As related in earlier chapters, all these movements have had an influence on the curriculum, but for present purposes it is to be noted that each employed the concept of unitary organization as a basis for curriculum planning and classroom teaching. Unlike Morrison's plan, the units referred to in the publications produced in the course of these developments were generally based on social functions, or on needs, interests, or life problems of learners, with subject matter to be selected as needed.

Thus the specific concepts associated with unitary organization held by an individual or a curriculum committee might have developed from Morrison's work and its interpretations in secondary education or from one of the writings or practices in the second group. Or perhaps a committee might attempt to use both approaches, the one basically employing a functional use of subject matter, the other an orientation of curriculum materials in terms of learners. In 1935 Caswell and Campbell listed nine different definitions of units and proposed two major classes of units, each with three subclasses.[2] More recent publications in the curriculum field have cited further definitions and have frequently proposed still additional ones and different classifications.[3] It is understandable that considerable confusion has existed in the philosophy and terminology of unitary organization, but it is perhaps more significant that the general idea of unitary organization caught on and gave a considerably

[2] Hollis L. Caswell and Doak S. Campbell, *Curriculum Development* (New York: American Book Company, 1935), pp. 404–406.

[3] See references at the end of this chapter, by Alberty, Lee and Lee, Leonard, and Smith, Stanley, and Shores.

broader base for fundamental curriculum planning than did the traditional subject-textbook, chapter-lesson, read-recite concept in organization of the curriculum. The relationship of unitary organization and curriculum planning is described in the following section.

Selection and Planning of Units

The student may feel that the concept of unitary organization introduces another element into an already complex picture of curriculum planning. How does unitary organization relate, for example, to design, scope, and sequence? to learning experience? to pupil-teacher planning? Perhaps these relationships will be made clearer by examining the logical order of steps in curriculum planning, as illustrated in Table 11:

1. Curriculum goals are determined.

2. The design or broad framework of the curriculum is outlined.

3. The scope of general areas and problems of living included in the curriculum is defined.

4. The principles of sequence suggesting the order of curriculum experiences are planned.

5. The organization of broad units is planned through the preparation or selection of resource *units.*

6. Specific *unit plans* for particular learning groups are made.

7. The learning group determines and carries on the learning experiences actually included (or possibly developed singly) in the *unit of work* as developed in the classroom.

Thus the term "unit" is used in three connections or steps in curriculum planning: first, the *resource unit* is a compilation of materials from which, second, an individual teacher draws suggestions for a *unit plan* which, third, is the basis for pupil-teacher development of the actual *unit of work* in the learning situation. All three steps are involved in the concept of unitary organization. We should note that such a logical process is not necessarily followed. Indeed the planning of a new unit may be a first step in a process of curriculum study which eventuates in a complete reorganization of goals, design, and general framework. Also, units may be planned without prior or later consideration of the broader aspects of curriculum planning, although such a procedure does not make for continuity and consistency of the curriculum of learners. But unit plans sometimes have to be made without access to resource units, and learning experiences selected in learning situations without advance planning.

In general, the selection and planning of units are determined by the design and general framework of the curriculum. Thus in a subject-centered curriculum the logical unitary organization is a division of

TABLE 11
The Logical Order of Steps in Curriculum Planning

WHO	DOES	WHAT? *(for example)*
A planning group representing citizens, boards of education, professional personnel, parents, and pupils	I. DETERMINES CURRICULUM GOALS decides on major goals to be sought by the schools:	Understanding of the responsibilities of American citizenship.
The system planning group	II. OUTLINES CURRICULUM DESIGNS develops the broad framework of the curriculum:	To use subject type of design and to include certain required subjects in social studies.
The system planning group	III. DEFINES THE SCOPE OF THE CURRICULUM indicates major areas and problems of living around which instructional units may ultimately be organized in relation to I and II:	The problem of participation in voting and other civic processes.
The system planning group	IV. DEFINES THE SEQUENCE OF THE CURRICULUM suggests levels at which emphasis may appropriately be given to each area or problem, or to aspects thereof:	For senior high school, voting in local, state, and national elections.
School planning groups	V. PLAN RESOURCE UNITS by levels or departments plan resource units for major areas or problems and aspects thereof:	A resource unit on "Voting."
Individual teachers	VI. MAKE UNIT PLANS make unit plans for each learning group.	A unit plan for an 11A American History class on "Voting in U.S. Presidential Elections."
The learning group	VII. DEVELOPS LEARNING EXPERIENCES plans and carries on learning experiences related to the unit plan, usually through units of work:	An experience in using voting machines in connection with the above-named unit or plan.

the subject involved: a period of history, a type of literature, a law of science, and so forth. If the curriculum design is based on areas of living, the unitary organization is logically derived by analysis of one or more areas in terms of the maturities of learners. If the design is an evolving one oriented in the experiences of learners, the unit would tend to be organized around the cluster point of experiences or problems and interests of a particular group of learners. However, we should note that a unitary organization of experiences not based on logical organization of subject matter might be planned within a subject design. Thus a unit involving much firsthand experience with the school store might be planned for an elementary group instead of separate units in arithmetic and social studies, and a unit on the history of transportation might be planned for a core, experience-centered curriculum. That is, the curriculum pattern influences the choice of units but does not necessarily restrict the nature of experiences included.

Another question of relationship is that of individual learning experiences to the unit. Logically, a unit is first chosen and experiences are planned to achieve the unit purposes. Thus the tenth-grade core teacher plans a unit related to the needs of children entering senior high school for orientation and adjustment, and includes various activities such as guided tours of the building, statements to the class by representatives of special-interest groups, introduction of the principal, the counselor, the librarian, and others. But such a unit might be developed because, for example, in undertaking an introductory unit on democratic organization the teacher discovers that the learners have no understanding of the school organization. Thus learning experiences may determine the choice of units, while the unit may determine the experiences to be included.

There may be confusion also as to whether a unit is a plan or a method. Actually, it is both. A unitary organization of experiences is developed (the unit plan), but the nature of the experiences involves a method of procedure in the actual unit of work. For example, a unit might be organized around a body of subject matter on the American Revolution, with the experiences included being primarily of the read-recite-test variety. Another unit might be organized around the meaning of American democracy to involve interviewing, attending group meetings, and committee discussions, as well as reading. However, we should note that the method of procedure is determined by the experiences planned rather than the unit idea, although some ideas are perhaps more adaptable to varied learning activities than others.

The relationship of advance planning and teacher-pupil planning is a critical problem in using unitary organization: How much shall be determined in advance? How shall pupils' interests and needs enter into the planning process? The principles of learning developed in Chapter 6 seem to provide the most satisfactory resolution of this problem. In general, experiences are more meaningful and effective when they have intrinsic value for learners. Hence maximum reference of the unit to learners' own goals is desirable. This is secured, first, by preplanning (the resource unit and unit plan) which takes into consideration learners' maturities, needs, and interests, and, second, by pupil planning of specific goals and experiences (the unit of work) to achieve the goal. Specifically, then, teachers need to plan in advance a unitary organization which can be modified in the learning situation by pupil participation in the day-by-day development of the unit of work. In this way, the teachers' more mature knowledge of the purposes and possibilities of the educational program is utilized, and then pupils' learning is facilitated by their participation, in accordance with their maturities, in planning and directing learning processes.

To summarize, the selection of units should be guided by previous planning of the over-all organization of the curriculum. This planning should give direction to the preparation of resource units. The preparation of these resource units and of plans for particular units of work should also be influenced by teachers' knowledge of such characteristics of desirable learning experiences as presented earlier in this chapter, because units are merely organizations of learning experiences. The final selection of a unit of work, and more particularly of the learning experiences it involves, should be made by the teacher and the learning group. Therefore, the problem of selecting and planning units of work is given further consideration in Chapter 13, "Planning and Developing Learning Experiences with Learners."

PREPARING RESOURCE UNITS

We believe that preparation of resource units is probably the most effective procedure other than a very critical evaluation and replanning of design (see Part 3), available for advance curriculum planning by groups of teachers. This procedure can definitely be translated into desirable learning experiences. Therefore consideration is given in this section to the nature, preparation, and use of resource units.

What Is a Resource Unit?

Resource units are typically developed for more than one learning group and may be used by teachers at different grade levels and in different subject areas. As the name implies, the resource unit is a "resource" from which teachers may draw materials to be used in unit plans for their particular learning groups. Klohr's comprehensive study of resource units employed the following definition: "The resource unit is defined in this study as a carefully planned series of suggestions centered in some broad problem, topic, or area of experience and organized to serve as a source of ideas, materials, and procedures to help a teacher in preplanning a learning unit." [4]

Further insight into the nature and use of resource units is provided by Klohr's summary of his interviews with 177 teachers and administrators in 26 secondary schools in which resource units had been used in curriculum planning. The summary of generalizations regarding resource units Klohr prepared by analysis of the statements made by these interviewees follows:

1. Resource units in use are proving to be highly effective in helping teachers in planning and guiding learning units.

2. Resource units developed at each of the planning levels—the state, the county, the city and the individual school—have distinct values recognized by the using teachers and administrators.

3. The degree of coordination and cooperation among the schools at the various planning levels is a significant factor in the effectiveness with which the resource units developed at these levels are used by teachers.

4. An effective resource unit includes a listing of many activities, suggested evaluation procedures, a carefully selected bibliography and list of teaching aids, and a well-planned description of the scope of the problem area. It also emphasizes many suggested procedures and techniques for planning and guiding learning experiences.

5. Provisions should be made for the frequent revision of resource units.

6. Participation in the development of resource units is a significant factor in the effectiveness with which they are used.

7. The quality of the in-service education program for teachers is a significant factor in the effectiveness with which any kinds of resource units are used.

8. Resource units are being used effectively to provide structure to general education areas of the curriculum by suggesting a general sequence of large problem areas and offering many suggestions for developing learning units in these areas.

9. Resource units may be used effectively to enrich the special

[4] Paul Robert Klohr, "A Study of the Role of the Resource Unit in the Curriculum Reorganization of Selected Secondary Schools" (unpublished doctoral dissertation; Columbus: Ohio State University, 1948), p. 11. The "learning unit" corresponds to what we call "the unit of work."

subject areas lying outside of general education or core areas of the curriculum.

10. Resource units may be used effectively to provide a basis for cooperative planning among teachers and to give direction to a program of supervision.

11. Resource units tend to be most effective when developed in a situation that fosters democratic participation and democratic leadership.

12. The quantity and quality of materials available in a school is a significant factor in the use of the resource unit.

13. The degree of administrative encouragement in a school is a significant factor in the use of the resource unit.

14. There are other organizations of curricular resource materials that are proving helpful as supplements to the use of the resource unit.[5]

Content of Resource Units

Examination of illustrative resource units indicates that the following materials are generally included:

1. Explanation of the unit problem
2. Statement of learning outcomes sought
3. Outline of subject matter appropriate to the problems and types being studied (problems, questions, content, etc.)
4. Suggested learning experiences and resources
5. Suggested evaluation procedures

In the Dade County (Florida) Schools, the following outline for preparing resource units was developed for use throughout the system:

I. *The Unit Problem*

(A paragraph or two explaining the central problem, question, need, or interest around which the unit was or can be developed.)

II. *Where—When—Why?*

(A paragraph stating the grade or grades in which the unit was taught or for which intended, the subjects included, and describing the situation in which the unit was or can be introduced.)

*III. *Desired Learnings Acquired or Hoped For*

(A list of concepts and specific attitudes developed by or planned for the unit—developed in such detail as appropriate to the subject matter involved.)

Ibid., pp. 221–223.

*IV. *Learning Experiences*

(A series of brief descriptions of the experience included in or planned for the unit, organized under [1] Experiences of the Entire Group, [2] Experiences of Small Groups or Committees, [3] Individual Experiences.)

*V. *Teaching-Learning Aids*

(Lists of specific aids actually used or definitely available, including [1] printed aids—books, magazines, pamphlets, [2] visual aids—films, film strips, slides, etc., [3] community resources, [4] other aids. Sufficiently definite information should be given that any teacher using the resource unit could find the exact page reference, or order the pamphlet, or book the film, or arrange the trip, etc.)

*VI. *Evaluation Techniques*

(A brief description of the means which were or could be used: [1] to determine whether the unit was successful and what changes might be made another time, and [2] to determine what progress was made by individual pupils. Thus this section might include such items as a list of questions used in an evaluative discussion, a description of any culminating, summarizing activity, sample test questions, and pupil check lists.)

*These sections might be arranged in columnar fashion in order to show the relationship between desired learnings, experiences, aids and evaluation techniques.

This outline has been followed by various curriculum committees and school faculty groups in the Dade County Schools in connection with extensive use of the resource unit technique in curriculum planning.

Who Prepares Resource Units?

Various practices prevail in school systems in regard to the responsibility for preparing resource units. Generally, the materials are prepared by groups of teachers, frequently with the help of librarians, curriculum consultants, and editorial assistants. These groups may be curriculum committees representing several schools or they may be faculty groups of individual schools, or both types of groups. Resource units are also prepared by national and state organizations, and by groups in local workshops (see the following section). Our own experience indicates that faculty groups within a single school can usually plan resource units more effectively than system-wide or other groups because the former can get together more easily, have in mind the needs and resources of their particular school, and move more easily from resource units of their own preparation to individual unit plans.

In the actual preparation of the resource units, such steps as the following are taken by the group responsible:

1. Either through committee discussion or by referral to a larger group of teachers, problems around which resource units need to be prepared are determined.

2. An attempt is made to find out what, if any, teachers may already be teaching units about such problems, and what, if any, written outlines, files, bibliographies, and the like, have already been prepared.

3. Such teachers may be asked to prepare the resource units, or members of the responsible group may be asked to organize resource units using the materials provided by these teachers.

4. For resource units desired and for which no materials are already available, members of the group may either undertake the job of writing these units or find individual teachers, departmental groups, or building committees willing to do the writing. In general, the preparation of the unit may be done more effectively on the basis of experience in teaching related units.

5. In writing the resource unit such a form as that illustrated earlier is agreed upon and followed. Use of one person, perhaps on a released-time basis, to do the final editing is essential.

Use of Resource Units

There is the danger that the resource unit, if used in its entirety and without adaptation to a particular situation, may have the weaknesses of the single textbook. However, used properly, the resource unit is of great advantage to teachers in developing unit plans and as a reference for materials and in some cases for subject matter. The usefulness of the resource unit is indicated by the growing number of resource units developed by curriculum planning groups and workshops, the widespread practice of maintaining files of resource units and materials in schools and school systems, and the publication of resource units by school systems and professional organizations.[6]

The teacher properly uses the resource unit as a reference from which he selects ideas that are appropriate for the particular group of learners and for the unit plan he is developing. It is to be noted that no one teacher would be likely to find it possible or desirable to plan and carry out with one group of learners all the experiences suggested in a resource unit. But any teacher at the appropriate grade level may find

---

[6] An extensive series of resource units, the "Problems in American Life Series," is sponsored by the National Association of Secondary School Principals and the National Council for the Social Studies and published by the parent organization, the National Education Association, Washington, D.C. Each unit includes a statement of the facts of the problem itself, as well as the usual resource unit contents.

some ideas worthy of exploration for a particular group. Resource units may also be used by groups of teachers. Specifically, the resource unit may be used in the following ways:

1. By the elementary school teacher in planning a large unit of work based on a social studies, science, or other problem and including experiences and drill in language arts and other skills.

2. By the secondary school teacher in a completely departmentalized program in planning an organization of subject matter and experiences, that is, a unit of work, which extends over a large number of class periods and is built around one major phase of the subject taught.

3. By the junior or senior high school core teacher in organizing a unit of work which is based on a social studies problem, for example, and includes experiences in language arts.

4. By a secondary school departmental group in planning phases of a large area or topic for consideration in different courses within the department.

5. By teachers from two or more secondary school subject areas in planning phases of a large area or topic for consideration by the different departments.

6. By elementary school teachers at different grade levels in planning phases of a large area or problem for consideration at different grade levels and in all-school programs and activities.

ILLUSTRATIVE RESOURCE UNIT: "WEIGHING THE NEWS"

The following illustrative resource unit is reproduced in abridged outline form (sections not reproduced are shown by bracketed notes) to illustrate the contents and possible utility of resource units. This unit was prepared[7] in connection with a county-wide curriculum study in language arts in the Dade County (Florida) Schools, and follows the Dade County outline form illustrated earlier in this chapter. In connection with this study, teams of language arts teachers in the individual secondary schools prepared various resource units. This particular unit is reproduced here because of its usefulness at several grade levels and in different subject combinations (it has been used by both junior and senior high school teachers in language arts and social studies in the Dade County Schools), and because it illustrates the variety of suggested learning experiences and resource materials which are included in resource units.

[7] The original unit was prepared by Blanche Wood and Vinola Woodward, Miami Jackson High School, Miami, Florida, and developed with the help of Flossie Drago by the Language Arts Instructional Planning Committee for county-wide use.

I. *The Unit Problem*

Too many stimuli are pressing upon us. It becomes necessary to weigh intelligently, to discard or to select quickly and accurately, and to do something about the impressions received from newspapers, magazines, radio, television, and word of mouth. The purpose of this unit is to help teachers organize plans for learners' thought and practice in evaluating the news.

II. *Where? When? Why?*

This unit was organized to be taught in the eleventh grade, but material has been included from the seventh-grade level upward. Subject matter in language arts, social studies, science and mathematics is included. The classroom teacher should be the judge as to when and where this unit can be taught most effectively.

III. *Desired Learnings Acquired or Hoped For*

A. Desired concepts

1. That the services rendered by free mediums of communication in a democracy are invaluable
2. That the freedom of news coverage is indispensable in a democracy (democracy vs. totalitarianism)
3. That only by mental alertness can one distinguish between sound and unsound reasoning and between assertion and proof
4. That a significant distinction exists between straight news coverage and that "slanted" by the opinion of the journalist or the commentator
5. That a distinction exists between impartial coverage and propaganda
6. That one must be acquainted with common propaganda devices in order that he may be on guard against such devices
7. That headlines and oral communication play a part in "slanting" the news
8. That a worthy citizen should develop an attitude of critical thinking
9. That every person should build standards by which he can properly evaluate mediums of communication
10. That advertising plays a significant role in present-day life
11. That a good newspaper has history and ethics

B. Desired growth in language arts

1. To facilitate and to improve both oral and written communication

2. To increase vocabulary and to improve ability to spell

3. To increase reading speed and comprehension

4. To motivate interest in reading

5. To develop the skill of critical listening

6. To distinguish between journalistic techniques and style, and literary techniques and style

C. Desired social outcomes

1. To foster the desire to become informed citizens

2. To foster the growth of independent thinking

3. To develop open-mindedness and the ability to see both sides of a question .

IV. *Learning Experiences*

A. Reading

1. Planning definite assignments in texts, resource books, magazines, newspapers, pamphlets

a. Emphasis should be placed on

(1) Methods of finding and collecting information

(2) Analysis of contents in news stories, editorials, feature articles, fiction for propaganda, headlines

b. Skills to be practiced

(1) Scanning

(2) Finding main thought quickly and accurately

(3) Recognizing important details

(4) Proofreading copy for student newspaper

c. Magazines for use

American Observer	*Good Housekeeping*
Atlantic Monthly	*Ladies' Home Journal*
Better Homes and Gardens	*Life*
Boys' Life	*National Geographic*
Collier's	*Nation's Business*
Coronet	*New York Times*
Cosmopolitan	*Newsweek*
Field and Stream	*Pathfinder*
Glamour	*Popular Mechanics*
Reader's Digest	*Popular Science*
Saturday Evening Post	*Time*
Saturday Review of Literature	*U. S. News & World Report*
Senior Scholastic	*Visual Digest*
Seventeen	*Vital Speeches*

2. Studying money values involved in the publishing business, in the radio and television industry, and in the advertising that is done through these mediums

   a. Using statistics

   b. Using charts

3. Recognizing today's leading journalists and politico-economic writers

4. Following the news reports of one event of international importance through a week, keeping clippings from different newspapers

5. Clipping editorials and finding news stories accounting for them   .

6. Studying editorial types, purposes, subjects, plan, style, reader appeal, attitude of writer, policy

7. Listing six to ten syndicated columns with sample of each from the daily papers

8. Comparing editorials from various magazines, recognizing the influence of their political or economic philosophies

9. Reading and summarizing reviews and criticisms of plays, motion pictures, books, radio-television programs

10. Clipping feature stories and commenting on the difference between news stories and features with regard to headlines (style and type), leads, and content appeal

11. Studying news services and their importance

12. Investigating well-known propaganda devices and finding examples in advertising

B. Speaking

1. Stories on subject of "Rumor"
   (Suggested topics: witchcraft, Orson Welles's "Man from Mars" broadcast, hurricanes, gossip at school, wartime motto "a slip of the lip may sink a ship," and folklore)

2. Playing "Gossip" to show how oral news (words) may be changed
   ("Gossip" is played by having a line of ten or more children. The first student whispers a sentence to the next, the second whispers to his neighbor, etc., until the last in line repeats aloud what he hears.)

3. Giving a demonstration of a correct conversation in contrast with gossip

4. Holding a discussion modeled on *America's Town Meeting of the Air*

Suggested topics:

a. Do consumers or business advertisers influence policies of magazines and newspapers?

b. How is our interpretation of the news influenced by prejudices and superstitions?

c. How may bias influence radio and news reports of sports?

d. Is communism or democracy winning the propaganda war?

e. What is the difference between critical thinking and cynical thinking?

5. Preparing a news broadcast for school or classroom
6. Interviewing editors, reporters, newscasters
7. Participating in class discussions after research on the following subjects:

a. Comparison of newspapers

b. Fallacies in advertising

c. Fallacies in political argument

8. Clipping cartoons and explaining meaning
9. After studying propaganda techniques, preparing a speech illustrating two or three propaganda techniques. Suggested subjects are a sales talk, a political appeal, trying to borrow father's car.

C. Writing

1. Writing original news stories, features, editorials, headlines
2. Editing a mimeographed paper
3. Outlining prepared discussions and reports
4. Practicing note taking on such topics as journalistic figures, history of journalism or radio, ethics
5. Practicing note taking while viewing film
6. Writing letters of inquiry, request, courtesy, such as

a. To *America's Town Meeting of the Air* for information or bulletins

b. "To the Editor." After studying make-up of papers and magazines, students may become interested in a controversial question in the "letter" section, or they may wish to express an opinion.

c. To friends about field trips

d. To thank for courtesies, and to thank outside speaker, librarians

7. Writing advertising copy for newspaper or magazine

8. Reporting field trip in newspaper style

9. Preparing committee plans for proposed projects, including materials needed

10. Preparing radio announcements: one slanted, the other sound advertising

11. Preparing statistical reports of trips

D. Listening and viewing

1. Analyzing radio and television shows (newsreels may be included)
   Suggested topics: kind of show, how slanted, popularity, with reasons

2. Inviting members of the staff of a local newspaper or school publication for talks

3. Viewing films (listed in Section V)

4. Listening to two programs of the same type

   a. A few recommended programs:
   "Columbia School of the Air"
   "Cavalcade of America"
   "Inter-American University of the Air"
   "One Man's Family"
   News commentators
   "American Portrait"
   "Lux Theatre of the Air"

   b. Judging the programs by this check list:

   (1) Material: Is it accurate and complete?
                      Is it unprejudiced?
   (2) Advertising: Is it completely honest?
                      Does it make exaggerated claims?
   (3) Program: Is it in good taste?
                      Is it realistic? natural? probable? distorted?
   (4) Diction: Is it good, clean-cut speech?
                      Is speech correct?
   (5) Announce-
       ments: Are commercial announcements brief and well mannered?
   (6) Judged as
       a whole: Excellent? Outstanding? Good? Adequate? Acceptable? Mediocre? Poor?

5. Listening to speaker in assembly program, a specific radio program, or a student giving a "propaganda" speech. Analyze for propaganda techniques.

E. Taking field trips

    1. Participating in field trips to local newspaper plants
       Allapattah News—1738 N. W. 35th Street
       Coral Gables Riviera Times—308 Aragon, Coral Gables
       Florida Sun—1859 Bay Road, Miami Beach
       Little River Shopper—222 N. E. 79th Street
       Miami Daily News—600 Biscayne Boulevard
       Miami Herald—200 S. Miami Avenue
       Miami Springs Shopper—503 Ludlum Drive, Miami Springs

       (Call offices to ask permission to visit and to inquire when papers are in the process of being printed)

    2. Using local library [List of libraries and addresses omitted.]

F. Planning other activities

    1. Preparing scrapbooks of collected material

    2. Displaying on bulletin board: examples of straight news articles, feature stories, editorials, cartoons, newspaper terms, syndicated materials, good and bad advertising, variety of sports, headlines, famous columnists

    3. Taking class opinion polls following reading of different versions of news events

    4. Drilling use and spelling of such words as the following as need and opportunity arise:

advertisement	beneficial	critical
propaganda	detrimental	cynical
analyze	skeptical	classified
analysis	naïve	articles
guaranteed	syndicated	factual
evaluation	column	opinion
economic	committee	political
economical	completely	scientific
gullible	scanned	irrelevant
research	statistics	analogy
acquainted	magazine	editorial
technique	sponsored	realistic
criteria	embarrassed	logical
ethical	glamour	weighing

    5. Preparing a chart of well-known propaganda devices, using illustrative material from pamphlets and advertisements

    6. Emphasizing the following skills: [The unit makes cross reference by items to a "Chart of Language Arts Skills" available to Dade County teachers.]

       a. Writing
       Using transitional words

Writing précis

Proofreading

   b. Speaking

Reading aloud

Conducting an interview

Reporting on a trip

   c. Listening

Evaluating what is heard

   d. Reading

Making use of key paragraph

Determining cause and effect

Using periodical indices

Reading newspaper bibliography

  G. Sample teaching unit plan: [This plan is omitted here and reproduced in the section on "Preparing Unit Plans" below.]

V. *Teaching-Learning Aids*

  A. Printed aids

    1. Library books [Omitted.]

    2. Textbooks [Detailed list with page references, omitted.]

    3. Magazine articles [Omitted.]

    4. Magazine articles, unsigned [Omitted.]

    5. Pamphlets [Omitted.]

    6. Newspapers

The *Miami Daily News* has agreed to supply all teachers with as many copies of the paper as they need, free of charge, for the purpose of this study. Address request to Mr. Tade Walsh, Circulation Director.

  B. Films [Annotated list omitted.]

  C. Free and inexpensive materials [Annotated list omitted.]

  D. Community resources [Omitted.]

VI. *Evaluation Techniques*

  A. Pupil evaluation

    1. Group evaluation

Symposium, followed by a forum, on an organized presentation of the complete unit, emphasis to be placed on the following suggested topics:

Services rendered by free mediums of communication in a democracy

What freedom of news coverage means in a democracy

How propaganda is used in a democracy

By what means I can, as a citizen, develop an attitude of critical thinking

Panel discussion: "To What Extent Has This Unit, 'Weighing the News,' Been Beneficial?"—the panel to be followed by a forum

Written objective tests with questions or statements contributed by the group and the final selection made by a student committee

2. Individual evaluation

   a. The student to write in the form of a letter a description of his participation in the unit

   b. The student to write an unsigned essay, including criticism, evaluation, and suggestions as to the extension and the improvement of this unit

   c. The student to answer the following questionnaire on magazines and newspapers: [Twenty-five-item questionnaire on reading habits omitted.]

   d. For film evaluation, students can be given such problems as the following one (related to a film on analyzing facts):

   At school a projector was to be bought. A school paper reporter had written that the projector was being paid for from the football funds. (The P.T.A. had planned to purchase the equipment.) Observations of those interviewed about the advisability of buying the projector follow. Identify the fallacies in each observation:

   Football player: "Why, they can't buy a projector! We don't have enough money to buy new uniforms."

   Projector operator at local theatre: "No, you shouldn't buy a projector. Do you know how much it costs to operate the one at the show? $400 a month for my salary alone!"

   Mrs. Butler, a housewife: "You don't need any more entertainment at school."

   Mary, a student: "I don't think we need a projector. My father didn't have one, and he's made a success."

B. Check list for teacher evaluation

   1. Have copies of the daily papers been provided for students to use in the classroom?

   2. Did you rely entirely on assignments for outside newspaper reading?

   3. Did you use the language of the newspaper, magazine, or radio as a basis of vocabulary study?

4. Did you plan a study of the many sections of the paper? What sections did you stress?

5. What methods did you follow in evaluations of newspapers and magazines and the differentiation between the conservative and the sensational?

6. What magazine content did you stress: stories, articles, editorials, reviews, poetry, cartoon, handicraft?

7. What aspects of radio and television did you stress?

8. Were social problems analyzed and social concepts developed?

9. Did your students' interest in news reading increase?

10. Did you draw comparisons between editorial comments or columns, and the opinions of the radio news commentator?

11. Did you give attention to advertising from the standpoint of consumers' needs, representation of merchandise, reliability of firm, evidence of propaganda?

C. Evaluation of pupil progress

1. Evaluation of subject matter learned

a. By observing student interest and effectiveness in oral and written activities

b. By evaluation tests, both objective and essay

2. Evaluation of social outcomes

a. By observing pupil progress in making discriminating choices of listening experiences

b. By observing pupil progress in placing a true value on things seen and things heard

c. By observing pupil progress in accepting social responsibility

PREPARING UNIT PLANS

As pointed out earlier, the planning of specific units of work is a task of the individual teacher in relation to the learning group (s) taught. This section deals with the nature of unit plans (frequently called teaching units), and describes methods of preparing unit plans with and without reference to resource units.

The Nature of a Unit Plan

A unit plan is simply an advance chart, outline, or prospectus of the unit of work the teacher hopes to develop with a class. It differs from the resource unit in at least three principal respects:

1. The unit plan is prepared specifically for one group of learners, and includes only those desired learnings, possible learning experiences, resources, and other materials which seem appropriate and feasible for the group concerned.

2. The unit plan involves a sequential arrangement not of concern in the resource unit; that is, the teacher planning the development of a unit of work in the learning situation must plan for the introduction, the full development, and the culmination of the unit.

3. The unit plan takes into consideration the role of pupil-teacher planning to an extent not necessary in the resource unit, since the latter includes all types of possible learning experiences and resources without particular attention to how and why they are finally selected for a particular learning group.

However the teacher's own unit plan is developed, the following items need to be provided for in planning:

1. Definition of the unit problem and desired outcomes in connection with its investigation.

2. Means of introducing the problem and carrying on pupil-teacher planning regarding the unit.

3. Learning experiences related to the problem, including lists of appropriate resources which are available.

4. Culminating activities for summarizing the experiences of learners.

5. Methods of evaluation that are applicable.

Unit Plans Based on Resource Units

If the teacher has a resource unit from which the specific unit of work is being planned, it may suffice merely to check sections of the resource unit which are appropriate. Some brief written outline is found desirable by many teachers as a guide to the unit of work. The resource unit may contain a sample unit plan, as in the preceding illustrative resource unit, and the teacher may prepare several unit plans following the form of the sample and utilizing materials from the resource unit by some plan of cross references. Such a unit plan is illustrated in the following example. This is a skeleton outline of the plan for a unit of work on "Getting Acquainted with Magazines," suggested for an eleventh-grade English class and prepared for the resource unit "Weighing the News":

The Unit Problem: The problem of this unit is how to become more discriminating in the choice and reading of magazines. Specific learnings planned for the unit of work are the following listed in Section III (of the resource unit): A–9, –10; B–1, –3, –4, –6; C–1, –2, –3.

Introducing the Unit: A questionnaire will be used to determine the magazines now used by pupils, and a summary of this questionnaire made a basis for class discussion of magazines. Learners will then be asked to become acquainted, or better acquainted, with one of the magazines listed in Section IV, A–1–c. Committees may be formed of persons interested in the same magazine. Through class discussion, a list of questions to be answered about each magazine will be formulated.

Developmental Activities: Committee activities should be based on the agreements reached in the introductory planning. In addition to committee reading, discussion, and preparation of reports, learning experiences of the entire class may be adapted from the following suggestions in Section IV: A–1, –8, –12; B–4; C–6; F–2, –5.

Culminating Activity: The major culminating activity should be the report of each committee on the magazine of its study. Careful planning by the entire class of the types of reports desired should come first. Some summary of the reports should be made, perhaps to include a statement of standards for selecting and evaluating magazines.

Evaluation Procedures: Several procedures included in Section V of the resource unit may be applicable. At least three procedures must be used: (1) a class discussion of what pupils think they learn in the unit; (2) another check, using the original questionnaire, on what magazines pupils read; and (3) individual evaluations of a particular magazine based on standards developed in class discussion.

Unit Plans Not Based on Resource Units

Many teachers do not have the advantage of resource units or other curriculum guides in preparing plans for many of their units of work. When these teachers are able to work with their colleagues in curriculum-planning activities, their plans, however actually written up, partake of the nature of resource units. Hence the real distinction is whether the individual teacher is able to work as one of a group in over-all curriculum planning, or whether all his planning must be done alone. In the latter event, his task is much more difficult, of course. The most helpful step he can take is that of preparing detailed unit plans which will provide for well-organized units of work. Care at this point will make for effective instruction and represents good curriculum planning even if done on a wholly individualized basis.

The following suggestions from the publication *How to Build a Unit of Work* may be helpful to teachers preparing unit plans without the help of resource units (note that the first four suggestions would be largely cared for by the preparation of a resource unit):

1. Survey the needs and interests which justify and make it significant. Are there any general needs and problems of life which make this study important? Are there community needs which might be helped? Do these children have need for the study and are they interested in it?

2. List important objectives or goals which might be achieved through this study.

3. Make an overview of the subject matter which might enter into the study, the kinds of experiences which would be good, and any ways in which different subjects could be drawn in or integrated with this unit.

4. List books and other materials for the children to use as well as some for teacher reference.

5. Plan possible ways of introducing the study and getting children interested in it.

6. Plan the working period, keeping in mind the fact that only part of the working plan can be arranged in advance because the children are to help plan it.

    a. Carrying on discussion and other activities which help the teacher find out what children know about the subject, their attitudes toward it, and what they are interested in.

    b. Planning the unit with the children and getting the work underway by listing questions on which information is wanted; making charts showing what to do; planning excursions, construction, and other activities; finding and listing sources of information, tools, and materials; and arranging committees to work on some of the questions or problems.

    c. Gathering information and ideas from books and other sources and sharing through discussions, reports, and other means. Carrying out the plans for excursions and other projects.

    d. Organizing the ideas gathered, checking the list of questions to see whether adequate answers have been found and to see that the children really understand the material they have been studying.

    e. Summarizing the total learnings in some way. It could be done through giving a program for parents or another group of children, writing an original play, painting a mural, or making a record for the class yearbook. Evaluating would be necessary to give the children an opportunity to consider the worth of the work they have been doing. There might be a group-made test on important points to be mastered.

7. Plan the evaluation of the total unit of work. Final evaluation would be concerned with two main points:

 a. Growth and changes which have taken place in the children.

 b. Individual strengths, weaknesses, and problems which need further attention.[8]

The following unit plan is illustrative of one prepared without reference to a resource unit or other curriculum guide giving some direction to, and also alternative suggestions for, the preparation of unit plans. This unit plan was adapted from materials prepared for a fifth-grade group.

UNIT: TRAVEL BY AIR, LAND, AND SEA

I. *Problems*

 A. How we are dependent on transportation in relation to our needs: food, clothing, shelter.

 B. How transportation has changed and is now changing rapidly.

 C. How people travel in other lands.

 D. The comparative uses, values, and characteristics of the three major types of transportation.

II. *Suggested Approaches:* stories, pictures, trips, experiences of children, and interests of children in aviation, boats, and automobiles.

III. *Development of the Unit*

 A. Travel by air: information.

  1. How men first learned to fly.

  2. Lighter than air: fire balloons, gas balloons, dirigibles and zeppelins.

  3. Heavier than air: airplane models; the first airplanes and their inventors: Maxim, Adler, Langley, Wright brothers; the first seaplane.

  4. Famous flights: by balloons, by dirigible, by airplanes and seaplanes.

  5. At an airport: the hangar; how a plane "takes off."

  6. How a plane flies.

[8] Ruth G. Strickland, *How to Build a Unit of Work* (U.S. Office of Education Bulletin, 1946, No. 5; Washington, D.C.: Government Printing Office, 1946), pp. 5–6.

B. Possible activities for air travel.

1. Tell stories about flights made by some of the class.
2. Tell stories about trips made to airports.
3. Make a frieze of air travel.
4. Find pictures of air travel.
5. Find stories of air travel and read to class.
6. Draw pictures for a book of travel.
7. Make a film for a motion-picture machine.
8. Write stories about famous flights.
9. Make model airplanes from wood.
10. Collect pictures of airplanes.
11. Visit an airport.
12. Make a model airport.

C. Travel by water: information.

1. The first boats: how man probably discovered boats; log, raft, dugout, canoe, kayak.
2. How sails might have been invented.
3. Egyptian and Phoenician boats.
4. Greek and Roman vessels.
5. Viking ships.
6. The caravels of Columbus.
7. Ships of early American settlers; packet ships, clipper ships.
8. Canal and river boats.
9. The first steamboats.
10. Famous ships: *The Half Moon, The Mayflower, Old Ironsides, The Clermont, The Titanic.*
11. Pirate ships.
12. Showboats on the Mississippi.
13. Boats on Long Island Sound: yachts, catboats, yawls.
14. Safety on the sea: signals, radio, compass, maps, charts, lifeboats, life preservers, lighthouses, buoys, pilots, coast guard.
15. Life aboard an ocean liner as told in the pictures and book *Full Steam Ahead.*

D. Possible activities for travel by water.

1. Make lists of kinds of boats we know.
2. Collect pictures of boats.
3. Make a frieze of travel by water.

4. Find stories about boats and read to class.

5. Learn the different parts of a boat.

6. Draw pictures for "Travel Book."

7. Make model boats from wood.

8. Visit an ocean liner.

9. Tell stories about voyages made by members of class.

E. Travel by land: information.

1. What transportation means: why people need to travel; what transportation is important.

2. The first traveler: the pack, the litter, the palanquin, the sedan chair.

3. Animals that help: the ox, the camel, the elephant, the donkey, the horse, the yak, the reindeer.

4. Moving loads without wheels: the drag, the sled, the travois.

5. The wheel: how it might have been discovered; the wheeled cart, the jinricksha, the chariot, the oxcart, the coach, the covered wagon, the stage coach, the horse car, the bicycle.

6. Faster ways of travel: the first steam locomotive, later locomotives, modern locomotives, trolley car, elevated train, automobiles.

7. Safety rules for land travel.

F. Possible activities for land travel.

1. Make a list of animals used for travel.

2. Make a frieze of land travel.

3. Find stories about land travel and read them to class.

4. Draw pictures for "Book of Travel."

5. Make models of ways of transportation from soap, wood, clay.

6. Collect pictures of animals, trains, etc.

7. Visit railroad station.

8. Learn safety rules for driving.

G. Books related to the unit [Omitted.]

IV. *Culminating Activities*

A. A transportation pageant, featuring models, friezes, pictures, and other projects prepared by the children.

B. Individual record books including drawings, written materials, clippings, postcards, maps, and other materials prepared by the pupil.

V. *Evaluation Activities*

    A. Informational summaries on these questions:

        1. Who made the first airplane?

        2. When did man first learn to fly?

        3. What makes an airplane stay up in the sky?

        4. What materials are used in making airplanes?

        5. Why can a balloon keep up in the air without an engine?

        6. How many kinds of airplanes are there?

        7. Why doesn't a dirigible need wings?

        8. What kind of boats did people have at first?

        9. How did people find out about boats?

      10. What did people use at first to make boats go?

      11. How did man find out about sails?

      12. Why did people use both sails and oars?

      13. Who invented the first steamboat?

      14. Why are steamboats better boats than sailboats?

      15. How many kinds of boats are there?

      16. What kinds of boats were used by the Eskimos? the Chinese? the Africans? the Indians?

      17. How are messages sent to and from a boat in distress?

    B. A class discussion of what pupils think they have learned.

    C. Teacher evaluation of individual record books and projects to determine pupil progress.

For Further Study

Alberty, Harold, *Reorganizing the High-School Curriculum*. Rev. ed.; New York: The Macmillan Company, 1953.

    Chapters XIV and XV deal with resource units in high schools and include illustrative materials.

Association for Supervision and Curriculum Development, National Education Association, *List of Outstanding Teaching and Learning Materials*. Washington: The Association, various dates.

    This list is published every few years by the Association as a guide to better materials produced by local school systems.

Bathurst, Effie G., and others. *The Place of Subjects in the Curriculum*. U.S. Office of Education Bulletin, 1949, No. 12. Washington, D.C.: Government Printing Office, 1949.

Describes a day with a modern fourth grade, analyzing how a visitor thinks it through as the day progresses. Summary section shows how subjects were being used in unit work.

Caswell, Hollis L., and Doak S. Campbell, *Curriculum Development*. New York: American Book Company, 1935.

See Chapter XV for a comprehensive analysis and classification of instructional units in 1935.

Consumer Education Study, National Association of Secondary School Principals, *Consumer Education Series*. Washington, D.C.: The Study, various dates.

A series of units in consumer education.

Denver Public Schools, *Manual for Using the Form for Planning and Developing an Instructional Unit*. Denver: The Schools, 1949.

This pamphlet is a guide to teachers in developing instructional units according to the form used in the Denver Schools. This form is reproduced as an appendix in the *Manual*.

Draper, Edgar M., and Gordon Gardner, "How to Construct a Resource Unit," *Clearing House*, 26:267–270 (January), 1952.

A brief analysis of the characteristics and divisions of a resource unit.

Hand, Harold C. (ed.), and others, *Living in the Atomic Age: A Resource Unit for Teachers in Secondary Schools*. Educational Research Circular No. 57. Urbana: Bureau of Educational Research, College of Education, University of Illinois, December 3, 1946.

A widely distributed and useful resource unit including considerable subject matter for teachers.

Hanna, Lavone, Neva Hagaman, and Gladys L. Potter, *Unit Teaching in the Elementary School*. New York: Rinehart & Company, Inc., 1954.

Discusses the value of unit teaching in a democratic elementary school system and describes techniques for planning, developing, and presenting the units.

Harap, Henry, *Social Living in the Curriculum*. Nashville: Division of Surveys and Field Services, George Peabody College for Teachers, 1952.

Reports the author's observations of classroom activities in programs designated as "social living" or core curriculum. Chapter 3 describes the "basic learning unit" and Part II describes practices in unit development at each grade with particular reference to classroom procedure.

Klohr, Paul R., "The Resource Unit in Curriculum Reorganization," *Bulletin*, National Association of Secondary School Principals, No. 171, 34:74–77 (May), 1950.

Brief report of a research study on the nature, organization, and uses of resource units.

Lee, J. Murray, and Dorris May Lee, *The Child and His Curriculum*. 2d ed.; New York: Appleton-Century-Crofts, Inc., 1950.

Chapter 7 is a comprehensive treatment of unit planning and development in the elementary school.

Leonard, J. Paul, *Developing the Secondary School Curriculum*. Rev. ed.; New York: Rinehart & Company, Inc., 1953.

Chapters XV–XVII deal with units of work and include many excerpts of units for illustrative purposes.

Mehrens, H. E. (ed.), *Adventures in Aviation Education*. Washington, D.C.: American Council on Education, 1951.

This compilation of descriptions of classroom work at all levels on aviation education gives many illustrations of effective teaching organization.

National Council for the Social Studies and National Association of Secondary School Principals, *Problems in American Life Series*. Washington, D.C.: National Education Association, various dates.

A series of resource units published periodically.

Noar, Gertrude, *Freedom to Live and Learn*. Philadelphia: Franklin Publishing & Supply Company, 1948.

Description of specific techniques for planning and developing instructional units, with illustrations of classroom procedure.

———, *The Junior High School—Today and Tomorrow*. New York: Prentice-Hall, Inc., 1953.

Part IV includes helpful resource materials for teachers.

North Central Association of Colleges and Secondary Schools, *Unit Studies in American Problems*. Boston: Ginn and Company, various dates.

A series of unit materials for high school classes in social studies.

Smith, B. Othaniel, William O. Stanley, and J. Harlan Shores, *Fundamentals of Curriculum Development*. Yonkers, N.Y.: World Book Company, 1950.

See Chapter 23, "The Unit Organization of Instruction," for an analysis and classification of units.

Strickland, Ruth G., *How to Build a Unit of Work*. U.S. Office of Education Bulletin, 1946, No. 5; Washington, D.C.: Government Printing Office, 1946.

Excellent guide for planning units of work for elementary school groups.

chapter 13

Planning and Developing
Learning Experiences with Learners

In Chapter 12 we dealt with the steps in curriculum planning that consisted of preparing resource units and unit plans. These steps, along with prior ones of planning the goals and the general organization of the curriculum, may be considered as "preplanning." In this chapter we shall deal with the planning that goes on by the learning group and the teacher in the classroom. The extent to which pupils actually participate in this planning depends on factors to be noted, but their likes and dislikes and other reactions are always important considerations in wise planning.

THE SELECTION OF UNITS OF WORK

Although resource units may have been prepared and consulted, and specific unit plans for the particular learning group may have been made, a definite point arrives when the decision must be reached as to what learning experiences come next. However much planning may have already been accomplished, the teacher needs to evaluate or re-evaluate possible units by certain basic criteria which weight heavily the needs and interests of learners. Although the characteristics of a good curriculum (Chapter 1) and of effective learning experiences (Chapter 12) are relevant, the orientation here is different. Consequently a brief statement of basic criteria for selecting units of work is given in this section.

The Unit of Work Should Be Based on a Significant Problem

Whatever the framework of the curriculum, a sound criterion for final selection of a unit of work is the significance of the problem which the learning experiences are to help solve. We believe that the concept of "problem" in itself implies an organizing center of greater significance than topic, theme, generalization, interest, felt need, or other source of unity. This belief is supported by Kight and Mickelson's experiment on problem-centered units as compared to subject matter–centered units. A problem-centered unit was considered to be one "based upon a real difficulty of the pupils" concerned, and the unit focused facts regarding the problem so "as to relate this information directly to the action which the pupils must take in order to overcome their difficulty or to solve their problem." A subject matter–centered unit was considered to be one "which does not have at its center a genuine pupil problem" and which "merely attempts to teach the facts in their logical relationship to each other." [1] The experiment, involving 1,415 pupils and twenty-four teachers in eleven different schools, showed that the problem-centered presentation resulted in the learning of more information, more rules of action, and more connections of rules of action with information. That is, this experiment indicates that a unit of work should be based on a problem of significance to learners. Some of the concluding recommendations made for curriculum organization by these investigators are of considerable relevance to the criterion we are discussing:

1. Organize each instructional unit, regardless of subject-matter field, around a clearly stated, genuine pupil problem.
2. Elaborate the major pupil problem into its sub-problem.
3. State the problem and sub-problems in each instructional unit in terms of something to do rather than something to learn.[2]

The Unit of Work Should Promote Breadth of Development

A desirable unit of work will include experiences of sufficient breadth and variety to hold the interests of boys and girls and develop needed competencies for dealing with the problems involved. One of the major values of unitary organization is the opportunity for pupils to work together on a problem of mutual interest. But if the problem is so narrowly defined as to make its solution a matter of individual study, there is no cooperative activity. It is difficult to imagine children doing any very meaningful cooperative activity in learning to use an index to a daily newspaper, for example, although this problem has significance to both society and learners. But the problem of publishing a class paper involves a variety of activities—planning, writing, editing, typing, reading proof, running a Mimeograph machine, assembling the paper, distributing cop-

[1] Stanford S. Kight and John M. Mickelson, "An Experimental Comparison of Problem Centered and Subject Matter Centered Types of Presentation of Units of Instruction" (unpublished doctoral dissertation; Los Angeles: University of Southern California, 1947), pp. 2–3.
[2] *Ibid.*, pp. 246–247.

ies. Involved in the latter example are many skills which will require practice, and the unit plan must include provision for such practice.

The Unit of Work Should Promote Continuity of Development

Reference to the curriculum framework and sequence is essential in selecting units of work if the unit is to relate progressively to the areas of
experience limiting the scope of the curriculum. Practice frequently neglects this criterion by planning for units which are highly repetitious
for learners.

Three general procedures are desirable in connection with the principle of continuity. The first was just stated—that is, the checking of proposed units against scope and sequence plans. In practice this may
involve planning a series of units in a general fashion for the year, or
at least securing from the previous teacher a list of the major units of
the preceding year. Second, one unit develops from another. That is, interests aroused or needs indicated in one series of experiences often point
the way to another series. Even so, the teacher should refer to the total
curriculum plan to make certain that some important areas and sequences are not being overlooked. If the second unit really develops from
pupils' interests and needs, we may safely assume there are no undesirable
repetitious learnings. Third, continuous cooperative planning of teachers is an important procedure for securing continuity. In a departmentalized program it is important to know how plans in one area relate to
those in another. In the elementary school each grade teacher needs conferences with the teacher of the preceding and following grades to secure
continuity in the experiences of particular children. Without application
of this criterion, it is possible to get some poor assortments of units, with
many gaps and undesirable overlappings.[3]

The Unit of Work Should Provide for Individual Differences

The unit plan should include a variety of learning experiences having
the characteristics stated in the preceding chapter, such as "meaningful
to learners," "appropriate to maturity of learners," and "flexible." A
good discussion, such as that shown in Plate 29, is one such experience.
So far as possible the plan should include some experiences which will
be meaningful and appropriate for each pupil. Then in developing the
unit, the teacher uses those planned experiences which are appropriate
and may need to plan others with the help of the class. The unit selected
should be sufficiently flexible that a learner who exhausts possible ap-

---

[3] See for an example of such an assortment: J. Murray Lee and Dorris May Lee,
The Child and His Curriculum (2d ed.; New York: Appleton-Century-Crofts, Inc.,
1950), pp. 226–27.

propriate learning experiences may be helped to select new problems and experiences. It should be emphasized that planning for individual differences is a larger problem than locating reading materials of different levels. Essentially the problem is to select units of work which permit such a variety of activities that each learner will be successful in achieving the unit purposes at his particular level of maturity.

PLATE 29. GOOD UNITS INCLUDE GOOD DISCUSSIONS. *Well-planned and -conducted discussions provide for interested participation by a maximum number of learners. (Courtesy of the Phoenix, Arizona, Union High School)*

The Unit of Work Should Utilize All Needed Available Resources

The planning of resources for attacking the unit problem is a challenging task for the creative teacher, who starts with the problem, analyzing the most desirable ways of attacking it, rather than starting with the resources, and analyzing the most effective ways to use them. Perhaps the teacher feels that the pupils could learn about the problem of selecting a vocation through talking with people who have had experience in various vocations under consideration; usually such persons can be found and persuaded to visit the class, or, better, the class can visit them at work. Films on many of these vocations can also be located. Some fathers might get materials from their business houses. Perhaps another teacher has had some work experience in a field of especial interest. Such re-

sources will likely be of considerably more interest and value to learners than textbook treatment, although the latter may be used, too, as a
check list of information.

When considering the selection of a unit of work, the teacher has to
weigh certain practical factors. First, other things being equal, the unit
of work for which adequate resources are most readily available is the
better choice. Second, as wide resources as possible should be utilized to
provide for the individual differences of learners. Third, the unit of
work which can be organized by reference to resource units or other
guides listing resources is a choice economical of the teacher's time. These
principles are considered in detail in Chapter 14.

The Unit of Work Should Provide for Evaluation and Modification

A justified criticism of many unit plans has to do with their inflexibility
in development. Flexibility is more likely if unit planning is regarded as
tentative, if there are alternative experiences, and if there is a definite
plan of frequent evaluation as the unit develops. In addition to having
a plan for evaluating the entire unit and learners' progress, it is desirable
to find out from time to time whether purposes are being achieved, pupils
are being challenged, and other criteria are being satisfied. Possibly the
most effective method is a periodic, perhaps daily, discussion of progress—in effect a session for pupil-teacher planning. Such a discussion
needs to be supplemented by teacher observations of individual and
group activities, of growth in skills, and interest indicators in discussion.
Probably the best assurance of adequate evaluation and subsequent modification of the unit of work is a considerable amount of group planning.
The following section deals with procedures of pupil-teacher planning,
which, if wisely employed, will assist in the development of units of
work that meet the criteria we have just presented.

PUPIL-TEACHER PLANNING

The assignment is the traditional method whereby the learning goal and
activity are communicated to pupils by the teacher. In pupil-teacher
planning, "assignments" are determined by the group. Teachers who
practice cooperative planning recognize the importance of this procedure in utilizing the interests and contributions of boys and girls. Group
planning gives an opportunity for learners to formulate questions and
problems of concern to them, to determine ways and means of answering
questions and solving problems of their own, and thereby to learn to
work together on matters that seem real.

Planning is not always a process which is definitely labeled as such when it is under way. In addition to periods when plans are made by the pupils and teacher there is frequent reference back to plans in order to make modifications or to take care of some exigency that was not foreseen. And the individual or small group engaged in carrying forward some investigation as originally planned with the total group may encounter a problem which was not anticipated and have to confer with the teacher on new plans. Thus planning in the classroom is occurring almost constantly and in relation to individuals and small groups as well as the total group.[4]

Descriptions of Pupil-Teacher Planning

The following descriptions of planning enterprises at different school levels may serve to indicate common elements.

Kindergarteners can help plan. This description of a kindergarten project is quoted from a teacher's diary included in *Toward Better Teaching,* the 1949 yearbook of the Association for Supervision and Curriculum Development:

> October 5—I called the children together for a talk today. (We talk, not really discuss, in the kindergarten.) First I told them that I was going home for the week end and that I had a plan. In my attic are many things we could have fun with—a doll bed big enough to get into, a stove with an oven that opens, a little sink with two faucets you can really get water out of because it has a water-tank on the back, and lots of other things—almost a car full.
>
> I asked them if they would be careful with my toys because I would like to bring them to this school when I drive down from the country Sunday. Such enthusiasm! Such sincere expressions of infinite care for the stove and the sink with the faucets! Such flashing of dark eyes and nodding of heads as they planned with me where would be a good place for the big bed and the doll's high chair, and where to keep the little broom and dustpan. Joy!
>
> October 8—I waited to unload the toys when the children arrived. They helped carry them up the two flights of stairs. I think the toys measured up to their week end of expectations because the children were thrilled.
>
> I think we have established a good friendly relationship between teacher and pupil. For example: when we were carrying in the toys, the cover of a box I was carrying slipped and out dropped aluminum muffin pans, jello molds, and a toy percolator. Polly Ruth looked at

[4] For many illustrations of cooperative planning in all-school and in classroom situations, see Alice Miel and associates, *Cooperative Procedures in Learning* (New York: Bureau of Publications, Teachers College, Columbia University, 1952)

the aluminum things, laughed up at me and said, "Well! Clumsy!"
I laughed and we both stopped and picked up the toys.[5]

Planning a primary story-writing period. In a primary room the day
began with each child's reporting any news item he chose. Some children
told about radio broadcasts they had heard the preceding afternoon, one
of a movie he had attended, several of interesting experiences of other
members of their households, and so forth. The teacher suggested before
the news reports that all the children listen for ideas about which they
might write stories. When the reports were finished, she asked, "Who has
an idea for a story?" One child responded that he wanted to write a story
about the dog which was reported as being ill, and the teacher asked him
what ideas he would include in the story and she wrote these ideas on the
board. Then another child said she wanted to write about the radio
broadcast several had heard, and again the teacher noted on the board
the ideas this child wanted in the story. The teacher then asked which children had no ideas for writing a story, and several children held up their
hands. One child suggested they write a story with the teacher, who
agreed. The teacher then asked the children who were ready to write
stories to go ahead at their seats, and the other children to come to a table
with her.

Starting a fourth-grade unit. The following excerpts from "A Day
with a Fourth Grade" are quoted from an Office of Education Bulletin,
The Place of Subjects in the Curriculum, to illustrate how a unit may
be introduced and group organization developed:

> Shortly after 9, at the teacher's suggestion, the children move their
> seats into an informal semi-circle for discussion.
> The teacher calls the group's attention to the problem which they
> planned yesterday—to gain more information to help them select
> wood for some things they want to make. She suggests that since this
> is one of their first experiences in working with wood, they may also
> want to try to find something about it that is interesting to study at
> some length.
> The children have brought to class samples of oak, walnut, hickory,
> white pine, and gumwood to add to the samples on the table.
> [There follows an extended discussion of the samples and of how
> the pupils can learn more about woods and forests.]

[5] Association for Supervision and Curriculum Development, National Education
Association, *Toward Better Teaching* (1949 Yearbook; Washington, D.C.: The Associa-
tion, 1949), p. 54. (Credited to Dorothea Krivicich, State Teachers College, Oneonta,
N.Y.) Reprinted by permission of the Association.

"Let's call the folks who want to study about forests Group One," says the teacher. "Now is there something else that you can see needs to be done? These children can work as Group Two."

"Well, somebody's got to finish labeling all the samples," says Andy. "Somebody that can spell the names right and make the letters so that we can all read them."

Most of the children decide that they want to be in Group One to study forests. Four others agree to do the labeling. The teacher suggests that Don and Edith, who have volunteered for Group One plan instead to use their time in finishing their report on a problem the class had been studying earlier. She urges one of the children who volunteers to label wood samples to join Group One, and a child who had not responded to join Group Two.

The children pass the samples of wood about the class. The pieces are cut in different ways. Some show the grain in cross sections. Others show lengthwise markings.

One of the children notices the rings of growth in a crosscut and asks what they are.

The teacher says that some of their books on science tell how a tree's trunk and stems are made with little tubes so that liquids can go up and down to carry food. Every year a new layer of tubes grows leaving last year's layer as part of the wood, forming rings of growth. In a cross section of the trunk you can see these rings. Children decide to select some of the pictures to throw on the screen.

She lays out several books, and then says, "Betty, you may want to borrow a book from someone in the fifth grade to answer some of your questions about the way trees grow."

The teacher asks the children to list the books where they may expect to find facts to help answer some of their other questions. Library books, geography and science books by different authors, encyclopedias, travel folders, some State and Federal bulletins with many pictures, and children's encyclopedias are mentioned.

James offers to share a book which has a chapter on logging. Some children use their textbooks, some use other books: to answer questions, to learn steps in a process, to get information from pictures, to prove a point, to locate information for committee use, or to get facts from maps and charts.

After most of the children have begun individual and small group work, the teacher suggests that, now, she would like to work with the children who were needing special help in reading. During this time the other members of the two groups can do some of the reading required to answer their questions.[6]

[6] Effie G. Bathurst and others, *The Place of Subjects in the Curriculum* (U.S. Office of Education Bulletin 1949, No. 12; Washington, D.C.: Government Printing Office, 1949), pp. 7–12.

Intermediate-graders plan to solve a problem. How a group of fourth- and fifth-grade children planned to save food in their school is related in the following description from *Toward Better Teaching:*

This year we decided to have the various grade children eat their lunches in one room, since the superintendent and cafeteria manager concluded that we didn't have the proper facilities or a safe room for a cafeteria. The two fourth and two fifth grades eat in the fifth-grade classroom with a teacher on duty for twenty minutes.

When it was my turn to be on duty, I decided to do something about the complaints of the fifth-grade teacher as to the condition of the room and the food that was being thrown away. I had had one of the groups as fourth-graders last year so I had them tell about our lunch time last year. The children told about putting their tables together so they could eat with their friends. They told how they talked quietly, so all groups could hear their group talking. They used paper towels for lunch mats to avoid leaving crumbs or water marks and to keep the other person's desk clean for his work in the afternoon. In cleaning up, each one swept the floor if any crumbs had fallen, threw away the paper towels, put the tables back in their proper places, and emptied the basket. "There wasn't a sign of a lunchroom when the other children and Mrs. Bach came back from their lunch," the children added.

I then asked the children why we should take care of this room as well and what we could do about the good food they were throwing away. I asked them if they had seen pictures of the Friendship Train. After talking about the train, the children realized that there were thousands of children in the world starving today. I asked them if they had ever been so hungry that they had to eat what they could find in a garbage can.

And so we planned what we could do to help alleviate this condition. A president was chosen and committees appointed to tell us "Why we should save our food."

When one of the suggestions made was a campaign in all the grades, I asked, "Can we get all the schools to help?" I knew our school was scheduled to make a recording for the series on the Stamford radio station, so I brought out the fact that one of the ways to reach all the schools would be the radio. That's how our Clean Your Plate Club started and the recording was made for the broadcast.

The recording was a dramatization of a boy asking, "Why shouldn't I throw my sandwich away if I want to?" Then he was taken to a Clean Your Plate Club meeting. He heard the meeting being called to order, the reports of the committee being read and discussed, and suggestions made as to how children can help other children and grown-ups too. It also included some good nutritional lunches and two original songs and poems. At the end the boy asked to be allowed

to join the club and decided to put his sandwich in the school refrig-
erator and not bring so much next time.

The various committees went to other grades in our school campaigning with pictures, posters, and talks, playing the recording and
getting other children to join the Clean Your Plate Club.[7]

Planning a junior high core unit. A junior high core class was observed while choosing its next unit. The teacher emphasized the desirability of all pupils helping and pointed out that some of them had lacked experience in planning earlier in the year and had failed to express their
ideas. The teacher then led a discussion of what makes a good unit, and
several ideas were agreed upon: that the unit should be about something
important and current, for example. Then suggestions for the unit itself
were made, some dozen in all, and each was checked against the agreements as to what makes a good unit. This narrowed the list to four
topics, and the teacher suggested that a committee of pupils interested in
each topic do some talking and reading about it and report back to the
class the next day. On the next day the discussion of the reports indicated
that one topic was not appropriate because of the lack of materials, that
two others were really larger problems than the teacher felt they could
tackle at this time, and that the fourth would make a very interesting
study. Following this decision, the discussion turned to a listing of questions that the pupils hoped to have answered and to planning for the first
reading to develop some background for further planning.

A tenth-grade group used socio-drama for evaluating and planning.
How a tenth-grade group used socio-drama to evaluate its own actions
and make suggestions for the future is described in the following account
from *Toward Better Teaching:*

> It was necessary for the instructor to be absent from school two days
> because of illness. One of the Basic Living classes openly rebelled
> against the substitute teacher on the second day; whereupon she called
> in the Dean of Boys to discipline the class.
>
> Upon the instructor's return he was informed by a few members of
> the class that all had not gone well during his absence. After many
> disconnected comments and explanations, the class was asked if they
> would like to dramatize the situation so that all of them together
> could analyze the various elements of the incident. This they readily
> agreed to do and did forthwith in a very realistic manner. As the socio-
> drama unfolded, a few questions were interjected to get the group
> thinking about the causes for the occurrence.

[7] Association for Supervision and Curriculum Development, *op. cit.,* pp. 201–202.
(Credited to Wilhelmina Bach, Stevens School, Stamford, Conn.) Reprinted by permission of the Association.

In the discussion after the socio-drama the following conclusions were reached:

1. The substitute teacher entered the room with a chip on her shoulder because of past experiences with some members of the group and immediately assumed a dictatorial attitude, as if expecting trouble.

2. The students immediately became so resentful that they refused to do anything she told them.

3. The Dean of Boys did the only thing he could do, back up the substitute teacher. (This was a student contribution, agreed to by a majority.)

4. The instructor was at fault in not preparing the substitute with adequate information concerning the class and work at the time.

5. The entire situation was very unfortunate and could have been avoided if the substitute had entered the class with a friendly attitude or at least a neutral one.

6. Emotions are very powerful and seem to constitute a chain reaction that leaves reason far behind.

7. Prejudice against individuals does not decrease of and by itself.[8]

Planning individual reading programs. In a senior high English class the teacher was observed to use cooperative planning techniques in organizing reading programs for his pupils. He explained at the beginning of the year that much of the work of the class would be on an individual basis and that each pupil would be encouraged to select and read the books in which he was interested. He gave the class no suggestions at that time and asked each pupil to spend some time and thought on selecting one book he would like to read. A few days later he asked what books had been selected and why. Following class discussion of the selections attention was directed to the question of how one goes about selecting good reading materials. Pupils were asked to re-evaluate their choices in the light of the discussion and then to write a brief statement of their reading interests with an indication of books they had read recently and other books related to their interests they would like to read. After the teacher had gone over these statements he had a personal conference with each pupil in which agreement was reached as to one or more books to be read.

Criteria for Effective Pupil-Teacher Planning

By identifying criteria for effective planning we may now look at the entire process and its elements in more detail.

[8] *Ibid.*, pp. 99–100. (Credited to Melvin J. Hetland, Battle Creek High School, Battle Creek, Mich.) Reprinted by permission of the Association for Supervision and Curriculum Development.

1. Pupil-teacher planning should identify appropriate purposes of learning experiences. In order to contribute to effective motivation of worth-while learning, the planning period must result in the identification of appropriate purposes. The dual connotation of "appropriate" should be again noted in this connection. That is, the purposes formulated should be appropriate to pupils' maturities and also to the philosophy of the school. When pupils propose purposes but lack skills to attack them, the teacher may have to point out that this is something for a later time. If the purposes suggested are irrelevant or undesirable he may have to explain why these are not good purposes to attack. If the fourth-graders in the example cited had proposed to learn to make furniture, the teacher would have shown that furniture making is a more mature job than could be undertaken. If a member of the English class selected for his reading a book which was not acceptable for the high school library because of obscenity, the teacher would be obliged to reject the selection because of an inappropriate reading purpose.

This criterion is a difficult one to apply. If the teacher says "No" too frequently, learners may decide that they really have no voice in decisions reached. If he fails to say "No," more inappropriate activity may result than can be justified. The ideal solution to the dilemma lies in the continuous use of the method of intelligence in the planning process. Where this method is carefully adhered to each proposal will be looked at critically on its own merits and rejected or accepted on the basis of the best evidence available. The role of the teacher is to see that the merits are examined and that the needed evidence is presented. Increasingly as the group becomes more adept in the method, decisions will be made on the basis of reason rather than on that of authority, and the teacher's presentation of reasons will be accepted on its merits rather than interpreted as a rejection of suggestions made by pupils.

2. The teacher should guide planning activities so that fundamental curriculum goals are served. The teacher must maintain a close relationship between the purposes and experiences identified in classroom planning and the general agreements of over-all planning groups regarding goals, scope, sequence, and related factors. In particular, in cooperative choosing of units of work and their emphases, he must keep before the learners the alternatives which are consistent with preplanning activities. For example, a fundamental curriculum goal typically identified by the curriculum planning group is that of command of communication skills. In classroom planning, it is possible to overlook the needs for sequential, progressive development of skills in reading, writing, speaking, and listening. The teacher is responsible therefore for ensuring a sufficient variety of learning experiences to give each learner opportunities to progress in these skills in accordance with his maturity. This means that the teacher must be exceedingly resourceful in locating varied materials and ingenious in suggesting opportunities for writing and speaking. How effectively this may be done was illustrated in the fourth-grade example on woods and forests taken from the Office of Education publication. Pupils were given guidance in choosing their groups, so that one child was asked to do labeling, another child was asked to borrow a fifth-grade book, a variety of books was laid out by the teacher, and a group that needed special help in reading was organized.

3. Pupils' judgment as to learning experiences should be based on adequate understanding of alternatives. The teacher's role in pupil-teacher planning is that of a leader as well as a resource person. As the leader he is responsible for seeing that the decisions reached represented genuine consensus based on analysis of alternatives presented. As the resource person, he is further responsible as the expert on the learning process for ensuring the adequate consideration of all desirable alternatives. Thus if the pupils propose going to a forest to study trees, the teacher must see that the difficulties, limitations, and possible results of the trip are understood in relation to comparable difficulties, limitations, and results of reading, movies, and other types of experiences. After careful consideration, if a trip instead of or in addition to other experiences seems desirable and feasible the teacher should cooperate in making the trip possible. However, he must also make sure that adult concerns of safety and costs are properly taken care of, and may have to eliminate from consideration proposed experiences because of such factors. In such cases, there needs to be careful explanation of the reasons for the elimination.

We recall, for example, the case of a seventh-grade core class engaged in a study of industries in a medium-sized city. The class proposed very enthusiastically a division into committees to visit several industries. The teacher found it necessary to explain several reasons why such a plan was impossible: (1) school rules did not allow groups of children to take excursions without a teacher; (2) parents would object to such a procedure; (3) transportation would be difficult; and (4) the industries would not permit this kind of visit. However, he proposed as an alternative that the entire class visit two or three sample industries, and that committees be organized to investigate special problems in connection with each and to present committee reports later. The alternative was enthusiastically received because it overcame the limitations of the pupils' suggestions and still provided for firsthand experiences and some committee activity.

4. Pupil-teacher planning should be developed in accordance with pupils' readiness for this type of activity. Children whose teachers from the first grade have utilized techniques of pupil-teacher planning will become increasingly competent in these techniques. If their experiences at home have included participation in family planning, they will be more ready for pupil-teacher planning when they come to school. On the other hand, children whose whole school and home experience have been in adult-dominated situations cannot suddenly exhibit judgment and skill in the democratic processes of pupil-teacher planning. As a matter of fact, teachers who have attempted to introduce cooperative planning procedures at higher grade levels have found frequent indifference if not resistance.

The teacher's first task in relation to cooperative classroom planning is to determine the learners' readiness for such planning. If the whole procedure of pupil-teacher planning is foreign to their experience, he will have to introduce the concept gradually. The group can plan a party, or a special program, or a trip. Later the teacher can show how a similar process may be followed in planning for a new unit. As rapidly as pupils show interest and competence the procedures may be extended to various elements of the school's program. Frequently, the transition can be made from some club or other extracurricular activity, for in these phases of the school program pupils usually have more responsibility for their own decisions. In some cases the class is organized as a club to ease the transition, and procedures of group organization are followed in an increasing number of activities. Thus one wonders if the Clean Your Plate Club described above might not have helped these pupils participate thereafter in classroom planning.

5. Plans should be modified as needs arise. This basic criterion of all effective planning is just as true in pupil-teacher planning. Its frequent violation is most evident in situations characterized by extreme laxity or extreme inflexibility on the part of the teacher. In the former situation, plans are modified by whim rather than by intelligent decision: in the latter the teacher is unwilling to change a plan for fear he will lose control of children's behavior. Where teachers are guided by intelligent concern for effective learning procedures, neither whims nor the customary disciplinary problems are likely to matter. Instead there is frequent checking of progress by such questions as these: Are the activities we are engaging in relevant to our purposes? In view of the unsatisfactory experience we had, should we give up this purpose and turn to another? Why are some learners seemingly bored and others frustrated? Is need for different types of experiences indicated?

6. The setting for pupil-teacher planning should encourage meaningful discussion and effective decision making. Although effective planning is done in crowded classrooms where there is little freedom of movement, such conditions militate against good planning. Desirable conditions include the following:

1. A seating arrangement which permits all participants to see each other.

2. As attractive, orderly, and comfortable physical environment as possible.

3. The maintenance of a record—at the blackboard, if possible—of decisions reached, with appropriate summaries from time to time.

4. As much freedom of movement as is needed by the learners and as is consistent with group welfare.

5. Rest or "stretching" periods as needed.

The Teacher's Task

To summarize, pupil-teacher planning is far more than, as sometimes satirized by critics, the teacher's asking pupils: "What do you want to do today?" Skillful guidance of the planning process is probably the most difficult and most important of all teaching tasks. The teacher must have done considerable advance planning in the light of the fundamental curriculum goals and framework. The plan must be introduced so capably that learners' reactions are considered in its modification and development. Each planning period must be so conducted as to identify appropriate purposes, to select activities which seem likely to serve curriculum goals, to base decisions on full understanding of alternatives, to keep plans on a flexible basis, and in general to encourage meaningful discussion and effective decision making.

Skill in teacher-pupil planning can be acquired through observation of skilled teachers and through conscious participation in planning. Every group of which the prospective teacher is a member gives an opportunity to observe and participate in planning. And in the teaching situation, the wise beginner will proceed carefully but definitely toward increasing the number and quality of learning experiences planned in accordance with such criteria as presented above.

MOVING TOWARD COOPERATIVE LEARNING

In Chapter 1 we pointed out the gap between practice and theory in regard to the recitation method of teaching in the later elementary and especially the secondary grades. In the foregoing sections of this chapter we have been concerned with a quite different function of the classroom, which we consider as "cooperative learning." These two functions are contrasted in Table 12. If, as we believe, the latter type of teaching is far preferable, how does the teacher move from reliance on recitation procedures to cooperative learning? Several suggestions follow.

Cooperative Point of View

In his publication entitled *Principles of Teaching,* Spears criticizes the whole recitation method because it "resembles a contest in which the teacher is pitted against the student." Specifically, he makes the following critical analysis:

1. Teachers' questions are used regularly for the purpose of catching students who have not done their homework. The daily recitation of numerous short questions is used to catch idlers as much as it is used to develop concepts from facts.

2. A student notes carefully the order in which the teacher goes up and down the classroom rows with her questions, in order to gird himself ahead of time for the specific points that may be asked when she gets to him.

3. In this question-answer contest, the student often has his book open before him and steals a look now and then in anticipation of the question about to come.

4. "Beating around the bush" in giving his answer is commonly resorted to by the student who doesn't know the answer to the question asked him, but who wants to retain his position in the teacher's scheme of things.

5. In following the assign-study-recite classroom procedure, the teacher often keeps grade book in hand, rating each effort or lack of effort in contest style.

6. Especially in the objective type of teacher's examination, it is not uncommon to find a trick question or two included, in an attempt to catch a student in his thinking.

7. Evaluating pupil progress, which is done at the end of the grading period, is a right retained by the teacher rather than a right shared with the pupils, again pitting the pupil against the teacher. Complaints about unfair marks are made by the bolder members of the class.

8. In preparing papers and notebooks outside of class, pupils use the work of their classmates freely, feeling that a bit of deception is fair as long as the teacher doesn't detect it.

Spears makes the following conclusions from this analysis:

This teacher-pupil contest conception of schooling has grown up most frequently in the classrooms and at the grade levels where the coverage of subject matter, the assign-study-recite method of teaching, and the marking system are all three overemphasized.

TABLE 12

Comparison of Two Functions of the Classroom

MAJOR CHARACTERISTICS OF

FEATURES OF CLASSROOM ORGANIZATION AND PROCEDURE	RECITATION FUNCTION	COOPERATIVE-LEARNING FUNCTION
Purpose of Activities	Acquisition of facts and skills	Solution of significant problems
Types of Activities	Questions and answers; reading and memorization	Discussion; planning; investigating; reporting; summarizing; evaluating
Who Makes Decisions?	Teacher	Group
Organizing Centers	Assignments made by teacher	Problems agreed on by group
Leader	Teacher	Chosen member of group, with teacher as guide
Grades—Motivation Devices	Grades, awards, failures used for motivation	Internal motivation through group planning
Use of Committees	To secure information assigned by teacher	To secure information desired by group
Use of Tests	To check mastery of subject matter	To diagnose difficulties and help in self-evaluation
Use of Individual Reports	To supplement "minimum-essentials" course	To provide group with needed information
Types of Materials	Textbooks; occasionally, workbooks	Books, magazines, newspapers, pamphlets, radio, etc.
Use of Materials	To master assignments—usually in textbooks	To secure information on problem from best sources available
Division of Period	To provide fixed amounts for recitation and study	To provide time as needed for group and individual activities
Seating	Fixed rows facing teacher	Flexible—to permit round-table discussions and group work
Use of Blackboard	For drill	For recording plans, problems, purposes, summaries

Source: William M. Alexander and J. Galen Saylor, *Secondary Education: Basic Principles and Practices* (New York: Rinehart & Company, Inc., 1950), p. 427.

The classroom is not an arena for jousting between teacher and pupil. It is headquarters for a co-operative program of work emphasizing meaningful activities of the pupils, the teacher being there to encourage and lead the pupils in such activities.

Teachers are not there to catch students. Students are not there to deceive teachers. Instructional methods that encourage the pupil-teacher contest are questionable.[9]

If the traditional classroom procedure exhibits the foregoing characteristics—and we feel that it does—the first step to correct the situation is for the teacher to accept his pupils as willing and cooperative rather than resisting and antagonistic. However lacking they may be in cooperativeness, that fact is probably due, it should be remembered, to their previous experiences, and the situation will not change until they have a different kind of experience.

Try Varying the Procedure

Most teachers and pupils accustomed to the recitation procedure would find a complete change-over too much. Hence the better plan is to introduce different procedures gradually. One important step is taken when learners are given a better chance to react to proposed plans, and later to suggest possible better learning activities. Perhaps they can be given a chance to plan a trip or a program or a debate. They may be encouraged to bring to class questions about current happenings in the school, community, and nation. Gradually a discussion procedure is substituted for the right-or-wrong, question-and-answer recitation. As these changes take place, homework becomes a matter of noting questions from the radio, television, and reading; the grade book disappears because there may be no absolute answer to the question; and the nature of tests, grades, papers, notebooks, and reports changes accordingly.

Use Different Materials

The problem of materials is treated more comprehensively in the following chapter, but we should note here the traditional marriage of uniform textbooks and the assign-study-recite teaching procedures. This marriage is of such long standing that one partner cannot be modernized without some effect on the other. Changing from recitation to cooperative learning involves changes in the use of the textbook, and the use of varied materials is frequently a major step toward abandonment of reliance on the basic textbook.

Although the teacher may feel more secure in continuing the use of

---

[9] Harold Spears, *Some Principles of Teaching*, pp. 62–64. Copyright 1947 by Prentice-Hall, Inc., New York. Reprinted by permission of the publisher.

basic textbooks, he encourages learners to find other sources. The pupil who finds a conflict between the text and some other book is encouraged and helped to reconcile the situation. Pupils are encouraged to supplement the text with library materials, and the learner who has difficulty with the text is guided to another source.

Practice Classroom Democracy

The essential step in developing a cooperative learning situation is to put democratic procedures to work in the classroom. The research study on "Classroom Democracy" cited in Chapter 1 defined the characteristics of a democratic classroom as follows:

A) There is evidence of pupil purposes.

B) Freedom exists through standards established by the group, for the group welfare.

C) Pupils participate in planning and evaluating their work.

D) In the curriculum there is emphasis upon pupil growth rather than upon subject matter acquisition *per se*.

E) Students are given the opportunity of governing themselves, with adult guidance.

F) There is an atmosphere of cooperation, of sharing, of helping, of group welfare.

G) A flexible classroom schedule exists.

H) Wholesome teacher-pupil, pupil-pupil, and teacher administrator relationships exist.

I) There is school-community cooperation.[10]

The revelation of this study—that the average class "democraticness" score was only 61 per cent when measured in a sample of schools by the above criteria—constitutes a challenge to teachers to try to develop classrooms which exhibit more completely the characteristics of a democratic organization.

DEVELOPING DAILY PLANS AND PROGRAMS

Daily planning by teachers is essential in the process of teaching that we are describing in this book, although formal lesson plans of the type still required in some schools may have quite limited value to the teacher. But if there is to be a cooperative planning period, there must be prior planning by the teacher of procedures to be followed, questions to be raised, and alternative plans that might be developed. If a unit of work is under

[10] Mary Beatrice Dalton, "Classroom Democracy—Functionally Defined and Measured" (unpublished doctoral dissertation; St. Louis, Mo.: Washington University, 1949), p. 5.

way records are needed of special enterprises and groups involved. The fact that a unit of work has been preplanned by the teacher and the fact that there is pupil-teacher planning do not eliminate the necessity of day-by-day planning for the teacher. In the following section, we shall note some of the common problems of daily planning.

Problems of Daily Planning

Certain types of problems for each day's work are relatively common at all grade levels and in both departmentalized and nondepartmentalized programs. The teacher in the departmentalized program simply has more pupils to plan for and as one result his planning is frequently in terms of the subject rather than in terms of the members of his classes.

Arranging facilities and resources. Because of the importance of the problem of resources for learning experiences we are dealing with it in some detail in Chapter 14. Here we may call attention to the wide variety of tasks that may be involved:

1. Securing books and other printed materials from the library or other sources
2. Checking on the availability of materials within the room
3. Selecting visual aids
4. Securing supplies for written work, art, construction activities, and so forth
5. Arranging for field trips
6. Arranging for speakers, visitors
7. Arranging for interviews
8. Arranging for use of special rooms at school: assembly, music, art, library, and so forth
9. Organizing the seating arrangement
10. Organizing exhibits, displays, special collections, bulletin boards
11. Checking on any special equipment needed
12. Arranging with other staff personnel for special contributions and cooperative activities

Not all of these tasks occur for every group or on every day, but some of them are involved each day for each group. Pupils may share some of these responsibilities, too, but the teacher's direction is essential.

Study of pupils' work and records. Because of the time-consuming nature of studying records, too little time is frequently given to this problem. In the nondepartmentalized organization or for home room or core classes, the teacher usually has pupils' cumulative records or is assumed to know about them if they are filed centrally. At the beginning of the year, particularly, he will need to study these records carefully to familiarize himself with individual backgrounds. In general, aimless reading of records is not very fruitful; a better procedure is to study each pupil's record fully, noting significant points for further observation or suggestions for particular action. Also, as questions arise about individual children's illnesses or interests or behavior it is frequently necessary to recheck records. Teachers who work in a departmentalized program generally study records as questions arise about individual pupils.

Study of records must frequently be supplemented by conferences with parents, other teachers, counselors, and other special service personnel. All this takes time and should be a definite part of the teacher's own schedule. Those who have planning periods within the school day frequently use this for study of records and for follow-up conferences with pupils and school personnel.

Pupils' work must also be examined if the teacher is to give helpful guidance. Although there is less "busywork" in the modern school, papers, letters, reports, drawings, and other types of purposeful written work are very important. For pupils to have maximum help, their work should be gone over by teachers with appropriate suggestions made for improvement. These suggestions are most effective when made soon after the work is completed. Also, depending on the reporting system in effect, time must be devoted to preparing evaluative statements. However, this job becomes one of summarizing progress if daily attention is given to pupils' progress. Notes for the cumulative record must be prepared, too, as particularly significant behavior is noted, or when other information called for by the record system is available.

Preparation of materials. Various materials need to be prepared from time to time for pupils. Special drill materials, lists of readings, outlines of units in progress, instructions for using equipment, progress tests, charts, and summaries of papers by pupils are all examples of the kinds of materials that teachers need to prepare. Although large classes and other factors are sometimes responsible for a heavy reliance on commercial workbooks and other materials, effective teachers do not rely on such sources alone but find time to locate or prepare materials adapted to the particular learners with whom they deal.

The teacher's own study. The teacher needs time each day to extend his own knowledge of the problems being dealt with in his class. Although the task becomes more significant as more complex subject matter is involved, even the teacher of young children must search for new stories, examine new books, investigate appropriate concepts in such fields as science. It is not to be implied that the teacher must "know all the answers," but the teacher's security and general ability is closely related to being well informed.

We do not mean to overemphasize the tasks of the teacher. We merely feel their scope and nature must be recognized both by the teacher and by those who set teacher loads. The teacher must be willing to give fully of his time and energy to the job, and the load must be set on a sufficiently reasonable basis to permit him to carry on an efficient job without undue pressure.

The Daily Program

The planning of a daily program is relatively simple for the teacher in a departmentalized program in which he has five or six classes of forty to fifty minutes in length. Yet the inflexibility of this schedule creates problems because plans for each class must be adapted to the fixed period. Planning an excursion, for example, becomes very complicated for, if possible at all, arrangements must be made for a longer period; hence conferences with other teachers, special dispensations, or similar tasks are involved. One of the problems in connection with the fixed period is determining a division, if any, between study and discussion and other activities. In view of the generally decreasing use of homework assignments, it is increasingly expected that all the work children do for the mathematics class, for example, will be done in the mathematics period. Accordingly, provision must be made for planning, summarizing, and evaluating activities within the time allotment. Instead of fixed divisions of time within the period, one whole session may be devoted to planning, several to study activities with short group sessions to note progress from time to time, and one or more periods devoted to summarization and evaluation.

The core curriculum presents still another type of daily program problem. Here there are two or three subjects—perhaps English, social studies, science. Should, then, the time be arbitrarily divided between these subjects? Such a program would not possess the characteristics of desirable core organization presented in Chapter 10. Instead, the better practice is again a flexible organization. Under this plan the English and the social studies periods are not generally labeled separately, for example, but time is provided as needed for discussion, reading, and writing, and other activities. The entire period is available if needed for a trip, for committee activity, or for any other purpose. The teacher's planning and guidance must provide for a balance of the various types of learning experiences included.

In the self-contained classroom of the elementary school, where the teacher has the group of learners throughout the school day, an almost completely flexible organization is possible. However, provision is usually made for physical education at a definite time and for any other activities such as art and music that involve the sharing of facilities or personnel with other groups. Some principles for planning the actual division of the day in the nondepartmentalized classroom (and the core room) are as follows:

1. A learning experience should continue as long as it seems profitable.

2. In general, as extended blocks of time as are suitable to children's maturities should be utilized.

3. Time of quiet and activity should be alternated with ample provision for physical activity for young children.

4. A balance of learning experiences should be provided over a period of several days rather than each day.

5. The daily program should include time for planning and sharing ideas, quiet study, drill and practice, creative and appreciative activities, recreation, and individual and small-group activities.

6. In terms of curriculum areas, the daily program should include provision for units of work which may be built around problems in social studies and science, for practice periods in various skills, for the appreciative areas (art and music), and for physical education. Usually the core organization of the secondary school includes only two or three of the following areas: social studies, language arts, science, and arithmetic.

Several of the foregoing principles are illustrated in the following description of a typical day in second grade in a Battle Creek, Michigan, elementary school. Although the activities included would be different (for example, less time for reading and more time for number skills) at upper-grade levels, the general organization of this daily program would apply at any elementary grade level:

8:30– 8:50   Get-acquainted and organization time

        a. Converse with children about activities in and out of school
        b. Children plan any special work
        c. Listen to service squad girl read stories
        d. Listen to classmates read stories

8:50– 9:00   Assembly time

        a. Greeting
        b. Morning prayer
        c. Songs

    d. News time
      1. Current news
      2. Check on people who are ill

9:00– 9:15   *Planning period*

    a. Review and evaluate preceding activities
    b. Plan activities of the day

9:15–10:15   *Language arts*

(Reading, Spelling, Writing, Written Language)
a. May be a discussion or study period
b. May consist of writing about some experiences we have had
c. Spelling words may be selected from experience story
d. Read from basal text
e. Silent reading for information
f. Word games
g. Letter writing
    This is a period where study habits are developed. There may be a study period for some and group recitation or discussion for others.

10:15–10:20   *Rest period*

10:20–10:40   *Physical education*

10:40–11:15   *Language arts, continued (sharing period)*

    a. Oral language and speech
    b. Evaluation of work
    c. Plan for afternoon activities
    d. Number experiences

11:15–12:30   *Noon*

12:30–12:50   *Get-acquainted time*

    a. Sign up for work-time activities
    b. Select and return library books (Thursday)

12:50– 1:50   *Science and social studies*

    a. Reading for information
    b. Planning group science activities
    c. Taking trips

    d. Reporting on excursions
    e. Reporting on science findings
    f. Solving number problems
    g. Developing new number experiences

1:50– 2:15   Music, singing, games, rhythms, dramatizations

2:15– 3:05   Work time

    a. Work on crafts and art—related to science activities
    b. Time for individual conferences and for help to small groups with special, specific difficulties
    c. Friday: story hour, concert hour, etc.

3:05– 3:15   Quick review of what we have done

    a. Forward look
    b. Clean-up
    c. Dismissal

ORGANIZING THE LEARNING SITUATION

Physical Arrangements

Unfortunately, every teacher cannot work in a large, airy, light classroom with movable furniture and adequate work space. Plate 30 illustrates the adaptation of a part of a room to the learning situation. Although new buildings are adding to the number of adequate rooms, the majority of American classrooms are probably still of the traditional type. In these more restricted situations the teacher's ingenuity may be severely taxed to find ways and means of making the room as attractive and as flexible as is consistent with the requirements of a good learning situation. However, ingenious teachers have found a great many devices for making their classrooms more attractive and flexible. Illustrative of these devices are a list of rich suggestions on "How Can We Make the Most of Inadequate Classroom Space?" contained in a recent publication of the Florida Program for Improvement of Schools. Although these suggestions were intended to apply to the art program, the following excerpts have wide utility:

> *Work Space:* Stationary desks that are much too small for art work are often one of our greatest handicaps in the average classroom. This can be overcome by using beaver board or corrugated boxes. Cut boards 18 x 24 inches or larger. Place the long end over front of desk. Mark the cardboard and slit it so that it will slip over the raised part of the desk. This will hold it in place and children will now have

PLATE 30. EFFECTIVE USE OF WALLS AND TABLES. *Organizing the learning situation involves the total classroom environment. (Courtesy of Gallatin, Tennessee, Public Schools)*

a working space for larger paper and a place for paint pans. Often the child will stand in the aisle to work.

Work Center: If we do not have large tables, table size areas can be made by getting mattress boxes and placing them over desk tops.

The Floor: (1) Newspapers placed on available classroom floor will provide space for large paintings. Large papers for the children to paint on can be placed on these. (2) Available hall space may be used in the same manner.

Cabinets: Attractive cabinets for storage space can be made out of orange crates or other wooden boxes. These can be painted a bright color and arranged in many interesting ways.

Files: (1) Files may be made out of orange crates with drawers to fit each section. This will give space for filing materials needed so often in a classroom. Pasteboard boxes may also be used for files. (2) The large corrugated box may be set up as the orange crate was.

Water: If a sink is unavailable, water in pails or large tin cans may be used, one for clean water and one for dirty water.

Blackboard: Blackboards may be used for display space. Paper or other materials may be used to cover blackboard if desired.

Bulletin Board: Keep bulletin boards attractive and interesting. The children will take great pride and become very efficient in taking this responsibility with the guidance of the teacher.

(1) Use interesting related materials. Change bulletins often.

(2) Pin all four corners down, so that materials will stay flat.

(3) If possible mount all pictures, clippings, or printed material. Use colored paper sometimes.

(4) Keep the bulletin board so that it has an orderly arrangement. Space so the things will not seem too crowded or have empty space.

Substitutes for Bulletin Boards: (1) If no bulletin boards are provided, old scraps of beaver board, celotex, plywood, large packing cases, etc., can be used. If space is limited, a series of small boards may be laced together with heavy cord, which can be folded and stored when not in use. Paint often improves the appearance of bulletin boards.

(2) Old picture frames may be refinished and used to display children's work. Change them often.

(3) Screens may be used where there are no bulletin boards. Materials for these can often be scrap materials from lumber yards, such as packing cases. Screens may be folded and put out of the way when not in use.

Picture Hanging: (1) Pictures should be hung at eye-level of the average person. Things hung in higher wall spaces should be decorative rather than pictorial.

(2) Hang picture in blackboard space rather than above or below it only for temporary use.

(3) Select pictures for fine quality and interest to children.[11]

Other suggestions for maintaining an attractive, flexible learning situation may also help. For example, screwed-down desks can usually be unscrewed and then arranged flexibly; if their top-heaviness makes frequent moving undesirable, arrange them in semicircular rather than straight rows. Also, if the classroom space permits, a small circle of desks may be arranged in one corner so that a committee or special work group may get together. If this is impossible but there are extra seats, one section of adjacent seats may be unassigned so that a group of learners may get together there. The attractiveness of any room may be increased by flowers, bright paint, and colorful posters and pictures. A clean blackboard helps greatly to make summaries, announcements, and so forth more legible and inviting. Change in exhibits, pictures, posters, and so forth, is just as desirable in the classroom as in any other room where people live day after day.

[11] Florida State Department of Education, *Art in the Lives of Florida Children* (Florida Program for Improvement of Schools, Bulletin No. 37; Tallahassee: The Department, January, 1950), pp. 61–67.

But not all the problems of physical arrangement are confined to the traditional classroom with its drab walls and fixed seats. In an article on "Immovable Movable Seats," Reeder states that, in the great majority of classrooms equipped with movable seats which he visits, "the handsome new movable seats and desks are placed in the beautiful straight rows so dear to the orderly schoolteacher's heart" and tells this story to illustrate the point:

> In one school on the day when the new movable furniture was delivered, one teacher waited after school until all the children had gone. Then she took a small pot of white paint and a brush. She arranged the chairs and tables in the old orderly rows; then she made a little circle with the white paint around the spot on the floor on which rested each leg of desk or chair. When the children arrived next morning, they were told in no uncertain terms that from then on each leg of each piece of furniture must be within its own proper circle or else the offender who had moved his desk or chair would get into serious trouble.[12]

Apparently there is more reason than the type of furniture for the maintenance of inflexible seating arrangements. Probably the real reason is the traditional practice of such seating bolstered by the argument of proper lighting. Teachers who have the advantages of flexible seating will need to overcome in their own minds as well as in those of learners the idea that classrooms must be organized around fixed seating arrangements. Considerable practice in planning flexible groupings, in adjusting desks for different purposes and to make use of light as it is available, may be necessary.

Group Organization

The classroom group is usually too large for effective communication. Although this is overcome in part as members become better acquainted, a first concern of the teacher is to identify the small groups which usually already exist because children have been together and have identified common interests. Even if they have not been together before, children are usually quick to form into small groups around some common relationship, frequently the neighborhood. Having identified these small groups, the teacher should move as rapidly as possible to develop one group.[13]

[12] Edwin H. Reeder, "Immovable Movable Seats," *Progressive Education*, 27:79 (January), 1950.
[13] See "Meeting the Needs of the Whole Child through Group Participation," *Teachers College Record*, 50:295–302 (February), 1949.

Rather than some standing organization, most teachers find preferable the designation of chairmen or other leaders for specific purposes. In this way, leadership may be rotated and any confusion eliminated as to the relative roles of pupil chairman and teacher. Thus a chairman may be elected for the home room period, for reporting sessions, for room business, or for club and other special programs. Others may be elected as recorders, observers, and reporters. Committees may be elected or appointed from time to time for the business functions of the group as in clubs or other social organizations: program plans, room maintenance, exhibits and displays, publications, funds, elections.

Perhaps the most difficult phase of group organization is that of the formation of small groups for specific learning experiences. In some situations interest is an adequate factor, and learners should be allowed to select their own groups. In others, particularly groups for special drill in skills, a stigma will be attached unless exceeding care is taken by teachers to avoid labeling "slow" groups. In the primary grades, where instruction in most skills is in small group situations, the problem can be met by refusal to label the groups and by some rotation of membership. As some children develop independent abilities, however, the group for special help becomes somewhat more obviously a slow group. Several devices for avoiding the stigma are possible: special help groups may be organized in a variety of skills rather than in a single, "special" group; children who do not need special help may be placed in the groups to help other children or the teacher but without embarrassment to the children; groups may have schedules so flexible that they will not be regarded as definite "classes."

A special problem is that of the remedial class in departmentalized programs. If the viewpoint is accepted that there are no uniform grade standards or other expectations for all children, there really can be no "remedial" instruction for the mass of slower learners. Some children develop more slowly than others and do not attain as high a level of skill, but forcing them through so-called "remedial" techniques will not substantially affect the situation. Olson reached this conclusion regarding forcing: "Under a forcing plan the teacher or parent, by urging, scolding, and setting up extrinsic awards, attempts to bring the child up to some preconceived standard of excellence. Such methods commonly fail and bring about bad social and emotional repercussions." [14] On the other hand, every effort should be made to diagnose the reasons for difficulty in reading or other skills. If there is a physical or emotional difficulty under-

[14] Willard C. Olson, *Child Development* (Boston: D. C. Heath & Company, 1949), p. 340.

lying the problem, considerable progress may be made through special help.

PLANNING DISCUSSION ACTIVITIES

One of the major learning experiences of modern classrooms at all levels is discussion. A democratic method of procedure commonly practiced in adult groups, it also has limitations obvious both in school classrooms and in these older groups. Most if not all limitations, however, result from inadequate experience of group members and can be met through more effective discussion situations throughout the school.

The first requirement of an effective discussion is a topic, problem, or question concerning which evidence or ideas can be brought from several sources and viewpoints. Thus, at least in the elementary or secondary school, the date of Columbus's discovery of America, the chemical composition of water, or the parts of speech are not suitable topics of discussion. The teacher long accustomed to question-and-answer recitation sometimes errs in making the transition to discussion procedures by assuming that facts previously questioned by "What?" "Who?" "When?" and "Where?" can become the subject matter of discussion by changing the question to "What do you think?" The topics suitable for profitable discussion must be such that questions as to their "why's," "wherefore's" and "therefore what's" will elicit intelligent responses, no one of which is usually the sole correct answer.

A second requirement is the interest of learners. As in any other learning experience, participation is based on motive and readiness. If the question for discussion is one which is associated with matters of concern to boys and girls, if their previous experiences have given some ideas regarding it, profitable discussion may result. In general, the nearer the problem and the more emotional interest attached to it the more real the discussion will be. For example, pupils become exceedingly involved in a discussion of a move from one school unit to another but completely disinterested in the history of the school system. The most effective way to secure interest is to have the question for discussion determined by the group, that is, to use the pupil-teacher planning techniques already discussed.

A third requirement, and it cannot be overemphasized, is skillful leadership. It is doubtful whether teachers should turn over the chairmanship of discussion experiences to pupils unless the latter are unusually mature and skillful. Since the success of the entire experience is so closely dependent on the quality of leadership, either the discussion may have un-

happy outcomes or the pupil chairman serves as a figurehead. The importance of teacher leadership is indicated by research studies showing that
monopoly of discussion by a few children is much more common under
pupil than teacher leadership.[15]

Some specific suggestions for the teacher-leader in discussion situations are as follows:

1. Keep as informal a situation as possible: have pupils keep seated
as they speak; have questions and comments addressed to each other
rather than to the teacher.

2. Use a blackboard freely to record points, questions, contrasts or
outlines, and be certain that writing is legible. If a pupil makes the blackboard record, go slowly enough to help him out.

3. Make sure that the question for discussion is thoroughly understood by everyone, and repeat it frequently. Interrupt pupils who digress
too much, and explain when comments are irrelevant.

4. Allow the class a good laugh occasionally.

5. Recognize each contribution by "That's a good point," "That's
good," or by similar comments.

6. Bring in questions and points that are being ignored.

7. Summarize frequently, and take the consensus when issues have
been discussed. Close each discussion by reviewing the question, major
points made, and the chief conclusions to be remembered.

We should emphasize that classroom experiences are not either "discussion or else" as sometimes indicated in descriptions of classroom
methods. Discussions have a very important place, but so do such experiences as reading and study, telling and listening, seeing and hearing. Discussions are most effective for problem-solving, planning, and evaluating
activities.

PLANNING INDIVIDUAL AND SMALL-GROUP ACTIVITIES

In the course of developing a unit, many learning experiences of individuals and small groups must be planned. In fact, all experiences
must be on individual or small-group bases except those of planning and
discussion by the total group. Some of the common types of activities carried on by individuals and small groups are these:

1. Securing information from published sources: books, magazines,
   newspapers, reference books, and so forth

2. Securing information from persons through interviews, conferences, and meetings

[15] See Arthur T. Jersild, *Child Psychology* (3d ed.; New York: Prentice-Hall, Inc.,
1947), p. 218.

3. Securing information from films, radio, and other audio-visual sources
4. Writing letters to secure information
5. Making posters, charts, graphs, exhibits, friezes, murals
6. Carrying on construction activities
7. Writing reports, summaries, minutes, digests, articles, editorials
8. Preparing for speeches, panel discussions, debates
9. Discussing in small groups the investigations being carried on

In planning these activities, learners should be guided in developing plans which are definite enough that they can be followed through. The teacher has to anticipate difficulties and give guidance in meeting them. Hence the teacher should be in position to consult with the individual or group at any time that help is needed. Also, plans should be made for daily conferences on progress so that unnecessary difficulties may be met.

Small-group activities will be aided by an efficient arrangement for using supplies, reference materials, the library, and other resources. The teacher should give special attention to the efficient and successful performance of responsibilities so that good work processes are developed.

Skill Development

A considerable part of the teacher's job with individuals and small groups is concerned with skill development. It is not appropriate to the purposes of this book to develop fully practices in skill development, but certain important principles are noted in the following paragraphs.

The teacher must be conscious of the status of skill development in every activity of the school program. There are skills other than reading, writing, and arithmetic: speaking, listening, social relations, use of tools, use of books, for example. Conscious attention to each of these is essential in developing the well-rounded person.

Teachers at every level of the school program must be concerned with skill development. Every teacher is a teacher of reading, for example, whether or not conscious effort is made to develop reading skill. The learner who meets frustration in learning because of improper guidance in reading has acquired a learning—to dislike reading—just as truly as has the primary child who learned to read properly and therefore to like reading. Similarly, each of the major skills is practiced throughout school and all teachers can help learners achieve increasing competence in them.

Learners cannot rightly be expected to acquire the same level in any skill at particular age and grade levels. The teacher is forced to recognize varying levels of competency in skills and to guide pupils in selecting experiences which are appropriate to their levels and which also may stimulate further development.

In recognition of the principle that skills develop best through meaningful experiences, teachers should be alert to every possibility in individual and group activities for developing readiness for new skills. Similarly, an adequate number of practice situations which have meaning for learners should be utilized.

Finally, and somewhat by way of summary, teachers should recognize that skills are not developed successfully without guidance. Supervised study, for example, which consists of pupils working on assignments at their desks and the teacher working on records is not an adequate form of guidance. The teacher needs to check with each pupil as frequently as possible on the process being followed and to suggest next steps. Particularly is individual guidance essential as new skills are being attacked.

RECORDING THE UNIT OF WORK

Some record of each unit of work completed is essential for two purposes: (1) for the information of other teachers of the same learners, that is, for the cumulative record or to be actually handed other teachers the next year or, in a departmentalized program, currently; (2) for reference by the teacher in planning a similar unit for another group. For the latter purpose a simple annotation of the original unit plan suffices, although such materials as the following may be more helpful at a later time:

1. A file kept by the teacher of daily plans, sample pupil papers, outlines, and related materials
2. A narrative, diary-like record kept by the teacher (or a pupil in more mature groups) and describing the development of the unit
3. A class summary of the unit
4. A recording of an oral summarizing session

Either of the latter three types of records may be used to inform other teachers of a unit of work. However, where the record is to be inserted in each pupil's cumulative record, as is sometimes the practice, a brief written summary by the teacher may be more practical. For this purpose such an outline as the following may be used:

1. Brief description of the unit: purpose, major problems, most significant learning experiences such as excursions and projects
2. List of materials read or audio-visual aids used by all
3. Skills developed through the unit
4. Evaluative evidence: tests, summary of opinions, and so on

PLANNING LEARNING EXPERIENCES NOT ORGANIZED IN
UNITS OF WORK

As already noted and as indicated by some of the illustrations in this chapter, not all learning experiences can or should be organized into large units of work. All-school activities, for example, such as assembly programs, athletic contests, festivals, social programs, and similar ones, may be related to units of work carried on in classrooms but definitely are developed outside the classroom. Also, many experiences in the classroom may need to be carried on without direct relationship to the experiences built around a unit problem. For example, systematic practice in skills is essential at every grade level, and frequently the sequential development of a skill such as arithmetic necessitates practice on processes other than those invoved in a unit of work at the time. In addition, special situations arise to provide opportunity for learning experiences that meet all the criteria for good experiences but at the same time are completely unrelated to current units of work.

We believe that the selection and planning of these learning experiences should be guided by the same criteria as those applied to experiences organized into units of work. With the exception of the last one (relationship to other units), each criterion we presented in Chapter 12 applies to any of the examples cited above.

One problem regarding the planning of learning experiences which occur outside unit organization and indeed outside classroom situations should be commented upon. In usual practice, responsibility for planning the "extra" activities is nominally in the hands of the faculty but actually is divided so that the physical education teacher handles athletics, individual sponsors have clubs, the English teacher is responsible for the publications, and so forth, with some activities planned by small faculty committees. As to be expected, there is little coordination among the faculty members, who seldom are able to review the entire school program. In the small school it would seem desirable for the entire faculty to plan the whole range of school activities, with responsibility for executing plans fixed after policies are determined. In the larger school, a representative council of the staff, with parent and pupil representation if possible, might undertake the coordination of the entire school program. Further consideration is given to council organization in Chapter 16.

For Further Study

Alberty, Harold, *Reorganizing the High-School Curriculum.* Rev. ed.; New York: The Macmillan Company, 1953.

Part III, "The Curriculum in Action," provides suggestions on teacher-pupil planning, teacher guidance, and handling of controversial issues.

Association for Supervision and Curriculum Development, National Education Association, *Toward Better Teaching*. 1949 Yearbook. Washington, D.C.: The Association, 1949.

Contains many fine illustrations of better teaching at various levels.

Cantor, Nathaniel, *Learning through Discussion*. Buffalo, N.Y.: Human Relations for Industry, 1951.

Deals with this question: "What takes place psychologically when a group of people, directed by a leader, meets to discuss a problem?"

————, *The Teaching-Learning Process*. New York: The Dryden Press, 1953.

Analysis of teacher-pupil interactions.

Cunningham, Ruth, and associates, *Understanding Group Behavior of Boys and Girls*. New York: Bureau of Publications, Teachers College, Columbia University, 1951.

Based on cooperative research in school situations, this book provides much insight into effective organization and procedure of learning groups.

Faunce, Roland C., and Nelson L. Bossing, *Developing the Core Curriculum*. New York: Prentice-Hall, Inc., 1951.

See especially Chapter 6, "The Core Class in Action," and Chapter 9, "The Role of the Teacher."

Harap, Henry, *Social Living in the Curriculum*. Nashville: Division of Surveys and Field Services, George Peabody College for Teachers, 1952.

Part II describes classroom work in social living observed by the author at each grade level. These descriptions suggest many procedures in good classroom planning and development of learning experiences.

Johnston, Edgar G., and Roland C. Faunce, *Student Activities in Secondary Schools*. New York: The Ronald Press Company, 1952.

This comprehensive treatment of student activities in secondary schools gives many suggestions for guiding learning in the activity program.

"Meeting the Needs of the Whole Child through Group Participation," *Teachers College Record*, 50:295–302 (February), 1949.

Analysis of the relation of group work to individual needs, and suggestions for group organization of varying types.

Miel, Alice, and associates, *Cooperative Procedures in Learning*. New York: Bureau of Publications, Teachers College, Columbia University, 1952.

This book presents concrete and helpful descriptions of actual practices in cooperative planning and working in classrooms. Based on wide experimentation, the publication is a rich source of help for teachers.

National Society for the Study of Education, *Adapting the Secondary-School Program to the Needs of Youth*. Part I, Fifty-second Yearbook of the Society. Chicago: The University of Chicago Press, 1953.

Section III analyzes problems of the classroom teacher in meeting the needs of youth through learning experiences.

————, *Learning and Instruction*. Part I, Forty-ninth Yearbook of the Society. Chicago: The University of Chicago Press, 1950.

Chapters IX–XII apply principles of learning to teaching at different levels; Chapter XIII describes "The School as a Learning Laboratory."

Rasey, Marie I., *This Is Teaching*. New York: Harper & Brothers, 1950.

Each chapter is written as a record of a session of a college seminar, conducted on a cooperative-planning, students' problems-centered basis. The book illustrates both such an organization for learning and how teachers solve problems in their own group.

"Role of Pupils in Cooperative Curriculum Development, The," *Teachers College Record*, 50:327–335 (February), 1949.

Analyzes basic assumptions defining the role of learners in curriculum planning.

Shull, W. Russell, *Techniques of Discussion with Teen-Agers*. Chicago: National Forum, Inc., 1951.

Developed as a guide for use of the publications of the National Forum Guidance Series, this monograph contains many helpful suggestions for discussion procedure.

Stratemeyer, Florence B., Hamden L. Forkner, and Margaret G. McKim, *Developing a Curriculum for Modern Living*. New York: Bureau of Publications, Teachers College, Columbia University, 1947.

See Chapter VI, "Developing the Curriculum with Learners," for suggestions on cooperative planning of experiences to help in the life situations learners face.

Thelen, Herbert A., "Human Dynamics in the Classroom," *Journal of Educational Research*, 6:30–55 (No. 2), 1950.

Applies a body of ideas about human dynamics to a set of policies for teaching.

Wiles, Kimball, *Teaching for Better Schools*. New York: Prentice-Hall, Inc., 1952.

An excellent source of modern principles of teaching at all levels.

chapter 14

Selection and Use of Resources for Learning

The selection and use of resources is an essential phase of the processes of planning and developing learning experiences. Although these processes were discussed in Chapters 12 and 13, we consider the problems of selecting and using resources sufficiently distinct to justify separate and more extended treatment.

THE NATURE OF LEARNING RESOURCES

As was pointed out in Chapter 6, learning occurs as an individual seeks to attain some goal of concern to him. In the process of goal seeking, that is, during the learning experience, the individual turns to one or more sources of help for successful attainment of the goal. This help may be information, ideas, formulas, or generalizations, contained in books or given by another person, or it may be an experience which the learner can observe as it happens or later through pictures, or it may be an environmental condition or facility to be studied firsthand. Whatever the source of help, it is a resource for the individual's learning. In other words, it is anything or anybody to which or to whom the individual turns for help in his goal-seeking activities.

The problem of resources would be relatively simple if individuals in the learning group could be assumed to have identical goals and identical backgrounds of experience. But we know that such identity does not exist, that even in a group of learners of about the same age and number of previous years in school the widest differences exist with respect to backgrounds and interests. Hence a single, identical resource for learning, such as a basic textbook, is not likely to be equally valuable for all learners in a particular group. There needs to be a variety of resources suitable to the range of interests and previous experiences of the learners, and adequate for such needs as obtaining data on a problem, learning how to locate information, and broadening interests and backgrounds.

Resources for learning must offer potential help for all learners, but the effectiveness of the resource is ultimately determined with respect to individual learners. For example, an encyclopedia, with its wealth of information, offers much potential help, but this resource is valueless for children unable to make proper use of an encyclopedia. To carry the example even further, individuals who turn to a specific article may receive quite different help even in answer to an identical question because their reading and understanding of the same information will vary according to their unique experiential backgrounds. No specific type of resource is equally valuable for all learners.

The range of possible tools for learning is as wide as that of known persons, objects, places, and processes. In general, anything that exists is a potential resource as pupils find their own experiences inadequate for the attainment of their goals. Any person, object, place, process, experiment, or demonstration may be of help to some individual in connection with some learning goal. Hence the problem of classification of resources is itself complex. For present purposes, the most usable classification is based on the form in which resources are available. Individual learners may find help through use of human, environmental, printed, and audio-visual resources. These four types are treated in this chapter.

THE TEACHER'S DILEMMA

If teachers could summon at will any aids needed by individual learners, the direction of learning might be much more rewarding. In practice, teachers are generally very limited through such factors as lack of facilities in the school, inaccessibility of resources outside the school, administrative regulations governing the use of even the available resources, and teachers' and pupils' own lack of facility in using a variety of learning aids. Hence instead of using the most suitable resource for each pupil, teachers frequently make use of a very limited number, usually printed ones and especially textbooks. It follows that individual learners vary widely in the extent of help they find in these resources and that teachers may find their work disappointing if not frustrating.

Confronted with the knowledge that wider resources would make for better knowledge and yet conscious of the lack of, or the inability to use, such resources, what is the teacher to do? At this point, certain general approaches to the problem may help:

1. Learn as much as possible about the variety of resources which may be used. Perhaps there are potentialities in the people and in the environment which are being overlooked.

2. Employ the resources which are available as effectively as possible. Possibly the problem is not only one of limited resources, but also one of ineffective use of those which are at hand.

3. Show that use of different aids does improve learning. Budgetary limitations and administrative regulations may be modified when there is justification. In this chapter we shall try to help teachers with such approaches by information and suggestions on the variety, values, and use of the possible resources to be considered in curriculum planning.

CHARACTERISTICS OF GOOD LEARNING RESOURCES

Although each of the following sections states specific principles for effective selection and use of the particular learning resources concerned, we should note that certain general criteria apply to all. These are briefly identified in the following paragraphs as a suggested basis of study and evaluation of all resources.

Relevancy

The first characteristic to be considered in selecting any learning aid is its relevancy to the goal-seeking activity involved. Thus one turns to the policeman to learn about his duties; to the dictionary to find the meaning of a word; to the microscope to examine the shape of bacteria. This seemingly obvious criterion of selection is abused, however, by such practices as these:

1. Use of textbooks and other printed materials as sole sources of information about problems which have materially changed since the materials were published

2. Use of films and other visual aids as time fillers and without relation to the subject at hand

3. Use of persons as speakers because they are entertaining without regard to their subject matter

4. Use of the same field trips from year to year without relation to particular units of work

Usability

The criterion of usability has at least two connotations of significance. First, the resources must be accessible at the time needed. The most relevant materials can be selected from book and film catalogues, but may not be usable because of lack of funds or time to secure them. The resource file may yield names of persons who can help on projects, but inquiry reveals that these persons are not available when needed. The problem of timing is a particularly complex one in relation to the selection of visual aids, which frequently must be ordered (on a rental basis) weeks in advance. Plate 31 shows a library which has arranged its materials to attract and interest its young patrons.

Second, a learning aid must be usable in terms of its appropriateness to the particular group. Relevant materials are available on almost any topic, but they may be appropriate only to mature readers. Similarly, competent persons may have a wealth of information bearing on boys and girls' questions but be completely unable to explain this information to children. The matter of appropriateness is ultimately an-

PLATE 31. WELL-ARRANGED MATERIALS ARE MORE USABLE. *Pupils use materials more readily when they are attractively arranged and displayed. (Courtesy of the El Paso, Texas, Public Schools)*

swered in terms of individual learners, and so far as possible teachers must select a range of resources which provides for each individual. This criterion is violated most generally in regard to instructional materials, the selection of which may be completely out of the teacher's hands. We shall discuss this problem more intensively in a later section of this chapter.

Accuracy

The resources for learning must give as accurate information as possible. This criterion is of especial significance in relation to printed sources, particularly pamphlet materials. However, films and even persons may also give inaccurate information. It should be noted that materials prepared with particular biases, such as those used for advertising, may be helpful resources, but the teacher is obliged to point out the biases and inaccuracies and to use any other available materials to show differing viewpoints.

Economy

Other things being equal, the most economical resource should be used. Often other things are not equal and teachers have difficulty in estimating the costs in time and money of different tools. However, good judgment will rule out using films when equally effective and more economical slides, pictures, or pamphlets are available; taking a group of learners to see a person who could come to the school; or sending an entire class to a set of reference books to check on the same topic when one person could present the information effectively. The principle of economy is violated, contrary to common assumption, by using the same materials for all members of a class. When perhaps half of the group finds these materials too difficult or too boring, the same funds would be better spent for materials written at different levels of interest and difficulty.

SELECTION AND USE OF HUMAN RESOURCES

Traditional concepts of learning and teaching fail to recognize the role of human resources. These concepts assign importance only to books and other inanimate objects as reservoirs of information which learners are to acquire. Observation of pupils taught under the influence of such concepts reveals great reliance on human beings, however. Pupils turn to the teacher, to their parents, and to each other for interpretations of what they read and see. Enthusiasm for learning is greatly increased in such a class when a visitor is invited to tell the children about some firsthand experience or when the latter have a chance to visit some person to get information. Perhaps the use of people is so obvious and commonplace that its importance in learning is simply overlooked in teaching-learning situations. If so, it may be profitable to identify clearly the types and utilities of various human resources to be called upon in learning situations.

The Teacher as a Resource Person

In order that teachers may study carefully their own role as a "human resource," attention is directed in this section to the concept of *the teacher as a resource person*. Traditionally, the teacher is an authority in the group—the assigner, lesson-hearer, tester, the final arbiter as to right and wrong responses in recitation and drill. The general point of view regarding teaching presented in this book conceives of the teacher as a resource person or helper rather than as a taskmaster and judge.

Observation of teachers in effective learning situations reveals some rather specific activities in relation to individual pupils which particularly characterize this helping role. Some of these activities are identified in the following paragraphs. The broader concept of teaching presented in Chapter 13 included description of many other types of activities through which teachers may exert a helping role for entire groups.

Helping individual pupils through finding appropriate activities. The boy or girl who is observed to be a nonparticipant in classroom activities is a challenge to the resourceful teacher. Such a teacher continues the search for something that will bring about this pupil's participation until a new book, a new leadership role, a different type of creative work, or some other device succeeds. The search may take a long time[1] and involve a great deal of creative ability,[2] but success in helping individual pupils is probably the most rewarding aspect of teaching. It is significant that many studies of pupil evaluation of their teachers indicate that pupils rate very high those teaching activities and traits which relate to the direct and personal help that these pupils received.

Providing the stimulus for individuals' creative activity. The resourcefulness necessary for guiding individuals' creative activity may be implied from a teacher's statement quoted in *Toward Better Teaching:*

> I suppose there is no one best way of beginning and promoting creative activity in a classroom. Certainly I have found none. With each group I must begin differently. That is because each group is a unit in itself. It is just as individual, just as unique, as the members comprising the group. Before we can create together, we have to arrive at a certain milestone in our journey together. I can never tell ahead of time just which one it will be. I always know when I get there, however.[3]

[1] For an interesting account of a two-year search for a way of interesting an elementary school pupil in physical education, see Association for Supervision and Curriculum Development, National Education Association, *Toward Better Teaching* (1949 Yearbook; Washington, D.C.: The Association, 1949), pp. 21–22. Credited to Evelyn Johnson, Ethical Culture School, New York City.

[2] For an account showing a teacher's resourcefulness in helping a child overcome his adjustment problems by making use of materials with which he was especially adept, also see *Toward Better Teaching*, pp. 23–25. Credited to Angela Mensing, University School, Indiana University, Bloomington, Ind.

[3] *Ibid.*, p. 135. Credited to Mary T. Johnson, Jenny Lind School, Minneapolis, Minn. Reprinted by permission of the Association for Supervision and Curriculum Development.

Serving as a source of information. The creative teacher does much more than interpret textbook statements or answer factual questions to which learners could secure answers elsewhere. He makes available to each boy and girl all the information from his own experience that may aid in the development of interests and understandings. His special studies in college and university, his travel, his work experience, his participation in community affairs are particularly useful items of experience. A breadth of experiences and facility in sharing these with others are highly desirable qualifications of teachers.

Suggesting a variety of sources of information. The teacher not only needs information to be shared with pupils; he must be competent to direct learners to the wide variety of sources they need to consult in pursuing their goals. Furthermore, he is uniquely able to make arrangements for the group to use many aids. The teacher occupies an important liaison position between pupils and librarians, school administrators, community agencies, and other resources. In fact, one of the essential services of teachers is that of directing individual learners to the most effective aids available in terms of the individuals' needs.

Pupils as Resources for Each Other

The importance of interpersonal relationships in learning has already been dwelt upon in this book. In general, we may conclude that the character of the relationships between the people involved in the learning situation has more to do with the nature and quality of learning than any other single factor. This conclusion challenges the teacher to arrange the human elements of the situation in such a way as to bring about optimum learning. To meet this challenge, he needs a maximum of information about pupils' likes and dislikes of each other as well as a maximum of skill in using this information to organize effective working groups. He needs insight into the changing emotional climate too. In addition to the use of interpersonal relations in motivation and in grouping, there are certain specific techniques whereby the teacher may help boys and girls serve as resources for each other. Some of these techniques are described in the following paragraphs.

Using pairs of learners. Many goal-seeking activities can be carried on by pairs of learners. Work by pairs is particularly effective for such purposes as the following:

1. Practice on some skill in which one learner can check the other: spelling; oral arithmetic drill; association of words and definitions; paraphrasing reading material; question-and-answer exercises

2. Explanation of processes by one learner who has mastered these to another who has not
3. Comparison of information about a particular topic or question from two or more sources
4. Checking each other's written materials such as tests, work type of exercises, maps, graphs, drawings
5. Preparing tabulations of class attendance, participation, money collections, and similar matters

Since poor choice of pairs results in ineffective work, it is most important that the teacher be on the alert to discover factors in pairings which make for unhappy or inefficient work together. Pupils' own choices are usually the best guides to initial pairings, although there may be frequent reason for change of pairs; also, the purposes for which learners are paired should result in different choices.

Using the unusual experiences of individual learners for helping others. Particularly with older children, the wide range of experiential backgrounds provides a variety of resources within the learning group. Travel and work experiences are particularly fruitful sources of information. The skillful teacher polls the class very frequently to find out which pupils have had experiences relating to people and places and processes under discussion, and draws out ideas, impressions, and information which stimulate and answer the questions of other pupils. Again insight into the interpersonal relations of the group is significant: too little or too much recognition of an individual may detract from the telling of his experience; overlooking some individual's experience may harm teacher-pupil relations.

Using special competences of individuals for helping others. The need for special competences in classrooms is as varied as the types of goal-seeking activities. In addition to the help that individuals can give because of their previous contacts with persons, places, and processes, many pupils have special skills which can be demonstrated to others. Thus special skills in music, art, writing, photography, woodwork, ceramics, athletics, dramatics, and all other "doing" areas of the school program are widely used to stimulate and guide development of skills on the part of other learners. Other competences and facilities of individuals which may be used to advantage for the entire learning group are: operation of special machines and tools; identification of unusual birds, plants, and other nature items; collections of a wide variety; training in various areas, such as art, that is far more specialized than the training offered by the school.

Use of special roles in group learning situations. Special competences are definitely to be considered in the selection of pupils for the
various roles in group discussion and other activities: chairman, recorder,
reporter, observer, and so forth. Although an important function of
group learning situations is to develop these competences in a maximum
number of learners, the wise teacher helps the group to develop standards for special roles which ensure adequate practice for pupils who demonstrate reasonable skill. The following account indicates that even third-
graders can acquire discrimination in the choice of other learners for
special roles:

> During this year about fourteen of our third-graders formed a
> "Book Club." These fourteen had become so proficient in their read-
> ing, both in oral reading and in comprehension, that it no longer
> seemed advisable to keep them in a supervised group.
>
> We met together and decided that each child could select stories
> to read to the group, that these stories should be as interesting as
> possible, and that we would meet daily to hear them. One of the chil-
> dren wanted to know how we could decide who was to read each day.
> Another suggested that we elect a chairman to decide this since her
> mother had been chairman of a grown-up club and had decided many
> things. The others agreed to elect a chairman for this purpose.
>
> The first election turned out to be one of those affairs where each
> votes for his best friend. The popular boy who had been chosen se-
> lected his readers for the following day and so we began.
>
> As time went on we learned that the harmony of the group depended
> a great deal on the chairman. If he were fair by giving each a chance
> to read, if he remembered a story that hadn't been finished, and if
> he were tactful when suggesting a story was too long, then our group
> had a pleasant and relaxing time. If he selected only a few of his
> close friends, and if he were abrupt in his suggestions, then the period
> became a waste of time and caused unhappy feelings. It was apparent
> that all enjoyed the pleasant meetings but none were content with
> the others. They began to realize that they could control the outcome
> of the meetings by careful selection of their leader.
>
> When the last election was held, remarks such as these were made:
> "Anne gives everybody a chance."
> "She always remembers when I haven't finished."

These were verbal evidences of the invisible criteria which had
evolved and proof that third-graders were beginning to recognize the
role of good leaders in promoting harmonious satisfying group experiences.[4]

---

[4] *Ibid.,* pp. 40–41. Credited to Joyce Williams, University School, Indiana University,
Bloomington, Ind. Reprinted by permission of the Association for Supervision and
Curriculum Development.

Use of learners for liaison with outside resources. Arrangements for use of community resources may frequently be expedited through help from individual learners. Thus, the teacher should be able to identify the pupil who can arrange through parents or other contacts for a particular resource person or a particular field trip. Although the teacher, the principal, or a class committee may conclude the final arrangements, a first inquiry made by a pupil who is personally connected with the adult involved may be both a good learning experience for this pupil and a help to the group.

School Personnel as Resources

Intelligent planning of learning experiences includes the selection and use of all school personnel who can help. The individual teacher can make use of his colleagues in at least two ways: first, in connection with their special responsibilities; second, by virtue of any unique resources their experiences provide.

As to special responsibilities, the possibilities of help depend on what personnel the school employs. Every school has an administrative head, the principal, who should be counted on to make community contacts, to secure facilities, and to help in arranging for the use of the school plant and its facilities. Every school has one or more persons responsible for custodial services, who can be most helpful in assisting with problems connected with various uses of the classroom and other building facilities. A school secretary, if there is one, may be an invaluable source of help in doing the telephoning, corresponding, and other tasks involved in preparing for learning experiences outside the school.

If available, other special personnel may be fully used. Specialists in various curriculum areas, such as music, art, and physical education, bring information and skill to the class, especially at the elementary school level. In the most effective learning situations, these specialists are called on to help with activities related to units of work under way. In the departmentalized secondary school, teachers may call on colleagues in other departments to help with understandings needed at particular times. Thus the history teacher may need to ask the art and music specialists to help answer questions concerning the development of art and music at different periods.

Guidance workers, health personnel, librarians, and other such specialists are of great utility to the classroom teacher. Counselors, social workers, and nurses ordinarily work with individual pupils, but these persons may also give effective help to the entire learning group when some problem upon which they are especially informed is under consideration. Thus the counselor may be called upon for help with studies of occupations, the nurse with those of disease, and the social worker with family problems of the community.

Departmentalization, time schedules, and the related machinery of the large school tend to restrict a free use of special personnel as described in the preceding paragraphs. The flexibility of the smaller school makes possible exchanges of classes and other plans of teachers for sharing their resources. The large school, with its greater number of special personnel and resources, sometimes operates on such a mechanical basis as to make such sharing difficult. The time of special personnel can be and usually is scheduled so that these people may work with learning groups on a rotating basis, but such schedules interfere when a particular group wants help from some specialist at once.

A major need for flexibility in scheduling is to use individual faculty members as speakers or as interviewees, and in other ways to induce them to share their personal travel, work, or other unique experiences with learning groups. Such flexibility is frequently made possible by combining classes, by using substitute teachers, by letting groups work by themselves, and by exchanging teachers (to share experiences with the other's group). A way to use special competences can usually be found. The teacher simply has to know what helps are available in the school personnel and to call on these in relation to definite needs of the learning group. A sort of catalogue—in other words, a resource file—of special interests and experiences of faculty members is needed in large schools.

Boys and girls other than those in the class for which the teacher is planning may be especially qualified to give help with some questions. It is splendid recognition for older children, as well as excellent stimulation for younger ones, to have the former meet with younger classes and tell of interesting experiences. Consultation of teachers at different levels may identify individual pupils with unusual experience, such as foreign travel, that may be so utilized.

Community People as Resources

The possibilities of using community people as resource persons are limited only by the special competencies of the local citizens, and the ingenuity of school personnel in utilizing these competencies. Some of the ways in which people from the community may be utilized are as follows:

1. To speak to classes about questions or problems under study
2. To be interviewed by one learner or a small group of learners to secure information to be reported to the total group
3. To demonstrate some process or skill of special interest to the learning group

4. To show movies, slides, or other visual aids about some place or process with which this person is intimately acquainted
5. To guide a group of learners on a field trip so as to explain what is observed
6. To meet with a class after a field trip or demonstration or film to answer questions
7. To present issues or a point of view about issues which are of significance in the community and of interest to learners
8. To give expert guidance in the presentation of a play, the preparation of a mural, the composition of a school song, or related projects in which technical competence is essential
9. To help organize community surveys and other projects requiring special knowledge of one or more aspects of community life
10. To serve as a counselor throughout some extended study of specific community resources or problems

As teachers seek to utilize such services, particularly close observance of several criteria already listed is important:

1. Community resource persons should be selected in terms of their helpfulness for specific learning goals. The teacher's major problem here is to know what persons may be helpful for what purposes. Curriculum planning groups can be very helpful in this connection by maintaining active inventories, probably as a card file such as that illustrated in Figure 3. Also, resource units may anticipate the types of services which will be needed from the community and suggest possible sources of these services.

2. The contributions of community resource persons should be appropriate to the maturity of learners. This criterion has special significance in regard to the use of people, for the best-informed person may not be able to communicate his information to learners. Teachers need to know whether or not the prospective resource person can talk with the age group concerned in such a way that learners' understandings will follow. Accordingly, the file of resource persons should include some information about the experience prospective persons have had with different age groups.

3. The use of resource persons should make for efficient expenditure of learners' time. Although it is conceivable that resource persons might be found in the community to help with virtually every goal undertaken by pupils, the time involved in consulting some of these persons might be more wisely spent if some other source of information were employed. The use of pupil committees for interviewing may frequently be more

(front)

COMMUNITY RESOURCE PERSONS

Last Name   Title   First Name   Initial

Home Address   Phone No.

Business Address   Phone No.

. . . . . .

Topic(s) on which can help:

How?

. . . . . .

Record of Use

Date   Grade or Area   Teacher   Comments

OVER

(reverse)

Record of Use (continued)

Date   Grade or Area   Teacher   Comments

FIG. 3. SAMPLE CARD FOR INVENTORY FILE OF COMMUNITY RESOURCE PERSONS

economical than field trips by the entire learning group, but a clear explanation by the teacher may be more economical than, and as effective as, a series of committee reports. That is, the teacher will have to plan for an equitable distribution of learners' time in relation to the importance of goals, accessibility of resources, and the relative utility of available resources, including people.

SELECTION AND USE OF ENVIRONMENTAL RESOURCES

Environmental resources—that is, *places*—may be classified for convience in terms of their location as resources in the school environment, in the community, and outside the community. Consideration is given in this section to the selection and use of these resources in curriculum planning.

Resources in the School Environment

Unfortunately, a great many schools have only the most meager facilities in building and grounds. At the other extreme, some modern schools have a variety of special and general-purpose rooms fitted to serve multiple-learning needs, as well as extensive outside spaces in playgrounds, gardens, and farming areas. The range of available resources in the school plants of America makes generalization impossible. We may note a brief classification of possibilities which teachers could use for checking their own school environment.

General classrooms. Every school, whatever its level, has classrooms which can be used by learning groups for activities requiring no special or immovable equipment. Thus the great majority of rooms in elementary schools are grade classrooms, and many, if not most, rooms in high schools are adaptable for instruction in curriculum areas such as social studies, language arts, and mathematics, which do not involve immovable laboratory and mechanical equipment. Suggestions regarding the maintenance of a good learning environment in such classrooms were given in Chapter 6. We may emphasize the point here that whether or not the few facilities—blackboard, bulletin board, blank walls—that the classroom environment offers are used effectively, depends very largely on the classroom teacher. The blackboard may be a very important aid if used for recording daily plans, summaries of discussions, and records of group agreements, and for illustrating problems and procedures. The bulletin board and blank walls offer space that can be used (see Plate 30, page 451) for displays to motivate goal-seeking activities and also to present information in clippings, charts, pictures, and the like, to answer learners' questions. How even the most barren of rooms may be made into a learning situation with rich resources is illustrated by the following description of the reconversion of a basement room:

> Hopeless indeed did the situation seem as we stood in the doorway of that gloomy basement room. The seats were fixed to the floor. The lighting was inadequate, with too much blackboard space absorbing what little light there was. The room, absolutely barren of even bulletin boards, was disgustingly dingy and dirty, and the floors were so oily they were out of the question for small children.
>
> The principal promised all possible cooperation and lost no time in supplanting the fixed seats with small round tables and a variety of small chairs salvaged recently from a condemned building. The janitor splashed on some paint and that was our send-off.
>
> Books which had been kept in a glass cupboard were put down within reach on bright new green and yellow shelves of a new book corner. A collection of cast-off dolls, with a little face-lifting and attention to new wardrobes, came to life for six-year-olds. Not only did the principal share the enthusiasm and interest for the project, but he contributed his efforts to making a new doll's bunk bed and doing some work in toy surgery. From the lid of a discarded sandbox and some blocks the group made a stage. Paint and murals decorated the extra blackboard space. Thus first-graders participated in improving the physical setup of their room. It became a place where they felt they belonged because they had helped to remake it.[5]

Special-purpose rooms. The traditional elementary school had no rooms other than general classrooms, toilets, an office, and perhaps an auditorium. In addition to the general classrooms and all-school facilities, the modern elementary school has rooms fitted for such purposes as instruction in art, music, gymnasium, and shop; library; movie projection (although general classrooms may be equipped for the use of visual aids, too); instruction of physically handicapped children; medical, dental, and psychological examination and treatment; kitchen and dining room for small groups; and museums. The teacher in such a school must know the possibilities of these special facilities, and provide for thorough orientation of learners in the use of facilities available to individuals and groups. Use of these rooms for learning purposes should be governed by the same criteria as apply to other resources; that is, the special facility should offer some utility for particular learning goals, a utility that can be more effectively and efficiently supplied than by some other source.

High schools typically have a larger proportion of rooms fitted for

---

[5] *Ibid.*, p. 30. Credited to Eleanor Crenan, Harvey Alter School, Rome, N.Y. Reprinted by permission of the Association for Supervision and Curriculum Development.

special purposes: science laboratories, greenhouses, homemaking rooms, industrial arts shops, and so forth. Unfortunately, these rooms are frequently so tightly scheduled for classes in the curriculum areas concerned as to be unavailable for learning groups from other classes wishing to use special equipment, such as microscopes or saws, for some unusual purpose. However, resourceful teachers can arrange with considerate colleagues for special help to individual learners and small groups during work periods of classes regularly scheduled in these facilities. Plate 32 illustrates the use of an unscheduled room.

PLATE 32. USE OF UNSCHEDULED ROOM FOR SMALL-GROUP WORK. *A high school committee uses the home economics kitchen during an unscheduled period. (Courtesy North Phoenix, Arizona, High School)*

All-school facilities. The facilities usually used without respect to class organization and curriculum areas are the assembly rooms or the auditorium, the cafeteria or the lunchroom, and the corridors. Use of these facilities may be planned for instructional purposes in addition to those provided by total school assemblies and meals. The assembly room may be used by small groups for practice in speech, preparation of skits, and other learning experiences in which a stage and other "props" are desired. The cafeteria offers at least two types of special resources: first, its physical arrangement provides for round-table work by small groups that may be impossible in general classrooms; second, the preparation, selection, service, and consumption of food are processes studied in various learning experiences which may be investigated firsthand through the cafeteria. Even corridors are resources for learning: if properly lighted, they provide space for exhibits and displays, and also for conferences by small groups.

Such uses of these facilities are possible only if the school's policy permits full-time utilization of the places concerned. In view of the limited facilities of classrooms, it seems completely wasteful to restrict the use of the auditorium to weekly assemblies, or of the lunchroom to the noon meal, or of the corridors to the passage of classes. Resourceful teachers and administrators schedule full use of all facilities with due concern for the protection of property and maintenance of good working conditions.

School grounds. An ideal urban school plant should probably include not only adequate playground space but enough gardens and other land for children to learn firsthand about the growth of flowers, vegetables, and small animals. Such space is rare, and school authorities sometimes exclude children from those portions of the school grounds which do bear grass and flowers. Any school ground available may be used for at least one learning experience: its proper care and beautification. Wherever there is some cultivation of plant life, learning groups have this as an additional resource. The playground is properly considered as a resource not only for developing physical skills but as a strategic opportunity for learning experiences in personal relationships. Weather conditions permitting, the school grounds may also be used as meeting places for learning groups; discussions around the grass may be even more interesting than around the classroom!

Resources in the Community

Although the range of resources varies in proportion to community size, all but very small rural communities have some community institutions, business houses, and other places of interest in connection with learning enterprises. The large community generally constitutes a rich reservoir of resources for learning groups at all levels, as Plate 33 suggests. To illustrate the variety of resources available in the large metropolitan centers we may note the types of places suggested for field trips in certain resource units prepared by groups of teachers in the junior high school core program in the Dade County Schools, Miami, Florida:

PLATE 33. PUPILS LEARN ABOUT TRAINS FIRSTHAND. *(Courtesy Florida State Department of Education)*

1. "Agriculture in Dade County"
   School farm
   Hydroponics farm
   Packing house
   Dairy
   Tropical garden
   Tropical food research laboratory
   Seed store

2. "Government of Dade County"
   Crime Commission
   Board of Commissioners
   Board of Public Instruction
   County Court
   Health Department
   Sheriff's office
   Tax Assessor's office
   Circuit Court
   Game and Fish Warden's office
   Tax Collector's office

3. "Our Latin American Neighbors"
   Consulate corps (various Latin American countries)
   Latin American organizations
   Airways (serving Latin America)
   Steamship companies (serving Latin America)
   Manufacturing companies (from Latin American imports)
   Banana dealers
   Coconut enterprises
   Coffee roasters and distributors
   United States Government Departments (serving Latin America)
   Parks (for Latin American animals, birds, plants, and flowers)

4. "Manufacturing"
   Apparel manufacturers
   Food manufacturers
   Industries dependent on wood
   Ceramics—Plastics
   Heavy industry

5. "Communication"
   Radio broadcasting stations
   Television station
   Newspaper plants
   Telephone office
   Telegraph office
   Stores selling radio and television sets
   Post office
   Theater offices

These resource units were prepared only for junior high school grades and only a few units or topics particularly closely related to community interests in Miami and in Dade County (which includes Miami) are cited above. Obviously, the entire range of resources in this large community is much broader. However, the foregoing list illustrates how curriculum planning may anticipate use of the community in relation to particular units of work as well as indicating the opportunities available in a large community.

Two major types of problems in planning for the selection and use of community resources merit particular consideration. First, there is the difficulty of identifying places to which learners may be taken or directed. This is especially difficult in larger communities and for teachers who are not acquainted with the community. Curriculum planning in many metropolitan areas includes the preparation of guides to excursions. The type of information customarily included in such a guide is illustrated in the following sample page from an elementary curriculum guide:

NATURAL HISTORY AND SCIENCE

Fairchild Tropical Garden, located on Old Cutler Road just south of Matheson Hammock, Phone 87-3022. Can accommodate large groups. Will have guide available only if planned well in advance. No admission charge. Botanical Gardens of special interest to upper grades. "Rambler," 10¢ per child, carries 18 per trip. Follows trails for a 45-minute excursion. Museum with palm products from foreign countries—Java, Hawaii, Bali, etc., 10¢ per child.

Humane Society, 2101 N.W. 95th Street, Phone 7-2217. No admission charges. Mr. Pusey or guide available most any time. Of interest in the study of pets, public services, kindness to animals, care of animals, etc.

Junior Museum of Miami, Biscayne Boulevard and 26th Street, Phone 2-6461. One class or small group attendance desired. No admission charges. Interesting displays of products, relics, costumes, etc., from foreign countries. Displays changed frequently. Some live animals—rabbits, white mice, turtles, snakes, etc.

Matheson Hammock Trails, located on Old Cutler Road opposite the entrance to Matheson Hammock Beach. No limit on number of children. No admission charges. No guides available. Beautiful trail walks through native Florida hammock land. Many trees and shrubs are labeled. Good spot for a bird walk too. Make this one of the attractions when you go to Matheson Park for a picnic. Phone 87-4010, Superintendent.

Monkey Jungle, 22 miles south of Miami on Dixie Highway. Phone: Perrine dial 81, then dial 7-3511. Make arrangements ahead of time and guide will be furnished. Admission for children, 15¢. Should have one adult for about 6 or 7 children. Accompanying adults within number required not required to pay. Of interest to most any grade level for study of animals, monkeys, apes.

Musa Isle Indian Village, 1700 N.W. 25th Avenue, Phone 4-9915. No admission charges. Can accommodate larger groups preferably in the spring or fall—not in the busy winter season. Guide is available at all times. Of interest to any age group to see the Seminoles in native dress, Seminole houses, utensils, handcrafts, alligator wrestling, small zoo animals, birds, etc.

North Miami Zoo, 800 N.E. 132nd Street, Phone 89-9379. Can accommodate large number of children. Will furnish guide if planned well in advance, and give a special show. Price of admission is 15¢. Numerous animals of interest—wild, trained, tame. Special animal acts if previous arrangements are made.

Parrot Jungle, located on South Red Road, Phone 87-3636. Make arrangements ahead of time. Visits by larger school groups not too well favored during the busy winter season. Admission for children is 25¢. Adults pay full price unless other arrangements can be made with supervising personnel at Parrot Jungle offices. Of interest to most grade levels. Bird life of all kinds.[6]

[6] Dade County Public Schools, *Elementary Curriculum Guide* (Curriculum Bulletin No. 2; Miami, Fla.: The Schools, August, 1951), p. 76.

In addition to, or in lieu of such a system-wide guide, many individual schools have their own inventories of possible field trips. For example, a card file including such information as that quoted might be maintained. The individual teacher may also very profitably keep for his future guidance some record of field trips actually taken.

A second group of problems has to do with administrative aspects of field trips. Some of these problems are briefly discussed in the following paragraphs.

Entire group or small groups? Some field trips may be advisedly taken by the entire group of learners and others only by small groups. Policies of both the places to be visited and of the school as well as the learning values involved have to be considered. In several of the instances cited above, committees of learners might investigate different possibilities. Thus in connection with the unit on manufacturing the entire group could be divided into committees, one on each type of manufacturing listed. The committee on apparel manufacturing, for example, could visit certain apparel plants, secure information on the basis of a prearranged schedule of questions, and report this information back to the total group. Other committees on other types of manufacturing would operate similarly. This type of field work would have the advantages of economy, but many learners would miss the values of firsthand experience, and the teacher's personal guidance of committee field trips would be lacking. In actual practice, the schools for which these resource units were prepared used both small and total learning groups for field trips. Usually, the factors of the learners' interests and the need for teacher guidance determined the issue.

Time. Elementary groups taught by one teacher throughout the school day can take field trips with little difficulty. In the departmentalized secondary school, the situation is much different. Relatively few worth-while field trips can be taken in the typical forty- to fifty-minute period. Core classes have an advantage; in fact, the greater flexibility of the longer period is one of the chief advantages of the core program. Under the one period for a subject schedule, various expedients are used, none of which is an adequate solution for every situation. In the final analysis, teachers and others concerned must decide whether interruption of other activities is justified by the purposes of a field trip, and, if so, make the necessary schedule adjustments.

Costs and transportation. Many school systems provide school buses for field trips. Where they are not available, arrangements for private cars or public carriers must be made. Too frequently learners have to pay for transportation and other costs of field trips. If field trips are as valuable learning resources as books, for example, they should be paid for as a cost of free public education. Where tax support does not cover the costs of field trips, parents may aid with transportation, or funds may be produced on a group basis to avoid burdens for economically less-favored pupils.

Liability. Although the laws concerning school liability vary by states, any teacher (or other person) is always liable for the consequences of negligence. Hence planning of field trips should include every possible precaution for safety and every possible guarantee against negligence.

Resources beyond the Local Community

The same principles apply to the use of learning resources at places outside as apply to those inside the community environment. Use of these

PLATE 34. OUTDOOR RESOURCES AID LEARNING. *The outdoors offers learning experiences at all times. (Courtesy of the Clear Lake Camp, Battle Creek, Michigan, Public Schools)*

outside places is of more importance in small than in large communities since the range of community resources, in general, is in proportion to community size. Schools in rural communities have rich resources in land and its products but poor resources in institutional facilities. Urban schools, however, lack the resources of nature, and utilize various facilities to provide them: school-owned or privately owned farms, school camps, and field trips to farms, camps, parks, and other natural resources. Schools in rural communities need to make extensive use of longer field trips to nearby urban centers for studies of industry and government.

The problem of costs becomes acute in planning for the use of resources involving extended transportation. Since schools do not ordinarily provide budgets for such purposes, learning groups must usually tax their members (or their parents) or raise funds. The former procedure incurs all the economic and social problems which free public education seeks to minimize among learners. A variety of fund-raising projects are used to avoid these problems, and some, such as farm projects, clean-up campaigns, and sales of school products, may provide useful learnings. Thus teachers may make use of the motivational aspects of a future learning project to stimulate more immediate worth-while activities. However, in view of the many inappropriate fund-raising projects also employed, the basic criteria of relevancy, usability, and economy need to be applied to the fund-raising activities as well as to the field trips supported. It is questionable, for example, whether games of chance, door-to-door sales of commercial products, and competition for cash contributions conform to these criteria.

In this connection we should note the frequent practice of school-sponsored contests of various sorts which provide trips for winning contestants. These contests need to be judged, first of all, on their own merits as learning experiences. Unless they produce important new learnings or stimulate many boys and girls in desirable learning activities which would not otherwise be undertaken, their intrinsic value is to be questioned. If they do have such values, these must still be appraised in the light of the possible frustrations to be experienced by losing contestants. And if the contest itself is considered as valuable, the award must be evaluated also. If only one or a very few individuals get to make the trip, only these individuals are being served directly although arrangements can be made to provide a maximum sharing of experience. Schools are more frequently willing to sponsor contests between learning groups, with the trip awarded to be taken by an entire group. Plans can be made for a series of annual contests between groups, with each winning group eliminated from future contests so that over a period of years each group has the advantage of the trip award.

The learning values of trips taken by athletic teams, debating squads, musical organizations, and other groups may be overlooked because of the concentration on the objectives of interschool competition. Perhaps high schools are truly letting "the tail wag the dog" when various school groups make extended trips for interschool competition but spend all their time in travel and in the actual competition. If one day must be given for this purpose, perhaps a second day should be given for well-supervised and planned visits to points of interest. Although such plans are sometimes made, the necessity of a minimum absence from school may be overstressed. Perhaps some schools might find it profitable to experiment with applying some funds previously expended for interschool competition to a broadened program of field trips for all youth.

These problems of curriculum planning for the use of distant resources should not detract from the potential value of extended field trips. An ideal curriculum plan would probably provide for a traveling school, for the limitations of physical location are highly restrictive factors in experience. If learners could travel at will, the learning advantages of firsthand experience could be utilized wherever needed. Since learners cannot travel at will, wise curriculum planning will utilize distant resources whenever relevant, usable, and economical. Experiences in visiting the state capital, great natural resources, industrial plants, and similar objectives of most extended trips, should be sought for a maximum number of learners.

SELECTION AND USE OF PRINTED RESOURCES

Printed resources are classified for present purposes as follows: textbooks; newspapers, magazines, and other current materials; free and inexpensive materials; classroom library materials; school library materials; printed resources in home and community. Principles and problems of curriculum planning in regard to each of these types of resources are discussed in the following paragraphs.

Textbooks

The most widely used of the printed resources is the school textbook. Unfortunately, it is virtually the only printed resource used in too many learning situations. The weakness in such situations is not one inherent in the textbook. The problem is that varied materials are needed to provide for the individual differences of learners and perhaps by enrichment and illustration to help all pupils understand better even the most authoritative and well-written textbook. Good teachers everywhere will probably agree with the American Textbook Publishers Institute's definition of a modern textbook as "an assistant teacher in print." [7] The major criticism to be made of the use of textbooks is that one such "assistant teacher" is not enough for the variety of needs, interests, and abilities of the typical learning group. The solution, however, is to increase the effectiveness of the use of this resource and, wherever possible, to add other resources—not to do away with a most important resource.

Practices in the selection of textbooks vary widely in the United States. It is not within the scope of this book to present all the arguments which can be advanced for and against the usual systems of selection. In general, it seems that a competent teacher should have freedom to decide whether the needs of the learning situation require the use of a basal textbook (that is, the same book for each pupil); and, if so, what additional materials are required; or, if not so, what materials must be available—co-basal textbooks (that is, sets of different books) or non-textbook materials. With freedom to make this decision, teachers may find it advantageous to select particular books from some list already screened or adopted. In practice, textbooks are sometimes chosen by state or local authorities and distributed to classrooms without any consultation of teachers' preferences on the foregoing questions. In such situations there may still be freedom for teachers to select additional materials or even to arrange exchanges.

Authors, professional committees, and school systems have prepared extensive lists of criteria, scoring sheets, and other guides for selecting textbooks. Although these may be valuable in making selections, the teacher needs more than anything else to keep in mind the unique needs, interests, and abilities of the particular group of learners involved and the general curriculum goals planned for this group. The criteria stated earlier in this chapter may be restated as follows in relation to the selection of textbooks:

Relevancy. What textbooks contain maximum material which will help learners understand the various problems anticipated in the curriculum plan for this group?

Usability. What textbooks are most appropriate to the reading le els and general interests of the various members of the learning group What textbooks are most usable in terms of mechanical, but highly important, features such as table of contents, study aids, illustrations, glossary, index?

[7] American Textbook Publishers Institute, *Textbooks in Education* (New York: The Institute, 1949), p. 5. This publication should be interesting and worth-while reading for all teachers.

Accuracy. What textbooks offer greatest assurance of objective, scholarly presentation of facts and their interpretation?

Economy. What system (single, multiple, series) of textbooks offers the most economy without sacrifice of the foregoing principles? What particular books are most economical for the system decided upon?

The major principle of planning for the use of textbooks is the same as that for any other resource, namely, that the resource should be used as a source of help (information, stimulation of ideas, directions, and the like) for learners' own goal-seeking activities. Certain applications of this principle in regard to textbooks follow:

1. The teacher must be thoroughly familiar with the organization and contents of the book, and should plan adequate opportunity for pupils to learn how to make the most satisfactory and economical use of its various features.

2. Some plan for using the textbook in relation to the sequence of learning problems rather than to the internal organization of contents should be developed. For example, in using a chronologically organized history text for units of work not following a chronological sequence, there may need to be developed both an analysis (by pages) of content keyed to the units and some skeleton of chronology (a time chart, for example) for cross reference.

3. In the event that more than one textbook in some curriculum area is used for a particular learning group, the teacher must know the particular features of each sufficiently well to ensure the distribution of books which is most appropriate to the learners concerned. Frequent exchanges of books and the use of more than one book by individual learners may need to be planned.

4. The modern textbook is replete with teaching and learning aids: study exercises, suggested learning experiences, tests, and so on. The teacher should devise ways and means of making the most effective use of these aids in accordance with the goals and other resources of the learning group.

5. The teacher has a particular function in guiding the use of textbooks in order to develop sound study practices. Simple, uniform page assignments violate principles of learning. When pupils are directed to a section of a textbook there needs to be careful attention to the proper use of the contents, including all graphic materials, of the section. For example, the relation of illustrations to textual material, the system of headings, paragraph structure, the significance of italics and boldface type, numbered lists, marginal glossaries, and other items may need

careful explanation and discussion in terms of the information being sought.

6. Use of the textbook in relation to other resources must be planned for. How the textbook material relates to a field trip or film or class discussion needs explanation if learners are to organize their learnings. Comparison of text contents with information in reference books and other sources should be planned to ensure the development of important learning processes.

Study and Testing Materials

In general such materials as problem workbooks and study guides have about the same advantages and limitations as textbooks. Curriculum planning should not assume the use of such materials on a uniform basis. Their major usefulness, along with teacher-prepared outlines, tests, and check lists, is in terms of the needs of individual learners. Thus some pupils need more practice than others in developing a skill and may profitably make use of work materials for drill. Tests and check lists may be very helpful to learners for evaluating their own progress and planning further learning steps. Since good evaluation is itself a learning process, any evaluative aid may be an aid to learning.

Adequate curriculum planning should include the preparation of such study and testing materials as may be needed in connection with specific units of work. In general, such materials are best prepared by the teacher for the particular learning group concerned, although the resource unit may include samples of possible materials.

Classroom Library Materials

Planning for the selection and use of materials for the classroom library must be done in terms of such practical factors as classroom storage space and facilities for materials, funds for the purchase of classroom materials, and school policies regarding the relationship of the central school library and classroom collections. Best practices usually make the following provisions:

1. Adequate shelves, cupboards, or other facilities permit the storage of such materials in the classroom as are appropriate to the learners and curriculum areas concerned.

2. The materials budget includes an allocation for classroom libraries sufficient to provide in each classroom the materials that are needed there on a relatively permanent basis, and an allocation for the central library sufficient to provide duplicate collections of items that may be desired in more than one classroom for an extended period.

3. Most, if not all, materials are acquired and accounted for by

the central library, which is also responsible for arranging transfers and loans from classroom to classroom.

Unfortunately, such provisions are lacking in many schools. Space in many classrooms is completely taken by desks and chairs. Many elementary schools have no sort of central library. School funds frequently provide no allocations or very inadequate allocations for classroom libraries. Under such conditions, teachers have to use the most feasible expedients. How one teacher overcame the problem of a lack of budget, and made an excellent learning experience out of the development of a classroom library, is described by this teacher in the following statement quoted in *Toward Better Teaching:*

> Knowing that materials for this class could not possibly be ordered in advance, I wrote on the booklist under the subject, General English: "Materials' rental fee to be decided upon in the classroom." Therefore, the group bought no books for my class before the opening of school.
>
> Thruout the early weeks, during the period of exploration, no materials were purchased. We called upon the resources of the library for reading material we used during the time of personal exploration.
>
> When goals were set and the group began to see that one text could not serve all, I took up the question of the materials' rental fee. I suggested that since we would need many different kinds of materials in our classroom, and since this material could not be prescribed in advance or bought at one time, we would need a common fund from which to buy our supplies.
>
> The group made decisions concerning the amount each would pay into the pool. They based their calculations upon the total amount they would pay for materials in any other English class where they would be required to buy an English handbook, a literature book, and a dictionary. They decided that three dollars would be a fair sum for each to pay into a common treasury to be used by all in a way the group saw fit.
>
> The budgeting of this money to buy materials to serve all needs was not easy. The amassing of materials became a cooperative experience for the group. They decided upon the magazines that they would order for the classroom library; they wrote their own letters of order. They went to the bookstores and selected many of their own books. Committees saw previews of movies at the university film library and made selections for the class. Groups were commissioned to select recordings at radio shops. The dispersing of materials was also an educational experience for those who set up the classroom library or made sales talks or arranged bulletin boards to advertise wares.
>
> Of course our meager seventy-two dollars would not have supplied

us adequately had we not found materials that did not have to be purchased.

I had in my classroom an accumulation of handbooks in English, of literature books, of dictionaries, of workbooks. A committee of pupils went thru the workbooks and clipped drill sheets on errors prevalent among the group. These sheets were filed according to error —verb forms, case, agreement—so that an individual might quickly select drills designed to meet his needs in mechanics.

The school library and the university library were generous in allowing us to borrow books and place them on our classroom shelves as long as they were needed by a number of the group. During the study of vocations, we had several shelves of vocational books in our room. However, since one of the aims of the group was to learn the effective use of the library, they did not bring to classroom shelves all of the books they needed. They went to libraries, within the school and without, to select their own reading material.

We made use of other sources of free material, distributed by radio broadcasting systems, by audio-visual education houses, by vocational centers, by state and national departments.

The group also made decisions concerning the dispersing of accumulated materials in the spring. It is significant that in late October the class decided to divide among themselves the materials they had amassed; in May, they decided to leave their materials to other classes that might use them profitably.[8]

The types of materials to be selected for a classroom library should be determined with respect to the criteria previously stated, as well as in accordance with such practical factors as those discussed above. The types of materials to be considered include:

Supplementary textbooks
General reference books
Any materials usually kept in school libraries
Current materials
Free and inexpensive materials
Materials from home and community

The classroom library is essentially a flexible collection of the materials useful in connection with particular purposes of the learning group. Classroom library materials are unique only in respect to location. More specific problems and principles regarding each type of material are discussed in other divisions of this section on "printed resources."

[8] Association for Supervision and Curriculum Development, *op. cit.*, pp. 71–72. Credited to Elizabeth Rose, Tuscaloosa High School, Tuscaloosa, Ala. Reprinted by permission of the Association.

School Library Materials

The school library can be an invaluable resource for learners. Here should be found adequate general reference books, current periodicals, a collection of books to give information on a wide variety of topics and to serve the great range of interests among learners, and perhaps files of "fugitive materials" arranged according to some topical index. Teachers and librarians need to do a great deal of cooperative planning to ensure the selection of materials which will serve the instructional needs of all learning groups, and also to ensure the equitable sharing of materials to meet these needs. Many aids in the form of annotated and graded lists of materials are available for the selection process.

Planning for the effective use of school library materials must anticipate available procedures. These procedures include the possibilities described in the following paragraphs.

Library orientation. Learning groups need frequent orientation to the use of the library, not only in general terms, but for specific instructional purposes. Both teachers and librarians are needed in these orientation activities.

Loan of materials to classrooms. When an entire class is working on an instructional unit for which most or all related materials are housed in the library, these materials can best be loaned as a classroom library collection to be used in the classroom. As pointed out already, practical factors sometimes make such an arrangement impossible.

Group reading periods in the library. Under some conditions, the entire learning group may spend some periods in the library in addition to orientation periods. When a unit is being initiated, there may be need to browse through materials in the library to identify questions and sources. Periods of free reading may be desirable for recreation, for the identification of pupil interests, and for the strengthening of independent reading habits. Ordinarily it is more convenient for everyone concerned to have the class spend such periods in the library than to move all the materials desired to the classroom.

Work by small groups in the library. Small groups at work on different problems in connection with some large unit will frequently need to search for information in library materials. Curriculum planning should establish procedures whereby such groups can work in the library during work periods of the total group.

Use of the library by individual pupils. As pupils are carrying on their goal-seeking activities, questions will arise whose answers will have to be found in library materials. More effective learning will result if the individual can consult a proper source in either the classroom or the school library at once, rather than have to wait for some scheduled library period. Also, schedules should facilitate reading of books and other materials for individual interests by arrangements for checking out books for use at home as well as in free reading periods.

Newspapers and Magazines

Newspapers and magazines may be kept in either or both the school library and the classroom library or may be secured only as occasion arises. Whatever the arrangement, the importance of these current materials, at both child and adult levels, should be recognized in curriculum planning. In the first place, a considerable share of the adult reader's time is spent in reading newspapers and magazines, and learners need to acquire facility and discrimination in selecting and using these materials. In the second place, current materials are valuable means of stimulating goal-seeking activities as well as important sources, in fact the major sources, of information on current topics.

The foregoing purposes for the use of current materials in the curriculum should be reflected in the plans made for their selection and usage. Thus as early as boys and girls can read adult newspapers and magazines—and they read them very early at home—these children need to be given help in the proper use of the materials. Proper planning of the use of newspapers and magazines for motivation of learning involves the preparation of interesting and appropriate displays. The frequently drab and uninteresting bulletin board with its assorted clippings and the disorderly magazine rack can be avoided by a little care and thought.[9] The use of magazines and newspapers as sources of information needs to be directed with careful attention to the criteria of *usability* and *accuracy*. That is, many adult newspapers and magazines are too mature for younger learners, and the bias of authors, reporters, and editors is always a possibility to be reckoned with.

Free and Inexpensive Materials

The term "free and inexpensive materials" is widely used to cover a great variety of pamphlets, bulletins, and monographs published by pro-

---

[9] See "The Room Display Area," in Lucien Kinney and Katharine Dresden (eds.), *Better Learning through Current Materials* (Stanford University, Calif.: Stanford University Press, 1952), for helpful suggestions on displays, bulletin boards, etc. This entire volume should be very helpful in the teacher's planning for effective selection and use of resources.

fessional, governmental, commercial, and various special-interest agencies. These materials are sometimes produced in the interest of the group concerned and may be somewhat one-sided. At the same time such materials are frequently rich resources both because of their attractive format and composition and their timeliness. Also, "one-sided" materials are resources for developing discrimination in reading. For all these reasons, the proper selection and use of free and inexpensive materials is an essential process of curriculum planning.

The problems involved in the use of these materials are so great that some school systems have adopted criteria for the selection of free and inexpensive materials. In some cases, materials must be screened by some committee before being used in the classroom. In the absence of such provisions, individual teachers should use some of the various services available as a guide to selecting free or inexpensive materials. Some of these services are as follows:

> *Standard Catalog for High School Libraries* with semi-annual supplements published by H. W. Wilson Company, New York, lists pamphlets under Dewey decimal classification.
> *Booklist,* published monthly by American Library Association, Chicago, includes lists of free and inexpensive materials and government publications.
> *NEA Journal,* published monthly, September–May, by the National Education Association, Washington, D.C., includes a section on free and inexpensive materials.
> *School Life,* published monthly, October–June, by the United States Office of Education, Washington, D.C., includes a section on government publications of special educational interest.
> *Educators' Index to Free Materials* published annually by Educators Progress Service, Randolph, Wisconsin, gives an annotated list of free charts, films, maps, exhibits, etc.
> *Free and Inexpensive Learning Materials,* published occasionally by the Division of Surveys and Field Services, George Peabody College for Teachers, Nashville, Tennessee, lists selected pamphlets and other materials by topics.

Various journals of professional organizations in subject fields also list free and inexpensive materials in the respective fields.

Probably the most important step in curriculum planning for the use of free and inexpensive materials is the actual examination of these materials by teachers. It is not surprising that learners find little usefulness in some materials for which this step is neglected.

Printed Resources in Home and Community

In curriculum planning teachers sometimes ignore the wealth of books and other printed materials available in home and community. The bookmobile is one such resource for many schools. Although materials at home cannot be relied on for all learners, full advantage should be taken of the home libraries in which some learners may have additional challenging and interesting reading. Also, learners may be encouraged to bring books and magazines to school for sharing with others.

PLATE 35. BOOKMOBILES BRING RESOURCES FOR LEARNING. *Pupils' reading can be aided by many types of library resources. (Courtesy of the Association for Supervision and Curriculum Development, National Education Association)*

Community libraries are rich resources for learning groups, particularly those for whom school libraries are inadequate or lacking. Usually arrangements can be made with community libraries to secure materials desired for pupils' use. In some communities, these materials may be loaned to teachers in considerable quantities, or arrangements may be made for an entire learning group to visit the library to withdraw materials. In any event individual learners can be encouraged to use the community library for special-interest purposes. A prerequisite to wise planning with respect to the community library is a firsthand knowledge of its resources by the teacher.

SELECTION AND USE OF AUDIO-VISUAL RESOURCES

A growing body of professional literature gives specific information about the many types of audio-visual resources available for school use.

(See appropriate references at the end of this chapter.) Most agencies which distribute such resources—distribution centers of school systems, museums, audio-visual libraries, film and other rental agencies—provide catalogues and other information to be considered in the selection and use of the materials concerned. Here we shall merely call attention to the variety of audio-visual resources to be considered in curriculum planning and certain applications of the basic criteria for selecting and using all resources.

Pictures, Slides, and Filmstrips

Collections of pictures, both in color and in black and white, may be prepared by pupils and teachers as useful resources for present and future learning. Pictures on a great variety of topics may be clipped from a number of popular magazines. To be usable, these pictures should be mounted, classified, and filed according to subject headings similar to the titles of units of work. Both classroom and central school collections are useful.

The criterion of *accuracy* is especially important in the selection of pictures, since distorted, one-sided, or untrue concepts may result from a single picture that fails to tell the whole story or misrepresents what it does tell. This caution is particularly applicable to the attractive pictures appearing in the advertisement sections of magazines. Series of pictures and contrasting pictures on the same topic are most hepful.

Slides may be prepared or rented or borrowed from distribution agencies. Like pictures, they have extensive utility in learning. Filmstrips are not as flexible as slides, since the former have to be shown in a fixed series but have the advantage over films in that the operator may pause to discuss any frame as the strip is projected.

Various types of projection equipment may be used for showing slides, filmstrips, and pictures on the projection screen. The opaque projector, which will project any flat object that fits into the projector, is a particularly usable resource. Children's own work as well as pictures and printed material may be used in this projector. Several types of equipment for projecting slides and filmstrips are available. Slides and filmstrips and equipment for their projection offer the advantage of considerable economy over motion pictures.

Exhibit Pieces

Collections, relics, specimens, models, and other items brought from home, bought from commercial agencies, or loaned by museums, serve valuable instructional purposes. Generally, these items are used in connection with the preparation of exhibits and displays, which serve both to stimulate learning and to provide information. Problems of space, storage, and preservation of these materials are sometimes acute. Unless a central school museum is practicable, probably it is best to prepare exhibits or displays when needed and then to return the pieces to the original sources.

Maps, Globes, and Charts

A great variety of maps, globes, and charts are available from commercial agencies. These need to be selected with particular concern for their practicability in the classroom situation as well as for their appropriateness to learners' maturity. Fixed equipment has the disadvantage of taking up needed space when not in use. Central school facilities for the storage of maps, globes, and charts seem desirable, provided these can be readily and easily moved into classrooms when need arises. Wise curriculum planning will make available a number of the most relevant, usable, and accurate maps, globes, and charts, and provide teachers with adequate information about the availability and use of these materials.

Motion Pictures

Possibly the most widely used—and also the most misused—audio-visual resource is the motion picture. Lack of careful planning and problems of distribution frequently result in the showing of films to learning groups without relation to the classroom experiences and maturity levels of the pupils. In fact, every criterion for selecting and using resources is violated by practices which permit the uneconomical use of learners' time in seeing films irrelevant to their goals, inappropriate to their interests, or inaccurate in film content. It clearly behooves teachers to plan carefully for the wise use of a most valuable resource which can so easily be completely misused.

The selection of films is helped by curriculum guides which suggest relevant film resources. In the absence of such guides, the teacher may be aided by annotated guides to films prepared by the distribution agencies. There is no adequate substitute for a preview of the film by the teacher concerned. In using the film, various steps may need to be planned for, but essentially they are like those in connection with any other learning experience: (1) the formulation of questions to be answered—that is, learning goals; (2) the goal-seeking activity of seeing the films; and (3) the reviewing of questions against information to evaluate the learning experience and plan the next steps. Properly used, the film is perhaps the resource which can give to the largest number of learners the most intelligible information on the greatest variety of problems in the shortest period of time. Hence we may well hope to see its proper use greatly expanded.

Recordings and Transcriptions

In addition to the usual phonograph records widely used in music and rhythms, several other types of recorded resources are available. Transcriptions of radio programs make possible the repetition of the program at more convenient times and as frequently as desired. Recordings of dramatizations, stories, poetry, and historical events are commercially available. Various recording devices owned by schools now make possible the recording of learners' own voices as well as of events in school and community. Tape recordings of classroom sessions, speeches, assembly programs, and the like, may serve many purposes. These resources offer excellent help for learning experiences in almost every curriculum area. University bureaus, schools, and school systems maintain libraries of records and recordings, frequently as a part of a complete resource center. If such libraries are not available, teachers will have to make selections from whatever listings they can find. Again, the curriculum guide should give maximum direction to the selection and use of recordings and transcriptions, along with other learning resources.

Radio and Television

Radio and television are resources of unique significance both because of their inherent values and because of their possible uses both in and out of school. Curriculum planning for in-school use has the practical problem of utilizing broadcasts at scheduled times which may or may not coincide with convenient times in the school schedule. The primary problem in directing out-of-school use is the difficulty of controlling learners' home schedules. Perhaps the major end to be sought with regard to out-of-school radio and television is cooperative planning with parents as to appropriate programs for children and youth.

The selection and use of in-school programs involves considerable day-by-day study of program announcements. Frequently some program can be found that bears directly on current units of work, and the daily program, especially in nondepartmentalized work, can be adjusted accordingly. Some school systems and broadcasting stations arrange programs in series for use in schools, and plans for instructional units may be built around such series. One effective way of using broadcasts (and telecasts) is through small groups or through individuals, who hear or see a program and report to the total learning group in the same way as might be done with respect to work in the library or a field trip. This plan is particularly useful for out-of-school programs.

HELPS IN SELECTING AND USING RESOURCES

The individual teacher may find it an impossible task to be thoroughly informed on all the resources dealt with in this chapter and hence may not be expected on his own initiative alone to make wise selection and adequate use of all resources. To help him, one or more of several plans may be provided.

The Resource Center

Some school systems group certain types of resources into one location or center. There the services of a coordinator of materials (sometimes audio-visual materials) may be provided, and there such facilities as the following are housed:

1. Collection of sample textbooks and library materials
2. Catalogues and other guides to other printed materials
3. Vertical files of "fugitive" materials
4. Professional reading materials
5. Sample supplies and equipment
6. Audio-visual aids distribution center
7. Informative materials about community resources
8. Space for demonstrations and experiments with new supplies and equipment

Such resource centers may even be possible in the larger individual school. Teachers who have access to such a center for selecting learning resources should be able to provide rich resources for their groups.

Curriculum Guides and Resource Units

As we noted earlier, one of the chief values of the written curriculum guide is its array of suggestions regarding learning resources. As also stressed in Chapter 12, the resource unit, dealing as it does with a single large problem, is primarily a guide to the learning experiences and resources related to the problem. Hence these printed helps, where available, should be relied upon as aids in selecting and using learning resources in relation to curriculum areas and units of work.

Guides to Specific Resources

In the absence of either or both the resource center and written curriculum guides, the teacher may receive help from various types of guides to specific resources. Thus audio-visual handbooks, guides to excursions, files of resource persons' names and addresses, and catalogues of museum and library collections may be very helpful. The difficulty in using such guides arises from the fact that a teacher has to consult so many different sources to learn about the possible resources available on a single topic. The resource unit offers the real advantage of a single list of the various related resources. Probably the best plan is a combination of resource units on single topics and of guides to specific resources regarding topics for which resource units are not available.

Evaluation Guides

Useful curriculum guides will probably include some type of check lists for evaluating resources. Various types of evaluative criteria and check lists are available in the professional literature, and some distribution agencies provide evaluation guides with each resource such as a film. The curriculum planning group and even the learning group should probably develop some type of guide for evaluating various resources. The form of such a guide is illustrated in Figure 4. Use of evaluative materials and discussions in connection with specific resources, especially field trips, speakers, films, and other resources occupying considerable time for an entire learning group, helps learners to organize their own learning and also provides guidance for future use of the resource by other groups.

For Further Study

American Textbook Publishers Institute, *Textbooks in Education*. New York: The Institute, 1949.

Traces the history of the textbook in American education and gives various items of information about textbooks.

Arbuthnot, May Hill, *Children and Books*. Chicago: Scott, Foresman & Company, 1947.

Analysis of books for children from two years through junior high school age. A very helpful aid for book selection.

Association for Supervision and Curriculum Development, National Education Association, *Toward Better Teaching*. 1949 Yearbook. Washington, D.C.: The Association, 1949.

————, *Creating a Good Environment for Learning*. 1954 Yearbook. Washington, D.C.: The Association, 1954.

These two yearbooks contain many fine illustrations of effective use of resources.

Bathurst, Effie G., *Where Children Live Affects the Curriculum*. U.S. Office of Education Bulletin, 1950, No. 7. Washington, D.C.: Government Printing Office, 1950.

Shows by illustrations how the community affects the curriculum.

Resource (Name, title, or other identifying information)

Grade or area for which evaluated   Name of person evaluating

Title (s) of unit of work or learning experience for which evaluated

EVALUATION

Criteria	Rating				
	EXCEL-LENT	GOOD	AVERAGE	POOR	UNDE-SIRABLE

I. RELEVANCY
  A. Relates to the unit
  B. Covers the unit broadly
  C. Is up-to-date
  D.
  E.
  etc.					

II. USABILITY
  A. Can be secured readily
  B. Appropriate for learners
  C. Can be used easily
  D.
  E.
  etc.					

III. ACCURACY
  A. Information seems true
  B. Bias is absent
  C. Avoids ambiguity
  D.
  E.
  etc.					

IV. ECONOMY
  A. Fits maximum number of learners
  B. Involves minimum waste of time in use
  C. Cost is consistent with potential value
  D.
  E.
  etc.					

FIG. 4.   FORM OF A CHECK LIST FOR EVALUATING LEARNING RESOURCF⁻
To be expanded and adapted for different types of resources

Dale, Edgar, *Audio-Visual Methods in Teaching*. Rev. Ed. New York: The Dryden Press, 1954.

A comprehensive treatment of the "why," "what," and "how" of audio-visual resources.

Department of Elementary Principals, National Education Association, *Elementary School Libraries Today*. Thirtieth Yearbook of the Department. Washington, D.C.: The Association, September, 1951.

Collection of articles on practices and problems in all phases of organizing and maintaining elementary school libraries.

Division of Surveys and Field Services, George Peabody College for Teachers, *Free and Inexpensive Learning Materials*. Nashville, Tenn.: The Division, various dates.

Annotated, classified list of materials; reissued every few years.

Florida State Department of Education, *The Audio-Visual Way*. Bulletin No. 22B. Tallahassee: The Department, January, 1948.

Good example of a comprehensive state bulletin on audio-visual resources.

Kinder, James S., *Audio-Visual Materials and Techniques*. New York: American Book Company, 1953.

A comprehensive treatment, replete with illustrations and specific suggestions, of the use of audio-visual resources.

Kinney, Lucien, and Katharine Dresden, *Better Learning through Current Materials*. 2d ed.; Stanford University, Calif.: Stanford University Press, 1952.

Very helpful suggestions on the selection and use of current materials, defined to include a wide range of resources. Based on experimentation in California.

Levenson, William B., *Teaching through Radio*. New York: Rinehart & Company, Inc., 1945.

Helpful materials on school broadcasts and the use of radio programs in the classroom.

Miles, John R., and Charles R. Spain, *Audio-Visual Aids in the Armed Services—Implications for American Education*. Washington, D.C.: American Council on Education, 1947.

Reviews the training aids used in the military service during World War II and summarizes their implications for civilian education.

National Society for the Study of Education, *Audio-Visual Materials of Instruction*. Part I, Forty eighth Yearbook of the Society. Chicago: The University of Chicago Press, 1949.

The educational values, uses, problems, and types of audio-visual materials.

———, *Education in Rural Communities*. Part II, Forty first Yearbook of the Society. Chicago: The University of Chicago Press, 1952.

See Chapter XI for an annotated list of publications, audio-visual materials, and other aids dealing with problems of rural schools.

Olson, Edward G., *School and Community Programs*. New York: Prentice-Hall, Inc., 1949.

Reports of successful practices in school and community relations, including use of many community resources.

Southern States Work Conference on Educational Problems, *Teaching Materials in the Modern School*. Gainesville, Fla.: The Conference, 1950.

Chapter I gives detailed suggestions for using a wide variety of instructional materials.

"The Textbook in America: A Symposium," *Saturday Review of Literature,* 35: 13–70 (April 19), 1952.

Collection of articles from various viewpoints regarding the place of the textbook in American education.

Walraven, Margaret Kessler, and Alfred L. Hall-Quest, *Teaching through the Elementary School Library*. New York: The H. W. Wilson Company, 1948.

Helps for elementary teachers in using library materials and facilities.

purpose of classroom research and experimentation is to determine problem solutions in which there can be a higher degree of confidence.

To summarize, classroom research and experimentation is the process of securing evidence regarding problems of a particular classroom, evidence based on tryout of procedures which are hoped will make for better education in these classrooms. Such experimentation is an essential step in curriculum planning and an important phase of the teacher's planning and execution of his responsibilities. Every successful teacher is constantly experimenting; the job of curriculum planning is to improve the quality of such experimentation and to increase the number of teachers interested and competent in experimentation. The teacher who experiments grows—he will do a better job of planning and teaching because he experiments.

The Steps in Classroom Experimentation

Four steps are involved in classroom experimentation: defining the problem; formulating a tryout solution; gathering data about the tryout solution; and reaching conclusions from the data. Each of these steps is briefly explained in the following paragraphs, and later illustrated by three examples of classroom experimentation.

Defining the problem. Although procedures are sometimes tried out without specific identification of the problem, there is invariably some reason behind experimentation. This reason—quite generally a dissatisfaction with the present situation—constitutes the background of the problem. To facilitate experimentation the reason needs to be stated as a specific question for investigation. Thus the teacher who wants to experiment with a new arrangement of pupils' chairs because he thinks discussion processes are poor may need to analyze the problem more carefully before stating possible solutions. Is the problem for investigation to determine the cause of the present situation regarding discussion, or what will produce a better situation? Is it desired to prove that some different seating arrangement is better or that it brings about better discussion? Or is it simply desired to find a seating arrangement in which the quality and extent of discussion is better without attempting to prove cause and effect?

Formulating a tryout solution. Once the specific question for investigation is identified, a tryout solution or hypothesis can be verbalized. Actually, the nature of the solution projected may determine the statement of the problem. In the example just cited we may assume that the teacher defined the problem as one of finding a seating arrangement in which the quality and extent of discussion would be improved. Thus the problem is not to establish that a single technique will or will not improve discussion but to find a situation in which discussion is improved. The formulation of a hypothesis is then a matter of selecting some seating arrangement for tryout. The teacher has a "hunch" that discussion will be better in some circular seating arrangement. To test this "hunch" he will need to state the proposed solution more definitely. As he considers the matter, he decides that better discussion would occur with a single row of chairs in a circular arrangement than occurs with the present seating arrangement in fixed rows. This is a possible solution that can definitely be tried out.

Gathering data about the tryout solution. In order for conclusions to be reached about the proposed solution to a problem, there must be evidence. Evidence or data gathering is at the heart of experimentation, and is usually the most difficult step. In the example we have been describing the teacher might be satisfied to draw evidence from sheer observation of discussion under the new arrangement. Although he might be content with such evidence, we would question the degree of confidence one could have in a conclusion based wholly on one person's observation. A more careful planning of his data gathering would involve planned observations of a specific nature under both seating arrangements. If he wished to reach generalizations applicable to other groups, the experiment would have to be planned so as to yield quantitative data that could be treated statistically to show significance of the results for the population of which this group is a sample. Thus data might be gathered about the range and extent of individual participation under both arrangements.

Reaching conclusions from the data. The process of reaching conclusions is difficult because of the frequent inadequacy of evidence. However, if sweeping generalizations are not sought, this step may be less complex than it is frequently feared to be. We may suppose that the teacher to whom we have been referring found that the usual number of participants in a discussion was increased by 25 per cent after the change of seating. His observations caused him to believe that the quality of and general interest in discussion was greater after the change in seating arrangement. Hence he concluded that his hypothesis was supported by the evidence: that with a single row of chairs in a circular arrangement better discussion occurred in this class than with the former seating arrangement. Note that this conclusion does not state that such an arrangement is better for other classrooms or for purposes other than discussion in this classroom. Neither does it state that the new seating arrangement was the one and only cause of the improved participation. But the conclusion represents a satisfactory solution of the original problem: to find a seating arrangement in which there was better discussion. The teacher may still be dissatisfied, and wish to find other seating arrangements. Or he may wish to investigate factors such as the understanding of group procedures, the use of standards of discussion, or the choice of leaders. If so, and the experimentally minded teacher will always be going from one conclusion to a new, related investigation, he again goes through the problem-defining, hypothesis-stating, data-gathering steps to new conclusions.

SELECTING PROBLEMS FOR EXPERIMENTATION

The teacher has no dearth of problems for experimentation, but sometimes overwork, complacency, frustration, or other factors cause him to ignore the myriad problems of the classroom. How he might go about recognizing these problems and identifying them for experimentation is treated in this section.

The Source of Problems

The basic source of problems is some type of dissatisfaction with existing conditions. The complacent, wholly satisfied teacher probably has little interest in experimentation; and probably his pupils have as little interest in effective learning! The teacher who is not wholly satisfied finds problems for experimentation by analyzing the bases of his dissatisfaction. This process is relatively simple when the dissatisfaction is real and definitely related to some causal factor, and relatively complex when the dissatisfaction is chronic and vague. Thus the teacher who is greatly disturbed by the showing of his pupils on an achievement test has a tangible dissatisfaction to analyze. But the teacher who rather vaguely suspects that his pupils might be learning more in general may have a very inadequate understanding of the factors to be investigated. The first teacher can start identifying the possible problems at once; the second one has first to determine whether there is any problem.

The nature of the dissatisfaction from which problems spring is a very important aspect of the process of experimentation. The following types of situations illustrate dissatisfactions which may cause teachers to initiate processes of experimentation.

Dissatisfaction from without. Experimentation is frequently stimulated by criticisms or other pressures from outside the learning situation.

Other teachers or supervisors or parents or even learners themselves may express criticisms which cause the teacher to begin some analysis and problem defining. Various pressure groups, frequently well intended although sometimes guided by selfish interests, may urge reforms or changes which suggest dissatisfactions. Boys and girls frequently communicate these dissatisfactions from without by citing statements of their parents, friends, and others regarding what the children should be doing or are failing to do. The teacher's in-service education activities may involve identification of many general criticisms by professional colleagues and authors with practices in his own classroom. If any of these criticisms motivate the teacher's own problem-solving activities there must sooner or later be some acceptance of the dissatisfaction as his own. Experimentation undertaken to prove that some outside critic is wrong is not likely to result in the identification of better practices, although there is always the chance that the critic might be found to be right and the teacher thus stimulated to accept the dissatisfaction.

Evidence of need for improvement. Probably the most effective stimulus of dissatisfaction is factual evidence that some classroom practice is wrong or poor. Surveys of parent and pupil opinion regarding some feature of classroom organization or curriculum planning may give specific evidence that there is need for improvement. Analyses of test results may indicate lack of expected or desired pupil progress or the work of pupils in higher grades that there had been ineffective learning earlier. Teacher evaluations by their pupils may suggest problems of self-improvement to the teachers. Checks of various types on learning goals may give results which are considered unsatisfactory. That is, any effort to evaluate the curriculum may give evidence of the need for improvement.

The teacher's own dissatisfaction. As already indicated, any criticism from the outside, as well as any evidence of the need for improvement, has to be identified as a stimulus to the teacher's own activity before effective experimentation can occur. But there are dissatisfactions which originate in the teacher's own reflections about the experiences of the learners he teaches. He may be dissatisfied with his acceptance by the group or by his inability to stimulate interest. He may be unhappy with an individual pupil's progress or about a specific learning experience of the group. He may sense a lack of interest in some particular curriculum area or type of learning experience, or a lack of attainment of some important goal. He may be frustrated by the lack of relationship between

school studies and out-of-school experiences or by the inadequate resources for learning. Any of these dissatisfactions, if not dismissed with
"But I can't do anything about it," may become a drive to experimentation of the most fruitful sort.

Identifying Possible Problems

The relationship between dissatisfactions and experimentation may be
more clearly revealed by analysis of specific examples. Here and in several subsequent sections of this chapter we shall describe in detail three
cases of classroom experimentation. Though based on our own experiences, these cases are presented so as to illustrate the principles we are
developing with the reader. Many actual instances of classroom experimentation may be known to the reader; descriptions of many others can
be found in the literature. A number of recent articles describing specific
instances are cited at the end of this chapter. Teachers who wish to engage in classroom experimentation can find a great deal of help through
learning about the experimentation of others.

The case of Teacher A. Teacher A was an elementary school
teacher, teaching a fourth-grade group. In her community there was a
great deal of criticism that the elementary schools were not teaching the
fundamental skills or the three R's. Although Teacher A did not accept
the criticism that the elementary schools were generally failing in this respect, she was quite sensitive to the complaints of certain parents that
their children were having difficulty. She felt that the group was doing
satisfactory work in the language skills, but she was conscious of the fact
that a number of children fell behind the group in arithmetic. Could it
be, she wondered, that these children were not being taught arithmetic
well? Why did they continually fail to complete their work in the fourth-
grade arithmetic textbook, in which all children had the same assignments and tests? Would their further development be so poor that they
would always have difficulty?

Teacher A, now having identified a dissatisfaction, began to analyze
the situation to seek some definite question for investigation. She gave
the entire class a standardized arithmetic test and learned that five children were virtual beginners in arithmetic, scoring below the norm for
second grade. Analysis of these children's tests and of their other work indicated that they had difficulties in counting and simple addition and
subtraction. She also found that they had difficulty in reading the problems in the textbook, they "hated" arithmetic, and they frequently disturbed other children during the period for arithmetic. Thus the phase of

the problem of the three R's that she identified was how to help these particular children overcome both their difficulties in specific skills and their emotional disturbance regarding arithmetic.

The case of Teacher B. Teacher B was a junior high school teacher assigned two classes of seventh-grade geography and three classes of seventh-grade English. He was interested in doing a good job with his classes and decided to use a simple check list to find out what his pupils thought of their classes. One of the questions to be checked was:

Is this class, as compared with others,
( ) Very dull
( ) Dull
( ) Average
( ) Interesting
( ) Very interesting

The responses to this question showed a range of answers, but he was quite concerned to find that less than one third of his pupils checked "interesting" or "very interesting." Over one third checked "very dull" or "dull." Something, he thought, was wrong. To explore the problem further, he asked the members of each group to have a discussion about what they considered "dull" about the class. Although the answers that came out in the discussion were varied, many of them had to do with the question-answer procedure whereby the classes were usually conducted. Pupils said: "We get bored going through the questions"; "We never have any discussion"; "We get tired of doing the same thing every day."

With this evidence, Teacher B decided his problem was to find some different way of carrying on learning experiences which would be considered more interesting by the pupils. He also got from the latter many suggestions as to procedures which would be more interesting.

The case of Teacher C. Teacher C was a senior high school history teacher. She was sincerely concerned about helping high school youth to understand the problems of contemporary America, but she also felt that she must first ensure their learning the facts of American history. In general she tended to a type of curriculum planning and classroom procedure which emphasized the importance of historical facts, but she worried about how little interest youth expressed in current affairs. Occasionally, she had discussion periods on current events, but pupils seldom revealed information on or interest in the topics which she felt were important.

Teacher C had well-organized unit plans based on the usual chronological organization of American history, and these were followed closely.

She wondered how she could teach these units on the past and cover the present, too, in the time available.

As she studied this problem, she began to question some of her original assumptions. Perhaps the past was not most important. Or perhaps it was not an "either-or" problem. Maybe, she reflected, there was a way to teach about the present without sacrificing the past. Her problem, she decided, was to find a way of organizing teaching units on some different basis which would provide for increased attention to current affairs and develop more understanding thereby.

Summary

Two essential phases of the selection of problems have been illustrated. First, there must be some kind of dissatisfaction from which the problem develops. A dissatisfaction may arise from outside forces, from examination of evidence regarding the learning situation, or from the teacher's own reflection. Whatever the source, there has to be conscious identification of something which is not satisfactory. That is, one does not rightly select a problem just to have one, but rather because there is some reason to believe there is a problem.

Once there is identification of a dissatisfaction, the problem for experimentation is selected by analyzing the dissatisfaction to determine a specific factor to be investigated. Thus, Teacher A's analyses regarding the "three R's" led to the identification of a group of children for whom she proposed to find a way of helping to learn arithmetic skills. Teacher B's study of the evidence from pupil evaluations of his class resulted in identifying the problem of planning learning experiences which would be more interesting to pupils. Teacher C's reflections on her teaching of American history in relation to pupils' interest in current affairs resulted in the identification of the problem of organizing units of work that would give increased attention to current affairs. For each the process of selecting the problem for investigation was a matter of considering various subproblems or factors related to the large dissatisfaction or problem and identifying one of these subproblems as *the* problem for investigation. That is, the process is one of narrowing the possible problems down to one for immediate investigation, although others may be attacked later. In this "narrowing" process such factors as the importance, relevancy, and maneuverability of each possible problem may be considered.

PLANNING TRYOUT SOLUTIONS

Inevitably in the reasoning one does about possible problems, the plausibility of solutions for each is considered too. That is, in actual curriculum planning teachers rarely select problems for experimentation and then quite separately explore hypotheses regarding these problems. The possible solution may influence greatly the selection of the problem for experimentation. For example, in defining his problem of finding more interesting learning experiences, Teacher B was undoubtedly quite sure that one or more particular types of learning experiences would be tried out. In fact, his "hunch" that more discussion activities would result in a more favorable evaluation of classroom procedure by pupils probably led him to define a problem for experimentation. Thus problem defining and solution proposing are closely related and are not usually considered as logically as the illustrations suggest.

Planning a Solution for the Arithmetic Problem (Teacher A)

Teacher A had already approached a possible solution of her problem through narrowing the problem to helping particular children. That is, a possible solution indicated was to work with these children as a special group. Probably she assumed this solution in defining her problem as she did. Her further analysis of the problem was then in terms of how to work with these children most effectively. Among the alternatives were special help periods for this group on the assignments given all pupils, special homework assignments, use of different materials. Teacher A rejected the first two alternatives because she felt that since the children were simply not able to work at the level of the others, no amount of additional time for such work would solve the problem. That is, she believed that these two solutions were less likely to succeed than the third.

Planning for the use of different materials presented several questions: What materials? When to use them? How? Teacher A decided to work with these children for six weeks or more in a special work period on problems she would devise for them, and to give them some lower-grade workbooks for drill during the arithmetic period of the other children. The hypothesis she was thereby formulating was this: The children concerned would make progress in specific arithmetic skills with less emotional disturbance by use of special materials in the kind of instructional arrangement described.

Planning a Solution for the Classroom Procedure Problem (Teacher B)

Teacher B took a cue from the discussion in his classes as to their dullness. Several pupils had mentioned that they thought the lack of discussion made the class procedure dull. Although various other procedures had been suggested, Teacher B felt that some type of discussion procedure would be the most likely alternative for experimentation. He decided that discussion procedures might be more appropriate to geography than to English. He also considered the question of whether to change procedures in both of his two geography classes and decided it would be better to experiment for the remaining three months of the year with a new procedure in one class only.

Teacher B felt that for the experimentation to be very fruitful, he should plan a definite discussion procedure. He consulted some descriptions in professional books and magazines dealing with discussion procedures and found that various organizational plans were possible. Since his room was large enough and had movable furniture, he decided to use a circular arrangement in seating the geography class which came to him the last period of the day. Also, he planned to use a pupil chairman and recorder for the discussion period, and to have prepared each day, as a basis for the next day's discussion, a list of questions related to the assigned readings. All of these plans were discussed with the class and several other suggestions from pupils were agreed upon: that there should be weekly rotation of chairmen and recorders; that time should be provided each day for reading on the questions chosen for discussion; that the questions for discussion might be revised at the beginning of each discussion period; that some pupil each day should be responsible for keeping a check on the participation in the discussion. Thus the solution or hypothesis to be tried out could be phrased thus: that the pupils in this particular geography class would find their classroom experiences more interesting when organized on a discussion basis according to the plans just described.

Planning a Solution for the Current Affairs Problem (Teacher C)

In her study of unit plans in American history, Teacher C discovered that a number of types were possible: the units based on chronological organization, which she was using; an occasional unit on current affairs; units organized on the "history backward" principle—beginning with the present problem and then developing its backgrounds; topical or functional units developed chronologically but always including attention to the topic in relation to the current situation; various combinations of chronological and topical units; and the use of current events periods in connection with any of the unit plans. Teacher C believed that each of these plans had advantages but decided that she could experiment most easily with the use of topical units since she could secure textbook materials organized on this basis. However, she decided to use a particular type of unit organization which would ensure attention to current affairs because she realized that topical units based solely on textbook materials might also never get to the present.

During the next semester she was to have three classes of first-semester and two classes of second-semester American history. Teacher C felt it would be impossible to plan a complete reorganization of her courses before the semester began, and decided to try to give more attention to current affairs in all classes in connection with the units already developed. She also decided to try out the topical plan completely in one of the second-semester classes. Since this class had already studied American history through the period of the Civil War, she planned a series of units on major American problems which had been persistent during the period after the Civil War: international relations, industrialization, political development, education, and others. She planned a unit organization which began with a comparison of "then and now" and thereafter followed a chronological outline of the developments from "then" to "now." In considering possible ways of studying the "now" with respect to each unit, Teacher C decided that it would save her time and also be interesting to the pupils to find their own sources of information on the "now." Regarding each topic selected she developed a series of pertinent questions about the "now," definite citations to reading on the "then," and an outline of related developments during the whole period. Thus the hypothesis which Teacher C was ready to try out was this: that increased attention to current affairs through the use of units of work developed as just described would develop more interest in and understanding of current affairs.

The Planning Process

Planning the tryout involves at least two major steps. First, a specific solution must be chosen from all those possible. Thus, Teacher A had to choose whether to try out a plan of special help periods, or special homework assignments, or use of special materials. Teacher B decided to experiment with discussion procedures instead of other alternatives to the question-and-answer procedure he usually followed. Teacher C selected experimentation with topical units rather than with some other type of unit plan. In making these choices the teachers were applying such criteria as the potential effectiveness, the feasibility, and the applicability of the various alternative solutions considered.

A second step is the refinement of the planned solutions. Decisions had to be reached by these teachers as to the precise specifications of the plan—that is, what kind of materials (A), discussion (B), and topical unit (C). Decisions also had to be reached as to when and where the solutions were to be tried out, and as to the use to be made of learners' ideas in further refinement of the plans.

GATHERING DATA

A third step in planning the tryout solution is planning for the data to be secured regarding the success of the tryout—that is, for the evidence. This planning will be described in connection with the following discussion of gathering the data.

Gathering Data about the Arithmetic Problem (A)

The type of data which Teacher A would need was indicated by her original analysis of the problem. The children with whom she planned to work had scored very low on a standardized achievement test, so she repeated this test after working with the group as planned for a period of six weeks. Her initial investigation had also shown that these children had difficulty in reading the textbook, so as she worked with the children in their lower-grade workbooks she had them note any unfamiliar words and from time to time also had them read to her problems in the regular textbook, noting their reading difficulties. She had learned, too, that these children "hated" arithmetic, so she asked their parents to keep note of their children's expressed attitudes regarding arithmetic. She had also been aware that these pupils frequently disturbed others during the arithmetic period, so she observed their behavior during both their own arithmetic period and that of the remainder of the class. Thus, as Teacher A carried on the experimentation with the arithmetic problem, data were being gathered to help her decide whether the experimentation helped.

Gathering Data about the Classroom Procedure Problem (B)

Teacher B's initial investigation also used techniques which he felt would be helpful in his data gathering, an evaluative check list and an evaluative discussion. So that he might make some comparison of results in the experimental class with those in the other classes, he gave the same check list to all classes at the end of the year and also had a discussion of the results in each class.

Teacher B felt that the pupils' participation in the discussion period would also indicate their interest. In addition to the check kept daily by a pupil of the number (not the names) of participants, Teacher B kept an informal record of pupils who became more interested participants, of pupils who monopolized the discussion, and of the periods in which the discussion digressed for an extended time from the agreed-upon questions and of other happenings which indicated lagging interest in the procedure. He also noted what progress was made by pupils in their skills of discussion leadership, problem selection, and summarization.

Gathering Data about the Current Affairs Problem (C)

Teacher C felt that she should collect evidence on the information and interest of her pupils on current affairs. Three types of data could be gathered: scores on current affairs tests; time devoted to reading and number read of newpapers and magazines, and time devoted to broadcasts on current affairs; and expressed interests of pupils in current affairs. Teacher C found a published test on current affairs which could be used at the beginning and end of the semester and planned to use this with all classes for purposes of comparison. She constructed a current affairs test related more directly to the unit plans developed for the experimental class, and gave this test at the end of the second semester to both second-semester classes. She also constructed a questionnaire to find out what magazine and newspapers were read by her pupils, what types of materials were read in these sources, and how much time was given weekly to such reading and to broadcasts on current affairs. This questionnaire was given to members of all her classes at the beginning and end of the semester. Teacher C also prepared a questionnaire for parents designed to find out what interests their children expressed at home on various current affairs, and had this filled out by parents of the pupils in the experimental class at the beginning and end of the semester.

Procedures in Gathering Data

The essential and implicit step in the data-gathering process is the actual experimentation. Related to this are all the observations made by the teacher and probably the pupils. As such observations are made with care and recorded for further reference, they become evidence to be evaluated. In addition, we have illustrated in the cases of Teachers A, B, and C how many other data may be gathered in reaching conclusions about the experimentation. Some of these data may be of a "before and after" type; some for comparing the experimental group with other groups; and some for supplementing the teacher's observations by opinions and facts from parents and other persons not involved directly in the learning situation. The important principle is that as much evidence as can be feasibly secured should be made available to give a reliable, factual basis for judgments to be reached regarding the success of the tryout solution of the problem. The teacher needs to keep in mind that the conclusions will merely deal with the group and the solution concerned and not with a wider problem but that they should be conclusions which are as well justified as the available data will permit.

REACHING CONCLUSIONS

The step of reaching conclusions has at least three phases: interpreting the data; making a judgment on the basis of the data; and determining questions which are not answered by or suggested by the data. These phases are illustrated by further reference to the cases of Teachers A, B, and C.

Reaching Conclusions about the Arithmetic Problem (A)

Teacher A's observations of the five children with whom she worked in arithmetic included the following points:

1. Over the six-week period these children gained considerable self-confidence in their arithmetic work.

2. Although these children had little difficulty in reading the lower-grade workbook, periodic checks indicated continued difficulty in reading the fourth-grade textbook.

3. They very infrequently disturbed other children, but they did show some sensitivity to being called a "special" group.

4. They made marked progress in the basic skills of counting, addition, and subtraction.

The parents said that their children no longer spoke of "hating" arithmetic, but the parents of three children said the latter wanted to get back into the regular arithmetic class.

Repetition of the standardized tests at the end of the six-week period revealed that each child had made more than six-months progress as measured by these tests. The teacher interpreted all these data to mean that the children had made substantial progress in overcoming their difficulties in arithmetic and some of the related emotional disturbance. Therefore she concluded that the use of the lower-grade workbook in a special work period of these children had been effective. At the same time she found that a new problem had apparently developed—the feeling that this "special" arrangement had a stigma. How, she then wondered, could she develop a situation in which these children would continue to gain self-confidence and skill and at the same time not feel they were "special" cases? And so Teacher A was off to defining another problem which might be a phase of further experimentation.

Reaching Conclusions about the Classroom Procedure Problem (B)

Over the semester Teacher B kept some notes and records of the discussion procedure which permitted the following observations at the end:

1. Several children who seemed to have no interest in the class at the beginning had become interested participants by the end.

2. Two pupils who tended to monopolize discussion in the beginning had become more interested in listening to others' statements and opinions.

3. As the class became more skillful in selecting questions for discussion, there was less digression from selected questions.

4. The quality of leadership in the discussion seemed more closely related to personal qualities than to experience in the procedure; that is, pupils who served as chairmen during the last few weeks were as likely to be poor chairmen as those who served at first.

5. Interest in the discussion seemed to vary with the skill of the chairman or with the intervening leadership of the teacher.

Teacher B interpreted the first three of these observations as evidence of the success of the procedure but felt that the latter two items simply raised questions for further study. Further evidence of interest in the discussion was given by analysis of the number of pupils participating orally: an average of 30 per cent participated daily during the first two weeks and an average of 60 per cent during the last two weeks.

Repetition of the evaluative check lists at the end of the year gave some interesting data. Whereas less than one third of the pupils had considered the class "very interesting" or "interesting" at the first use of the check list, almost two thirds of the pupils in all classes now so rated his classes. Could it be, he wondered, that in attempting to make one class more interesting he had used some of the techniques with other classes, too? However, three fourths of the experimental class rated the class as "interesting" or "very interesting" and no pupil said the class was "dull" or "very dull." Hence Teacher B concluded that his tryout solution was correct, that is, that pupils in the experimental class had found their experiences more interesting. He did not feel that the evidence warranted any conclusion that the procedures used in this class were better than those used in the other classes, but he did feel that the procedure might be tried in all his classes to see if interest would be improved in all as in the one.

In addition to the questions for further study which were suggested by the data, the evaluative discussions in each class produced others. For example, pupils in a geography and an English class both taught by Teacher B asked why they couldn't have a double period so that they could carry on an interesting discussion longer? Many pupils suggested that discussion procedures could be used in English as well as in geography classes. And pupils insisted that discussion would be better if they kept a good chairman instead of the weekly rotation plan. All of these questions could lead to further experimentation by Teacher B.

Reaching Conclusions about the Current Affairs Problem (C)

Teacher C's observations during the semester indicated that the learners in the experimental group were developing much more interest in and information on current affairs. These observations were confirmed by the following data:

1. The median score on the published current affairs test was substantially higher at the end than at the beginning of the semester.

2. The parents' questionnaire showed that most pupils expressed more interest at home on current affairs at the end than at the beginning of the semester.

3. The average amount of time given to reading current newspapers and magazines and listening to broadcasts on current affairs increased considerably.

Teacher C's analysis of the data for the experimental group in comparison to those for other classes revealed little evidence that she considered conclusive. Some gain on the published current affairs test was made by all classes, and without applying statistical methods she was unable to decide whether the slightly larger gain of the experimental class was significant. Likewise, she could not be certain that on the test she had constructed the larger median score made by the experimental class as compared with the other second-semester class really proved anything. She did feel that the considerably increased attention to newspapers, magazines, and broadcasts by members of the experimental class, as compared with the almost negligible changes in this respect by other classes, showed that the experimental units had produced more reading and listening than might have occurred otherwise. However, Teacher A considered the chief significance of the results of the questionnaire on reading and listening habits to be in the great range it revealed in the reading and listening habits of students. She was also concerned about the lack of discrimination on the part of many in the selection of newspapers, magazines, and broadcasts. How, she wondered, could more reading and listening be further encouraged and how could students be helped to become more discriminating?

Thus Teacher C could conclude that the greater attention to current affairs given through the new teaching units did develop more interest in and understanding of current affairs by the members of the class con-

cerned. At the same time she had to recognize many further related problems on which she was unable to make any generalizations.

Making Generalizations

Throughout this section, in fact throughout this chapter, we have attempted to emphasize the fact that the teacher's experimentation should
not be expected to result in generalizations concerning larger popula-
tions than those included in the experiments. In other words, as we see it,
the individual teacher's research and experimentation is primarily concerned with solving problems of teaching and curriculum planning for
the learning group he teaches. However, the need for generalizations to
help with future learning groups both of his own and other teachers is
recognized. Two ways of arriving at such generalizations may be noted.
One is the use of statistical procedures which make possible predictions
as to the possibility that a given result may occur elsewhere. In general,
the use of such procedures is difficult for the individual teacher and
usually quite inconclusive with only a single experimental group.[3] Second, cooperative research may increase the number of classrooms in
which the same experimentation is going on. Concurrence of results in a
number of cases facilitates the making of generalizations with, and under
some circumstances without, statistical processes. Further attention is
given to cooperative research in the next section.

THE ROLE OF TEACHERS IN CURRICULUM RESEARCH
AND EXPERIMENTATION

Although teachers have important contributions to make to curriculum
research and experimentation through their individual classroom researches, they may also help through working with each other to plan
cooperative research. The effectiveness of classroom research and experimentation is increased by cooperative planning and also by arrangements whereby the same problem is attacked in several classrooms.
Through such arrangements more people and more situations are involved, these people can help each other, and more adequate generalizations may ultimately be reached. Although the term "cooperative research" is more frequently applied to intersystem and university-school
arrangements (see Chapter 16), cooperative research can be planned by
any school faculty or curriculum committee. Teachers have a particularly important role to play in curriculum improvement through participation in such planning.

[3] See Corey, *op. cit.,* Chapter VII, "Action Research, Statistics, and the Sampling
Problem."

Every problem facing the curriculum planning group is an opportunity for research, and every proposed solution a hypothesis for investigation. The success of curriculum planning, as stated before, depends very largely on the extent to which classroom experimentation takes place. Under cooperative planning procedures, the burden of proposing experimentation does not rest with the individual teacher alone although he may propose hypotheses. The real responsibility is that of the planning group: to identify teachers interested in carrying forward experimentation and to give them help and recognition comparable to that supplied by the sponsoring organization or institution in programs of cooperative research. We believe that many curriculum problems can be solved by more widespread participation of teachers in the type of curriculum research we have been describing. The school staff which is experimenting is a growing staff and will offer a better program as it experiments and grows.

The Need for More "Action" Research

In Chapter 1 we analyzed in some detail the need for curriculum planning which would remedy the shortcomings of present curriculum practice. Throughout this book we have presented principles and practices of such planning. We must note, however, that in many instances we have been unable to state that the effectiveness of particular plans was supported by research. In general, many if not most of the problems of curriculum planning are still unanswered by research findings. Many of the difficulties which are experienced in making curriculum improvement might be substantially reduced if there were guidance and support of a definite body of curriculum research findings.

There have been many national investigations, studies by state and local systems, and individual researches of considerable significance. The fact remains, however, that research is either unable to answer some problems of curriculum planning or is inadequate to effect needed improvement of the curriculum. Curriculum research has too frequently been carried on in situations removed from classroom practice or patterned to meet conventional research requirements rather than classroom needs. Both large-scale studies and individual teacher-researchers have sometimes failed to affect practices. Hence, the need for more research is particularly acute with respect to a kind of research that can affect curriculum practice and will be publicized to those concerned. A summary of a conference on curriculum research sponsored by the Association for Supervision and Curriculum Development, National Education Association, in 1951, stated that "cooperative action research" should have the following characteristics:

The purpose should be to improve [curriculum] practice.

The problem to which a research is devoted should be one of importance that exists in an actual school (or school-community) situation.

The persons who regularly work in the situation should actively conduct the research, sometimes with advice from technical experts and other persons.

The purpose of a research should be to determine whether a particular practice results in the consequences anticipated (the hypothesis).

Evidence should be systematically secured and interpreted in order for generalizations to be reached regarding the success of a practice.

The organization, development, interpretation, and use of findings of the research should be a joint undertaking of the group of persons who are actively interested in the problem and who associate themselves together for its solution.[4]

The only difference between the kind of research described above and the descriptions of classroom research and experimentation contained earlier in this chapter is the former's emphasis on cooperation by several persons. But both cooperative research patterns and individual classroom researches involve the teacher's leadership. That is, "action" research in the curriculum area is classroom research and experimentation, and through cooperative endeavor this research may take on more significance. We may note now how individual teachers, all teachers, may help to meet the need for such research.

How Teachers May Help

The obvious fact is that teachers may help meet the need for curriculum research by carrying it on. Specifically, teachers may promote the development of more comprehensive research findings by such activities as the following:

1. By attacking their individual curriculum problems through a research approach as described in this chapter.

2. By planning research projects as a phase of planning in curriculum committees, building faculties, and other groups.

3. By reporting findings of their research to their colleagues.

4. By writing articles reporting their findings, for publication in state and national journals.

5. By joining with other teachers in carrying on cooperative research projects.

[4] William M. Alexander, "ASCD's Role in Cooperative Curriculum Research," *Educational Leadership,* 9:473 (May), 1952.

6. By asking for help from others when facilities for carrying on a research project are not immediately available.

7. By questioning practices and proposals for curriculum change that are not supported by evidence or designed to secure evidence.

8. By talking freely about the dissatisfactions they have with existing curriculum practices.

Results to Teachers

There is evidence that teachers who do engage in such activities find the experience satisfying. Some of the articles cited at the end of this chapter report teachers' satisfaction with specific research and experimentation projects. For example, the report of their study by Farley and Overton included the following observation:

> We would like to stress our conviction that the chief value of what we did does not necessarily lie in its results, which are tentative at best, but in the methods that we used to test a belief. By using similar techniques, any teacher in any classroom can examine his assumptions, thus escaping from the reign of guesswork and tradition which has hampered the development of better techniques of teaching. Experimentation such as we attempted is time-consuming, and, at times, frustrating, but both of us are convinced that the results, both direct and incidental, are highly rewarding.[5]

From his study of the reactions of teachers who had participated in a number of cooperative action research projects in Springfield, Missouri, Wann drew the following conclusions:

1. Study of professional problems will be vital to teachers if it enables them to study, at firsthand, their own problems and if it helps them to see solutions to those problems.

2. Teachers consider it very desirable to have a framework for study and to be systematic in seeking evidence to prove or disprove their ideas.

3. Professional study will provide a satisfying experience for teachers if it is focused on children and if it enables teachers to gain new insights into reasons for children's behavior.

4. Methods used in professional study should provide for cooperative attack on problems, and they should provide for growth, on the part of the participants, in the skills of cooperative endeavor.

5. Teachers see more value and more possibilities for participation in study if it is closely related to regular classroom work and if it employs procedures in which change is inherent.

[5] Edgar S. Farley and Harvey Overton, "Improving Discussion as a Means of Improving Understanding," *School Review*, 59:409 (October), 1951.

6. Cooperative action research, as conducted in Springfield, embodies many of the characteristics of study which teachers consider desirable.[6]

A statement by the teachers concerned, in a report of a cooperative research project in Battle Creek, Michigan, on "How Cooperating Teachers Feel about Cooperative Research" cited various problems and advantages and concluded with this paragraph:

> Some of our greatest satisfactions have been found in the classroom. The experimental and research approach to building a better learning situation brings us into a closer relationship with students, sharpens our observations of their behavior and enables us to see developmental changes throughout the year more clearly. We find it highly satisfying to help groups locate their problems and work on solutions to them, and in this process, observe them develop better social attitudes, assume responsibilities, learn to work together to understand one another. And finally, there is great satisfaction in knowing that each member of the cooperating group is engaged in an activity whose major goal is to find better solutions to some of the innumerable problems in education.[7]

Our own experience indicates that teachers with intellectual curiosity and initiative are generally happier when they are working to solve their problems through the best techniques available. Such teachers will carry on classroom research and experimentation when conditions permit. In the following section attention is turned to appropriate conditions and particularly to the role of teachers in creating and maintaining these conditions.

CONDITIONS ESSENTIAL TO EFFECTIVE CLASSROOM RESEARCH

Although administrators are usually blamed for the absence of needed conditions for research and other purposes, we believe that all school personnel must help to create and maintain desired conditions. Several essential conditions for effective classroom research and experimentation which a school faculty could help develop are described in this section.

[6] Kenneth Douglass Wann, "Teacher Participation in Action Research Directed toward Curriculum Change" (unpublished doctoral project; New York: Teachers College, Columbia University, 1950), pp. 86–87. Used by permission of Professor Wann. For a summary of this study, see the article by Wann cited at the end of this chapter.

[7] Hubert M. Evans (ed.), "Cooperative Research and Curriculum Improvement," *Teachers College Record*, 51:474 (April), 1951.

Respect for Experimentation.

Unfortunately, some situations discourage experimentation. Teachers who have grown accustomed to particular routines of work are sometimes very critical of suggested experiments which might challenge the efficacy of these routines. Criticisms of this sort are frequently directed to newcomers who would try out different procedures. Research and experimentation do not flourish very well side by side with reverence for traditional procedures, revered not because of their proved effectiveness but because of their long existence.

Another obstacle is the well-entrenched notion that teachers "can't experiment with the public's money" or "with other people's children." A similar attitude toward research in medicine would have denied us all the modern medical developments which have so greatly increased the well-being and the life span of the American people. Furthermore, the blind, continued use of educational methods which are not supported by research data is much more open to question than the effort to determine methods which can be supported. Thinking parents would undoubtedly prefer to have their children taught by teachers who are continually seeking more effective procedures than by teachers who year after year use the same procedures without bothering to look for evidence of success or failure.

Teachers and other school personnel who recognize the dynamic nature of educational processes have respect for research and experimentation. They know this is the most defensible method of curriculum change. Accordingly, they welcome ideas which challenge current practice and give support and encouragement to efforts in research and experimentation. Reports of research are sought and recognition is given to those who produce the reports. Instead of suspicion and fear of experimentation, there are respect and encouragement. In such situations, experimentation thrives.

Reliance on Evidence in Decision Making

A respect for experimentation implies that evidence is relied upon. However, an individual teacher might respect the right of another to carry on research and still reach his own decisions on the basis of suppositions. To emphasize the necessity of a reliance on evidence by all who do curriculum planning, we note here some aspects of decision making in which evidence should be sought.

Decisions are made almost continually in the learning situation: What do we do next? When do we turn to something else? When do we work as individuals? as small groups? as a total group? Who will do this and who will do that? Obviously it is not possible to carry on a research study every time such a question has to be answered. Almost as obviously, however, these questions need to be answered by such facts about the alternatives as are available. And when teachers lack facts from their own previous experience or that of others it may be time to explore the possibility of a research study which would give the facts. Continual reference to the "why" of decisions develops a pattern of thinking which helps and even stimulates research and experimentation.

Many decisions regarding so-called administrative problems which have great significance for curriculum planning also need to be based on evidence. Problems regarding the assignment of teachers and pupils, the size of classes, the use of facilities, and other matters need to be approached as experimentally as those concerning curriculum plans and instructional organization. In general, these administrative problems, too, are conditioned by factors within the individual school situation and therefore should be solved by those concerned with full attention to the facts of the situation.

Throughout this book we have been dealing with problems of curriculum planning by the individual teacher and groups of teachers. Implicit in all this discussion is the problem-solving approach that relies on evidence as the criterion for evaluating curriculum plans. Teachers who go about curriculum planning thoroughly and conscientiously can find no other basis for making judgments. And the evidence to be relied upon must generally come through processes of research and experimentation.

Cooperative Ways of Working

Classroom research and experimentation is difficult in situations where experience or interest in cooperative endeavor is lacking. It is not enough that one's colleagues respect experimentation; sometimes it is essential that they and others give a helping hand. Cooperation in research and experimentation means, for example, willingness to waive routine procedures, helping with facilities and giving time, sharing in planning and evaluating, and sometimes helping in time-consuming jobs.

Research projects are rarely initiated as the result of a single person's thinking. As noted earlier, they frequently spring from dissatisfactions expressed by persons other than the teacher concerned or are revealed by evidence available to the teachers. For these dissatisfactions to become the basis of positive action, there is needed a spirit of friendly give-and-take in faculty, teacher-parent, and teacher-pupil discussions which will encourage mutual problem-defining activities, in short, an atmosphere similar to the one suggested in Plate 36. Such a spirit is present in groups accustomed to frequent discussion and planning sessions where ideas are evaluated for their own worth rather than in terms of their source. Teachers who can freely express their self-criticisms, their problems, and their ideas in faculty planning groups are much more likely to carry on effective classroom research and experimentation than teachers who feel it necessary to conceal their feelings. The creation and

PLATE 36. PLANNING TOGETHER FOR COOPERATIVE RESEARCH. *Parents and teachers can plan problems for cooperative study. (Courtesy of the Baltimore Public Schools)*

maintenance of groups in which there can be friendly identification of problems and exploration of problem solutions is a responsibility of each member of the group. That is, every teacher can help develop research and experimentation by cooperative participation in discussions with other school personnel.

Cooperative ways of working, as already suggested, also involve specific help from many sources in connection with classroom research and experimentation. Pupils may need to help the research effort by adjusting themselves to different procedures and sometimes by gathering and summarizing facts about an experiment. Parents may need to fill out questionnaires or keep records or give other assistance that would not be called for otherwise. Other teachers may be asked to help in tabulating data, or to take a class temporarily to relieve a teacher doing a special task in an experiment, or to give information about the performance of learners. Librarians, secretaries, custodians, principals, and others may be involved in all sorts of unusual assignments if research and experimentation is being conducted. But all this help comes readily if there is genuine respect for experimentation and if cooperative ways of working are already established.

Facilities for Research and Experimentation

Even with ideal attitudes and working relationships, teachers will find research and experimentation difficult unless there is provision of time and other facilities. Wann's study cited earlier revealed that teachers felt their chief difficulties in carrying on research were lack of time, lack of skill in conducting research, and unsatisfactory arrangements for communication with cooperating teachers. His analysis suggested the following conclusions:

1. If interest in research on professional problems is sufficiently high, teachers will accept difficulties as challenges and not as barriers to progress.

2. Because teachers see lack of time for study as a serious problem, those who work with teachers should strive to relieve time pressure whenever possible.

3. Since time pressure seems to be related to skill in research, one way to relieve time pressure is to help teachers achieve as rapidly as possible the skills necessary to successful study.

4. It is important that teachers see relationships between their research activities and the goals they have set and that they be able to see progress toward these goals.

5. Careful consideration should be given to the time set for planning meetings with teachers and to the length of the meetings.

6. It is important to teachers that sufficient time be allotted to planning in order that problems can be adequately discussed and in order that each person can gain a clear understanding of what is to be done.

7. Teachers need much help with the skills involved in observation and recording of children's behavior.

8. Teachers need much help with the use of projective devices.

9. Persons who work with teachers will need to provide very direct leadership in analyzing and interpreting data which teachers gather if the maximum benefits are to be derived from the research.

10. Much attention should be given to developing better methods of communication between groups and individuals in order that there can be a beneficial interchange of ideas.[8]

It appears that faculty groups and administrators wishing to encourage research and experimentation will need to provide for at least three major types of facilities briefly described in the following paragraphs.

Time and meetings. Although a limited amount of experimental work can be and is done under the usual time schedules, the planning of research projects, the collection and summarization of data, and the communication of information usually involve considerably more time than is generally available to a teacher engaged in full-time teaching. More time is needed both for the individual teacher's activities and for group planning and sharing periods (for cooperative research). Two types of provisions are frequently made to facilitate these activities: (1) for teachers working on a departmentalized schedule, a reduced number of periods assigned to direct teaching so that the additional period(s) can be used for research purposes; (2) for such teachers in lieu of the foregoing provision and for elementary teachers not on a departmentalized schedule, arrangements whereby substitute teachers, or other helpers, relieve the teacher for agreed-upon periods of time during which he works on the research problem. In cooperative projects of an entire faculty, arrangements for days or parts of days without children being in school may be necessary.

Materials and clerical assistance. Inevitably the gathering of evidence involves the use of tests, questionnaires, or other data-securing instruments. The preparation of these materials, their checking, and their tabulation require supplies and clerical assistance. Frequently an investment by the school in clerical help for this purpose is more economical and better for learners than expecting teachers to do the routine work.

Experimentation may also involve expenditures for different types of instructional materials. When the budget is prepared it should provide ample funds for the purchase of such materials as may be required for research and experimentation as teachers and learners explore new resources for learning.

Consultative assistance. A major difficulty in research and experimentation is the limitation of the teacher's own experience and knowledge. Although this is overcome in part by cooperative planning, fre-

---

[8] Wann, *op. cit.*, pp. 152–153. Used by permission of Professor Wann.

quently the faculty planning group lacks persons experienced in research procedures. Persons from within and without the school system may render exceedingly helpful assistance at all stages of research and experimentation. Probably one of the chief advantages to the school system in participating in some cooperative research program (see Chapter 16) is the availability of consultative help in the program. In the absence of such a program, the individual school and teacher can frequently find helpful resources in experienced teachers, consultants employed by the local system and the state, nearby college and university instructors, and other sources.

For Further Study

Alexander, William M., "ASCD's Role in Cooperative Curriculum Research," *Educational Leadership,* 9:471–477 (May), 1952.

Reports planning of the Association for Supervision and Curriculum Development toward cooperation in expanding curriculum research activities in schools.

Banks, Tressa, and others, "We Tested Some Beliefs about the Biographical Method," *School Review,* 59:157–163 (March), 1951.

Report of a cooperative research project by a group of high school teachers.

Barr, Avril S., Robert M. Davis, and Palmer O. Johnson, *Educational Research and Appraisal.* Philadelphia: J. B. Lippincott Company, 1953.

Comprehensive treatment of usual research procedures in education.

Caswell, Hollis L., "Research in the Curriculum," *Educational Leadership,* 7:438–445 (April), 1950.

Emphasizes the need for, and suggests means of providing, more curriculum research.

Corey, Stephen M., *Action Research to Improve School Practices.* New York: Bureau of Publications, Teachers College, Columbia University, 1953.

The one comprehensive treatment of action research in education. Includes materials from several articles by Corey and others cited in the present chapter, and also a helpful chapter on "Action Research, Statistics, and the Sampling Problem" (Chapter VII).

Cunningham, Ruth, and Alice Miel, "Frontiers of Educational Research: In Elementary School Curriculum Development," *Journal of Educational Research,* 40:365–372 (January), 1947.

Lists problems of curriculum change and describes techniques for research dealing with these problems.

Draper, Edgar, "Curriculum Research: Biggest Responsibility of Every Teacher," *Clearing House,* 24:387–392 (March), 1950.

Describes types of research which can be conducted by classroom teachers.

Evans, Hubert M. (ed.), "Cooperative Research and Curriculum Improvement," *Teachers College Record,* 51:408–474 (April), 1950.

Detailed report of a cooperative research project in Battle Creek, Michigan.

Farley, Edgar S., and Harvey Overton, "Improving Discussion as a Means of Improving Understanding," *School Review,* 59:403–409 (October), 1951.

Report of a classroom research project by these two teachers.

Foshay, A. Wellesley, and James A. Hall, "Experimentation Moves into the Classroom," *Teachers College Record,* 51:353–359 (March), 1950.

Summary of a group discussion on problems and procedures of classroom experimentation.

Good, Carter V., A. S. Barr, and Douglas E. Scates, *Methodology of Educational Research.* New York: Appleton-Century-Crofts, Inc., 1942.

Standard text on scientific research procedures in education.

Horace Mann–Lincoln Study Group, "Recommended: Group Research for Teachers," *Teachers College Record,* 50:108–113 (November), 1948.

Describes a classroom research project carried forward by teachers in the Horace Mann–Lincoln School, New York City, and cites values of such research by a group of teachers.

Mackenzie, Gordon N., "Frontiers in Educational Research: In Secondary School Curriculum Building," *Journal of Educational Research,* 40:356–364 (January), 1947.

Suggests plan of cooperative research for secondary school curriculum planning.

Peters, Charles C., *Teaching High School History and Social Studies for Citizenship Training.* Coral Gables, Fla.: The University of Miami Press, 1948.

Report of an experiment in DAC ("democratic, action-centered education") carried forward with thirty-five experimental groups in high school social studies classes.

Smith, Mary Neel, "Action Research to Improve Teacher Planning Meetings," *School Review,* 60:142–150 (March), 1952.

Report of a cooperative research project by a junior high school faculty in Denver, Colorado.

Thelen, Herbert A., "Engineering Research in Curriculum Building," *Journal of Educational Research,* 41:577–596 (April), 1949.

Describes social engineering and some of the problems of group processes, structure, and productivity which are involved.

———, "Interaction Research Methodology," *Journal of Social Issues,* 6:56–76 (Nov. 2), 1950.

Describes a methodology for studying human interaction.

Wann, Kenneth D., "Teachers as Researchers," *Educational Leadership,* 9:489–495 (May), 1952.

Report of a research study on teachers' attitudes toward cooperative action research.

Whitney, Frederick Lamson, *The Elements of Research.* 3d ed.; New York: Prentice-Hall, Inc., 1951.

Includes a chapter on each type of research, and additional materials on various problems of scientific research.

Zirbes, Laura, "Gaps in Curriculum Research," *Educational Leadership,* 7:187–192 (December), 1949.

Describes areas in which curriculum research is needed and suggests approaches to undertaking such research.

————, "Our Research Responsibilities," *Educational Leadership,* 9:485–588 (May), 1952.

Plea for "voluntary participation in cooperative evaluation of some significant phase of school practice in an undefensive, honest quest for improvement."

part 5

HOW SHALL CURRICULUM PLANNING
BE ORGANIZED AND EVALUATED?

The preceding parts of this book have dealt directly with the problems and processes of planning for better curriculums, and only indirectly with the improvement of the planning process itself. Up to this point we have been presenting materials to help those who plan the curriculum, whoever these persons are and however they may be organized, in doing their job. In this final part we turn our attention to ways and means of organizing for the job and of determining how well it is done. These are the essential steps, we believe, in improvement of the planning process.

As we see it, the most critical problem in curriculum planning is that of securing more widespread and more cooperative participation on the part of all concerned. Especially critical is the need for more informed participation by all school personnel. As those who direct the learning experiences of boys and girls in school learn themselves how to do a better job of cooperative planning, we are confident that pupils, parents, and laymen in general will be given more and better opportunity to participate. Hence the primary task of organization for curriculum planning is that of stimulating and coordinating the participation of school personnel. Accordingly our chapter (16) on organization is devoted to the problems and procedures of cooperative participation in curriculum planning.

In the final analysis, the planning process can be improved only as there is evidence of need for improvement and as actions are taken accordingly. As we point out in Chapter 17, planning and evaluation are really complementary processes. Hence this, the final, chapter of our book describes specific procedures for evaluating curriculum planning in order to secure evidence on which further planning may be based.

chapter 16

Organizing for Cooperative Participation
in Curriculum Planning

One source of difficulty in improving curriculum planning in individual schools and school systems is securing the cooperation of those involved. Even teachers sometimes seem to feel that their sole job is to plan and carry on an effective program of instruction within their respective classrooms. Although we recognize fully the importance of this job, we also see the teacher's responsibility as extending beyond the immediate tasks of guiding the learning of particular groups of children and youth. We feel that each teacher should have a contribution to make, and a responsibility to make it, to the total program of the school. Furthermore, we are equally certain that the curriculum of a particular group of learners may be planned better as a result of the teacher's participation in cooperative planning, study, and experimentation with other school personnel. Similarly, we believe that school administrators, school specialists, and laymen have a contribution to make, as well as an obligation to make it, to curriculum planning. In this chapter, therefore, we describe characteristics and types of organization to effect cooperative participation in curriculum improvement.

Since this book is primarily concerned with curriculum planning as an important phase of the professional educator's job, we do not deal extensively here with the role of laymen in curriculum planning. As already stated in Chapter 2, we firmly believe that laymen have an important role to play. However, our present purpose is to describe ways and means of securing the participation of all concerned rather than to again define the respective roles of teachers, administrators, laymen, and others. Readers are referred to Chapter 2 and also to various references at the end of the present chapter for further information on the roles of various groups of participants.

TYPES AND LEVELS OF COOPERATIVE PARTICIPATION

The term "curriculum program" is ordinarily used to define a group of more or less related efforts within a particular school or school system to bring about general improvement of the curriculum.[1] For convenience in dealing with these efforts, we group them as follows: (1) curriculum planning for a particular school, (2) curriculum planning for a particular group of schools comprising a school "system," (3) inservice education, (4) cooperative experimentation and research, and (5) programs of professional organizations. It should be noted that these groupings merely describe points of orientation and are not mutually exclusive, since curriculum planning, for example, may result in or be initiated by in-service education, cooperative experimentation, and studies of professional organizations. But this classification may be useful in planning for participation in organized curriculum improvement. In this section the characteristics of effective cooperative participation in all such efforts are described, and later sections discuss each type of cooperative participation. First, however, we should note the various levels of curriculum planning.

Levels of Curriculum Planning

Four levels of curriculum planning may be identified. Of first importance is the teachers' own planning—both with and without pupils—of the curriculum of his particular group of learners. It is at this level that curriculum planning directly affects the experiences of learners. Regardless of how sound planning at other levels may be, it serves little purpose unless it is implemented at the classroom level. Curriculum planning at this level is basically a matter of making choices within a flexible curriculum framework. This is the level with which Part 4 of this book dealt.

Second, there is the school unit level. The building faculty, perhaps together with pupils and parents, is responsible for planning the total program of the school for effecting desired learnings. Here planning may proceed through the total faculty, departmental and grade groups, special committees, and cooperative school councils.

Third, there is the system level. Such representative or composite groups of status leadership as may be designated are responsible for planning general policies concerning the programs of all the schools for effecting desired learnings. Representative councils, departmental and grade groups, special committees, individuals or groups having particular interests, and sometimes the whole group may carry on this planning, with the legally responsible body, the board of education, having final responsibility. There may be a hierarchy of planning groups at this

[1] See Hollis L. Caswell, "Development of Organized Curriculum Programs," Chapter 3 in Hollis L. Caswell and associates, *Curriculum Improvement in Public School Systems* (New York: Bureau of Publications, Teachers College, Columbia University, 1950), for a careful analysis of the development and current procedures of curriculum programs.

level; that is, the local district may need to work out plans consistent with those of the county school authorities and the county with those of the state. All these plans may be affected by state laws and regulations of the state board of education, as described in Chapter 3.

Fourth, there is a level we may classify as external. Although having no legal or administrative relationship to the school, an accrediting association may have considerable influence on local curriculum planning. Through research studies and publications and curriculum materials, professional associations frequently contribute very directly to local planning groups. Also, curriculum planning which affects local groups indirectly but sometimes quite forcibly is done by various organized groups throughout the nation who seek to influence what is taught in school in relation to their interests. They may work through direct publications and speakers and films for schools, or through pressure on legislatures, boards, school curriculum planning groups, and textbook writers. Although the processes of curriculum planning are fundamentally the same at each level, it is important to keep these distinctions in mind since the nature of participation is somewhat different from level to level.

The teacher may participate in each level of planning. He is the planner at the first, one of the group of planners at the second, and is represented if not personally involved at the third. His participation at the latter two levels may be in connection with in-service education activities and cooperative experimentation and research in addition to membership on faculty planning groups. So far as the fourth level is concerned, participation is usually as a consumer of materials from the various groups, although he may work actively with professional organizations in curriculum planning. Participation at the second and third levels and in connection with some activities at the fourth level is described subsequently in this chapter.

THE NATURE OF COOPERATIVE PARTICIPATION

Whatever the type of program, one element of unity exists in all sound efforts to improve the curriculum: the cooperative activity of educational workers. Whether the point of attack in curriculum improvement be developing a course of study, planning a workshop, arranging a series of observations and demonstrations, or establishing a curriculum council, the common denominator is that of group study and action.

Curriculum Planning—A Group Process

Curriculum planning has become a group process rather than a matter for supervisors or research directors alone. The group concerned is composed of teachers and others. Thus, a curriculum improvement program is fundamentally an opportunity for pooling efforts and ideas rather than for accepting something developed from the outside. True, in practice, programs are sometimes organized in central offices and local school personnel have little opportunity to plan their nature. These kinds of programs are generally those which effect very little change in the classroom practices of the schools. The chief trend in the curriculum improvement efforts of the past two or three decades has been to bring about an increasingly close identification of improvement goals with teacher problems and thus to effect curriculum improvement through cooperative goal-seeking activities of groups of teachers and other school workers. Because of this trend, attention is given here to the characteristics of effective group planning for curriculum improvement.

Viewed as just stated, the curriculum program becomes one of learning as well as action for all who participate. All types of curriculum improvement efforts carried forward as cooperative goal seeking have in-service education values. Hence participation in all organized curriculum programs should be viewed by both educators and laymen as an opportunity not only to contribute to the school program but to increase their understandings.

A Central Goal

It cannot be emphasized too strongly that the one and only goal of curriculum improvement efforts must be the improvement of the experiences learners have through the school program. Thus in-service education is merely a means to an end—more effective planning and guidance of learning experiences. Each type of curriculum improvement effort must be finally evaluated by the contribution it makes to helping develop improved learning experiences.

We must note, too, that fundamental curriculum improvement is made in the learning situation. The immediate efforts to plan and guide this situation are those of the teacher. Because of this fact we have devoted Part 4 of this book to consideration of the immediate tasks of the teacher in connection with learning situations. Again, however, we should note that the teacher's work in planning and guiding learning experiences, locating and using resources, and evaluating learning should proceed in accordance with school and system plans. Participation in making these plans helps in the more immediate jobs of the learning situation.

Characteristics of Effective Group Planning

As previously stated, the distinguishing characteristic of current efforts to effect curriculum improvement is that of cooperative planning of educational workers and others. That is, effective curriculum programs employ techniques of effective group planning. Modern curriculum leaders are greatly helped by analyses of group processes in general. However, criteria for planning by curriculum groups have to be applied in accordance with the factors just described, that is, in the light of the types of improvement activities utilized, the levels at which curriculum planning occurs, and the central goal of improved learning experiences. In consideration of these factors, certain criteria of organized curriculum improvement efforts are described in the following paragraphs. Such principles indicate means whereby the participant in curriculum improvement may evaluate the organization and also indicate goals which he may assist the group to attain. The criteria presented here are those of adequate organization, common goals, group decisions, effective communication, and able leadership.

Adequate organization. In her analysis of the conditions of effective group endeavor, Miel mentions organization as of first importance, and suggests the following characteristics of a desirable organization in general:

1. It is functional.
2. It facilitates widespread participation and a free-flowing type of interpersonal relationships.
3. It fulfills a constructive social purpose that is the group's own purpose.
4. It provides for continuity of problem-solving.
5. It provides for necessary coordination among groups.[2]

With regard to organization for curriculum improvement, three principles seem of fundamental importance. First, the organization should provide for coordination of various improvement efforts at different levels. Sometimes school faculties within the same system are trying to attack the same problems but are unaware of what the others are doing. Exchange of experiences would be helpful. In some systems efforts to organize in-service education activities by central and school unit groups come into conflict. In others the central planning groups dominate the curriculum program to such an extent that the school units do

[2] Alice Miel, *Changing the Curriculum: A Social Process* (New York: Appleton-Century-Crofts, Inc., 1946), p. 64. Reprinted by permission of Appleton-Century-Crofts, Inc., publishers.

little planning of their own. Such practices can be avoided by careful planning of an organization so that the central group receives reports, promotes exchange of experiences, stimulates participation, and organizes programs to help local school units as needed.

The second principle follows: in the organization, the local school unit should have major responsibility for planning its own program. Since the sole purpose of curriculum planning is to bring about an improved school program, that program should be planned in large part by the planning group nearest the learners. The system-wide group can serve the coordinating function indicated, but the initiative in program planning should come from the local unit. Thus members of each school planning group should seek help on, and report to the central council, problems unique to the school unit.

Third, the organization of each curriculum group should itself be based on sound principles of group organization. That is, the functions of the group, of leaders and members, should be definitely fixed, and democratic practices in the conduct of discussion, in the discharge of individual responsibilities, and in the relation of majorities and minorities should be followed.

Common purposes. Whatever the planning group and the problem, the common goal of improved learning experiences is central. However, this goal will be variously interpreted, and even when points of view are in harmony, there may be many subgoals that provide agenda for various groups. The same underlying purpose of effective and cooperative group behavior applies for the curriculum planning group as for the classroom learning group.

The concept of common goals is implicit in group organization; that is, the basis of group organization must be some common problem, need, interest, or goal. Group planning is simply a matter of clarifying and solving goals. This process is clearly defined by Benne, Bradford, and Lippitt as follows:

> Put briefly, group thinking and discussion refer to the entire process by which a group of people surveys the problems facing it, clarifies these problems, selects a problem which the group comes to feel is important and which it can hope to solve, formulates an acceptable common solution, devises ways in which the solution may be tried and decides upon the trial. In certain cases, where the group remains together after the trial of the solution, evaluation of the success of the problem-solution as thought through and tried and rethinking of the problem insofar as it remains unsolved and of other related problems are integral parts of the process of discussion. Group thinking and

discussion, as used in this treatment, are focused upon the definition and solution of common problems by a group of people. They are, therefore, oriented in some degree at all stages toward action, designed to solve the problem or problems being discussed. They move continually toward the clarification of goals, the definition of barriers to these goals and the devising of action to reach the goals through overcoming the barriers as studied and defined. The purpose of discussion involves, therefore, the remolding of habits, attitudes, understandings and ways of working of members appropriate to the problem being confronted and the solution devised. Though people do discuss in order to serve one or another stage of this process only, e.g., definition of common problems, clarification of goals, etc., the functions of these "partial" discussions are best seen in relation to the process of problem definition and solution as a whole.[3]

The criterion of common goals is frequently overlooked by representative groups whose members are concerned with their personal goals rather than with the common goals of groups represented. Also individuals may not be willing to subordinate personal concerns in order to attack concerns on which others agree. Hence the problem of securing genuine consensus as to goals is a perplexing one for the group leader. The participant in curriculum planning may help greatly by clear definition of goals, earnest efforts to recognize mutuality of goals if existent and to ignore personal goals not shared by others, and careful instruction of representatives or, if he is the representative, careful adherence to instructions.

Group decisions. It follows that group goals must be achieved by group decisions if there is to be continued identification of the individual with goal attainment. The analysis of group planning by Benne, Bradford, and Lippitt emphasizes the nature and importance of group decisions in the following paragraphs:

> A group becomes a group fully only as it forms a common purpose and decides on a course of action appropriate to that purpose. Common decision is, therefore, an important measure of the maturity of a group. And groups achieve this maturity only through successful experience in making decisions together. Decision is the bridge between the discussion of alternatives together with the choice of one of these and action. Any group discussion oriented to action is left dangling and incomplete if it does not culminate in decision.

[3] K. D. Benne, L. P. Bradford, and R. Lippitt, "Stages in the Process of Group Thinking and Discussion," in Kenneth D. Benne and Bozidar Muntyan, *Human Relations in Curriculum Change* (New York: The Dryden Press, 1951), pp. 68–69. Reprinted by permission of the authors.

There is growing evidence also that it is through decision in a group setting that individuals most effectively modify their attitudes and conduct in ways indicated by the meanings of facts and ideas discussed. All of the objectives of group discussion, previously noted, are, therefore, best served by a group's pushing thought and discussion through a group decision. The group must answer the question individually and collectively, "What do our discussion and thinking commit us to do?" [4]

It is important that the participants in curriculum planning be fully cognizant of the limitations of their decision-making powers. The limits should be set in the determination of goals which are attainable by the group. However, curriculum planning groups frequently assume responsibility for decisions which concern individuals or schools or groups not represented in the planning group. As a result, the decision is either resented or disregarded. Also, groups are sometimes frustrated by not understanding what decisions they can make. "Shouldn't the superintendent (or the supervisor or the principal or someone else) decide this?" is a frequent question. Accordingly, there should be clear understanding of the group's functions and limitations. Sometimes the group may lack authority to make a policy decision but is asked to make a recommendation to the policy-making body. In such cases, the planning group is still making a decision, that is, as to what to recommend, and the process is the same.

Effective communication of ideas. Careful analysis of typical curriculum programs suggests that both in the planning group and in the implementation of plans in the curriculum of learners, a major block to action is the failure of those concerned to understand each other. Group decisions are impossible unless all concerned have an opportunity to express their ideas and have them understood, and to understand the ideas of others. Even face-to-face communication breaks down because of semantic difficulties. Written communications eliminate opportunity for discussion and are an inadequate basis for curriculum planning at all levels. In group situations, factors such as poor facilities, overaggressive or reticent members, ambiguous terms, and time limits present difficulties.

The effectiveness of communication depends very directly on the quality and universality of participation. Communication is a two-way process, and all curriculum planners are obligated to express their lack of understanding when oral or written statements of planning groups or individuals are not clear. The effectiveness of the two-way process is greatly increased by participation in the formulation of common goals

[4] *Ibid.,* p. 80. Reprinted by permission of the authors.

and the determination of common goals and group decisions. In addition, cooperation in careful listening to statements from representatives and in careful reading of minutes and reports of meetings is essential, along with expression of disagreement or requests for clarification.

Able leadership. The major test of able leadership in group planning is the cooperative and democratic performance of the leader. This type of performance recognizes that every individual in the group is a potential leader who may at any point direct group thinking by his questions, observations, and suggestions. The leader by designation or status provides every opportunity for all the potential leadership within the group to exert itself. At the same time he must be able to give personal direction to the group enterprise when his own direction is indicated as being essential. The skills needed by the group leader were summarized by one of us as follows in another publication:

1. Maintaining a good physical and social environment
2. Securing frank and full expression of ideas
3. Providing resources to supplement those within the group as needed
4. Expressing faithfully for the group agreements or decisions reached
5. Assisting in the maintenance of adequate records
6. Discriminating between relevant and irrelevant suggestions and proposals
7. Delegating responsibilities to other members of the group
8. Summarizing progress from time to time for the group
9. Reporting appropriate actions, recommendations, or requests from other groups concerned with the same problems
10. Suggesting alternative courses of actions when group proposals are not inclusive
11. Determining the consensus when needed [5]

In addition to possessing these skills of a good group leader, the curriculum leader needs the ability to coordinate the efforts of all groups working on curriculum improvement. His experiences must be sufficiently broad, his contacts with groups sufficiently thorough, and his personal leadership sufficiently strong that he can direct curriculum planning to decisions based on intelligent consideration of all related problems and solutions.

[5] William M. Alexander, "The Role of Leadership in Curriculum Planning," Chapter X in Virgil E. Herrick and Ralph W. Tyler (eds.), *Toward Improved Curriculum Theory* (Chicago: The University of Chicago Press, 1950), pp. 107–108. Also see Gordon N. Mackenzie, Stephen M. Corey, and associates, *Instructional Leadership* (New York: Bureau of Publications, Teachers College, Columbia University, 1954).

ORGANIZING THE INDIVIDUAL SCHOOL FOR
CURRICULUM PLANNING

In the school whose staff becomes concerned about better curriculum
planning, some organization for this purpose is needed. This organization may differ from general faculty organization, or the organizations
for school operation and for curriculum planning may be identical. Certain features of any school organization designed for effective curriculum planning are described in this section.

Determining Curriculum Goals

Effective activity in planning the curriculum is directed toward specific
curriculum goals (see Chapter 7). Granted that schools have some common curriculum goals, the organization of a system-wide program which
assumes and starts with a set of goals uniform for all schools is inconsistent with a sound conception of curriculum planning. The problem
becomes one of defining procedures whereby the individual school may
determine goals for its own curriculum planning which are consistent
with those stated by system-wide groups or become parts of the system-
wide statement.

For the school unit to determine a curriculum goal, problems of the
entire school should be identified with participation by a maximum number of those persons affected by and able to evaluate the school's program. Goal-defining activities need to be pursued through an organized
process that will ensure the selection of goals which represent the best
thinking of all concerned about the program of the school as a whole. To
carry on such an organized process, the following groups are proposed:

1. *A school-community council* designed to provide maximum representation of each neighborhood served by the school, and organized to
secure maximum communication with parents and other citizens about
school needs.

2. *A student council* organized around the basic pupil groups (grade
rooms, core rooms, or home rooms) within the school, to give all learners
opportunity to propose and react.

3. *A staff council* organized on a representative basis if the staff (including nonteaching personnel) is large or including the entire staff if
small.

4. *An executive council* to include representatives of the foregoing
groups (with a parent or teacher representing student councils in elementary schools, if this seems more feasible) and perhaps a representative from any system-wide planning group.

The proposed councils, which are described in more detail in the next section, would have as a continuing function the making of suggestions and criticisms regarding any and all phases of the school's program. These criticisms and suggestions might be based in part on prepared questions, inventories, and evaluation instruments such as those described in Chapter 17, proposed by the faculty planning group. However secured, all evaluative statements and improvement proposals would be reviewed by the executive council. From time to time proposals might be referred back to all groups for consideration. The final definition of a particular goal for curriculum planning would be made by the executive council on the basis of careful study as to the comprehensiveness, appropriateness, and practicability of the goal, as well as on the basis of the interests of the groups concerned.

School Councils

No phase of the organization seems more essential than that of the various councils. These groups provide for the expression of opinion by all persons directly concerned with the school, for proposals, evaluation, and agreement as to planning goals, and for communication as to practices within the school. A desirable organization of councils and other groups involved in the school's curriculum planning is illustrated in Figure 5.

Among various plans for organizing school-community councils, that of neighborhood representation seems of widest applicability. For the small elementary school, this may become a matter of selection of a representative from each block. For the large high school, representation may be secured through the feeder school groups. For the consolidated school, representatives may be chosen from each district within the area. Such plans should reduce the possibility of councils which represent only one economic and social group within the community.

As already pointed out, practice seems agreed that student councils should be representative of such units within the school as will provide representation for all students and an opportunity for discussion within these units of proposals to and from the council. In the elementary school these units are the general classrooms, and in the secondary school the core rooms or home rooms.

As also stated earlier, the staff council may include all school personnel in the small school. If the group is too large for effective work together, some organization may be devised to provide representation of such staff units as exist: grades or departments, office personnel, special service personnel, and custodial personnel. The functions of the council should be clearly defined as proposing, evaluating, and the like, and not as policy making. In those schools in which the faculty serves both as the

STEP 1 – PLANNING CURRICULUM PURPOSES AND POLICIES

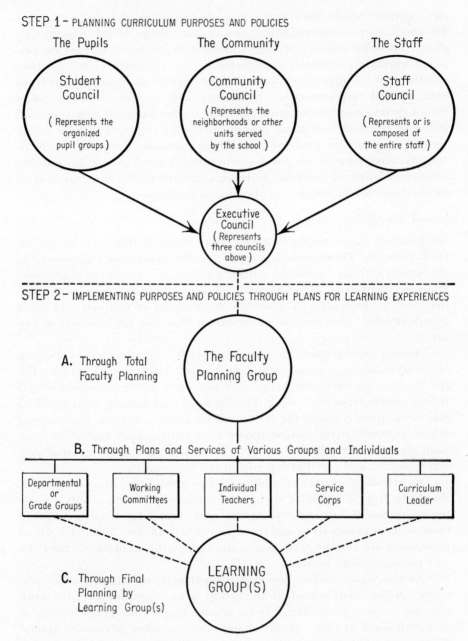

FIG. 5. ORGANIZATION OF THE INDIVIDUAL SCHOOL FOR CURRICULUM PLANNING

staff council and the faculty planning group, as defined in this section, discussions should be labeled as one or the other. However, the groups would not be identical if the council does include all school personnel.

Additional councils may be organized as there is need. Particular goals or the presence of one or more strong interest groups in the community may create the need for special councils. Thus councils from business or industry or welfare interests or of school graduates may be helpful as advisory groups.

Coordination of the activities of these councils may be effected by the executive council mentioned earlier. The functions of this representative council are to expedite communication between the three councils and between the councils and the faculty planning group, to secure consensus on improvement goals, and to serve as a liaison between the councils and the faculty planning group. In general, it would seem appropriate for the curriculum leader of the school to serve as an adviser to this representative council, or as its chairman.

Faculty Planning Group

It seems neither possible nor desirable for parents, pupils, laymen in general, and teachers to participate identically in every step of curriculum planning. Neither is it believed that advisory and decision-making groups or goal-determining and planning groups can be sharply distinguished. Parents and pupils participate in making plans as they propose needs, criticisms, and goals, and they participate in making plans work as they provide their services and enthusiasm. At the same time, a major share of planning and executing devolves on the technician, the teacher. There must be times when proposals are sifted down to specific plans for organizing the all-school program and for organizing instruction in every classroom. It is at this point that the teaching personnel of the school who direct this program and the instruction in these classrooms must make specific decisions and take specific actions, even though these decisions and actions may be later modified by further planning on the part of all concerned, including nonteaching personnel, parents, and pupils.

The organization of the faculty planning group should generally be determined by the faculty itself. In the small school the entire faculty constitutes the natural planning group. In the larger school some organization may be needed to provide a representative planning group. In the latter case the nature of representation depends on the organization of the faculty. Grade or departmental chairmen provide for a type of status representation. If the former are not elected by their groups, elected representatives to the planning group may be chosen. In such a situation, conflicts may arise as to the function of elected representatives and appointed chairmen—conflicts which may lead to desirable reorganization of the grade or departmental system. Another type of organization for planning in the large school cuts across departmental and grade lines by setting up some arbitrary division of the total group into committees of the same size whose members are chosen at random. Each small group designates its own representative to the central group, and this representative serves primarily as a liaison person. Whatever the organization for planning, it may be desirable for the curriculum leader of the school to serve as chairman or factotum and for the representative group to have full authority to establish such working committees and services corps as are required by agreed-upon plans.

Working Committees

Assignments to committees are usually made for such purposes as preparing materials, gathering data, making arrangements, proposing detailed plans. Some assignments may be made to individuals, others to committees. A particular job may be done best by the librarian, or the counselor, or a group of parents, or a committee including persons of varied competences. Ideally, the central planning group should be able to call on any person within the individual school, the community, or the system-wide organization to do a job for which that person is best qualified. In practice, the assignments have to be made to those who are qualified, available, and willing, and sometimes must go undone because such persons are not at hand. A major function of the curriculum leader is that of knowing the qualifications, availability, and willingness of persons who may be called upon.

Service Corps

Every school concerned with curriculum improvement needs to organize service corps of pupils, parents, and laymen in general for various services. A service corps of parents may be helpful for such differing purposes as informing other parents, arranging parent-teacher conferences, directing pupil activities while teachers confer, guiding special pupil activities in which a parent's competences are better than the teacher's, conducting out-of-school experiences of learners, preparing publicity materials.

Service corps of pupils are widely used for such services as the following:

1. Supervising younger children when parents visit the school
2. Repairing books, equipment, furniture
3. Operating movie projectors and other audio-visual equipment

4. Preparing school exhibits and decorations
5. Serving as ticket sellers and collectors and ushers for school programs
6. Conducting surveys in the community for information needed by the school
7. Caring for school grounds and gardens
8. Maintaining athletic fields
9. Operating duplicating machines
10. Providing telephone-answering and messenger service
11. Assisting in cafeteria, library, and other special centers
12. Operating school stores, snack bars, and similar facilities

Citizens of the community in general help in connection with improving school facilities, making arrangements for out-of-school learning experiences, and serving as speakers and consultants. A well-maintained register of available community persons and services seems desirable in any school program. In the larger school, a formal organization of service corps may be needed. In general, however, these services are of a nature which require flexibility and frequent procurement for a particular, nonrecurring function. In any school the curriculum leader would seem the logical organizer and procurer of these services.

The Curriculum Leader

Organized efforts toward curriculum planning in an individual school require the stimulation, coordination, and direction of an individual leader. It is questionable whether the usual devices for providing this leadership are adequate.

For the school which can afford an additional person, either of two procedures solve the problem: (1) designation of an administrative assistant to the principal to give the latter adequate time for curriculum leadership; or (2) designation of a qualified person as curriculum coordinator. In schools that cannot afford additional personnel, various less satisfactory possibilities are available. A competent teacher or other person may be released part time from other duties. The principal's function may be reorganized so that he can give maximum time to curriculum leadership. A librarian or counselor competent in the curriculum field might serve part time as a curriculum leader. A curriculum coordinator might be shared by several schools. In the large system one curriculum coordinator might be assigned to each district to work with the high school and its feeder elementary schools. If none of these possibilities are feasible, such a relationship may be hoped for with the central curriculum staff as will provide guidance and leadership to the individual school in terms of its goals

Meetings for Curriculum Planning in Individual Schools

The simplest organization for curriculum planning is the small, virtually autonomous building faculty in the one-building school system. Here there is no problem which cannot be settled by the total group and no problem which requires reference to the policies of other buildings to those of the system. On the other hand, there are lacking the facilities for planning which may come from membership in a larger system and from the wider competences of more people.

Faculty meetings. Unfortunately, building faculty meetings are not always used for productive curriculum planning. Frequently, announcements, the establishment of new administrative routines, or exhortations by the building principal constitute their only purpose. The meetings of building faculties within larger systems sometimes must—or at least do—give all their time to regulations, instructions, or requests from the central office. Even when there is time for curriculum planning, lack of skillful leadership and resulting disinterest in participation may result in poor use of the time. In such situations, faculty members may rightfully resent faculty meetings and so these opportunities to plan more adequate school programs are wasted. Among methods widely used to improve the quality and productivity of meetings are the following:

1. Holding meetings at a time when teachers are not already tired
2. Providing a social period before or after meetings
3. Planning agenda by representative committees or by contribution of suggestions of all members
4. Arranging a sequence of meetings on particular curriculum problems
5. Elimination of announcements by including them in duplicated bulletins
6. Observance of the general principles of good discussion procedures, such as adherence to definite problems, preliminary identifications of data relating to the problems, frequent summarization of suggestions and conclusions, evaluation of the process by the group or by a designated representative (observer)

Typically, the principal serves as chairman of faculty planning sessions; hence here is an excellent place to test and also train his leadership abilities as well as those of any other faculty member who may have special functions. In some schools the chairmanship is rotated among different faculty members. The faculty planning committee may provide leadership from its members or from the faculty at large. Frequently much of the time of larger faculties is devoted to reports from subgroups (departments, grade meetings, or committees). A recorder may or may not be utilized, although sound procedure suggests the need of some record. Meetings are generally held after school, but variations include meetings before school, at noon, in the evening, on Saturday, and longer, less rushed meetings by early dismissal of pupils.

Department meetings. In larger secondary schools and in elementary school faculties organized departmentally, considerable planning is done through the departmental groups, organized around the broad fields (science, social studies, and so forth). Unless this kind of planning is coordinated through the general faculty group or some representative coordinating council, each department is likely to proceed without reference to the other, with resulting inconsistencies and conflicts in plans. In accordance with its subject basis of organization departmental planning sometimes makes grade or course placements of subject matter, agrees on "minimum essentials," and prepares tests and other materials. More significant purposes can be served through exchange of experiences, arrangements for sharing of materials, planning of experimentation and research, development of resource units, relating of departmental projects to school purposes, and similar tasks.

The departmental organization is usually headed by a department chairman or head, who may be given a lighter teaching load in order to carry on the duties involved. Meetings occur in about the same pattern as the general faculty meetings, although some high schools are able to arrange a common planning period for members of small departments. In small systems with only two or three schools on a departmentalized basis—for example, one junior high and one senior high—the departmental group may include all teachers of the subjects concerned. In such cases, even more emphasis is likely to be given to the subjects than to the unique needs of the school unit's pupil population.

Grade level meetings. In larger elementary schools, the general faculty meeting may be broken down into primary and intermediate meetings or even into meetings of first-grade teachers, second-grade teachers, and so forth. The characteristics of these meetings generally parallel those of departmental groups. The danger in these meetings, too, is that the functions and problems of the entire school may be lost in the concentration on problems considered unique to the level concerned.

Building committees. Building committees are organized to deal with a great variety of problems, including both those of a temporary nature such as American Education Week and those of a continuing type such as visual aids. Larger buildings also utilize various types of general planning committees such as those already described. Such general committees or councils may serve very helpful functions in planning general faculty meetings, proposing curriculum studies, reviewing reports of subgroups, and so forth.

The problem of special committees is one which most larger faculties may well consider very carefully. If the committee is given more or less independent authority, as is frequently true, does there result a lack of desirable participation in dealing with the problems concerned? Problems of communication and coordination also challenge school leadership.

Relationship with the System Organization

At least three major types of relationships of the individual school are needed with the system as a whole. In the first place, school systems are increasingly maintaining central councils on instruction which are primarily representative of the individual units and which serve as clearinghouses for preparing statements of curriculum goals and plans of design, scope, and sequence. The representative has an exceedingly important function in serving as a liaison between school planning and central planning. He must report faithfully the thinking of each group to the other and represent his school faculty fairly in the establishment of system-wide policies in such a council as shown on page 558.

In the second place, the individual school needs full access to all services and facilities of the central staff. The curriculum leader needs to bring to bear on local curriculum problems the best facilities available through the consultative services, the materials collections, and the in-service education programs provided by the central staff. In the third place, individual units may profit greatly from the exchange of experience and from the joint planning for identical goals. Particularly is an arrangement desirable whereby faculties and perhaps community councils of elementary and secondary schools in the same district may come together from time to time for joint planning.

Characteristics of a Good School Organization

Underlying the various procedures and processes presented in this section are certain convictions that we have as to the essential characteristics of a good school organization for curriculum planning. These characteristics are summarized as follows:

1. Curriculum planning efforts are organized in terms of goals which result from the considered thinking of all persons directly affected

and which represent general agreements as to jobs to be accomplished by the school.

2. No sharp lines are drawn between pupil, parent, layman, and teacher participation in curriculum planning, but each person and each group are utilized in terms of their potential contributions bearing on the goals sought.

3. Although many jobs may be of a very narrow nature, each job assigned a committee or an individual is in terms of the needs of the total program. Final decisions as to policies, jobs, and specific changes are made with reference to the program of the school as a whole rather than by departmental or special-activities groups.

4. An atmosphere of cooperative planning and evaluation pervades all groups and the school as a whole.

5. A continuing search is made by all concerned to identify services, materials, facilities, and persons who can contribute to curriculum planning.

The following section gives consideration to organization for cooperative planning on a system-wide basis. The foregoing principles are believed to apply to system-wide organization also.

COOPERATIVE PLANNING FOR THE SYSTEM

The organization for system-wide planning varies, of course, with the size of the system. If there are less than a hundred teachers, a considerable part of the planning may be done in the system-wide faculty group. Certain types of other groupings may be effectively used in systems of any size, however: coordinating councils, advisory councils, curriculum working committees, and special-interest groups. In many school systems the major share of curriculum planning is done by departmental and grade groups, considered here as types of special-interest groups. Many special assignments may also be delegated to individual staff members: research, writing, compilation of materials. However, such special assignments should be and usually are made at the requests of particular groups who are responsible for fundamental planning.

System-Wide Faculty Meetings

In larger systems, general faculty meetings are too large and unwieldy to be useful in curriculum planning. They do provide opportunities for the explanation of plans made by smaller groups, the presentation of points of view, and similar purposes, but little discussion back and forth can be expected in the audience type of situation. In systems small enough that free discussion can take place in faculty meetings, curriculum decisions and recommendations may be made through discussion and action of the total group.

Plans for general faculty meetings vary. Increasingly school systems are arranging preschool conferences which usually include one or more general meetings. The latter provide excellent opportunities for presenting plans that may have been made during the preceding year. In medium-sized and small systems some regular series of meetings, held perhaps monthly, may include presentations of curriculum problems and plans. Meetings dominated by one or more speakers are not regarded as useful except to present points of view and to stimulate ideas or comments on current plans and experimentation. Frequently early dismissal of children is used to provide for system-wide meetings. Responsibility for these meetings is frequently shared by the school administration and the local teachers' association, with planning in the hands of a representative committee.

Coordinating Council

As school systems seek means of decentralizing curriculum responsibility, an agency for coordinating planning in local units becomes very desirable. For this purpose, some type of group representing each local unit is necessary. This group is responsible for exchanging information between schools, for recommending policies to the local units where uniformity is desired, for organizing in-service education programs, for preparing for the administration recommendations bearing on instructional problems, and for similar functions.[6]

In systems having some twenty-five or fewer units (individual schools) the organization of such a council is relatively simple. One elected representative from each unit plus one or more representatives of the central administrative and supervisory group make a council that is small enough for effective action. In larger systems councils may be organized for different levels, but this makes for failure to plan for the total scope of the curriculum. Another plan is to maintain a large representative body for general reporting and reviewing of problems and policies, with a smaller steering committee responsible for much detailed planning. Still another possibility in very large systems is a district organization, each district including a high school and its feeder schools.

---

[6] For descriptions of illustrative councils, see the reports of curriculum programs in these sources: Caswell and associates, *op. cit.,* Chaps. 6–14; and the Association for Supervision and Curriculum Development, National Education Association, *Action for Curriculum Improvement* (1951 Yearbook; Washington, D.C.: The Association, 1951), Chaps. IV–V; Ronald Doll and others, *Organizing for Curriculum Improvement* (New York: Bureau of Publications, Teachers College, Columbia University, 1953).

Each such district may have a planning council, with some type of central interlocking committee.

The choice of representatives to such a council is a very significant problem for effective participation of teachers in system-wide planning. It is essential that the representative be a liaison between the local unit and the coordinating council, not a legislator or an executive. With this criterion in mind, the following principles are suggested for the selection of representatives from the individual school units:

1. The representative should be elected by the staff, following careful consideration of the functions of the council and its members.

2. The representative should be one in whose ability to report honestly back and forth from unit to council, the staff has confidence.

3. The representative should understand as well as possible the total program of the local unit.

4. The representative should be subject to recall by a majority vote of the local unit.

5. Each representative should serve for a term of one year, with midyear elections in approximately half the units to provide for some continuity in the council.

The relationship of the curriculum council to other aspects of the system-wide organization is shown in Figure 6. As to the council's operation, frequently the curriculum director or assistant superintendent in charge of instruction or other designated curriculum leader serves as chairman, although a unit representative may be chosen. The choice of a recorder or secretary is very important, since the records of council meetings ordinarily form the basis of reports to the units. Publication of the reports to all staff members is a useful device for keeping the council close to them. Meetings are sufficiently extended to provide for full discussion, many school systems providing released time through the employment of substitutes or through other means allowing for meetings of a half day or more in length.

Curriculum Working Committees

As coordinating councils function, a great many problems arise which need more careful study than can be given by the entire council. Such problems are usually referred to small working committees, whose functions and perhaps membership are designated by the council. The membership of these subcommittees may or may not be confined to the council; use of nonmembers increases both the number of participants in system-wide planning and the range of abilities that may be utilized.

Illustrative of the kinds of curriculum jobs which may be assigned

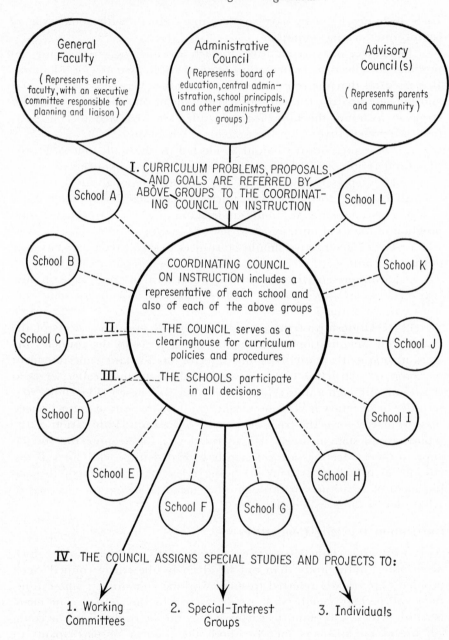

General
Faculty

(Represents entire
faculty, with an executive
committee responsible for
planning and liaison)

Administrative
Council
(Represents board of
education, central admin-
istration, school principals,
and other administrative
groups)

Advisory
Council (s)

(Represents parents
and community)

I. CURRICULUM PROBLEMS, PROPOSALS, AND GOALS ARE REFERRED BY ABOVE GROUPS TO THE COORDINAT- ING COUNCIL ON INSTRUCTION

School A

School L

School B

School K

COORDINATING COUNCIL ON INSTRUCTION includes a representative of each school and also of each of the above groups

School C

II.____THE COUNCIL serves as a clearinghouse for curriculum policies and procedures

School J

III.____THE SCHOOLS participate in all decisions

School D

School I

School E

School H

School F

School G

IV. THE COUNCIL ASSIGNS SPECIAL STUDIES AND PROJECTS TO:

1. Working
Committees

2. Special-Interest
Groups

3. Individuals

FIG. 6. ORGANIZATION OF THE SCHOOL SYSTEM FOR CURRICULUM IMPROVEMENT

to subcommittees are the following ones reported in a description of the functions over a two-year period of the Battle Creek (Michigan) Council on Instruction:

1. Planning an arts and crafts workshop
2. Developing the conference method of reporting to parents in the elementary schools
3. Revision of junior high reports to parents
4. Preparation of new cumulative records
5. Selection of tests for city-wide testing
6. Preparation of curriculum guides in social studies, arithmetic, language arts, and science
7. Planning of an annual summer workshop
8. Preparation of approved lists of supplies and books
9. Organization of system-wide study groups in music and reading
10. Preparation of resource units, bibliographies, and sample daily programs[7]

The relationship of the committees, council, and local units was described as follows in this report:

> For almost each of these projects some committee responsible to the council did much of the actual work involved. . . . The essential function of the Council in each case was a clearing-house one. Through the Council the building faculties were informed of committee work, were able to raise questions and propose problems, and were thus in better position to effect changes as recommended by committees.[8]

Advisory Councils

Various advisory or other councils having lay and sometimes staff and pupil members are frequently used in modern school systems. At least three patterns of organization are evident. First, the coordinating council may itself include lay and pupil representatives and perhaps serve the primary function of advising a steering committee or the administration. Second, there may be one advisory council which advises the administration, the curriculum council, and other groups who refer problems to the former or to whom the advisory council may propose problems. Third, there may be various advisory councils including one on curriculum. We ourselves question confusing the coordinating and advisory functions as is done in the first pattern. The job of central curriculum planning and coordination is a technical one in which lay and pupil

[7] See William M. Alexander, "Improving Instruction in Battle Creek, 1946–49," Chapter 6 in Caswell and associates, *op. cit.*, pp. 123–125.

[8] *Ibid.*, p. 125.

representatives cannot, we feel, make very significant contributions. Their helpfulness is in proposing problems at the school level, in serving on central advisory councils, and in giving reactions to general policies and plans. Whether the second or third pattern described above is used should probably depend on the size of the system. In a small system one council may serve effective functions with respect to all problems; in the larger one a council concerned solely with curriculum matters may be very helpful.

The representation on the advisory council is usually chosen to provide a cross section of opinion of all those concerned with the schools. Thus, in addition to administration, staff, and pupil representatives, such groups as parent associations, churches, labor, business, industry, women's organizations, and civic societies may be represented.

Special-Interest Groups

In most school systems various special-interest groups engage in some type of curriculum planning. If there is not some plan for the coordination of curriculum planning, one may find that there is considerable work done by organized departmental and grade level groups that is quite inconsistent with general school purposes and even with facilities. This difficulty occurs most frequently at the secondary level where the departments (English, social studies, mathematics, science, homemaking, industrial arts, and so forth) vie with each other in prescribing requirements, setting schedules, demanding budgetary appropriations, and so on. Formally organized groups in primary education, intermediate education, the secondary subject departments, counseling, supervision, and administration may involve the participation of each staff member in at least one such group. Purposes may include both social and professional ones, but curriculum planning is generally on the agenda.

Under the leadership of coordinating councils, the nature and the program of such groups may be considerably modified. They may be encouraged to carry on a study of problems before the council, and to present problems and recommendations to the coordinating council or perhaps to the advisory council. Frequently the special-interest group is a logical one for in-service education activities; special workshops, extension courses, or consultative services may be arranged. Also, the council may stimulate the development of different types of groupings based on common problems rather than on levels or subjects: for example, human relations, pupil-teacher planning, reading, and so forth. In order for there to be coordinated curriculum planning centered in the local school unit, it is frequently necessary to challenge the responsibilities assumed by subject and grade groups for developing uniform policies for the system. At the same time their facilities for bringing about interunit and interpersonal understanding and exchange are such as to merit teacher participation.

Special Assignments for Individuals

As indicated earlier, some of the specific jobs of curriculum planning at the system level (and also the local unit) may be such as to require intensive study by a qualified individual. For example, a frequent problem for study at the secondary level is that of dropouts. The nature of such a study might be planned by the high school faculty or by the system's coordinating council, and the final data might provide a basis for curriculum planning to reduce dropouts. But in between plans and final data there is a job of intensive research to identify dropouts and their whereabouts, their reasons for leaving school, and other factors. This is a job which might well be assigned to one qualified person. Such special assignments are made either to personnel holding related jobs (for example, the research or guidance director) or, if there are no such employees, to teachers who may be relieved of their regular jobs for the period required or given special summer employment.

In the systems which provide for special assignments to individuals to write, carry on research, and so forth, teachers who have related interests should make their qualifications known to the appropriate administrator. Frequently, administrators with inadequate central staffs have great difficulty in locating qualified persons to work on special assignments. Among the types of jobs which can be done well through the assignment of individual teachers or other personnel for periods of intensive work, are the following:

1. Writing of resource units on the basis of group plans, suggestions, and materials
2. Preparing, administering, and summarizing various kinds of instruments for evaluative purposes
3. Using interviews and other techniques to secure information from pupils, parents, laymen, and teachers for use in curriculum planning
4. Making intensive investigations of community and other resources to be used on an expanded scale
5. Heading discussions, or serving as a consultant in various faculty groups, on some curriculum issue of which the individual has made a special analysis
6. Writing tentative drafts of sections of comprehensive curriculum guides for review by appropriate committees
7. Carrying on specific fact-finding studies and surveys of a wide variety as bases for curriculum planning activities

A Desirable Organization for the System

Features of desirable organization for curriculum planning at the system level have been indicated throughout this section. These features are incorporated in a proposed organization for a small or medium-sized system in Figure 6. Criteria for a desirable organization may be summarized as follows:

1. Individual school units should be encouraged and facilitated by a central coordinating agency to develop curriculum plans appropriate to their pupils and communities.

2. Curriculum planning by departmental and grade groups and other special-interest groups should be coordinated through the central coordinating agency and subject to implementation as desired by individual units.

3. Centrally planned policies should involve participation of all concerned and should be subject to review and modification by individual school units in accordance with the first criterion.

4. Once general policies are established or problems identified cooperatively, the most efficient means possible of implementing plans and solving problems should be utilized.

5. The plan of organization should be continuously evaluated and modified as needs arise.

PARTICIPATION THROUGH IN-SERVICE EDUCATION ACTIVITIES

A widespread development in the past two decades has been the great increase in the number of teachers who, following initial employment, participate in some type of in-service education activity, that is, continued education on the job. Along with the increase in participation has been considerable change in the nature of in-service education. As continued professional study is coming to be regarded as a part of the teacher's job, many school systems are requiring periodic participation. That is, these systems require for continued employment that staff members engage in some approved type of in-service education every few years or oftener. Many school systems organize their own in-service activities, and others offer various incentives for teachers' study in summer sessions, extension courses, and other means. In some cases teachers' employment is extended through part or all of the summer, and in-service programs are provided during the period that children are not in school. In this section attention is given to certain activities which are widely used for in-service education.

PLATE 37

PLATE 38

PLATES 37 AND 38. TEACHER WORKSHOP ACTIVITIES. *In workshops teachers learn to direct pupils' creative activities by carrying on these activities themselves. (Courtesy of the Broward County, Florida, Public Schools [top] and of the Elizabeth, New Jersey, Public Schools [bottom])*

Workshops

The beginning of a considerable modification of summer sessions and college course procedures was made in 1936 when a group of teachers from schools participating in the Eight-Year Study of the Progressive Education Association came together at Ohio State University in the first so-called "workshop" to work with consultative assistance on curriculum problems. Three workshops were sponsored the following summer and five in 1938 by the same organization. The idea of a workshop in contrast to the traditional college-course pattern took hold and in succeeding years a wide variety of workshops have been organized throughout the United States. Also, the idea has been so popular that a great many courses and conferences have been renamed "workshops" without substantial modification of procedures. At the same time many courses and conferences have been improved through the use of workshop techniques.

The distinguishing characteristics of the workshop may be summarized as follows:

1. Participants work on problems that are related by association in the same school system, or in a cooperative study, or by preliminary definition.

2. The problems are attacked through individual and group activities during an intensive period not limited by the inflexible schedule characteristic of the college course.

3. Consultants are selected in terms of their competences to deal with the problems identified by the participants, and work as advisers and resource persons rather than as lecturers.

4. A total program for the workshop is arranged by the participants to provide for a breadth of learning experiences, a balanced personal life, and as tangible results with respect to the problems as possible. These provisions are indicated in the following illustrative schedule of a typical workshop day.

9:00–10:00	*General session* Group singing Announcements Address by a staff member
10:00–10:30	*Meeting of teams from individual schools* (At coffee hour)
10:30–12:00	*Work session, problems groups*
12:00– 1:00	*Lunch*
1:00– 2:30	*Conference period* (committees; work in resource centers; appointments with consultants)
2:30– 3:30	*Work session, problems groups*
3:30– ?	*Recreational activities* (sports, arts and crafts, cards, etc.)

Three general types of workshops can be identified. First, organizations sponsoring various types of curriculum studies bring together representatives from participating schools to consider common problems. This was the basis of the first workshops sponsored by the Progressive Education Association and was the same plan subsequently used by such groups as the Commission on Teacher Education of the American Council on Education, the National Commission on Teacher Education and Professional Standards of the National Education Association, the Horace Mann–Lincoln Institute of School Experimentation and particularly by various state curriculum programs, as in Michigan, Florida, Wisconsin, and Illinois, where series of workshops in local centers and institutions have been developed. Second, many organizations and institutions have utilized short periods (a few days to a few weeks) to bring together invited or representative personnel for the consideration of a single professional problem. Thus school systems very frequently designate representatives to a workshop sponsored by the state department of education to consider some important problem of state-wide concern, or to a workshop sponsored by a state or national professional organization or by a teacher-education institution to consider some problem of general professional significance. The emphasis here is on developing an action program for the profession rather than on the specific, common problems of the systems represented. Third, and perhaps of more direct relationship to curriculum improvement, many city and county school systems hold annual workshops for their own personnel. These local workshops follow various patterns, but usually involve the cooperation of some institution which may grant college credit, arrangements to cover or reduce the expenses of participants, and the identification of problems of the system as the centers of attention. Some systems now provide such workshops as a part of the teacher's employment period, whereas others offer the workshop on a voluntary basis with participation perhaps stimulated by credit requirements.

Study Groups

In many individual schools and school systems formal and informal opportunities are provided for the continuing study of curriculum problems. Thus, educational aims or child development or teaching procedures may be the theme of a series of meetings of the local faculty, or of cross-sectional groups throughout a city system, or of a joint parent-teacher group. Frequently, leadership in the organization of such groups is taken by professional organizations. The program committee of the local branch of the Association for Childhood Education, or of the local teachers' association, or of the principals' club, for example, may arrange a series of lecture-discussions, panels, or other types of programs around some common theme.

Such study groups may be organized wholly on a voluntary basis or as a part of an organized curriculum program. In some systems, study groups are organized centrally for new teachers or other groups whose members are expected to participate. In the more formally organized study programs, provision may be made for credit on salary-schedule requirements or for released time or for other inducements.

Certain characteristics seem to make for successful study groups: (1) participation of group members in the identification of problems and the planning of procedures and programs, (2) appropriate times and places for group meetings, (3) relatively small groups of ten to twenty-five, (4) varied types of programs, with ample provision for group discussion, and (5) clear channels for presenting recommendations to larger groups, representative councils, or administrative bodies. Probably the term "study group" describes a procedure rather than an organization, since a series of faculty meetings or committee meetings or an extension course might have similar characteristics. The procedure, however, is an accepted one that may be quite significant in developing mutual understanding and solutions to common problems.

Organized Courses

Probably the most frequent type of in-service education is still participation in organized college courses. Degree, certification, and board requirements make mandatory the accumulation of credits in many systems, and even in others the salary schedule offers incentives for course work.

Although degree and other requirements may define the nature of the courses to be taken, increasing flexibility is noted in the courses offered on an in-service basis. Many teachers are able to take off-campus courses in their own or neighboring districts during late afternoons, evenings, and Saturdays. A great variety of courses are available in college summer sessions. Many off-campus courses are organized around problems of the enrollees, and frequently are arranged for by the local administration or the curriculum council to help with local probems. In some school systems teachers are now given guidance in their choice of summer session courses so that new insights and ideas may be brought back to the local faculty. Indeed, teachers are sometimes asked to attend a particular summer session on a salaried, expense, or scholarship basis in order to develop some competence needed in the local situation.

Possibly as a result of the workshop movement teachers have increasing opportunity to make their in-service courses practical and valuable. With the insight that experience gives into one's own curriculum problems, teachers who participate actively in defining problems and procedures for their courses may find themselves engaging in exceedingly well-motivated and productive learning activities.

Organized Visitation and Other In-Service Activities

The traditional practice of a fixed number of "visiting days" in many school systems has been replaced by plans for visitation which ensure a clearer definition of the reasons and results of the visit. When teachers observe others for well-defined purposes with full opportunity to discuss their observations and draw conclusions cooperatively there may be important educational values. Accordingly, supervisory programs increasingly provide for invitations to teachers to visit others for such purposes as the following ones identified by Melchior: (1) observation of a closely similar situation—age level or subject matter area—for a particular phase of the work for more inclusive purposes; (2) observation of a grade level below or above the one being taught by the visiting teacher, for purposes of continuity of the curriculum and teaching procedures; and (3) observation of a class in a subject matter area other than the visitor's, to see how subject matter is related.[9]

Another type of organized visitation is the visit of a group of teachers to a particular situation in their own or another community. Haskew has described the planned visitation of a group interested in a particular problem as an "educational clinic." [10] The advantage of this plan lies in the follow-up discussion which is facilitated by the observations of a number of persons. Whatever the purpose and type of visit, certain steps are essential: (1) the clear identification of a problem for which observation of another teacher or teachers can help; (2) the selection (with the help usually of the principal or supervisor) of the situation or situations in which observation may be expected to help; (3) definite arrangements with each teacher to be visited as to the time of the visit and the type of activity to be observed; and (4) following the visit, a conference between the visitor and the host. The follow-up conference may be much more successful if a third person, the principal or supervisor if possible, who has also visited the same situation, may participate.

We consider in-service education as a process of learning in regard

[9] William T. Melchior, *Instructional Supervision* (Boston: D. C. Heath & Company, 1950), p. 365.
[10] L. D. Haskew, "The Educational Clinic—A Means for Curriculum Change," *Educational Leadership*, 7:227–230 (January), 1950.

to the actual teaching problems of the teacher. In the light of this definition, a great many additional in-service educational opportunities may
be identified:

1. Conferences with supervisors or others following their observations
   of the teacher at work
2. Observation of a demonstration by another teacher or supervisor
3. Study of professional publications bearing on problems of concern
4. Travel to secure firsthand information about processes, places, and
   people included in the scope of the curriculum
5. Participation in professional meetings and conferences
6. Attendance at programs of a general educational nature
7. Practice to attain greater proficiency in activities such as music,
   art, sports, or others in which the teacher lacks skills to guide
   youngsters
8. Study of the community and its institutions

In addition to all the procedures discussed and listed in this section, the
teacher's participation in curriculum councils, faculty meetings, and
other approaches to curriculum improvement has in-service educational
values.

In-Service Education and Curriculum Planning

The chief criteria for the in-service educational value of any activity are
these: (1) Does the activity relate to a definite problem recognized by
the participant? (2) Does the experience involved make a positive contribution to ability to deal with the problem? (3) Does the activity promote general professional growth and thus the curriculum of learners?
As in learning of all types, the answers to such questions have to be
reached for each individual if sound conclusions of an evaluative nature
are to be made. However, the increasing participation of educational
workers in these in-service educational programs and activities seems to
attest to the validity of this approach to improvement.

For curriculum planning, the great significance of the in-service
educational program is the provision it makes for cooperative attack of
school personnel on curriculum problems. That is, an organized program
of in-service education is in effect a program of curriculum improvement. In many school systems a workshop or other in-service activity is the starting point for fundamental curriculum improvement.
We believe that the reason lies in the cooperative participation these activities generally demonstrate. Participation in continuous curriculum
planning may and frequently does follow.

COOPERATIVE RESEARCH AND EXPERIMENTATION

A considerable amount of curriculum experimentation and research (see Chapter 15) is carried forward on an intersystem basis, usually with the leadership or sponsorship of some organization or teacher-education institution. The Eight-Year Study of the Progressive Education Association was an early and important program of this type. Similar large-scale programs have been carried forward by the Commission on Teacher Education of the American Council on Education, the Sloan Foundation, the Southern Association of Colleges and Secondary Schools, the Stanford University Studies in Social Education and Language Arts, the Bureau for Intercultural Education, the Horace Mann–Lincoln Institute of School Experimentation, and other organizations. Several of these programs are described in references listed at the end of this chapter. Usually there is some joint definition of problems by the cooperating institutions, some agreement as to how each unit will approach the problem, and arrangements for exchange of experiments and sharing of consultative assistance. Examples of national, regional, and state cooperative programs are described in the following paragraphs.

Horace Mann–Lincoln Institute of School Experimentation

For several years the Horace Mann–Lincoln Institute of School Experimentation, Teachers College, Columbia University, has carried on cooperative studies with school systems designated as "cooperating field laboratories." These systems have included Battle Creek, Michigan; Denver, Colorado; Glencoe, Illinois; Kansas City, Missouri; Montgomery County, Maryland; New York City; Philadelphia; Springfield, Missouri; West Orange, New Jersey; and others. The Institute's own description of "The Way We Work" includes the following statements:

> Our experimentation has to do with problems significant *both* to the cooperating field group and to the members of the Institute staff.

> Experimentation is most valid and most likely to lead to practical results when it relates intimately to matters of personal and professional concern to the experimenters. In all the field situations in which Institute staff members are now working, the research under way represents mutuality of interest and shared effort.

> Most of the cooperative experimentation is of the *action* or *operational research* type.

> The problems attacked experimentally grow out of the field situation in which the cooperative studies are undertaken. An attempt is made to design these studies so as, first, to discover and test the

worth of practices initiated to improve the learning experiences of boys and girls in the local situation, and, second, to formulate generalizations of wide applicability.

The Institute staff spends a considerable amount of its time working directly with school people in the cooperating field laboratories.

For most effective cooperative experimentation the persons involved must spend a great deal of time in a face-to-face working group. In 1949–50 each full-time Institute staff member engaged in cooperative experimentation spent approximately 50 days in the field.

The public school system and the Institute share the cost of experimentation.

The public school system meets the cost of providing (1) substitute teachers so that the research teams may have time for their experimentation; (2) new materials; (3) workshop and conference attendance; and (4) similar items necessitated by experimentation. The Institute pays the salaries and travel expenses of its staff.[11]

In addition to the direct influence of the program of the Institute in the cooperating field situations, an impressive list of Institute publications are designed to report its studies to the profession in general. The brochure just cited listed the following completed publications in addition to a list of publications planned:

Books and Monographs	*Publication Date*
Child Development and the Curriculum Arthur T. Jersild and associates	1946
Developing a Curriculum for Modern Living Florence B. Stratemeyer, Hamden L. Forkner, Margaret G. McKim, and associates	1947
How to Construct a Sociogram The Staff	1947
Guide to Cooperative Planning in Education The Staff	1947
Teacher's Role in Pupil-Teacher Planning The Staff	1947
Children's Interests Arthur T. Jersild, Ruth J. Tasch, and associates	1949
Joys and Problems of Child Rearing Arthur T. Jersild and associates	1949

[11] *Horace Mann–Lincoln Institute of School Experimentation, Teachers College, Columbia University* (New York: The Institute, 1951), p. 4. Reprinted by permission of the Bureau of Publications, Teachers College, Columbia University.

Books and Monographs (continued)

Parents and Teachers View the Child	1949
Charlotte Del Solar	
Cooperative Research and Curriculum Improvement	1950
Hubert Evans (editor)	
Understanding Group Behavior of Boys and Girls	1951
Ruth Cunningham and associates	

Films	*Release Date*
Learning through Cooperative Planning	1948
Alice Miel and associates	
We Plan Together	1948 [12]
Alice Miel and associates	

The Southern Association's Cooperative Study in Elementary Education

The Southern Association's Cooperative Study in Elementary Education is an example of a regional program designed to stimulate and assist local research and experimentation. Although not planned as a research program of the type just described, the Cooperative Study has involved cooperative effort in the South in the improvement of elementary education through processes of research and experimentation in local elementary schools. The study was supported by special grants from the General Education Board through 1951 and some of its activities have since been continued by the Southern Association of Colleges and Secondary Schools. The study functions through state committees in each of the southern states. Four publications issued by the Cooperative Study have had wide use:

> *Good Schools for Children* (a pictorial brochure on desirable characteristics of elementary schools)
> *Education of Elementary School Personnel* (statement of principles for local programs of teacher recruitment, selection, education, and welfare)
> *Evaluating the Elementary School—A Guide for Cooperative Study* (a study guide for school faculties and others to use in evaluating and planning elementary school programs)
> *Promising Practices in Elementary Schools* (verbal and pictorial descriptions of good teaching and curriculum practices throughout the region) [13]

[12] *Ibid.*, p. 5. All of these publications are published by the Bureau of Publications, Teachers College, Columbia University, as are the following Institute publications pertinent to curriculum planning which have been issued since the above list: Alice Miel and associates, *Cooperative Procedures of Learning* (1952); Stephen M. Corey, *Action Research to Improve School Practices* (1953); Gordon N. Mackenzie, Stephen M. Corey, and associates, *Instructional Leadership* (1954).

[13] All these publications are published by the Southern Association of Colleges and Secondary Schools, 316 Peachtree Street, N.E., Atlanta, Georgia.

In addition to the payment of dues, the following responsibilities are assumed by cooperating schools:

Initiating a school improvement program within the local district, and furnishing the state committee with an occasional progress report.

Furnishing personnel to work with the state committee in developing a coordinated program of school improvement in the state.

Sharing promising practices with other cooperating school systems.

Helping in providing materials for and suggesting revisions of regional publications.

Sending representatives to state and regional workshops and conferences.

Cooperating in regional activities developed by the Central Coordinating Committee.[14]

The Illinois Secondary School Curriculum Program

An interesting pattern of a state program of curriculum research and improvement was initiated in Illinois in 1947 under the joint sponsorship of the Illinois Secondary School Principals' Association, the State Department of Public Instruction, and the College of Education, University of Illinois. The conditions under which schools and their staffs might participate in the study indicate the expectation of cooperative activity aimed at program improvement, as well as in part the nature of participation:

1. The board of education must approve participation in the ISSCP.

2. The school must make available enough of the time of the teachers concerned so that reasonable participation is possible. It is too much to expect teachers who are presently busy and overworked to participate effectively in an experimental program. Boards of education will, we hope, be willing to make this adjustment, in view of the extra services that they are obtaining without cost from the teams of consultants.

3. The schools must be willing to permit teachers who have participated in curriculum projects to spend a number of days each year in workshops, in meetings with teachers in other schools, and in helping generally to show other teachers how the projects were conducted. In this way, we hope that a substantial group of teachers who have participated in the program will, in time, be available to assist other

[14] "A Recommendation Regarding the Relationship of Elementary Schools to the Southern Association of Colleges and Secondary Schools" (Atlanta, Ga.: The Southern Association of Colleges and Secondary Schools, May 31, 1952), p. 2. Mimeographed. (Adopted by the Association in December, 1952. See the Association's 1953 brochure entitled *A New Program for the Improvement of Elementary Schools.*)

schools and thus increase the number of schools that are putting cur-riculum improvements into operation.

4. The schools should be willing to serve as observation centers. The Committee believes that one of the best ways to improve practice is to have teachers observe improved practice.

5. The schools to be used as developmental centers should be located at numerous points throughout the State, thus making it possible for teachers and administrators to visit these schools with a minimum amount of driving.

6. The schools should welcome a visit, prior to starting a program, by a small committee whose responsibility would be to try, in cooperation with local school officials, to ascertain whether or not the school should be used as a developmental center.

7. The school should provide, for members of the local school staff, funds for travel connected with curriculum improvement work.[15]

Subsequently a large number of schools entered the program, data were gathered concerning practices and problems, new programs were introduced, and several bulletins on findings and practices were published.

Cooperative Studies within School Systems

Persons who participate in such programs as described frequently are able to enjoy very fine professional experiences as a result. Participation in conferences, workshops, and publications is common. In addition to these professional opportunities, there is the possibility of personal satisfaction in making contributions to educational knowledge. Hence it is usually considered a privilege rather than an extra duty to participate in intersystem studies. These same privileges may be made available by the school system for interschool studies.

Every problem facing the system's curriculum planning committee is an opportunity for research, and every proposed solution a hypothesis for investigation. The success of curriculum planning, as noted in Chapter 15, depends very largely on the extent to which classroom experimentation takes place. Under cooperative planning procedures, the burden of proposing experimentation does not rest with the teacher, although he may propose hypotheses. The real responsibility is that of the planning group to identify schools and teachers interested in carrying forward experimentation and in giving them help and recognition comparable to that supplied by the sponsoring organization or institution in such intersystem studies as described.

[15] *Guide to the Study of the Curriculum in the Secondary Schools of Illinois,* Illinois Secondary School Curriculum Program, Bulletin No. 1 (Springfield, Ill.: State Superintendent of Public Instruction, August, 1948), p. 24. Reprinted by permission of the Superintendent.

PARTICIPATION IN PROFESSIONAL ASSOCIATIONS

No analysis of cooperative participation in organized curriculum improvement can rightfully overlook the leadership of professional organizations. Their programs for curriculum and general educational progress are of great importance in contemporary American education.

In some local systems lacking adequate administrative and supervisory leadership the impetus and indeed the program for curriculum study and improvement come from the local teachers' association. In several states, programs of cooperative curriculum study have been sponsored by state professional organizations. At the national level, organizations such as the National Society for the Study of Education, the Progressive Education Association, the John Dewey Society, the Association for Childhood Education, and the Association for Supervision and Curriculum Development of the National Education Association carry on effective leadership through publications, sponsorship of research studies, and organization of conferences to bring about general curriculum improvement. Organizations such as the National Council of Teachers of English, the National Council for the Social Studies, the National Council of Teachers of Mathematics, and others in special fields have rendered curriculum services through studies, publications, and conferences.

A particularly important project in cooperative curriculum research was initiated in 1951 by the Association for Supervision and Curriculum Development of the National Education Association. A summary of the discussions of this project held at an ASCD Curriculum Research Conference in Chicago, November, 1951, and at the annual convention of the Association in Boston, February, 1952, pointed out the following implications for teacher participation:

> One of the heartening points of emphasis in the Chicago and Boston discussions was that concerning the need for recognition and help to the large number of teachers and other educational workers carrying on classroom research and experimentation. As stated over and over again, these are the persons on whom we must count and to whom we must extend a helping hand if curriculum research activities are significantly expanded. According to reports made at these conferences, there are many teachers and others carrying on research as described in this article who do not think of their evidence-gathering activities as being research. Yet their studies, shared with others and perhaps refined by cooperative planning, might be of real significance in curriculum improvement.
>
> To give such teachers and others recognition and help and to make their research and experimentation of wider utility, such suggestions as these have been made:

Invite wider participation of teacher-researchers in ASCD membership, in conference programs, and in publications and other projects.

Maintain inventories of significant classroom research under way.

Encourage total school experimentation and the affiliation of schools engaged in experimentation for purposes of mutual exchange of ideas.

Emphasize classroom research projects in all publications dealing with research.

Encourage studies of provisions for teacher participation in research.[16]

Participation in improvement programs sponsored by professional organizations may include the following types of activities: (1) membership in appropriate organizations: (2) cooperation in questionnaires and other types of surveys and studies; (3) use of publications; (4) attendance at meetings and participation in programs; (5) preparation of materials for publication in official journals, yearbooks, and special reports or bulletins; (6) service on committees and in offices. The success of programs of these organizations depends on just such participation spread as widely as possible.

FACTORS WHICH FACILITATE PARTICIPATION

In closing this analysis of opportunities for participation in programs of curriculum improvement it is appropriate to identify the factors or conditions which seem to make for wide and effective participation. Our own observations indicate that the following factors are most critical:[17]

1. Teachers who are imaginative, open-minded, energetic, self-critical: teachers, like the learners they teach, must want to learn if participation is to be real.

2. A pattern of administrative procedure and quality of administrative leadership which encourage individual initiative: teachers and others cannot participate effectively in curriculum programs unless they have faith that the results of their work will be accepted and implemented by administrative officials.

3. Clearly defined groups and procedures for planning curriculum

---

[16] William M. Alexander, "ASCD's Role in Cooperative Curriculum Research," *Educational Leadership*, 9:476 (May), 1952.

[17] See, for an extensive study of such factors, J. Galen Saylor, *Factors Associated with Participation in Cooperative Programs of Curriculum Development* (New York: Bureau of Publications, Teachers College, Columbia University, 1941).

improvement: without such groups and procedures participation may be aimless and wasted.

4. Facilities and time for experimentation, planning, and study: a reasonable teaching load, adequate facilities in materials and working quarters, and time for cooperative planning are essential.

5. Provision of adequate local consultative services of a competent and permissive type: such services are essential in helping individuals overcome the limitations of their experience.

6. Full opportunity for interchange of experience: arrangements for exchange of personnel, interschool councils and bulletins, and reciprocal visits are helpful.

7. Recognition of successful effort: the incentive of salary and other advancement, scholarships, opportunities for writing and speaking, leaves of absence, and expenses for professional meetings may greatly encourage continued participation.

For Further Study

Alexander, William M., "Organizing the Individual School for Curriculum Improvement," *Teachers College Record,* 52:278–286 (February), 1951.

Describes a plan of organizing the individual school for curriculum improvement.

American Association of School Administrators, *American School Curriculum.* Thirty-first Yearbook. Washington, D.C.: National Education Association, 1953.

See Chapter IV, "Mobilizing for Curriculum Improvement"; Chapter IX, "Home and Community Influence Instruction"; and Chapter X, "Building Public Understanding."

Association for Supervision and Curriculum Development, National Education Association, *Action for Curriculum Improvement.* 1951 Yearbook. Washington, D.C.: The Association, 1951.

See for descriptions of participation in various phases of curriculum improvement.

Benne, Kenneth D., and Bozidar Muntyan, *Human Relations in Curriculum Change.* New York: The Dryden Press, 1951.

Helpful source book of readings on the role of human relations in curriculum change.

Caswell, Hollis L., and associates, *Curriculum Improvement in Public School Systems.* New York: Bureau of Publications, Teachers College, Columbia University, 1950.

Contains detailed descriptions of curriculum programs in nine school systems.

Corey, Stephen M., *Action Research to Improve School Practices.* New York: Bureau of Publications, Teachers College, Columbia University, 1953.

Excellent guide to cooperative participation in action research. Based on the cooperative studies carried forward by the Horace Mann–Lincoln Institute of School Experimentation.

Denver Public Schools, *Human Relations in Action: Pupils, Parents, and Teachers Work Together*. Denver: The Schools, 1952.

Report of experiences in the elementary schools of Denver in the study of human relations. Part II gives many illustrations of cooperative planning and study by parents, teachers, and principals.

Doll, Ronald A., Harry A. Passow, and Stephen M. Corey, *Organizing for Curriculum Improvement*. New York: Bureau of Publications, Teachers College, Columbia University, 1953.

Analysis of patterns of organization for curriculum improvement.

Guide to the Study of the Curriculum in the Secondary Schools of Illinois. Illinois Secondary School Curriculum Program, Bulletin No. 1; Springfield, Ill.: Superintendent of Public Instruction, August, 1948.

This initial bulletin in the Illinois Secondary School Curriculum Program describes means of securing participation in the Program.

Haskew, L. D., *The Educational Clinic*. Washington, D.C.: American Council on Education, 1949.

Description of educational clinics as means of continued education of school personnel.

Iowa ASCD Chapter, *Time and Funds for Curriculum Development*. Washington, D.C.: Association for Supervision and Curriculum Development, National Education Association, 1951.

Report of survey of provision of time and funds by school systems, for curriculum development.

Kelley, Earl C., *The Workshop Way of Learning*. New York: Harper & Brothers, 1951.

This report of a Wayne University workshop for teachers describes workshop procedures and their implications for teaching.

Mackenzie, Gordon N., Stephen M. Corey, and associates, *Instructional Leadership*. New York: Bureau of Publications, Teachers College, Columbia University, 1954.

Outgrowth of three years of cooperative experimentation in the Denver, Colorado, Schools in conjunction with the Horace Mann–Lincoln Institute.

Melchoir, William T., *Instructional Supervision*. Boston: D. C. Heath & Company, 1950.

Gives 35 "Illustrations of Practice" to describe supervisory programs and activities. Teacher participation in curriculum study and in-service education is well illustrated.

Miel, Alice, *Changing the Curriculum: A Social Process*. New York: Appleton-Century-Crofts, Inc., 1946.

Fundamental analysis of curriculum development as a process of change in people.

National Citizens Commission for the Public Schools, *How Can We Organize for Better Schools?* New York: The Commission, 1953.

This guidebook for citizens' school committees answers these questions: "Do we need a citizens' committee?" "What kind of committee do we need?" "How should we organize our committee?" "How should our committee operate?" "How can we keep our committee going?"

Prall, Charles E., and C. Leslie Cushman, *Teacher Education In-Service.* Washington: American Council on Education, 1944.

Report of the in-service programs of schools which cooperated in the national study of teacher education sponsored by the American Council on Education.

Saylor, J. Galen, *Factors Associated with Participation in Cooperative Programs of Curriculum Improvement.* New York: Bureau of Publications, Teachers College, Columbia University, 1941.

Comprehensive study of factors in the Virginia state program.

Sharp, George, *Curriculum Development as Re-education of the Teacher.* New York: Bureau of Publications, Teachers College, Columbia University, 1951.

Investigates the thesis that the curriculum develops basically as the result of the development of teachers' personalities.

Stinnett, T. M. (ed.), *The Teaching Profession Grows in Service.* Washington, D.C.: Commission on Teacher Education and Professional Standards, National Education Association, 1949.

This report of the National Conference on the Professional Growth of Teachers in Service is a helpful guide to planning in-service education programs.

Strauss, Bert, and Frances Strauss, *New Ways to Better Meetings.* New York: The Viking Press, 1951.

Leads for making meetings, committees, conferences, and so forth, *produce* more effectively.

Utterback, W. E., *Group Thinking and Conference Leadership.* New York: Rinehart & Company, Inc., 1950.

Use of discussion techniques and skills in community relations and classrooms with emphasis on the role of the discussion leader.

chapter 17

Evaluating Curriculum Planning

In previous chapters of this book we have considered the various problems and processes of curriculum planning. In connection with most, if not all, of these problems and processes attention has been directed to evaluative procedures. In this final chapter we shall examine the total process of evaluating curriculum planning.

THE RELATIONSHIP OF EVALUATION AND PLANNING

In the simplest terms, to evaluate is "to determine the value of." The evaluation of curriculum planning is the determination of the value of that planning. Thus evaluation is one phase of the total process of curriculum planning, for we recognize and emphasize the necessity of constant revision of plans in the light of evidence regarding the need for change. Such evidence is secured through evaluative procedures. Inasmuch as the dynamic nature of the curriculum makes curriculum planning a continuous process, evaluation must be continuous also.

Evaluation and planning are really complementary processes. We plan the curriculum to achieve educational values. Our planning is based on evaluation of existing plans in terms of their relevance to these values, and our subsequent evaluation determines the relevance of new plans to whatever values are held, and then we plan further. We plan on the basis of evaluation and we evaluate on the basis of planning; evaluation without planning or planning without evaluation is incomplete and hence unwise.

Evaluation is frequently the weakest link in this chain of curriculum planning. After the planning is done is not the time to decide to evaluate. Because evaluation is frequently approached as hindsight only, evidence is frequently inadequate as to the success of changes made. Skeptics and critics of curriculum change are not answered very well when school personnel say that they "think" the new practice is better, but that they forgot to plan ways and means of comparing "before" and "after" or of collecting other evidence. Both to protect ourselves in making change and to assure sound steps in planning, we need to incorporate procedures of evaluation in every curriculum plan.

As complementary processes, planning and evaluation rarely occur as completely discrete steps. In usual practice these processes are occurring somewhat simultaneously. A group of teachers carrying on curriculum planning are almost continuously referring back and forth to plans and judgments. Virtually every step in a plan involves the making of a judgment, an evaluative process. That is, we plan as we evaluate and we evaluate as we plan. The integrality of the relationship is further indicated by the fact that the process of curriculum planning includes planning the evaluation of its results. And evaluation procedures must inevitably themselves be evaluated.

These various relationships are possibly responsible for considerable confusion in the use of the terms involved. Evaluation is used by some writers to include the whole process of planning. We ourselves believe that the somewhat narrower definition we have given creates less confusion and provides a basis for understanding the relationship between the total process of planning and one of its major phases, evaluation.

To summarize, planning and evaluation are complementary processes which should occur almost simultaneously and continuously. This does not mean, however, that evaluation itself cannot be planned. The worth of planning is determined in part by the soundness of the judgments on which it is based. Although plans and judgments are being made together, there are still discrete procedures which may be planned to ensure sound judgments. In general, these procedures, in relation to curriculum planning, are of two types: those which evaluate planning as a process, and those which evaluate planning through its results. These procedures are considered in the following two sections; a concluding section deals with the development of a program of continuous evaluation of curriculum planning.

EVALUATING THE PLANNING PROCESS

At least three aspects of the process of curriculum planning may be identified for purposes of evaluation: first, the over-all planning of goals, design, scope, and sequence; second, the planning of learning experiences; and, third, the organization for planning. Since we have already dealt with each of these aspects, in this section we shall merely review possible approaches to their evaluation. Later in this chapter (see Table 13) there is presented a check list for evaluating the process of curriculum planning in an individual school.

Evaluating Over-all Curriculum Planning

Part 3 dealt with procedures for over-all curriculum planning. In these chapters desirable principles for defining the goals, design, and general framework of the curriculum were identified. The usual procedure for evaluating the process of planning or making these definitions is that of determining whether such desirable principles were followed. That is, to evaluate over-all curriculum planning the evaluating group simply asks: Did we use, or are we using, desirable principles in defining curriculum goals? the design of the curriculum? the general framework? What we consider "desirable principles" may be reviewed by reference to Chapters 8–11. Whether or not these particular principles are accepted by the planning group, the first step in evaluation is to determine desirable principles of planning. This process may involve extended experimentation and evaluation of the results of planning, or it may be more simply done through accepting the principles proposed by competent authority or established by the research of others. However arrived at, these principles, restated as necessary to be applicable, become criteria for evaluating planning processes. The second step is to apply these standards, and the third is to interpret the results of such application.

To illustrate the evaluative procedure just described, note the following as sample criteria of over-all curriculum planning:

1. One essential source of curriculum goals is analysis of contemporary community problems.

2. Experimentation with new curriculum designs should be one provision of the design planned for.

3. One essential consideration in defining the scope of the curriculum is that of the persistent social functions.

4. One major factor in defining the sequence of the curriculum is analysis of the developmental needs of learners.

If a typical high school faculty reviewed its over-all curriculum planning activities in the light of the above criteria, the following facts might be revealed:

1. The curriculum goals of the school are not planned by direct reference to contemporary community problems.

2. The system of required and elective subjects makes impossible any experimentation with another curriculum design.

3. The planning of subjects does not consider directly the persistent social functions.

4. The sequence of courses taken is based primarily on tradition without reference to the developmental needs of learners.

If such negative findings were determined by application of evaluative criteria, the obvious interpretation to be made is that the process of curriculum planning needs change to include more consideration of desirable principles of over-all planning.

To summarize, the evaluation of over-all curriculum planning as a process can be a relatively simple matter of critical analysis. One determines desirable principles of over-all planning, and this may be the difficult step; one ascertains whether these principles have been followed; and one then decides whether the facts indicate that different procedures in over-all planning are needed.

Evaluating the Planning of Learning Experiences

Several of the preceding chapters dealt with various phases of the planning of specific learning experiences: resource units and unit plans (Chapter 12); classroom planning (Chapter 13); resources for learning experiences (Chapter 14); and classroom research and experimentation (Chapter 15). In each of these chapters desirable characteristics of planning in relation to the phase concerned have been stated directly or may be implied from the analysis. For example, Chapter 12 includes a statement of the characteristics of good units of work, and Chapter 15 presents an analysis of three examples of classroom research and experimentation. The evaluative steps might again be the acceptance, with such modification as needed, of these desirable characteristics as criteria, then their application, and the interpretation of findings. That is, the procedure is similar to that described in the preceding section: (1) determination of criteria for planning; (2) examination of the procedures actually employed on the basis of the criteria; and (3) interpretation of the findings.

It should be noted here that the explanation of these evaluative procedures as such simple and logical steps is based on two assumptions. First, it is assumed that the group doing the evaluating is the same as the group doing the planning. Therefore the step of securing evidence regarding how planning was done is primarily a matter of reflection by the people who did the planning. If others do the evaluating, this step may be much more difficult. Second, it is assumed that the process of determining criteria is simplified by adapting those that have been proposed in published form. If the evaluative procedure involves the development and validation of standards by other means, this step may be considerably more complex. We believe that the planning group should do its own evaluation, but that this group may accept or adapt criteria developed by others if these criteria appear applicable and valid. In general, it seems desirable that any set of criteria developed outside the situation be carefully evaluated in the light of the situation and modified so as to apply if used at all.

Evaluating the Organization for Planning

In our chapter (16) on organization for curriculum planning we suggested the following essential characteristics of a good school organization:

1. Curriculum planning efforts are organized in terms of goals which result from the considered thinking of all persons directly affected and which represent general agreements as to jobs to be better accomplished by the school.

2. No sharp lines are drawn between pupil, parent, layman, and teacher participation in curriculum planning, but each person and each group are utilized in terms of their potential contributions bearing on the goals sought.

3. Although many jobs may be of a very narrow nature, each job assigned a committee or an individual is in terms of the needs of the total program. Final decisions as to policies, jobs, and specific changes are made with reference to the program of the school as a whole rather than by departmental or special-activities groups.

4. An atmosphere of cooperative planning and evaluation pervades all groups and the school as a whole.

5. A continuing search is made by all concerned to identify services, materials, facilities, and persons who can contribute to curriculum planning.

Subject to the two assumptions explained in the preceding section, we believe that the planning-evaluating group might evaluate its organization for planning in terms of the above characteristics or some modification thereof.

EVALUATING THE RESULTS OF CURRICULUM PLANNING

The procedure of evaluating curriculum planning as a process makes an important assumption: that a good process will have good results. A parallel assumption would be that good planning procedures by the medical personnel of a health clinic would result in sound treatment of all patients. By and large, we would agree that efficient and comprehensive planning of case histories, examinations, diagnoses, and treatments would make for better treatment of patients than haphazard planning. At the same time, before going to such a clinic for treatment we would probably make some inquiry as to the nature and results of the treatment previous patients had been given. That is, we would want to test the goodness of clinical planning by its results, that is, the treatments. Similarly, neither the teaching profession nor the public would be likely to accept the curriculum as good simply because we had determined that good planning procedures had been used. We would want to know how good were the results of planning, that is, the curriculum itself.

Many procedures are available for evaluating the results of curriculum planning. One procedure is that of evaluating written curriculum guides. Because "paper curriculums" may be so very different from the actual curriculum of learners, we feel this procedure is more unrealistic than the evaluation of planning as a process. Certainly physicians would not evaluate a colleague's work sheerly on the basis of his written prescriptions. We also believe that certain other procedures are either too impractical or too unrelated to the real results sought to justify their use by curriculum planning groups in general. These procedures include the experimental comparison of different curriculums, which focuses on comparative factors in plans rather than on the goodness of a particular plan for the learning group; the analysis of factors influencing the curriculum, which helps, but does not evaluate directly, curriculum planning; and the determination of what results curriculum planning has on teacher growth and similar indirectly affected factors, which again evaluates factors only hypothetically related to the real results sought by curriculum planning. We ourselves believe that the following four procedures can be used effectively by curriculum planning groups to evaluate the results of their activities: (1) appraisal of pupil progress; (2) follow-up studies of learners; (3) studies of opinions regarding the curriculum; and (4) cooperative evaluation by the faculty. Each of these procedures is described in a subsequent section.

Appraisal of Pupil Progress

The test we would be most concerned about in relation to medical planning is that of the results to the patient. Similarly, the fundamental test of curriculum planning is its results on learners. This, according to Caswell, is the "ultimate criterion":

> The ultimate criterion for testing all curriculum work is improvement in the experiences of pupils. No matter how elaborate a program may be or how enthusiastic the staff, unless in the end the experiences of pupils are changed so that educational outcomes are better than before, the work cannot be considered successful. It is extremely difficult to apply this ultimate criterion, and every school system should have a carefully conceived plan of evaluation in con-

tinuous operation to secure as reliable evidence as possible upon which to base judgment.[1]

Other bases for evaluation are described by Caswell as "subordinate criteria." Thus all of the approaches to evaluation reviewed in the previous section, and the plan of cooperative evaluation to be described in a subsequent section, would be classified as "subordinate." Use of these procedures is frequently essential, however, because of the difficulty noted by Caswell in applying the criterion of effects on learners.

A major source of difficulty in evaluating curriculum planning through the "ultimate criterion" is that of distinguishing between changes in learners which result from school experience and those which result from other influences. This difficulty is particularly acute in appraising changes in attitudes and general behaviors, which can be affected by so many factors. Furthermore, these changes are more difficult to measure than changes in skills. However, these difficulties can be overcome at least partially by a well-planned program of appraisal. The major elements of such a program follow the same three steps in evaluation as previously illustrated. Attention is given to these steps in the following paragraphs.

Determination of goals in terms of desired behavior of learners. However goals may be stated in the process of curriculum planning, they need to be expressed in terms of the behavior (that is, the way an individual *acts*) of learners, for purposes of appraisal. For example, the goal of "understanding the responsibilities of American citizenship" (see Table 11, page 400) may need to be broken down into such specific pupil behaviors as the following.

> To understand the significance in American life of voting, paying taxes, law obedience, and other responsibilities of citizenship
> To observe accepted standards of courtesy in playing and working with other persons
> To carry one's share of responsibility for maintaining a good working situation in the classroom

Curriculum planning processes should result in at least three types of goal statements which influence the appraisal of pupil progress. First, as we noted in Chapter 7, over-all planning should determine major goals sought in curriculum planning. These goals are the basic guides or criteria for appraising pupil progress at all levels. Second, the planning for scope and sequence of the curriculum should result in some identifica-

[1] Hollis L. Caswell and associates, *Curriculum Improvement in Public School Systems* (New York: Bureau of Publications, Teachers College, Columbia University, 1950), pp. 98–99. Reprinted by permission of the Bureau of Publications, Teachers College, Columbia University.

tion of goals or subgoals to be emphasized at particular levels. Teachers at a particular level use this selection of goals as criteria for appraising the progress of their pupils. For example, over-all planning might identify as a major curriculum goal "facility in the use of communication skills" and allocate, in the curriculum framework, emphasis in the primary grades to the area of beginning reading. Plans for appraising pupil progress in the primary grades would therefore include means of appraising skill in reading. Third, the teacher's planning for a particular learning group involves the selection of units of work, each having specific learning goals. Thus, the first-grade teacher's unit of work on "Our School Helpers" includes as a desired learning the recognition of such words as "school," "teacher," and "nurse," and plans for appraising progress will provide for tests of the recognition of these words.

Securing evidence regarding the desired behaviors. The application of behavior goals as criteria involves the accumulation of evidence. The traditional method of appraisal, the written test, is only one of many ways of securing evidence regarding pupil behavior, and is actually one of the most unreliable with respect to many types of behavior. Among the techniques for getting data about the behavior of learners are the following:

1. Case studies—comprehensive studies of individuals usually made for analysis of causes rather than of the nature of behavior

2. Conferences—with parents, other teachers, employers, and so on, to secure data regarding an individual's behavior in situations not observed by the teacher

3. Diaries and logs—kept by learners and analyzed by the teacher to secure various items of information

4. Group evaluation of individuals—through rating scales and sociometric techniques to secure evidence from his peers of an individual learner's acceptance and performance

5. Interviews with learners—to get information about their performance, understanding, and other items of behavior

6. Inventories of many types—to give information about such items as personality traits, outside activities, reading and listening habits, and use of time

7. Observation of pupils—in various situations to determine behavior of a specific nature

8. Performance tests—including creative work, group productions, physical skills, and similar items of behavior best tested through observation of performance

9. Pictures, still and motion—for later observation of performance, appearance, and so on

10. Rating scales—used by teacher, pupils, and others to estimate behavior on specific traits such as courtesy, speech, and legibility of handwriting

11. Recordings—of individual voices and group discussions for later analysis

12. Records of many types—achievement, anecdotal, attendance, autobiographical, cumulative, disciplinary, health, library, participation (in activities, discussion, elections, and so on), stenographic (of group proceedings), tests, and time studies

13. Self-analyses—made by learners on check lists, rating scales, questionnaires, problem situations, and general questions

14. Written tests—standardized, teacher-made, group-made, to test information and skills

The chief problem in securing evidence is to select the proper technique to appraise the actions under consideration. The teacher's familiarity with many types of techniques is essential. Further information about these techniques is available in the professional literature, and several helpful references are cited at the end of this chapter.

Interpreting the evidence. Once learners' behavior has been appraised in terms of the goals sought, there must still be careful analysis of appraisal results for judgments to be reached about the goodness of curriculum planning. Two major issues to be considered in the interpretation of appraisal results are these:

1. Are the results good (or bad) enough to make possible a judgment regarding curriculum planning? In order to meet this issue squarely, two preliminary steps are desirable. First, some basis of comparison of one set of appraisal results with another is needed. That is, to determine progress on a skill, for example, it is necessary to have an initial measure of performance and one or more subsequent measures. Second, some norm of expected progress should be set. Although this step may be difficult, and it may even be impossible to establish quantitative norms for some behavior goals, the teacher can usually have in mind some relative standard of desirable progress for the group and for individuals. If some measures of progress are established and some standard exists for appraising these measures, then one can answer the foregoing question. To indicate that this issue is not necessarily a statistical problem, the following illustration is relevant:

A high school faculty had been very disappointed with elections to the student council because of the mediocre leadership elected to office (an initial judgment). In planning for the next year, plans were made for the study of elections in several classes and for different procedures in the choice of candidates, campaigning for office, and conduct of elections. The following year the faculty was pleased with the superior leadership elected to office (a subsequent appraisal) and concluded in discussion that its planning had been successful (an interpretation of the findings).

2. Can the appraisal results be attributed to curriculum planning? About the only satisfactory resolution of this issue is to study the possibilities of other factors having affected the results. For example, in the preceding illustration the faculty might have engaged in some discussion to determine whether the popularity of the students elected the second year, or the disappointment occasioned the student body by the poor leadership chosen the previous year, or other factors, might have brought about the more favorable election. If all possible factors could be eliminated other than the planning described, then the results would undoubtedly be attributed to planning. Frequently, however, all other factors cannot be eliminated, and the planning group must simply come to the best judgment the facts permit. Sometimes this amounts to a conclusion that progress was good (or bad) regardless of what factors were at work, and planning should continue (or be revised) to make whatever contributions it can to pupil progress.

The difficulty of satisfactorily resolving such issues causes us to reiterate the fact that the appraisal of pupil progress is as difficult as it is a desirable approach to evaluating curriculum planning. This approach is most satisfactorily used along with others. Thus, if the planning group's appraisal of its own processes is favorable, and if the appraisal of pupil progress is also favorable, the tendency would be to interpret the results as confirming the goodness of curriculum planning. We turn now to certain other approaches to evaluating the results of curriculum planning which may be considered along with the appraisal of pupil progress.

Follow-up Studies of Learners

The term "follow-up study" is generally applied to studies made of youth who finish or leave high school. However, we believe that the general purpose and technique of these studies is applicable at any grade level for evaluating curriculum planning. A follow-up study designed to secure evidence about the value of school experiences, and therefore their planning, is essentially an appraisal of pupil progress. It differs from the types of appraisal we have just described in that these are concerned with appraising progress during or at the end of a planned series of experiences, whereas a follow-up study focuses attention on progress *after* the experiences are past. Several types of follow-up studies useful

for evaluating curriculum planning are described in the following paragraphs.

Studies of school graduates. The most common type of follow-up
study is that made by a high school to determine what its students do
after graduation. These studies may or may not be developed so as to
give data which bear directly on the quality of curriculum planning.
Even information about the occupations followed by graduates has considerable implications for high school curriculum planning. In fact, major revisions of the traditional college-preparatory high school curriculum
have been stimulated by data showing the relatively small proportion of
high school graduates who enter college.

Follow-up studies of high school graduates may serve more specific
purposes than identifying occupational placement. Among the specific
data that are secured to help in curriculum planning and evaluation are
the following:

1. Various items concerning college adjustment and success, such as
marks, social activities, special interests and honors, and disciplinary records, which give the high school curriculum planning group some basis of
evaluating the preparation of youth for college

2. Estimates by employers of graduates' success on the job, which
give information relative to the success of planning for vocational preparation

3. Information concerning various aspects of graduates' postschool
living such as leisure activities and family life, which may be considered
in evaluating the planning of the program of general education

4. Estimates by graduates as to the success of their school experiences
(see the following section on studies of opinions)

5. Information from graduates or others about their continuation of
interests pursued while in school, for consideration in planning of
special-interest phases of the high school program

6. Surveys of graduates' difficulties in various particulars such as
communication skills, social adjustment, and military service, in connection with studies of specific phases of curriculum planning

Such follow-up studies have promise of great value in curriculum
planning, for they may reveal major deficiencies in the curriculum.
When considerable inconsistencies are found between the afterschool activities of graduates and those to which curriculum planning was directed, it can at least be concluded that planning was not adequate to
overcome whatever other factors may have exerted stronger influence.
In the face of such a conclusion, the need for more and better planning
would seem obvious.

Studies of dropouts. Two types of studies are commonly made of learners who leave school before the end of the terminal year. First, studies of dropouts are usually concerned with determining the reasons why learners leave school. In many individual schools, such studies are frequently very illuminating as to the failure of curriculum planning to provide for the needs of youth. National studies have been impressive even through showing the number of youth who do leave school before completion and thus raising serious questions about the real universality of "universal" secondary education.

Second, data regarding dropouts may be secured for the same purposes, other than college preparation, as for school graduates. A series of youth studies of great significance carried forward in the 1930's by the American Youth Commission was concerned with youth who had and who had not completed high school.[2] Other significant studies of youth have been made under the auspices of the New York Regents' Inquiry[3] and the Occupational Adjustment Study of the National Association of Secondary School Principals.[4]

Some of the techniques of these studies might be used by any curriculum planning group desiring evaluative information from learners who have left school. Two major difficulties in getting data should be noted: (1) the problem of locating these dropouts and of getting them to respond to inquiries; and (2) the problem of getting reliable information. Both difficulties may be partially met through the use of interviews rather than questionnaires. "Exit interviews" are frequently had with dropouts, for example. Although more difficult to arrange, follow-up interviews also may be desirable.

The kinds of information available from dropouts have valuable implications for curriculum planning: Why did they leave? What kinds of occupational choices did they make? What bearings did their previous schooling have on their postschool employment? What kinds of school experience do they wish they had remained for? These and similar questions if answered by or for enough learners and through procedures which assure a degree of reliability, should be of real value to the curriculum planning-evaluating group.

Studies of learners at subsequent levels. Although not usually termed a "follow-up study," inquiries and analyses of learners' successes

[2] See American Youth Commission, *Youth and the Future* (Washington, D.C.: American Council on Education, 1942), and Howard M. Bell, *Youth Tell Their Story* (Washington, D.C.: American Council on Education, 1939).

[3] See Ruth E. Eckert and Thomas O. Marshall, *When Youth Leave School* (New York: McGraw-Hill Book Company, Inc., 1938).

[4] See Edward Landy, "Occupational Adjustment and the School," *Bulletin,* National Association of Secondary School Principals, No. 93, 24:1–154 (November), 1940.

and difficulties at subsequent levels are commonly made. Unfortunately, these studies are frequently inadequate and are sometimes influenced by the bias of the curriculum planning group at the subsequent level. That is, there is sometimes a tendency to blame low scores on achievement tests on poor teaching and planning at the previous level without real study of the factors involved.

Studies of learners at subsequent levels have particularly promising uses in the elementary school or other levels where an entire learning group remains relatively intact from one year to the next. In such situations the teacher at the lower level can formulate an evaluative pattern which will answer questions of concern with some assurance that the data secured are relevant. For example, a grade teacher might plan a follow-up evaluative study through such steps as the following:

1. List learning goals in which continued progress is expected from grade to grade: for example, ability to work effectively as a group.

2. Design a schedule of information to be supplied by the teacher at the next level, which would reveal gaps or inadequacies in a learning group's progress regarding these goals; for example, difficulty of the group in adjusting to a new leader.

3. Through conference with the subsequent teacher, arrange to secure the information planned for.

4. Receive and interpret this information with respect to its significance for further curriculum planning: for example, noting the need for arranging with the next teacher to work with the group occasionally before the change of teachers occurs.

Studies of pupil progress at subsequent levels may also be fruitful in connection with individual learners. Good curriculum planning at the classroom level involves planning for individuals. Teachers may evaluate the quality of this planning through arranging with subsequent teachers for exchange of data regarding individual pupils. The further progress of the pupil for whom special learning experiences were planned to help him overcome disabilities, or the pupil whose special interests were provided for, or the pupil to whom special help was given with his adjustment problems, may be of real value to the teacher in planning for other learners.

Studies of later progress in special areas. Curriculum planning groups in special areas, particularly in the vocational field, make considerable use of follow-up studies. Business-education departments, for example, give great weight in curriculum planning to employers' estimates of the deficiencies of employees trained in these departments. Similarly, information is widely secured in such fields as industrial arts, agriculture, art, music, and athletics.

Follow-up studies may also be made of special-interest activities of a somewhat less technical nature. Inquiries of homemakers as to the relevance of school instruction in homemaking to their needs are as pertinent to curriculum planning in homemaking as employers' ratings of stenographers are to planning in business education. Follow-ups of learners who go to college may well include analyses of the persistence of interest and competence in debate, dramatics, journalism, recreational activities, photography, radio, and similar special interests. Follow-up studies in the community can be made to determine the persistence of leadership training as revealed through offices held in local government, churches, civic clubs, and the variety of community organizations.

Studies in special areas are sometimes exploited to give certain departments an overly important place in school curriculum planning. Thus a survey of graduates in business education may create a demand for various specialized courses in business English, speech, mathematics, and so forth. Hence it is important that the evaluation program be planned as a whole so that its different phases may be appraised in terms of their importance to the total problem of curriculum planning.

Use of Opinion Polls

Opinion enters into any program of evaluation. Even the appraisal of pupil progress through objective tests involves the use of teacher opinion in evaluating test results. Typical procedures usually are too greatly influenced by opinions of individual pupils, teachers, parents, citizens, or individual pressure groups, which are not carefully weighed as chance, sample, or biased opinions. The interpretation of opinion is a complex problem of considerable significance; a complete analysis of it is, of course, beyond the scope of this book. It is helpful to note Hand's analysis of three "psychic deluders" as serious limitations of the usual use of personal observations and other opinions: " (1) the influence of unrepresentative opinions; (2) the reluctance of people to be frankly critical; and (3) the influence of the observer's opinions and interests." [5] In his useful book on public opinion polling regarding schools, he describes representative sampling, anonymous responses, and expertly worded questions as means of overcoming these limitations.[6]

Opinion polls attempting to avoid the "psychic deluders" are employed for a variety of purposes in educational work. National opinion

---

[5] Harold Hand, *What People Think about Their Schools* (Yonkers, N.Y.: World Book Company, 1948), p. 26.
[6] *Ibid.*, p. 31.

polling agencies conduct general polls on educational issues. Professional organizations use polls in connection with their interests. School surveys frequently poll opinions of pupils, parents, and school personnel. State and local school systems use polls to sample or survey opinion on various issues. Individual schools and even individual teachers use "opinionnaires" for many purposes. In relation to curriculum planning, opinion polls may be classified as polls on specific curriculum issues, polls on an individual school's program, and polls on the bases and results of curriculum planning. These types are described in the following paragraphs.

Polls on specific curriculum issues. In the process of curriculum planning, some issue or issues frequently assume considerable interest. One technique of evaluating past practices in connection with an issue is to take an opinion poll of those in the best position to make a judgment. For example, curriculum planning in some systems is substituting parent teacher conferences for periodic written reports to parents of elementary school children. Although these changes may be discussed in curriculum councils and parent meetings, criticisms may develop from individual parents after the conferences are instituted. At this point, an opinion poll may be a very useful device for determining whether these critics are representative of all the parents or whether they are simply a small but vocal minority. It should be noted that a poll after the conferences are instituted is likely to give much better-informed opinions than one taken beforehand.

Similarly, polls of parent opinion may be taken regarding any issue which develops in curriculum planning. It is exceedingly important that parents have enough information about the issue to express an informed opinion. For this reason, the opinion inventories are frequently distributed in parent meetings or personally by school personnel or other parents or are accompanied by carefully worded statements of explanation. The nature of the issue should determine whether a comprehensive survey or a sample survey is needed. Thus a representative sample of opinion might be satisfactory to determine parent opinion as to student government policies of the school but as nearly a complete expression of parents concerned as possible would be necessary in connection with evaluating a field trip by one learning group. In the former case, the general trend of parent opinion is most significant; in the latter, parent appraisal of the specific results to individual learners is desired. Even in the former case, some information about the responding parents might be essential to drawing conclusions from the sample opinions; for example, whether or not the parent himself had participated in student government activities while in school might make a difference.

The same precautions need to be observed in taking polls and interpreting their results regarding specific issues as in connection with any use of opinion polls in evaluation. Some of the more important of these precautions are as follows:

1. If a sample survey is indicated, there should be adequate planning of the sample to ensure that the results will be representative of the total population.

2. If a comprehensive survey is indicated, every possible step should be taken to get complete returns.

3. If the opinion may be influenced by the fact that the respondent's identity is known, the poll should be made completely anonymous.

4. The respondents should be supplied adequate background for expressing opinions.

5. The wording of every item should be as simple and specific as possible.

6. All directions should be given as clearly as possible.

7. The form or interview schedule should be tried out several times before its final use.

8. The questions and responses should be constructed in such a way as to facilitate tabulation and summarization.

Polls on an individual school's program. Polls of pupil, teacher, and parent opinion may give very helpful evidence regarding the total program of an individual school. Although such polls give information that needs to be consulted in curriculum planning, as usually constituted they appraise the status of the curriculum without reference to a set of values whereby the opinions may be evaluated. Polls designed to give this more complete information are discussed in the next section.

A number of published instruments are available for securing opinions relative to an individual school's program.[7] For example, the Illinois Inventory of Parent Opinion asks certain personal facts "in order to report the main body of the survey findings intelligently," and then in Part I asks a series of thirty-six questions to discover parent satisfactions and dissatisfactions with the school, and in Part II, eight questions to determine parent opinions on certain educational issues.[8] Although such inventories have wide application and utility, an individual school-evaluating group may find it advantageous to develop instruments which ask questions about unique features of the school concerned.

[7] See Harold G. Shane and E. T. McSwain, *Evaluation and the Elementary Curriculum* (New York: Henry Holt and Company, 1951), pp. 437–443, for a selected, annotated list of evaluative devices and materials for use in appraising the general educational program of the elementary school.

[8] See Hand, *op. cit.*, pp. 153–169. This inventory is also published separately by the World Book Company, Yonkers, N. Y.

A poll of opinions regarding a school's total program gives many leads for evaluating curriculum planning. Specifically, such a poll gives one set of evidence as to the results of curriculum planning, that is, the curriculum. As already noted, this evidence may be without reference to any standard designated by the respondents, but nevertheless it tells what the respondents think is good and bad about the present curriculum. From such evidence from parents, for example, the curriculum planning-evaluating group should be able to answer questions of the following types:

1. Are parents satisfied or dissatisfied with the curriculum? To what extent and in what particulars?

2. Are the expectations of parents' desires for their children confirmed or denied? To what extent and in what particulars?

3. Do or do not parents understand what the school is trying to do for their children? To what extent and in what areas?

4. In what curriculum areas do parents believe their children's experiences are adequate and inadequate?

5. What are the handicaps to curriculum improvement recognized by parents? What handicaps do they fail to recognize?

6. What suggestions do parents offer which should be considered in curriculum planning?

The answers which analysis of opinion polls gives to these questions should be a very important phase of the evaluation of curriculum planning. Although it is not suggested that parent satisfaction or dissatisfaction is an adequate criterion alone, certainly this is a very important factor. If parents are dissatisfied, it is time for the curriculum planning group to take complete stock of itself. As a check, such questions as the preceding ones may also be answered by analysis of polls of pupil, teacher, and general lay opinion of the school's program. Possibly the most effective use of opinion polls in a total school program is the analysis of opinions of such different groups to determine points of agreement and explanation of disagreements between the groups.

Polls on bases and results of curriculum planning. Polls may also be developed so as to secure opinions both as to desirable bases of curriculum planning and as to how the school's curriculum is appraised with respect to these bases. For example, use of such a question as the following would give information of this type:

1. Do you think our school should provide sex information?_____Yes _____No

   If "Yes" above, do you think our school's program of sex education is adequate? _____Yes _____No

This general plan of evaluation is employed in the comprehensive study of opinion used in the Illinois Secondary School Curriculum Program. This plan, called the "Follow-Up Study," is described in the following excerpt from one of the publications of the Program:

1. PROBLEMS OF HIGH SCHOOL YOUTH

This is the title given to the list of real-life problems of youth around which the entire study centers. . . . It contains 56 real-life problems of youth variously subsumed under the headings of "Earning a Living," "Developing an Effective Personality," "Living Healthfully and Safely," "Managing Personal Finances Wisely," "Spending Leisure Time Wholesomely and Enjoyably," "Taking an Effective Part in Civic Affairs," "Preparing for Marriage, Homemaking and Parenthood," and "Making Effective Use of Educational Opportunities."

These problems stem from the postulated "Basic Needs of High School Youth" which are set forth in the *Guide to the Study of the Curriculum in the Secondary Schools of Illinois.* The lay and professional groups who are cooperating in the Illinois Secondary School Curriculum Program have indicated that meeting these basic needs is the task of the secondary school. . . .

2. WHAT DO YOU THINK?

This is the title of a questionnaire designed for anonymous use by teachers, pupils, parents, and "non-parent" patrons of the school. This questionnaire contains each of the 56 real-life problems of youth given in the basic formulation (see Paragraph 1 above). The respondent is asked to indicate whether or not he thinks the secondary school should help pupils with each problem. If this reply is in the affirmative, the respondent is asked to tell how important it is for the school to provide such help.

Obviously, the use of this questionnaire will enable the local administrator or curriculum director to secure an estimate of the "attitudinal given" which he confronts as he moves to unite more adequately teachers, pupils, parents, and other patrons in support of a school program geared to the real-life problems of youth. Data secured by its use will tell him what proportions of each group favor or oppose the introduction or strengthening, as the case may be, of each type of problem-centered content into the curriculum. The data will also afford him an estimate of the relative intensities of the views of each group included in the canvass of opinion. This instrument is to be used anonymously to attain increased validity.

The results secured by the "What Do You Think?" questionnaire may be used as the basis for group discussion of the purposes of the secondary school.

3. HOW MUCH REAL-LIFE HELP DID THEY GET?

This questionnaire is designed for anonymous use by teachers. It includes all of the 56 problems listed in the basic formulation (see Paragraph 1 above). In reference to each problem, the respondent is asked to tell how much of the help that the students needed he thinks was typically received by those in the last graduating class.

The data yielded by this instrument thus afford a composite of the teachers' estimates of the extent to which the school is already meeting these real-life problems of youth. Any appreciable discrepancy between (a) their views concerning what the school *should* be doing, as revealed by their replies in the "What Do You Think?" questionnaire, and (b) their judgments of the *actual accomplishment* of the school, as revealed by their replies in the present instrument, may be taken as a rough but useful measure of the willingness of the faculty group to make curricular changes of the types indicated.

4. WHAT HAS BECOME OF THE MEMBERS OF YOUR HIGH SCHOOL CLASS AND WHAT ARE THEY DOING?

This questionnaire is one of three designed for use with graduates of the school. The instrument is designed to find out what proportions of the relatively recent graduates are already experiencing each of the real-life problems included in the basic formulation. In pretesting this questionnaire in a city of about 70,000 it was found that from one-half to all of the "one-year-old" graduates had already encountered all but one (parenthood) of the 56 real-life problems included in the basic formulation (see Paragraph 1 above). As would be expected, this finding underscored, for pupils, teachers, and patrons alike, the need for secondary schools to deal adequately with the real-life problems in question.

The central purpose underlying the use of this questionnaire is precisely that of securing factual evidence which can be used to persuade a larger proportion of the pupils, teachers, and school patrons of the necessity of thus functionalizing the high school curriculum.

5. HOW MUCH WERE YOU HELPED BY YOUR HIGH SCHOOL?

This is the second of the three follow-up questionnaires to be used with graduates. The respondent is asked to tell how much of the help that he needed in reference to each of the 56 real-life problems (see Paragraph 1 above) he received from his high school. The composite replies of the graduates thus afford another appraisal of the adequacy of the school's program—an appraisal which pupils, teachers, and patrons can be expected to take seriously. Consequently, this appraisal can be expected to facilitate the work of curriculum development.

6. HOW WELL EQUIPPED ARE YOU FOR EFFECTIVE LIVING?

This is the third questionnaire to be used with graduates. The respondent is asked to estimate how effectively he is meeting the various problems included in the basic formulation (see Paragraph 1 above). Since effective living is the object of—and hence the real test of—education, it is apparent that the appraisal afforded by the use of this instrument can be expected to be decisive in enabling pupils, teachers, and patrons to conclude intelligently regarding the adequacy of the present program of the school.[9]

Two significant features of the Illinois Program's pattern of opinion polls should be noted:

1. Opinions regarding the effectiveness of the curriculum are related to certain real-life needs of youth, regarding the importance of which opinions are also secured.

2. Opinions are secured from separate polls of pupils, teachers, parents, and school graduates, as appropriate to the pattern of study, and the returns are used by discussion groups in reaching recommendations as to curriculum change. Thus, the poll is only a step in the Follow-Up Study.

Curriculum planning groups might develop similar patterns for appraising results of their activities. The general procedure to be followed is this:

1. Through opinion polls (the Illinois questionnaires, other published instruments, or instruments prepared locally), determine the opinions of respondents as to: (a) what bases, such as appropriate life needs of youth, of curriculum planning should be employed; and (b) what provisions the curriculum makes for the bases of curriculum planning considered important.

2. By analysis and interpretation of the returns, decide what bases for curriculum planning seem appropriate and acceptable and what curriculum provisions seem adequate and inadequate.

3. Modify previous curriculum planning as necessary in the light of this analysis and interpretation (step 2).

Cooperative Evaluation by the Faculty

The general procedure of cooperative faculty evaluation was described in the earlier section on evaluation of the process of planning. This pro-

[9] Kenneth B. Henderson and John E. Goerwitz, *How to Conduct the Follow-up Study* (Circular Series A, No. 51, Illinois Secondary School Curriculum Program, Bulletin No. 11; Springfield, Ill.: Superintendent of Public Instruction, August, 1950), pp. 11–13. The questionnaires appear in the appendix of this publication and may be reproduced.

cedure of faculty development and application of criteria and faculty interpretation of the findings seemed the most usable one available for evaluation of the planning process. The same general plan of procedure may be used to evaluate the results of curriculum planning. The steps involved are described in the following paragraphs.

Development of evaluative criteria. The development of criteria for evaluating the curriculum is best accomplished through extensive and continuing curriculum study and planning. As system-wide and school planning groups are studying and reaching decisions on questions of curriculum goals and designs they are also stating principles which can be converted into evaluative criteria.

Planning groups confronted by the necessity of developing a statement of evaluative criteria for appraising the curriculum can choose from at least three alternative procedures. First, they may simply adopt some statement of criteria already in existence. For example, many secondary school faculties have made use of the *Evaluative Criteria* prepared by the Cooperative Study of Secondary-School Standards, organized in 1933. This guide includes a section (D) on "Program of Studies" which gives specific criteria, arranged as check lists and with a scoring device, covering the following points:

General principles
Curriculum development procedures
Programs of studies
    Extent of offerings
    Nature of offerings
General outcomes of the program of studies
    Former pupils and graduates
    Present pupils
Special characteristics of the program of studies
General evaluation of the program of studies[10]

This guide also includes evaluative criteria for each curriculum area, the pupil activity program, library services, and guidance services, as phases of the educational program.

Many other statements of criteria for evaluating the curriculum are available. A different type of pattern is illustrated by the relatively simple check list on the curriculum as a whole that we presented in Chapter 1 of this book. Another type is the rating scale based on categories of learners' needs published under the auspices of the National Association

[10] See Cooperative Study of Secondary-School Standards, *Evaluative Criteria,* (Washington, D.C.: The Study, 1950), pp. 47–54.

of Secondary School Principals.[11] A publication of the Southern Association's Cooperative Study in Elementary Education does not list criteria as such but suggests study questions that may be restated as criteria for evaluating an elementary school program.[12] Several state departments of education have also developed criteria or scales for school evaluation.

Although the planning-evaluating group might choose from any of the above-described statements as well as many others, an alternative procedure seems preferable. This is for the group to develop its own standards following careful study of such statements as have been described. If this alternative is chosen, such factors as the following can be better provided for in the statement:

1. Criteria can be included which apply specifically to the curriculum of the schools concerned.

2. Criteria can be stated in such definite terms that they can be applied.

3. Criteria can be used which reflect the group's agreement as to values sought in the curriculum.

Still a third method retains some of the values of a pattern of evaluation which emerges from curriculum study and planning and also solves partially the time problem this pattern involves. This alternative is an evaluative study during which criteria are formulated. Such a study is made, for example, by the elementary school faculty which works through the Southern Association's guide described above. This plan is really a step in a total curriculum planning program but makes specific provision for the development and use of criteria in connection with planning. Thus through actually evaluating its curriculum, a school faculty may develop the criteria as it goes along and at the same time apply them and interpret the findings into new plans.

Application of the criteria. The term "cooperative evaluation" implies that the cooperating individuals will work together in applying the criteria. This may be done through group discussion completely but is more efficiently achieved by a combination of activities. In connection with many criteria facts have to be secured, and there may be needed extensive fact-finding investigations by individuals and small groups. It may even be desirable to assign individual standards to teams of staff

---

[11] William L. Ransom, "How Well Does Your High School Rate on the Imperative Needs of Youth?" *Bulletin* of the National Association of Secondary School Principals, No. 164, 33:8–46 (October), 1949. Reprints are available from the Association, Washington, D.C.

[12] See Cooperative Study in Elementary Education, Southern Association of Colleges and Secondary Schools, *Evaluating the Elementary School: A Guide for Cooperative Study* (Atlanta, Ga.: The Association, 1951), pp. 51–200.

members to secure needed evidence. Total group sessions then serve the functions of appraising the data for their adequacy and validity.

The process of applying criteria may be illustrated by the "Check List for Appraising a School's Curriculum" on pages 14–15. Criterion 1A, for example, is: "The school program includes opportunity for pupils to participate in the government and other institutional functions of the school." The individual or team responsible for securing evidence on this item would need to find out how many pupils participated in government and other institutional functions (such as intercommunication, social activities, and maintenance) of the school, and what the nature of the participation was. When these data are reported to the total staff, judgments can be reached by the group as to whether the facts are reliable, accurate, and complete.

Interpreting the findings. If the facts reported in connection with the criterion just cited are accepted and indicate that only a small proportion of pupils have any real participation in institutional functions, the staff would probably decide that the curriculum is poor or inadequate in this particular. Then or later it would further interpret the facts by reaching some conclusions as to means of increasing participation. Thus the interpretation of findings involves, first, judgment as to the goodness of the curriculum in relation to the criterion concerned, and, second, preliminary decisions as to a plan of action in the light of the judgment.

PLANNING FOR CONTINUOUS EVALUATION

As noted earlier, evaluation should be a continuous phase of the entire process of curriculum planning. Steps to be taken in connection with this phase are described in this concluding section.

Recognition of the Nature and Importance of Evaluation

The first essential in the planning of a program of continuous evaluation is the recognition by all concerned of the necessity of evaluation as a basis as well as a result of planning. Early in this chapter we noted the "hindsight" fallacy in much evaluation. Two other common errors regarding evaluation must in particular be clarified by planning groups. One fallacy is that evaluation has reference only to the measurement of pupil progress. Traditional evaluative programs have operated under this concept and have consisted almost exclusively of various procedures for appraising pupil progress. Furthermore, these procedures have generally assumed a static curriculum and the measures of pupil progress have been intepreted only as an evaluation of pupil achievement with reference to this curriculum. Such programs are not considered as appraisals of curriculum planning, or as bases for further such planning. In these programs, tests are simply given periodically, pupil progress is estimated, and the curriculum remains unchanged.

A second fallacy is that evaluation is a process applying to the total school program but carried on very intermittently, frequently by persons not working in the school. This is the practice of evaluation usually operating in accreditation and survey procedures. At the secondary school level it has been most widely practiced through use of the *Evaluative Criteria* of the Cooperative Study of Secondary-School Standards. Although the use of this guide has probably been a significant improvement over the traditional high school "inspection" for accreditation purposes and has involved faculty participation, the evaluative study concerned frequently consists of a period of intensive work by the faculty, a review by a visiting committee, and a return thereafter to customary planning procedures. Thus the procedure may not provide for continuous evaluation nor does it necessarily affect curriculum planning.

An adequate concept of evaluation should include such items of belief and practice as the following:

1. The curriculum planning process should include provision for getting evidence by sound procedures of evaluation carried on continuously.

2. Curriculum planning should be evaluated by the planners, including all teachers, with such assistance from consultants, parents, and others in a position to help as possible. As indicated by Plate 39, pupils can help evaluate, too.

3. Evaluative data, such as test results and follow-up studies, do not within themselves constitute an evaluation, but are important as bases for the judgments reached by the persons best able to evaluate curriculum planning.

Formulation of Criteria for Evaluation

As indicated throughout this chapter, evaluations are always made with reference to some set of criteria, stated or implied. That is, when we determine the value of anything, we must have some measure of value or a criterion. We say the day is hot or cold in terms of some criterion of temperature; and we say that pupils' learning is good or poor in terms of some criterion of learning. A faculty committed to a program of continuous evaluation must come to agreement as to a set of measures or criteria for its curriculum planning.

Each of the approaches to evaluation described in this chapter has involved the development or the assumption of criteria. And each of the approaches suggested for evaluating the planning process involved the development of a set of criteria or the adaptation of criteria that we or others have stated. In connection with the approach to evaluating the results of planning through the appraisal of pupil progress, we pointed out that standards would be needed in the form of learning goals stated in terms of pupils' behavior. Even follow-up studies and opinion polls are

PLATE 39. STUDENT COUNCILS CAN HELP EVALUATE THE SCHOOL. *Council members help the faculty identify problems and proposals for school planning. (Courtesy of the Durham County, North Carolina, Public Schools)*

useful in evaluation as their data are viewed in the light of some predetermined measures. The approach of cooperative faculty evaluation is primarily a process of developing and applying criteria. This is the approach to evaluation which seems most profitable and feasible, but should, in our judgment, be planned as a total pattern which involves the securing of data through some of the other approaches suggested.

The general process of cooperative faculty evaluation through the use of evaluative criteria was described in a previous section. We may note here certain additional suggestions regarding the nature of such criteria. First, we believe that the statement should include a section on evaluation of the planning process. A possible check list for evaluation of the process is shown in the accompanying table. It is to be noted that the organization for planning is included as a part of the process. Second, we believe that the statement should include a section on the curriculum. An illustrative check list which might be used for this purpose was presented in Chapter 1. Third, we believe that the statement should include a section on criteria for evaluating the evaluation program itself. Such a statement might be prepared on the basis of the desirable characteristics of an evaluation program, summarized in the final section of this chapter.

TABLE 13

A Check List for Evaluating the Process of Curriculum Planning in an Individual School

	IS PRACTICE SATISFACTORY?	
CRITERIA	Yes	No
Organization for Planning		
1. All groups concerned (community, pupils, and staff) participate in planning curriculum purposes and policies.		
2. The faculty planning group is ultimately responsible for implementing purposes and policies through plans for learning experiences.		
3. Each specific job of curriculum planning assigned an individual or group is assigned and reviewed by the total faculty planning group.		
4. The services of individuals and groups in preparing curriculum plans and materials are organized to facilitate final adaptation and planning by the learning group.		
5. Some competent individual is designated and functions as coordinator of curriculum planning.		
Steps in Planning		
1. Curriculum plans are designed to accomplish agreed-upon goals.		
2. The framework of the curriculum is tentatively outlined and understood by the faculty planning group as a basis for making more specific curriculum plans.		
3. Resource units are planned in sufficient number and breadth to give direction and assistance to the planning of individual teachers.		

TABLE 13 *continued*

CRITERIA	IS PRACTICE SATISFACTORY?	
	Yes	No

Steps in Planning continued

4. The teacher's preparation of unit plans gives first consideration to total faculty agreements regarding areas of emphasis as
indicated by over-all curriculum plans and resource units.

5. The ultimate initiation and classroom development of units
of work involve cooperative planning with learners.

Ways of Working

1. A systematic set of procedures for evaluating curriculum
planning is in operation.

2. Changes in the procedures of curriculum planning are based
on evidence as to the need for change.

3. The help of each group and individual involved in curriculum
planning is utilized in terms of potential contributions rather
than status.

4. Each job of planning assigned to and accomplished by an
individual or group is evaluated and accepted or modified by
reference to the goals and needs of the total school program.

5. Group planning activities are so conducted as to direct the
creative abilities of all involved toward the goals sought.

6. Group decisions are made on the basis of careful consideration of issues and alternatives.

7. An atmosphere of cooperative planning and evaluation pervades all planning groups and the school as a whole.

Providing for Essential Evaluative Data

We believe that any program of continuous evaluation should include
provision for at least four types of evaluative data described in the following paragraphs.

Appraisal of pupil progress. The many means of appraising pupil
progress were listed earlier in this chapter. Not all of these are feasible or
even necessary in the individual school, but we believe that at least three
types of data on pupil progress are essential: (1) evidence of individual
progress with respect to each unit of work undertaken by the learning
group; (2) evidence of individual and group progress on whatever
basic skills are considered appropriate for development with the learning
group involved; and (3) evidence of individual progress with respect to
learning goals not included in (1) and (2), such as special interests and
general growth characteristics.

Follow-up studies. Such follow-up studies as are feasible for the individual school should be included. Follow-up studies at the next level

could be made possible in any school situation through the initiative of individual teachers.

Polls of parent opinion. Although large-scale parent polls may not be possible in many situations, some device can usually be utilized for securing a measure of parent expression. In the elementary school the grade teacher can readily solicit parent opinion on issues of planning for the learning group. In the secondary schools the home room teacher can usually reach parents easily.

Teacher check lists. Although faculty group discussion is essential at various stages in planning and evaluation, there may also be need to secure individual teacher judgments on the curriculum through check lists, "opinionnaires," and similar instruments. It may be an expedient procedure to have the total statement of criteria developed in the form of a check list, which can be completed individually (anonymously if necessary to secure critical responses), with summaries providing a basis of group discussion.

Arranging Group Sessions on Evaluation

As just suggested, it may be expedient for some evaluating to be done on an individual teacher basis. Also, some of the evaluative data has to be secured on a school-wide basis and carefully summarized prior to the application of criteria and the interpretation of findings. At appropriate times, however, the members of the faculty planning-evaluating group need to come together to review critically curriculum planning in the light of the data and according to basic criteria. Such sessions are particularly desirable at the end of each school year, although more frequent sessions are helpful. It seems obvious that any school group can do a better job of planning if at least once each year this group meets for an extended session, preferably of several days, to examine critically the processes and results of its planning activities. For this reason, an increasing number of schools provide postschool planning and evaluating periods, when faculty groups can work together without the routine of usual school activities.

Essential Characteristics of an Evaluation Program

To summarize this section, we propose the following as the essential characteristics of a program for continuous evaluation of curriculum planning:

1. The integral relationship of curriculum planning and evaluation

should be clearly understood by all persons who participate in planning the school program.

2. Changes in the procedures of curriculum planning and in overall curriculum plans should be based on evaluative evidence.

3. The planning of learning experiences for all learning groups should include provisions for evaluation by the groups and their teachers of the experiences.

4. A systematic set of procedures for securing evaluative evidence should be in operation.

5. These procedures should be based on values agreed upon by all who participate in curriculum planning.

6. Evidence should be secured regarding (a) the progress of pupils *during* the period concerned toward specific curriculum goals; (b) the progress of pupils *after* completing phases of the curriculum; and (c) the opinions of parents and teachers bearing on curriculum planning.

In concluding this book, we wish to reiterate our conviction that curriculum planning is the job of all who work for the education of children and youth. We believe that full and wise participation in this essential phase of education is a fundamental step toward improving the curriculum and the living of boys and girls. This book has been written to help in the job.

For Further Study

American Association of School Administrators, *American School Curriculum.* Thirty-first Yearbook. Washington, D.C.: National Education Association, 1953.

Chapters XI and XII deal with evaluation. The latter chapter offers many suggestions as to techniques, including various published instruments, for evaluating "the school's total effectiveness."

Association for Supervision and Curriculum Development, National Education Association, *Action for Curriculum Improvement.* 1951 Yearbook. Washington, D.C.: The Association, 1951.

Chapter VII, "Evaluating Improvement Programs," gives illustrations of evaluation techniques and develops guiding principles.

Bell, Howard M., *Youth Tell Their Story.* Washington, D.C.: American Council on Education, 1938.

See for techniques used in a large-scale survey of youth conditions and attitudes.

Caswell, Hollis L., and associates, *Curriculum Improvement in Public School Systems.* New York: Bureau of Publications, Teachers College, Columbia University, 1950.

Chapter 5 presents a check list for evaluating curriculum programs.

Cooperative Study in Elementary Education, Southern Association of Colleges and Secondary Schools, *Evaluating the Elementary School.* Atlanta, Ga.: The Association, 1951.

Guide for a comprehensive study of an elementary school program by its faculty. Develops principles of evaluation, but is prepared as a workbook to be completed by the study group.

Cooperative Study of Secondary-School Standards, *Evaluative Criteria.* Washington, D.C.: The Study, 1950.

Criteria (including a manual of instructions) which have been widely used in evaluating secondary schools.

Hand, Harold C., *How the Illinois Secondary School Curriculum Program Basic Studies Can Help You Improve Your High School.* Circular Series A, No. 51; Bulletin No. 13. Springfield, Ill.: Superintendent of Public Instruction, May, 1951.

Guide to materials and techniques of the Illinois Basic Studies for improvement of secondary schools.

————, *What People Think about Their Schools.* Yonkers, N.Y.: World Book Company, 1948.

Helpful handbook on specific techniques for polling public opinion on school problems. Includes sample inventories of parent, pupil, and teacher opinion.

Henderson, Kenneth B., and John E. Goerwitz, *How to Conduct the Follow-up Study.* Circular Series A, No. 51; Bulletin No. 11. Springfield, Ill.: Superintendent of Public Instruction, August, 1950.

Explanation of procedures for the study of pupil, parent, and teacher opinions regarding the high school program. Includes the instruments used in the Illinois studies.

Lee, J. Murray, and Dorris May Lee, *The Child and His Curriculum,* 2d ed.; New York: Appleton-Century-Crofts, Inc., 1950.

Chapter 15, "Evaluating Changes in the Child," also enumerates the essential elements of an evaluation program.

Leonard, J. Paul, *Developing the Secondary School Curriculum.* Rev. ed.; New York: Rinehart & Company, Inc., 1953.

Chapter XVIII describes the steps and techniques of a program for evaluating learning.

————, and A. C. Eurich (eds.), *An Evaluation of Modern Education.* New York: Appleton-Century-Crofts, Inc., 1942.

Reviews many research studies to give an evaluation of modern education.

Ransom, William L., "How Well Does Your High School Rate on the Imperative Needs of Youth?" *Bulletin,* National Association of Secondary School Principals. No. 164, 33:8–46 (October), 1949.

Check list for evaluating a school's provisions for meeting the ten imperative needs of youth as set forth in the Educational Policies Commission's 1944 publication, *Education for All American Youth*.

Shane, Harold G., and E. T. McSwain, *Evaluation and the Elementary Curriculum*. New York: Henry Holt & Company, 1951.

Comprehensive treatment of procedures for evaluating the elementary school and its various curriculum areas.

Weston, Grace, and others, *Democratic Citizenship and Development of Children*. Detroit: Citizenship Education Study, 1950.

Guide to evaluating citizenship education in terms of criteria for democratic living based on the developmental characteristics and needs of boys and girls.

Wood, Ben D., and Ralph Haefner, *Measuring and Guiding Individual Youth*. New York: Silver Burdett Company, 1948.

Discussions among members of school and community regarding individual differences, measurement instruments, and guidance procedures.

Yauch, Wilbur A., *How Good Is Your School?* New York: Harper & Brothers, 1951.

Although written as a handbook for parents, this book would be helpful to any teacher as an interpretation of modern elementary education and as a basis for evaluating the school. Chapter XV gives a check list for parents' use in visiting and evaluating a school.

Wrightston, J. Wayne, "Trends in Evaluation," *Educational Leadership*, 8:91–95 (November), 1950.

Brief analysis of how modern evaluative devices have developed

INDEX

Index